Alcoholism and Substance Abuse in Diverse Populations

Alcoholism and Substance Abuse in Diverse Populations

SECOND EDITION

EDITED BY

Gary W. Lawson

and

Ann W. Lawson

8700 Shoal Creek Boulevard
Austin, Texas 78757-6897
800/897-3202 Fax 800/397-7633
www.proedinc.com

8700 Shoal Creek Boulevard
Austin, Texas 78757-6897
800/897-3202 Fax 800/397-7633
www.proedinc.com

Originally published as *Alcoholism and Substance Abuse in Special Populations.*

Library of Congress Cataloging-in-Publication Data
Alcoholism and substance abuse in diverse populations/edited by Gary W. Lawson and Ann W. Lawson.—2nd ed.
p. cm.
Previously published under title: Alcoholism & substance abuse in special populations.
ISBN 978-1-4164-0439-2
1. Alcoholism—United States—Prevention. 2. Drug abuse—United States—Prevention. 3. Alcoholism—Treatment—United States. 4. Drug abuse—Treatment—United States. I. Lawson, Gary. II. Lawson, Ann W.
HV5292.A386 2010
363.290973—dc22 2010027664

Art Director: Jason Crosier
Designer: Nancy A. Meador
This book is designed in Charlotte LET and Minion.

Printed in the United States of America

1 2 3 4 5 6 7 8 9 10 19 18 17 16 15 14 13 12 11 10

We would like to thank our many patients and students, who over the years have taught us so much about substance abuse and issues of diversity. Without them, this book would not have been possible.

Contents

About the Editors

Gary W. Lawson, PhD, CAS, is a professor of clinical psychology at Alliant International University, California School of Professional Psychology, in San Diego, California. He is a licensed psychologist with a private practice in La Jolla, California, and an internationally known author, consultant, and trainer in the field of addiction.

With over 36 years of experience as a psychologist, he has written more than 50 articles and chapters and has published eight books in the field of substance abuse; he has also served as coeditor of *Family Dynamics of Addiction Quarterly.* His books include *Alcoholism and the Family: A Guide to Treatment and Prevention* (2nd ed.); *Alcoholism and Substance Abuse in Special Populations; Adolescent Substance Abuse: Etiology, Treatment and Prevention; Clinical Psychopharmacology: A Guide for Nonmedical Psychotherapists;* and *Essentials of Chemical Dependency Counseling* (3rd ed.).

He is a certified addiction specialist, a fellow in the American Orthopsychiatric Association, and is a diplomate in professional chemical dependency counseling. He has worked in the addictions field for 39 years and has experience with each of the populations represented in this book. He specializes in working with the reluctant-to-recover.

Ann W. Lawson, PhD, CAS, is a professor and coordinator of clinical training for the marriage and family therapy programs at Alliant International University, and is in private practice in San Diego. She is a licensed marriage and family therapist and a certified addiction specialist; she is also a diplomate in professional chemical dependency counseling.

She is a clinical member and approved supervisor of the American Association for Marriage and Family Therapy and is the past president of the California Division of the American Association for Marriage and Family Therapy.

She is a nationally known author, journal editor, consultant, and speaker. Her publications include *Essentials of Chemical Dependency Counseling* (3rd ed.); *Alcoholism and the Family: A Guide to Treatment and Prevention* (2nd ed.); *Alcoholism and Substance Abuse in Special Populations;* and *Adolescent Substance Abuse: Etiology, Treatment and Prevention.* She has also served as coeditor of *Family Dynamics of Addiction Quarterly.*

She is the founder and former director of the Children From Alcoholic Families Program, Lincoln, Nebraska, and former director of the Addiction Counselor Training Program at U.S. International University.

About the Contributors

Martin Adam, MSW, qualified as a social worker at the University of Edinburgh in 1987 and completed his MA in marital and family therapy at Alliant International University in San Diego, California, in 2003. He now lives and works in Edinburgh, Scotland. He works part-time as a social worker with people affected by HIV and part-time in the Family Therapy Team at Couple Counselling Lothian.

Matthew Berlin, PsyD, is a licensed psychologist who received his doctorate degree in psychology with an emphasis in marital and family counseling in 2002 from Alliant International University. He is currently working as a therapist for Fred Finch Youth Center, where he specializes in working with severely emotionally disturbed foster and group home children and adolescents and their families. Dr. Berlin practices utilizing a behavior–cognitive approach, as well as a solution-focused approach, narrative therapy, and attachment therapy, among other modalities. Dr. Berlin treats issues such as physical and emotional abuse, separation and attachment from family of origin, prenatal substance exposure, intergenerational substance abuse, adolescent substance abuse, sexual abuse, and domestic violence, as well as other child- and family-related issues.

Jodi Bunting Stanley, PsyD, received her doctorate from Alliant International University in 2008, specializing in chemical dependency treatment. She is a program therapist at the San Diego Center for Children's Discovery Valley Day Treatment School, where she specializes in adolescent substance abuse.

Lisa A. Cox-Romain, PhD, is a professor and counselor at Palomar College in San Marcos, California. She earned her PhD in organizational psychology in 1999 and an MS in organizational management and development in 1997 at the California School of Professional Psychology. She holds an MEd in educational counseling from the University of San Diego and is currently working toward a marriage and family therapy degree with an emphasis in chemical dependency at Alliant International University. She has owned and operated sober living homes for women and children and specializes in domestic and workplace violence. Currently, she is the interim director at the Career Center in Counseling Services; she also teaches alcohol and drug studies, psychology, child development, and counseling courses at Palomar College.

Barbara R. Cunningham, PsyD, is a licensed marriage and family therapist who has a private practice in San Diego. She received a doctorate in psychology with a specialization in marital and family therapy from Alliant International University in 2006. After graduating, she taught as an adjunct professor at Alliant's San Diego campus, teaching classes such as Parent–Child Therapy, Developmental Aspects of Aging, Marriage and Family Therapy Techniques, and Marriage and Family Theories. Dr. Cunningham utilizes a resiliency-based Bowen Family Systems approach in treating couples, individuals, and families, especially those suffering from marital or relationship distress, physician impairment, sexual abuse, violent loss, and grief. Her Web page is www.Cunninghamtherapy.com.

Thuy-Phuong Do, MA, is currently a doctoral student in the clinical psychology program at the California School of Professional Psychology at Alliant International University. She has over 10 years of experience teaching and counseling people with various physical and sensory disabilities. She has published several book chapters on the topic of communication and disability, and has taught at San Diego State University in the speech communication department. She has also spoken as an expert moderator at numerous conferences on the topic of life and disability.

Helena Dano Dow, PsyD, MFT, is a licensed marriage and family therapist in private practice and a member of the adjunct faculty at Alliant International University and Chapman University. A native of Albania, she has worked with clients of diverse backgrounds, including those who suffer from substance abuse or alcohol addiction. Under the instruction of Drs. Ann and Gary Lawson, Dr. Dow has developed a deeper understanding of substance abuse issues as they pertain to therapy and an appreciation of the work and research that need to be conducted in this area of mental health treatment.

Arthur J. Farkas, PhD, is the cofounder, along with his wife, Judith A. Salinger, MFT, CAS, of Lasting Recovery (www.lastingrecovery.com), an intensive outpatient substance abuse treatment program based in San Diego. Arthur is a former associate professor of family and preventive medicine at the University of California, San Diego, Medical School, and has published over 40 papers on substance abuse.

J. D. Friedman, PsyD, completed his doctorate in clinical psychology at the California School of Professional Psychology at Alliant International University's San Diego campus, after graduating from Columbia University with a Bachelor of Arts degree. He spent 6 years working in sports journalism and television production for FOX Sports–New York, which piqued his interest in professional athletes and substance abuse.

Susanne Friedrich, Dipl. Psych., is currently working toward her psychotherapy license in behavioral therapy in Dresden, Germany. As a Fulbright student, she was enrolled in the doctoral program at Alliant International University, where she obtained a certification in chemical dependency treatment in 2001. She has studied psychology in Leipzig, Germany, and has held a diploma in psychology since 2003. For her thesis, she investigated personality features and the social situation in relation to alcohol abuse in a group of homeless individuals in Germany. She has worked in Germany at several rehabilitation clinics designed for the treatment of substance abuse and psychosomatic diseases.

Veronica Gutierrez, PhD, is an assistant professor at Alliant International University. Her specialty areas include family, couple, and child therapies, as well as working with diverse populations such as Latinos, sexual minorities, and individuals with HIV/AIDS.

A. Thomas Horvath, PhD, ABPP, is president and founder of Practical Recovery, a self-empowering (non-12-step, non-disease-oriented) addiction treatment system (practicalrecovery.com). He is also president (since 1995) of SMART Recovery (smartrecovery.org), as well as a past president of the American Psychological Association's Division on Addictions (Division 50) and the San Diego Psychological Association.

Nick Curtis Jackson, PhD, is a professor in the Department of Counseling, Educational and Developmental Psychology at Eastern Washington University. He earned his PhD in developmental psychology at the University of Kansas in 1994. In addition to substance abuse issues among older adults, he studies lesbian, gay, bisexual, and transgendered discrimination in acute and long-term care facilities. Before joining the faculty of Eastern Washington University in 1996, he served as the director of two adult family homes for persons with Alzheimer's and other forms of dementia. He continues to serve family caregivers of persons with Alzheimer's as a volunteer for the Inland Northwest Alzheimer's Association.

Gary R. Lewis, PhD, is a clinical and forensic psychologist currently working at Richard J. Donovan California State Men's Correctional Facility in San Diego. He also works in the field of HIV/AIDS research and is a current member of the APA-sponsored Behavioral and Social Scientist Volunteers. In addition to specializing in the fields of forensics and substance abuse, he works with members of the gay, lesbian, bisexual, and transgender community who are dealing with abuse suffered in childhood.

Ron J. Llewelyn, PsyD, is the clinical manager for the Domestic Violence and Mental Health Team at Cornerstone Counseling Center in Salt Lake City, Utah, and a graduate professor at the University of Phoenix and Argosy University. His research interests are in psychological assessment, psychodynamic psychotherapy, and the treatment of post-traumatic stress disorder.

Melissa Malakoff, PsyD, is a registered clinical psychologist completing her post-doctoral fellowship at Rady Children's Hospital's Chadwick Center for Children and Families, where she provides therapy services for children and families affected by trauma. Her past work experience includes an internship at San Diego State University's Counseling and Psychological Services, where she provided a variety of counseling services, including those to students who violated the university's alcohol and drug policy. She also served as an intern and psychological assistant at Home Start, Inc., where she provided in-home therapy to families affected by abuse, neglect, and domestic violence. Her first practicum in graduate school was at St. Vincent de Paul Village, where she worked with homeless adults, many of whom were dually diagnosed.

Micah J. Mann, MA, LADC, is a licensed substance abuse counselor in Connecticut. He received his master's degree with a specialization in chemical dependency from United States International University. Micah has worked in the criminal justice field as a substance abuse therapist. He is currently a project coordinator for substance abuse research at the University of Connecticut Health Center and is an adjunct instructor at a local college.

Colleen J. Mullen, MFT, is a licensed marriage and family therapist and a doctoral candidate at Alliant International University. She teaches in the undergraduate program at Alliant International University and in the Alcohol and Other Drug Studies certificate program at San Diego City College. She has served as the director of rehabilitation services at the Salvation Army Adult Rehabilitation Center of San Diego and as a team leader with the Telecare ACT program. At Telecare ACT, she supervised an outpatient treatment team serving the severely and persistently mentally ill population of San Diego, the majority of whom were dually diagnosed. Her areas of interest involve chaos theory and nonlinear dynamical systems, addiction assessment and relapse prevention counseling, and underprivileged populations. She is currently a working member of the start-up team for the School Violence Prevention Institute at Alliant International University and is in private practice in San Diego.

Emily Naughton Lindley, MA, is a licensed marriage and family therapist in San Diego. She received a master's degree in marriage and family therapy from the University of San Diego in 2004. She is currently a doctoral student at Alliant International University, working toward her PsyD in marital and family therapy. In her private practice, she is specializing in the treatment of anxiety disorders.

P. Clayton Rivers, PhD, is professor emeritus in the Department of Psychology at the University of Nebraska–Lincoln. From 1972 to 2002, he conducted alcohol training in the clinical psychology training program and worked closely with community agencies. He spent a year as a postdoctoral fellow in alcohol use and abuse at Harvard Medical School and Massachusetts General Hospital. In 1979, he spent a year in New Zealand assisting that country in establishing alcohol assessment centers and training personnel in intervention, prevention, and treatment approaches.

Duane E. Rogers, PsyD, is a licensed marriage and family therapist who practices in San Diego. He has worked in the field of chemical dependency since 1972. He directed the San Diego County Employee Assistance Program (EAP) and later developed a private

EAP company. He has worked as a group facilitator in the California Physician Diversion Program since 1982, running ongoing groups for physicians, dentists, pharmacists, and other licensed health professionals with addiction or mental health issues. He has also worked as the self-referral therapist for the State Bar Court Lawyer Assistance Program in San Diego since 1990. Practice specialties include recovery groups for impaired health and legal professionals, and individual, family, and couple relational and addiction issues. Duane also holds a professional degree in public health (MPH).

Cynthia G. Scott, PhD, received her doctorate in counselor education from Southern Illinois University–Carbondale in 1989. She is an associate professor in the Clinical Mental Health Counseling Program at the University of North Florida in Jacksonville, Florida, where she has worked for 14 years. During that time, she has served as director for both the Addictions Counseling Program and the Rehabilitation Counseling Program. Prior to that, Dr. Scott served for 5 years as the director of the Graduate Program in Substance Abuse Counseling at the University of Iowa, during which time she also maintained a private practice in Cedar Rapids. Her areas of specialty and interest include chemical and behavioral addictions and how they relate to family systems, addiction as a disability, and group theory and practice.

Jillian Sokoloff, MA, has her master's degree in marriage and family therapy from California School of Professional Psychology at Alliant International University. She graduated with honors from Dowling College. She spent 3 years working with children with developmental disabilities after receiving her associate's degree in early childhood education. Jillian plans to focus her career on working with recovery resistance and chemical dependency issues.

Preface

It has been 21 years since we published *Alcoholism and Substance Abuse in Special Populations*, the first edition of this book. We have learned a great deal during that time in our clinical and academic work. And, a lot has changed in the field of addictions, including the terminology we use. Today, *diverse populations* more accurately describes the populations represented here. For who is to say who is "special"? The word *diversity* both captures the social reality of our world and celebrates the myriad differences among us. Yet it is very difficult to accurately define *diverse population*. Perhaps that is one reason we have taken so long to publish a second book on the topic. There are benefits to having a spouse working in the same field as you do. One of those is that you can easily share experiences and ideas on a daily basis. We have spent a great deal of time in our lives discussing various clinical issues, including the difficulties involved in categorizing people who have substance abuse problems. For example, if you are a woman, you could also be a Black woman or a Native American woman. You could at the same time be a professional athlete or a doctor or a child of an alcoholic. Which of those categories is most important with regard to substance abuse prevention or treatment? This new book examines the issues involved in the etiology, treatment, and prevention of alcoholism and other types of substance abuse among specific populations. It is important to recognize that each chapter attempts to be discrete and point primarily to the issues involved in a specific population. However, any single substance-abusing client might have issues that are addressed in more than one chapter. And, some populations have a great deal in common with each other, for example, adolescents and those who are elderly. First, both are often involved in major life-changing events. Adolescents are leaving school and going into a completely new environment, perhaps to a new location far from home. Elderly people are retiring from work, often moving to a new location. Both groups are faced with the challenge of adapting to changing hormones. Such life experiences can be stressful.

The populations represented in this book were chosen either because of their high risk for substance abuse problems in relation to the general population, as with Native Americans and adolescents, or because of a lack of resources available to provide up-to-date, appropriate information, as in the chapter on those who resist 12-step treatment and the chapter on individuals with disabilities. Chapter 13, "A Systems Treatment for the Impaired Physician Family," both examines the risk factors associated with physicians and offers a systems approach to treatment that is applicable to any population. This approach, which views addiction as rooted in multigenerational family processes, best represents our personal view.

Each of the contributors is uniquely suited to address the specific population discussed. In most cases, the contributors have had personal experience working with their specific populations in clinical settings. In several cases, the contributors are members of the population they are writing about, giving them special insight into the issues involved. The reader may choose to use the book to research a specific population; however, we feel that the book will be most beneficial to those working in the field of substance abuse if they read it in its entirety. As in the first edition of the book, each contributor has carefully reviewed the existing literature on a specific population in order to include the most current and useful substance abuse information regarding that population. The amount of literature available varies considerably across populations; each author has made a concerted effort to provide the most complete and up-to-date information possible. In addition, each chapter contains a reference list, which gives the reader a means of pursuing further reading in any given area. Of particular interest are the many Web sites and electronic documents provided in these pages. There seems to be almost no limit to the useful information you can find on the Web. Unfortunately, there is also no limit to the misleading, useless information available on the Web. We have attempted to help the reader by providing reliable sites. In addition to the reference lists, most of the chapters include a section entitled "Resources," which lists useful organizations and their contact information.

Although the contributors were given latitude to write their chapters as they saw fit, they were each provided with a brief outline to follow. Therefore, most chapters have the same structure. For example, most chapters begin with a review of demographic information, substance abuse rates, and kinds of substances abused by the specific population.

The underlying approach to the etiology, treatment, and prevention of substance abuse is likewise consistent across chapters. The majority of the contributors have had close professional contact with us and share similar beliefs. They are likely to believe that alcoholism and other types of substance abuse are multifaceted problems that should be examined from physical, social, and psychological perspectives. They are further likely to believe that the family—both the family of origin and the nuclear family—plays a major role in the cause, or etiology, of substance abuse and that treatment and prevention efforts are best undertaken with the family fully involved. As the editors of this volume, we feel that the message regarding the role of the family is an important one and cannot be overstated.

Although there have been enormous strides in knowledge and attitudes regarding substance abuse, we are just beginning to comprehend the significance of substance abuse problems with regard to our society and our world. Substance abuse problems are emerging as major political and economic issues, offering many challenges for those working in the field. It becomes ever more important that we learn from, yet not be bound by, our past. We must understand and use the information provided by research and clinical experience to guide us in planning programs to prevent and treat substance abuse. The significant progress made over the past 60 years in identifying and understanding substance abuse has not been equaled in the areas of treatment and prevention. It is time, we believe, to develop programs designed for specific populations that can be proven over time to be effective in reducing or even eliminating these most pressing of problems involving addiction and abuse. We hope this book will be a step in that direction.

Gary W. Lawson
Ann W. Lawson

CHAPTER 1

A Rationale for Planning Treatment and Prevention of Alcoholism and Substance Abuse for Specific Populations

Gary W. Lawson

A key concept underlying this book is that as clinicians, we must approach the treatment and prevention of substance abuse, including alcoholism, from a viewpoint that considers diversity issues. The members of specific populations tend to have shared characteristics that have been shown empirically to affect etiology, treatment, and prevention. For many in the field, this emphasis on diversity calls for a new way of thinking about alcoholism and substance abuse. Since formal treatment programs were first offered for addictions in this country, we have provided what I call "McTreatment." One treatment program is a lot like the next. But, unlike fast-food hamburgers, consistency across programs is not necessarily a good thing. Different programs need to address different issues. For example, a program that is effective with homeless veterans would not necessarily work well with rich athletes. And so on. Although, as Vega and Cortes (2005) point out, the use of terms such as *special populations* or *diverse populations* may result in overgeneralizations, it is useful to look at populations in these terms to maximize treatment effectiveness.

Research on addiction treatment and prevention supports differentiated treatment, but has been slow to drive changes in programs. There are many complex reasons for this, but the fact remains: You can examine treatment programs in any part of the country, and although the physical settings may differ, the programs consist mostly of the same elements. The first goal is to get the alcoholic/addict to dry out (which is logical). Then, while the person is sober, the next goal is to get him or her to admit to his or her addiction while also admitting that his or her life has become unmanageable and out of control—which may or may not be useful, depending on the individual. This treatment approach usually involves group therapy, 12-step self-help meetings, and individual therapy, where these ideas are presented over and over until the client has accepted them. Clients are given the AA *Big Book* (Alcoholics Anonymous, 1976); they are encouraged to begin reading it and to write down a list of people they need to make amends to because of their behavior. It should be noted here that reading the *Big Book* and making a list of people we may have offended is something anyone who can read and write can do, any time they choose, in the absence of a formal treatment program, for free. People can also attend any of the thousands of 12-step self-help meetings offered each day in this country—also for free (though a small donation is sometimes encouraged). If any of these things are helpful, people should be encouraged to do them, whether they are in a formal treatment program or not. In most programs, if patients don't find the 12 steps or the *Big Book* or the idea that they have "lost control" helpful, they are told by staff and fellow patients that they are "in denial" or "resistant to treatment." Group pressure is applied to "help" them "get with the program"; if they do not, they are sometimes asked to leave the program and to come back when they are "ready for help." This seems to be a bit like telling depressed patients to "cheer up," and if they don't, you won't see them until they are ready to "cheer up!"

I have counseled thousands of alcoholics and drug addicts during the past 35 years. The majority of them have been in one or more treatment programs at some point. With few exceptions, they described their experience in terms similar to those above. Yet each individual case is very different. People become addicted or abuse substances for a variety of reasons, just as they recover from addictions for a variety of reasons. For an excellent account of one alcoholic couple's experience in treatment and their somewhat unorthodox approach to recovery, the reader is encouraged to read the book *Phoenix in a Bottle,* by Lillian and Murdoch MacDonald (2005). It is an inspiring personal account of their struggle to overcome alcohol addiction, and it illustrates the point that people's experiences with addiction and recovery are not all the same.

There are several reasons why most treatment programs are similar and not necessarily based on research. First, the majority of addictions counselors are paraprofessionals (Lawson, Lawson, & Rivers, 2001). They have not been trained to read research studies in scientific journals on addictions and to apply the research findings to their programs. Second, as I discovered in a recent review of state requirements, only a few states require a master's degree for addiction counseling certification. Many states do not even require a bachelor's degree for certification as a drug or alcohol counselor. Yet all other mental health professionals are required to have at least a master's degree and some direct clinical supervision. This situation would seem to imply that it takes less education and training to treat addictions than it does to treat other mental and emotional problems, which, given the complexity of addictive behaviors, seems unlikely. Nonetheless, many mistakenly believe that all that is necessary for people to treat addictions effectively is to have been addicted themselves and to have been through a recovery process of some kind.

Third, mental health professionals who don't specialize in addictions have had very little training in addictions. They often see addicts or alcoholics in their practice but do not have the training to recognize addiction—at least not as the primary problem. Many such mental health professionals refer addicts to those who specialize in the field; but again, these are mostly nonprofessionals or paraprofessionals. Perhaps referrals are made because many professionals perceive addictive disorders as difficult to work with. Patients are often noncompliant and resistant to treatment. That belief is inconsistent with the idea that it is not necessary to have an advanced degree to treat addictions. In fact, addictive disorders may be some of the most complex and difficult problems humans deal with. This issue will be discussed further in Chapter 3, on dual diagnosis.

Fourth, the non- or paraprofessional status of most addictions counselors is part of what has been called the "apprenticeship model" (Lawson et al., 2001). This training model translates into "Learn to counsel like I do and you can become one of 'us'. Don't question what you are taught; the teacher is the expert. Learn to do counseling like the expert." Professionals with advanced degrees, by contrast, are trained in the scientific model and are taught to question everything. They are taught to look for evidence regarding what works and what does not work. They are taught to use best practices that are based on empirical evidence. The two approaches to training are not very compatible. However, with the cost of treatment rising, and as managed care companies become more involved in treatment programs, there will be an increasing need to offer evidence-based treatments (Bernal & Saez-Santiago, 2006). There will also be an increasing need to offer programs that address diversity issues (Ida, 2007; Sue, 2006).

In order to develop a model for the treatment or prevention of any disorder, it is useful to understand the etiology, or cause, of the disorder. There are at least three important types of risk factors to consider in the etiology of addictive behaviors: physiological, sociological, and psychological (Lawson & Lawson, 1998). However, there is little agreement among researchers and scientists regarding the etiology of addictions, and most theories are based on a single one of these three factors. It is unclear how much of a role each factor plays in the development of addictive behaviors. It is likely that the percentage is different for each individual. For example, some might have more of a genetic risk, and others might have more of a sociological or psychological risk.

Factors in the Etiology of Addiction

All three aspects—physical, social, and psychological—should be considered in combination in developing plans for the prevention and treatment of alcoholism, other substance abuse, and other addictions. From a physiological or genetic perspective, it has been clearly shown that alcoholism and other addictive disorders have a genetic component. Cotton (1979) was one of the first to provide a review of empirical support for this idea, with his review of vast amounts of research. Later, Goodwin, Schuckit, and others produced many studies indicating the genetic factors involved in addictions (Searles, 1991). More physiological research is available for alcohol addiction than for other types of substance abuse or addictions.

Sociological factors, whether they are related to culture, the family, peer groups, fellow workers, or several of these in combination, have a great deal to do with the risk that a person will abuse drugs or alcohol (Cahalan, 1970). The psychological makeup of an individual, which can be defined as the personality and emotional stability of the person, also plays a major part in the likelihood that the individual will use or abuse drugs or alcohol (Lawson & Lawson, 1998).

Before we examine these three factors and their specific roles in treatment and prevention, a clear definition of what it is to be treated or prevented is in order. Many terms are used to describe the behavior involved in a person's destructive relationship with a chemical or a behavior: *alcoholism, substance abuse, problem drinking, drug abuse, drug dependence,* and *addiction,* among others. Although the conditions for which these terms stand include subtle or even major differences, they all have a common denominator: They exist when an individual is in a relationship with a chemical substance (e.g., alcohol) or a behavior (e.g., gambling) to the extent that there are continuing difficulties, of any kind, in that person's life as a result of using the chemical substance or exhibiting the offending behavior. It has been recognized more and more in the treatment field that the mere removal of a substance or a particular behavior does not always improve the situation or the life of the abuser or addict. Other problems in the person's life may even get worse. These life difficulties can be physical problems, relationship problems, social problems, work-related problems, or any other type of problem. A typical example of this would be what many AA members refer to as a "dry drunk." This is someone who stops drinking but continues to behave in ways that are detrimental to both self and others. In part, this phenomenon may have to do with the increasingly large number of people who are mandated by the court or a probation officer to attend self-help meetings such as AA, regardless of the usefulness of attending. In such cases, people are often attending meetings but not "working the program," as they say in AA.

Using a drug, drinking alcohol, gambling, and shopping excessively are all behaviors. It is often a secondary or related behavior, rather than the drug-using behavior, that causes most of the problems for the individual or those around him or her (e.g., driving drunk, fighting); thus, the behavior that results from the drinking is what causes the problems that motivate the individual to seek treatment. An individual may not seek treatment if his or her excessive behaviors don't result in obvious problems. If you can afford to gamble or binge shop, for example, you are less likely to seek treatment. If you gamble with the rent money, steal other people's money to support your gambling habit, or run up credit cards you can't pay off, you are more likely to go into treatment.

The problems ultimately addressed in treatment or prevention thus result from behaviors. In most cases, these behaviors cause problems not only for the individuals using or abusing drugs or alcohol, or those with other addictive behaviors, but also for those around them. At times, alcoholics or drug users may be unaware of the degree of difficulties they are causing the significant people in their life. Sometimes even the family or others close to the user are unaware of the negative effect the behavior has on the social or family system they live in. In those cases, part of the role of the therapist is to create awareness in the family of the current and potential negative consequences of the addictive behavior. However, it is equally important for the therapist to examine what may appear to the user to be the positive consequences of the addictive behavior, and to do this in a culturally sensitive way that accounts for differing values around what acceptable behavior is in the world in which the individual lives. This systems view of behavior is important in the planning of strategies to help the patient change the addictive or abusive behavior. The concept of considering both positive and negative consequences of substance abuse is discussed later in this chapter and throughout this book. First, we should examine why some are reluctant to admit that alcoholism and other substance abuse are behaviors with social and psychological causes rather than a disease that people "get" or have, like cancer. The best example of this reluctance can perhaps be found in the field of alcoholism.

Not all those working in the field of alcoholism want to admit that alcoholic drinking is primarily a behavior. Many prefer to see alcoholism as a disease; rarely, though, does one hear addiction to heroin or addiction to cigarettes referred to as a disease. There are many historical reasons why treatment professionals, as well as alcoholics themselves, would be reluctant to admit that alcoholism and other types of substance abuse are behaviors. Dr. Alfred Smith, a psychiatrist who spent 15 years seeking a biological cause for alcoholism, stated before the National Safety Congress in Chicago, "It's a terrible disappointment to me to finally face up to the fact that alcoholism is a behavioral disorder" (quoted in Vogler & Bartz, 1982, p. 8). It is understandable why someone who spent so much time and effort looking for a biological cause for alcoholism would be disappointed to find so little evidence of its existence. It is also understandable that such a person would be disappointed to realize that social factors, environment, and the psychological makeup of the individual, not biological causes, are the primary factors in alcoholism, substance abuse, and other addictive behaviors.

An important corollary of seeing alcoholism as a behavioral disorder is that the individual has control over the behavior. This implication is threatening to those who have convinced themselves that they are not responsible for their past behavior because they had a "disease" with a biological basis. There may never be agreement among professionals with regard to the etiology of addictive behaviors. There are far too many economic, social, and personal considerations involved for a simple answer. But an excellent example of the type of conflict that exists in the field of addictions is the Supreme Court decision during the '80s relating to alcoholism as a disease (cited in *Traynor v. Turnage, 1988*). The Supreme Court denied an alcoholic veteran's claim that he had a disease and therefore was entitled to disability payments. This is an issue that volumes have been written on; yet it seems we are no closer to a resolution than we were 21 years ago, when this book was first published.

Davis (1987) stated, "Therapists are ill-advised to take sides on the issues of cause versus effect when it comes to alcoholism" (p. 5). Whether one takes sides or not, it is important with regard to the plans developed for treatment or prevention to understand the dynamics of the disorder to be treated or prevented. If the disorder is misunderstood, treatment or prevention planning may be negatively affected. For example, a misunderstanding of excessive drinking or drug use as purely maladaptive (as opposed to having both maladaptive and adaptive aspects), with a single ultimate cause, either biological or psychological, may lead to therapeutically ineffective moral exhortations and scare tactics, a punitive legal approach, and generally aversive therapeutic approaches, such as the use of disulfiram (Antabuse), apomorphine injections, or videotaped self-contradiction. Therapeutic approaches based on an ultimate-cause hypothesis rather than on a multicausal hypothesis have led therapists to apply uniform therapies to all "addicts." These therapeutic approaches may lead to short-term improvements, but they usually result in relapse and increased frustration for both the therapist and the patient. Working with this model can have the added negative effect of separating control of the behavior from behavioral contingencies (Davis, 1987; Lawson et al., 2001). In other words, patients feel there are no logical reasons for their behavior and that they have no control over their actions. The attitude that some external, unknown factor "made me do it" is likely to lead only to a continuation of the behavior and a feeling of helplessness on the part of the patient.

As an alternative to this approach, a behavioral–adaptive model that emphasizes finding what seems to be adaptive and reinforcing for the drinking, drug taking, or other addictive behavior is recommended. Davis (1987) offered the following three hypotheses:

1. The abuse of alcohol has adaptive consequences. (No implication is made that adaptive means "good" or "moral" or necessarily desirable.)
2. These adaptive consequences are sufficiently reinforcing to serve as the primary factors maintaining a habit of drinking, regardless of what underlying causation there may be.
3. The primary factors for each individual differ and may be operating at an intra-psychic level, intra-couple level, or at the level of maintenance of homeostasis in a family or wider social system. (p. 17)

If we accept these hypotheses as reasonable, we can see that a therapist who knows which factors are likely to motivate a specific population to abuse drugs or alcohol will be at an advantage when planning treatment or prevention for a given individual. It would further seem likely that a therapist who bases plans for treatment on risk factors pertaining to one group may not be successful using the same risk factors to plan treatment for a different group. For example, the adaptive consequences for a male drinker may not be the same as those for a female drinker, and the adaptive consequences for an individual with a disability are unlikely to be the same as those for a high-performance athlete. It is also likely that individuals in some groups (e.g., African Americans, women, Native Americans) might have some adaptive consequences in common.

The remaining chapters of this book provide information on physiological, sociological, and psychological risks for drug- or alcohol-abusing behavior, as well as the adaptive consequences of this type of behavior, for a variety of specific populations. With this information, the therapist or prevention specialist will be better equipped to design treatment and prevention strategies based on the needs most often seen in that specific group. Reading about the risk factors associated with these populations may also help therapists understand possible risk factors in groups not covered here.

It would be ideal to plan treatment for each individual after considering his or her specific needs. From a practical standpoint, however, this is difficult. There are only a limited number of treatment providers, and there are many, many people who need treatment. Planning for specific groups is the next best approach. With the limited amount of funds available for prevention programs, it makes sense to target spending for programs for populations that are at high risk.

Characterizing Individuals and Assessing Their Needs

There is no "typical" chemically dependent person, and there is no specific personality type, family history, socioeconomic situation, or stressful experience that has been found to predict categorically the development of chemical dependency (Lawson et al., 2001). However, in assessing or diagnosing the chemically dependent person, it is best to systematically cover the important aspects of the three areas mentioned earlier: physiological, sociological, and psychological. Some of the major aspects in each area are addressed below and are presented in Table 1.1.

Physiological Factors

In assessing the physiological nature of the problem, it is important to determine if physical addiction is present. Obtaining a detailed history of drug or alcohol use is often appropriate at this beginning point in treatment. If physical addiction is present, the first order of treatment will be to detoxify the individual. This is usually done under the supervision of a medical practitioner; therefore, a referral will be necessary if the therapist is not a physician. This is also a good time to rule out other addiction-related or physical diseases or disorders. Other aspects of a physical nature that need to be ruled out are underlying psychopathological problems such as chronic depression, schizophrenia, or other mental disorders that are likely to respond to psychotropic medications. (For more detailed information on this topic, see Chapter 3, on dual diagnosis.)

Finally, it is useful to assess the individual's family background to determine if there is a history of substance abuse. If there is a history of alcoholism or substance abuse in the parents or grandparents, a physical predisposition to the condition may be present. There is little or nothing of a physical nature that can be done to reduce a potential predisposition, but it may be helpful to suggest to clients or patients that they should take precautions to ensure that the sociological and psychological areas of their lives do not introduce undue risk or pressure for them to abuse drugs or alcohol. This type of communication is similar to that which is often shared with patients who have a family history of heart disease, high blood pressure, or diabetes.

Table 1.1
Factors to Consider in the Etiology, Treatment, and Prevention of Alcoholism and Substance Abuse

Physiological factors	Sociological factors	Psychological factors
Physical addiction	Ethnic and cultural characteristics	Social skills
Disease or physical disorders	Family background	Emotional level
Related medical problems	Education	Self-image
Inherited risk	Employment	Attitude toward life
Mental disorders	Peer relationships	Defense mechanisms
(with physiological causes)		Mental obsessions
		Decision-making skills

Sociological Factors

Sociological factors are related to the interactions between the individual and those around him or her, including interactions with the family of origin, the nuclear family, and the extended family. Education, or the lack of it, is often an important factor with regard to a person's self-image. Employment history, peer group, and cultural or ethnic background are all very important factors. These characteristics are all related to the motivation the person is likely to have to change the offending behavior.

Sociological factors determine not only whether people will drink but also how people will view themselves after drinking. In a review of a 33-year prospective study of alcoholism, Vaillant and Milofsky (1982) found data suggesting that ethnicity (in this instance, southern European) and the number of alcoholic relatives accounted for most of the variance in adult alcoholism.

Tarter and Schneider (1976) identified 14 sociological variables that have an impact on an individual's decision to start, continue, or stop drinking. These are (a) childhood exposure to alcohol and drinking models, (b) the quantity of alcohol that is considered to be appropriate or excessive, (c) drinking customs, (d) the type of alcoholic beverage used, (e) the levels of inhibition considered safe, (f) the symbolic meaning of alcohol, (g) the attitude toward public intoxication, (h) the social group associated with drinking, (i) the activities associated with drinking, (j) the amount of pressure exerted on the individual to drink and continue drinking, (k) the use of alcohol in the social or private context, (l) the individual's mobility in changing drinking reference groups, (m) the duration of the drinking, and (n) the social rewards or punishments for drinking.

Four "parent types" have also been identified as producing high-risk offspring. These are the alcoholic or drug-addicted parent; the rigid, teetotaling parent; the over-demanding (and perhaps overachieving) parent; and the overprotective parent (who may have come from a dysfunctional family) (Lawson & Lawson, 1998). A complete social history would include asking about these parent types, and a good treatment plan would involve dealing with the effects these parent types have had on the patient.

Psychological Factors

Among the major psychological factors involved are the individual's emotions or feelings and personality. A person's personality is loosely measured by how that person interacts with his or her environment, what his or her defense mechanisms are, and what rules he or she abides by. These psychological factors are often directly related to sociological factors. For example, an individual may develop certain methods of coping with stress or may learn to withdraw from stress altogether after growing up in a family where there was a great deal of stress. On the other hand, an individual who grew up in a family where there was very little stress might not handle stress well at all in his or her later life.

Among the psychological aspects to look for are mental obsessions, emotional compulsions, a poor self-image, negative attitudes, rigid defense systems, and delusions. Problem areas include low identification with viable role models; low identification with family; and inadequate interpersonal skills, including communication, cooperation, negotiation, empathy, listening, and sharing. Another psychosocial problem is inadequate systemic skills, or the inability to respond to the limits inherent in a situation (responsibility) and the inability to adapt behavior constructively to a situation in order to get needs met (adaptability). Irresponsibility, refusal to accept the consequences of behavior, and scapegoating are all expressed when there is a weakness in this area. There are also inadequate judgment skills, which include the inability to recognize, understand, and apply appropriate meanings to relationships. Weaknesses in judgment are manifested as crises in sexual, natural, consumer, and drug and alcohol environments and as repetitive self-destructive behavior (Glenn, 1981).

Treatment and Prevention

When clients come in or are sent in for treatment for an alcohol or substance abuse problem, they need to change something in their lives. Usually, that something begins with their behavior. Next, they need to change the way they think about their behavior, and finally, they need to change the way they feel. In prevention work, a specific behavior or a series of behaviors and ways of thinking and feeling are what change. The behavior may be using drugs, drinking alcohol, gambling, or fighting. The thinking may not be based in reality and the feelings may play a major role in behavior. For example, an individual might say, "I feel sad, hurt, lonely" (or any number of negative emotions). The use of drugs may provide temporary relief, so the related belief is, "Drug use is the way to solve my problems." A number of factors and dynamics are involved for each individual.

Three things can change in an individual: behavior, thinking, and feeling. That is, you can change your behavior, your thinking (or way of looking at certain things), or the way you feel about something. These are interrelated. How you think is related to how you feel, and vice versa. How you behave is related to how you feel and think. The job of treatment is to facilitate change. The job of prevention is to guide change.

What makes a person change his or her behavior, thinking, or feeling? What can a therapist do to help the client or patient change? One way to help people change is to help them and their family become aware of the consequences of the drinking, drug use, or other specific behavior. This does not always work, but sometimes it does, and it may be the simplest way to facilitate change. If the receiver of the information holds the person providing the new information in high esteem, this interchange could increase the likelihood of a change. For example, a physician telling a patient about a major health risk from a behavior could have enough effect on the patient to help him or her to change that behavior (Peele, 2004). A wife making it clear during therapy that she will leave her husband if he drinks again might lead to a change in his behavior. But, if he wants to end the relationship, he might respond to her ultimatum by continuing to drink. To avoid making major mistakes in therapy, the therapist should find out all he or she can about what is motivating a given behavior. For example, if an alcoholic is drinking to kill himself (suicide on the installment plan), the therapist who knows this can avoid statements to the patient such as "If you keep drinking you are going to die." That is exactly the consequence the patient wants.

As a therapist and educator in the field of addiction treatment, I have asked many hundreds of recovering alcoholics and drug addicts why they decided to change. All of them had an answer, and all of them knew of something that caused them to change. When a man with a 15-year history of drug and alcohol abuse who had been sober for 3 years was asked why he stopped using, he said, "Because my 10-year-old son asked me to." When asked why he had not stopped much earlier, when his parents and wife had asked him to, he said, "Because they were the reason I was using." For this man, it took his son's request to motivate him to change his behavior.

For each person, there is a reason (and perhaps many reasons) he or she is using, and there are also reasons or perhaps just one reason he or she would be willing to stop using. For the therapist, the task is to identify these reasons. The clues to what will cause change in the present are found in the past of the individual. What was it that caused the person to think, feel, and behave the way he or she did to begin with? By knowing that, a therapist can plan events to change what is necessary. For change to be lasting, the precipitating event or motivation to change needs to be as powerful or meaningful as the event or events that caused the person to behave, think, or feel the way he or she did to begin with. For example, individuals who have low self-esteem because they were adopted, and who feel that they were unwanted and unloved by their natural parents, might be able to change those feelings by meeting the natural parents and finding out what happened to make the natural parents give them up. It might not be enough for a therapist to say, "I'm sure your parents loved you." The experience of actually meeting the natural parents might change the individuals' self-esteem by changing the way they think and feel about why their natural parents gave them up. After meeting the natural parents, they can say to themselves: "I was lovable and my parents loved me, but given the circumstances, they were unable to keep me. So, I'm not unlovable after all."

Diversity Issues and Evidence-Based Therapy

There is some disagreement among professionals regarding what addiction treatment should involve and how it should be evaluated. It has been suggested that the slogan "Treatment Works," although it has many advantages, should be replaced because it simplifies a complex problem and implies some things that just are not true (White, 2005). There are many approaches to treatment, in many different settings (Wilbourne & Miller, 2003). Some approaches are widely used yet lacking in scientific validation (Miller & Hester, 1986). Others have support from a substantial number of scientific studies (Siegel, Haugland, & Schore, 2005), yet are not well accepted in the addiction treatment community (Kreek & Vocci, 2002).

The remainder of this book attempts to present to the reader information on different treatment approaches, in the context of a focus on diversity issues that might affect the alcoholism or other addictions in a given population. This information should be useful in the planning of treatment or prevention programs for members of specific groups. Some chapters (e.g., Chapters 4 and 13) focus more on current approaches to treatment and prevention. Other chapters address characteristics that are specific to the population they are discussing. All of the chapters include a reference list, and most of the chapters include a section at the end that lists helpful resources. For additional resources related to diversity issues and evidence-based therapy, see the appendix.

In addition to diversity issues and evidence-based practice, a focus on the patient's family is key to treatment planning. For me, treatment planning always includes the family in some manner, even if just as a way of understanding the systemic factors involved and how they impact the case. The events that mold individuals can almost always be traced to the family in some way. If the family is included in the treatment and prevention process, the chances of success will be greatly increased. A number of family treatment books are available (Barnard, 1981; Davis, 1987; Juhnke & Hagedorn, 2006; Lawson & Lawson, 1998; Stanton & Todd, 1982); the addiction counselor should read them all.

The remaining chapters in this book are diverse in their viewpoints and presentations of issues for specific populations. Readers are advised to keep an open mind, use the information that is useful, and reflect on the viewpoints that do not support their own.

References

Alcoholics Anonymous. (1976). *Alcoholics anonymous: The story of how many thousands of men and women have recovered from alcoholism* (3rd ed.) New York: Alcoholics Anonymous World Services. (Popularly known as the *Big Book*)

Barnard, C. (1981). *Families, alcoholism, and therapy.* Springfield, IL: Thomas.

Bernal, G., & Saez-Santiago, E. (2006). Culturally centered psychosocial interventions. *Journal of Community Psychology, 34,* 121–132.

Cahalan, D. (1970). *Problem, drinkers: A national survey.* San Francisco: Jossey-Bass.

Cotton, N. S. (1979). The familial incidence of alcoholism: A review. *Journal of Studies on Alcohol, 46,* 98–116.

Davis, D. (1987). *Alcoholism treatment: An integrated family and individual approach.* New York: Gardner.

Glenn, S. (1981, February). *Directions for the 80s.* Paper presented at the Nebraska Prevention Center, Omaha.

Ida, D. J. (2007). Cultural competency and recovery within diverse populations. *Psychiatric Rehabilitation Journal, 31,* 49–53.

Juhnke, G. A., & Hagedorn, W. B. (2006). *Counseling addicted families: An integrated assessment and treatment model.* New York: Routledge.

Kreek, M., & Vocci, F. (2002). History and current status of opioid maintenance treatments. *Journal of Substance Abuse, 23,* 93–105.

Lawson, A. W., & Lawson, G. W. (1998). *Alcoholism and the family: A guide to treatment and prevention* (2nd ed.). Austin, TX: PRO-ED.

Lawson, G. W., Lawson, A. W., & Rivers, C. (2001). *The essentials of chemical dependency counseling* (3rd ed). Austin, TX: PRO-ED.

MacDonald, L., & MacDonald, M. (2005). *Phoenix in a bottle.* Cambridgeshire, UK: Melrose Books.

Miller, W. R., & Hester, R. K. (1986). The effectiveness of alcoholism treatment: What research reveals. In W. R. Miller & N. Heather (Eds.), *Treating addictive behaviors: Process of change* (pp. 121–174). New York: Plenum Press.

Peele, S. (2004). *Seven tools to beat addiction.* New York: Three Rivers Press.

Searles, J. S. (1991). The genetics of alcoholism: Impact on family and sociological models of addiction. *Family Dynamics of Addiction Quarterly, 1,* 8–21.

Siegel, C., Haugland, G., & Schore, R. (2005). The interface of cultural competency and evidence-based practices. In R. E. Drake, M. R. Merrens, & D. Lynde (Eds.), *Evidence-based mental health practice: A textbook* (pp. 273–299). New York: Norton.

Stanton, M. D., & Todd, T. (1982). *The family therapy of drug abuse and addiction.* New York: Guilford Press.

Sue, S. (2006). Cultural competency: From philosophy to research and practice. *Journal of Community Psychology, 34,* 237–245.

Tarter, R. E., & Schneider, D. V. (1976). Models and theories of alcoholism. In R. E. Tarter & A. A. Sungleman (Eds.), *Alcoholism: Interdisciplinary approaches to an enduring problem* (pp. 202–210). Reading, MA: Addison-Wesley.

Traynor v. Turnage, 485 U.S. 535 (1988).

Vaillant, G. E., & Milofsky, E. S. (1982). The etiology of alcoholism: A prospective viewpoint. *American Psychologist, 37,* 494–503.

Vega, R. R., & Cortes, D. E. (2005). Diverse drug abusing populations. In R. H. Coombs (Ed.), *Addiction counseling review: Preparing for comprehensive, certification and licensing examinations* (pp. 129–147). Mahwah, NJ: Erlbaum.

Vogler, R., & Bartz, W. (1982). *The better way to drink.* Oakland, CA: New Harbinger.

White, W. (2005). Treatment works: Is it time for a new slogan? *Addiction Professional, 3*(1), 22–28.

Wilbourne, P., & Miller, W. (2003). Treatment of alcoholism: Older and wiser? *Alcoholism Treatment Quarterly, 20*(3/4), 41–59.

CHAPTER 2

An Overview of Women, Alcohol, and Their Treatment

Helena Dano Dow

This chapter is a literature review of women and alcoholism. It is clear from this review that the etiology of alcoholism in women differs from that of men, physically, socially, and psychologically. However, alcoholism has traditionally been viewed as a male disorder, and the criteria for diagnosis and treatment have been based on male characteristics. There is thus a need for gender-specific treatment that will better meet the needs of women with alcoholism.

First, the chapter provides some facts about women and alcohol in the United States. A history of female alcoholism, including views from earlier times to the present, is provided. Some of the reasons regarding why women drink are explained, along with the consequences of such drinking. Furthermore, the consequences of female drinking on women's children, as well as the effects of familial alcoholism on women, are explored. Some barriers to treating women with substance abuse problems are described, along with some counseling approaches and techniques designed specifically for their treatment. Finally, some women's organizations and hotlines are provided for further contact and additional information.

Women and Alcohol

It is estimated that of 15.1 million alcohol-abusing and alcohol-dependent individuals in the United States, approximately 4.6 million are women (G. Williams, Grant, Harford, & Noble, 1990). The growing body of research on drinking patterns among women generally shows that women drink less than men (Wilsnack, 1996), exhibit more psychiatric comorbidities (Brady & Randall, 1999), and metabolize alcohol differently than men (Frezza, Di Padova, Pozzato, Terpin, Baroana, & Lieber, 1990). Because of these drinking and metabolic differences, the effects of alcohol on the cognitive and motor abilities in women cannot necessarily be generalized from those observed in men (Sullivan, Fama, Rosenbloom, & Pfefferbaum, 2002). Based on the findings that women drink less than men, drink for a shorter period of time than men, and yet display comparable cognitive deficits, it has been hypothesized that women are especially vulnerable to the toxic effects of alcohol (Glenn, Parsons, Sinha, & Stevens, 1988).

National surveys indicate that alcohol use is more prevalent among men than women in the United States, and that men are much more likely than women to drink in ways that are harmful. In one national survey of 19- to 30-year-olds, 45% of men and 26.7% of women reported heavy drinking (defined in that study as five or more drinks on one occasion) within a 2-week period, and 7.4% of men and 3% of women reported daily drinking (Chen, Dufour, & Yi, 2005). Another survey yielded similar results regarding the greater rate of alcohol consumption among men as compared to women (National Institute on Alcoholism and Alcohol Abuse [NIAAA], 1998). In this survey, 34% of women reported consuming at least 12 standard drinks during a 1-year period as compared with 56% of men. Among drinkers surveyed, 10% of women and 22% of men consumed two or more drinks per day on average. In addition, men were found to be more likely than women to become alcohol dependent (Grant & Arria, 1995).

Women's drinking patterns and alcohol-related problems vary across age groups. Women's drinking is most common between ages 26 and 34 and among women who are divorced or separated. Binge drinking (i.e., consumption of five or more drinks per occasion on 5 or more days in the past month) is most common among women ages 18 to 25 (Su, Larison, & Ghadialy, 1997). Recent research indicates that alcohol and drug use has dramatically increased among college students and women of childbearing age (King, Burt, Malone, McGue, & Iacono, 2005; Mohr et al., 2005).

In a review of the literature, Gomberg (1996) examined drinking problems among alcoholic women categorized as young (in their 20s and 30s), middle-aged (ages 40 to 59), and older (age 60 and over, or age 55 and over, depending on the study). She found that young alcoholic women were more likely than nondrinkers of the same age to be victims of assaults and to have problems with nonprescription drugs, drinking and driving, and other legal problems. Middle-aged alcoholic women were more likely than non-alcoholic women of the same age to use prescribed psychoactive medication. Loss of important life roles, including the loss of a partner due to death, separation, or divorce; job loss; and children leaving home, was found to be associated with problem drinking among middle-aged women. However, it is unclear whether alcohol abuse is a result of the role loss, or the role loss resulted from the alcohol abuse. Wilsnack (1996) stated that more research is needed to explain the association between role loss and alcohol abuse and dependence. According to Gomberg's (1996) review, the literature suggests that although alcohol consumption tends to decrease as age increases, drinking and alcohol problems vary more among older women than within other age groups, and that women may be more likely than men to begin drinking after age 40.

Alcohol problems and drinking patterns among women also vary by ethnicity. Among racial groups, women's drinking is more prevalent among Whites, although African American women are more likely to drink heavily (NIAAA, 1998). Caetano and Kaskutas (1995) concluded that African American women are more likely to abstain from drinking than White women and Latinas. However, African American women suffer more social consequences from drinking than White women, and the incidence of social consequences from drinking among Latinas is almost three times higher than the incidence for White women (Caetano, 1997). An association, according to Caetano, exists between alcohol outlet density and the violent victimization of Latinas. An *outlet* is a place where alcohol may be legally sold for the buyer to drink either there or elsewhere. *Density* refers to the number of alcohol outlets in a given area (Alcoholic Beverage Outlet Density Regulation to Reduce Excessive Alcohol Consumption, 1997). A study done in Cleveland showed that blocks that have more bars have higher crime rates for murder, rape, assault, robbery, burglary, grand theft, and auto theft. Adding one bar to a block would result in 3.38 crimes committed on that block in a year. It would increase the risk of murder taking place on that block by 5%, and other crimes of any type by 17.6% (Runcek & Maier, 1991). Gilbert, Mora, and Ferguson (1994) found that Mexican American women in Los Angeles who obtained professional jobs drank more than those in other types of jobs; however, there was little evidence of alcohol-related problems such as drinking and driving among the women in the study. According to Wilsnack (1996), among Latinas and Asian women, drinking increased as levels of acculturation increased.

A number of studies indicate that among non-White minorities, Native American women of certain tribes drink the most, African American and Latina women are in the middle, and Asian American women drink the least. This includes heavy drinking, which is considered more than five drinks a day at least once a month (NIAAA, 2002).

As with other ethnic groups, Native American women tend to drink less then men and report fewer incidents related to violence and arrests (May, 1989). High rates of abstinence are found among women from tribes where social norms or tribal policies prohibit drinking among women (Wilsnack, 1996).

Among African Americans, a strong commitment to religious values and church participation has been accompanied by a lack of tolerance for consuming alcohol (Herd, 1996). African American women have been found to participate in religious activities to a higher degree than African American men (Taylor, Mattis, & Chatters, 1999).

Compared with Latino men, Latinas show higher rates of abstaining from alcohol and relatively low rates of heavy drinking. The results of a national survey of 4,462 Hispanic Americans of Cuban ($n = 620$), Mexican ($n = 2,467$), Puerto Rican ($n = 619$), and Central and South American ($n = 756$) origin indicated that almost 46% of the Cuban women, 43% of the Mexican American women, and 44% of the Puerto Rican women reported abstaining from alcohol (Nielson, 2000).

The lower rates of alcohol use and problem drinking among Asian American women are connected not only to their cultural norms, but also to a biological factor that affects their ability to metabolize alcohol, which is usually manifested as facial flushing (Chan, 1986). Most Asians possess a gene, inactive aldehyde dehydrogenase (ALDH2-2), which is one of several variants of the gene that produces aldehyde dehydrogenase (ALDH), one of two enzymes involved in alcohol metabolism. This gene causes Asians to metabolize alcohol differently than people who don't have this gene (Cook & Gurling, 2001). However, cultural and social norms have also been found to be significant in determining alcohol consumption among Asian Americans (Nakawatase, Yamamoto, & Sasao, 1993).

The research on drinking patterns among lesbians is very scarce, and the studies that do exist use small samples and are difficult to generalize from. According to Hughes and Wilsnack (1997), the existing literature suggests that lesbians may drink more and have disproportionately more alcohol problems than heterosexual women. In addition, alcohol consumption and related problems may not decrease as much with age among lesbians as among heterosexual women. However, Hughes and Wilsnack caution that the available studies tended to be based on convenience samples of lesbians attending bars and other venues.

History of Female Alcoholism

In 17th- and most of 18th-century America, drinking alcoholic beverages was not considered wrong or dangerous. Men and women both consumed alcohol on many special occasions. It was from 1776 to 1926 that the societal outlook on alcohol consumption changed toward viewing alcohol as a "demon." By the end of the 19th century, to drink and get drunk was identified with the lower class and with immigrants. There was strong support during this time for abstinence, especially among middle- and upper-class Protestants, and particularly among women (Levine, 1980). Women who used alcohol were viewed as being promiscuous, prostitutes, or of a lower status in society. The American Temperance Society, established in 1826, focused on the issue of men's drinking, not women's. With the decline in the temperance movement, the repeal of Prohibition, and the change in the status of women, drinking patterns among women changed (Fillmore, 1984).

Reports from the clinical literature in the 1930s indicate that the number of women admitted to treatment for alcoholism increased among hospitalized samples during that decade. In the 1940s and 1950s, very few articles were written on the subject of female drinking, at least in part because of the firmly established belief that alcoholics were primarily men (Fillmore, 1984). Jellinek's (1947) study developed the first prevalence estimates of female alcoholism. Jellinek reported alcoholism among women, but it was quite infrequent compared to alcoholism among men, with a ratio between 5:1 and 6:1. It is likely that Jellinek significantly underestimated the number of female drinkers, possibly because women were seen as upholders of society's morals (Gomberg, 1976). M. W. Johnson (1965), in his study of doctors, revealed that doctors believed that alcoholic women had loose sexual morals, had more psychosexual conflicts, and were more likely to get into social difficulties than alcoholic men.

It was not until 1970s, however, that alcohol problems among women were recognized as a widespread phenomenon. The Comprehensive Alcohol Abuse and Alcoholism Prevention, Treatment, and Rehabilitation Act of 1976 gave special consideration to treatment and prevention grants related to women. Yet, in the late 1970s and early 1980s, increases in heavy drinking and alcohol abuse among women were not reported. It is difficult to determine the degree to which reported numbers reflect actual numbers as opposed to the tendency to underestimate the problem in women.

Some research indicates that drinking among women has increased since the emergence of the Women's Movement. The passage of the 1976 act was not sufficient to mitigate emerging social and workforce issues. There are more women in the workforce, which increases role expectations related to balancing work and family and may increase stress. These added expectations could increase psychological distress, which in turn might lead to increased drinking among more women. Furthermore, working outside of the home may provide more opportunities and social situations to drink (Cho & Crittenden, 2006).

Views on Contemporary Women's Drinking

Alcoholism in women is still stigmatized in current American culture. Substance use among females is more highly stigmatized than among males (Grella & Joshi, 1999). Women who drink continue to be seen as sexually promiscuous and neglectful of their partners and children (Carter, 1997).

Women continue to suffer greater social and emotional consequences for drinking and continue to experience more discrimination compared with alcoholic men, due to "sex-biased attitudes" (Carter, 1997, p. 473). Carter (p. 472) noted that historically, "alcoholism in women has been linked to the absence of femininity, sexual misconduct, and parental neglect." According to Lex (1994), although lack of control is negatively attributed to men, it is far more stigmatizing for women, who are supposed to be docile, submissive, and responsible, and to "avoid unrestrained behavior" (p. 216). According to Carter, this attitude toward women with alcoholism remains prevalent. Also, Norris (1994) pointed out that myths surrounding female alcoholism and promiscuity place women at increased risk for sexual assault and rape. Women who drink in bars are considered by many college men as being sexually promiscuous, and as a result, targets for sexual aggression (Martin & Hummer, 1989). Women who are under the influence of alcohol are also held more accountable for their actions relative to sexual assault than are men, even in cases where both parties are equally intoxicated. Such situations are less likely to be considered rape (Stormo, Lang, & Stritzke, 1997).

In a study conducted with male and female college students, based on both actual incidents and hypothetical examples, the use of alcohol implied consent in a rape situation and drastically altered attitudes toward both the assailant and the victim, wherein the male was frequently not held responsible for his behavior and the blame was placed solely on the female victim (Norris, 1994).

Men, especially married men, are more likely than women to receive support from families and friends to enter alcohol treatment (Beckman & Amaro, 1986); women, especially those with children, tend to experience more shame than men and worry about losing custody of their children (Brienza & Stein, 2002).

Why Do Women Drink?

Research indicates that women drink for a variety of reasons. Many women drink in response to the multiple losses they experience throughout of their lifetime (Gomberg, 1996). In general, losses include divorce or death of parents; inconsistent, unavailable, or neglectful behavior of parents that is due to their own alcoholism; or a sense of disconnection from themselves and others due to family abuse and violence (Cirillo, 1994). According to Gomberg (1996), women drink mostly in response to divorce, empty nest syndrome, and widowhood. The strong stigma associated with alcoholism in women often leads to feelings of guilt and shame for their "inadequacy to fulfill their roles as wife, mother, and sexual partner" (Beckman, 1994, p. 208).

Many women who have suffered sexual, emotional, or physical abuse may develop posttraumatic stress disorder (PTSD) and use alcohol to self-medicate this disorder. It is estimated that women with PTSD are 1.4 times as likely as other women to develop alcoholism and drug dependency (Dansky, Saladin, Brady, Kilpatrick, & Resnick, 1995). More recently, Gatz et al. (2005) asserted that an individual with PTSD is three times more likely to have a substance abuse problem than are those without PTSD. In some cases, women drink to alleviate tension in anticipation of potential intimate encounters. In many cases, alcohol-abusing women experience sexual dysfunction prior to drinking and are quite ambivalent about sex (Beckman, 1994). Because of the deleterious effects of alcohol on sexual functioning, a woman may continue to drink as a way to cope with increased feelings of inadequacy and begin a downward spiral (Norris, 1994).

Gomberg (1996) identified stress and distress as prevalent factors in the development of women's alcoholism. Childhood sexual abuse has been linked to women's alcoholism (Beckman, 1994). It is estimated that somewhere between 30% and 80% of alcoholic women were victims of incest (Gomberg, 1996). As a result of such experiences, women develop anxiety, depression, poor self-esteem, difficulty trusting others, internalized anger and hostility, and other self-destructive behavior, and they drink to manage negative internal psychological states (Grayson & Nolen-Hoesksema, 2005; Langeland & Hartgers, 1998). Whereas alcohol-abusing women tend to internalize their feelings, alcoholic men more often channel their feelings outward in the form of aggressive behavior (Langeland & Hartgers, 1998; Lex, 1994).

In a study of homeless women in residential alcohol treatment, Sacks, McKendrick, and Banks (2008) reported that of 146 homeless addicted women, "sixty-nine percent of the women reported exposure to childhood physical, sexual or emotional abuse; the majority reported multiple forms of abuse" (p. 90). Eighty-nine percent reported lifetime abuse. They spoke of a lifelong pattern of abuse, trauma, and retraumatization. They also reported disruption in their family background, including parents with mental illness, a low level of education, unemployment, frequent moves, separation, and divorce. The women who reported childhood abuse did not improve as much as the other women in terms of "psychological functioning ($p < .001$), substance abuse ($p < .01$), or continuing trauma exposure ($p < .01$)" (p. 90).

In a hospital-based treatment program with 19 lesbian and 39 heterosexual women, all of the lesbian women reported childhood physical and/or sexual abuse, compared to a little over half of the heterosexual women (Ross & Durkin, 2005). There were also higher rates of depression and borderline personality disorder among the lesbian women. The authors suggested viewing these findings with caution because of the small sample size.

A family history of alcoholism places women at increased risk for becoming alcoholic (Gomberg, 1996). In addition to abuse and neglect, these women learn to deny their own needs and feelings, are hyperresponsible, blame themselves for the problems of others, and lack an outlet for expressing their pain (Finkelstein, 1993). The stress experienced by female children of alcoholics can lead them to self-medicate through drinking (Gomberg, 1996).

Consequences of Alcohol

Chronic alcohol abuse exacts a greater physical toll on women than on men. Although alcohol problems are more common in male trauma patients, women with alcohol problems are just as severely impaired, have at least as many adverse consequences of alcohol use, and have more evidence of alcohol-related physical and psychological harm (Gentilello et al., 2000). Research suggests that women are more vulnerable than men to alcohol-related organ damage, trauma, and legal and interpersonal difficulties.

Cirrhosis and Liver Damage

The risk for developing cirrhosis increases with increasing alcohol consumption for both genders; however, both sets of data support the hypothesis that women are more susceptible to alcohol-induced cirrhosis than are men at each consumption level (Deal & Galaver, 1994). According to a study by Mezey, Kolman, Diehl, Mitchell, and Herlong (1988), women with alcoholic hepatitis and cirrhosis were found to have consumed less alcohol per body weight per day than men. Also, women with alcoholic pancreatitis were found to have shorter drinking histories than men with alcoholic pancreatitis. In a study of trauma center patients, Gentilello et al. (2000) found that women were significantly more likely than men to have liver disease. Mann, Smart, and Govoni (2003) also found that although males have higher rates of cirrhosis mortality than women overall, proportionately more alcohol-dependent females die from cirrhosis than do alcohol-dependent males.

Several reasons have been found for gender differences in alcohol liver disease. One reason has to do with females achieving a higher concentration of alcohol in the blood than men after drinking equivalent amounts of alcohol (Redgrave, Swartz, & Romanoski, 2003). A study of over 13,000 men and women in Europe found that the risk of developing alcohol-related liver disease was significantly higher among women than men, regardless of the alcohol intake (Becker et al., 1996). Further, the level of alcohol dehydrogenase, which is an enzyme associated with alcohol metabolism, may be lower in females than in males (Baraona et al., 2001).

Brain Damage

Women have been found to be more vulnerable than men to alcohol-induced brain damage (Sohrabji, 2003). For example, a study of alcoholic and non-alcoholic men and women's gray and white matter volumes indicated that the women were more significantly affected by alcoholism than the men (Hommer, Momenan, Kaiser, & Rawlings, 2001).

Heart Disease

In an attempt to determine whether women's response to alcohol is different from men's, 50 asymptomatic alcoholic women, 100 asymptomatic alcoholic men, and 50 female nonalcoholic controls were studied. The results indicated that although the mean lifetime dose of alcohol in female alcoholics was only 60% of that in male alcoholics, cardiomyopathy (a degenerative disease of the heart muscle) was as common in female alcoholics as in males. The authors suggested that women may be more susceptible than men to the toxic effects of alcohol on the heart muscle (Urbano, Estruch, Fernandez, Pare, & Rubin, 1995).

Breast Cancer

Alcohol consumption is associated with a linear increase in breast cancer incidence in women over the range of consumption reported by most women. A pooled analysis of several studies conducted over the course of 11 years in Canada, the Netherlands, Sweden, and the United States with a total of 322,647 women, 4,335 of whom had a diagnosis of incident invasive breast cancer, indicated that breast cancer risk was significantly elevated (by 9%) for each 10 grams (approximately one third of a standard 1-ounce alcoholic drink) per day increase in alcohol intake for intakes up to 60 grams (approximately 2.1 ounces) per day (Smith-Warner et al., 1998).

Suicide

Lisansky-Gomberg (1989), in her study of suicide risk among women with alcohol problems, compared 301 alcoholic women ages 20 to 50 with a control group of non-alcoholic women matched for age and socioeconomic status of family of origin. The findings indicated that 40% of alcoholic women attempted to commit suicide, compared to 8.8% of non-alcoholic women, and that younger alcoholic women were twice as likely (50.5%) as older alcoholic women to commit suicide. A study of 313 female suicide deaths occurring in New Mexico between 1990 and 1994 among women between the ages of 14 and 93 indicated that alcohol or drugs were present in 65.5% of the victims at the time of autopsy (L. Olson et al., 1999).

Traffic Accidents

Women are less likely than men to be involved in fatal alcohol-related traffic accidents. However, from 1977 to 1997, the number of male drivers involved in alcohol-related fatal traffic accidents decreased 31%, while the number of females drivers involved in alcohol-related fatal accidents increased 12% (Yi, Stinson, Williams, & Bertolucci, 1999).

Criminal Behavior

An estimated 4 in 10 women who committed violence were perceived by the victim as being under the influence of alcohol or drugs at the time of the crime. An estimated 25% of women on probation, 29% of women in local jails, 29% of women in state prisons, and 15% of women in federal prisons were under the influence of alcohol at the time of the offense (Greenfield & Snell, 1999). Gomberg (1990) compared problem-drinking females (n = 30) with a control group with no drinking problems (n = 137) matched by age. About 50% of the problem-drinking group reported throwing things or hitting their partners. This group was also more likely than the control group to report losing their tempers after drinking. There was a difference found in age, with the 20- to 29-year-olds being more likely to report physical violence.

Finally, a meta-analysis by Bushman and Cooper (1990) of 30 laboratory-based studies addressed the question of whether women are more aggressive toward men or toward other women. They noted that the sex of the target did influence alcohol-related aggression. When intoxicated, both men and women behaved more aggressively toward a female target.

Fetal Alcohol Syndrome

Fetal alcohol syndrome (FAS) in the United States is estimated to occur in 0.5 to 2 cases per 1,000 live births (Centers for Disease Control and Prevention, 2002). Rates of FAS are more widespread among high-risk populations, such as Southwestern Plains Indians living on reservations, whose rate is reported to be 9.8 per 1,000 live births (May & Gossage, 2001). Research has shown that even small levels of alcohol consumed during pregnancy may affect the fetus in damaging ways. In pregnant women, alcohol is not only carried to all organs and tissues of the fetus, but also carried to the placenta, where it easily crosses through the membrane separating maternal and fetal blood systems. In this way, alcohol is transported directly to the fetus and to all its developing tissues and organs. The liver of the fetus cannot process alcohol at the same rate as the adult liver. High concentrations of alcohol stay in the fetus longer, often for up to 24 hours; in fact, the unborn baby's blood alcohol concentration is even higher than the mother's during the second and third hour after a drink is consumed. Children born with FAS have abnormalities in three specific areas: growth, central nervous system, and facial characteristics. The first trimester of pregnancy appears to be the most critical time for potential damage to the fetus. Alcohol may affect the way cells grow and arrange themselves as they multiply. The brain is particularly sensitive to alcohol, which diminishes the number of cells growing in the brain. As a result, the brain is smaller and often its neurons are found in the wrong places, which explains the overall retarded growth and low birthweight in babies with FAS. During the second trimester, miscarriage is a major risk. During the third trimester, alcohol can impair the normal rapid and substantial growth of the fetus (Streissguth, 1997).

Research also indicates that prenatal exposure to alcohol increases the risk for disorders such as depression and negative self-cognitions in offspring (H. C. Olson et al., 2001). Exposure to alcohol by a fetus may also result in long-term neurocognitive disorders, such as problems with executive functions (e.g., poor organizational skills, difficulties in impulse control, and poor decision-making skills), as well as mental disorders and maladaptive behaviors that make it difficult for these individuals to be self-sufficient and independent (Streissguth & O'Malley, 2000). May et al. (2005) reported risk factors associated with FAS, including heavy periodic drinking that results in high blood-alcohol concentration, smoking, and the use of other drugs. They found higher rates of FAS among Black women, Native American women, women from low socioeconomic status groups, and women with alcoholic male partners.

The Effects of Alcoholism on Female Sexual Functioning

The illness of alcoholism and drug addiction makes the loss of sexual intimacy inevitable. As communication in general breaks down, sexual communication and sexual activity suffer as well. As alcoholism or drug addiction progresses, loving expressions of warmth and tenderness tend to decrease. At the same time, resentment increases dramatically. As a result, alcohol and drug addiction usually results not only in physical, mental, emotional, and spiritual alienation, but also in sexual alienation (Marlin, 1990). In addition, women alcoholics tend to experience high levels of guilt, low self-esteem, and a general loss of a sense of power in their lives. All of these factors psychologically inhibit alcoholic women from enjoying their sexuality (McIntyre & Livingston, 1983).

In the early stage of alcoholism, alcohol depresses the control centers of the brain, which may increase a woman's sexual desire and create more ease in initiating sexual experiences. Alcohol also dilates the blood vessels and can enhance one's sense of sexual well-being, warmth, and sexual adequacy (Livingston & McIntyre, 1984). During the middle stage of alcoholism, other sexual changes are likely to develop. Sexual desire may diminish due to a decrease in testosterone, an important hormone that mediates sexual desire and functioning. Also, the woman in the middle stage of alcoholism is likely to notice reduced lubrication, and her capacity to experience orgasm is impaired. Alcoholic women reported that they can be sexual but that no matter what they do or try, it is difficult or impossible to reach orgasm. In the late stage of alcoholism, major physiological changes have occurred within the woman's body. She may notice that her menstrual cycle is irregular and unpredictable. If there is severe liver damage, the liver metabolizes less estrogen, which may result in the total cessation of ovulation and menstruation. In addition, the vaginal walls may atrophy or shrink, resulting in very little lubrication (McIntyre & Livingston, 1983).

Over time, the psychological effects of alcohol disrupt the sexual response cycle and lead to sexual dysfunction. This dysfunction typically develops throughout the middle and late stages of alcoholism, although in many cases the problems are not apparent until after the alcoholic has stopped drinking and is in recovery. The dysfunctions that are most commonly found in alcoholic women are inhibited desire, orgasmic dysfunction, dyspareunia, and vaginismus (McIntyre & Livingston, 1983). According to the *Diagnostic and Statistical Manual of Mental Disorders–Fourth Edition, Text Revision* (American Psychiatric Association, 2000), *dyspareunia* is recurrent genital pain caused by sexual activity. *Vaginismus* is a conditioned pain caused by involuntary spasm of the muscles around the lower third of the vagina, resulting from the association of sexual activity with pain and fear.

Violent Victimization

Women's alcohol use is associated with violent victimization of women and girls (Brienza & Stein, 2002). Research indicates that there is a relationship between childhood physical and sexual abuse and later alcohol problems in the general population. Some of the evidence suggesting such a relationship comes from studies of women with histories of childhood sexual abuse attending treatment for mental health problems. These studies have generally indicated higher rates of alcohol abuse in women with a history of childhood sexual abuse (Pribor & Dinwiddie, 1992; Swett & Halpert, 1994). Two studies conducted in early 1980s, one by Covington (1982) and the other one by Schaeffer, Evans, and Sterne (1985), showed that women with alcohol and substance abuse problems were more likely to have been abused. Within the group of women who had been abused, the histories were different. In the women who reported histories of abuse occurring earlier in life, at age 5 years or younger, the abuse was more frequent and continued for a longer period of time. Covington also found that the abuse in these younger girls was more violent and was carried out by more than one person.

Wilsnack, Vogeltanz, Klassen, and Harris (1997) interviewed 1,099 women as part of a national survey to examine the relationship between childhood sexual abuse of women and their use of alcohol. The results indicated that women who had been sexually abused as children were significantly more likely than non-abused women to report intoxication, alcohol dependence symptoms, and problem consequences of drinking during the 12 months prior to the study. That research corroborates studies of clinical populations. For example, earlier work by B. A. Miller, Downs, and Testa (1993) indicated that of 148 women studied, 47% in treatment for alcoholism and 44% of women with alcohol problems in treatment for issues other than alcoholism had experienced severe childhood sexual abuse. The same study uncovered a childhood history of severe paternal violence in 45% of women in alcoholism treatment and in 40% of women with alcohol problems in treatment for issues other than alcoholism, as compared with 13% of women in a random household sample. A study conducted by B. A. Miller and Downs (1993) explored the impact of family violence on the use of alcohol by women. According to this study, women with alcohol problems reported experiencing higher rates of family violence as children, including more severe violence by the father and more childhood sexual abuse, as well as significantly higher levels of violence by partners, than did women without alcohol problems. Similarly, Clark and Foy (2000) studied the relationship between battering severity and alcohol use among battered women. In a sample of 78 battered women, three forms of trauma exposure—childhood physical abuse, childhood sexual abuse, and domestic violence—were examined in relation to alcohol use. Both battering severity and childhood sexual abuse were positively correlated with alcohol use. Multiple regression analysis showed that childhood sexual abuse was the stronger predictor when colinearity was controlled.

The relationship between alcohol use and adult women's violent victimization is complex. Leonard (1993) suggested a relationship between alcohol and partner abuse. According to Cantor (1993), alcoholic women have been found to be significantly more likely to have experienced negative verbal conflict with spouses than non-alcoholic women. They have also been found to be significantly more likely to have experienced a range of moderate and severe physical violence. Kaufman Kantor and Strauss (1987) found that husbands who binge drink are three times more likely to abuse their wives than are husbands who abstain. According to a U.S. Department of Justice study, two thirds of partner abuse victims (those abused by a current or former spouse, boyfriend, or girlfriend) reported that alcohol has been a factor in the abuse; the offender was drinking in three out of four cases; and about half of alcohol-related violent incidents reported to police involved current or former spouses, boyfriends, or girlfriends of the offenders (Greenfield, 1998). In their review of about 25 studies, Hamilton and Collins (1981) found alcohol to be most relevant to wife beating, where it was present in one quarter to half of all such events. The most common pattern was for only the husband to be drinking or for both parties to have consumed alcohol; it was uncommon for only the wife to have been drinking.

B. A. Miller and Downs (1993) also found that women with alcohol problems were more likely than women without alcohol problems to have been assaulted by an intimate partner. Also, women who were intoxicated at the time of the assault were more likely to have had consensual sex before the assault than women who were sober (Davis, George, & Norris, 2004). Kaufman Kantor and Asdigian (1997) found that husbands were more likely to assault their wives when both spouses were heavy drinkers. Ullman (2003) reported that half of all acquaintance-related sexual assaults involved drinking by the victims. Women's drinking also increased their chances of being assaulted (Testa, Livingston, & Collins, 2000). According to Lammers, Schippers, and van der Staak (1995), women with drinking problems may enter into traumatic and violent relationships or may use alcohol to deal with a relationship in which they feel powerless.

Use of alcohol and illicit drugs by a male spouse or boyfriend increases the likelihood of his sexual aggression. Alcohol and drug use may facilitate miscommunication and resentment and reduce the ability to take into account the consequences of aggressive actions. Furthermore, men are more likely than women to associate alcohol use with a decreased ability to manage anger and with increased feelings of superiority over others. For several reasons, women who use illicit drugs or alcohol are at higher risk of experiencing sexual abuse. An intoxicated woman may be less able to defend herself against an assault and may be more likely to become aggressive herself, leading her partner to respond with physical aggression (Fernaughty, Farris, & Bruce, 2001).

In a review of the literature, B. A. Miller (1996) found that the relationship between women's alcohol use and their violent victimization may be bidirectional: Sometimes alcohol use comes first, and sometimes violent victimization comes first. Several studies in this review indicated that women with alcohol problems had suffered criminal victimization before they started drinking. However, B. A. Miller also found research regarding women who had been drinking at the time that they were victimized, especially in the case of sexual assault. These findings may be complicated by the context in which the alcohol use and violent incidents occur. For example, other lifestyle factors may lead to both problem drinking and violent victimization, in which case there would not be a causal link between drinking and victimization in either direction. Kaufman Kantor and Asdigian (1997) addressed the relationship between victims' and perpetrators' alcohol use. They found that although husbands were more than twice as likely as wives to have been drinking at the time of a violent assault, alcohol-related wife assaults were more likely when both partners were heavy drinkers. They advanced several theories regarding the relationship between alcohol and spousal abuse, including the idea that when men experience the alcohol-related physical sensations of arousal, such as increased heartbeat, they may be more likely than women to "misattribute" such feelings as increased aggression and dominance, which may in turn lead to violence. Like B. A. Miller, Kaufman Kantor and Asdigian (1997) concluded that more research is needed to clarify the nature of the association between women's alcohol use and their violent victimization.

Alcohol and Domestic Violence

A number of theories have addressed the link between partner abuse and alcohol. According to disinhibition theory, alcohol interferes with the brain's normal tendency to suppress violent behavior (Bushman, 1997). This means that when the brain functions normally, aggressive behavior is inhibited, or blocked. Alcohol may "disinhibit" or remove the block against aggressive behavior. Another theory holds that drinking behavior may be influenced by an individual's beliefs about alcohol-related effects on the self and others—such as a belief in disinhibition theory. With such a belief system, a partner abuse episode may be excused when the batterer is drunk (Gelles, 1987).

Additional research indicates that beliefs about alcohol's effects are quite complex. A national survey by Kaufman Kantor and Asdigian (1997) indicated that people hold a range of beliefs about alcohol. The researchers spoke with both men and women who had assaulted their partners. In this study, women were less likely than men to have perpetrated partner abuse. Male perpetrators were significantly more likely than female perpetrators to subscribe to the belief that alcohol use leads to losing one's temper and behaving impulsively. The study also supported the theory that when men experience alcohol-related physical sensations of arousal such as increased heart rate, they may misinterpret such feelings as increased aggression or dominance. Women are less likely to make such a connection, possibly because of socialization. Notably, Stets and Strauss (1990) found that men underreport perpetrating partner abuse, and female domestic violence victims tend to sustain more severe injuries than male victims.

According to Bushman's (1997) meta-analysis, the indirect cause model offers an alternative explanation of the relationship between alcohol and violence. According to this model, alcohol consumption has a psychopharmacological effect on behavior. It causes psychological, emotional, and cognitive changes that may lead to aggressive behavior such as partner abuse.

Effects of Maternal Drinking on Children

In studying the differences between the effects of alcoholic mothers and fathers on their children, Fox (1962) suggested that an alcoholic mother is more damaging to children than an alcoholic father because of her impairment as a nurturer and caregiver and her overdependency upon her children for her self-esteem as she withdraws from the outside world to hide her drinking. Seixas (1977) later came to a similar conclusion. According to these two researchers, alcoholic mothers caused more damage than alcoholic fathers because the children's maturation and development through Eriksonian stages of growth were hindered by the mothers' neuroticism and lack of ego development. The children of these mothers learn to expect unreliability, inconsistency, ineptitude, and general disorganization, and as a result develop denial, lack of trust, emotional withdrawal, and lack of respect for authority. On several scales measuring maternal attitudes, Krauthamer (1979) found that alcoholic mothers displayed significantly more ambivalent, confused, and inconsistent attitudes toward their children than did nonalcoholic mothers, regardless of social class. Krauthamer concluded that these behaviors were more the result of the drinking than of underlying personality disorders and could be reversed with cessation of excessive alcohol use. Krauthamer also reported that children of alcoholic mothers were more distrustful, rigid, reserved, submissive, dependent, and emotionally distant than control children.

More recent studies have confirmed the adverse consequences that maternal drinking has on children. For example, Conners et al. (2003) examined the life circumstances and experiences of 4,084 children affected by maternal addiction to alcohol or other drugs. They collected the data from mothers at intake into 50 publicly funded residential substance abuse treatment programs and concluded that children whose mothers abuse alcohol or other drugs are at increased risk for physical, academic, and socioemotional problems. Studies of adolescents raised by alcoholic mothers have yielded similar findings. For example, Ohannessian et al. (2004) found that the adolescent's avoidance of the mother when she was drinking or using drugs, as well as maternal anger during drinking or drug-using episodes, was significantly associated with adolescent alcohol dependence, conduct disorder, and major depressive disorder. In contrast, adolescent avoidance of the father and paternal anger during drinking or drug-using episodes was not related to any of these adolescent diagnoses, suggesting that maternal, and not paternal, substance use may be more closely linked to psychological problems in adolescents. In addition, more children and adolescents with heavy prenatal alcohol exposure, but without FAS, were reported to meet criteria for conduct disorder. They were also reported to be at a lower developmental level with respect to their moral reasoning about their affiliation with others and at higher risk for delinquency (Schonfeld, 2003).

The Effect of Familial Alcoholism on Women

Research indicates that women are greatly affected by familial alcoholism (Prescott, Neale, Corey, & Kendler, 1997). Of the estimated 28 million American adults who are children of alcoholics, slightly more than half are female (Lex, 1991). The estimated prevalence of alcoholism in female adult children of alcoholics is 5% to 10%, compared with a prevalence in the general female population of 0.1% to 1.0% (Goodwin, 1991).

Searles (1988) attributes high rates of alcoholism found in adult children of alcoholics to both environmental and genetic vulnerability, as well as disturbed family interaction patterns caused by drinking or other psychopathology. Parental alcoholism is environmentally transmitted to children. For example, children model parental use of alcoholism as a coping mechanism. Women are more likely to report alcoholic parents and alcoholic relatives. Maternal alcoholism increases the risk of alcohol dependence in female offspring, so female adult children of alcoholics may be more affected by parental alcoholism if their mothers were alcoholic (Lex, 1991). A number of researchers have concluded that early exposure to familial alcoholism places individuals at greater risk of alcoholism, substance abuse, and related problems than those who were not so exposed (Goodwin, 1991; Prescott et al., 1997; Windle, 1996).

Corrigan (1980) found that female alcoholics are more likely than other women to have grown up in unstable family environments, with greater disruption occurring as a result of separation and divorce, economic distress, abuse or neglect, or placement of the child outside of the home. In general, the quality of child care experienced by these women was poor, discipline was erratic or lax, and the demands on the child were inappropriately low or high.

In a study of alcoholic women in treatment done by Kinsey (1966), the women described their mothers as difficult to please, strict, dominant, and emotionally distant, while the fathers were remembered as warmer, but weaker. In a study by Jones (1971), mothers of both boys and girls who later became adult alcoholics were viewed as sour, disagreeable, and dissatisfied. The girls described high levels of family conflict and excessive dependence on their families during adolescence.

Similar conclusions were reached in a study done by Zucker and Devoe (1975) in which problem-drinking adolescents described their parents as unconcerned, neglectful, and arbitrary in discipline. Girls, however, reported greater distress over lack of affection and nurturance from their parents than did boys.

In a literature review about alcohol and drug abuse among female adolescents, Waite-O'Brien (1992) stated that "girls are more likely to drink if their relations with their parents are unsupportive, alienated, or hostile" (p. 371). She also distinguished between boys' and girls' drinking: "When there is tension at home, boys are likely to drink in ways that are rebellious and acting out," whereas girls "tend to drink to get drunk" (p. 371). Other studies have shown that mothers' drinking contributes to their daughters' delinquent behaviors. Widseth and Mayer (1971) reported that delinquent adolescent girls who were excessive drinkers generally had drinking mothers, while abstainers had abstinent mothers. No association with the father's drinking patterns was found.

Furthermore, delinquent daughters of problem-drinking mothers were also much more rejecting of them and ran away more frequently than daughters of problem-drinking fathers.

In a 20-year longitudinal study involving a subsample of families with one or two alcohol-abusing parents, D. Miller and Jang (1977) found that sons were heavier drinkers than daughters, irrespective of which parent was alcoholic, but the daughters were heavier drinkers if the mother was an alcoholic.

C. Williams and Klerman (1984) concluded that the early family life of problem-drinking adolescents and of women who later become alcoholic was characterized by impaired parent–child relationships and separations, neglect, erratic discipline, and poor parenting. According to Williams and Klerman, female alcoholics' experiences in their families of origin may be re-created in their families of procreation, continuing the cycle of familial disruption and alcoholism into the next generation.

These findings are supported by a number of studies showing that alcoholic women have a higher prevalence of husbands with drinking problems than do women in general, and their husbands may play an important role in the maintenance of their problem drinking by drinking with them (Corrigan, 1980). Similarly, Rimmer and Winokur (1972) concluded that alcoholics and problem drinkers look for those who have family backgrounds and drinking patterns similar to their own.

Barriers to Treatment for Alcoholic Women

Several obstacles to the treatment of alcoholic women are related to myths, stereotypical thinking, and stigmatization associated with women who abuse alcohol. One of these myths is that women are intrinsically more difficult to treat (Copeland & Hall, 1992). However, several studies indicate that treatment that addresses concerns specific to women is still relatively rare. According to Walitzer and Connors (1997), alcohol treatment has traditionally been male oriented. Collins (1993) noted that this orientation applies to types of services provided as well as to the availability of inpatient facilities and treatment groups. Treatment approaches have thus typically neglected issues that are specific to women with alcohol problems, which in turn has negatively affected treatment outcomes.

Another barrier to treatment for women who abuse alcohol is the stigma attached to them. In reaction to this stigma, women are less likely to access agencies that are seen to be alcohol identified (Hingson, Scotch, & Culbert, 1980). Furthermore, they are more likely to experience friends or relatives being obstructive rather than supportive of their accessing treatment (Beckman & Amaro, 1986). Some of these women experience shame and guilt, which prevents them from seeking treatment, while others deny they have a drinking problem, sometimes focusing on physical symptoms that they attempt to address in other settings (Beckman, 1994). Therefore, they either delay seeking help regarding their alcoholism or seek help from physicians or mental health services that do not offer alcohol treatment services. Diagnosis and treatment of alcoholism are further impeded by the fact that many doctors and counselors are less effective in diagnosing women than they are in diagnosing men (Beckman, 1994). Blume (1997) noted that the less the alcoholic woman resembles the mythical "sexually immoral woman," the less likely it is for her to be correctly diagnosed.

There has been increasing concern regarding alcoholic elderly women and their reluctance to seek treatment. Brennan, Moos, and Kim (1993) reported that, like women in the younger age groups, they do not refer themselves to alcohol-identified treatment agencies. The younger women, particularly those with families, however, may well be in contact with health services for other family members if not for themselves, whereas older women may remain unaffiliated and therefore untreated for longer (Dunham, 1986).

Obligations to children, family, and work may also keep women from seeking treatment, a source of pressure that did not affect male alcoholics seeking treatment or remaining in a treatment facility (Blume, 1997; Hanke & Faupel, 1993). Many women who abuse alcohol have no alternative care for their children and often drop out of treatment when there is a problem with their children. They are also afraid that they will be considered to be unfit parents, and their children will be taken away. Some laws define parental alcohol abuse as child abuse and neglect (Blume, 1997).

Laws related to substance abuse and pregnancy can also be a barrier to treatment. Some state laws include criminal consequences for women who are abusing drugs or alcohol during pregnancy. Attorneys representing pregnant and parenting women have reported that at least 200 women in more than 30 states have been arrested and criminally charged for drug use during pregnancy (Paltrow, 1998).

Economic concerns are another barrier to treatment. Addicted women are often poor, unemployed, lacking in employable job skills, single, divorced, or separated, and isolated from social support systems (Finnegan, 1991). Although both men and women are affected by the lack of insurance coverage for alcohol treatment, women are more likely than men to be underemployed and therefore underinsured (Blume, 1997).

Studies indicate that the spouses and cohabitating partners of alcoholic women significantly affect their drinking habits as well as their treatment outcomes. Lewis, Haller, Branch, and Ingersoll (1996) found that partner opposition is one major barrier to women entering treatment and involving those partners in treatment. On the other hand, partner involvement in treatment is associated with more positive treatment outcomes for both alcoholic women and men (Berger, 1981).

Furthermore, partner and relationship issues have been found to precipitate relapse for women in recovery (Connors, Maisto, & Zywiak, 1998). Thundal and Allebeck (1998) reported that poor communication with a spouse was strongly associated with alcohol dependence and abuse for Swedish women. Jennison and Johnson (1997) found that good spousal communication mitigated expected adverse drinking outcomes in adult women of alcoholic parents. Collins (1993) reported that another significant barrier to treatment for alcoholic women is that the majority of participants in support group settings are male, and discussion tends to focus on issues and situations that often do not relate to the issues women consider important. For example, women were found to place greater importance on their family and couple relationships and to be more likely than men to state marital instability and family problems as reasons both for problem drinking and for seeking treatment (C. Williams & Klerman, 1984). In addition, many women who abuse alcohol have had a history of sexual and physical abuse that can prevent them from seeking treatment unless the program provides opportunities for women to work through psychological sequelae in a safe, gender-sensitive environment (Copeland & Hall, 1992).

Gender-Specific Treatment

Historically, alcoholism has been seen as a male disorder, and criteria for diagnosis and treatment were based on male characteristics (Vannicelli, 1984). Although this area needs to be further researched, the available literature confirms that gender-specific treatment is most effective; the etiology of alcoholism in women, whether physical, social, or psychological in nature, differs from that in men (Walitzer & Connors, 1997).

Dahlgren and Willander (1989) compared Swedish women in a gender-specific treatment program to a control group of women in a traditional mixed-gender program. They found that women in the gender-specific program stayed in the program an average of 8 months, whereas the ones in the traditional program stayed an average of 5 months. Thirty-five percent of the women in the gender-specific program reported improved relationships with their children, compared with 12% of the control group. The women in the gender-specific program also had fewer deaths, less alcohol consumption, less need for inpatient care due to relapse, higher job stability, and greater maintenance of child custody.

In mixed-gender treatment programs, men and men's issues tend to dominate discussions (Hodgins, El-Guebaly, & Addington, 1997). Thus there is a need for women-only groups where women can discuss issues that they would not be able to touch on in mixed-gender groups. This does not mean that the treatment used for men cannot be used for women; programs for women should address their specific needs (Hanna, Hanna, Giordano, & Tollerud, 1998).

The fact that a family history of alcoholism significantly affects women's drinking suggests the importance of using family-oriented approaches in the treatment of alcoholic females. Early on, the family was recognized as the place through which alcohol addiction could be transmitted across generations. This view was clearly expressed by MacNish (1835), who stated, "Drunkenness appears to be in some measure hereditary. We frequently see it descending from parents to their children. This may undoubtedly often arise from bad example and imitation, but there can be little question that, in many instances, it exists as a family predisposition" (p. 61). According to Cotton (1979), women with a first-degree relative with alcoholism are two to four times more likely to abuse alcohol.

Until about 12 years ago, however, very few drug treatment programs and fewer alcohol treatment programs involved spouses or other family members in the treatment of the identified patient, according to Lawson (1994). She identified a number of dynamics responsible for this reluctance to utilize family therapy in the treatment of alcohol abuse: Alcohol counselors may not have training in family therapy approaches; they may believe that family therapy is opposed to Alcoholics Anonymous (AA); they may see it as incompatible with the disease concept of alcoholism; they may be unsupported by their employers in their efforts to use family therapy; and the family may be unavailable or unwilling to participate.

Stanton (1997) found that family therapy approaches have an average retention rate of 66%, which is nearly twice that of individually focused treatment. Furthermore, longer lasting recovery is more probable when partners are involved (Zweben & Pearlman, 1983). In a study of 48 women who remained in treatment for 5 months, Zlotnick, Franchino, St. Claire, Cox, and St. John (1996) found that significantly more women who received family therapy services as part of outpatient treatment remained abstinent than did those who did not receive family therapy. The usage of this approach was found to improve communication, employment, and parenting, even if the alcoholic was not totally abstinent.

Trepper, McCollum, Dankoski, Davis, and LaFazia (2000) presented a model as an adjunct treatment for women in intensive outpatient drug and alcohol treatment. It integrates several family therapy models to focus on both current patterns of couple interaction and the multigenerational legacy of these patterns. The model is delivered in two formats: Systemic Couple Therapy (SCT) and Systemic Individual Therapy (SIT) (Wetchler, Nelson, McCollum, Trepper, & Lewis, 1994). SCT is conducted with both partners attending sessions with the therapist. In SIT, the focus remains on couple interaction, but only the woman attends sessions. The same underlying theoretical model informs both formats. The model uses structural and strategic family therapy concepts to define and understand current dysfunctional couple relationship patterns, with a particular focus on the patterns surrounding drug use. Elements of Bowen Family Systems Theory are also used to understand the roots of these patterns in past generations and especially in the families that the two partners grew up in. "The only definite statement the chemical dependency field can make is that chemical dependency and other addictions run in families, generation after generation, and more in some families than others" (Lawson & Lawson, 1998, p. 73). By understanding the present in light of the past, both partners are able to see the problems they are experiencing not simply as personal failures, but also as reflections of what each partner learned in his or her family of origin.

A pilot study showed that this model adds two important dimensions to alcohol treatment. First, it addresses family issues that the agency wishes to include as part of the regular treatment but has been unable to include because of time constraints. Second, agency staff involved in the study observed significant benefits from the focus on family issues. The advantages of using this model were also indicated by the number of women in treatment who benefited from it. Over two thirds of the women (71%) reported an increase in satisfaction with their relationship as measured by the Marital Satisfaction Scale (Roach, Frazier, & Bowden, 1981). On the Emotional Cut-Off Scale (McCollum, 1991), 63% of the women showed an improvement (lower score) in their relationships with their families of origin. The women who completed the treatment program improved not only on relationship factors but also in their individual symptomatology (Trepper et al., 2000).

In a study of married or cohabitating women drug abusers, women were randomly assigned to a behavioral couples therapy treatment that consisted of group, individual, and behavioral couples therapy, or to an intensive individual treatment that consisted of group and individual counseling (Winters, O'Farrell, Fals-Stewart, Birchler, & Kelley,

2002). The behavioral couples therapy group had fewer days of substance use; longer periods of abstinence; lower levels of alcohol, drug, and family problems; and higher satisfaction in their relationships. However, at the end of 1 year posttreatment, there were no significant differences between groups in relational satisfaction or number of days of substance use.

Behavioral Marital Therapy (BMT) has proven to be successful in helping couples with an alcoholic spouse. This therapy combines a focus on the drinking with work on more general marital relationship issues. BMT uses two alcohol-focused methods: (a) a behavioral contract between alcoholic and spouse to maintain Antabuse ingestion and (b) alcohol-focused spouse intervention that consists of rearranging reinforcement contingencies in the family to decrease family member behaviors that trigger or enable drinking and to increase positive reinforcement for sobriety (O'Farrell, Cutter, Choquette, Floyd, & Bayog, 1992).

Alcohol Behavioral Couple Therapy (ABCT), as presented by Epstein and McCrady (2002), consists of intervening at multiple levels: with the drinking individual, with the individual's partner, with the relationship as a unit, with the family, and with the other social systems in which the individual is involved. At the individual level, treatment helps the client identify individual psychological problems associated with drinking, reinforcers for increased and decreased drinking, negative consequences of drinking, and beliefs and expectations about drinking and its consequences. The second set of interventions revolves around helping the partner learn a variety of coping skills to deal with drinking and abstinence. Alcohol-focused couple interventions, the third set of interventions, focus on the interactions between partners around alcohol and other issues, as well as their communication and problem-solving skills. The treatment also incorporates general reciprocity enhancement interventions to increase the overall reward value of the relationship. The fourth set of interventions focuses on other social systems in which the drinking individual and the partner are involved. Clients are helped to identify situations and persons associated with heavy drinking, as well as social situations that would be supportive of abstinence or decreased drinking. Some clients are encouraged to attend AA or other programs, such as Self-Management and Recovery Training (SMART; Epstein & McCrady, 2002).

SCT is a brief, couple-focused therapy model designed to treat female substance users (Wetchler et al., 1994). Based on family systems concepts utilizing aspects of structural, strategic, and transgenerational family therapies, it is used in conjunction with an individual substance abuse treatment program (Wetchler et al., 1994).

SCT has 12 sessions and is conceptualized in three stages: (a) creating a context for change, (b) challenging behaviors and expanding alternatives, and (c) consolidating change. Stage 1 is concerned with joining with the substance-abusing woman and her partner. As explained in the section on barriers to treatment, women in many cases do not seek treatment because of the stigma they face, as well as other barriers. Therefore, joining with them is very important. Assessment is also a component of the first stage and incorporates several other parts: (a) problem definition, which is concerned with the couple's view of the problem; (b) individual assessment (mental status exam), which helps therapists to be aware of any dual-diagnosis issues that may impact treatment; (c) identification of interpersonal sequences surrounding substance abuse, which is concerned with pinpointing interactions and behaviors that occur before and after the drug-abusing behavior; and (d) multigenerational family system assessment, which examines transgenerational patterns that maintain the substance abuse (Wetchler et al., 1994).

The second stage, challenging behaviors and expanding alternatives, aims at changing unhealthy couple behaviors surrounding the drug use and assists them in building problem-solving and communication skills. The main aspects of this stage are as follows:

(a) *conducting couple negotiation*, which is the cornerstone of SCT and which assists the couple to negotiate in spite of high levels of marital conflict,
(b) *altering dysfunctional couple sequences*, which involves identifying a problem-maintaining sequence and finding a way to alter it, developing a homework assignment for the couple to do outside the session, assisting each partner to focus on how to alter his or her own behavior versus that of his or her partner, and changing the sequence of substance abuse as early in the pattern as possible, and
(c) *neutralizing family-of-origin themes and patterns*, which includes three main interventions: discussion of similar patterns between the couple and each partner's family of origin, discussion of transgenerational information to facilitate a stuck negotiation process, and efforts to have the couple respond differently with their families of origin (Wetchler et al., 1994).

The third and final stage of SCT, consolidation, focuses on consolidating the changes the couple has made and also helping them develop a clear understanding about what they have accomplished. The couple is helped to see what they have achieved, to recognize that they have control over their lives, and to realize that they have the tools to resolve similar problems in the future (Wetchler et al., 1994).

AA has been shown to be an important tool and a healing place for many women struggling with alcoholism, in spite of the debate regarding AA's concept of powerlessness. For example, according to Rhodes and Johnson (1994), admitting powerlessness is not helpful for women in a patriarchal society, in which they have experienced continuous oppression and powerlessness. Adding another admission of powerlessness, according to this view, is not helpful (Kasl, 1992), especially in the context of a program where individuals seek empowerment and transformation (Herndon, 2001).

However, according to other authors, such as Bateson (1972), AA's concept of powerlessness constitutes a paradoxical metaphor in that "the experience of defeat not only serves to convince the alcoholic that change is necessary; it is the first step in that change ... to be defeated by the bottle and to know it is the first 'spiritual' experience" (p. 313). It is through this metaphor of powerlessness as connectedness that group and personal narratives transform from a competitive stance into a complementary relationship with people who have similar struggles with addiction (van Wormer & Davis, 2003). Riessman (1985) referred to this reauthoring experience as "self-help-induced empowerment." It is important to understand this alternate view of powerlessness to avoid oversimplifying and misinterpreting AA language in terms of oppression, discrimination, and victimization instead of perceiving it as a language of transformation (van Wormer & Davis, 2003).

Matheson and McCollum (2008) found that the idea of powerlessness appears to be most helpful for those women who say that they hit "rock bottom" before entering recovery. This means they felt their addiction was so severe that they were unable to function any longer without stopping their drug or alcohol use. For these women, the idea of powerlessness was often very real to them while they were actively using, and it was not difficult to embrace once they decided to quit. The concept of powerlessness is now associated with feelings of relief and calmness. However, for women who felt their lives were successful except for a few areas where drugs and alcohol were problematic, the concept of powerlessness was more difficult to accept. These are women who may not have felt they had "hit bottom" but for whom their addiction was having a significantly negative impact only on certain areas of their life. These women found it difficult to initially understand the notion of powerlessness unless they only focused on the areas of their lives where they felt drugs and alcohol were a significant problem.

Family Involvement

In a review of couple and family interventions for use with alcohol abusers and alcoholics, O'Farrell et al. (1992) identified three general stages of recovery: (a) the initial commitment to change (recognizing that the problem exists), (b) the change itself (stopping abusive drinking), and (c) the long-term maintenance of change. O'Farrell et al. also noted that interventions directed toward helping the non-alcoholic partner to change have proven useful in motivating the alcoholic to seek help.

Research indicates that the interventions directed toward the non-alcoholic spouse and other non-alcoholic family members have proven useful in motivating the alcoholic to seek help. Sisson and Azrin (1986) investigated the effect of family members' involvement in a reinforcement program. The involvement of non-alcoholic family members in this program, designed to teach interactionally based behavioral contingency skills for coping with the alcoholic, resulted in significantly more alcoholics entering treatment than a did a more traditional program for family members that consisted of family education, individually oriented supportive counseling, and referral to Al-Anon. This approach does not use confrontation. Rather, the spouse is taught to request that the alcoholic seek counseling at a time when the alcoholic is motivated to stop drinking (O'Farrell et al., 1992).

Unilateral Family Therapy (UFT) is an intervention with the spouse to improve spousal coping, reduce drinking by the alcohol abuser, and promote treatment entry for the alcohol abuser (Thomas & Santa, 1982). A programmed confrontation by the spouse at home with the alcoholic is the last part of this method. The confrontation is used only when previous steps in therapy have failed to change the alcoholic's drinking (O'Farrell et al., 1992).

The Johnson Institute intervention procedure involves three to four educational and rehearsal sessions with family members prior to confronting the alcoholic about his or her drinking, and strongly encouraging treatment entry (V. E. Johnson, 1986). During this intervention, the counselor aids the spouse in confronting the alcoholic about the negative effects of his or her drinking and asking the alcoholic to enter treatment (O'Farrell et al., 1992).

Women's Organizations

Women for Sobriety "New Life" Program is an organization of women for women. It is dedicated to helping women overcome alcoholism and other addictions. This organization recognizes women's emerging roles and their need for self-esteem and self-discovery in order to successfully meet the many challenges associated with women's lives today. Women for Sobriety (WFS) is not affiliated with AA. Members of WFS sometimes belong to AA, but each organization has its individual purpose and is a separate entity. Members of WFS live this philosophy: Forget the past; plan for tomorrow; live for today. Membership in WFS requires a desire to stop drinking and a sincere desire for a "new life." More information on Women for Sobriety may be found on the Web (http://www.womenforsobriety.org).

The Hazelden Women and Children's Recovery Community consists of a cluster of apartment units where women who have been drug free and sober for several months can live with their children in a safe, supportive environment. The women receive support services that help enhance their recovery and help them learn the skills needed to achieve family, financial, and career goals. Many services and activities are provided for children. Women residents receive continuing-care support, such as a 12-step group and other individual and group meetings. They also support each other by sharing rides, child care, friendship, and sobriety. Please see the Resources list at the end of this chapter for contact information for the Hazelden Women and Children's Recovery Community. To learn about the Child Protection/Alcohol and Drug Partnership Act, a bill introduced into Congress in 2003 but not passed into law, visit the Child Welfare League of America's Web site.

References

Alcoholic Beverage Outlet Density Regulation to Reduce Excessive Alcohol Consumption. (1997). *Guide to Community Preventive Services Website.* Centers for Disease Control and Prevention. Retrieved November 25, 2008, from www.thecommunityguide.org/alcohol

American Psychiatric Association. (2000). *Diagnostic and statistical manual of mental disorders* (4th ed., text rev.). Washington, DC: Author.

Baraona, E., Abittan, C. S., Dohmen, K., Moretti, M., Pozzato, G., Chayes, Z. W., Schaefer, C. & Lieber, C. S. (2001). Gender differences in pharmacokinetics of alcohol. *Alcoholism: Clinical and Experimental Research, 25,* 502–507.

Bateson, G. (1972). *Steps to an ecology of mind.* Chicago: University of Chicago Press.

Becker, U., Deis, A., Sorensen, T. I., Gronbaek, M., Borch-Johnsen, K., Muller, C. F., et al. (1996). Prediction of risk of liver disease by alcohol intake, sex, and age: A prospective population study. *Hepatology, 23,* 1025–1029.

Beckman, L. J. (1994). Treatment needs of women with alcohol problems. *Alcohol, Health, and Research World, 18,* 206–211.

Beckman, L. J., & Amaro, H. (1986). Personal and social difficulties faced by women and men entering alcoholism treatment. *Journal of Studies on Alcohol, 47,* 135–145.

Berger, A. (1981). Family involvement and alcoholics' completion of a multiphase treatment program. *Journal of Studies on Alcohol, 42,* 517–521.

Blume, S. B. (1997). Women and alcohol: Issues in social policy. In S. C. Wilsnack & R. Wilsnack (Eds.), *Gender and alcohol* (pp. 462–477). New Brunswick, NJ: Rutgers Center of Alcohol Studies.

Brady, K., & Randall, C. (1999). Gender differences in substance use disorders. *Psychiatric Clinics of North America, 22,* 241–252.

Brennan, P. L., Moos, R. H., & Kim, J. Y. (1993). Gender differences in the individual characteristics and life contexts of late middle-aged and older problem drinkers. *Addiction, 88,* 781–790.

Brienza, R. S., & Stein, M. D. (2002). Alcohol use disorders in primary care: Do gender-specific differences exist? *Journal of General Internal Medicine, 17,* 387–397.

Bushman, B. (1997). Effects of alcohol on human aggression: Validity of proposed explanations. In M. Galanter (Ed.), *Recent developments in alcoholism: Vol. 13. Alcoholism and violence* (pp. 227–243). New York: Plenum Press.

Bushman, B., & Cooper, H. (1990). Effects of alcohol on human aggression: An integrative research review. *Psychological Bulletin, 107,* 341–354.

Caetano, R. (1997). Prevalence, incidence and stability of drinking problems among whites, blacks and Hispanics: 1984–1992. *Journal of Studies on Alcohol, 58,* 565–572.

Caetano, R., & Kaskutas, L. (1995). Changes in drinking patterns among whites, blacks and Hispanics: 1984–1992. *Journal of Studies on Alcohol, 56,* 558–565.

Cantor, G. (1993). *Refining the brushstrokes in portraits of alcohol and wife assaults* (Research Monograph No. 24). Rockville, MD: National Institute on Alcohol Abuse and Alcoholism.

Carter, C. S. (1997). Ladies don't: A historical perspective on attitudes towards alcoholic women. *Affillia, 12,* 471–478.

Centers for Disease Control and Prevention. (2002). Fetal alcohol syndrome—Alaska, Arizona, Colorado, and New York, 1995–1997. *Morbidity and Mortality Weekly Reports, 51*(20), 433–435.

Chan, A. W. K. (1986). Racial differences in alcohol sensitivity. *Alcohol and Alcoholism, 21,* 93–104.

Chen, C. M., Dufour, M. C., & Yi, H. Y. (2005). Alcohol consumption among young adults ages 18–24 in the United States: Results from the 2001–2002 NESARC survey. *Alcohol Research and Health 28*(4), 269–280.

Cho, Y. I., & Crittenden, K. S. (2006). The impact of adult roles on drinking among women in the United States. *Substance Use and Misuse, 41,* 17–34.

Cirillo, J. M. (1994). Differential treatment: Considerations for the female alcoholic. In J. A. Sechzer, S. M. Pfafflin, F. L. Denmark, A. Griffin, & S. J. Blumenthal (Eds.), *Women and mental health* (pp. 83–99). New York: New York Academy of Sciences.

Clark, A., & Foy, D. (2000). Trauma exposure and alcohol use in battered women. *Violence Against Women, 6*(1), 37–48.

Collins, R. L. (1993). Women's issues in alcohol use and cigarette smoking. In J. S. Baci, G. A. Marlatt, & R. J. McMahon (Eds.), *Addictive behaviors across the lifespan: Prevention* (pp. 274–306). Newbury Park, CA: Sage.

Comprehensive Alcohol Abuse and Alcoholism Prevention, Treatment, and Rehabilitation Act Amendments of 1976, 42 U.S.C. § 4552 (1976).

Conners, N. A., Bradley, R. H., Mansell, L. W., Liu, J. Y., Roberts, T. J., & Burgdorf, K. (2003). Children of mothers with serious substance abuse problems: An accumulation of risks. *American Journal of Drug and Alcohol Abuse, 29*(4), 743–758.

Connors, G., Maisto, S., & Zywiak, W. (1998). Male and female alcoholics' attributions regarding the onset and termination of relapses and the maintenance of abstinence. *Journal of Substance Abuse, 10,* 27–42.

Cook, C. C. H., & Gurling, H. H. D. (2001). Genetic predisposition to alcohol dependence and problems. In N. Heather, T. J. Peters, & T. Stockwell (Eds.), *International handbook of alcohol dependence and problems* (pp. 257–279). Chichester, England: Wiley.

Copeland, J., & Hall, W. (1992). A comparison of predictors of treatment drop-out in a specialist women's and two traditional mixed-sex treatment services. *British Journal of Addictions, 87,* 883–890.

Corrigan, E. M. (1980). *Alcoholic women in treatment.* New York: Oxford University Press.

Cotton, N. (1979). The familial incidence of alcoholism: A review. *Journal of Studies on Alcohol, 40,* 89–116.

Covington, S. (1982). Sexual experience, dysfunction, and abuse: A descriptive study of alcoholic and non-alcoholic women, Unpublished doctoral dissertation, Union Graduate School, Cincinnati.

Dahlgren, L., & Willander, A. (1989). Are special treatment facilities for female alcoholics needed? A controlled 2-year follow-up study from a specialized female unit (EWA) versus a mixed male/female treatment facility. *Alcoholism: Clinical and Experimental Research, 13*(4), 499–504.

Dansky, B., Saladin, M., Brady, K., Kilpatrick, D., & Resnick, H. (1995). Prevalence of victimization and post-traumatic stress disorder among women with substance use disorders: Comparison of telephone and in-person assessment sample. *International Journal of the Addictions, 30,* 1079–1099.

Davis, K. C., George, W. H., & Norris, J. (2004). Women's response to unwanted sexual advances: The role of alcohol and inhibition conflict. *Psychology of Women Quarterly, 28,* 333–343.

Deal, S. A., & Galaver, J. (1994). Are women more susceptible than men to alcohol-induced cirrhosis? *Alcohol, Health and Research World, 18,* 189–191.

Dunham, R. G. (1986). Noticing alcoholism in the elderly and women: A nationwide examination of referral behavior. *Journal of Drug Issues, 16,* 397–406.

Epstein, E. E., & McCrady, B. S. (2002). Couple therapy in the treatment of alcohol problems. In A. S. Gurman & N. S. Jacobson (Eds.), *Clinical handbook of couple therapy* (pp. 597–628). New York: Guilford Press.

Fernaughty, A. M., Farris, C., & Bruce, S. R. (2001). Sexual coercion and substance use among drug-using women: An event analysis. *Contemporary Drug Problems, 28,* 463.

Fillmore, K. M. (1984). "When angels fall": Women's drinking as cultural preoccupation and as reality. In S. C. Wilsnack & L. J. Beckman (Eds.), *Alcohol problems in women: Antecedents, consequences, and intervention* (pp. 7–36). New York: Guilford Press.

Finkelstein, N. (1993). Treatment programming for alcohol and drug dependent pregnant women. *International Journal of Addiction, 28,* 1275–1309.

Finnegan, L. (1991, January). *The clinical management of pregnant, drug-dependent women.* Workshop presented at the NIDA National Conference on Drug Abuse Research and Practice, An Alliance for the 21st Century, Washington, DC.

Fox, R. (1962). Children in the alcoholic family. In W. C. Bier (Ed.), *Problems in addiction: Alcoholism and narcotics* (pp. 71–96). New York: Fordham.

Frezza, M., Di Padova, C., Pozzato, G., Terpin, M., Baroana, E., & Lieber, C.S. (1990). High blood alcohol levels in women: The role of decreased gastric alcohol dehydrogenase activity and first-pass metabolism. *New England Journal of Medicine, 322*(2), 95–99.

Gatz, M., Russell, L. A., Grady, J., Kram-Fernandez, D., Clark, C., & Marshall, B. (2005). Women's recollections of victimization, psychological problems, and substance use. *Journal of Community Psychology, 33*(4), 479–493.

Gelles, R. (1987). *The violent home.* Newbury Park, CA: Sage.

Gentilello, L., Rivara, F., Donovan, D., Villaveces, A., Daranciang, E., Dunn, C., & Ries, R. (2000). Alcohol problems in women admitted to a level I trauma center: A gender-based comparison. *Journal of Trauma: Injury, Infection, and Critical Care, 48*(1), 108–114.

Gilbert, M., Mora, J., & Ferguson, L. (1994). Alcohol-related expectations among Mexican-American women. *International Journal of Addictions, 29*(9), 1127–1147.

Glenn, S., Parsons, O., Sinha, R., & Stevens, L. (1988). The effects of repeated withdrawals from alcohol on the memory of male and female alcoholics. *Alcohol and Alcoholism, 23,* 337–342.

Gomberg, E. S. L. (1976). Alcoholism in women. In B. Kissin & H. Begleiter (Eds.), *Social aspects of alcoholism* (pp. 117–165). New York: Plenum Press.

Gomberg, E. S. L. (1990). Alcoholic women in treatment report of violent events. *Alcoholism: Clinical and Experimental Research, 14,* 312.

Gomberg, E. S. L. (1996). Women's drinking practices and problems from a lifespan perspective. In J. Howard, S. Martin, P. D. Mail, M. E. Hilton, & E. D. Taylor (Eds.), *Women and alcohol: Issues for prevention research* (NIH Publication No. 96-3817, pp. 185–214). Bethesda, MD: National Institute on Alcohol Abuse and Alcoholism.

Goodwin, D. (1991). The etiology of alcoholism. In D. Pittman & H. White (Eds.), *Society, culture and drinking patterns reexamined* (pp. 598–608). New Brunswick, NJ: Rutgers Center of Alcohol Studies.

Grant, B., & Arria, A. (1995). Prevalence and correlates of alcohol use and DSM-IV alcohol dependence in the United States: Results of the National Longitudinal Alcohol Epidemiologic Survey. *Journal of Studies on Alcohol, 58*(5), 464–473.

Grayson, C. E., & Nolen-Hoeksema, S. (2005). Motives to drink as mediators between childhood sexual assault and alcohol problems in adult women. *Journal of Traumatic Stress, 18*(2), 137–145.

Greenfield, L. (1998). *Alcohol and crime: An analysis of national data on the prevalence of alcohol involvement in crime* (Bureau of Justice Statistics Report No. NCJ-168632). Washington, DC: U.S. Department of Justice.

Greenfield, L., & Snell, T. (1999). *Women offenders.* Washington, DC: U.S. Department of Justice.

Grella, C. E., & Joshi, V. (1999). Gender differences in drug treatment careers among clients in the national Drug Abuse Treatment Outcome Study. *American Journal of Drug and Alcohol Abuse, 25,* 385–406.

Hamilton, C. J., & Collins, J. J., Jr. (1981). The role of alcohol in wife beating and child abuse: A review of the literature. In J. J. Collins Jr. (Ed.), *Drinking and crime: Perspectives on the relationship between alcohol consumption and criminal behavior* (pp. 253–287). New York: Guilford Press.

Hanke, P. J., & Faupel, C. E. (1993). Women opiate users' perceptions of treatment services in New York City. *Journal of Substance Abuse Treatment, 10,* 513–522.

Hanna, C. A., Hanna, E. J., Giordano, F. G., & Tollerud, T. (1998). Meeting the needs of women in counseling: Implications of a review of the literature. *Journal of Humanistic Education and Development, 36,* 160–170.

Herd, D. (1996). The influence of religious affiliation on socio-cultural predictors of drinking among black and white Americans. *Substance Use and Misuse, 31,* 35–63.

Herndon, S. L. (2001). The paradox of powerlessness: Gender, sex, and power in step groups. *Women and Language, 24*(2), 7–12.

Hingson, R., Scotch, N., & Culbert, A. (1980). Recognizing and seeking help for drinking problems: A study in the Boston metropolitan area. *Journal of Studies on Alcohol, 41,* 1102–1117.

Hodgins, D. C., El-Guebaly, N., & Addington, J. (1997). Treatment of substance abusers: Single or mixed gender programs. *Addictions, 92,* 805–820.

Hommer, D., Momenan, R., Kaiser, E., & Rawlings, R. (2001). Evidence for a gender-related effect of alcoholism on brain volumes. *American Journal of Psychiatry, 158,* 198–204.

Hughes, T., & Wilsnack, S. C. (1997). Use of alcohol among lesbians: Research and implications. *American Journal of Orthopsychiatry, 67*(1), 20–36.

Jellinek, E. M. (1947). Recent trends in alcoholism and alcohol consumption. *Quarterly Journal of Studies in Alcohol, 8,* 1–42.

Jennison, K. M., & Johnson, K. A. (1997). Resilience to drinking vulnerability in women with alcoholic parents: The moderating effects of dyadic cohesion in marital communication. *Substance Use and Misuse, 32,* 1461–1489.

Johnson, M. W. (1965). Physicians' views on alcoholism with specific reference to alcoholism in women. *Nebraska State Medical Journal, 50,* 380.

Johnson, V. E. (1986). *Intervention: How to help someone who doesn't want help: A step-by-step guide for families and friends of chemically dependent persons.* Minneapolis, MN: Johnson Institute Books.

Jones, M. C. (1971). Personality antecedents and correlates of drinking patterns in women. *Journal of Consulting and Clinical Psychology, 36,* 61–69.

Kasl, C. D. (1992). *Many roads, one journey: Moving beyond the 12 steps.* New York: HarperCollins.

Kaufman Kantor, G., & Asdigian, N. (1997). Gender differences in alcohol-related spousal aggression. In R. Wilsnack & S. C. Wilsnack (Eds.), *Gender and alcohol: Individual and social perspectives* (pp. 312–334). New Brunswick, NJ: Rutgers Center of Alcohol Studies.

Kauffman Kantor, G., & Strauss, M. (1987). The "drunken bum" theory of wife beating. *Social Problems, 34*(3), 214–231.

King, S. M., Burt, S. A., Malone, S. M., McGue, M., & Iacono, W. G. (2005). Etiological contributions to heavy drinking from late adolescence to young adulthood. *Journal of Abnormal Psychology, 114*(4), 587–598.

Kinsey, B. A. (1966). *The female alcoholic: A social psychological study.* Springfield, IL: Thomas.

Krauthamer, C. (1979). The personality of alcoholic and nonalcoholic upper middle class women. *International Journal of the Addictions, 14,* 639–644.

Lammers, S., Schippers, G., & van der Staak, C. (1995). Submission and rebellion: Excessive drinking of women in problematic heterosexual partner relationships. *International Journal of Addictions, 30,* 901–917.

Langeland, W., & Hartgers, C. (1998). Child sexual and physical abuse and alcoholism. *Journal of Studies on Alcohol, 59,* 336–350.

Lawson, A. W. (1994). Family therapy and addictions. In J. A. Lewis (Ed.), *Addictions: Concepts and strategies for treatment* (pp. 211–232). Gaithersburg, MD: Aspen.

Lawson, A. W., & Lawson, G. W. (1998). *Alcoholism and the family: A guide to treatment and prevention* (2nd ed.). Austin, TX: PRO-ED.

Leonard, K. (1993). Drinking patterns and intoxication in marital violence: Review, critique, and future directions for research. In S. Martin (Ed.), *Alcohol and interpersonal violence: Fostering multidisciplinary perspectives* (NIH Publication No. 93-3496, pp. 253–280). Rockville, MD: National Institute on Alcohol Abuse and Alcoholism.

Levine, H. G. (1980). Temperance and women in 19th-century United States. In O. J. Kalant (Ed.), *Alcohol and drug problems in women: Research advances in alcohol and drug problems* (Vol. 5, p. 26). New York: Plenum Press.

Lewis, R., Haller, D., Branch, D., & Ingersoll, K. (1996). Retention issues involving drug-abusing women in treatment research. In E. Rahdert (Ed.), *Treatment for drug exposed women and children: Advances in research methodology* (NIDA Research Monograph 165). Rockville, MD: National Institute on Drug Abuse.

Lex, B. W. (1991). Some gender differences in alcohol polysubstance users. *Health Psychology, 10,* 121–132.

Lex, B. W. (1994). Alcohol and other drug abuse among women. *Alcohol Health and Research World, 18,* 212.

Lisansky-Gomberg, E. S. (1989). Suicide risk among women with alcohol problems. *American Journal of Public Health, 79*(10), 1363–1365.

Livingston, C., & McIntyre, M. (1984). Sexuality and alcoholism. In N. F. Woods (Ed.), *Human sexuality in health and illness* (pp. 415–433). St. Louis, MO: Mosby.

MacNish, R. (1835). *Anatomy of drunkenness.* New York: William Pearson.

Mann, R. E., Smart, R. G., & Govoni, R. (2003). The epidemiology of alcoholic liver disease. *Alcoholism, Research and Health, 27,* 209–219.

Marlin, E. (1990). *Relationships in recovery: Healing strategies for couples and families.* New York: Harper & Row.

Martin, P. Y., & Hummer, R. A. (1989). Fraternities and rape on campus. *Gender and Society, 3,* 457–473.

Matheson, J. L., & McCollum, E. E. (2008). Using metaphors to explore the experience of powerlessness among women in 12-step recovery. *Substance Use and Misuse, 43,* 1027–1044.

May, P. A. (1989). Alcohol abuse and alcoholism among Native Americans: An overview. In T. D. Watts & R. Wright, Jr. (Eds.), *Alcoholism in minority populations* (pp. 95–119). Springfield, IL: Thomas.

May, P. A., & Gossage, J. P. (2001). Estimating the prevalence of Fetal Alcohol Syndrome: A summary. *Alcohol Research and Health, 25,* 159–167.

May, P. A., Gossage, J. P., Brook, L. E., Snell, C. L., Marais, A., Hendricks, L. S., Croxford, J. A., & Vijoen, D. L. (2005). Maternal risk factors for fetal alcohol syndrome in the Western Cape province of South Africa: A population-based study. *American Journal of Public Health, 95*(7), 1190–1199.

McCollum, E. E. (1991). A scale to measure Bowen's concept of emotional cutoff. *Contemporary Family Therapy, 13*(3), 247–254.

Mezey, E., Kolman, C., Diehl, A., Mitchell, M., & Herlong, H. (1988). Alcohol and dietary intake in the development of chronic pancreatitus and liver disease in alcoholism. *American Journal of Clinical Nutrition, 48*(1), 148–151.

Miller, B. A. (1996). Women's alcohol use and their violent victimization. In J. Howard, S. Martin, P. Mail, M. Hilton, & E. Taylor (Eds.), *Women and alcohol: Issues for prevention research* (NIH Publication No. 96–3817, pp. 239–260). Bethesda, MD: National Institute on Alcohol Abuse and Alcoholism.

Miller, B. A., & Downs, W. R. (1993). The impact of family violence on the use of alcohol by women. *Alcohol Health and Research World, 17*(2), 137–143.

Miller, B. A., Downs, W., & Testa, M. (1993). The impact of family violence on the use of alcohol by women. *Alcohol Health and Research World, 17*(2), 137–142.

Miller, D., & Jang, M. (1977). Children of alcoholics: A 20-year longitudinal study. *Social Work Research and Abstracts, 13*(4), 23–29.

Mohr, C. D., Armeli, S., Tennen, H., Temple, M., Todd, M., Clark, J., & Carney, M. A. (2005). Moving beyond the keg party: A daily process study of college student drinking motivations. *Psychology of Addictive Behaviors, 19*(4), 392–403.

Nakawatase, T. V., Yamamoto, J., & Sasao, T. (1993). The association between fast-flushing and alcohol use among Japanese Americans. *Journal of Studies on Alcohol, 54,* 48–53.

National Institute on Alcoholism and Alcohol Abuse. (1998). *Drinking in the United States: Main findings from the 1992 National Longitudinal Alcohol Epidemiological Survey* (NLAES) (U.S. Alcohol Epidemiologic Data Reference Manual, Vol. 6.). Bethesda, MD: Author.

National Institute on Alcohol Abuse and Alcoholism. (2002). Alcohol and minorities: An update. *Alcohol Alert* (Report No. 55). Rockville, MD: Author.

Nielsen, A. L. (2000). Examining drinking patterns and problems among Hispanic groups: Results from a national survey. *Journal of Studies on Alcohol, 61,* 301–310.

Norris, J. (1994). Alcohol and female sexuality: A look at expectancies and risks. *Alcohol Health and Research World, 18,* 197–201.

O'Farrell, T. J., Cutter, H. S. G., Choquette, K. A., Floyd, F. J., & Bayog, R. D. (1992). Behavioral marital therapy for male alcoholics: Marital and drinking adjustment during the 2 years after treatment. *Behavior Therapy, 23,* 529–549.

Ohannessian, C. M., Hesselbrock, V. M., Kramer, J., Bucholz, K. K., Schuckit, M. A., Kuperman, S., & Nurnberger, J. L. (2004). Parental substance use: Consequences and adolescent psychopathology. *Journal of Studies on Alcohol, 65*(6), 725–730.

Olson, H. C., O'Connor, M. J., & Fitzgerald, H. E. (2001). Lessons learned from study of the developmental impact of parental alcohol use. *Infant Mental Health Journal, 22,* 271–290.

Olson, L., Huyler, F., Lynch, A. A., Fullerton, L., Werenko, D., Sklar, D., & Zumwalt, R. (1999). Guns, alcohol, and intimate violence: The epidemiology of female suicide in New Mexico. *Crisis: The Journal of Crisis Intervention and Suicide Prevention, 20*(3), 121–126.

Paltrow, L. M. (1998). Punishing women for their behavior during pregnancy: An approach that undermines the health of women and children. In C. L. Wetherington & P. M. Roman (Eds.), *Drug addiction research and the health of women* (pp. 467–501). Rockville, MD: National Institute on Drug Abuse.

Prescott, C., Neale, M., Corey, L., & Kendler, K. (1997). Predictors of problem drinking and alcohol dependence in a population-based sample of female twins. *Journal of Studies on Alcohol, 58,* 167–181.

Pribor, E. F., & Dinwiddie, S. H. (1992). Psychiatric correlates of incest in childhood. *American Journal of Psychiatry, 149,* 455–463.

Redgrave, G. W., Swartz, K. L., & Romanoski, A. J. (2003). Alcohol misuse by women. *International Review of Psychiatry, 15,* 256–268.

Rhodes, R., & Johnson, A. (1994). Women and alcoholism: A psychosocial approach. *Affilia, 9,* 145–156.

Riessman, F. (1985). New dimensions in self-help. *Social Policy,* 7, 41–45.

Rimmer J., & Winokur, G. (1972). The spouses of alcoholics: An example of assertive mating. *Disorders of Nervous System, 33,* 509–511.

Roach, A. J., Frazier, L. P., & Bowden, S. R. (1981). *Handbook for marriage and family therapy.* New York: Brunner Mazel.

Ross, C. A., & Durkin, V. (2005). Childhood trauma, dissociation and alcohol/other drug abuse among lesbian women. *Alcoholism Treatment Quarterly, 23*(1), 99–105.

Runcek, D., & Maier, P. (1991). Bars, blocks, and crimes revisited: Linking the theory of routine activities to the empiricism of "hot spots." *Criminology, 29*(4), 725–753.

Sacks, J. Y., McKendrick, K., & Banks, S. (2008). The impact of early trauma and abuse on residential substance abuse treatment outcomes for women. *Journal of Substance Abuse Treatment, 34,* 90–100.

Schaeffer, S., Evans, S., & Sterne, M. (1985). Incest among women in recovery from drug dependency: Correlation and implication for treatment. In M. Plant (Ed.), *Women and alcohol: Contemporary and historical perspectives* (pp. 268–269). New York: Free Association Books Ltd.

Schonfeld, A. M. G. (2003). Moral judgment and reasoning in children and adolescents with prenatal alcohol exposure. *Dissertation Abstracts International, 63*(8), 3937B.

Searles, J. S. (1988). The role of genetics in the pathogenesis of alcoholism. *Journal of Abnormal Psychology, 97,* 153–167.

Seixas, J. (1977). Children from alcohol families. In N. Estes & M. Heinemann (Eds.), *Alcoholism: Development, consequences, and interventions* (pp. 193–201). St. Louis, MO: Mosby.

Sisson, R. W., & Azrin, N. H. (1986). Family-member involvement to initiate and promote treatment of problem drinkers. *Journal of Behavior and Experimental Psychiatry, 17*(1), 15–21.

Smith-Warner, S., Spiegelman., D., Yaun, S., Brand, V. D., Folsom, A., Goldbohn, R., et al. (1998). Alcohol and breast cancer in women: A pooled analysis of cohort studies. *Journal of the American Medical Association, 279*(7), 535–540.

Sohrabji, F. (2003). Neurodegeneration in women. *Alcohol Research and Health, 26*(4), 316–318.

Stanton, M. (1997). The role of family and significant others in the engagement and retention of drug-dependent individuals. In L. Onken, J. Blaine, & J. Boren (Eds.), *Beyond the therapeutic alliance: Keeping the drug-dependent individual in treatment* (NIDA Research Monograph No. 165, pp. 157–180). Rockville, MD: National Institute on Drug Abuse.

Stets, J., & Strauss, M. (1990). Gender differences in reporting marital violence and its medical and psychological consequences. In M. Strauss & R. Gelles (Ed.), *Physical violence in American families: Risk factors and adaptations to violence in 8,145 families.* New Brunswick, NJ: Transaction.

Stormo, K. J., Lang, A. R., & Stritzke, W. G. K. (1997). Attributions about acquaintance rape: The role of alcohol and individual differences. *Journal of Applied Social Psychology, 27,* 279–305.

Streissguth, A. P. (1997). *Fetal alcohol syndrome: A guide for families and communities.* Baltimore: Brookes.

Streissguth, A. P., & O'Malley, K. (2000). Neuropsychiatric implications and long-term consequences of fetal alcohol spectrum disorders. *Seminars in Clinical Neuropsychiatry, 5*(3), 177–190.

Su, S., Larison, C., & Ghadialy, R. (1997). *Substance use among women in the United States* (SAMHSA Analytic Series A-3). Rockville, MD: Substance Abuse and Mental Heath Services Administration.

Sullivan, E., Fama, R., Rosenbloom, M., & Pfefferbaum, A. (2002). A profile of neuropsychological deficits in alcoholic women. *Neuropsychology, 16*(1), 74–83.

Swett, C., & Halpert, M. (1994). High rates of alcohol problems and history of physical and sexual abuse among women inpatients. *American Journal of Drug and Alcohol Abuse, 20,* 551–556.

Taylor, R. J., Mattis, J., & Chatters, L. M. (1999). Subjective religiosity among African Americans: A synthesis of findings from five national samples. *Journal of Black Psychology, 25,* 524–543.

Testa, M., Livingston, J. A., & Collins, R. L. (2000). The role of women's alcohol consumption in evaluation of vulnerability to sexual aggression. *Experimental and Clinical Psychopharmacology, 8,* 185–191.

Thomas, E. J., & Santa, C. A. (1982). Unilateral family therapy for alcohol abuse: A working conception. *American Journal of Family Therapy, 10,* 49–60.

Thundal, K., & Allebeck, P. (1998). Abuse of and dependence on alcohol in Swedish women: Role of education, occupation and family structure. *Social Psychiatry and Psychiatric Epidemiology, 33,* 445–450.

Trepper, T. S., McCollum, E. E., Dankoski, M. E., Davis, S. K., & LaFazia M. A. (2000). Couples therapy for drug abusing women in an inpatient setting: A pilot study. *Contemporary Family Therapy, 22*(2), 201–221.

Ullman, S. E. (2003). A critical review of field studies on the link of alcohol and adult sexual assault in women. *Aggression and Violent Behavior, 8*(5), 471–486.

Urbano, M., Estruch, R., Fernandez, S., Pare, J., & Rubin, E. (1995). The greater risk of alcoholic cardiomyopathy and myopathy in women compared with men. *Journal of the American Medical Association, 274*(2), 149–154.

Vanicelli, M. (1984). Treatment outcomes of alcoholic women: The state of art in relation to sex bias and expectancy effects. In S. C. Wilsnack & L. J. Beckman (Eds.), *Alcohol problems in women* (pp. 369–412). New York: Guilford Press.

van Wormer, K., & Davis, D. R. (2003). *Addiction treatment: A strengths perspective.* Pacific Grove, CA: Thomson Brooks/Cole.

Waite-O'Brien, N. (1992). Alcohol and drug abuse among female adolescents. In G. W. Lawson & A. W. Lawson (Eds.), *Adolescent substance abuse: Etiology, treatment and prevention* (pp. 367–379). Gaithersburg, MD: Aspen.

Walitzer, K. S., & Connors, G. J. (1997). Gender and treatment of alcohol related problems. In R. W. Wilsnack & S. C. Wilsnack (Eds.), *Gender and alcohol* (pp. 445–461). New Brunswick, NJ: Rutgers Center of Alcohol Studies.

Wetchler, J. L., Nelson, T. S., McCollum, E. E., Trepper, T. S., & Lewis, R. A. (1994). Couple-focused therapy for substance-abusing women. In J. A. Lewis (Ed.), *Addictions: Concepts and strategies for treatment* (pp. 253–262). Gaithersburg, MD: Aspen.

Widseth, J. C., & Mayer, J. (1971). Drinking behaviors and attitudes toward alcohol in delinquent girls. *International Journal of the Addictions, 6*(3), 453–461.

Williams, C., & Klerman, L. (1984). Female alcohol abuse: Its effect on the family. In S. C. Wilsnack & S. L. Beckman (Eds.), *Alcohol problems in women: Antecedents, consequences and interventions* (pp. 280–312). New York: Guilford Press.

Williams, G., Grant, B., Harford, T., & Noble, B. (1990). Population projection using DSM-III criteria: Alcohol abuse and dependence. *Alcohol Health and Research World, 13*(4), 366–370.

Wilsnack, S. C. (1996). Patterns and trends in women's drinking: Recent findings and some implications for prevention. In J. Howard, S. Martin, P. D. Mail, M. E. Hilton, & E. D. Taylor (Eds.), *Women and alcohol: Issues for prevention research* (NIH Publication No. 96–3817, pp. 19–63). Bethesda, MD: National Institutes of Health.

Wilsnack, S. C., Vogeltanz, N. D., Klassen, A. D., & Harris, T. R. (1997). Childhood sexual abuse and women's substance abuse: National survey findings. *Journal of Studies on Alcohol, 58,* 264–271.

Windle, M. (1996). On the discriminative validity of a family history of problem drinking index with a national sample of young adults. *Journal of Studies on Alcohol, 57,* 378–386.

Winters, J., O'Farrell, T. J., Fals-Stewart, W., Birchler, G. R., & Kelley, M. L. (2002). Behavioral couples therapy for female substance-abusing patients: Effects of substance use and relationship adjustment. *Journal of Consulting and Clinical Psychology, 70*(2), 344–355.

Yi, H., Stinson, F., Williams, G., & Bertolucci, D. (1999). *Trends in alcohol-related fatal traffic crashes in the United Sates, 1975–1997* (NIAAA Surveillance Report No. 49). Bethesda, MD: National Institute on Alcohol Abuse and Alcoholism.

Zlotnick, C., Franchino, K., St. Claire, N., Cox, K., & St. John, M. (1996). The impact of outpatient drug services on abstinence among pregnant and parenting women. *Journal of Substance Abuse Treatment, 13,* 195–202.

Zucker, R. A., & Devoe, C. I. (1975). Life history characteristics associated with problem drinking and antisocial behavior among adolescent girls. In R. D. Wort, G. Winokur, & M. Roff (Eds.), *Life history research in psychopathology* (Vol. 4, pp. 109–134). Minneapolis: University of Minnesota Press.

Zweben, A., & Pearlman, S. (1983). Evaluating the effectiveness of conjoint treatment of alcohol complicated marriages: Clinical and methodological issues. *Journal of Marital and Family Therapy, 9,* 61–72.

Resources

Al-Anon for Families of Alcoholics
800-344-2666
www.al-anon.alateen.org
www.alanon-alateenservicesnc.org

Alcohol and Drug Abuse Crisis Line
800-234-0420

Alcohol and Drug Helpline
1-800-821-4357
24-Hour Toll Free Helpline
888-435-7711

Alcohol and Drug Abuse Hotline
800-729-6686
800-331-2900

Alcoholics Anonymous (AA) World Services, Inc.
212-870-3400
http://www.aa.org

Child Welfare League of America
www.cwla.org
www.hhs.gov/programs/cb/pubs/cm04
www.childwelfare.gov

Christian Crisis Drug and Alcohol Hotline
866-642-9271
www.cchotline.org

Hazelden Women and Children's Recovery Community
800-257-7810
www.hazelden.org

HOPE LINE
800 NCA-CALL (800-622-2255)
(24-hour affiliate referral)
http://www.ncadd.org

National Association for Children of Alcoholics
1-888-554-2627
http://nacoa.macrovolt.com
www.shoutinginside.com

The National Council on Alcoholism
1-800-NCA-CALL (800-622-2255)
http://www.niaaa.nih.gov

National Institute on Alcohol Abuse and Alcoholism (NIAAA)
310-443-3860
niaaaweb-r@exchange.nih.gov

National Council on Alcoholism and Drug Dependence (NCADD)
212-269-7797
national@ncadd.org

National Help and Referral Line for People Affected by Alcohol and Drug Abuse
800-ALCOHOL (800-252-6465)
www.aa.org/lang/en/aasite_finder
.cfm?origpage=72

National Organization for Fetal Alcohol Syndrome (NOFAS)
900 17th Street, NW, Suite 910
Washington, DC 20006
(800) 66-NOFAS (800-666-6327;
or 202-785-4585)
Fax: 202-466-6456
http://www.nofas.org

Rimrock Foundation
800-227-3953
www.rimrock.org

Substance Abuse and Mental Health Services Administrations (SAMHSA) Treatment Facility Locator
800-662–HELP (800-662-4357)
http://www.findtreatment.samhsa.gov

Prevline
http://www.health.org

Recovery Works Resource Center
http://www.addictions.org/recoveryworks

Treatment Resources: Addiction and Behavioral Health Directory
info@treatment-resources.com

CHAPTER 4

Substance Abuse and Psychopathology

Dually Diagnosed Patients

P. Clayton Rivers, Colleen J. Mullen, and Melissa Malakoff

Currently, integrated, comprehensive treatment programs for comorbid disorders provide interventions and support over a long period and include stage-wise motivational interventions (Santa, Elizabeth, Wulfert, & Nietert, 2007). They also typically include components of assertive outreach, case management, group interventions, individual counseling, and family interventions (Drake et al., 1998; Grella & Stein, 2006; Whisman, 2008).

It is gratifying to find integrated, comprehensive, comorbid treatment programs in the substance abuse literature, but such programs are still a "gold standard" that is not fully realized in most alcohol and drug programs (Mueser, Noordsy, Drake, & Fox, 2003). One of the major reasons for this is that most treatment personnel in this country are trained in a single care modality (i.e., either mental health or substance abuse) (Drake, O'Neal, & Wallach, 2008). The treatment philosophies, program structures, and even the length of care vary greatly between mental health and substance abuse treatment orientations. There is a push for practitioners to now be versed in the treatment language for both mental health and substance abuse in order to provide the comprehensive treatment necessary.

Substance abuse agencies are now focusing on mental health issues in their substance-abusing clients, and mental health agencies are more aware of substance abuse by their clients. Despite these attempts at integration, there are more "partial programs" from both mental health and substance abuse orientations than there are comprehensive, integrated programs. Because the treatment is not comprehensive, clients who need both mental health and substance abuse services can still get stuck in a "revolving door" from one type of treatment program to another. For example, mental health agencies treat the mental health disorder and release the client with medication. When the medication runs out, the patient turns to substance abuse and is eventually referred to a substance abuse agency. That agency sobers the client up. This process, with its inattention to the interactive effects of prescribed medications and illicit drugs, can lead to hallucinations, delusions, depression, and other behaviors that result in the patient being taken back to the mental health agency. This pattern, or variations of it, is often repeated time after time by dually diagnosed patients. Orlin, O'Neill, and Davis (2004) note that it is a mistake to treat all patients as if they were in a single diagnostic category. There should be a distinction between the two types of clients with dual diagnoses: those with a primary psychiatric disorder and those who are primarily chemical abusers.

Mueser et al. (2003) reviewed four types of models explaining the comorbidity between substance abuse and psychiatric illness. The *common factor* model suggests that the risk for psychiatric illness and substance abuse increases due to exposure to one or more independent factors. "These factors can be familial (genetic) factors, antisocial personality disorder, or neurobiological dysfunction," among others (Mueser et al., 2003, p. 9). *Secondary psychopathology models* posit that long-term psychiatric disorders are caused by substance abuse and would not have developed otherwise. Similarly, *secondary substance abuse models* state that substance abuse is caused by primary psychiatric illnesses (Mueser et al., 2003). Finally, *bidirectional models* propose that several different factors may contribute to the development and maintenance of dual disorders. "An individual who is biologically vulnerable to psychiatric illness may begin using substances while socializing with peers. This could trigger the psychiatric disorder. Once the psychiatric illness begins, the person may continue to use substances" to cope with symptoms (Mueser et al., 2003, p. 13).

Dual-diagnosis patients constitute a diverse population in terms of both diagnoses and the way professionals must respond to their presenting problems. This chapter focuses on the conjoint occurrence of the following problems: (a) substance abuse and anxiety disorders, (b) substance abuse and affective disorders, and (c) substance abuse and sociopathy. Obviously, the list could be extended to all types of mental health problems and various combinations of substance abuse. These mental health–substance abuse pairings were selected because sufficient clinical and research data have been compiled in these areas, and treatment approaches have been developed for them. In addition to focusing on these specific pairings, the chapter discusses special issues in treating patients with dual diagnoses in general, noting similarities and differences between the two types of disorders as well as outlining critical steps in the assessment and treatment process.

Anxiety and Substance Abuse

There is general agreement that problems associated with alcohol use and anxiety co-occur, but the reasons for this association are still being debated (Grella & Stein, 2006; Kushner, Abrams, & Borchardt, 2000). Kushner et al. list writings that have focused on the co-occurrence of alcohol abuse and anxiety. They note that the co-occurrence of specific anxiety disorders and substance abuse disorders are often erroneously grouped together when in fact different types of anxiety call for different clinical approaches. There is likely to be some value in diagnostic specificity, they suggest, when comorbidity is considered. This is because there are substantial differences (e.g., base rate, treatment responses) between anxiety disorders and substance use disorders. Significant differences in comorbidity rates have been documented for both classes of disorders (Kushner et al., 2000).

Bolo (1991) notes there has been an increased interest in the coexistence of drug and alcohol abuse and various anxiety disorders. Panic disorders, agoraphobia, and posttraumatic stress disorder (PTSD) have been highlighted in the literature, perhaps because of the large number of veterans with PTSD and co-occurring substance abuse problems. Generalized anxiety disorder, social phobia, simple phobia, and obsessive–compulsive disorder have received less attention, yet they can be just as debilitating. Bolo also notes that most of the research he reviewed focused on alcohol; few studies focused on anxiety and its comorbidity with other drugs.

The Epidemiologic Catchment Area Study (Regier, Narrow, & Rae, 1990) indicated that individuals with any anxiety disorder had a 50% increase in the odds of being diagnosed with a lifetime alcohol use disorder and were 1.5 times more likely to be diagnosed with alcohol abuse or dependence. More specifically, those with panic disorder were 3.3 times more likely and those with obsessive–compulsive disorder were 2.5 times more likely to be diagnosed with alcohol abuse or dependence. The National Comorbidity Survey Analysis indicated that if men and women were diagnosed as having an anxiety disorder, they were also likely to have an alcohol dependence disorder (Kessler, Crum, Warner, Schulenberg, & Anthony, 1997; cited in Kushner et al., 2000). The odds of being diagnosed with alcohol dependence almost tripled in females suffering from panic disorders. The odds in males with panic disorders nearly doubled. The risk for alcohol dependence was also higher in males and females having social phobia, simple phobia, and agoraphobia. Generalized anxiety disorder sufferers were also more likely to have an increased probability of being diagnosed with alcohol dependence or abuse (males having a 3.9 and females a 3.0 times greater probability when compared with the population at large). Kushner et al. concluded that the presence of most anxiety disorders doubles or quadruples the risk for alcohol and drug dependence, and that dependence on alcohol and drugs versus abuse is most strongly associated with anxiety problems.

Kushner et al. (2000) present three hypotheses in their attempt to explain these relationships. One possible explanation, the "self-medication" hypothesis, is that anxiety promotes alcohol use and abuse because of the anxiety-reducing effects of alcohol. It is presumed that alcohol, a central nervous system depressant, reduces the level of anxiety in an anxious person. Thus alcohol reduces negative symptoms, in turn leading to increased use by means of positive reinforcement. That is, drinkers find that alcohol rescues them from an aversive state—being highly anxious—by relaxing them. Multiple pairings of alcohol intake and reduction of aversive levels of anxiety lead to conditioning the individual to drink more alcohol.

A second hypothesis is that abusive use of drugs or alcohol leads to the development of the anxiety disorder. High levels of anxiety are caused by chronic alcohol or drug use and may be generated by the syndrome associated with withdrawal from alcohol and drugs. This second hypothesis is more likely to be utilized by those substance abuse researchers who study comorbidity of mental health and substance abuse disorders (Kushner et al., 2000).

A third causal position discussed by Kushner et al. (2000) is that there is an unknown factor that contributes to both the "self-medication" and "withdrawal" motives for drinking or using drugs. At present, this causal connection is difficult to specify. However, it is safe to assume that alcohol "works" to reduce the symptoms of anxiety, at least in the beginning phase of use.

Diagnosis and Treatment Issues

An excellent source for diagnostic and treatment suggestions for dealing with clients diagnosed with both substance abuse and anxiety disorders is a book written by Evans and Sullivan (2001). These authors note that several pathologies fall under the umbrella of anxiety disorders, and discuss several ways of conceptualizing those disorders. One way to conceptualize multiple anxiety disorders is the "trigger." In a simple phobia, for example, a snake might be the trigger; in agoraphobia, it would be the absence of an escape route. In generalized anxiety disorder, there is no trigger; the individual feels anxious all the time. Evans and Sullivan note that

> the diagnostic criteria for a generalized anxiety disorder include (1) excessive anxiety and worry occurring for more days than not for at least 6 months about a number of events or activities; (2) difficulty controlling the worry; (3) association of the anxiety and worry with three or more of the following symptoms: restlessness or feeling keyed up or on edge; being easily fatigued; difficulty in concentrating or the mind "going blank"; irritability; muscle tension; and sleep disturbance. (Evans & Sullivan, 2000, p. 115)

The reader is also encouraged to review the *Diagnostic and Statistical Manual of Mental Disorders–Fourth Edition, Text Revision* (DSM-IV-TR; American Psychiatric Association [APA], 2000) for the other diagnostic features of the various anxiety disorders. It is currently available on the Web by subscription at apa.org.

Evans and Sullivan (2001) suggest numerous strategies for dealing with the anxious client who is also a substance abuser. These include the following:

1. Teach the person with an anxiety disorder anxiety management techniques, such as relaxation procedures like Jacobson's Progressive Relaxation, which can help the client learn to relax the whole body.
2. Help the client challenge his or her "fear arousal" thoughts.
3. Encourage aerobic exercise.
4. Encourage the client to consult with the therapist and to "borrow the therapist's brain" as a first step in making a plan to deal with stress.
5. Wait until the client has anxiety management skills before beginning graded exposure to the feared situation or object (in the case of phobia) and prevention of the avoidance response.
6. Use a gentle but firm pressure to nudge clients with anxiety disorders to take one step at a time. For instance, have the client focus on what is being said and then repeat the material to help improve concentration.
7. Use medication if the anxiety is severe or the client shows little response to relaxation training. Medications should have a low probability of abuse. Research has shown that buspirone (trade name Buspar), "in combination with relapse preven-

tion psychotherapy, improve[s] outcomes on both anxiety and drinking measures" (Kranzler, 1996, cited in Evans & Sullivan, 2001, p. 120). Caution is in order here since medication may not be the best available treatment. Panic disorder, for example, has been shown to be more effectively treated with cognitive behavior therapy.

8. Use a team-oriented approach. For example, medical/psychiatric interventions should emphasize abstinence and the non-use of addictive medications. Both mental health and substance abuse personnel should be sensitive to those suffering from agoraphobia and panic attacks and not expect them to attend large Alcoholics Anonymous (AA) groups. Smaller AA groups or individual therapy may be better. Heavy use of caffeinated beverages such as coffee, tea, or colas can lead to increased tension and produce more anxiety symptoms. So, consumption needs to be monitored and reduced as necessary.

Affective Disorders and Substance Abuse

Alcohol and Depression

The relationship between affective disorder and alcoholism has been studied extensively (O'Sullivan, 1984). The positive relationship between affective disorder and alcoholism can be inferred from the finding of a high incidence of affective disorders in the families of alcoholics (Winokur, Clayton, & Reich, cited in Mayfield, 1985; Winokur, Reich, Rimmer, & Pitts, cited in Mayfield, 1985). There is also a high rate of suicidal attempts and contemplation with both affective disorder and alcoholism. As O'Sullivan (1984, p. 379) notes: "Studies reporting on the prevalence of affective disorder in alcoholic populations give ratio rates of 5 of 9, or slightly over 50% while conversely 8 of 36 or just over 20% of bi-polar individuals are said to exhibit coexisting alcoholism." Other researchers (e.g., Zimberg, 1985) have provided somewhat different figures. Addiction to substances other than alcohol and the relationship of these addictions to depression have been less well researched.

The Epidemiologic Catchment Area Study (Regier et al., 1990) indicated that 32% of individuals with any affective disorder also had a substance use disorder. Twenty-seven percent of individuals with major depressive disorder and 50% of individuals with bipolar disorder met criteria for a substance use disorder. The National Comorbidity Survey (Kessler at al., 1997) showed that 53% of women and 28% of men with alcohol dependence disorder met criteria for major depression, and 6% of both women and men were diagnosed with a manic disorder.

Diagnosis and Treatment

An association has been established between depression and alcoholism for a relatively long time, particularly in terms of suicide (East, cited in Mayfield, 1985; Sullivan, cited in Mayfield, 1985). Recently, a more direct relationship has been established between alcoholism and affective disorder. Before launching into those studies, we outline some differences in how alcohol abuse can be associated with depression. First, relatively consistent test data suggest that alcohol abuse leads to elevated scores on the depression scale of the Minnesota Multiphasic Personality Inventory (MMPI; Hathaway & McKinley, 1940) and the Beck Depression Inventory (Beck, Ward, & Mendelson, 1961). However, in the majority of cases, the score on the depression scale declines as the individual begins to recover from the toxic state of alcohol abuse. This indicates that alcohol abuse itself may bring on depression. This depression clears up as individuals begin to cope with the toxic state of alcohol abuse and resolve their guilt over the harm they may have done to significant people in their lives. These individuals typically show no history of depression. The type of depression that usually occurs in reaction to the physical and psychological consequences of drinking is reactive, or exogenous, depression.

Endogenous depression can be defined as depression that is not related to a precipitating event, does not seem to be improved by a change in the person's situation, and reoccurs over the person's lifetime. There is sometimes, but not always, a family history of depression that can be readily documented. Two types of endogenous depression are identified in the psychiatric literature. The first type, unipolar depression, refers to a disorder that is expressed by deep depression and melancholia. Persons may, over their life span, move several times from a mood that would be classified as "normal" to severe depression.

Evans and Sullivan (2001) have outlined the DSM-IV-TR diagnostic signs of depression. The major features of depression are a deeply sad, blue, or irritable mood that lasts for most of the day over the course of at least 2 weeks. The DSM-IV-TR indicates that at least five or more additional symptoms are necessary for making the diagnosis of depression, including either the first or the second of the following features: (a) depressed or irritable mood most of the day and almost every day, (b) markedly diminished interest or loss of pleasure, (c) significant unplanned weight loss or significant unplanned weight gain, (d) insomnia or hypersomnia, (e) psychomotor agitation or retardation almost every day, (f) fatigue or loss of energy every day, (g) feelings of worthlessness or guilt; (h) inability to concentrate or inability to make decisions, and (i) thoughts of death and suicidal ideation without a plan, or suicide attempts, or a specific plan for committing suicide.

The second type of endogenous depression is called "bipolar depression" and has been referred to in earlier classification schemes as manic-depressive disorder. Individuals show a typical cycle of moving from normal affect to manic-like behavior where they sleep very little, are very active, talk and move constantly, and show a rapid shift in ideas and verbal material. They are so active that they may exhaust the onlooker. They also may have grandiose schemes and be temporarily amusing to the people with whom they interact, although eventually they push the limits too far and are perceived as rude and insensitive. This part of the cycle is then followed by depression. The depression cycle is the same as or similar to unipolar depression. Sometimes it may show a typical pattern of going from normal behavior to mania and then depression. Finally, the person will return again to a normal mood state.

Depression has been shown to be associated with alcoholism. Studies at the beginning of the 20th century showed a high rate of alcoholism among those who had committed suicide (East, cited in Mayfield, 1985; Sullivan, cited in Mayfield, 1985). More recent research has tended to confirm those findings (e.g., Robins, Murphy, Wilkinson,

Gassner, & Kayes, 1959, cited in Mayfield, 1985). Curran, Flynn, Kirchner, and Booth (2000) found that among 298 men from a Veterans Administration (VA) hospital inpatient substance treatment program, those classified as mildly to moderately depressed on the Beck Depression Inventory at 3 months posttreatment were nearly 3 times more likely to relapse to alcohol use over the follow-up period as compared to nondepressed men. Men who were severely depressed were nearly 5 times more likely to relapse.

Mayfield (1985) notes that the co-occurrence of alcoholism and affective disorder is a more recent finding. For example, Mayfield and Coleman (1968) found alcoholism in 26% of their bipolar patients. For individuals whose primary diagnosis was alcoholism, Mayfield (1985) reported less striking but still reliable co-incidences of about 7% to 9% who were also diagnosed as having an affective disorder.

One of the major hypotheses regarding affective disorders and alcoholism is that the two conditions may reflect the same underlying problem in different ways, that is, expressed as alcoholism in men and as depression in women. This hypothesis has been generated from the research noted above on family co-incidences of alcoholism and depression. As Mayfield (1985) indicates, Winokur and his colleagues used the research on concurrence of depression and alcoholism "to devise a hypothetical subdivision of unipolar affective disorder" (Mayfield, 1985, p. 71), including

1. depressive spectrum disease, a serious unipolar depression occurring in a person with a first-degree relative suffering from either alcoholism or antisocial personality disorder, with or without a first-degree relative with unipolar depression;
2. familial pure depressive disease, occurring in an individual with a first-degree relative suffering only from unipolar depression; and
3. sporadic depressive disease, occurring in the absence of any psychiatric illness among first-degree relatives.

Depressive spectrum disease suggests a common underlying familial attribute that may be expressed as either unipolar affective disease or alcoholism.

There has also been research on the role of alcohol abuse in relationship to bipolar affective disorder. One of the important studies in this area was done by Mayfield and Coleman (1968). In a group of 59 patients with cyclic affective disorders, they found that 20% of that group drank excessively. They also found that drinking was associated with mood swings. Contrary to what might be expected, they found that increased drinking was associated with elation, not depression. When depression occurred, drinking in general decreased. An increase in drinking was predominant in the elation cycle. Other researchers have also found this type of association between affect and alcohol. Thus the notion that alcohol abuse by people suffering from bipolar disorder is an attempt to cope with a severely depressed mood is likely erroneous. Our personal clinical experience suggests that many bipolar individuals drink when their manic symptoms become intolerable (e.g., lack of sleep). Then, shortly after they begin drinking, the manic phase turns quickly into a depressive phase.

Many people use alcohol to alter their mood state. It simply works for them. If the self-reports of drinkers can be accepted, alcohol does modify mood. Moderate social drinkers, when intoxicated in a laboratory setting, show improved mood at low levels of alcohol intoxication. However, this change in mood does not appear to be euphoric and seems to be below the positive affect changes reported for cocaine or amphetamines. At high levels of intoxication, there is a deterioration of mood.

These findings do not support the notion that the alcoholic drinker abuses alcohol to reach a euphoric state. Indeed, research on alcoholics suggests that alcoholics in laboratory settings have deterioration in mood (i.e., become more depressed and anxious) under chronic heavy alcohol intake (Mendelson, 1964). Mood changes have been observed to proceed to the point of a severe depressive syndrome with suicidal ideation. A question arises: Why do alcoholics who suffer this depressive affect continue to drink? One possibility is that although they are not experiencing euphoria from their drinking, they may be relieved from dysphoria (a sense of melancholia or sadness—depression); that is, they are returning to a more moderate and midrange mood state. Laboratory research provides some degree of support for this possibility (Mayfield & Allen, 1967). The participants in Mayfield and Allen's studies showed profound improvement in most mood factors after mildly acute intoxication. While these findings suggest that alcohol can have positive effects on severely depressed people, they also suggest that those participants who had a history of excessive drinking showed much less improvement than did individuals who had never been excessive drinkers. More recently, the National Comorbidity Survey indicated that 24% of the men and 48.5% of the women who had a lifetime prevalence for alcohol dependence also had a lifetime prevalence for major depression (Kessler et al., 1997).

Pharmacotherapy for Depressed Alcoholics

Having a dual diagnosis usually means a longer period of treatment than would be the case for a person with only one of the problems, and this is especially true in regard to alcoholism. In addition, there is concern about the use of psychotropic drugs as a part of alcohol treatment; such drugs should not be used at all if their use can be avoided. Despite these concerns, pharmacotherapy has been used effectively with depressed alcoholics. It is important to remember that the alcoholic should be sober and abstinent before any psychotropic drugs are prescribed.

Overall, Brown, Williams, and Neil (1973) found that phenothiazine and tricyclic antidepressants in low dosages might be of assistance for the neurotic, or reactive (exogenous), depression so often seen in alcoholics. These two types of medication were more effective than diazepam in producing symptom relief in separate groups of detoxified alcoholics with anxiety–depression syndrome. This is an important finding since many people feel that the prescribing of minor tranquilizers is not a realistic treatment option in view of the drugs' addiction potential. In general, research has not supported the initial enthusiasm for treating depressed alcoholics with antidepressants (O'Sullivan, 1984).

A similar finding seems to have been established for the use of lithium carbonate in the treatment of depression in alcoholics. While this treatment does seem to be effective with patients who have a primary affective disorder, it is not useful with reactive depression. Severe depressive disorders occur only occasionally in alcoholics. When these disorders do occur, the pattern of using lithium treatment is similar to that followed in treating non-alcoholics with an affective disorder (O'Sullivan, 1984).

When treating the alcoholic with depression, the clinician should have as specific a description of the client as possible. Mayfield (1985) outlined four subtypes of depression in alcoholics:

1. depression developed in reaction to chronic intoxication (disappears promptly upon cessation of drinking)
2. suicidal/reactive depression
3. depression that might be called "characterological depression," which is long-standing and independent of life events ("normally" a depressed individual)
4. severe affective disorder, or endogenous depression

Medication may be helpful only for the last type, severe affective disorder (Mayfield, 1985).

Comprehensive Treatment of Mood Disorders With Alcoholics

O'Sullivan (1984) outlines the preferred ordering of treatment with the dual diagnosis of alcoholism and depression. He suggests that control over problem drinking takes priority in the early phase of treatment. Only after the alcoholic is abstinent can a true picture of the underlying pathology emerge and be dealt with over time. Once abstinence has been accomplished, the type of treatment offered will depend on many factors, including the patient's capacity for insight, the intactness of the personality, and the presence or absence of intellectual impairment. O'Sullivan suggests obtaining a collateral history from a significant other to help deal with the issue of the patient's denial or memory lapses. The use of family members and other possible sources of support is also encouraged. Support from others is particularly helpful in dealing with the reactive depression found in alcoholics suffering from guilt related to drinking-associated actions. Support is especially important when the alcoholic is forced to deal with these guilt feelings without the numbing effects of alcohol.

Blume (1985) discusses dealing with depression in the group psychotherapy session, suggesting that the therapist make an effort to draw people out slowly so they can express their feelings, including crying or mourning, if appropriate. She notes that depressed persons are usually very quiet in the group. Once the depression and its possible causes are expressed, the group can sympathize with and comfort depressed participants. The group can then assist such patients win a series of small victories to help them gain a sense of mastery over their lives and their environments. A helpful question once the depression begins to lift is "Do you deserve to be happy?" Once the patients admit they have that right, the leader can ask each of them to go to each member, make eye contact, and repeat: "I deserve to be happy." According to Blume, "not guilty" is an excellent motto for some depressed people in such group sessions.

While the presence of reactive depression is frequent in both male and female alcoholics, the presence of a major affective disorder is much more common in female alcoholics. For example, Zimberg (1985) reported that only 5% or fewer of male alcoholics have major affective disorders, while 25% to 50% of female alcoholics may suffer from this type of problem. He suggested treatment with lithium carbonate for these patients. A similar finding regarding the rates for severe affective disorders in women was made by Tamerin (1985).

One result of depression in female alcoholics is a syndrome called "inhibited sexual desire." Powell (1985) outlines ways of treating this disorder. His techniques are included here because some of them are quite effective in dealing with depression in general in both men and women. Powell suggests that the therapist intervene to disrupt depression in a number of ways:

- *behavioral interventions:* increasing positive reinforcers, dealing with learned helplessness, reducing stress, and teaching problem-solving skills
- *affective interventions:* dealing with anger, resentment, and guilt; reducing passivity and distrust; and dealing with negative self-fulfilling prophecies
- *cognitive interventions:* eliminating negative thoughts, teaching thought-stopping techniques, reframing myths and cognitions, and dealing with boredom
- *systematic relational interventions:* modifying relationships and role expectations, changing destructive interactions, and reducing tendencies toward being a workaholic

Other Drugs and Depression

Several studies have shown a strong association between alcohol and depression. Mayfield (1985) concluded that there is little empirical evidence of an association between the use of other "recreational" drugs and depression, though this is contrary to what one would predict from substance abuse theories. Both psychodynamic and behavioral theories hold that most drugs are used in a manner similar to alcohol; that is, they meet similar psychodynamic needs or serve as reinforcers of behavior.

There has been more research on alcohol use and abuse, relative to other drugs, because it is so pervasive, and it is possible that no relationship between other drugs and depression has been established simply because sufficient research is yet to be done. Here, we examine the currently available research and clinical/theoretical thinking concerning opiate and non-opiate drug abuse and depression.

Opiates

Opiate abuse has been more widely studied than any other drug use except for alcohol, probably because most opiate abusers, like most alcoholics, use only one addictive drug. Opiate abusers are also more often what Mayfield (1985) calls a "captive audience." For example, over the past 50 years, there has been extensive research on opiate abusers at the Lexington Federal Narcotics Hospital.

When the same research strategies used for alcoholics are followed with opiate abusers, that is, looking at depression rates in opiate abusers or looking at opiate abuse in depressed psychiatric patients, the findings are not persuasive. For example, Mayfield and Coleman (1968) concluded that few opiate abusers are found in diagnosed depressives. Valliant (1966) followed New York addicts over 12 years who were treated at the Lexington Federal Narcotics Hospital and found few subjects with a clearly definable affective disorder.

Blatt, Rounsaville, Eyre, and Wilber (1984) found a more positive relationship between opiate abuse and depression. Working from a psychodynamic framework, they used the Depressive Experience Questionnaire to assess depression in 86 drug abusers. Of that group, 36 men and 11 women were primarily addicted to opiates. Data from these participants suggest that depression is a central issue for opiate addicts.

Kosten, Rounsaville, and Kleber (1986) examined the effect of depression on relapse to opioids. Results of the Schedule for Affective Disorders and Schizophrenia (SADS; Endicott & Spitzer, 1978) interview conducted at treatment admission revealed that 26% of those addicted to opiates met criteria for major depressive disorder. However, no significant relationship was found between depression and relapse during the 2.5-year follow-up period.

Blatt et al. (1984) found that the opiate addicts were significantly more depressed than a group of poly-drug users who were not yet opiate addicted. Their data also indicated that the elevation in depression by opiate addicts focused primarily on issues of self-criticism, guilt, and shame. Issues of dependency and feelings of rejection, abandonment, and neglect do not appear to be common in depressed opium addicts.

Charney, Paraherakis, Negrete, and Gill (1998) looked at 75 individuals in substance abuse treatment who were given a clinical interview for the *Diagnostic and Statistical Manual of Mental Disorders–Fourth Edition* (DSM-IV; 1994) at intake and at 3 months into the treatment program. The individuals were also administered the Beck Depression Inventory and the Hamilton Rating Scale for Depression (HAM-D; Hamilton, 1960) to assess for depression. Surprisingly, the researchers found at the 3-month follow-up that individuals diagnosed with depression or with high scores on the HAM-D at intake abstained from their primary substance of abuse for longer than those without a diagnosis of depression or with low scores on the HAM-D.

Thus, the scant literature regarding the association of depression and opiate abuse has produced mixed findings. A common thread is that the depression found in opiate addicts seems to be reactive, or exogenous, rather than the result of a major affective disorder. Apparently, severe depression does not occur more frequently in opiate addicts than in the population at large.

Non-Opiates

Well-designed studies on non-opiate drug abusers who have affective disorders are even more scarce and inconclusive than those for opiate addicts (Mayfield, 1985). The studies that have been directed at establishing correlations between type of drug use and type of psychopathology have not indicated a high coincidence of affective disorder and substance abuse. McLellan and Druley (1977) found an interesting differential association of diagnosis and type of drug abused. They systematically interviewed patients admitted to psychiatric wards with a questionnaire designed to detect substance abuse. They found that 50% of the patients had initially been missed in the diagnostic process and should have had a substance abuse diagnosis. A comparison was made between patients' psychiatric diagnoses and their type of drug abuse. The following relationships were found:

1. Barbiturate use had a high association with depressive diagnosis and a low association with schizophrenia.
2. Alcohol and heroin abuse had about the same association with depression as in the general population.

3. Amphetamine and hallucinogen abuse was highly correlated with paranoid schizophrenia.

McKay et al. (1997) found that individuals diagnosed with depression were significantly less likely to relapse to cocaine use. However, Alterman et al. (2000), Brown et al. (1998), and Carroll, Nich, and Rounsaville (1995) found no evidence of a relationship between depression and cocaine relapse.

Treatment Issues

As with research on the possible association between depression and drug use, there is scant literature on how to proceed in treatment with depressed people who are addicted to drugs other than alcohol. Generally, inpatient drug treatment lasts longer and has a more comprehensive focus than does the typical alcohol treatment program of 28 to 30 days. Drug treatment programs thus allow more time to be spent with the patient as well as allowing a longitudinal monitoring of mood. These programs usually place an emphasis on "habilitating" the patient. This approach implies a more client centered, personalized regime and comprehensive attention to behaviors the patient must modify. The clinician helps the patient handle extreme mood swings (both positive and negative), which are seen by some as relapse inducing (see Baker, 1987), and to build a value structure that is more consistent with that of society in general. The patient must also learn to deal with life without drugs, and that alone can be a major loss for the longtime user. These types of changes are difficult when there is not a major concern with depression. When depression is present, more time in a supportive atmosphere is needed. In addition, the wise and judicious management of psychotropic medication may be necessary.

Sociopathy and Substance Abuse

We begin by defining the term *sociopathy.* This diagnostic category is often vaguely defined; the situation is further complicated by the way sociopathy is viewed in relation to substance abuse by different researchers.

Definitions and Descriptions of Sociopathy

The terms *psychopath* and *sociopath* (often used interchangeably) have evolved over the history of abnormal psychology. While a review of that history is beyond the scope of this chapter, a review of the clinical profile presented by Cleckly (1941) is useful in understanding the general characteristics of abnormal behavior. These characteristics include

- superficial charm and high intelligence
- absence of delusions and other signs of irrational thinking

- absence of nervousness or psychoneurotic tendencies
- unreliability
- untruthfulness and insincerity
- lack of remorse or shame
- inadequately motivated antisocial behavior
- poor judgment and failure to learn from experience
- pathological egocentricity and incapacity for love
- general poverty in major affective relations
- specific loss of insight
- unresponsiveness in general interpersonal relationships
- threats of suicide, rarely carried out
- sex life impersonal, trivial, and poorly integrated
- failure to follow any life plan

In Robins et al.'s (cited in Mayfield, 1985) definition of sociopathic personality, criteria included (a) chronic failure to conform with social norms, (b) a failure to maintain close interpersonal relationships, (c) a poor work record, (d) participation in illegal activities, (e) problems maintaining social support, (f) sudden changes in plans, and (g) a low frustration tolerance.

Diagnosis and Treatment

The DSM-IV-TR (the prevailing psychiatric diagnostic system in the United States) does not contain a sociopathic category. The DSM-IV-TR does specify diagnostic criteria for antisocial personality disorder, which places a greater emphasis on observable behaviors being used to develop consistent diagnosis of the disorder across different clinicians. These criteria include the following:

A. There is a pervasive pattern of disregard for and violation of the rights of others occurring since age 15 years as indicated by three (or more) of the following:
   1. Failure to conform to social norms with respect to lawful behaviors as indicated by repeatedly performing acts that are grounds for arrest
   2. Deceitfulness, as indicated by repeated lying, use of aliases, or conning others for personal profit or pleasure
   3. Impulsivity or failure to plan ahead
   4. Irritability and aggressiveness, as indicated by physical fights or assaults
   5. Reckless disregard for safety of self or others
   6. Consistent irresponsibility, as indicated by repeated failure to sustain consistent work behavior or honor financial obligations
   7. Lack of remorse, as indicated by being indifferent to or rationalizing having hurt, mistreated or stolen from another

B. The individual is at least 18 years old

C. There is evidence of Conduct Disorder with onset before 15 years

D. The occurrence of antisocial behavior is not exclusively during the course of schizophrenia or a manic episode. (APA, 2000, pp. 645–650)

Across time, the substance abuse literature has documented a consistent relationship between sociopathic behavior (or antisocial behavior, as it is currently called) and substance abuse. Kay (1985) included all violations of socially approved behaviors, even if these behaviors did not involve breaking rules and laws, in his discussion of substance abuse and sociopathy. He pointed out in his review of the literature that an association has been established between substance abuse and both thrill seekers and habitual criminals. Another common finding is that the Psychopathic Deviate (Pd) scale on the MMPI has been frequently elevated in substance abusers. When this scale was factor analyzed, several independent factors were established. For example, Monroe, Miller, and Lyle (cited in Kay, 1985) derived six major independent factors from Pd scale items on the MMPIs of alcoholics. These were intrapunitiveness, denial of shyness, hypersensitivity, impulse control, emotional deprivation, and social maladaptation. In another study (H. E. Hill, Haertzen, & Davis, 1962), criminals, opiate addicts, and alcoholics had remarkably similar profiles on the MMPI, with only an elevation of the Depression scale score discriminating the two addict groups from the criminal group. In general, the findings suggested that most substance abuse groups have an elevated Pd scale score on the MMPI.

Alcohol and Sociopathy

Barry (1974) indicates that sociopathy has been associated with alcohol abuse in research spanning several decades, pointing out that sociopathy is a rather vague and poorly established psychodiagnostic category. Sociopathy is, he suggests, manifested by a variety of irresponsible, impulsive, and destructive actions. He also notes that the chronic, excessive drinking by the alcoholic is one of the antisocial behaviors and is associated with many others. For example, alcoholism is found in 43% of felons (Goodwin, Crane, & Guze, 1971). Sociopathy characterizes a much higher proportion of alcoholic than nonalcoholic felons (Barry, 1974). Abusive drinking has also been associated with antisocial behavior in young Black men (Robins et al., cited in Mayfield, 1985).

Kissen (1977) suggests that character disorders, including antisocial behavior, account for 70% to 80% of the psychopathology seen in alcoholics. He also notes that alcoholics have a tendency to score high on the Pd and mania scales of the MMPI (see H. E. Hill et al., 1962). However, Kissen (1977) states that if the items on the Pd scale that pertain to acute alcoholics are omitted, the level of sociopathy for alcoholics is not significantly different from that of normal individuals. He doubts that alcoholics are as psychopathic as has been generally concluded, especially since most of the antisocial behavior occurred under the influence of alcohol, a psychotoxic drug.

Kissen's (1977) suggestion concerning the MMPI Pd scale would indicate that the endorsement of the items by chronic alcohol abusers does not mean that they are sociopathic in the traditional sense of the term. However, at the same time, Kissen reports that the consistency in finding certain personality characteristics in alcoholics suggests there may be some reliability to the diagnosis of character disorder for alcoholics.

The antisocial personality he describes shows a mild to moderate level of socially oppositional behavior, depending on the degree of psychopathology. In most respects, these patients exhibited the major aspects of character disorders; for example, they were immature, impulsive, and showed a low frustration tolerance, a high degree of hostility, and a tendency to act out. Many of these individuals came from families with a high incidence of antisocial behavior, broken homes, alcoholism, and low socioeconomic status.

A similar description for antisocial personality (with the possible exception of low socioeconomic status) has been given by several researchers. Zucker (1987) found, in preliminary results, that married couples in which one spouse had been arrested for driving while intoxicated (DWI) differed in significant ways from community control families. For example, "alcoholic" fathers (those arrested for DWI) and their wives reported a high incidence during their adolescence of delinquent activity (e.g., truancy, joyriding, shoplifting); overaggression (e.g., fighting in school, beating up people, killing animals); and school-related antisocial behavior (e.g., suspension from school, cursing at teachers). In adulthood, these same alcoholic fathers and their wives reported more job-related antisocial behavior (e.g., being fired for absenteeism, having three or more jobs per year). They also reported more trouble with the law (e.g., taking part in robberies, resisting arrest) than did community control couples.

Morgenstern, Langenbucher, Labouvie, and Miller (1997) found that approximately 58% of a sample of substance abusers in treatment met criteria for at least one personality disorder. Antisocial personality disorder was the most prevalent personality disorder, with 23% of the sample meeting criteria. Borderline personality disorder was the most prevalent among women (36%), and antisocial personality disorder was the most prevalent among men (26%). Similarly, Tomasson and Vaglum (2000) examined the association between cormorbid Axis I disorders and relapse at 16 and 28 months posttreatment in alcoholics with antisocial personality disorder. Eighty-seven percent of individuals relapsed during the follow-up period.

Zucker (1987) reviewed data from the Epidemiologic Catchment Area Study to establish the relation of alcohol-related diagnoses to other psychiatric diagnoses. The data showed that alcohol-related diagnoses were most likely to be associated with antisocial personality, followed by manic episodes, drug abuse or dependence, and to a lesser but still significant degree, by major depressive episodes. These data are important because the sample was not a treatment-based one, and hence the selectivity that surrounds treatment-based samples was avoided.

Both of the findings by Zucker (1987) suggest that alcohol abuse and antisocial behavior are closely associated. A study by Hoffman, Loper, and Kammier (1974) compared the MMPI profiles of freshmen at the University of Minnesota with their later profiles while in treatment for alcoholism. As freshmen, these prealcoholics showed elevation on the Pd scale and the hypomania scale, suggesting that they were more gregarious, impulsive, and nonconforming than their peers who were not prealcoholics. The onset of alcoholism later in life led to a somewhat different picture, with clear evidence of subjective distress in addition to the psychopathy noted while they were students.

This study suggests that there may be behaviors and personality factors that can precede alcohol abuse in at least some alcoholics. According to S. Y. Hill, Steinhauer, and Zubin (1987), research by Jones (1968, 1971), Jessor and Jessor (1977, 1978), and Kandel (1978, 1980) indicated that addicts' behavior during adolescence (specifically, greater independence, rebelliousness, and failure to value conventional institutions) is related to alcohol and drug abuse in adulthood.

Mueser et al. (2006) found that among 178 dually diagnosed clients, those with adult antisocial personality disorder only (no conduct disorder as a child) had the most severe drug abuse, the most extensive homelessness, and the most numerous sexual partners, followed by the "full" antisocial personality disorder group (conduct disorder as a child and antisocial personality disorder as an adult), compared to those with no antisocial personality disorder or conduct disorder history, as well as those with conduct disorder only. Clients with "full" antisocial personality disorder had the most criminal justice involvement, especially with regard to violent charges and convictions.

Treatment of Alcohol Abuse and Sociopathy

The relationship of alcohol abuse and sociopathy can be seen in a number of ways. The descriptions are often confusing. It is difficult to decide exactly what the relationship is between substance abuse and sociopathy. Are some patients sociopathic and alcoholic? Do other patients develop sociopathic behaviors in reaction to substance abuse? It is likely that at least these two basic co-occurrences are present in populations needing alcohol and/or psychiatric treatment. When the sociopathic behavior is in reaction to alcohol abuse, much of the sociopathic problem is dealt with as a normal function of the alcohol treatment programs followed in this country. As Kissen (1977) notes, many of the items endorsed by chronic alcohol abusers on the MMPI that produced elevated Pd scores can be seen as being related to alcohol abuse itself.

It is possible to see some of the philosophy and steps of Alcoholics Anonymous (AA) as directed toward dealing with sociopathic behavior in the alcoholic. For example, the emphasis on total honesty is directed at changing the deceit and dishonesty many alcoholics have engaged in while drinking. Steps 2 and 3 deal with the alienation of alcoholics and encourage them to seek support from outside themselves, offering the emotional support of the group as well as God in dealing with their tendency to go it alone. Step 4 recognizes the rationalization of alcoholics and encourages them to see and accept themselves as they are. Jellinek (1983), in discussing the chronic phase of drinking and the prolonged intoxication of the alcoholic, stated: "This latter drinking behavior meets with such unanimous rejection that it involves a grave social risk. Only an originally psychopathic personality or a person who had later in life undergone a psychopathological process would expose himself to such risk" (p. 22). One way to see sociopathy is as a method to defend oneself against guilt and social pressure from other people; Step 8 of AA has the alcoholic make restitution to those he or she has harmed.

Tournier (1990) believes that AA's philosophy and methods have come to dominate alcohol treatment approaches in the United States. Whether Tournier's assertions are correct or not, it is true that honesty (not lying to or deceiving either yourself or others) is an important part of most alcohol treatment programs in the United States. The point here is that inherent in virtually all U.S. alcohol treatment programs are procedures to deal with "sociopathic" behavior, particularly as it is associated with alcohol abuse. The use of the group to confront the alcoholic's dishonesty can be seen as a means of dealing with sociopathic behavior. However, this aspect of treatment might also be seen simply as an attempt to break dysfunctional behavior patterns that have developed as a function of alcohol abuse. The use of group pressure, among other characteristic methods used in alcohol treatment, does not seem to be directed at deep characterological changes, which would require more intense and longer treatment.

It should be noted, too, that some researchers have cautioned against too much confrontation with alcoholism. For example, Wallace (1985) suggests using only the minimal amount of confrontation needed for change in the alcoholic. He states that heavy confrontation might lead to less internal change in the person being treated. Individuals with alcohol problems placed under heavy confrontation may rebel or decide to conform just to avoid the heavy confrontation; that is, they might simply tell the group what it wants to hear in order to stop the confrontational behavior. Neither of these postures leads to internal value change, which some researchers feel is crucial in the recovery of the alcoholic (e.g., Wallace, 1985). Other researchers (Landfield & Rivers, 1975; Rivers & Landfield, 1985) have observed that heavy confrontation leads to an arousal of general defensive behavior in the client.

Many, if not most, patients in alcohol treatment may not need a level of confrontation that would be seen as necessary with individuals who have shown the development of sociopathic behavior over the life span. The director of a major alcohol treatment center in the Midwest related that perhaps 20% of the alcoholics who arrived at his freestanding, nonprofit, third-party-payment treatment center need a heavily confrontational approach (W. Leipold, personal communication, 1978). Generally, the focus of treatment seemed to be on restoring self-esteem and getting people to accept more responsibility for their behavior. The first part of this treatment approach is not served well by heavy confrontation and personal attacks on the individual.

Clearly, some alcoholics may need the more confrontational treatment. These individuals may be more frequent patients in some alcohol treatment programs, particularly those where referrals have come through the criminal justice system, or the person is in prison. It is also possible that many alcoholics who show high rates of recidivism in traditional alcohol treatment programs may need a program with heavier confrontation and one that restricts and structures their activity to a greater degree. The question is, What should be done in these programs where the sociopathic behavior is more resistant to change? The U.S. Department of Health and Human Services (1995) publication entitled *Assessment and Treatment of Patients With Coexisting Mental Illness and Alcohol and Other Drug Abuse* provides several useful suggestions regarding the diagnosis and treatment of clients presenting with substance abuse and sociopathy. This manual suggests using the following assessment instruments: the Minnesota Multiphasic Personality Inventory (MMPI), the Millon Clinical Multiaxial Inventory (MCMI; Millon, 1977), the Hare Psychopathy Checklist–Revised (PCL-R; Hare, 2003), and the CAGE questionnaire (Ewing, 1984).

The DHHS (1995) manual also notes that when antisocial clients encounter a life crisis, they can become physically aggressive, so the therapist should be especially cautious in interactions with such clients. The therapist should avoid angry confrontations during stressful periods. The aim for many of these clients is not to change them so that they have empathic and loving personalities. A more modest and realistic goal is to use individual therapy and counseling to guide the patient to follow society's basic rules and constraints. This goal can be accomplished, in part, by the use of individual counseling. In this setting, the therapist can point out the patient's errors in thinking without the possible humiliation that might occur in group treatment.

Three key concepts constitute a viable strategy for working with antisocial clients: *corral, confront, consequences*. The DHHS (1995) publication discusses each of these concepts. The concept of corraling refers to coordination; it

> means coordinating with other professionals, establishing a system of communications with the patient, contracting patients to be responsible for their AOD (alcohol or other drug) use in the recovery program, monitoring information about the patient and working toward specific goals. Patients may benefit by signing agreements to comply with the treatment plan and by receiving written clarification of what is being done and why. Interventions and interactions should be linked to original treatment goals. (p. 64)

The concept of confrontation involves being direct without being abusive:

> In confronting antisocial patients, therapists can be direct without being abusive. They can be clear in pointing out antisocial thinking patterns. They can remark on contradictions between what patients say and what patients do. Random AOD testing is essential for monitoring patients. Honest reporting of AOD use should be an active part of treatment. (p. 64)

The concept of consequences is discussed as follows:

> Patients should bear the consequences of their behavior. For instance, violation of probation or rules should be recorded. Patients who are offenders should be encouraged to report behavior that violates probations, thus taking responsibility for their own actions. Positive consequences that demonstrate to patients the benefits of appropriate behavior should also be designed and incorporated into the treatment plan. Financial incentives and opportunities for power or recognition can be a key element of treatment. (p. 64)

Sociopathy and Other Drugs

Many of the same factors hold for sociopathic abusers of other drugs as for the sociopathic alcoholic. One aspect of drug abuse that tends to increase the probability of sociopathic behavior is its association with criminal behavior. Since the purchase of most drugs is illegal without a physician's prescription, drug abusers are typically forced into illegal behaviors to obtain various mood-altering chemicals. In addition, the expense of maintaining an addictive drug habit (e.g., heroin, cocaine) can lead to stealing and fraud. Under these conditions, it is easy to rapidly acquire a lifestyle that is antisocial and that operates against traditional life patterns. This lifestyle is difficult to change because it involves people with core values that are antithetical to those held by mainstream society.

Kay (1985), in his description of the Houston VA program, states that adequate therapy for sociopathic substance abusers must begin with behavioral and/or chemical inhibition of their antisocial behavior. In keeping with this belief, the Houston program has incorporated the following practices:

- daily collection of urine, with random testing of commonly abused drugs
- confrontation by members of the therapeutic community to reduce rule violations
- confrontation in therapy groups to inhibit common nonproductive transactional analysis games

This program also uses lithium and neuroleptics to inhibit behavior. These medications are not popular in the program, according to Kay. Unfortunately, he did not relate whether it was the staff or the patients who disliked the drugs' use.

Kay (1985) uses the term *hypophoria* to describe the absence of a positive mood (euphoria), rather than the word *dysphoria*. He suggests that some people might drink or use drugs because they wish to obtain a positive mood state. Kay's concept *psychopathic state* incorporates the idea of a variable mood or feeling state (including euphoria and dysphoria) that may be acute or chronic (if chronic, it is equivalent to a psychopathic personality). A psychopathic state is often related to the chronic use of psychoactive drugs (or drug-induced psychopathic state), which has a better prognosis than does a chronic psychopathic state associated with either a major mood disorder or persistent antisocial behavior. As Kay noted, the treatment of sociopathy associated with substance abuse is tied to the degree to which external control is needed to help abusers inhibit some of their behaviors. Those who have severe sociopathic and drug problems will have to be treated while imprisoned, or at least under strict limitations. He also suggested that physiological medical drug interventions might need to be developed in the future.

Some Special Issues in Treating the Dually Diagnosed Patient

In treating those with both mental health and substance use disorders, it is important to recognize how these two types of disorders are similar to each other. Orlin et al. (2004) cite the following similarities between the effects of mental health and substance use disorders (pp. 113–114):

1. impairment in many or all areas of functioning
2. loss of control
3. persistence and relapse
4. denial as a primary defense
5. social isolation
6. inattention to physical health
7. extremes in behavior
8. impact on family

It is important for both mental health and substance use workers to not feel intimidated in the face of the challenges involved with dually diagnosed clients. The professionals in each of these different fields can use their knowledge about their own field to understand the various issues presented by the client. Horvath (2007) suggests that mental health clinicians can understand addictive behavior because it is universally human. He explains that we are all hardwired for food, sex, and the attention of others. These are all pleasurable experiences that all humans crave. Therefore, addiction can be understood without specialized training in the addictions field. The mental health clinician can apply his knowledge of the human mind, along with consultation with substance abuse experts, to successfully treat substance-addicted individuals.

As noted earlier, the DHHS (1995) manual examines a number of considerations for treating the dually diagnosed patient. These include three basic treatment models used to treat comorbid patients. In the *sequential system*, the patient first participates in mental health treatment and then is treated for substance abuse, or vice versa. Mueser et al. (2003) describe the sequential system as ignoring individual clients' and larger systems' needs while adhering to artificial boundaries set by treatment programs. They assert that this type of system does not recognize that dual disorders are interactive and cyclical.

The *parallel system* is one in which the patient is treated in mental health and substance abuse programs at the same time (DHHS, 1995). However, different professionals provide services and, due to administrative regulations, collaboration between mental health and substance abuse professionals is rare (Mueser et al., 2003).

Finally, in the *integrated system*, the patient is treated in a single, unified, comprehensive treatment program. In this system, both mental health and substance abuse problems are treated at the same time and by the same staff, who are competent in both mental health and substance abuse treatment (DHHS, 1995). Services address the many areas of functioning that are impaired in dually diagnosed clients. Treatment professionals assertively encourage clients to become engaged in the process. Clients are actively involved in treatment and are made aware that the clinicians' primary goal is to reduce the harmful effects on the client. Clinicians use motivation-based treatment to help clients utilize their true desire to change their behavior. It is also important to note that multiple therapeutic models are used in order to tailor treatment to each individual client (Mueser et al., 2003). Such comprehensive programs should be planned to engage clients, to accommodate various levels of severity and disability, to be able to deal with various levels of compliance and motivation, and to meet the needs of patients in different phases of treatment (DHHS, 1995).

Regardless of which treatment model is employed, assessment of the presenting problems is a critical first step in treating the dually diagnosed client. Mueser et al. (2003) identify five steps of assessment needed to understand the client's mental health and substance abuse symptoms, as well as to identify treatment needs:

1. *Detection*—If the client is presenting with mental health symptoms, it is important to identify whether he or she is also experiencing substance use problems. Since substance abuse is often not recognized in patients with severe mental illness, clinicians should be inclusive in their assessment.
2. *Classification*—Using the DSM-IV-TR (APA, 2000) criteria for substance use disorders, classify the nature of the client's symptomology. Determine whether the client meets DSM-IV-TR criteria for substance use or substance

dependence, and whether the client is psychologically or physically dependent on the substance(s). Clients who meet DSM-IV-TR criteria should be further assessed, and those who do not should be monitored for future problems.

3. *Functional assessment*—Conduct an assessment of the client, focusing on the role that substance use plays in the client's life. The clinician should be able to obtain a full understanding of the client's adjustment in all areas of life, including "psychiatric symptoms, physical health and safety, psychosocial functioning, and substance use" (Mueser et al., 2003, p. 50).

4. *Functional analysis*—Synthesize the information obtained from the functional assessment. During this stage, the clinician gains an understanding of the role that substance use plays in the client's life and identifies factors that contribute to continued substance abuse. Focus on obstacles to achieving harm reduction or sobriety. It is extremely important to note that substance use often meets particular needs that a client has, despite negative consequences the client experiences. It is also important for the clinician to understand that effective treatment will involve helping the client to find other ways of meeting those needs.

5. *Treatment planning*—The client and clinician develop a treatment plan focusing on the problems and goals that were identified in the earlier steps. The clinician must understand the client's level of motivation to meet the goals in the plan and to identify potential obstacles so that the client has strategies to use when encountering these obstacles.

Mueser et al. (2003) also recommend helpful assessment instruments to use in each stage of assessment. These include the following (p. 51):

Stage	Instrument
Detection	Dartmouth Assessment of Lifestyle Instrument (DALI; Rosenberg, 1998)
Classification	Alcohol Use Scale–Revised (AUS-R; Mueser et al., 2003)
	Drug Use Scale–Revised (DUS-R; Mueser et al., 2003)
Functional assessment	Functional Assessment Interview (Mueser et al., 2003)
	Drug/Alcohol Time-Line Follow-Back Calendar (TLFBC; Sobell & Sobell, 1992)
Functional analysis	Payoff Matrix (Mueser et al., 2003)
	Functional Analysis Summary (Mueser et al., 2003)
Treatment planning	Substance Abuse Treatment Scale–Revised (SATS-R; Mueser et al., 2003)
	Individual Dual-Disorder Treatment Plan (Mueser et al., 2003)
	Individual Treatment Review (Mueser et al., 2003)

Orlin et al. (2004) encourage using an assessment form that looks at several areas of the client's history. The clinician notes the client's history in both psychiatric and substance use/abuse areas, creating a column for each of the two areas so that the specific effects on each area can be fully understood. Orlin et al. recommend nine areas of history, as follows (p. 108):

1. age of onset and circumstances
2. treatment history
   a. hospitalizations/detoxifications
   b. outpatient treatment involvement (include rehabilitation and residential programs)
   c. medications prescribed (include compliance, length of time)
      i. helpful/not helpful to patient
3. periods of remission—length of time and circumstances
4. triggers for return of symptoms/use of substances
5. positive consequences of illness(es) for patient
6. negative consequences of illness(es) for patient
7. patient's understanding of illness(es)—does he or she see connections?
8. family history of illness(es)
9. family responses to patient's illness(es)

Horvath (2007) notes that during the assessment phase, it is extremely important to inquire about what you, as a clinician, do not know. This helps to clarify all of the client's presenting problems. Horvath also stresses the importance of asking about the quantity and frequency of the client's substance use. If the client is vague, it is helpful to use the "high/low" question. For example, the clinician asks the client how many beers he or she drinks on a day when he or she drinks a lot. The clinician can give the client an option (i.e., "36 beers, or 3 beers?") in order to help the client approximate.

Horvath (2007) also emphasizes the importance of asking the client about high-risk situations and or the typical time of the day when he or she uses. This allows the client to see the problem as something to deal with for a set amount of time (i.e., a 4-hour period after work) rather than a problem that he or she has to deal with all day.

Treatment programs must focus on the following four stages of dual-diagnosis treatment: (a) the engagement stage, (b) the persuasion stage, (c) the active stage, and (d) the relapse prevention stage. Each of these stages will be briefly discussed. Mueser et al. (2003) note that case management is extremely important throughout all stages of treatment. Therefore, the role of the case manager will be discussed in relation to each stage.

Engagement Stage

Treatment engagement refers to initiating and sustaining the patient's participation in the treatment process. For example, a patient can be engaged in treatment by offering him or her social services like food, shelter, and medical services. Removing barriers to treatment by making the treatment program easier to access and by offering the convenience of both night and day programs will increase the likelihood that more patients will participate. Engagement can also be improved by offering seemingly unconnected services like child care, transportation, job skills counseling, and recreational activities.

Many times, engagement of clients can be difficult when the aim of treatment is total abstinence or full recovery from their mental health disorder. This is a far-fetched goal for many clients, as they cannot imagine a life without substance use, and full recovery from their mental health disorder might not be possible. Orlin et al. (2004) note that programs have had more success using the principle of harm reduction, as opposed to abstinence, as an initial treatment goal. The client is more likely to engage in treatment when he or she can identify the negative effects of the substance use and/or psychological disorders and realize a desire to minimize or reduce those effects.

Horvath (2007) suggests the following five techniques to help engage the client in the treatment process:

1. *Cost–benefit analysis:* Ask the client to identify specific costs, as well as benefits, to substance use. Addiction is a repetitive behavior where the costs outweigh the benefits and the person experiences a craving. If someone can develop a selfish reason to reduce or quit using, he or she will likely be successful.
2. *Coping with craving:* Educate clients on the properties of anxiety:
   a. Anxiety is time limited. Have the client recall a time when he or she had the urge to drink or use, but he or she didn't. Ask the client what happened during and after this time.
   b. Anxiety doesn't physically force someone to drink or use. Ask the client whether the anxiety he or she feels actually makes him or her put the glass to his or her mouth.
   c. Anxiety is distracting, but not harmful. Ask the client about a time he or she has had a craving and what he or she feels. Point out that he or she does not endure any physical harm, just discomfort.
3. *Eliciting psychological reactance:* People with addictions often respond successfully to people telling them they won't be able to reduce use or quit. If the clinician questions the client's ability to reduce use or quit, the client will likely rise to the challenge and prove his or her dedication to changing his or her behavior.
4. *Not using labels:* Do not label the client as having a disease. This creates a stigma and removes him or her from being able to be treated as others are for behavioral problems.
5. *Using the harm-reduction perspective:* Natural recovery is the primary treatment for addictive behavior. Treatment should be considered an adjunct to a naturally occurring process. The initial goal is to prevent further harm to the client and possibly move closer to the long-term or ultimate goal of reduction or cessation of use.

During the engagement stage, the clinical case manager should have access to the client on a regular basis. The clinician should promote an open and honest environment in which the client can openly discuss mental health and substance use issues (Mueser et al., 2003).

Persuasion Stage

While the working relationship is developing, the client may not initially acknowledge or understand his or her substance use or mental illness symptoms. This is characteristic of the persuasion stage (Brunette & Drake, 2006). The clinical case manager's role is to help the client understand everything about his or her psychiatric illness and substance use/abuse disorder. The clinician should help the client to become motivated to change behaviors to be able to manage his or her substance use and mental health condition.

Active Stage

Once the client develops a working relationship with the clinician and acknowledges that substance use is a problem, he or she is in the active stage. During this stage, the client decides to reduce or stop use and begins to build a support system (Brunette & Drake, 2006). The clinician's role is to assist the client in gaining the skills necessary to change the client's behavior. The clinician can help the client by coordinating the various areas of care so that there is collaboration in working to reach treatment goals (Mueser et al., 2003).

Relapse Prevention Stage

During the relapse prevention stage, the clinician focuses on shifting the responsibility from the clinician and other professionals to the client. The client is, of course, encouraged to remain connected to professional support, but is also expected to rely on the support of community members, friends, family, and other supporters he or she has identified throughout the treatment process (Mueser et al., 2003).

The ABC Model of Psychiatric Screening

Because patients change over time and their needs change, there should be constant diagnosis and reassessment of what interventions are needed. One way of understanding the complexity of this process is to look at the areas of functioning included in the ABC Model of Psychiatric Screening. While this model is used as a screening process, it is also associated with behaviors that can suggest deviations from normal functioning and the degree of that deviation across time.

Appearance, Alertness, Affect, and Anxiety

Appearance: general appearance, hygiene, and dress
Alertness: level of consciousness
Affect: elation or depression, gestures, facial expression, and speech
Anxiety: anxiety level (nervous, phobic, panicky?)

Behavior

Movements: rate (hyperactive, hypoactive, abrupt, constant?)
Organization: coherent and goal oriented?
Purpose: bizarre, stereotypical, dangerous, or impulsive?
Speech: rate, organization, coherence, and content

Cognition

Orientation: person, place, time, and condition
Calculation: memory and simple tasks
Reasoning: insight, judgment, problem solving
Coherence: incoherent ideas, delusions, or hallucinations?

The Use of Self-Help Groups With Dually Diagnosed Clients

Dual diagnosis plays an important role in the use of self-help groups. Paranoid patients may feel threatened by the typical AA group. Persons suffering from anxiety may be too anxious to participate. In recent years, "Double Trouble" support groups have been developed. These groups are specifically set up to serve people with dual diagnoses. Evans and Sullivan (2001, p. 39) describe how they use self-help and support groups:

> We strongly urge our dually diagnosed clients *to attend self help recovery groups.* These groups offer readily available, free social support, which can help dually diagnosed clients to maintain not only abstinence but also psychiatric stability. Moreover, these groups also help these individuals with such problems as social isolation, poor social skills, low rates of productive behavior, and disturbed patterns of thinking that are associated with their disorders. Some AA and NA [Narcotics Anonymous] sponsors are remarkably tolerant and accepting of the special issues and needs of the dually diagnosed. In the larger metropolitan areas there are also now Dual Recovery and Double Trouble 12-step groups. Others have developed special self-help groups that are a blend of 12 step and group therapy that serve as a substitute or transition group for the dually diagnosed persons (e.g., Hastings-Vertino, 1996).

Summary

This chapter has examined the relationships between alcohol or other drug abuse and the psychiatric diagnosis of anxiety disorders, affective disorders, and sociopathy. Relevant issues of etiology, assessment, treatment, and research were reviewed for each diagnosis.

Assessments, treatment plans, and staffing problems must be examined in light of the complexities involved in dual diagnoses. Whether a clinician is working in the mental health field or the substance abuse field, awareness of dual diagnosis is especially crucial when medications are being used with chemically dependent patients. Rigid approaches must be avoided; flexibility in policies, programs, and treatment professionals is essential to improving the prognosis for this population.

Dual-diagnosis patients are unique in the field of chemical dependency. As a specific population, they have emerged as a complex and difficult group to treat. The etiology of these dual diagnoses is not thoroughly understood. In some cases it appears that the psychiatric problem preceded the chemical abuse. In other cases the reverse is true. Some patients may be medicating psychiatric symptoms with chemical abuse, while others may be experiencing psychiatric symptoms that are secondary to substance abuse.

Dual-diagnosis patients are often misdiagnosed, undertreated, or shifted between mental health and chemical dependency treatment units. To reduce treatment failures with this population, mental health professionals and substance abuse counselors must be cross-trained in both disciplines, and treatment programs should be designed to meet their multiple needs. Even in the absence of cross-training, professionals from the mental health and substance abuse fields can make strides toward coordinated treatment by cultivating an awareness of the complexities inherent in dual diagnosis.

References

Alterman, A. I., McKay, J. R., Mulvaney, F. D., Cnaan A., Cacciola, J. S., Tourian, K. A., et al. (2000). Baseline prediction of 7-month cocaine abstinence for cocaine dependence patients. *Drug and Alcohol Dependence, 59,* 215–221.

American Psychiatric Association. (1994). *Diagnostic and statistical manual of mental disorders* (4th ed.). Washington, DC: Author.

American Psychiatric Association. (2000). *Diagnostic and statistical manual of mental disorders* (4th ed., text rev.). Washington, DC: Author.

Baker, T. B. (1987). The motivation to use drugs: A psychobiological analysis of urges. In P. C. Rivers (Ed.), *Alcohol and addictive behavior: Vol. 34. Nebraska Symposium on Motivation* (pp. 257–323). Lincoln: University of Nebraska Press.

Barry, H. (1974). Psychological factors in alcoholism. In B. Kissen & H. Begleiter (Eds.), *The biology of alcoholism* (Vol. 3, pp. 83–107). New York: Plenum Press.

Beck, A. T., Ward, C., & Mendelson, M. (1961). Beck depression inventory (BDI). *Archives of General Psychiatry, 4,* 561–571.

Blatt, S. J., Rounsaville, B., Eyre, S. L., & Wilber, C. (1984). The psychodynamics of opiate addiction. *Journal of Nervous and Mental Disease, 172,* 342–352.

Blume, S. B. (1985). Group psychotherapy in the treatment of alcoholism. In S. Zimberg, J. Wallace, & S. B. Blume (Eds.), *Practical approaches to alcoholism psychotherapy* (2nd ed., pp. 73–107). New York: Plenum Press.

Bolo, P. M. (1991). Substance abuse and anxiety disorders. In M. S. Gold & A. E. Slaby (Eds.), *Dual diagnosis in substance abuse* (pp. 45–46). New York: Marcel Dekker.

Brown, R. A., Monti, P. M., Myers, M. G., Martin, R. A., Rivinus, T., Dubreuil, M. E., et al. (1998). Depression among cocaine abusers in treatment: Relation to cocaine and alcohol use and treatment outcome. *American Journal of Psychiatry, 155,* 220–225.

Brunette, M., & Drake, R. E. (2006). *Integrated dual disorders treatment workbook.* Retrieved May 8, 2007, from http://mentalhealth.samhsa.gov/cmhs/communitysupport/toolkits/cooccurring/workbook/

Carroll, K. M., Nich, S., & Rounsaville, B. J. (1995). Differential symptom reduction in depressed cocaine abusers treated with psychotherapy and pharmacotherapy. *Journal of Nervous and Mental Disease, 181,* 436–443.

Charney, D. A., Paraherakis, A. M., Negrete, J. C., & Gill, K. J. (1998). The impact of depression on the outcome of addictions treatment. *Substance Abuse Treatment, 15,* 123–130.

Cleckly, H. (1941). *The mask of sanity.* St. Louis, MO: Mosby.

Curran, G. M., Flynn, H. A., Kirchner, J., & Booth, B. M. (2000). Depression after alcohol treatment as a risk factor for relapse among male veterans. *Journal of Substance Abuse Treatment, 19,* 259–265.

Drake, R. E., Mercer-McFadden, C., Mueser, K. T., McHugo, G. J., & Bond, G. R. (1998). Integrated mental health and substance abuse treatment for patients with dual disorders. *Schizophrenia Bulletin, 24,* 589–609.

Drake, R. E., O'Neal, E., & Wallach, M. (2008). A systematic review of psychosocial research on psychosocial interventions for people with co-occurring severe mental and substance use disorders. *Journal of Substance Abuse Treatment, 34*(1), 123–138.

Endicott, J., & Spitzer, R. L. (1978). A diagnostic interview: The schedule for affective disorders and schizophrenia. *Archives of General Psychiatry, 35,* 837–844.

Evans, K., & Sullivan, J. M. (2001). *Dual diagnosis* (2nd ed.). New York: Guilford Press.

Ewing, J. A. (1984). Detecting alcoholism: The CAGE questionnaire. *JAMA, 252,* 1905–1907.

Goodwin, D. W., Crane, J. B., & Guze, S. B. (1971). Felons who drink. *Quarterly Journal of Studies on Alcohol, 32,* 136–147.

Grella, C. E., & Stein, J. A. (2006). *Impact of program services on treatment outcomes of patients with comorbid mental and substance use disorders.* Washington, DC: American Psychiatric Association.

Hamilton, M. (1960). A rating scale for depression. *Journal of Neurology, Neurosurgery and Psychiatry, 23,* 56–62.

Hare, R. D. (2003). *The psychopathy checklist* (2nd ed). Toronto: Multi-Health Systems.

Hastings-Vertino, K. A. (1996). STEMSS (support for mental and emotional serenity and sobriety): An alternative to traditional forms of self-help for the dually diagnosed consumer. *Journal of Addictions Nursing, 8,* 20–28.

Hathaway, S. R., & McKinley, J. C. (1940). A multiphasic personality schedule (Minnesota): I. Construction of the schedule. *Journal of Psychology, 10,* 249–254.

Hill, H. E., Haertzen, C. A., & Davis, H. (1962). An MMPI factor analytic study of alcoholics, narcotic addicts and criminals. *Quarterly Journal of Studies on Alcoholism, 23,* 411–431.

Hill, S. Y., Steinhauer, S. R., & Zubin, J. (1987). Biological markers for alcoholism: A vulnerability model. In P. C. Rivers (Ed.), *Nebraska Symposium on Motivation: Vol. 34. Alcohol and addictive behavior* (pp. 208–256). Lincoln: University of Nebraska Press.

Hoffman, H., Loper, R. G., & Kammier, M. L. (1974). Identifying future alcoholics with MMPI alcoholism scales. *Quarterly Journal of Studies on Alcohol, 35,* 490–498.

Horvath, A. (2007, February). *Treatment for addictive behavior.* Paper presented at Alliant International University, San Diego, CA.

Jellinek, E. M. (1983). Phases of alcohol addiction. In D. A. Ward (Ed.), *Alcoholism: Introduction to theory and treatment* (2nd ed., pp. 14–24). Dubuque, IA: Kendall/Hunt.

Jessor, R., & Jessor, S. (1977). *Problem behavior and psychosocial development: A longitudinal study of youth.* New York: Academic Press.

Jessor, R., & Jessor, S. (1978). Theory testing on longitudinal research on marijuana use. In D. Kandel (Ed.), *Longitudinal research on drug use* (pp. 41–71). Washington, DC: Hemisphere.

Jones, M. C. (1968). Personality correlates and antecedents of drinking patterns in adult males. *Journal of Consulting and Clinical Psychology, 32,* 2–12.

Jones, M. C. (1971). Personality antecedents and correlates of drinking patterns in women. *Journal of Consulting and Clinical Psychology, 36,* 61–69.

Kandel, D. B. (1978). *Longitudinal research on drug use: Empirical findings and methodological issues.* Washington, DC: Hemisphere.

Kandel, D. B. (1980). Drug and drinking behavior among youth. In A. Inkeles, N. J. Smelser, & R. H. Turner (Eds.), *Annual review of sociology* (Vol. 6). Palo Alto, CA: Annual Reviews.

Kay, D. C. (1985). Substance abuse in psychopathic states and sociopathic individuals. In A. Alterman (Ed.), *Psychopathology and substance abuse* (pp. 91–119). New York: Plenum Press.

Kessler, R. C., Crum, R. M., Warner, L. A., Schulenberg, J., & Anthony, J. C. (1997). Lifetime co-occurrence of DSM-IIIR alcohol abuse and dependence with other psychiatric disorders in the National Comorbidity Survey. *Archives of General Psychiatry, 54,* 313–321.

Kissen, B. (1977). Medical management of the alcoholic patient. In B. Kissen & H. Begleiter (Eds.), *The biology of alcoholism* (Vol. 3, pp. 53–103). New York: Plenum Press.

Kosten, T. R., Rounsaville, B. J., & Kleber, H. D. (1986). A 2.5 year follow-up of depression, life crises, and treatment effects on abstinence among opioid addicts. *Archives of General Psychology, 43,* 733–738.

Kushner, M. G., Abrams, K., & Borchardt, C. (2000). The relationship between anxiety disorders and alcohol use disorders: A review of major perspectives and findings. *Clinical Psychology Review, 20,* 149–171.

Landfield, A. W., & Rivers, P. C. (1975). An introduction to interpersonal transaction and rotating dyads. *Psychotherapy: Theory, Research and Practice, 12,* 366–374.

Mayfield, D. (1985). Substance abuse in the affective disorders. In A. Alterman (Ed.), *Psychopathology and substance abuse* (pp. 69–90). New York: Plenum Press.

Mayfield, D., & Allen, D. (1967). Alcohol and affect: A psychopharmacological study. *American Journal of Psychiatry, 123,* 1346–1351.

Mayfield, D., & Coleman, L. L. (1968). Alcohol use and affective disorder. *Diseases of the Nervous System, 29,* 467–474.

McKay, J. R., Alterman, A. I., Cacciola, J. S., Rutherford, M. J., O'Brien, C. P., & Koppenhaver, J. (1997). Group counseling versus individualized relapse prevention aftercare following intensive outpatient treatment for cocaine dependence: Initial results. *Journal of Consulting and Clinical Psychology, 65,* 778–788.

McLellan, A. T., & Druley, K. A. (1977). Non-random relation between drugs of abuse and abusers. *Journal of Psychiatric Research, 13,* 179–184.

Mendelson, J. H. (1964). Experimentally induced chronic intoxication and withdrawal in alcoholics. *Quarterly Journal of Studies on Alcohol, 25*(Suppl. 2), 65–70.

Millon, T. (1977). *Millon clinical multiaxial inventory, manual.* Minneapolis: National Computer Inventory and Computer Systems.

Morgenstern, J., Langenbucher, J., Labouvie, E., & Miller, K. J. (1997). The comorbidity of alcoholism and personality disorders in a clinical population: Prevalence and relation to alcohol typology variables. *Journal of Abnormal Psychology, 106*(1), 74–84.

Mueser, K. T., Crocker, A. G., Frisman, L. B., Drake, R. E., Covell, N. H., & Essock, S. M. (2006). Conduct disorder and antisocial personality disorder in persons with severe psychiatric and substance use disorders. *Schizophrenia Bulletin, 32,* 626–636.

Mueser, K. T., Noordsy, D. L., Drake, R. E., & Fox, L. (2003). *Integrated treatment for dual disorders: A guide to effective practice.* New York: Guilford Press.

Orlin, L., O'Neill, M., & Davis, J. (2004). Assessment and intervention with clients who have coexisting psychiatric and substance-related disorders. In S. L. A. Straussner (Ed.), *Clinical work with substance-abusing clients* (pp. 103–124). New York: Guilford Press.

O'Sullivan, K. (1984). Depression and its treatment in alcoholics: A review. *Canadian Journal of Psychiatry, 29,* 289–384.

Overall, J. E., Brown, D., Williams, J. D., & Neil, L. T. (1973). Drug treatment of anxiety and depression in detoxified alcoholic patients. *Archives of General Psychiatry, 29,* 218–221.

Powell, D. J. (1985). Management of sexual dysfunctions in alcoholics. In S. Zimberg, I. Wallace, & S. B. Blume (Eds.), *Practical approaches in alcoholism psychotherapy* (2nd ed., pp. 213–237). New York: Plenum Press.

Regier, D. A., Narrow, W. E., & Rae, D. S. (1990). The epidemiology of anxiety disorders: The epidemiologic catchment area (ECA) experience. *Journal of Psychiatric Research, 24,* 649–667.

Rivers, P. C., & Landfield, A. W. (1985). Personal construct theory and alcohol dependence. In E. Button (Ed.), *Personal construct theory and mental health* (pp. 169–181). Beckenham, Kent, England: Croom Helm.

Rosenberg, S. D. (1998). Dartmouth Assessment of Lifestyle Instrument (DALI): A substance use disorder screen for people with severe mental illness. *American Journal of Psychiatry, 155*(2), 232–238.

Santa, A., Elizabeth, J., Wulfert, E., & Nietert, P. (2007). Efficacy of group motivational interviewing (GMI) for psychiatric inpatients with chemical dependence. *Journal of Consulting and Clinical Psychology, 75*(5), 816–822.

Sobell, L. C., & Sobell, M. B. (1992). Timeline follow-back: A technique for assessing self-reported ethanol consumption. In J. Allen & R. Z. Litten (Eds.), *Measuring alcohol consumption: Psychosocial and biological methods* (pp. 41–72). Totowa, NJ: Humana Press.

Tamerin, J. S. (1985). The psychotherapy of alcoholic women. In S. Zimberg, J. Wallace, & S. B. Blume (Eds.), *Practical approaches to alcoholism psychotherapy* (2nd ed., pp. 259–279). New York: Plenum Press.

Tomasson, K., & Vaglum, P. (2000). Antisocial addicts: The importance of additional axis I disorders for the 28-month outcome. *European Psychiatry, 15*(8), 443–449.

Tournier, R. E. (1990). Alcoholics Anonymous as treatment and ideology. In D. A. Ward (Ed.), *Alcoholism: Introduction to theory and treatment* (pp. 341–350). Dubuque, IA: Kendall/Hunt.

U.S. Department of Health and Human Services. (1995). *Assessment and treatment of patients with coexisting mental illness and alcohol and other drug abuse.* Rockville, MD: Author.

Valliant, G. E. (1966). A 12 year follow-up of New York narcotic addicts. *Archives of General Psychiatry, 15,* 599–609.

Wallace, J. (1985). Critical issues in alcoholism therapy. In S. Zimberg, J. Wallace, & S. B. Blume (Eds.), *Practical approaches to alcoholism psychotherapy* (2nd ed., pp. 37–49). New York: Plenum Press.

Whisman, M. A. (Ed.). (2008). *Adapting cognitive therapy for depression: Managing complexity and comorbidity.* New York: Guilford Press.

Zimberg, S. (1985). Principles of alcoholism psychotherapy. In S. Zimberg, J. Wallace, & S. B. Blume (Eds.), *Practical approaches to alcoholism psychotherapy* (2nd ed., pp. 27–83). New York: Plenum Press.

Zucker, R. A. (1987). The four alcoholisms: A developmental account of the etiologic process. In P. C. Rivers (Ed.), *Nebraska Symposium on Motivation: Vol. 34. Alcohol and addictive behavior* (pp. 27–83). Lincoln: University of Nebraska Press.

Resources

http://users.erols.com/ksciacca/

http://www.nlm.nih.gov/medlineplus/dualdiagnosis.html

http://www.helpguide.org/mental/dual_diagnosis.htm

http://www.nami.org/

http://www.mentalhealthamerica.net/

CHAPTER 4

Individuals Seeking Non-12-Step Recovery

A. Thomas Horvath and Jillian Sokoloff

Alcoholics Anonymous, the original 12-step recovery support group, was founded in 1935, and is commonly known as AA. Participation in AA involves completing 12 steps of recovery in order to stop drinking permanently. Although primarily a U.S. phenomenon, AA has established a recovery model, the 12-step approach, that is recognized around the world (Alcoholics Anonymous, 1976; Humphries, 2004). AA has a worldwide membership of approximately 2 million. Dozens of other 12-step groups have emerged since 1935, the largest of which is Narcotics Anonymous. The 12-step approach is the dominant recovery approach in the United States.

A significant number of individuals prefer a non-12-step ("alternative") recovery approach. An addiction service provider will encounter many people who for various reasons object to the 12-step approach. To practice competently and ethically, addiction service providers need a basic understanding of this population and the non-12-step methods available for helping them. Imagine that a 12-step-oriented provider at an addiction treatment center concludes his evaluation of a middle-aged client with the following summary:

> Clearly you are an alcoholic. Alcoholism runs in your family. Your drinking is progressing. As your physician has told you already, alcohol is beginning to destroy your body. The only hope for you is to begin treatment. We will give you a trial of intensive outpatient treatment, but if your current abstinence does not last, we will send you for a 28-day residential stay, with continuing care of some type after that. Most importantly, you need to attend Alcoholics Anonymous meetings daily, starting today. If you do not accept your disease and turn your life over to a higher power, you will soon die of this disease. I know you have been to AA before. It's time to take AA seriously.

For the client who accepts these recommendations wholeheartedly, there is hope for ongoing recovery. However, many—perhaps most—will object to these recommendations for one or more reasons. What objections might be made?

"I don't believe it's a disease."

"Maybe it's a disease, but if I take that approach I feel so hopeless! I would just give up, having a disease I could never get rid of. I need to find some other way to think about it."

"I don't believe in a higher power."

"I am not powerless. I chose to drink and now I'm choosing to stop. I may need some outside help, but I'm not going to get it from a group that essentially is telling me I'm stupid."

"I refuse to go to group meetings. I want to do this in private sessions."

"I'm too nervous to go to meetings. It's hard enough talking to you."

"I believe God helps those who help themselves. I'm not going to turn this problem over to him. I'll deal with it myself."

"I want to do this on my own, in my way. I don't need a group or sponsor telling me what to do."

"I can't explain it, but those meetings just don't help."

"Those meetings just make me want to drink more."

"I refuse to adopt a program that I can't graduate from."

"I may drink too much. You could even call me a drunk. But I'll never call myself an alcoholic."

"I think I can learn to control my drinking. I don't believe I have to stop entirely."

"I've looked into the history of AA. It started in 1935 and really hasn't changed since. I want an approach that is based on the latest science."

"I have no faith in AA. I kept seeing on Monday night the people I saw in the bar on Saturday night."

"I'm Jewish. They end the meeting with the Lord's Prayer. Then they try to tell me that prayer is for anyone. That really offends me. I won't go back."

"I had a sponsor the last time. She tried to take over my entire life. It really confused me. I'd rather deal with a professional this time."

"My real problem isn't drinking, it's [depression, anxiety, my job, my marriage, my boss, etc.]. That's what I want to work on. Those meetings won't help my real problem."

"I'm a [Buddhist, Jehovah's Witness, Muslim, Christian Scientist, etc.]. The 12-step approach is so different from my own view of spirituality that it would just interfere with it. I need another approach."

"They say my higher power can be anything I want, even a doorknob. I don't believe it. It's bait and switch. Once I agree to a higher power, they are going to work me until I accept the Judeo-Christian god, hook, line, and sinker. Have you ever read

Chapter 4 of the Big Book, 'We Agnostics'? It's blatant proselytizing. I know where they are headed. I'm not going there again."

"I've been to several meetings. They are filled with people who are so down and out! They are not my type of people. What am I going to learn from a homeless guy who sleeps under a bridge and goes to three meetings a day?"

"Every time the subject of AA comes up when I meet some AA member, all they want to do is persuade me what a great program it is. Thankfully they don't know I have already been to meetings or they would really strong-arm me! It looks to me like AA is just another addiction. I know it's better than drinking, but I want to overcome my addictions once and for all, not start a new one."

"Yes, I went to one meeting years ago, but I saw someone I knew and snuck out before she saw me. I'm pretty well known in this town. Unless you think I'm going to drive 100 miles to go to meetings—which I'm not going to do—there is no way I'll set foot in a meeting again. It's not worth the risk to my reputation. I've kept my drinking problems private. I'm going to keep my recovery private too."

These objections are stated here more articulately and assertively than many clients would be able to state them. Client thoughts about attending 12-step groups may need to be inferred from subtler comments or signs, or from their overt behavior (such as not attending meetings despite promising to do so). This chapter provides some options for responding to objections to 12-step attendance.

Defining the Population That Seeks a Non-12-Step Approach

Addictive behavior is widespread, apparently a major phenomenon of modern life. If we consider the three most widespread addictive behaviors—overeating, drinking, and smoking—the majority of U.S. residents have at least one significant addictive behavior. Significant addictive behavior is understood here as not necessarily meeting *Diagnostic and Statistical Manual of Mental Disorders–Fourth Edition* (DSM-IV; American Psychiatric Association, 1994) diagnostic criteria for a diagnosis, but nevertheless resulting in noticeable negative effects on the individual.

Most individuals with significant addictive behavior have no serious intention of changing (although they may have much wishful thinking). Most who intend to change have no interest in seeking organized outside help (treatment services or a support group). Because human beings are very social creatures, it is unlikely that a person would be able to make major changes in behavior without some outside help. However, casual social support is not usually at the same level of organization or focus as organized outside help, which roughly divides itself, in the case of addiction recovery, into treatment services and support groups.

The population of interest in the present chapter can be defined as individuals who aim to change one or more addictions, who want organized outside help (treatment or a support group), and who are seeking (or would prefer) treatment or support that is not 12-step based. There appear to be no surveys that estimate how large this population is. Such an estimate is complicated by the fact that in the United States, but not in most other countries, common public knowledge and cultural norms have so highly incorporated the 12-step approach that many individuals who might prefer a non-12-step approach do not even realize the possibility of its existence. It may take decades for this situation to change.

We will not be able to survey how many individuals seek a non-12-step approach until there is "information parity" about recovery approaches, combined with similar ease of access to all approaches. By information parity, we refer to widely held knowledge that there are many recovery approaches. Ease of access is also important; if the alternative group is an hour's drive away, but the 12-step group is down the street, the preference for the alternative may be outweighed by the convenience of the closer meeting. There are reasons to believe that if information parity and relative ease of access existed in the United States, the majority of those seeking organized outside help would seek an alternative approach. These reasons include the relatively minor role the 12-step approach plays in other countries and the observation that despite the nearly universal awareness of the 12-step approach in the United States, the vast majority of those who might benefit from 12-step groups do not attend. One explanation is that most who do not attend are in denial about their problems. Another explanation is that if information parity and ease of access were as good as in other countries, more people might seek help. Indeed, in the United States, addiction rates are relatively high compared to rates in other countries.

Individuals may object to 12-step recovery for many reasons. These individuals do not appear as a group to have any other factors in common, although some subgroups can be identified, for example, atheists, those who have religious orientations not viewed as compatible with the 12 steps, those who believe that addiction is not a disease, those who experience discomfort in groups, and so forth.

Legal Issues

Beginning in 1996, federal appeals courts began ruling that the government cannot require an individual to attend 12-step meetings (Apanovitch, 1998; Peele, Bufe, & Brodsky, 2000). The basis of these rulings is the judgment that the 12 steps constitute a religious exercise. The establishment clause of the U.S. Constitution's First Amendment states, "Congress shall make no law respecting an establishment of religion, or prohibiting the free exercise thereof." As of this writing, these rulings apply in the 2nd Federal Circuit Court of Appeals (New York, Connecticut, and Vermont), the 3rd Circuit (Pennsylvania, New Jersey, Delaware, and the Virgin Islands), the 7th Circuit (Wisconsin, Illinois, and Indiana), and the 8th Circuit (Arkansas, Missouri, Iowa, Minnesota, Nebraska, South Dakota, and North Dakota). The U.S. Supreme Court declined to hear an appeal of the 2nd Circuit case.

These judicial decisions apply to addiction service providers who work in one of the above states and are employed by the government or an agent of the government. In particular, these decisions apply in the correctional system, with inmates, probationers, and parolees. These decisions prohibit requiring these individuals to attend 12-step groups or 12-step-based treatment. It remains acceptable to require support group or treatment attendance, provided these requirements can be met by attendance in alternative approaches.

Treatments Available to Individuals Seeking Alternative Approaches

Treatment for those who seek an alternative approach is relatively difficult to find, mostly because of the predominance of 12-step approaches. In a recent survey (Roman & Blum, 1997), 93% of U.S. addiction service providers indicated that they had a 12-step orientation. The Internet has made access to information about alternatives easier, but the availability of alternative treatments has been slow to develop. Two commercial addiction portals include a category for these providers: www.sober.com ("alternative programs") and www.soberrecovery.com ("alternatives to 12-step").

Other resources for finding alternative treatment are university-affiliated clinics and members of the Association for Behavioral and Cognitive Therapies (formerly known as the Association for Advancement of Behavior Therapy, www.abct.org). In a university setting, the focus for such treatment approaches tends to be on research, though, so even if a client finds an attractive program, he or she might not be able to actually participate in it. A great irony of U.S. addiction treatment is that the 12-step approach predominates, but the evidence of its efficacy is greatly outweighed by the evidence of efficacy for some other approaches. Nevertheless, as noted, these empirically supported alternatives are not readily available.

Two comprehensive addiction treatment outcome reviews are recommended. First, the opening chapter of *Handbook of Alcoholism Treatment Approaches* summarizes that book's review of nearly 400 randomized controlled clinical trials through the year 2000 for treatment of alcohol problems (Miller & Hester, 2003). Miller and Hester concluded that "there is no single superior approach for all individuals ... treatment programs and systems should be constructed with a variety of approaches ... different types of individuals may respond best to different treatment approaches" (p. 10). Second, in comparing the scientific evidence about treatment outcomes with standard U.S. practice, Miller, Wilbourne, and Hettema (2003, p. 41) concluded that "the negative correlation between scientific evidence and treatment-as-usual remains striking, and could hardly be larger if one intentionally constructed treatment programs from those approaches with the least evidence of efficacy." In a ranking of treatments according to efficacy, 12-step-oriented treatment ranked 37th, and AA ranked 38th. This ranking took into account the number of studies of each treatment, the scientific quality of these studies, the outcomes (how well did the treatment work?), and the severity of the population treated. The treatments with a strong research base are not household words (like AA): brief intervention, motivational enhancement, community reinforcement, behavioral self-control training (a moderation approach), social skills training, and behavioral marital therapy, to list a few near the top of the list.

A review of the efficacy of treatments for drugs other than alcohol (National Institute on Drug Abuse, 1999) lists 13 principles of treatment, the first of which is that "no single treatment is appropriate for all individuals" (p. 1) and the last of which is that "participation in self-help support programs during and following treatment often is helpful in maintaining abstinence" (p. 3). The review also lists support groups clients might attend, including both 12-step groups and SMART Recovery, an alternative support group discussed in the following section.

Alternative Support Groups

Given the predominance of AA and other 12-step approaches, familiarity with the 12 steps and 12 traditions of AA has been a reasonable expectation for addiction service providers. Given the frequency of client objections to AA, as well as the proliferation of alternatives (which is likely to continue), however, service providers would do well to have enough information to answer basic client questions and facilitate client exploration. This chapter aims to provide that level of information. Five secular alternative support groups are described, presented in order of longevity: Women for Sobriety, Secular Organizations for Sobriety/Save Our Selves, Moderation Management, SMART Recovery, and LifeRing Secular Recovery. Not covered are Rational Recovery, which ceased offering support groups in 1999, and groups that have a non-12-step religious or spiritual orientation (16-step groups; Overcomers Outreach; Overcomers in Christ; the Calix Society; and Jewish Alcoholics, Chemically Dependent Persons, and Significant Others).

In spite of their alternative status, the five organizations described in this chapter are similar to 12-step groups in several basic ways. All are nonprofits and request donations. All are self-supporting. All but one (Moderation Management) are abstinence oriented. All have extensive reading lists and an online presence. And, like 12-step groups, these five groups have little or no scientific evidence of effectiveness. However, the ultimate justification of a support group will not be established by a controlled trial, but by whether people attend and find relief from their addictions. By the attendance standard, 12-step groups, and AA in particular, are hugely successful. It remains to be seen whether any of these five alternative groups will generate similar levels of attendance. However, all five have a reasonable expectation of continuing existence.

The alternative approaches are substantially different from 12-step programs. All the alternatives are relatively recent, with Women for Sobriety, founded in 1976, being the oldest. None emphasize belief in a higher power. All leave matters of spirituality and religion up to each participant. None have sponsors. All support appropriate professional treatment. None expect lifetime attendance. All appeal primarily to higher functioning individuals, although lower functioning individuals are not excluded. All have true discussion meetings (as opposed to the sequential monologues of 12-step groups, or speaker meetings). Compared to AA, all are very small; most communities do not have a face-to-face meeting for even one of the five alternative approaches described in this chapter.

The primary differences among the alternative approaches are their stands on addiction as a disease. At one end of the continuum, Women for Sobriety takes a disease approach. At the other end of the continuum, Moderation Management and SMART Recovery view addictive behavior as learned maladaptive behavior. LifeRing Secular Recovery and Secular Organizations for Sobriety/Save Our Selves are somewhere in between.

For providers familiar with the 12-step approach, the lack of explicit religious or spiritual guidance in these alternatives may be troubling. For many participants in these alternative organizations, however, the lack of a religious or spiritual component is liberating. Also, even though these groups do not have an explicit spiritual focus, participants do appear to take a substantial interest not just in the (often cognitive behavioral) mechanics of recovery, but also in the ultimate aspects of human life.

Another noticeable difference from 12-step meetings is that the level of consistency across meetings is not as high. For instance, at different meetings of the same organization, one might hear the facilitator take a stronger or weaker view regarding the biological (disease) aspects of addictive behavior. The facilitators of these groups, for good or ill, have a much more powerful influence on how meetings are run than is typical in 12-step meetings. Those considering a particular organization need to be advised that the facilitator is probably as important as the organization's documents in determining the nature of the group.

Alternative groups frequently articulate some kind of critique of 12-step groups. For example, a group's literature or facilitator might point out how 12-step groups have strayed in some significant aspects from what is written in AA's fundamental document, the *Big Book* (Alcoholics Anonymous, 1976). According to the *Big Book,* for instance, AA members should accept the advice of their physicians regarding psychiatric medications. In practice, however, many 12-step groups frown on medication use and even, in some cases, professional addiction treatment. Similarly, as some alternative groups have noted, the *Big Book* actually takes a positive view of moderate alcohol use for those not yet alcoholic (pp. 20–21), but this fact is unlikely to be mentioned in AA meetings. In fact, medication, professional treatment, and moderation are likely to be taboo topics in AA meetings. In an alternative support group, by contrast, these topics tend to be discussed freely.

It would be unreasonable to insist that addiction service providers have detailed information about all available support groups, but they should know some basic information about at least some groups, such as the Web site address and whether the group meets locally. Clients can then read about the group and possibly attend meetings online if the group does not meet locally. Further, service providers should look at the Web sites and familiarize themselves with each group's basic text and guiding principles. For more in-depth information on alternative treatment approaches, the reader is referred to Horvath (2005) and McCrady, Horvath, and Delaney (2003).

Women for Sobriety

Jean Kirkpatrick founded Women for Sobriety (WFS; www.womenforsobriety.org) in 1976. She wanted to address what she perceived to be the unique concerns of women alcoholics, including self-value, self-worth, guilt, and humiliation. Kirkpatrick had had personal experience as an AA member, and she felt that the recitation of the harm caused by drinking was good for the men, because it seemed to help prevent relapse, but not necessarily good for her as a woman because it seemed like a constant reminder of her shortcomings. Recitations about the harm caused by drinking seemed to make self-acceptance even harder for her. She also felt that AA was not sensitive to how society's view of women, and especially alcoholic women, can make recovery more difficult. She suggested that AA might be good for helping a woman achieve initial sobriety, but from that point forward a woman needed a different approach. Kirkpatrick died in 2000 at the age of 77. She achieved sobriety in her 50s, relying in part on the ideas of the Unity Church, Emerson, and Thoreau. She incorporated these ideas, as well as the principles of cognitive behavioral therapy, health promotion, and peer support, into WFS.

General Principles of the WFS "New Life" Acceptance Program

1. I have a life-threatening problem that once had me.
   I now take charge of my life. I accept the responsibility.
2. Negative thoughts destroy only myself.
   My first conscious act must be to remove negativity from my life.
3. Happiness is a habit I will develop.
   Happiness is created, not waited for.
4. Problems bother me only to the degree I permit them to.
   I now better understand my problems and do not permit problems to overwhelm me.
5. I am what I think.
   I am a capable, competent, caring, compassionate woman.
6. Life can be ordinary or it can be great.
   Greatness is mine by a conscious effort.
7. Love can change the course of my world.
   Caring becomes all-important.
8. The fundamental object of life is emotional and spiritual growth.
   Daily I put my life into a proper order, knowing which are the priorities.
9. The past is gone forever.
   No longer will I be victimized by the past, I am a new person.
10. All love given returns.
    I will learn to know that others love me.
11. Enthusiasm is my daily exercise.
    I treasure all moments of my new life.
12. I am a competent woman and have much to give life.
    This is what I am and I shall know it always.

13. I am responsible for myself and for my actions.
    I am in charge of my mind, my thoughts, and my life.
    (http://womenforsobriety.org/)

Secular Organizations for Sobriety/Save Our Selves

Jim Christopher founded Secular Organizations for Sobriety/Save Our Selves (SOS; www.sossobriety.org) in 1985. He achieved sobriety in 1978 through AA, but quickly separated from it because he wanted a recovery approach based on personal responsibility rather than reliance on a higher power. In 1985 he wrote "Sobriety Without Superstition" for *Free Inquiry*, a leading secular humanist publication. The response to the article was so positive that he founded SOS.

General Principles of SOS

All those who sincerely seek sobriety are welcome as members in any SOS Group.

SOS is not a spin-off of any religious or secular group. There is no hidden agenda, as SOS is concerned with achieving and maintaining sobriety (abstinence).

SOS seeks only to promote sobriety amongst those who suffer from addictions. As a group, SOS has no opinion on outside matters and does not wish to become entangled in outside controversy.

Although sobriety is an individual responsibility, life does not have to be faced alone. The support of other alcoholics and addicts is a vital adjunct to recovery. In SOS, members share experiences, insights, information, strength, and encouragement in friendly, honest, anonymous, and supportive group meetings.

To avoid unnecessary entanglements, each SOS group is self-supporting through contributions from its members and refuses outside support.

Sobriety is the number one priority in a recovering person's life. As such, he or she must abstain from all drugs or alcohol.

Honest, clear, and direct communication of feelings, thoughts, and knowledge aids in recovery and in choosing nondestructive, nondelusional, and rational approaches to living sober and rewarding lives.

As knowledge of addiction might cause a person harm or embarrassment in the outside world, SOS guards the anonymity of its membership and the contents of its discussions from those not within the group.

SOS encourages the scientific study of addiction in all its aspects. SOS does not limit its outlook to one area of knowledge or theory of addiction.
(http://www.sossobriety.org/overview.htm)

Suggested Guidelines for Sobriety

To break the cycle of denial and achieve sobriety, we first acknowledge that we are alcoholics or addicts.

We reaffirm this truth daily and accept without reservation the fact that, as clean and sober individuals, we cannot and do not drink or use, no matter what.

Since drinking or using is not an option for us, we take whatever steps are necessary to continue our Sobriety Priority lifelong.

A quality of life—"the good life"—can be achieved. However, life is also filled with uncertainties. Therefore, we do not drink or use regardless of feelings, circumstances, or conflicts.

We share in confidence with each other our thoughts and feelings as sober, clean individuals.

Sobriety is our Priority, and we are each responsible for our lives and our sobriety. (http://www.sossobriety.org/overview.htm)

Moderation Management

Audrey Kishline founded Moderation Management (MM; www.moderation.org) in 1993, after moderating her drinking for several years. She had found it difficult to get support for the goal of moderation, despite substantial scientific literature supporting the effectiveness of moderation approaches. In the spring of 2000, Kishline, driving with a high blood alcohol level, killed two passengers in an oncoming car and subsequently served time in prison. Most media reports of the event omitted mentioning that she had left MM about 2 months before the crash and become an AA member. It would not appear to be reasonable to blame either MM or AA for her drunk driving.

Assumptions of MM

Problem drinkers should be offered a choice of behavioral change goals.

Harmful drinking habits should be addressed at a very early stage, before problems become severe.

Problem drinkers can make informed choices about moderation or abstinence goals based upon educational information and the experiences shared at self-help groups.

Harm reduction is a worthwhile goal, especially when the total elimination of harm or risk is not a realistic option.

People should not be forced to change in ways they do not choose willingly.

Moderation is a natural part of the process [of recovery] from harmful drinking, whether moderation or abstinence becomes the final goal. Most individuals who are able to maintain total abstinence first attempted to reduce their drinking, unsuccessfully. Moderation programs shorten the process of "discovering" if moderation is a workable solution by providing concrete guidelines about the limits of moderate alcohol consumption. (http://www.moderation.org/)

Nine Steps Toward Moderation and Positive Lifestyle Changes

1. Attend meetings or online groups and learn about the program of Moderation Management.
2. Abstain from alcoholic beverages for 30 days and complete Steps 3 through 6 during this time.
3. Examine how drinking has affected your life.
4. Write down your life priorities.
5. Take a look at how much, how often, and under what circumstances you had been drinking.
6. Learn the MM guidelines and limits for moderate drinking.
7. Set moderate drinking limits and start weekly "small steps" toward balance and moderation in other areas of your life.
8. Review your progress and update your goals.
9. Continue to make positive lifestyle changes and attend meetings whenever you need ongoing support or would like to help newcomers. (http://www.moderation.org/)

The MM Limits

Strictly obey local laws regarding drinking and driving.

Do not drink in situations that would endanger yourself or others.

Do not drink every day. MM suggests that you abstain from drinking alcohol at least 3 or 4 days per week.

Women who drink more than three drinks on any day, and more than nine drinks per week, may be drinking at harmful levels. (See Note 2 below for definition of a "standard" drink.)

Men who drink more than 4 drinks on any day, and more than 14 drinks per week, may be drinking at harmful levels. (http://www.moderation.org/)

Notes

1. Blood alcohol concentration (BAC) charts are available at MM meetings.
2. Standard drink: one 12-ounce beer (5% alcohol), one 5-ounce glass wine (12% alcohol), or $1\frac{1}{2}$ ounces of 80-proof liquor (40% alcohol).

SMART Recovery

SMART (www.smartrecovery.org) was incorporated in 1992 as the Rational Recovery Self-Help Network. It operated as a nonprofit affiliate of Rational Recovery Systems, founded by Jack Trimpey. In 1994, SMART Recovery ended its affiliation with Rational Recovery. The separation occurred because of different perspectives about the recovery program to be offered. The SMART Recovery board, having a substantial number of behavioral health professionals, wanted to offer a program based on scientific evidence about what is effective in addiction recovery that would evolve as the evidence evolved. At present, SMART Recovery primarily incorporates cognitive behavioral and motivational enhancement techniques for change.

SMART Recovery Purposes and Methods

1. We help individuals gain independence from addictive behavior.
2. We teach how to
   - enhance and maintain motivation to abstain,
   - cope with urges,
   - manage thoughts, feelings, and behavior, and
   - balance momentary and enduring satisfactions.
3. Our efforts are based on scientific knowledge, and evolve as scientific knowledge evolves.
4. Individuals who have gained independence from addictive behavior are invited to stay involved with us, to enhance their gains and help others.
   (http://www.smartrecovery.org)

LifeRing Secular Recovery

LifeRing Secular Recovery (LSR; www.unhooked.com) began in 1999 when a federal court ruled that Secular Organizations for Sobriety (SOS) could not use that name in northern California. SOS meetings in that region adopted the name LSR. LSR evolved into an independent organization and ratified its bylaws in 2001. Groups in other regions of the United States have since affiliated with LSR. This organization utilizes the "Three-S" philosophy, which is shorthand for the fundamental principles of LifeRing Recovery: Sobriety, Secularity, and Self-Help.

The "Three-S" Philosophy

Sobriety. "Sobriety" can mean different things in dictionaries, but in LifeRing it always means abstinence. The basic membership requirement is a sincere desire to remain abstinent from alcohol and "drugs." LifeRing welcomes alcoholics and addicts without distinction, as well as people involved in relationships with them. Please look elsewhere for support if your intention is to keep drinking or using, but not so much, or to stop drinking but continue using, or stop using but continue drinking. The successful LifeRing participant practices the Sobriety Priority, meaning that nothing is allowed to interfere with staying abstinent from alcohol and "drugs." The motto is "we do not drink or use, no matter what."

Secularity. LifeRing Recovery welcomes people of all faiths and none. You get to keep whatever religious beliefs you have, and you are under no pressure to acquire any if you don't. Neither religion nor anti-religion normally comes up in meeting discussion. Participants' spiritual or religious beliefs or lack thereof remain private. Participants are free to attend both LifeRing and Twelve-Step meetings, but LifeRing supports recovery methods that rely on human efforts rather than on divine intervention or faith healing.

Self-Help. Self-help in LifeRing means that the key to recovery is the individual's own motivation and effort. The main purpose of the group process is to reinforce the individual's own inner strivings to stay clean and sober. LifeRing is a permanent workshop where individuals can build their own personal recovery plans. Cross-talk is permitted within limits set by each meeting. LifeRing does not prescribe any particular "steps" and is not a vehicle for any particular therapeutic doctrine. LifeRing participation is compatible with a wide variety of abstinence-based therapeutic or counseling programs. (http://www.unhooked.com/lsr/three_s_philosophy.htm)

Clinical Considerations

In *Handbook of Alcoholism Treatment Approaches: Effective Alternatives,* Miller and Hester (2003, p. 11) commented, "Because research has provided few reliable guidelines about how best to match people to different approaches, clients themselves are important resources in choosing from the menu of options. They know a great deal about themselves and their own level of motivation for different approaches to change." Their statement is informed by a review of nearly 400 treatment trials. That review also indicated that both 12-step treatment and 12-step groups were rather low on a list of treatment approaches ranked according to efficacy. Thus it does not seem sensible to insist that a client attend 12-step treatment or 12-step groups if that person is unmotivated to do so.

The introduction to this chapter listed various objections to attending 12-step groups or 12-step-based treatment. If a client offers objections to the 12-step approach, or any other approach, it is worth discussing those objections in the hope that the information elicited will result in the formulation of a more effective treatment plan. Some objections may be based on simple misunderstandings and thus be easily corrected. Others may provide direct access to the client's deepest beliefs and values, which are unlikely to change in one or a few clinical interviews. The provider will be more effective at enhancing motivation and supporting treatment adherence by maintaining an open mind about what the final recovery plan will look like, rather than attempting to impose his or her will upon the client. An individualized approach to recovery would suggest that there are as many recovery plans as there are individuals in recovery. Fletcher (2001) reviewed the histories of 222 individuals who had maintained recovery for at least 5 years, using a variety of recovery methods.

We are not opposed to including 12-step groups in recovery planning. There are numerous advantages to attending 12-step groups, provided the client does so willingly. The groups are very easily accessible (e.g., they are listed in every U.S. phone book); they draw a large attendance (increasing the chances that the client will find one or more persons who can provide a suitable model of recovery); and attendance is likely to be well supported by friends, family, other 12-step members, and treatment professionals.

Neither are we opposed to some providers offering 12-step treatment exclusively. Although treatment systems need to provide options, and those providing evaluations and recommendations need to present all alternatives in recovery planning, it is legitimate for a provider to say: "If you wish to pursue a 12-step based program, we can provide that here. We have an excellent one. It is the only approach we offer. I've mentioned the other options you have to consider. At some of those facilities you could try more than one approach, or even have a blended program, but here we exclusively do 12-step. It's now up to you to decide where you want to start."

Because clients can return to treatment a number of times, a provider open to hearing about strong negative feelings toward 12-step groups or 12-step providers will regularly hear them. In these cases, listening may provide an opportunity for catharsis. How much catharsis to allow may be difficult to determine. Too little catharsis, and the client may not be fully receptive to pursuing a new treatment approach. Too much catharsis can turn into an avoidance of the recovery work needed. Alternative support groups need to monitor this issue closely because many participants assume the group is a trauma support group for their negative 12-step experiences rather than a recovery group for their current addiction problems.

For providers whose recovery orientation has been primarily or exclusively a 12-step one, the proposals in this chapter may be troubling. One option for such providers is to consider a new overarching framework of recovery based on the principles of natural recovery and harm reduction. The 12-step approach can then fit under this framework, at least in the provider's work with clients. It is understood that if a provider has personal recovery plans, these remain a highly personal matter.

Both treatment and support groups can be viewed as extensions of the naturally occurring process of addiction recovery, often termed "natural recovery," which refers to recovery from addiction without attendance in treatment or support groups. It appears that natural recovery is the predominant route to recovery for all addictions (Klingemann, 2001; Peele, 2004). It is certainly true for cigarette smoking. Those who attend treatment or a support group are often the ones who struggle the most. Treatment and support can be viewed as helping the client do more of, or do a better job at, the processes of change that are already in operation (to some degree). From this perspective, there is little in treatment that goes beyond natural recovery. As the French surgeon Ambroise Paré (1517–1590) famously remarked: "I treated him, but God healed him."

Addiction service providers would do well to be similarly humble. Thus the provider might ask, What outside assistance would promote the movement toward recovery, the natural recovery, already occurring? How can this assistance be provided without also impeding natural recovery? As physicians learn, "First, do no harm."

Harm reduction refers to the recognition that a client is often not ready to make a full commitment to recovery, but may consider partial change. If the provider supports these changes, the provider may at least be helping to reduce the harm the client is exposed to. In time, small changes added together may amount to full or nearly full recovery. Harm reduction is the opposite of insistence on abstinence, residential treatment, or some other major change. Harm reduction can also be viewed as the recognition of the clinical reality that most clients are not ready for major change. The provider can align with the level of motivation the client currently has, and hope to make greater progress later. By insisting on too much at once, the clinician may alienate the client.

Within a harm reduction perspective, understanding the natural recovery that is already occurring can guide the provider to recommendations and actions that support that natural recovery, and build a relationship that can nurture more changes in the future. In this manner, providers can work with clients and not against them (Miller & Rollnick, 2002). As suggested in this chapter, knowledge about non-12-step treatment and support groups is an important component for dealing with a substantial portion of clients the addiction service provider will see.

References

Alcoholics Anonymous. (1976). *Alcoholics anonymous: The story of how many thousands of men and women have recovered from alcoholism* (3rd ed.) New York: Alcoholics Anonymous World Services. (Popularly known as the Big Book)

American Psychiatric Association. (1994). *Diagnostic and statistical manual of mental disorders* (4th ed.). Washington, DC: Author.

Apanovitch, D. P. (1998). Religion and rehabilitation: The requisition of god by the state. *Duke Law Journal, 47*(4), 785–852. Available at http://www.law.duke.edu/journals/dlj/articles/dlj47p785.htm

Christopher, J. (1985). Sobriety without superstition. *Free Inquiry.* Available at http://www.secularhumanism.org/index.php?section=library&page=jchristopher_26_5

Fletcher, A. (2001). *Sober for good: New solutions for drinking problems—Advice from those who have succeeded.* Boston: Houghton Mifflin.

Hester, R. K., & Miller, W. R. (Eds.). (2003). *Handbook of alcoholism treatment approaches: Effective alternatives* (3rd ed.). Boston: Allyn & Bacon.

Horvath, A. T. (2005). Alternative support groups. In J. H. Lowinson, P. Ruiz, R. B. Millman, & J. G. Langrod (Eds.), *Substance abuse: A comprehensive textbook* (4th ed., pp. 599–609). Philadelphia: Lippincott, Williams & Wilkins.

Humphries, K. (2004). *Circles of recovery: Self-help organizations for addictions.* Cambridge: Cambridge University Press.

Klingemann, H. K. (2001). Natural recovery from alcohol problems. In N. Heather, T. J. Peters, & T. J. Stockwell (Eds.), *International handbook of alcohol dependence and problems* (pp. 649–662). New York: Wiley.

McCrady, B. S., Horvath, A. T., & Delaney, S. I. (2003). Self-help groups. In R. K. Hester & W. R. Miller (Eds.), *Handbook of alcoholism treatment approaches: Effective alternatives* (3rd ed., pp. 165–187). Boston: Allyn & Bacon.

Miller, W. R., & Hester, R. K. (2003). Treating alcohol problems: Toward an informed eclecticism. In R. K. Hester & W. R. Miller (Eds.), *Handbook of alcoholism treatment approaches: Effective alternatives* (3rd ed., pp. 1–12). Boston: Allyn & Bacon.

Miller, W. R. & Rollnick, S. (2002). *Motivational interviewing: Preparing people for change* (2nd ed.). New York: Guilford Press.

Miller, W. R., Wilbourne, P. L., & Hettema, J. E. (2003). What works? A summary of alcohol treatment outcome research. In R. K. Hester & W. R. Miller (Eds.), *Handbook of alcoholism treatment approaches: Effective alternatives* (3rd ed., pp. 13–63). Boston: Allyn & Bacon.

National Institute on Drug Abuse. (1999). *Principles of drug addiction treatment.* Washington, DC: Author. Available at http://www.drugabuse.gov/PDF/PODAT/PODAT.pdf

Peele, S. (2004). *Seven tools to beat addiction.* New York: Three Rivers Press.

Peele, S., Bufe, C., & Brodsky, A. (2000). *Resisting 12-step coercion: How to fight forced participation in AA, NA or 12-step treatment.* Tucson, AZ: See Sharp Press.

Roman, P. M., & Blum, T. C. (1997). *National treatment center study summary report.* Athens: University of Georgia Press.

Secular Organizations for Sobriety. (2006). *An overview of SOS: A self-empowerment approach to sobriety.* Retrieved September 10, 2006, from http://www.sossobriety.org/overview.htm

Resources

LifeRing
www.unhooked.com/

Moderation Management
www.moderation.org/

Secular Organizations for Sobriety (Save Our Selves)
www.sossobriety.org

SMART Recovery
www.smartrecovery.org/

Women for Sobriety
www.womenforsobriety.org/

CHAPTER 5

Substance Abuse and Misuse Among Older Adults

Risk Factors, Treatment, Prevention, and Future Directions

Nick Curtis Jackson

The number of older adults in the United States is expected to grow dramatically into the early to middle part of the 21st century. Substantial increases in life expectancy, from approximately 47 years in 1900 to close to 80 by the year 2000, coupled with the birth of the Baby Boom generation (1946–1964), have led to the prediction that up to 30% of the population will be composed of persons 65 years old and older by the year 2025. Even greater growth is expected in the population of very old persons. The U.S. Census Bureau has estimated that 1 out of every 12 Americans will be over 80 years old in the year 2050, with 1.2 million persons 100 years old or older (U.S. Census Bureau, 2001).

The long-expected growth of the older adult population in the United States is already being realized; the year 2006 marked the 60th birth year of the oldest Baby Boomers. Those who are already financially able and ready have opted for early retirement, and with this transition into older adulthood, are beginning to face many of the joys and challenges associated with the transition. Some of these joys include freedom from daily career commitments, the ability to travel, more leisure time with family and friends, and time to pursue hobbies and other interests delayed by intensive work schedules. Some of the challenges of the transition include the loss of a sense of meaning associated with one's career, the stress of financial planning in one's later years, the loss of friends and family members who are also older, and the health-care challenges that often ensue as one reaches the later years of life.

While the lives of older adults in the United States generally have been and will continue to be rich, lively, and adventurous, a portion of this population has resorted to using substances as a means of coping with the many challenges that accompany later life. Some researchers have even suggested that improvements in the quality of life for the elderly, such as greater disposable income, better overall health, and more leisure time, can lead to heavier drinking, for example (e.g., Watts, 2007).

Another portion of the older population has continued to abuse substances from earlier years of life as a means of coping with ongoing life challenges. Those who do not deliberately seek substances such as alcohol and illicit drugs to ward off the new and continuing stresses of older adulthood may fall prey to prescription or over-the-counter substance misuse or abuse.

Despite the obvious challenges older adults face, clinicians have not typically targeted them as an at-risk group; substance abuse has generally been considered a problem for adolescents and younger adults (Reid & Anderson, 1997). Thus, the methods for detecting, diagnosing, and treating older adults for substance abuse have mostly been designed for the young. Further, symptoms of abuse easily detected among younger adults are not as easily detected among elders because abuse symptoms are often mistaken for symptoms of illnesses and disorders in older adulthood, such as balance problems, sensory deficits, and dementia or delirium (Atkinson, 1990; Atkinson, Ganzini, & Bernstein, 1992). Another reason for the difficulty in diagnosis is that older people may live in greater isolation than younger adults (Atkinson et al., 1992). Further complicating matters is the tendency of some families to hide substance abuse of their older loved ones either because they are embarrassed or because they feel that older adults, nearing death, should be allowed to indulge in unhealthy practices they enjoy (Atkinson et al., 1992). Also, some families may believe that alcohol is healthy and so may not be disposed to recognize abuse when it occurs.

This chapter reviews a sample of the literature on substance abuse and misuse among older adults, including treatment and prevention strategies that have been demonstrated to successfully avert abuse and misuse of alcohol, medication, and illegal drugs. O'Connell et al. (cited in Watts, 2007) found that older adults can benefit from treatment as much as younger people. Olsin (cited in Goldberg, 2005) noted that older adults are most amenable to treatment in facilities that are tailored to and knowledgeable about the needs of older substance abusers. The chapter concludes with a discussion of directions for future research and treatment in anticipation of a higher incidence of substance abuse and misuse as Baby Boomers and their children reach older adulthood in the early to middle part of the 21st century.

Alcohol Abuse

Prevalence

There has been some divergence in reports of the prevalence of alcohol use and abuse in the United States, but researchers generally agree that drinking declines with age, that a greater percentage of older men drink than older women, and that separated and divorced older adults have greater dependence problems than widows and widowers (Bucholz, Sheline, & Helzer, 1995; Ganzini & Atkinson, 1996). However, in a review of longitudinal studies on alcohol abuse, Reid and Anderson (1997) cited studies that reported declining consumption with age (Adams, Garry, Rhyne, Hunt, & Goodwin, 1990; Temple & Leino, 1989), stable consumption with age (Ekerdt, De Labry, Glynn, & Davis, 1989), and increased consumption with age (Gordon & Kannel, 1983). Estimated percentages of overall alcohol abuse prevalence in the United States are varied, ranging from .6% to as much as 10% (Glantz, 1983; Liberto, Oslin, & Ruskin, 1992; Reid & Anderson, 1997; U.S. Department of Health and Human Services [DHHS], 2005). A 1992 report from Congress estimated that 2.5 million older Americans had alcohol-related problems (U.S. House of Representatives, 1992).

Many researchers have speculated about the reasons for lower incidence and prevalence of alcohol use and abuse among older adults compared to younger and middle-aged adults. Foos and Clark (2003) hypothesized that alcohol use and abuse in the elderly are underreported due to the isolation that sometimes accompanies older adulthood (also see Ganzini & Atkinson, 1996; Lawson, 1989). Foos and Clark noted that alcoholics often die before reaching older adulthood owing to such complications as cirrhosis of the liver and Kosakoff's syndrome (also see Moos, Brennan, & Mertens, 1994). Also, it is possible that among those elders who grew up during Prohibition (1920–1933), the strong anti-alcohol sentiment prevailing at that time might have had the effect of reducing alcohol use in that cohort (Ganzini & Atkinson, 1996). Elders in this cohort might also be more ashamed to report excessive alcohol consumption (Ganzini & Atkinson, 1996). Finally, Atkinson et al. (1992) suggested that clinicians may play a role in underreporting excessive drinking among older adults because they often fail to view older adults as an at-risk group for alcohol abuse. Supporting this claim, Curtis, Geller, Stokes, Levine, and Moore (1989) found that physicians were not as likely to diagnose alcohol abuse in older adults as they were in younger adults, and that when physicians did diagnose older adults, they were less likely to refer them for treatment. It is also possible that such underreporting could be a function of physicians, confusing symptoms of alcohol abuse with symptoms of disorders or diseases characteristic of older adulthood.

The literature on the prevalence of alcoholism in older adulthood distinguishes between early- and late-onset abuse. Early-onset alcoholics are those who started drinking in early to middle adulthood and have continued to drink into late adulthood. This group comprises two thirds of the population of older alcoholics (Dupree & Schonfeld, 1996; Institute of Alcohol Studies, 2007). Late-onset alcoholics are those who began drinking in older adulthood and are believed to drink in response to the stressors associated with older adulthood (Horton & Fogelman, 1991; Schutte, Brennan, & Moos, 1998). Reid and Anderson (1997) noted that the data on incidence of late-onset alcohol use disorders may vary depending upon how "late" is defined, but they cited prevalence percentages ranging from 11% to 33% of older alcoholics (Adams & Waskel, 1991; Brennan & Moos, 1991). Atkinson, Tolson, and Turner (1990) reported that among a sample of patients age 60 years and older who were being treated for alcoholism, the prevalence of late-onset alcoholism ranged from 29% to 68%. In the Epidemiologic Catchment Area (ECA) study (Eaton et al., 1989), incidence of late-onset alcoholism among persons age 65 years and older was 1.2 per 100 for men and .27 per 100 for women.

Information about the prevalence of alcohol dependence in older adulthood by gender, ethnicity, and type of residence (community-residing versus institution-residing) is also available. In one report, alcohol abuse and dependence were found to be four times more common among older men than older women (1.2% vs. .3%) (Grant, Adams, & Reed, 1984). The highest rate of alcoholism appears to be for widowers who are age 75 years and older (Glass, Prigerson, Kasl, & Mendes de Leon, 1995; Gurland, 1996). The ECA study reported that 1-year prevalence of alcohol abuse among people age 65 and older was 3.1% in men and .46% in women (Helzer, Burnam, & McEvoy, 1991). It should be noted, however, that the lower prevalence among women might be a function of underreporting. The current cohort of older women would have been exposed to rather severe societal disapprobation regarding alcohol use, with such use in women being widely associated with prostitution and moral lassitude. In response, women might experience greater shame and thus a greater reluctance to report problems with alcohol (see Chapter 2 of this volume).

Research findings on alcohol abuse in older adults by ethnicity are somewhat inconsistent. There is general agreement that older White Americans have higher rates of alcohol dependence than older African Americans (National Institute on Alcohol Abuse and Alcoholism [NIAAA], 1995). However, Gomberg and Zucker (1998) reported that among low-income older adults, African Americans have significantly more problems with alcohol dependence than other ethnic groups. Jackson et al. (1998) noted that alcohol use decreases with age among White Americans, but increases with age among African Americans. Further complicating these reports, Helzer et al. (1991) found that older African Americans have higher rates of alcohol dependence than older Hispanics and that older Hispanics have higher rates than older White Americans. They also found that Hispanic females have lower rates of dependence than older Whites and African Americans. Gomberg and Nelson (1995), in a comparison of older African American and White male alcoholic patients, found that African American men consumed larger quantities of alcohol, were more likely to prefer drinks with a high alcohol content, tended to drink publicly more often, and suffered more health consequences.

Researchers are in general agreement that older residents of institutional settings such as nursing homes are more likely to abuse or to have abused alcohol than community-residing older adults. As early as the late 1970s, researchers reported a higher incidence of alcohol dependence among nursing home residents, psychiatric patients, and patients on medical wards than among community-residing elders (Schuckit & Miller, 1976; Zimberg, 1979); research throughout the 1980s and 1990s supported these findings (see Adams, 1997; Horton & Fogelman, 1991). Adams and Cox (1997) speculated that greater alcohol dependence among long-term care residents in recent years might reflect a trend toward using such settings as short-term alcohol rehabilitation centers. Atkinson et al. (1990) hypothesized that late-onset alcohol dependence might be encouraged in some retirement communities in which social drinking is encouraged. Joseph (1997) estimated problem drinking to be as high as 49% among nursing home residents, and Joseph, Ganzini, and Atkinson (1995) identified 11% of Veterans Administration nursing home admissions as alcohol dependent. Reports of the incidence of alcohol dependence among older patients in hospitals, utilizing standardized screening instruments and admissions data, range from 6% to 23% (Council on Scientific Affairs, American Medical Association, 1996; Curtis et al., 1989; Mangion, Platt, & Syam, 1992; Simon, Epstein, & Reynolds, 1968). Reports of alcohol dependence in hospital emergency departments are strikingly consistent, with estimates at 14% to 15% of older adult admissions (Adams, Magruder-Habib, Trued, & Broome, 1992; Council on Scientific Affairs, American Medical Association, 1996; Tabisz, Badger, Meatherall, & Jacyk, 1991). Reports of incidence among geriatric psychiatry patients are also fairly consistent. Speer and Bates (1992) identified 23% of hospitalized geriatric psychiatry patients as alcohol dependent, while the Council on Scientific Affairs of the American Medical Association estimated incidence of dependence at 20% in geriatric psychiatric wards.

A few somewhat dated studies have focused on the rate of alcoholism among community-residing older adults. For example, Goodwin et al. (1987), in a study of 270 community-residing adults age 65 years and older, found that 17% had more than two drinks per day. Maddox (1988) summarized a study by the National Institute of Mental Health that sampled 8,000 community-residing adults over 60 years old. The range of self-reported alcoholism prevalence was .9% to 4.6% for men and .1% to .7% for women. Meyers, Hingson, Mucatel, and Goldman (1982) interviewed 928 noninstitutionalized older adults and found that 53% reported abstaining from alcohol use, 5% reported having previous alcohol abuse problems, and 1% reported having a current drinking problem. Brennan and Moos (1990) found that community-dwelling problem drinkers aged 55 to 65 reported more negative life events, chronic stress, and lack of social resources than nonproblem drinkers in this age range.

Karlamangla, Zhou, Reuben, Greendale, and Moore (2006) tracked 14,127 adults ages 25 to 74 at baseline over 22 years to determine demographic trends related to smoking and drinking alcohol. They discovered that heavy drinking at the reference age of 56.5 years was related to being unmarried, not graduating from high school, receiving an income lower than the median, and smoking. Getting married and quitting smoking were associated with a lower probability of heavy drinking. Further, they found that drinking levels for both men and women declined with age, but the decline was slower in men.

Alcohol Abuse Risk Factors and Effects

Risk factors for alcohol use and effects of alcohol abuse can be categorized into biological/physiological risk factors and effects, the effects of alcoholism on cognition, and psychosocial risk factors and effects. Research on risk factors and effects of alcohol use are presented together here because in many cases researchers have not clearly distinguished between risk factors and effects.

The physiological process of aging itself, or primary aging, is perhaps the greatest risk factor for alcohol abuse in older adulthood because it increases one's sensitivity to alcohol. Reid and Anderson (1997) noted that the composition of the body is altered with age in that equivalent amounts of substances such as alcohol produce higher concentrations in the bloodstream. For example, a 1-ounce drink consumed by a 60-year-old produces a blood alcohol concentration 20% greater than the same amount consumed by a younger adult (Ganzini & Atkinson, 1996; Reid & Anderson, 1997; Vestal et al., 1977). An age-related decrease in body water, which dilutes alcohol, presents increased risk for intoxication in spite of the ability of older adults to metabolize and eliminate alcohol as efficiently as younger adults (Dufour & Fuller, 1995). Further, unlike younger adults, older adults do not become more tolerant of alcohol as they consume it (Kalant, 1998). Thus, older adults can develop alcohol problems even when their consumption rate remains stable.

Primary aging, when combined with alcohol dependence, also presents risk for a number of physical injuries and conditions. For example, as with the general population, risk for injuries from automobile crashes is significantly increased with alcohol use among older adults (Waller, 1998). Since increased use of prescription medications often accompanies older adulthood, there is also greater potential for adverse interactions with alcohol consumption that result in long-term disability (Korrapati & Vestal, 1995). Older alcohol users are also at greater risk for falls than older nonusers because the cerebellum, which decreases in volume with age, regulates gait, posture, and balance (Malmivaara, Heliovaara, Knekt, Reunanen, & Aromaa, 1993; Reid & Anderson, 1997). Because older women are at risk for osteoporosis, those who drink are especially vulnerable to hip fractures (Bikle, Stesin, Halloran, Steinbach, & Recker, 1993; Council on Scientific Affairs, American Medical Association, 1996; Schnitzler, Menashe, Sutton, & Sweet, 1988). However, Reid and Anderson (1997) cited several studies of community-residing older adults that reported no increased risk of falls or injuries from falls with alcohol use (see Grisso et al., 1991; Nelson, Sattin, Langlois, DeVito, & Stevens, 1992; Nevitt, Cummings, Kidd, & Black, 1989; Tinetti, Speechley, & Ginter, 1988).

While alcohol consumption among older adults affects their cognitive functioning differently than it affects younger adults, the degree and the permanence of cognitive impairment among older adults who drink has not been well established. It has been widely assumed that persons who abuse alcohol for an extended period are more susceptible to dementia, with some studies reporting prevalence estimates of alcoholism as high as 21% to 24% among dementia cases (Carlen et al., 1994; Smith & Atkinson, 1995). Several other researchers have claimed that alcohol dependence in older adulthood is directly associated with prolonged cognitive impairment and dementia (e.g., I. Grant et al., 1984; Pfefferbaum, Rosenbloom, Crusan, & Jernigan, 1988). However, while *Diagnostic and Statistical Manual of Mental Disorders–Fourth Edition* (American Psychiatric Association, 1994) criteria for an alcohol-induced dementia diagnosis have been established, they are not specific enough to rule out other causes. Aging and alcohol use have similar effects on the brain in that both decrease its volume (Harper et al., 1998), so it is difficult to distinguish between natural aging effects on cognition and effects of alcoholism on cognition in older adulthood. In a report by the National Institute on Alcohol Abuse and Alcoholism (NIAAA, 1998), it was speculated that long-term alcohol use might cause changes in the cerebellum and frontal lobes, which could hasten the effects of aging on cognition. In support of this claim, Pfefferbaum, Sullivan, Mathalon, and Lim (1997) found that older alcoholics had more brain tissue loss than younger alcoholics, despite similar total alcohol use. Atkinson et al. (1992) stated that neuro-psychological deficits in chronic alcoholics are magnified with age. Other researchers have hesitated to link older adult alcoholism directly with cognitive impairment. For example, Reid and Anderson (1997) cited two studies that indicated no age–alcohol effects on a variety of cognitive performance tasks (Collins & Mertens, 1988; Yesavage, Dolhert, & Taylor, 1994). Further, Reid et al. (2006) conducted a study of 760 men ages 65 and older and found that individuals who drank at a light or moderate level (seven or fewer drinks a week) actually performed better on cognitive tasks than those who never drank or who were former drinkers.

Depression and other psychiatric disorders have been identified as psychosocial risk factors for alcoholism, as coexisting with alcohol use, or as an effect of alcohol use among older adults. For example, Grant and Harford (1995) found that older alcoholics were three times more likely to exhibit major depressive disorder than older non-alcoholics. Grabbe, Demi, Camann, and Potter (1997) found that moderate and heavy older drinkers were 16 times more likely to commit suicide than older non-alcoholics. Moos, Brennan, and Schutte (1998) found that 30% of a sample of 5,600 older alcoholics had concurrent psychiatric disorders. Psychiatric disorders in older adulthood are often assumed to be linked to the theme of loss that accompanies the older adulthood experience and the stress it causes. The link between loss, stress, and alcoholism, however, has been difficult to demonstrate. Atkinson et al. (1992) pointed out that while loss may ultimately be experienced by all older adults, substance abuse occurs in only a small percentage of the older adult population. The role that stress plays in alcoholism as a function of older adult loss remains an enigma.

As one might assume, there is an inverse relationship between reports of family alcoholism and the age of onset of alcoholism. In other words, it is more likely that early-onset drinking, rather than late-onset drinking, is linked to the experience of family alcoholism. Atkinson (1984) indicated that 41% of late-onset alcoholics reported familial alcoholism, while 86% of early-onset alcoholics reported familial alcoholism. Family members may play a role in late-onset alcoholism, however, by frequently providing alcohol to the older family member or by becoming drinking partners with the family member (Atkinson et al., 1992).

Approach, Assessment, and Diagnosis of Alcohol Abuse in Older Adults

A sound approach to working with older adults who have become dependent on alcohol always involves the clinician's sensitivity to the distinct needs of older patients. For example, the cohort of older adults who came of age during Prohibition experienced a nationwide stigma associated with alcohol use. Individuals in this cohort might be reluctant to share their personal history of alcohol use (Reid & Anderson, 1997). There might also be an impression among members of this age group that psychological and psychiatric care are reserved for persons with mental illness, such as schizophrenia, and that care is only provided in institutional settings such as state hospitals. For these and other cohort-based reasons, clinicians should approach the therapeutic relationship with the older alcoholic from this cohort gently. Examples of strategies for a gentle approach include introducing oneself as a helper or friend rather than a clinician, psychologist, or psychiatrist, and building a strong rapport with the patient while gradually introducing the topic of alcohol dependence.

Other needs of older adults are not cohort based, but are due to the primary aging process. For example, all older adults, to some degree, experience sensory deficits that impair hearing, vision, and other sensory functions. Older adults also experience slower processing speed as a function of primary aging. In the process of building rapport, administering assessments and diagnostic tests, and providing treatment, the clinician should proceed slowly and frequently seek feedback from the older patient about how he or she is experiencing treatment delivery.

The assessment of alcohol dependence among older adults is complicated by the potential coexistence of problems that mimic symptoms of dependence. For example, Reid and Anderson (1997) noted that symptoms of alcohol dependence, such as depression, isolation, and confusion, might be caused by other problems associated with the aging process. Other examples of problems, the effects of which are similar to the effects of chronic alcohol use, include dementia, loss of balance, and sensory deficits. To assist clinicians with the initial informal assessment of alcohol dependence among older adults and help them rule out other problems, Lichtenberg (1994) provided a list of nonspecific presentations that include the following:

- general health problems: poor grooming, incontinence, myopathy, falling, accidental hypothermia, seizures, malnutrition, diarrhea, unexplained bruises or burns, peptic ulceration, heart and liver disease, chronic obstructive pulmonary disease
- interpersonal problems: confusion, aggression, termination of family relationships
- alcohol problems: being preoccupied with drinking, drinking rapidly, using alcohol as medicine, drinking alone, and protecting alcohol supply

Additionally, Beresford, Blow, Brower, Adams, and Hall (1988) provided a list of general features of alcohol addiction that might assist clinicians in their initial assessment of dependence:

1. tolerance: the need to increase drinking by 50% to achieve the same effect (however, older adults may not increase tolerance)
2. withdrawal: symptoms that ensue 6 to 12 hours after blood alcohol level has decreased, such as higher blood pressure, low-grade fever, sweating, nausea, and anxiety
3. loss of control over drinking behavior
4. social decline

The clinical interview reveals the particulars of the patient's life that further assist in the assessment process, including personal history, family relationships, and frequency and pattern of drinking behavior. Clinicians are advised to seek information about current social problems with family and friends, impaired social networks, solitary drinking, binge drinking, depression, and coordination problems (Gomberg, 1982). They are also advised to seek information about past patterns of drinking behavior, not only to distinguish between early- versus late-onset dependence, but also to detect intermittent histories of drinking that suggest the use of alcohol as a problem solver (Gomberg, 1982). Shame is a common theme of the clinical interview with the older alcoholic, so clinicians are encouraged to build rapport not only with the patient, as mentioned previously, but also with members of the patient's social network, such as family, friends, and caregivers, who might be able to detect and possibly explain alcohol-related behavior (Atkinson et al., 1992; Ganzini & Atkinson, 1996). These observers of the patient's behavior patterns and personal history may offer valuable insight to assist with diagnosis and subsequent determination of effective treatment. Home visitation may also be a useful tool in the clinical interview (Atkinson et al., 1991). In the home environment, the clinician can speak with the patient and family members/caregivers in the setting where they are most comfortable, observe behavior of the patient and family/caregivers where problem drinking is most likely to occur, and observe any general features of the home environment that might encourage dependence. For example, limited accessibility may hinder the resident from going outdoors and prevent potential "gatekeepers" such as mail carriers, oil delivery personnel, electricity meter readers, and other visitors from observing behaviors of older residents that might be cause for concern (see Raschko, 1990).

Formal assessment and screening tools such as the DSM-IV and other tools that were designed through work with younger and middle-aged adults have generally been deemed inappropriate for use with older adults. The DSM-IV criteria include increased tolerance to the effects of alcohol over time, but because of the physiological processes associated with aging, older adults may not experience increased tolerance with continued use of alcohol (U.S. Department of Health and Human Services [DHHS], 2005). Other DSM-IV criteria are related to the impact of substance abuse on typical tasks of young to middle adulthood such as parental treatment of children and work performance, which generally are not relevant to the life situation of older adults.

Two examples of assessment instruments that several researchers have identified as appropriate standardized tools for use with older adults are the Michigan Alcohol Screening Test (MAST; Selzer, 1971) and the CAGE (Ewing, 1984). The MAST is a 25-item instrument developed to provide a consistent and quantifiable method to detect alcohol dependence (Selzer, 1971). Pokorny, Miller, and Kaplan (1972) selected 10 of the 25 questions on the MAST to develop the Brief MAST. Internal consistency for the Brief MAST was reported at .8 and .6 on samples of alcoholics at all ages. The Brief MAST contains the following questions:

1. Do you feel that you are a normal drinker?
2. Do friends and relatives think you are a normal drinker?
3. Have you ever attended AA?
4. Have you ever lost friends or girlfriends/boyfriends because of drinking?
5. Have you ever gotten into trouble at work because of drinking?
6. Have you ever neglected your obligations, your family, or your work for 2 or more days in a row because you were drinking?
7. Have you ever had delirium tremens, severe shaking, heard voices, or seen things that were not there after drinking?
8. Have you ever gone to anyone for help about your drinking?
9. Have you ever been in a hospital because of drinking?
10. Have you ever been arrested for drunk driving after drinking?

Four or more "yes" answers on the Brief MAST suggest possible alcoholism (Pokorny et al., 1972). While item 6 addresses neglect of work, which may not be applicable to older adults, it also addresses neglect of general obligations and family, which is applicable to older adulthood. Item 5 is the only question that is exclusively about work. All other questions in the Brief MAST are as applicable to older adults as they are to younger adults.

The CAGE questionnaire contains four simple questions about attitudes and behaviors associated with the respondent's drinking:

C: Have you ever felt you ought to cut down on your drinking?
A: Have people annoyed you by criticizing your drinking?
G: Have you ever felt bad or guilty about your drinking?
E: Have you ever had a drink first thing in the morning to steady your nerves or get rid of a hangover?

Two "yes" responses indicate possible alcoholism, while three or four "yes" responses indicate certain alcoholism (Ewing, 1984). The CAGE has demonstrated good generalizability when applied to older adult populations (Reid & Anderson, 1997).

Finally, laboratory tests can be used as a diagnostic and assessment tool to reveal information about blood alcohol level, alcohol content in urine, and long-term physiological effects of alcoholism. Liver disease, peripheral polyneuropathy, and cerebellar ataxia are examples of physiological effects that are revealed through laboratory diagnostic procedures (Ganzini & Atkinson, 1996). A blood alcohol level of more than 150 mg per 100 ml is evidence for tolerance and physical dependence if the patient presents with relatively normal mental status (Ganzini & Atkinson, 1996). Atkinson et al. (1992) suggested that toxicological examinations of urine, blood, and breath are the most useful laboratory tests for diagnosing alcohol dependence.

As mentioned previously, alcohol dependence may be more difficult to diagnose among older adults than among younger adults. Reid and Anderson (1997) offered three suggestions for clinicians to deal with the difficulty of diagnosis. First, they stated that brief advice is appropriate even without certain diagnosis; the clinician should follow this by suggesting a 1-month trial of abstinence as long as the patient is not at risk for withdrawal. Second, Reid and Anderson suggested referral to a specialist or appropriate agency for assessment. At this appointment, the clinician should explain the need for another opinion in order to avoid misdiagnosis. Referral should be formal and tracked to reduce the risk of the patient not following through. Third, a record of clinician concerns should be made even when no action is taken, and care should be taken to avoid nonessential sedative-hypnotics or other psychoactive drugs (Reid & Anderson, 1997).

Alcohol Abuse Management and Treatment

Before a clinician chooses a particular strategy or combination of strategies for treatment, it is important to consider general recommendations that have been deemed useful. According to Ganzini and Atkinson (1996) and Smyer and Qualls (1999), the clinician should follow three general goals for treatment: (a) to stabilize and reduce the consumption of alcohol, (b) to treat medical and psychiatric comorbidity, and (c) to reduce the risk of relapse through psychosocial changes and social interventions. Gomberg and Zucker (1998) noted that patients in elder-specific programs are more likely to complete treatment, while Ganzini and Atkinson suggested that in mild cases of dependence, the only social intervention needed might be the clinician's advice to cut down on alcohol. A person who has more pervasive alcohol problems should receive outpatient psychosocial treatment and attend Alcoholics Anonymous (AA) meetings (if the person objects to AA, the clinician might suggest alternatives; see Chapter 4 of this volume). In more serious cases, patients should be referred to an inpatient alcoholism treatment unit (Ganzini & Atkinson, 1996). Nirenberg, Gomberg, and Cellucci (1998) offered a list of general considerations and recommendations for treatment of older adult alcohol abusers:

1. Treatment effects may be realized more slowly for elders, so more patience is needed.
2. The age differential between therapist and client is an important consideration because of possible embarrassment of disclosure to younger persons.
3. Therapists should work with the family of the older abuser.
4. The dignity of the older person must be considered at all times.

Finally, Dupree and Schonfeld (1996) identified six recommendations for treatment of older alcohol abusers based on a review of available approaches:

1. Emphasize age-specific group treatment with supportive approaches and avoidance of confrontation.
2. Focus on negative emotional states, such as depression, loneliness, and overcoming losses.
3. Teach skills to rebuild social support networks.
4. Employ staff interested and experienced in working with older adults.
5. Develop links with aging and medical services for referral to treatment and out of treatment, as well as case management.
6. Develop the pace and content of treatment appropriate for older adults.

Researchers have generally recommended conservative approaches to detoxification with older adults due to the physiological changes associated with older adulthood and the greater possibility of comorbidity with age (Reid & Anderson, 1997). Older adults generally take longer to withdraw from alcohol dependence and are likely to have more withdrawal symptoms, such as insomnia, cognitive impairment, and hypertension, during detoxification (Brower, Mudd, Blow, Young, & Hill, 1994; Reid & Anderson, 1997). In comparing 26 older patients with a mean age of 65 who were undergoing detoxification to 24 younger patients with a mean age of 29, Liskow, Rinck, Campbell, and DeSouza (1989) found that the older group had more withdrawal symptoms. Brower et al. found that the duration of withdrawal symptoms was greater among older patients than younger patients (9 vs. 6.5 days). Finally, in a study of 216 patients age 65 years and older undergoing detoxification, Finlayson, Hurt, Davis, and Morse (1988) found more serious medical conditions and more dual diagnoses compared to younger groups. Examples of dual diagnoses included dementia, delirium, and affective disorders. Additionally, 15% of the patients were dependent on prescription tranquilizers, narcotic analgesics, or sedative-hypnotics (Finlayson et al., 1988).

A variety of treatment approaches for alcohol dependence have been identified for use with older adults. In some cases, the approaches were originally designed for use with younger adults and have been adapted for use with elders, while others have been specifically designed for older adults. Research on treatment approaches indicates that older adults are at least as likely to benefit from treatment as younger adults (Atkinson, 1990; NIAAA, 1998), and at least one study has shown that adults are more likely than younger adults to complete treatment programs. Atkinson et al. (1990) observed a group of older male veteran alcohol abusers during a 1-year treatment program specifically designed for older adults. Fifty-seven percent of the men completed the program versus 27% of a group of younger men who participated in a treatment program designed for their age group.

Examples of types of treatment approaches include self-management programs, brief physician intervention, and community outreach programs. Self-management treatment approaches with older adults have generally been successful and have shown low rates of relapse (Dupree & Schonfeld, 1996). Dupree and colleagues (Dupree, Broskowski, & Schonfeld, 1984; Dupree & Schonfeld, 1996) described a behavioral self-management strategy that encourages the patient to assert progressively greater control over his or her drinking behavior; this approach stands in contrast to the psychotherapeutic approach, which focuses primarily on establishing a therapeutic relationship with a clinician. Teaching the self-management approach entails three general stages: (a) Conduct a functional analysis of the patient's drinking behavior by identifying antecedents, patterns of drinking behavior, and consequences of drinking behavior; (b) teach the patient to recognize situations that prompt excessive consumption of alcohol; and (c) teach effective coping skills specific to the antecedents that prompt the consumption. Throughout this process, the clinician maintains a passive role, reinforcing the patient's efforts to follow the self-management approach but not directly reinforcing abstention from alcohol (Dupree et al., 1984; Dupree & Schonfeld, 1996). Reid and Anderson (1997) cited several studies that have demonstrated the effectiveness of brief physician intervention with older adults who abuse alcohol and summarized the steps of brief intervention that have proved successful. The steps include (a) providing feedback to the patient who articulates concern about his or her alcohol consumption; (b) providing advice to the patient about reducing the consumption of alcohol; and (c) following up with the patient to monitor his or her consumption (Reid & Anderson, 1997). As a final example of individual treatment approaches, Graham et al. (1995) described a community outreach project in Toronto, Canada, that provided assistance to help keep older adults in their own homes, improve their physical and emotional health, and reduce or eliminate substance dependence. The project significantly reduced substance abuse and improved other areas of the older adults' lives.

Three examples of group treatment strategies include intervention, group and family therapy, and formal rehabilitation. *Intervention* is a term that has been used to describe an emergency management approach wherein a clinician schedules a confrontation between the alcohol abuser and key members of his or her social support network (Lichtenberg, 1994). The purpose of the intervention is to help the alcohol abuser overcome his or her denial of the problem and seek treatment (Atkinson, 1985; Lichtenberg, 1994). The concept is based on the idea that group confrontation is a more powerful tool than individual confrontation. Ganzini and Atkinson (1996) suggested including only one or two participants, while Lichtenberg suggested three to six persons with a meaningful relationship to the alcoholic. Ganzini and Atkinson also cautioned that young family members should not be involved in the intervention.

For those older adults who were youths during Prohibition, the group intervention process might not be as effective; the severe stigma associated with alcoholism during that era might make public disclosure particularly uncomfortable and unproductive. Increasing numbers of older adults born into later cohorts have been participating in group and family therapy programs such as AA in recent years (Gomberg & Zucker, 1998). Recommendations for the composition and structure of group treatment for elders include arranging a group of peers from the same cohort in a slow-paced and supportive environment (Kofoed, Tolson, Atkinson, Toth, & Turner, 1987), using shared reminiscence, and involving family members to improve member retention (Atkinson et al., 1992). There is some evidence that older adults remain in group treatment longer than younger adults and that older adults whose family members join them in treatment stay in treatment longer than their same-age peers who are not accompanied by family (Atkinson et al., 1992).

Formal rehabilitation programs offer multiple intervention strategies, including individual and group therapy, education, and 12-step programs (Reid & Anderson, 1997). Outcome research suggests that late-onset older alcoholics respond better to rehabilitation than early-onset older alcoholics and that late-onset abusers have better attendance, but researchers have not found significant differences between the two groups in their completion of rehabilitation programs or in relapse after treatment (Reid & Anderson, 1997). As with other treatment approaches, age-specific treatment appears to be more effective in rehabilitation than mixed-age treatment (Atkinson, 1985; Kofoed et al., 1987).

Prevention of Alcohol Abuse Among Older Adults

Research on the effects of long-term abuse and neglect of the human body have yielded sound preventive approaches to offsetting and in some cases virtually eliminating risks for such health problems as diabetes mellitus, melanoma, and lung cancer. Identifying preventive solutions for alcohol abuse in older adulthood, however, remains challenging because definitive risk factors for abuse have been difficult to verify through research. Researchers generally recommend that older adults experiencing stress in the form of loss, social status change through retirement, and change in health status seek some type of counseling because of the assumed link between stress and alcohol abuse (Gomberg & Zucker, 1998; Lawson, 1989; Reid & Anderson, 1997). Atkinson et al. (1992) and Brody (1982) went so far as to recommend that employers take the initiative to prevent problems such as substance abuse through preretirement planning that assures meaningful and constructive roles for employees in post-retirement life. Research has not yielded sound evidence, though, of a direct link between stress in older adulthood and substance abuse. Given that people throughout the life course respond to stressful life events with varying degrees of stress and that people have a variety of means at their disposal for coping with stress other than drinking, establishing a direct link between stress and alcohol abuse appears to be a daunting task.

Researchers have, nonetheless, offered a variety of recommendations for alcohol abuse prevention that may be useful. Alexander and Duff (1988) recommended that prevention programs be provided in retirement communities. Gomberg and Zucker

(1998) recommended that volunteers in home-delivered meal and other community-based programs be educated to detect signs of substance abuse. The Gatekeeper Program, developed by Raschko (1990) and based in Spokane, Washington, actually trained community volunteers and community professionals, such as mail carriers, electricity and natural gas meter readers, oil delivery personnel, and others, to identify older adults living in their homes who might be at risk for such problems as falls, malnutrition, and substance abuse and to contact the appropriate community agencies, which could then approach the older adults and provide services as appropriate.

In an extensive discussion of preventive approaches, Lawson (1989) divided prevention activities into three areas to target the physical, social, and psychological risk factors associated with alcohol abuse. Physical risk factors for substance abuse include such changes as the sensory deficits and lost mobility that ultimately accompany older adulthood. For these risk factors, Lawson recommended that physicians spend more time understanding their patients and respond to their needs with appropriate treatment while monitoring their use of medications. The main social risk factor that Lawson identified was isolation. She suggested that community agencies that serve older adults (a) provide opportunities for engagement in older adulthood such as volunteer work, (b) provide activities that are meaningful, and (c) link older adults with people at various stages in the life course, such as children in day care settings and adolescents volunteering for human service agencies. Finally, Lawson identified psychological risk factors stemming from social risk factors, for example, depression experienced as an effect of the loss of one's spouse. For this, Lawson recommended providing meaningful activities and challenging older adults to learn new skills, such as dancing or a new language. Lawson also recommended that older adults experiencing loss seek grief counseling either individually or in a group setting.

Medication Misuse

The etiology and treatment of medication misuse is quite different from the etiology and treatment of alcohol abuse. Only a small percentage of older adults are dependent on alcohol, and older adults are not as likely to abuse alcohol and other illicit substances as younger adults (Gomberg & Zucker, 1998; Smyer & Qualls, 1999). A much larger percentage of older adults are dependent upon medications, and older adults are more likely to misuse medications than younger adults. And, whereas a wide variety of treatment programs have been designed to treat alcohol abuse, few treatment programs beyond basic physician monitoring and patient compliance training have been designed for medication misuse. A useful distinction can be made between the terms *abuse* and *misuse*, in this context. *Abuse* refers to the overuse of a substance, whereas *misuse* refers to a variety of inappropriate uses, including underuse, erratic use, and overuse (Peterson, Whittington, & Beer, 1979). Abuse of medications may represent an attempt to cope with stress, whereas misuse is thought to be due to errors by a physician in the prescription process and the older adult's failure or inability to effectively manage a prescribed medication regimen (Lawson, 1989; Peterson et al., 1979).

Misuse of medications is considered particularly dangerous in older adulthood because of the physiological changes associated with older adulthood and the increased risk for side effects that accompanies misuse in older adulthood. Avorn and Wang (2004) warned that with increased age, adults have a decreased capacity to metabolize and excrete drugs and that side effects such as lethargy, fatigue, anxiety, and depression are a common result of toxic dosages. Dupree and Schonfeld (1996) noted that pharmacokinetics—the ability to absorb, distribute, metabolize, and eliminate drugs—is altered by age, and that the changes in lean to fat body ratio that accompany older adulthood decrease liver and renal function, resulting in impaired elimination of waste. These physiological conditions, coupled with the greater likelihood of coexisting illnesses and the potential for drug interactions with multiple prescription and over-the-counter medications (Avorn & Wang, 2004), place older adults at considerable risk for adverse side effects.

While the reported prevalence of alcohol abuse is relatively low among the current older adult cohort compared to other age groups, use of prescription and nonprescription medications by older adults is high compared to the rate in other age groups. Twenty-five percent of the medications consumed in the United States are taken by adults 65 years and older (Whitbourne, 2005), giving this age group the highest overall rate of drug intake (Schaie & Willis, 2002; Smyer & Downs, 1995). In a survey of over 6,000 community-residing older adults, Willcox, Himmelstein, and Wollhandler (1994) estimated that 32% were taking at least one medication that was inappropriate for their age.

While older adults (65 and older) currently make up only 12% to 13% of the U.S. population, they consume 30% to 35% of all prescription medications (Avorn & Wang, 2004; Grossberg & Grossberg, 1998; Health Care Financing Administration, Office of National Cost Estimates, 1990). They use prescription medications three times as frequently as the general population (DHHS, 2005), and 34% of older adults take three or more prescribed medications (Lemme, 2002; Park & Kidder, 1996). In a review of 100 medical records of patients 65 and older, Finlayson and Davis (1994) found that approximately 33% became dependent on prescription medications after they turned 60. Psychoactive drugs and benzodiazepines tend to be prescribed for older adults much more frequently than for younger adults, with older women more likely than older men to use psychoactive drugs (DHHS, 2005) and with benzodiazepines prescribed for older adults more frequently than for younger adults, and for longer periods (Shorr, Bauwens, & Landefeld, 1990). In a study of community-residing older persons taking benzodiazepines longer than 1 year, Mellinger, Balter, and Uhlenhuth (1984) found that over 70% were older than 50 and over 30% were older than 65. Prevalence of nonprescription medication use among older adults is estimated to be even greater than prescription medication use (DHHS, 2005), with 30% to 40% of all nonprescription drugs being consumed by older adults (Coons, Hendricks, & Sheahan, 1988; Dupree & Schonfeld, 1996) and with older adults more likely than younger adults to take over-the-counter drugs (Gomberg & Zucker, 1998; Korrapati & Vestal, 1995). Kofoed (1984) reported that 69% of people 60 years old and older use nonprescription drugs and that 40% of them use nonprescription drugs daily (cited in Lawson, 1989).

The physiological changes associated with primary aging constitute the greatest risk factor for misuse of medications among older adults—just as they are the greatest risk factor for alcohol abuse. As mentioned previously, pharmacokinetics (the absorption, distribution, metabolism, and excretion of drugs; Gomberg & Zucker, 1998) and pharmacodynamics (the physiological and psychological effects of pharmacokinetics; Gomberg & Zucker, 1998) are significantly altered with the aging process. Older adults' ability to absorb, distribute, metabolize, and excrete drugs is significantly slowed and limited, thus placing them at greater risk than other age groups for drug toxicity, drug interactions, enhanced drug effects, cognitive dysfunction, and other inadvertent consequences. Drugs tend to have greater effects on older adults and tend to stay in the body longer before they can be broken down and excreted (Lawson, 1989; Schaie & Willis, 2002; Vollhardt, Bergener, & Hesse, 1992). There is evidence that older adults have increased response to benzodiazepines and frequently have adverse reactions to psychoactive drugs (Gomberg & Zucker, 1998; McCormack & O'Malley, 1986). Buildup of psychoactive medications can increase symptoms of other disorders, such as cognitive dysfunction and cardiovascular/pulmonary disorders (Atkinson et al., 1992). Because drugs stay in the body longer and older adults tend to take multiple prescription and nonprescription medications, the potential for adverse side effects from drug interactions is high.

Other risk factors for misuse of medications include poor medication regimen management, chronic pain and other symptoms associated with aging, psychosocial risk factors, and polypharmacy and drug interactions due to the availability of nonprescription medications. Older adults with even normal forgetfulness may not manage their medications properly, resulting in underuse, overuse, or erratic use (DHHS, 2005). This may happen in spite of physicians' attempts to monitor medication use and provide explicit instructions for medication amounts and schedules. Prescription and nonprescription medications are frequently used to reduce symptoms associated with secondary aging (i.e., diseases and disorders associated with the aging process) (Lawson, 1989), and chronic pain has been cited as the most common reason for prescription drug dependence among the elderly (Dupree & Schonfeld, 1996). Consistent with the literature on psychosocial risk factors for alcohol abuse, researchers have cited problems such as insomnia, marital and family problems, retirement, depression, death of a spouse, and depression as risk factors for medication abuse (Dupree & Schonfeld, 1996), although the evidence is limited. Finally, the potential for polypharmacy and drug interactions among older adults taking prescription medications grows higher with each additional prescribed medication, and the potential is even greater among older adults taking psychoactive prescription medications and among those continuing to take nonprescription medications in combination with prescription medications. The risk of adverse effects from medications increases 15% for persons taking two medications daily and rises to 50% to 60% for persons taking five medications daily (Lemme, 2002; Schwartz, 1997). Further, physicians may be unaware of or misinformed by their patients about additional nonprescription medications they are taking in addition to prescription medications.

Prescription Medication Misuse and Abuse

The most commonly prescribed drugs for physical problems among older adults include cardiovascular medications, diuretics, antibiotics, and analgesics (Gomberg & Zucker,

1998). The most commonly prescribed drugs for psychological problems among older adults include sedative-hypnotics, such as benzodiazepines, and psychotherapeutic drugs, such as antidepressants and stimulants (Gomberg & Zucker, 1998). While information on the adverse effects of medications for strictly physical problems is sparse, the literature on the adverse effects of psychoactive medications such as psychotropics and benzodiazepines is extensive. Several studies have discussed the abuse potential and negative side effects of psychoactive drugs (Reid & Anderson, 1997; Solomon, Manepalli, Ireland, & Mahon, 1993; Zhan et al., 2001). Zhan et al. identified psychotropics such as amitriptyline and benzodiazepines as being among the most commonly prescribed inappropriate drugs. The inappropriate use of psychoactive medications is exacerbated by the alarming prevalence of their use among older adults. Over 300 million prescriptions for psychoactive drugs are written in the United States per year (Salzman, 1992; Schaie & Willis, 2002). Schaie and Willis estimated that over 55% of older patients in mental hospitals receive psychoactive medication. One out of four community-residing older adults is taking psychoactive medications at any given time (Reid & Anderson, 1997). Gomberg and Zucker (1998) noted that in virtually every country for which information on drug usage is available, older adults and women are more frequent users of psychoactive medication than any other group.

Research on the prevalence of psychotropic medication use and side effects is also extensive. Psychotropic medications have been identified as the most commonly prescribed drugs taken by older adults next to hormone replacement, cardiovascular drugs, analgesics, GI medications, and hypoglycemic agents (Avorn & Wang, 2004; Schappert, 1999). Older adults residing in hospitals are especially vulnerable to the overprescribing and misprescribing of psychotropics. Avorn and Wang estimated that more than one third of older patients in general hospital settings receive psychotropics. Over twice as many older hospital patients receive psychotropic/antipsychotic medication as do outpatients (Antonijoan, Barbonoj, Torrent, & Jane, 1990; Avorn & Wang, 2004). As many as one third of physician visits with older patients result in the prescription of drugs with psychiatric effects (Ancill, Embury, MacEwan, & Kennedy, 1988; Avorn & Wang, 2004). Use of psychotropics among nursing home residents is also extensive and is often found among residents for whom alternative medications have not been identified. For example, residents with a primary diagnosis of probable Alzheimer's disease or related dementia have traditionally been given psychotropic medication for excessive wandering and abusive behavior toward staff and other residents because of the sedating and calming effect of psychotropics, not for any ability to improve cognitive functioning. Frequent use in these settings has been well documented, with as many as one third of residents receiving psychotropics (Avorn & Wang; Wancata, Benda, Meise, & Muller, 1997). Long-term-care-facility surveys of drug use have also revealed practices among practical registered nurses such as high use of psychotropics, absence of stop dates on psychotropic prescriptions, and extended use of psychotropics without clinical drug reviews (Avorn & Wang, 2004).

Avorn and Wang (2004) listed several potential side effects of psychotropic drug use among older adults that result from the unique pharmacodynamics and pharmacokinetics of aging. Older adults may experience sedation from psychotropics when the hypnotic effects of the drug persist into the day after the drug was taken; alternatively, they may experience insomnia due to drugs administered during the daytime.

Insomnia can lead to feelings of isolation and confusion, especially among nursing home residents with dementia (Avorn & Wang, 2004). The potential for confusion among older adults who use psychotropics is high when they are used alone, but is even higher when they are used with additional psychotropic or other drugs. Older adults may also experience falls and fractures as a result of orthostatic hypotension, where the blood supply to the brain is reduced from psychotropic use (Avorn & Wang, 2004). Cardiac side effects have been reported with neuroleptic medications, and extrapyramidal symptoms, including extreme restlessness, involuntary movements, and uncontrollable speech, are sometimes experienced among persons who take psychotropics for prolonged periods (Avorn & Wang, 2004).

Benzodiazepines are prescribed for the treatment of insomnia, anxiety, pain, and insomnia (Ganzini & Atkinson, 1996). Their effectiveness diminishes with continued use, so progressively greater dosages must be taken to maintain effectiveness (Ganzini & Atkinson, 1996). Atkinson et al. (1992) reported that of the sedative-hypnotic agents, benzodiazepines lead to the most problems in older adults.

The frequency of benzodiazepine prescriptions increases significantly with age (O'Malley, Judge, & Crooks, 1980; Woods, Katz, & Winger, 1992). Women are believed to be more likely than men to use benzodiazepines, but not all studies have indicated gender distinctions (Ganzini & Atkinson, 1996). Physicians frequently prescribe benzodiazepines for older adults for extended periods (American Psychiatric Association, 1990; Ganzini & Atkinson, 1996), and use of several benzodiazepines at once is not uncommon for older adults. Multiple use can happen when the physician does not share information about the dangers and when physicians and other health-care providers do not ask patients about other medications they are taking (Atkinson et al., 1992).

Epidemiologic studies and studies focusing on noninstitutional settings have identified characteristics of benzodiazepine users and demonstrated the disproportionate use of benzodiazepines among older adults. Long-term benzodiazepine users tend to be older, tend to suffer from chronic illnesses such as cardiovascular disease and arthritis, and report more psychological distress than non-users (Uhlenhuth, DeWit, Balter, Johanson, & Mellinger, 1988). Ganzini and Atkinson (1996) cautioned that self-report data used for epidemiologic studies might actually underestimate drug use, citing Sullivan et al. (1988), who found that the reported figure of 14% prevalence in a Liverpool study was low compared with national prescription audits. Studies of benzodiazepine use among residents of long-term care settings have yielded prevalence estimates of approximately 25% (Beardsley, Larson, Burns, Thompson, & Kamerow, 1989; Ganzini & Atkinson, 1996). Multiple studies have shown that a high percentage of nursing home residents receive benzodiazepines on a daily basis (Ganzini & Atkinson, 1996).

Complications arising from long-term benzodiazepine use include dependence and the discontinuance effects associated with dependence, as well as both acute and chronic side effects resulting from toxicity. Some researchers report that dependence can result from regular use after 6 to 12 months (Ganzini & Atkinson, 1996), while others report that dependence may occur in as few as 4 to 6 weeks (Atkinson et al., 1992). Discontinuance effects are experienced by an estimated 15% to 44% of long-term benzodiazepine users (Atkinson et al., 1992). They include recurrence and rebound symptoms as well as true withdrawal. Recurrence symptoms involve the reemergence of the original anxiety for which the drug was taken and longer lasting anxiety (Atkinson et al., 1992). Rebound symptoms also involve reemergence of the original symptoms, but with greater intensity. Examples of rebound symptoms include anxiety, insomnia, concentration problems, and restlessness (American Psychiatric Association, 1990). True withdrawal involves the emergence of novel symptoms for which the drug was not originally prescribed (American Psychiatric Association, 1990).

Chronic toxicity is most likely to occur among older adults who have developed tolerance for benzodiazepines after long-term use (Atkinson et al., 1992). They are at greater risk for toxicity than younger adults because they do not clear benzodiazepines as quickly and because repeated use produces higher concentrations of the drug in the bloodstream (Ganzini & Atkinson, 1996). Examples of side effects from toxicity include a range of cognitive and psychomotor irregularities. Balance problems, impaired memory and attention, increased reaction time, drowsiness, delirium and dementia-like symptoms, and impaired arousal are all possible indicators (American Psychiatric Association, 1990; Atkinson et al., 1992; Ganzini & Atkinson; Greenblatt & Shader, 1991; Pomara, Deptula, Singh, & Monroy, 1991). In general, long-term benzodiazepine use is associated with poor physical health (Ganzini & Atkinson, 1996). Cognitive impairments resulting from long-term use of multiple benzodiazepines are worsened by the fact that older adults from the current cohort are less inclined to seek help from mental health professionals than younger adults (Ganzini & Atkinson, 1996; Mellinger et al., 1984).

As noted, suggestions for management and treatment of prescription medication misuse are not nearly as well developed as those for alcohol abuse. They generally fall under the categories of patient compliance training and guidelines for the health-care provider. The almost exclusive focus on compliance training may be partly justified by the fact that older adults are not as likely as other age groups to comply with physician instructions involving medication (Schaie & Willis, 2002). Adults in their 70s are twice as likely to not comply with medication instructions as adults in their 40s. Examples of mistakes among older adults include 4% taking medications in the wrong sequence or at the wrong time, 10% taking the wrong amount, 17% self-medicating, and 47% omitting the medication altogether (Schaie & Willis, 2002). There are several possible explanations for noncompliance. One is that common use of multiple medications among older adults increases the risk for poor compliance with drug regimens (Avorn & Wang, 2004). Underuse may occur because the patient simply forgets to take his or her medication or because the patient decides to save medication for future use (Avorn & Wang, 2004). Overuse might occur because the patient believes that taking more of the drug will hasten recovery from the illness (Avorn & Wang, 2004). Another factor contributing to noncompliance is poor communication, such as lack of information from the clinician about the need for the medication or unclear directions from the clinician or pharmacist (Avorn & Wang, 2004).

Avorn and Wang (2004) presented thorough guidelines for physicians to enhance older patient compliance and better assure that patients are receiving appropriate dosages at the prescribed intervals. They suggested that no medication be prescribed without a discussion of its purpose, expected effects, and potential side effects, and they provided a list of questions for the physician to ask the patient and him- or herself before prescribing the medication:

1. Does the patient have sensory, cognitive, or literacy problems?
2. How many physicians does the patient consult?
3. Can the patient manage and tolerate an additional drug?
4. How should the standard dose be modified?
5. What side effects are likely to occur and what interactions?
6. What dosage is best for the patient and can the patient administer the dosage?
7. Is the patient alone and is special packaging required? Is it necessary to arrange supervision of the drug regimen?
8. Can the patient afford the regimen prescribed?
9. What monitoring is necessary to evaluate outcomes and adjust the regimen accordingly?

Avorn and Wang also offered guidelines that may help clinicians maximize patient benefits from medication use:

1. Become familiar with altered physiology in primary aging as well as significant changes that come with secondary aging.
2. Use drug therapy only after a thorough diagnostic workup demonstrates that this approach is appropriate.
3. Never assume that symptoms are a function of aging without seeking a treatable underlying cause.
4. Choose the agent and dose appropriate for altered characteristics of the older adult patient.
5. Identify early the subjective or behavioral goals for the use of psychoactive medication and periodically perform systematic assessment of how well the goals have been met.
6. Closely monitor how the patient is using prescribed medications and be alert to signs of poor compliance.

Given the nature of prescription drug utilization, it makes sense that most or all of the suggestions for its management would be directed to the health-care provider. Still, specific treatment programs directed toward the patient are more likely to be effective, just as specific treatment programs involving the alcohol abuser are more effective than simple physician monitoring and advice.

Nonprescription Medication Misuse

Misuse of nonprescription medications commonly utilized by older adults for the treatment of various ailments would not seem to be as great of a concern as prescription medication misuse, mainly because nonprescription medications are not as powerful as prescription medications. Nonetheless, their wide availability and affordability, the tendency of older adults to use them in combination with other nonprescription and prescription medications, and the trend toward over-the-counter access to potentially harmful drugs that were recently accessible only through prescription (Avorn & Wang, 2004) raise concern about their misuse. In an early study, Kofoed (1984) reported that 69% of persons 60 years old and older used nonprescription drugs and that 40% used them daily. Even physicians who inspect the medication history of their patients and follow the guidelines for appropriate prescribing practices noted above have little or no control over a patient's decision to withhold information about nonprescription drug use (Avorn & Wang, 2004). Mismanagement of multiple nonprescription drugs or a combination of nonprescription drugs is likely to result in one or more adverse drug reactions (Ganzini & Atkinson, 1996). Older adults sometimes fail to read warning labels and directions on nonprescription drug containers and are often unaware of any adverse effects they may have (Conn, 1991).

Perhaps the most obvious reasons for misuse of nonprescription drugs are their wide availability and their relatively low cost compared with prescription drugs (Coons et al., 1988; Lemme, 2002). There are several other factors that may account for their greater use by older adults. For example, older adults may resort to nonprescription medications because of bad experiences with health-care professionals (Lawson, 1989). Atkinson et al. (1992) cited lack of access to quality medical care, poverty, and reluctance to admit that one is ill as possible reasons for misuse. Interestingly, studies also show that nonprescription drug use is positively correlated with higher education level (Conn, 1991; Ganzini & Atkinson, 1996).

Examples of types of nonprescription medications commonly used by older adults include analgesics, antihistamines, laxatives, and caffeine. Analgesics such as aspirin, acetaminophen, ibuprofen, and naproxen sodium are believed to be the most commonly used nonprescription medications, with estimates at 33% to 50% of all older adults using such drugs (Conn, 1991; Ganzini & Atkinson, 1996). Roumie and Griffin (2004) noted that older adults' long-term use of analgesics at higher than recommended doses might result in harmful effects such as gastrointestinal hemorrhage and cardiovascular or renal toxicity. Lawson (1989) noted that drugs such as aspirin and acetaminophen can cause acute metabolic disturbances and stomach bleeding. Antihistamines such as Benadryl may be used by older adults as sedative-hypnotics. The risks associated with their use include paradoxical excitement, urinary retention and constipation, blurred vision, impaired heat dissipation, and acute toxic delirium (Atkinson et al., 1992; Lawson, 1989). Laxatives are believed by some to be the most commonly misused nonprescription medication by older adults (Conn, 1991; Ganzini & Atkinson, 1996), with greater misuse suspected among older women than men (Atkinson et al., 1992). Laxatives can cause diarrhea, malabsorption syndromes, and dehydration (Lawson, 1989). While nonbeverage caffeine use by older adults is not nearly as common as the use of other medications (Ganzini & Atkinson, 1996), older adults are at greater risk than younger adults for adverse effects because of their altered physiology. High doses of caffeine and subsequent buildup in the older adult's system can cause insomnia, headaches, tremors, and even mild delirium (Atkinson et al., 1992). Lawson also reported that caffeine overuse can contribute to anxiety disorders, cardiac dysrhythmia, gastric disease, and osteoporosis.

Illegal Drugs

Older adults' use of illegal substances such as marijuana, cocaine, heroin, and LSD is uncommon in the current cohort, with older criminals and long-term heroin addicts identified as the most likely to use these drugs (Atkinson et al., 1992; Dupree & Schonfeld, 1996; Lawson, 1989). In addition to surveys of community-dwelling and institutionalized older adults, surveys of older homeless persons and records of drug arrests also support this claim (Atkinson et al., 1992; Ganzini & Atkinson, 1996). Regier et al. (1988) found that fewer than .1% of older adults met *Diagnostic and Statistical Manual of Mental Disorders–Third Edition* (American Psychiatric Association, 1980) criteria for illicit substance dependence (DHHS, 2005). Studies on younger adults show that the majority of illicit drug users are in their late teens and early 20s (Whitbourne, 2005), with fewer than 1% of people 35 and older reporting use of marijuana or cocaine (Dupree & Schonfeld, 1996; Substance Abuse and Mental Health Services Administration [SAMHSA], 1994a, 1994b).

While the current cohort of older adults is unlikely to abuse illicit substances, the Baby Boomers may be more likely to use such drugs. Generally, use of illicit drugs is expected to increase as an effect of the Baby Boom generation reaching retirement, just as the use of alcohol is expected to increase (DHHS, 2005). The high probability of morbidity and mortality among long-term heroin addicts prevents most of them from reaching older adulthood, but there is some evidence that this group is also growing (Gomberg & Zucker, 1998). For example, Pascarelli (1985) found that the percentage of methadone program patients who were 60 years old and older rose from .005% in 1974 to 2% in 1985. A trend toward increased survival rate of long-term heroin users might be attributed to the hygienic use of needles and syringes (Atkinson et al., 1992).

Little research has been conducted on the types of illegal substances used by older adults and the adverse effects of those substances (Gomberg & Zucker, 1998). The variety of drugs that older adults may take include marijuana, opioids, hallucinogens, and psychostimulants such as amphetamines and cocaine (Atkinson et al., 1992). Generally, adverse effects of short-term and long-term illegal drug use include delirium, dementia, intoxication, and delusional and mood disorders (Atkinson et al., 1992). Older adults who are dependent on illegal drugs tend to be socially withdrawn and to hide their use of drugs from others (Des Jarlais, Joseph, & Courtwright, 1985).

The only illegal drug used by older adults that has been extensively researched is heroin. In fact, opioid use was once associated with aging. Historical examples of abuse include opium smoking among older Chinese men prior to the 1930s and British older adults before 1960 (Atkinson et al., 1992; Bean, 1974; Deely, Kaufman, Yen, Jue, & Brown, 1979). Use of heroin by older adults has since declined significantly. Older heroin addicts represent only 2% to 3% of older adults who have been admitted to treatment programs for some type of substance abuse (Atkinson et al., 1992; Ganzini & Atkinson, 1996; Pascarelli, 1985). SAMHSA (1994a) found that only 1.8% of heroin and morphine abuse reports in U.S. city hospital emergency departments were of people older than 55 years old. The low incidence of initial heroin use after the age of 25 to 30 years can be partially explained by the high mortality rate of illegal drug users, as well as imprisonment of drug users, which prevents their inclusion in research (Atkinson et al., 1992; Des Jarlais et al., 1985).

Discussion and Future Directions

This final section includes discussion of distinguishing between the causes and effects of alcohol use, cohort differences, research methodology, predictions regarding future use, and the service needs of older adults.

Distinguishing Between Cause and Effect

As noted, it is often difficult to distinguish between causes and effects of alcohol abuse. While pharmacokinetics and pharmacodynamics are obvious physiological risk factors for substance abuse, it is difficult to determine whether psychological factors, such as depression, are risk factors or effects of abuse. For example, B. F. Grant and Harford (1995) found that older alcoholics were more likely to exhibit major depressive disorder than older non-alcoholics, but the disorder was not identified as a cause or effect of abuse. Diagnostic instruments to detect psychosocial causes and effects of substance abuse might assist clinicians in designing effective treatment plans. For example, a clinician who is able to identify depression resulting from loss of a spouse as a reason for a patient's alcohol abuse might plan a different course of treatment than a clinician who identified depression as a function of the drinking itself.

Determining the degree to which alcohol abuse impairs cognitive functioning in older adulthood has also been challenging for researchers. As mentioned previously, while researchers such as I. Grant et al. (1984) and Pfefferbaum et al. (1988) have claimed that alcohol dependence in older adulthood is directly associated with prolonged cognitive impairment and dementia, researchers such as Collins and Mertens (1988) and Yesavage et al. (1994) found no alcohol effects on cognitive performance tasks with older adults. The dispute between such researchers might be resolved through a refinement of diagnostic instruments. For example, DSM-IV criteria for alcohol-induced dementia are not specific enough to rule out other causes. A refinement of DSM-IV criteria to rule out causes such as Alzheimer's disease, vascular dementia, AIDS-related dementia, and dementia resulting from Parkinson's disease is warranted.

Cohort Differences

Treatment of older adults with substance abuse problems requires a cohort-sensitive approach—one that takes into account the culture in which the particular cohort of older adults grew up. For example, those who were youths during Prohibition may be influenced by the strong stigma associated with alcohol abuse during that period; they may be less likely to benefit from group programs in which public sharing is prominent. They may also tend to be somewhat suspicious of professional psychological services, believing it is better to go it alone. Baby Boomers, by contrast, may be less likely to be suspicious of psychological services, having grown up in an era when accessing such services was commonplace. Baby Boomers are also more likely to benefit from a group setting. As noted earlier, participation of persons 50 and older in group therapy and AA programs has increased in recent years (Gomberg & Zucker, 1998), suggesting greater acceptance of such services among adults just beginning to enter older adulthood. Finally, having grown up in an era when alcohol and illicit drug use was relatively widespread, Baby Boomers may be more likely than the previous generation to use alcohol as well as illicit drugs such as marijuana and cocaine.

Methodological Considerations

Researchers studying substance abuse in older adulthood have identified several methodological problems. Substance abuse questionnaires and diagnostic instruments are typically designed for younger adults, including questions that are irrelevant to older adults (Adams, 1997). Further, whether in the clinical or the research setting, it is easy to confuse the symptoms of substance abuse with symptoms of other disorders and diseases encountered in older adulthood. Finally, the observed low prevalence of substance abuse in older adulthood may be an artifact of the lower survival rate of long-term substance abusers.

Few have criticized research designs per se, yet most of the studies cited in this chapter were conducted using a basic cross-sectional research design as opposed to a longitudinal or sequential design. Generally, this approach to age-focused research raises concerns because it does not enable the researcher or the reader to tease out the effects of age from the effects of history or cohort. This methodological limitation is coupled with the fact that the current older adult cohort was raised during Prohibition, a cultural milieu that might have the effect of suppressing self-reports of alcohol or other substance abuse. These methodological concerns raise serious questions regarding the extent to which the currently reported lower incidence of alcoholism in older adulthood is a function of age or cohort. Further, researchers generally assume that substance utilization among older adults who were raised during the Prohibition era was lower when they were younger adults, but there is little evidence of this; few longitudinal data were gathered for the current older adult cohort when they were young. Future studies should utilize longitudinal designs, or, more ideally, sequential designs, which combine the benefits of longitudinal and cross-sectional designs. Only then will researchers be able to distinguish between substance abuse as a function of age and substance abuse as a function of cohort.

In their recommendations for future research, Atkinson et al. (1992) offered a list of alcoholism-related themes that they believed deserved special attention:

1. improved methods for determining older adult alcohol consumption and early identification of cases,
2. clarification of the relationship between late-onset and relapsing varieties of alcoholism and life stress and coexisting mental disorders, and
3. studies of prevalence, management, and prevention of problem alcohol and prescription psychoactive use in nursing homes and other long-term care facilities.

Some studies of the prevalence and management of alcohol and prescription psychoactive use in long-term care facilities have been conducted since Atkinson et al. (1992), but the relationship between late-onset alcoholism and life stress or coexisting mental disorders remains a mystery. Further, the present review of the literature yielded little regarding improved methods for determining older adult alcohol consumption and early identification beyond instruments such as the MAST and the CAGE. Both of these challenges could be addressed with the creation of new diagnostic instruments or the refinement of existing instruments that more specifically measure such phenomena as the behavioral effects of life stress and the circumstances that evoke life stress.

Predicting Future Use and Service Needs

Researchers generally assume that use of illicit substances such as marijuana and cocaine will be greater among future generations of older adults because Baby Boomers and their children are more likely to have used these substances as adolescents and young adults than the current cohort of older adults. A 2005 DHHS report indicated that health-care expenditures are expected to rise dramatically as a result of greater alcohol and illicit drug dependence among aging Baby Boomers, attributing this greater dependence to greater consumption and acceptance of alcohol and drug use in this cohort.

There is also reason to suspect that future older adults will be just as likely as current elders to abuse or misuse prescription and nonprescription medications. The greater incidence of use of these substances among current older adults does not appear to be cohort related, but rather a response to the affordability and availability of a wide variety of legal substances to treat a wide variety of ailments. The trend toward greater availability of more powerful medications that were once available only through prescription is cause for alarm in future years, as older adults will likely continue to consume more of these medications than any other age group.

Management programs for prescription and nonprescription medication regimens are therefore highly recommended. The current scarcity of formal programs to assist older adults with the management of medications compared to the wide availability of formal treatment programs for older adults who are dependent on alcohol or illicit drugs is disconcerting; the development of such programs will become even more important as the next generation of older adults uses even more prescription and nonprescription drugs. The growing cost of prescription medications also makes it more likely that older adults will use nonprescription drugs as a substitute for prescription drugs. Formal programs geared toward assisting older adults with medication management will therefore need to be developed and marketed to both physicians and older adults.

A current trend in long-term care and community-based services for older adults is the synthesis of a variety of community-based and institutional services to better meet the needs of community-residing older adults. Community-based services once provided through Area Agencies on Aging as a provision of the Older Americans Act of 1965, such as home-delivered meals, congregate meals, transportation services, and home visitation programs, are gradually becoming integrated with services traditionally offered exclusively through long-term care settings such as home health care and skilled care. For example, in small communities, home-delivered meals may be prepared and delivered by long-term care facilities that serve as the only resource for community-based services in the area.

Such a blending of services, once offered separately by social service providers and medical care providers, may serve as a model for an integration of services offered for the older adult who is struggling with substance abuse or misuse. An example of this might be the long-term care setting that continues to offer long-term skilled care but also offers short-term rehabilitation to older adults who are alcohol dependent. Short-term physical rehabilitation and sub-acute care are becoming the norm in long-term care facilities; a portion of the care provided could be devoted to substance dependence rehabilitation. Another example of this synthesis might be a home health care service in which the professional who visits the older adult in the home is not a nurse, but a clinical psychologist who provides psychotherapy or self-management training to the homebound older adult who is alcohol dependent. Such services will help meet the needs of 21st-century older adults, who will most certainly depend upon services as much as, and possibly more than, the current cohort of elders.

References

Adams, S. L., & Waskel, S. A. (1991). Late onset of alcoholism among older midwestern men in treatment. *Psychological Reports, 68,* 432–434.

Adams, W. L. (1997). Interactions between alcohol and other drugs. In A. M. Gurnack (Ed.), *Older adults' misuse of alcohol, medicines, and other drugs: Research and practice issues* (pp. 185–205). New York: Springer.

Adams, W. L., & Cox, N. S. (1997). Epidemiology of problem drinking among elderly people. In A. M. Gurnack (Ed.), *Older adults' misuse of alcohol, medicines, and other drugs: Research and practice issues* (pp. 1–23). New York: Springer.

Adams, W. L., Garry, P. J., Rhyne, R., Hunt, W. C., & Goodwin, J. S. (1990). Alcohol intake in the healthy elderly: Changes with age in a cross-sectional and longitudinal study. *Journal of the American Geriatrics Society, 38,* 211–216.

Adams, W. L., Magruder-Habib, K., Trued, S., & Broome, H. L. (1992). Alcohol abuse in elderly emergency department patients. *Journal of the American Geriatrics Society, 40,* 1236–1240.

Alexander, F., & Duff, R. W. (1988). Social interactions and alcohol use in retirement communities. *Gerontologist, 28*(5), 632–636.

American Psychiatric Association. (1990). *Benzodiazepine dependence, toxicity and abuse: A task force report of the American Psychiatric Association.* Washington, DC: Author.

American Psychiatric Association. (1994). *Diagnostic and statistical manual of mental disorders* (4th ed.). Washington, DC: Author.

Ancill, R. J., Embury, G. D., MacEwan, G. W., & Kennedy, J. S. (1988). The use and misuse of psychotropic prescribing for elderly psychiatric patients. *Canadian Journal of Psychiatry, 33,* 585–589.

Antonijoan, R. M., Barbonoj, M. J., Torrent, J., & Jane, F. (1990). Evaluation of psychotropic drug consumption related to psychological distress in the elderly: Hospitalized vs. nonhospitalized. *Neuropsychobiology, 23,* 25–30.

Atkinson, R. M. (Ed.). (1984). *Alcohol and drug abuse in old age.* Washington, DC: American Psychiatric Press.

Atkinson, R. M. (1985). Persuading alcoholic patients to seek treatment. *Comprehensive Therapy, 11*(11), 16–24.

Atkinson, R. M. (1990). Aging and alcohol use disorders: Diagnostic issues in the elderly. *International Psychogeriatrics, 2*(1), 55–72.

Atkinson, R. M., Ganzini, L., & Bernstein, M. J. (1992). Alcohol and substance-use disorders in the elderly. In J. E. Birren, R. B. Sloane, & G. D. Cohen (Eds.), *Handbook of mental health and aging* (2nd ed., pp. 515–555). New York: Academic Press.

Atkinson, R. M., Tolson, R. L., & Turner, J. A. (1990). Late versus early onset problem drinking in older men. *Alcoholism, 14*(4), 574–579.

Avorn, J., & Wang, P. (2004). Drug prescribing, adverse reaction, and compliance in elderly patients. In C. Salzman (Ed.), *Clinical geriatric psychopharmacology* (4th ed., pp. 23–47). Philadelphia, PA: Lippincott, Williams & Wilkins.

Bean, P. (1974). *The social control of drugs.* New York: Wiley.

Beardsley, R. S., Larson, D. B., Burns, B. J., Thompson, J. W., & Kamerow, D. B. (1989). Prescribing of psychotropics in elderly nursing home patients. *Journal of the American Geriatrics Society, 37,* 327–330.

Beresford, T. P., Blow, F. C., Brower, K. J., Adams, K. M., & Hall, R. C. W. (1988). Alcoholism and aging in the general hospital. *Psychosomatics, 29*(1), 61–72.

Bikle, D. D., Stesin, A., Halloran, B., Steinbach, L., & Recker, R. (1993). Alcohol-induced bone disease: Relationship to age and parathyroid hormone levels. *Alcoholism: Clinical and Experimental Research, 17*(3), 690–695.

Brennan, P. L., & Moos, R. H. (1990). Life stressors, social resources, and late-life problem drinking. *Psychology and Aging, 5*(4), 491–501.

Brennan, P. L., & Moos, R. H. (1991). Functioning, life context, and help-seeking among late-onset problem drinkers: Comparisons with nonproblem and early-onset problem drinkers. *British Journal of Addiction, 86,* 1139–1150.

Brody, J. A. (1982). Aging and alcohol abuse. *Journal of the American Geriatrics Society, 30*(2), 123–126.

Brower, K. J., Mudd, S., Blow, F. C., Young, J. P., & Hill, E. M. (1994). Severity and treatment of alcohol withdrawal in elderly versus younger patients. *Alcoholism: Clinical and Experimental Research, 18*(1), 196.

Bucholz, K. K., Sheline, Y. I., & Helzer, J. E. (1995). The epidemiology of alcohol use, problems, and dependence in elders: A review. In T. Beresford & E. S. L. Gomberg (Eds.), *Alcohol and aging* (pp. 19–41). New York: Oxford University Press.

Carlen, P. L., McAndrews, M. P., Weiss, R. T., Dongier, M., Hill, J. M., Menzano, E., Farcnik, K., Abarbanel, J., & Eastwood, M. R. (1994). Alcohol-related dementia in the institutionalized elderly. *Alcoholism: Clinical and Experimental Research, 18*(6), 1330–1334.

Collins, W. E., & Mertens, H. W. (1988). Age, alcohol, and simulated altitude: Effects on performance and breathalyzer scores. *Aviation, Space, and Environmental Medicine, 59*(11), 1026–1033.

Conn, V. S. (1991). Older adults: Factors that predict the use of over-the-counter medication. *Journal of Advanced Nursing, 16*(10), 1190–1196.

Coons, S. J., Hendricks, J., & Sheahan, S. L. (1988). Self medication with nonprescription drugs. *Generations, 12*(4), 22–26.

Council on Scientific Affairs, American Medical Association. (1996). Alcoholism in the elderly. *Journal of the American Medical Association, 275*(10), 797–801.

Curtis, J. R., Geller, G., Stokes, E. J., Levine, D. M., & Moore, R. D. (1989). Characteristics, diagnosis, and treatment of alcoholism in elderly patients. *Journal of the American Geriatrics Society, 37,* 310–316.

Deely, P. J., Kaufman, E., Yen, M. S., Jue, A., & Brown, E. (1979). The special problems and treatment of a group of elderly Chinese opiate addicts in New York City. *British Journal of Addiction, 74,* 403–409.

Des Jarlais, D. C., Joseph, H., & Courtwright, D. T. (1985). Old age and addiction: A study of elderly patients in methadone maintenance treatment. In E. Gottheil, K. A. Druley, T. E. Skoloda, & H. M. Waxman (Eds.), *The combined problems of alcoholism, drug addiction, and aging* (pp. 201–209). Springfield, IL: Thomas.

Dufour, M., & Fuller, R. K. (1995). Alcohol in the elderly. *Annual Review of Medicine, 46,* 123–132.

Dupree, L. W., Broskowski, H., & Schonfeld, L. (1984). The Gerontology Alcohol Project: A behavioral treatment program for elderly alcohol abusers. *Gerontologist, 24*(5), 510–516.

Dupree, L. W., & Schonfeld, L. (1996). Substance abuse. In M. Hersen & V. B. Van Hasselt (Eds.), *Psychological treatment of older adults: An introductory text* (pp. 281–297). New York: Plenum Press.

Eaton, W. W., Kramer, M., Anthony, J. C., Dryman, A., Shapiro, & Locke, B. Z. (1989). The incidence of specific DIS/DSM-III mental disorders: Data from the NIMH Epidemiologic Catchment Area program. *Acta Psychiatrica Scandinavica, 79*(2), 163–178.

Ekerdt, D. J., De Labry, L. O., Glynn, R. J., & Davis, R. W. (1989). Change in drinking behaviors with retirement: Findings from the normative aging study. *Journal of Studies on Alcohol, 50*(4), 347–353.

Ewing, J. A. (1984). Detecting alcoholism: The CAGE questionnaire. *Journal of the American Medical Association, 252*(14), 1905–1907.

Finlayson, R. E., & Davis, L. J., Jr. (1994). Prescription drug dependence in the elderly population: Demographic and clinical features of 100 inpatients. *Mayo Clinic Proceedings, 69,* 1137–1145.

Finlayson, R. E., Hurt, R. D., Davis, L. J., Jr., & Morse, R. M. (1988). Alcoholism in elderly persons: A study of the psychiatric and psychosocial features of 216 inpatients. *Mayo Clinic Proceedings, 63*(8), 761–768.

Foos, P. W., & Clark, M. C. (2003). *Human aging.* Boston: Allyn & Bacon.

Ganzini, L., & Atkinson, R. M. (1996). Substance abuse. In J. Sadavoy, L. W. Lazarus, L. F. Jarvik, & G. T. Grossberg (Eds.), *Comprehensive review of geriatric psychiatry II* (2nd ed., pp. 659–692). Washington, DC: American Psychiatric Press.

Glantz, M. D. (1983). Drugs and the elderly adult: An overview. In M. D. Glantz, D. M. Peterson, & F. J. Whittington (Eds.), *Drugs and the elderly adult: Research issues* (NIDA Report No. 32, pp. 1–3). Rockville, MD: National Institute on Drug Abuse.

Glass, T. A., Prigerson, H., Kasl, S. V., & Mendes de Leon, C. F. (1995). The effects of negative life events on alcohol consumption among older men and women. *Journal of Gerontology, 50B*(4), S205–S216.

Goldberg, R. J. (2005). Late-life alcohol abuse: Finding solutions to a hidden medical problem. *Brown University Geriatric Psychopharmacology Update, (9)*1, 5–6.

Gomberg, E. S. L. (1982). Alcohol use and alcohol problems among the elderly. In *Special population issues* (DHHS Publication No. ADM 82-1193, pp. 263–290). Washington, DC: U.S. Government Printing Office.

Gomberg, E. S. L., & Nelson, B. W. (1995). Black and white older men: Alcohol use and abuse. In T. Beresford & E. S. L. Gomberg (Eds.), *Alcohol and aging* (pp. 307–323). New York: Oxford University Press.

Gomberg, E. S. L., & Zucker, R. A. (1998). Substance use and abuse in old age. In I. H. Nordhus, G. R. VandenBos, S. Berg, & P. Fromholt (Eds.), *Clinical geropsychology* (pp. 189–204). Washington, DC: American Psychological Association.

Goodwin, J. S., Sanchez, C. J., Thomas, P., Hunt, C., Garry, P. J., & Goodwin, J. M. (1987). Alcohol intake and a healthy elderly population. *American Journal of Public Health, 77*(2), 173–177.

Gordon, T., & Kannel, W. B. (1983). Drinking and its relation to smoking, BP, blood lipids, and uric acid: The Framingham study. *Archives of Internal Medicine, 143,* 1366–1374.

Grabbe, L., Demi, A., Camann, M. A., & Potter, L. (1997). The health status of elderly persons in the last year of life: A comparison of deaths by suicide, injury, and natural causes. *American Journal of Public Health, 87*(3), 434–437.

Graham, K., Saunders, S. J., Flower, M. C., Timney, C. B., White-Campbell, M., & Pietropaolo, A. Z. (1995). *Addictions treatment for older adults: Evaluation of an innovative client-centered approach.* New York: Haworth.

Grant, B. F., & Harford, T. C. (1995). Comorbidity between DSM-IV alcohol use disorders and major depression: Results of a national survey. *Drug and Alcohol Dependence, 39,* 197–206.

Grant, I., Adams, K. M., & Reed, R. (1984). Aging, abstinence, and medical risk factors in the prediction of neuropsychologic deficit among long-term alcoholics. *Archives of General Psychiatry, 41,* 710–718.

Greenblatt, D. J., & Shader, R. I. (1991). Benzodiazepines in the elderly: Pharmacokinetics and drug sensitivity. In C. Salzman & B. D. Lebowitz (Eds.), *Anxiety in the elderly: Treatment and research* (pp. 131–145). New York: Springer.

Grisso, J. A., Kelsey, J. L., Strom, B. L., Chiu, G. Y., Maislin, G., O'Brien, L. A., Hoffman, S., & Kaplan, F. (1991). Risk factors for falls as a cause of hip fracture in women. *New England Journal of Medicine, 324,* 1326–1331.

Grossberg, G. T., & Grossberg, J. A. (1998). Epidemiology of psychotherapeutic drug use in older adults. *Clinics in Geriatric Medicine, 14*(1), 1–5.

Gurland, B. (1996). Epidemiology of psychiatric disorders. In J. Sadavoy, L. W. Lazarus, L. F. Jarvik, & G. T. Grossberg (Eds.), *Comprehensive review of geriatric psychiatry II* (2nd ed., pp. 3–41). Washington, DC: American Psychiatric Press.

Harper, C., Sheedy, D., Halliday, G., Double, K., Dodd, P., Lewohl, J., & Kril, J. (1998). Neuropathological studies: The relationship between alcohol and aging. In E. S. L. Gomberg, A. M. Hegedusand, & R. A. Zucker (Eds.), *Alcohol problems and aging* (pp. 117–134). Bethesda, MD: National Institute on Alcohol Abuse and Alcoholism.

Health Care Financing Administration, Office of National Cost Estimates. (1990). National health expenditures, 1988. *Health Care Financing Review, 11*(4), 1–41.

Helzer, J. E., Burnam, A., & McEvoy, L. T. (1991). Alcohol abuse and dependence. In L. N. Robins & D. A. Regier (Eds.), *Psychiatric disorders in America: The Epidemiologic Catchment Area study* (pp. 81–115). New York: Free Press.

Horton, A. M., & Fogelman, C. J. (1991). Behavioral treatment of aged alcoholics and drug addicts. In P. A. Wisocki (Ed.), *Handbook of clinical behavioral therapy with the elderly client* (pp. 299–315). New York: Plenum Press.

Institute of Alcohol Studies. (2007). Alcohol and the elderly. *IAS Fact Sheet.* Retrieved May 9, 2007, from www.ias.org.uk/resources/factsheets/elderly.pdf

Jackson, J. S., Williams, D. R., & Gomberg, E. S. L. (1998). Aging and alcohol use and abuse among African Americans: A life-course perspective. In E. S. L. Gomberg, A. M. Hegedusand, & R. A. Zucker (Eds.), *Alcohol problems and aging* (pp. 63–82). Bethesda, MD: National Institute on Alcohol Abuse and Alcoholism.

Joseph, C. L. (1997). Misuse of alcohol and drugs in the nursing home. In A. M. Gurnack (Ed.), *Older adults' misuse of alcohol, medicines, and other drugs: Research and practice issues* (pp. 228–254). New York: Springer.

Joseph, C. L., Ganzini, L., & Atkinson, R. M. (1995). Screening for alcohol use disorders in the nursing home. *Journal of the American Geriatrics Society, 43*(4), 368–373.

Kalant, H. (1998). Pharmacological interactions of aging and alcohol. In E. S. L. Gomberg, A. M. Hegedusand, & R. A. Zucker (Eds.), *Alcohol problems and aging* (NIAAA Research Monograph No. 33). Bethesda, MD: National Institute on Alcohol Abuse and Alcoholism.

Karlamangla, A., Zhou, K., Reuben, D., Greendale, G., & Moore, A. (2006). Longitudinal trajectories of heavy drinking in adults in the United States of America. *Addiction, 101,* 91–99.

Kofoed, L. L. (1984). Abuse and misuse of over the counter drugs by the elderly. In R. M. Atkinson (Ed.), *Alcohol and drug abuse in old age* (pp. 50–59). Washington, DC: American Psychiatric Press.

Kofoed, L. L., Tolson, R. L., Atkinson, R. M., Toth, R. L., & Turner, J. A. (1987). Treatment compliance of older alcoholics: An elder-specific approach is superior to "mainstreaming." *Journal of Studies on Alcohol, 48*(1), 47–51.

Korrapati, M. R., & Vestal, R. E. (1995). Alcohol and medications in the elderly: Complex interactions. In T. Beresford & E. S. L. Gomberg (Eds.), *Alcohol and aging* (pp. 42–55). New York: Oxford University Press.

Lawson, A. W. (1989). Substance abuse problems of the elderly: Considerations for treatment and prevention. In G. W. Lawson & A. W. Lawson (Eds.), *Alcoholism and substance abuse in special populations* (pp. 95–113). Austin, TX: PRO-ED.

Lemme, B. H. (2002). *Development in adulthood* (3rd ed.). Boston: Allyn & Bacon.

Liberto, J. G., Oslin, D. W., & Ruskin, P. E. (1992). Alcoholism in older persons: A review of the literature. *Hospital and Community Psychiatry, 43*(10), 975–984.

Lichtenberg, P. A. (1994). *A guide to psychological practice in geriatric long-term care.* New York: Haworth Press.

Liskow, B. I., Rinck, C., Campbell, J., & DeSouza, C. (1989). Alcohol withdrawal in the elderly. *Journal of Studies on Alcohol, 50*(5), 414–421.

Maddox, G. L. (1988, Summer). Aging, drinking and alcohol abuse. *Generations,* pp. 14–16.

Malmivaara, A., Heliovaara, M., Knekt, P., Reunanen, A., & Aromaa, A. (1993). Risk factors for injurious falls leading to hospitalization or death in a cohort of 19,500 adults. *American Journal of Epidemiology, 138*(6), 384–394.

Mangion, D. M., Platt, J. S., & Syam, V. (1992). Alcohol and acute medical admission of elderly people. *Age and Ageing, 21,* 362–367.

McCormack, P., & O'Malley, K. (1986). Biological and medical aspects of drug treatment in the elderly. In R. E. Dunkle, G. J. Petot, & A. B. Ford (Eds.), *Food, drugs, and aging* (pp. 19–27). New York: Springer.

Mellinger, G. D., Balter, M. B., & Uhlenhuth, E. H. (1984). Prevalence and correlates of the long-term regular use of anxiolytics. *Journal of the American Medical Association, 251*(3), 375–379.

Meyers, A. R., Hingson, R., Mucatel, M., & Goldman, E. (1982). Social and psychological correlates of problem drinking in old age. *Journal of the American Geriatrics Society, 30*(7), 452–456.

Moos, R. H., Brennan, P. L., & Mertens, J. R. (1994). Mortality rates and predictors of mortality among late-middle-aged and older substance abuse patients. *Alcoholism: Clinical and Experimental Research, 18*(1), 187–195.

Moos, R., Brennan, P., & Schutte, K. (1998). Life context factors, treatment, and late-life drinking behavior. In E. S. L. Gomberg, A. M. Hegedusand, & R. A. Zucker (Eds.), *Alcohol problems and aging* (NIAAA Research Monograph No. 33, pp. 261–279). Bethesda, MD: National Institute on Alcohol Abuse and Alcoholism.

National Institute on Alcohol Abuse and Alcoholism. (1995). *Prevalence and population estimates of DSM-IV alcohol abuse and dependency by age, sex, and ethnicity, United States, 1992.* Retrieved January 23, 2010, from psycnet.apa.org

National Institute on Alcohol Abuse and Alcoholism. (1998). Alcohol and aging. *Alcohol Alert,* no. 40.

Nelson, D. E., Sattin, R. W., Langlois, J. A., DeVito, C. A., & Stevens, J. A. (1992). Alcohol as a risk factor for fall injury events among elderly persons living in the community. *Journal of the American Geriatrics Society, 40,* 658–661.

Nevitt, M. C., Cummings, S. R., Kidd, S., & Black, D. (1989). Risk factors for recurrent nonsyncopal falls: A prospective study. *Journal of the American Medical Association, 261*(18), 2663–2668.

Nirenberg, T. D., Gomberg, E. S. L., & Cellucci, T. (1998). Substance abuse disorders. In M. Hersen & V. B. Van Hasselt (Eds.), *Handbook of clinical geropsychology* (pp. 312–330). New York: Plenum Press.

Older Americans Act of 1965, 42 U.S.C. § 3057b (1965).

O'Malley, K., Judge, T. G., & Crooks, J. (1980). Geriatric clinical pharmacology and therapeutics. In G. S. Avery (Ed.), *Drug treatment: Principles and practice of clinical pharmacology and therapeutics* (2nd ed., pp. 158–181). New York: Adis Press.

Park, D. C., & Kidder, D. P. (1996). Prospective memory and medication adherence. In M. Brandimonte, G. O. Einstein, & M. A. McDaniel (Eds.), *Prospective memory: Theory and applications* (pp. 369–390). Mahwah, NJ: Erlbaum.

Pascarelli, E. F. (1985). The elderly in methadone maintenance. In E. Gottheil, K. A. Druley, T. E. Skoloda, & H. M. Waxman (Eds.), *The combined problems of alcoholism, drug addiction, and aging* (pp. 210–214). Springfield, IL: Thomas.

Peterson, D. M., Whittington, F. J., & Beer, E. T. (1979). Drug use and misuse among the elderly. *Journal of Drug Issues, 9*(1), 5–26.

Pfefferbaum, A., Rosenbloom, M., Crusan, K., & Jernigan, T. L. (1988). Brain CT changes in alcoholics: Effects of age and alcohol consumption. *Alcoholism: Clinical and Experimental Research, 12*(1), 81–87.

Pfefferbaum, A., Sullivan, E. V., Mathalon, D. H., & Lim, K. O. (1997). Frontal lobe volume loss observed with magnetic resonance imaging in older chronic alcoholics. *Alcoholism: Clinical and Experimental Research, 21*(3), 521–529.

Pokorny, A. D., Miller, B. A., & Kaplan, H. B. (1972). The brief MAST: A shortened version of the Michigan Alcoholism Screening Test. *American Journal of Psychiatry, 129*(3), 342–345.

Pomara, N., Deptula, D., Singh, R., & Monroy, C. A. (1991). Cognitive toxicity of benzodiazepines in the elderly. In C. Salzman & B. D. Lebowitz (Eds.), *Anxiety in the elderly: Treatment and research* (pp. 175–196). New York: Springer.

Raschko, R. (1990). The gatekeeper model for the isolated, at-risk elderly. In N. L. Cohen (Ed.), *Psychiatry takes to the streets: Outreach and crisis intervention for the mentally ill* (pp. 195–209). New York: Guilford Press.

Regier, D. A., Boyd, J. H., Burke, J. D., Jr., Rae, D. S., Myers, J. K., Kramer, M., Robins, L. N., George, L. K., Karno, M., & Locke, B. Z. (1988). One-month prevalence of mental disorders in the United States: Based on five Epidemiologic Catchment Area sites. *Archives of General Psychiatry, 45*, 977–986.

Reid, M. C., & Anderson, P. A. (1997). Geriatric substance use disorders. *Medical Clinics of North America, 81*(4), 999–1016.

Reid, M. C., Van Ness, P. H., Hawkins, K. A., Towle, V., Concato, J., & Guo, Z. (2006). Light to moderate alcohol consumption is associated with better cognitive functioning among older male veterans receiving primary care. *Journal of Geriatric Neurology, 19*(98). Retrieved January 23, 2010, from Sage Publications database: jgp.sagepub.com/cgi/content/absract/19/2/98

Salzman, G. (1992). *Clinical geriatric psychopharmacology* (2nd ed.). Baltimore: Williams and Wilkins.

Schaie, K. W., & Willis, S. L. (2002). *Adult development and aging* (5th ed.). Upper Saddle River, NJ: Prentice Hall.

Schappert, S. M. (1999). Ambulatory care visits to physician offices, hospital outpatient departments, and emergency departments: United States, 1997. In *Vital health statistics* (Series 13, National Health Survey Report No. 143, pp. 1–39). Hyattsville, MD: Division of Health Care Statistics, National Center for Health Care Statistics.

Schnitzler, C. M., Menashe, L. Sutton, C. G., & Sweet, M. B. (1988). Serum biochemical and haematological markers of alcohol abuse in patients with femoral neck and intertrochanteric fractures. *Alcohol and Alcoholism, 23*(2), 127–132.

Schuckit, M. A., & Miller, P. L. (1976). Alcoholism in elderly men: A survey of a general medical ward. *Annals of the New York Academy of Sciences, 273*, 558–571.

Schutte, K. K., Brennan, P. L., & Moos, R. H. (1998). Predicting the development of late-life late-onset drinking problems: A 7-year prospective study. *Alcoholism: Clinical and Experimental Research, 22*(6), 1349–1358.

Schwartz, J. B. (1997, Spring). Medications in the elderly: The good news and the bad news. *Newsletter of Buehler Center on Aging* (McGaw Medical Center, Northwestern University), *13*(1), 1–2.

Selzer, M. L. (1971). The Michigan Alcoholism Screening Test: The quest for a new diagnostic instrument. *American Journal of Psychiatry, 127*(12), 1653–1658.

Shorr, R. I., Bauwens, S. F., & Landefeld, C. S. (1990). Failure to limit quantities of benzodiazepine hypnotic drugs for outpatients: Placing the elderly at risk. *American Journal of Medicine, 89*, 725–732.

Simon, A., Epstein, L. J., & Reynolds, L. (1968). Alcoholism in the geriatric mentally ill. *Geriatrics, 23*, 125–131.

Smith, D. M., & Atkinson, R. M. (1995). Alcoholism and dementia. *International Journal of the Addictions, 30*(13–14), 1843–1869.

Smyer, M. A., & Downs, M. G. (1995). Psychopharmacology: An essential element in educating clinical psychologists for working with older adults. In B. G. Knight, L. Teri, P. Wohlford, & J. Santos (Eds.), *Mental health services for older adults: Implications for training and practice in geropsychology* (pp. 73–83). Washington, DC: American Psychological Association.

Smyer, M. A., & Qualls, S. H. (1999). *Aging and mental health*. Malden, MA: Blackwell.

Solomon, K., Manepalli, J., Ireland, G. A., & Mahon, G. M. (1993). Alcoholism and prescription drug abuse in the elderly: St. Louis University grand rounds. *Journal of the American Geriatrics Society, 41*, 57–69.

Speer, D. C., & Bates, K. (1992). Comorbid mental and substance disorders among older psychiatric patients. *Journal of the American Geriatrics Society, 40*, 886–890.

Substance Abuse and Mental Health Services Administration. (1994a). *Annual emergency room data 1992: Data from the Drug Abuse Warning Network (DAWN)* (Series 1, No. 12-A, DHHS Publication No. [SMA] 94-2080). Rockville, MD: SAMHSA, Office of Applied Studies.

Substance Abuse and Mental Health Services Administration. (1994b). *Annual medical examiner data 1992: Data from the Drug Abuse Warning Network (DAWN)* (Series 1, No. 12-B, DHHS Publication No. [SMA] 94-2080). Rockville, MD: SAMHSA, Office of Applied Studies.

Sullivan, C. F., Copeland, J. R. M., Dewey, M. E., Davidson, I. A., McWilliam, C., Saunders, P., Sharma, V. K., & Voruganti, L. N. P. (1988). Benzodiazepine usage amongst the elderly: Findings of the Liverpool community survey. *International Journal of Geriatric Psychiatry, 3,* 289–292.

Tabisz, E., Badger, M., Meatherall, R., & Jacyk, W. R. (1991). Identification of chemical abuse in the elderly admitted to emergency. *Clinical Gerontology, 11*(2), 27–38.

Temple, M. T., & Leino, E. V. (1989). Long-term outcomes of drinking: A 20-year longitudinal study of men. *British Journal of Addiction, 84,* 889–899.

Tinetti, M. E., Speechley, M., & Ginter, S. F. (1988). Risk factors for falls among elderly persons living in the community. *New England Journal of Medicine, 319,* 1701–1707.

Uhlenhuth, E. H., DeWit, H., Balter, M. B., Johanson, C. E., & Mellinger, G. D. (1988). Risks and benefits of long-term benzodiazepine use. *Journal of Clinical Psychopharmacology, 8*(3), 161–167.

U.S. Census Bureau. (2001). *The 65 years and over population: 2000.* Retrieved January 23, 2010, from U.S. Census Bureau Web site: http://www.census.gov/prod/2001pubs/c2kbr01-10.pdf

U.S. Department of Health and Human Services. (2005). *Mental health: A report of the Surgeon General.* Bethesda, MD: U.S. Public Health Service.

U.S. House of Representatives. (1992). *Alcohol abuse and misuse among the elderly* (H.R. Rep. No. 852, 102nd Congress, 2nd Session). Washington, DC: Author.

Vestal, R. E., McGuire, E. A., Tobin, J. D., Andres, R., Norris, A. H., & Mezey, E. (1977). Aging and ethanol metabolism. *Clinical Pharmacology and Therapeutics, 21*(3), 343–354.

Vollhardt, B. R., Bergener, M., & Hesse, C. (1992). Psychotropics in the elderly. In M. Bergener, K. Hasegawa, S. I. Finkel, & T. Nishimura (Eds.), *Aging and mental disorders: International perspectives* (pp. 194–211). New York: Springer.

Waller, P. F. (1998). Alcohol, aging, and driving. In E. S. L. Gomberg, A. M. Hegedus, & R. A. Zucker (Eds.), *Alcohol problems and aging* (pp. 301–320). Bethesda, MD: National Institute on Alcohol Abuse and Alcoholism.

Wancata, J., Benda, N., Meise, U., & Muller, C. (1997). Psychotropic drug intake in residents newly admitted to nursing homes. *Psychopharmacology, 134,* 115–120.

Watts, M. (2007). Incidences of excess alcohol consumption in the older person. *Nursing Older People, 18*(12), 27–30.

Whitbourne, S. K. (2005). *Adult development and aging: Biopsychosocial perspectives* (2nd ed.). Hoboken, NJ: Wiley.

Willcox, S. M., Himmelstein, D. U., & Woolhandler, S. (1994). Inappropriate drug prescribing for the community-dwelling elderly. *Journal of the American Medical Association, 272*(4), 292–296.

Woods, J. H., Katz, J. L., & Winger, G. (1992). Benzodiazepines: Use, abuse, and consequences. *Pharmacological Reviews, 44*(2), 151–347.

Yesavage, J. A., Dolhert, N., & Taylor, J. L. (1994). Flight simulator performance of younger and older aircraft pilots: Effects of age and alcohol. *Journal of the American Geriatrics Society, 42*(6), 577–582.

Zhan, C., Sangl, J., Bierman, A. S., Miller, M. R., Friedman, B., Wickizer, S. W., & Meyer, G. S. (2001). Potentially inappropriate medication use in the community-dwelling elderly: Findings from the 1996 Medical Expenditure Panel Survey. *Journal of the American Medical Association, 286*(22), 2823–2829.

Zimberg, S. (1979). Alcohol and the elderly. In D. M. Peterson, E. J. Whittington, & B. P. Payne (Eds.), *Drugs and the elderly: Social and pharmacological issues* (pp. 28–40). Springfield, IL: Thomas.

Resources

http://www.newlifestyles.com/resources/articles/Substance_Abuse.aspx

http://www.usatoday.com/news/health/2005-01-21-senior-addicts_x.htm

http://www.ndsn.org/mayjun98/trends2.html

http://alcoholism.about.com/cs/elder/a/aa981118_2.htm

CHAPTER 6

Issues of Addiction and Abuse Among African Americans

Cynthia G. Scott, Lisa A. Cox-Romain, and Jodi Bunting Stanley

Chemical and behavioral abuse and addiction both impact, and are impacted by, ethnicity, diversity, and disability. In this chapter we explore the physical, sociological, and historical complexity of addiction-related problems that are unique to African Americans. We also examine, through the lens of African American culture, substance abuse, available treatment options, and prevention initiatives.

To begin, it is important and unsettling to note that the difference in life expectancy between African Americans and White Americans continues to be substantial (U.S. Census Bureau, 2004–2005). African American males who were born in 2001 have a life expectancy of 68.6 years. The life expectancy of White males born in 2001 is 75. Gender differences prevail as well. The current life expectancy for African American females is 75.5 years; that of White females is 80.2 years (Freid, Prager, MacKay, & Xia, 2003).

Further, drug addiction is the single most significant social, economic, and public health problem for African Americans (Dei, 2002). Not surprisingly, individuals who are particularly affected include those from urban, lower socioeconomic, and limited-resource communities. What is surprising, however, is that African Americans consume fewer drugs than White Americans, yet they are more likely to suffer greater negative social and health consequences (Belgrave & Allison, 2006). In general, minority groups in the United States not only experience disproportionately high numbers of alcohol- and other drug-related health problems, but also are typically underserved when it comes to accessing available treatment (Blume & Garcia de la Cruz, 2005; Schmidt, Greenfield, & Mulia, 2001).

African Americans frequently lack access to treatment, most often because of socioeconomic factors, which typically translates to having little or no insurance coverage. Interestingly, however, even when treatment is accessible, many African Americans find the choices aversive or unappealing. "Since treatment modalities often are developed within majority culture in the U.S., the models may not be relevant to the needs of potential clients from minority cultures" (Blume & Garcia de la Cruz, 2005, p. 45). There are also foundational and conceptual issues inherent in addiction that transcend culture. These will be highlighted in the discussion on treatment.

The demographic information on African Americans is illuminating. According to U.S. Census Bureau figures for 2000 (http://www.census.gov/), African Americans comprise roughly 12.9% of the U.S. population (including 0.6% who report being "Black in addition to one or more other races"). Between 2000 and 2003, the population growth rate of African Americans exceeded that of the national population growth rate by approximately 0.5%. While the majority of growth has occurred through natural increase, a small portion of the increase has occurred through immigration. African Americans emigrating to the United States typically come from Caribbean or African nations. In recent years, people emigrating to the United States from African countries have done so primarily to escape civil unrest and because of the impact of the Immigration and Naturalization Diversity Program (Kaiser Permanente National Diversity Council, 2003).

In 2000, the median age of African Americans was 30.6 years—31.7 for women, and 28.5 for men. Because of the burgeoning birth rate of African American children, it is estimated that the African American population may grow to nearly 23% of the total U.S. population by 2015. In the absence of major changes in the current patterns of arrest and incarceration, this increase will have a significant impact on rates of arrest and incarceration for drug-related crimes. African Americans are more likely to be investigated for and charged with drug use, possession, and trafficking than any other ethnic group. Even though African Americans account for just fewer than 13% of the population, they account for 32.5% of state and local drug-related arrests (U.S. Sentencing Commission, 2002). Drug arrests are one of the primary reasons why the percentage of African Americans in prison has increased so dramatically over the past 2 decades. Since the "war on drugs" was declared in the 1980s, prison populations have tripled, especially in federal institutions, where 57% of those incarcerated are there for drug-related offenses (Nunn, 2002). The higher arrest rates for African Americans cannot be accounted for by greater drug use, as more drug users are White (Belgrave & Allison, 2006). These higher arrest rates may, in part, be attributable to how police pattern their primary arrest target zones. "Police are more likely to concentrate their arrests in socially disorganized neighborhoods where drug dealing is at a street level" (Nunn, 2002, p. 321).

African Americans have some interesting and unique health challenges, both generally and in relation to their drug use. First, as African Americans age, they contract more alcohol-related diseases than any other group in the population (Kochanek, Murphy, Anderson, & Scott, 2004). The age-adjusted alcohol-related death rate for African Americans was found to be 10% higher than that of the general population. African Americans, who are typically underrepresented in the population at large, continue to be overrepresented in reported health statistics. They are disproportionately more vulnerable to diseases such as hypertension, diabetes mellitus, end stage renal disease, stroke, liver disease, cardiovascular disease, cerebral vascular disease, and cancer, as well as autoimmune, pulmonary, and infectious diseases. They also experience higher rates of suicide, homicide, and violent behavior (U.S. Census Bureau, 2004–2005).

Additionally, African Americans have the highest lung cancer mortality rate in the population (Haiman et al., 2006). Interestingly, while more African American males smoke than do White males, they smoke far fewer cigarettes per day (Stellman et al., 2003). Their absorption rate per cigarette, however, is 30% higher than that of Whites, and they metabolize nicotine more slowly. African American males are 50% more likely to develop lung cancer. The lung cancer rate is about equal in African American and White females (Pérez-Stable, Herrera, Jacob, & Benowitz, 1998).

One possible explanation for the disparity in lung cancer vulnerability rates between African American and White males is that many more African Americans smoke mentholated cigarettes than Whites—75% versus 25%. Menthol is a substance that triggers the cold-sensitive nerves in the skin without actually providing a drop in temperature, and has also been shown to inhibit nicotine metabolism, which causes an increased exposure to nicotine (Benowitz, Herrera, & Peyton, 2004). Williams et al. (2007) reported that serum nicotine levels were higher in smokers of menthol compared to nonmenthol cigarettes. Mustonen, Spencer, Hoskinson, Sachs, and Garvey (2005) found that high cotinine levels (a metabolite of nicotine) and smoking menthol cigarettes may lead to higher toxin intake, which contributes to increased disease risk. However, their findings also suggest that the relationship between the number of cigarettes consumed and salivary cotinine is more complex than previously believed. Thus, it is not sufficient to look at race alone; researchers need to look at race and gender concurrently, as well as the type of cigarette consumed. Further, the menthol cigarette's cooling and numbing properties may permit larger puffs and deeper inhalations, making it easier for one to hold smoke in the lungs for a longer period of time. This obviously increases the exposure to nicotine, as well as the many other carcinogens that are activated when combustion occurs.

Crack cocaine has had a devastating impact on many African American communities. First appearing in the mid-1980s, crack cocaine is a pellet-like smokable form of cocaine that is far cheaper, yet is more addictive, than powdered cocaine (Weil & Rosen, 2004). As addiction to crack cocaine began to rise in African American communities, so, too, did crime, family disruption, and disease (Belgrave & Allison, 2006; Substance Abuse and Mental Health Services Administration, 2002). When the use of crack cocaine became a nationwide epidemic in the 1980s and 1990s, there was great fear that prenatal exposure to it would produce many disabilities in children. However, the findings of researchers who have systematically followed children who were exposed to crack cocaine before birth suggest otherwise. So far, it appears that the long-term effects of exposure on children's brain development and behavior are relatively small. Cocaine does slow fetal growth, and exposed infants tend to be smaller at birth, with smaller heads. But as these children grow, brain and body size appear to catch up. Poor parenting, poverty, and stresses like exposure to violence are far more likely to damage a children's cognitive and psychological development (*"Crack Babies,"* 2009).

African Americans have been deeply impacted by HIV and AIDS as well, which are both closely tied to drug use, among other things. According to the U.S. Census Bureau (2004–2005), 35.1% of African American males had AIDS in 2001, compared to 4.6% of White males, 13.2% of African American females, and 1.0% of White females.

African American women and their children are at greater risk from alcohol- and other drug-related health problems as well, particularly during pregnancy. African American women who use during pregnancy are more susceptible to cardiac disease, hepatitis, and anemia. Infants of African American women who used alcohol and other drugs during pregnancy are more prone to sudden infant death syndrome as well (Guntheroth & Spiers, 2006).

Fetal alcohol syndrome (FAS) and fetal alcohol effects (FAE) are two of the most damaging and permanently debilitating disabilities for children who are exposed to alcohol before birth. FAS, also known as fetal alcohol spectrum disorder (FASD), is not a single birth defect, but a cluster of problems including distinctive facial features (e.g., small eyes; an exceptionally thin upper lip; a short, upturned nose; and a smooth skin surface between the nose and upper lip), heart defects, joint deformities, slow physical growth before and after birth, vision and hearing difficulties, small head circumference and brain size (microcephaly), mental retardation or delayed development, and abnormal behaviors such as a short attention span, hyperactivity, poor impulse control, extreme nervousness, and anxiety (Fetal Alcohol Syndrome, n.d.).

Children with FAE typically lack the distinct facial features of children with FAS and usually have normal IQs. Unfortunately, however, these children are often plagued by damage to the brain that results in a number of behavioral problems, often resulting in trouble in school and with the law, as well as difficulty developing effective social skills. Thus they look "normal" (i.e., they have an invisible disability) but do not behave normally. Often, society has unrealistic expectations about their capabilities without providing them adequate support (Mauro, n.d.).

Finally, fetuses exposed to nicotine are often born prematurely and with low birthweight, whether premature or not. This is most often due to intrauterine growth retardation (Kaiser Permanente National Diversity Council, 2003).

Regarding mental health, epidemiologic studies have demonstrated few differences in the lifetime prevalence of mental illness across ethnicity. However, compared to Whites, African Americans have been shown to be at increased lifetime risk for phobias and somatization and at lower risk for depression and cognitive disorders among those age 45 and older (Robins et al., 1984). Further, African Americans experience lower rates of affective disorders and comorbidity (Kessler et al., 1994). Research has also indicated that African Americans report lower levels of happiness and higher levels of serious personal problems. Overall, however, they report greater life satisfaction (Neighbors & Jackson, 1996).

Young African Americans and Substance Abuse

Young African Americans (i.e., those aged 12 to 20) have their own unique vulnerabilities related to using alcohol and other drugs. The following discussion and demographic information illuminate some of the problems that African American youth experience.

Alcohol is the single most widely used drug by young African Americans, yet their consumption appears to be far less than that of young Whites. According to the 2004 National Survey on Drug Use and Health (Substance Abuse and Mental Health Services Administration, 2004), in a 30-day period, 19.1% of young African Americans used alcohol, compared to 32.6% of young Whites. Regarding binge drinking (i.e., five or more drinks on the same occasion on at least 1 day in the past 30 days), only 9.9% of young African Americans reported binge drinking, as compared to 22.8% of their White counterparts. In spite of the lower rates of alcohol consumption, young African Americans show a higher prevalence for alcohol-related problems than Whites. Alcohol use contributes to the three leading causes of death among African American youth between the ages of 12 and 20: homicide, unintentional injury (including vehicular crashes), and suicide (Center on Alcohol Marketing and Youth, n.d.).

Marijuana continues to be a popular drug of choice for young African Americans (Partnership Attitude Tracking Teens Study, 2003). While marijuana use has declined among White adolescents, the rate of use remains unchanged for young African Americans. One out of six 12- to 17-year-old African Americans reported using marijuana at least once in their lifetime. In Jamaica, young female members of the Rastafarian Church consider marijuana to be "wisdom weed" (Huffman, 2004).

In 2002, 14.3% of African American high school students smoked cigarettes. White high schoolers were more than twice as likely to smoke. African Americans were less likely than Whites to report their smoking (Griesler, Kandel, & Davies, 2002). Smoking rates for White and African American middle school students was roughly equivalent (10.4% for Whites, 9.4% for African Americans).

African American History: Its Impact on Drug and Behavioral Addictions

African American history has great depth, breadth, and complexity. A brief summary is presented here as it relates to drug use and addiction. This history cannot and must not be overlooked as a confounding factor in patterns of addiction.

For purposes of definition, *African Americans* in the United States are typically thought to be descendants of those individuals who were abducted from Africa, brought to America, and enslaved between the 17th and 19th centuries (Kaiser Permanente National Diversity Council, 2003). President Abraham Lincoln issued the Emancipation Proclamation in 1862.

The United States as a nation has come a long way since this most shameful part of its past, yet African Americans' seemingly endless struggle for these rights to be realized—socially, socioeconomically, and educationally—continues to impact them deeply. While African Americans are as diverse as any ethnic group in terms of their many demographic features and differences, it is safe to say that the shadow of enslavement and the continual impact of that shadow, as well as the long and often discouraging fight against racism and for civil rights, always hovers, never too far from the surface for many. This in turn impacts how they sometimes view and respond to the world. This history understandably affects many African Americans' attitudes as well as their coping strategies, including their use of alcohol and other drugs. While alcohol and other drug use is a choice for coping with stress used by many people across many cultures, its prevalence as a coping strategy for many African Americans is especially widespread. A historical perspective on patterns of drug use among African Americans, particularly indigenous Africans, helps to shed light on the use and abuse patterns of African Americans in the United States today.

Humans have been making and consuming alcohol almost from the beginning of their existence. "If any watery mixture of vegetable sugars or starches is allowed to stand long enough in a warm place, alcohol will make itself" (Kinney & Leaton, 1978, p. 4). African tribes used fermented corn and millet to create what they thought to be a sacred drink, using it both in social interactions and as a product of trade for food and other necessities. Many tribes made wine from locally tapped palm trees and used it for social and religious ceremonies (James & Johnson, 1996). Some tribes brewed beer as well, viewing it as an integral part of social interactions among tribal males; they also used it as an offering to the gods as well as a reward to those who had worked the land (Gordon, 2003). Some tribes in Southern Africa used cannabis as well (Ambler, 2003).

African enslavement began in Europe as early as 1399, long before Columbus. The first Africans to be brought to the New World were taken to Virginia in 1619, where they were traded for food and supplies. By 1661, labor was in short supply, and slavery was soon legalized. Slaves had no personal rights, and now, by law, they were fated to lives of both servitude and ignorance (W. H. James & Johnson, 1996). By the 1700s, alcohol came to be used as currency in trading enslaved Africans, and in fact was used to purchase between 5% and 10% of all West Africans (Ambler, 2003). Over time, the slave trade became inextricably linked to alcohol production. Molasses and sugar from the British and Spanish West Indies were shipped to New England, where they were distilled into rum. The rum was then sent to Africa, where it was exchanged for enslaved Africans. Enslaved Africans were, in turn, shipped to the West Indies in order to work in the fields that yielded the very products that were eventually used for their purchase (James & Johnson, 1996).

According to Suggs and Lewis (2003), during the era of slavery, the social drinking patterns of enslaved African Americans consisted mostly of weekend, holiday, and celebratory use. The extreme work demands placed on them from dawn to dusk left little time for recreational drinking. The "masters" often offered them alcohol as a cheap reward for obedience and hard work, especially during harvest time.

After the Civil War, African Americans became more involved in the Protestant Church (Maffly-Kipp, 2001). The doctrines of the church forbade the use of alcohol and other drugs. After the signing of the Emancipation Proclamation in 1862, African American churches of many denominations grew significantly, and all promoted either abstinence from or moderation in the use of spirits.

However, during this same postwar period, many African Americans migrated to the North, most often to urban areas, in search of employment. Men had to leave their families behind while they searched for work because the cost of moving them was prohibitive. Even after finding employment, they seldom had enough money to move their families, and so the families lived perpetually in limbo, with the mother and children still being influenced by the oppressiveness and racism of the postwar South, and their husbands living without their families, in the harsh urban areas of the North. For many, exposure to urban life was accompanied by heavier drinking. Not surprisingly, many African Americans began to use alcohol to cope with the countless problems of daily living, most of which were a direct result of both poverty and the merciless impact of postwar racism. They had gained their "freedom," but many were not prepared for, and were deeply traumatized by, the tumult that accompanied the end of the Civil War in both the North and the South.

Interestingly, during this period, opium—one of the first non-indigenous drugs to become a part of 19th-century culture—became widely popular. Chinese immigrants, who were brought to the United States primarily to build the transcontinental railroad, migrated across the country, bringing their opium-smoking habits with them. In the early to mid-1800s, opium and its preparations were easily obtainable and subject to no regulatory controls (James & Johnson, 1996). The peak of opiate dependence in the United States occurred around 1900, when the number of individuals addicted was estimated at close to 250,000 in a population of 76 million. This rate has never again been equaled (Musto, 2001).

World War I galvanized the African American community. African Americans saw an opportunity to make America truly democratic by ensuring full citizenship for all. African American soldiers, who continued to serve in segregated units, began to protest against racial injustice, both on the home front and abroad. Both African Americans and Whites in the newly formed National Association for the Advancement of Colored People (NAACP) and other organizations led the crusade against discrimination and segregation in the United States ("World War I and Postwar Society," n.d.).

The United States faced World War II, and again, African Americans fought for their country. African Americans did not return from World War II with the illusion that they would be able to participate equally in America's political and economic arenas, as they had after World War I. African Americans continued to fight against discrimination both at home and abroad.

Prior to 1930, illegal drug use in the United States was primarily limited to exconvicts and criminals. By the 1930s, however, African Americans had become disproportionately represented in the population of addicted individuals, most from urban areas. African American clubs and bars burgeoned, and with this expansion came increased opportunities to use alcohol and other drugs (James & Johnson, 1996).

Heroin and marijuana use increased in African American communities during the 1940s and 1950s. However, this paled in comparison to the increase in alcohol consumption in both rural and urban African American communities, where excessive use was generally tolerated because of the oppressive and stressful circumstances under which many African Americans lived. There were few treatment options; African Americans were barred from Alcoholics Anonymous during this period (Belgrave & Allison, 2006).

The 1950s and 1960s ushered in the era of the Civil Rights Movement. African Americans fought for racial equality and desegregation, and the Civil Rights Act was passed into law in 1964. It was a landmark piece of legislation that outlawed racial segregation in schools, public places, and employment. Conceived to help African Americans, the bill was amended prior to passage to protect women, and explicitly included White Americans. It also created the Equal Employment Opportunity Commission (Lawson, 1991).

During this same period, however, organized crime took control of the drug markets. With the poverty rate for African Americans hovering at approximately 30% (U.S. Census Bureau, 2004–2005), many younger African Americans began to participate in drug preparation and trafficking in order to make money (Belgrave & Allison, 2006).

During the 1970s, 1980s, and 1990s, cocaine became wildly popular, and crack cocaine became the drug of choice for many lower socioeconomic groups, particularly African Americans, because it was far less expensive than cocaine in powdered form. As previously noted, its impact on many African American communities was and continues to be devastating. Just as devastating, however, was the impact of the Anti-Drug Abuse Act of 1986, which made possession of crack cocaine—the form of the drug that was and continues to be widely sold in inner-city, predominantly African American neighborhoods—punishable with far tougher sentences than possession of powdered cocaine.

African American Family Systems

Every family both is subsumed by larger systems and subsumes smaller systems within it. The health or ill-health of any family system is dependent on how well that system operates—the risk and protective factors within the family. Risk factors include addiction and dependency.

In thinking about families and family systems, it is important to be clear about what exactly constitutes a system. A *system* is a set of elements that operate in inter-action with one another. Each element in the system is affected by whatever happens to any of the other elements. Systems are composed of three elements: objects, attributes, and relationships among the objects within an environment (Littlejohn, 1978). Within any family, the *objects* consist of the individual family members. The *attributes* may include family and individual goals, energy, attitudes, ethnic composition, and a myriad of other characteristics. The *relationship among objects* is descriptive of how family members communicate with and about each other. The environment includes the surroundings that both shape and are shaped by the family. Family therapists are most concerned with looking at the relationship between the "objects," or family members. It is the interaction between the family members that best reflects the dynamic nature of families (Hecker, Mims, & Boughner, 2003).

Historically, American society has defined *family* in a fairly restricted, Eurocentric manner, typically thinking of family as a *nuclear* family consisting of a mother, a father, and their children. Systems theory, however, examines families from a far broader perspective, so that a family system may include stepfamilies, foster families, single-parent families, cohabiting families, three-generational families, grandfamilies, families with gay parents, and biologically unrelated families.

These complex family systems are also composed of subsystems—smaller, self-contained but interrelated systems within the larger system. For instance, the parents in a family comprise a parental subsystem that has its own set of rules, boundaries, and goals. Siblings, stepsiblings, and half-siblings are all constituents of the sibling subsystem. The concept of hierarchy refers to the fact that any complex system is also a subsystem of a higher order system, which, in turn, is a subsystem of yet another higher order system. For instance, one's religious community, medical community, and business community are also subsystems of the town or city, and each town or city is a smaller element of other larger systems (e.g., state government, the American Medical Association, etc.).

Another important subsystem is the *personal* subsystem and its components. Individuals possess unique biological, psychological, and social components that not only encapsulate them as individuals but also impact and are impacted by the other subsystems and systems (Kantor & Lehr, 1976).

The heterogeneity of African American families, which is related to their value systems, lifestyles, and social class structure, makes it impossible to characterize them in a uniform fashion. The sociocultural, economic, and community contexts in which families live have strong implications for how each family functions and raises children. As an aggregate, African Americans have a rich and diverse cultural heritage, and their beliefs about family, faith, and kinship are deeply woven into their cultural identity.

Hill (1998) defined the African American family as a household related by blood, marriage, or function that meets the family's *instrumental* and *expressive* needs. *Instrumental needs* include those that are basic to survival, such as clothing, shelter, and food. The *expressive needs* include emotional support and nurturing.

The family *network* can include both biologically related members and nonbiological members, and is characterized as an *extended* family. The *extended family* consists of a system of functionally related individuals who live in different households. The *immediate family* consists of individuals who reside in the same household, regardless of the number of generations living there. *Fictive kin*, defined as members of the family who are neither biologically related nor related through marriage but who feel and function like family, are often included as members of African American families (Scott & Black, 1989).

African American families are often extended and multigenerational, with a cooperative and collective family structure (Wilson et al., 1995). The family network can include not only the immediate and extended family members but also friends, neighbors, church members, and fictive kin.

Spiritual and religious beliefs are interwoven into almost every aspect of African American life. These beliefs influence family and social relationships, political considerations, employment and educational decisions, community involvement, basic physical and emotional well-being, and coping skills (Mattis, 2000). There is also a high level of spiritual and religious activity in most African American communities. African Americans are more likely than Whites to have prayed, read the Bible, and attended church in any given week. Attending church is an important ritual for many African Americans. The typical Sunday service is 70% longer than those attended by Whites, and church attendance is approximately 50% greater in African American churches than in White churches (Barna Group, 2005).

During the centuries of enslavement in the United States, slave masters used Christianity as a way to control enslaved Africans and keep them submissive, teaching them that Christianity would save their souls and provide them with a joyful afterlife as long as they were obedient while here on Earth. While many enslaved Africans adopted Christian beliefs, they adapted the religion to more accurately depict their native African spirituality, organizing their own worship services and meeting in secret places in order to sing, preach, and pray. Christ became a liberating figure for them, as they felt strengthened by his resolve and found hope in his resurrection (Lincoln & Mamiya,

1990). Within their own churches, they felt respected and in control of their destiny. Even today the church remains a place where African Americans can achieve status and influence irrespective of their socioeconomic standing (Belgrave & Allison, 2006).

Generally, there has been a steady rise in the number of single-parent households in the United States, but disproportionately so for African Americans. In 2002, 16% of White American families were headed by a single mother, compared to 48% of African American families (Fields, 2003). It is important to note that the reasons for the burgeoning rate of single-parent, and most particularly, single-mother households is different for Whites than it is for African Americans. For White females, there has been an increase in the divorce rate and a decrease in the rate of remarriages. For African American females, the increase is more often due to the large number of never-married mothers, who as a group tend to have less economic stability and are likely to be younger and less educated than married women. Poverty among children is highest among those who live in single-mother families. They are four times more likely to be poor than African American children who live with two parents (Hogan & Lichter, 1995).

A small percentage (5%) of African American children live with single fathers, who tend to be less economically disadvantaged and have more support in the household, as 80% of these men report residing in a subfamily, in a cohabiting relationship, or with a related adult. Thus, African American single-parent males seldom have the sole responsibility for child rearing that African American single-parent females do.

African American children are also more likely to live in a home where a grandparent is present than are White American children (U.S. Census Bureau, 2004). In about 11% of these households, grandparents are the primary caregivers for at least one grandchild.

Marriage rates have declined for both African Americans and Whites. However, White women are twice as likely to remarry as African American women (Kreider & Simmons, 2003). There are several explanations for the declining marriage rate of African Americans. Economics is a foundational factor. A. D. James (1998) noted that declines in male economic viability contribute to decreased marriage rates. When economic opportunities are good, both men and women tend to marry, and they marry earlier. Thus, declines in marriage among African Americans may be due to a poor labor market for men; unemployment makes them less attractive as potential marriage partners. Second, African American women have become more economically independent and do not have to depend on a spouse to meet their economic needs. Third, gender ratios have changed. There are more available women than men as marriage partners.

African Americans are also more likely than Whites to separate or divorce, and they wait longer between separating and divorcing (Bramlett & Mosher, 2002). African American women are also less likely to remarry than White women. The probability of remarrying after 5 years of divorce is 58% for White women and 32% for African American women.

African American men identify their ability to provide for their families as a key role, and their concerns about not being able to fulfill the role of provider are often associated with marital difficulties (Veroff, Douvan, & Hatchett, 1995). African American men have often been stereotypically vilified as husbands because of the perception of their lack of family involvement and financial irresponsibility. Unfortunately, much of the research substantiates this portrayal (Taylor & Johnson, 1997). However, research on middle-income fathers indicates that African American men are actively involved in socializing and providing for their children (McAdoo, 1988). Further, older men and those with higher personal incomes are more likely to be positive role models and good providers than those who are younger or who have lower socioeconomic status (Taylor, Leashore, & Toliver, 1988). Interestingly, Bowman and Forman (1997) found that while African American fathers had more personal income and less financial stress than mothers, they perceived greater difficulty being good providers for their children.

Belgrave and Allison (2006) noted that the research focus on African American families has moved from a deficit-based view to a strengths-based view in the last several decades. Hill (1998) defined family strengths as those attributes that enable families to meet both the needs of its members and the external demands made on the family. Some family strengths that are typical of African American families are an orientation toward high achievement, a strong work ethic, flexibility of family roles, strong familial bonds, and a strong religious orientation.

Thus, African American families have unique characteristics within the culture, but each family is a system in and of itself. In conceptualizing African American families using the template of systems theory, each one possesses all the characteristics of the elements (i.e., the objects, attributes, and relationship among objects) that operate in interaction with one another, each element being influenced by and influencing the other elements in the system.

Treatment

African Americans comprise the largest minority culture population in the United States. Unfortunately, to date, little research has focused on culturally sensitive substance abuse treatment or, especially relevant for the African American community, how prejudice and racism can be addressed effectively in treatment to better help clients. Issues of discrimination and racism and their impact on addictive behaviors have been discussed throughout the chapter. Not surprisingly, epidemiologic research suggests that racism can be a contributing factor to increased psychopathology, including addiction (Carter, 1994; Wingo, 2001). Prejudice and racism often entail a financial disadvantage, and the two combined can significantly increase the risk for addictive disorders, as well as relapse back into unhealthy behaviors once they have been stopped (Brewer, Catalano, Haggerty, Gainey, & Fleming, 1998).

One of the primary shortcomings of research related to effective treatment and relapse prevention has been testing whether they are effective with minority populations. Little is known about what is most predictive of relapse in minority cultures such as the African American community, which has such a markedly different worldview, values, and family and social organizational structures compared to those of the majority culture (Blume & Garcia de la Cruz, 2005). For example, individualism, with its emphasis on "self" and "autonomy," is the primary worldview of the majority culture in the United States, whereas collectivism, with an emphasis on "interdependency" and "relationships," is the primary worldview of most minority cultures. The majority culture in the United States typically views time and history as linear and progressive; many from minority cultures view time and history as cyclical and recurring (Gaines et al., 1997; Sue & Sue, 2003a). Gender roles may also be conceptualized differently. Such roles may vary according to birth order, which may dictate specific expectations for children within the family structure (Gushue & Sciarra, 1995; Sue & Sue, 2003b, 2003c). Since family life tends to be at the core of many ethnic minority cultures, as it is in most African American communities, roles and relationships can have a far greater influence than they might otherwise have by the standards of the majority culture, with its emphasis on the individual.

Moreover, ethnic minority cultures often have value systems that are markedly different from those of the majority culture. For instance, since relationships are highly valued in many minority cultures, social ideals such as honor, respect, and role in the community are of great import, and develop within the context of service to others rather than as a result of personal achievement. "Self" is frequently defined by one's relationship with and role in the community. "Autonomy" is a foreign concept to many people from minority cultures because interdependence is so highly valued and so intrinsically a part of the value system of the culture (Sue & Sue, 2003a).

Many ethnic minority communities also place great importance on spoken traditions; stories and shared histories take on great meaning. Additionally, the preferred pace, or rhythm, of life may be slower than is often is in the fast-paced majority culture in the United States.

Even though research and treatment about addiction has evolved appreciably, most traditional treatment programs still do not effectively address the impact of racism on addiction, which may cause clinicians to overlook a potentially toxic stressor (Rhodes & Johnson, 1997) and one that is highly likely to undermine success in treatment. Clinicians who treat African Americans need to equip themselves with a solid understanding of African American history, always looking through the lens of the cultural differences, the atrocities of racism, and the trauma that continues to reverberate throughout African American communities, not only from centuries of enslavement but also from a cultural heritage that was in large part stolen from them. Many African Americans share a history of family trauma and dysfunction, oppression, and economic disadvantage, as well as strong, deeply rooted spiritual beliefs: "God will bring us through anything." Using this as a cultural framework from which to approach treatment will help clinicians optimize the potential for successful treatment (Mental Health Center of Dane County, 2003).

However, more is needed to optimize success, and this is true about people of any culture. As noted earlier, African Americans are less likely than Whites to seek treatment for addiction-related disabilities, and they often find the available options aversive or unappealing, in large part because most have been developed within the White majority culture, which often renders them culturally irrelevant (Blume & Garcia de la Cruz, 2005). Nevertheless, addiction involves inseparable biological and behavioral components, many of which transcend culture (Leshner, 2001). Addictive behaviors do have special characteristics related to the social contexts in which they originate, but there are a host of fundamental biopsychosocial factors that are relevant to all individuals, irrespective of culture. If these are not addressed in treatment, the chances of long-term success will be greatly reduced.

Addiction and the Brain

Research on the relationship between brain chemistry and the addictive process is compelling. Identifying what happens in the brain when a drug is inhaled, injected, or eaten, understanding why it leads to compulsive drug seeking, and then learning how to disrupt that process is considered by many to be the last best hope for a permanent solution to addiction.

The most enlightening revelation about addiction may be that scientists now regard it as a *brain disease* that develops over time as a result of an *initially* voluntary use of drugs that becomes increasingly habitual. Habitual use causes changes in the brain's "reward" pathway, which lies in the primitive region of the brain known as the limbic system. Dopamine is the primary neurotransmitter involved in the pleasure pathway (Leshner, 1997, 2001). All mood-altering drugs, from prescription medications to heroin to tobacco to caffeine, increase levels of dopamine in the brain. Importantly, the effect of the increase in dopamine is *also believed to underlie their reinforcing effects* (Di Chiara & Imperato, 1988; Koob & Bloom, 1988). Although each drug activates it in a somewhat different way, addictions center on alterations in the reward pathway.

Another important consideration is that the reward pathway is the brain system that governs *motivated* behavior. This is a key concept related to treatment that will be discussed later. While addiction experts are divided on the following point, many believe the reward pathway also figures in behavioral addictions such as compulsive eating, exercise, gambling, and sex.

Powledge (1999) noted that addiction as a brain disease is "triggered by frequent use of drugs that change the biochemistry and anatomy of neurons and alter the way they work" (p. 513). The changes represent a "desperate attempt of the brain to carry on business-as-usual—to make neurons less responsive to drugs and so restore homeostasis—while under extreme chemical siege" (p. 513).

Further, drug craving that is triggered by cues (known as cue reactivity), such as the sight, smell, and other sensory stimuli associated with a particular drug, is central to addiction, and poses an ever-present threat to sustained success. While it is clear that brain chemistry underlies "cue-induced" craving, studies have shown that with repeated drug exposure to neutral stimuli paired with the drug (conditioned stimuli), neurons begin to increase dopamine by themselves, which is an effect that could well underlie drug-seeking behavior (Volkow et al., 2006). Understanding the mechanisms of cue-induced craving will result in more accurate and successful treatment strategies.

Cognitive Impairment

The effect of alcohol and other drugs on the brain's ability to process information is another important confounding factor in treatment, and something that is often either overlooked or not given due importance. For instance, the majority of individuals who abuse alcohol eventually experience some degree of cognitive impairment (Goldman, 1990, 1995), and there is strong clinical evidence of a relationship between the degree of cognitive impairment and one's ability to participate in treatment (Bates et al., 2002). Thus, one might enter treatment but be cognitively unable to participate—to grasp and retain information—for weeks, sometimes months. For some people, at least some degree of cognitive impairment may be irreversible (Goldman, 1990). Not surprisingly then, cognitive impairment may result in reducing the amount of time one stays in treatment or remains abstinent (Aharonovich, Nunes, & Hasin, 2003).

Determinants of Relapse and Relapse Prevention

Learning the skills of relapse prevention is foundational to effective long-term outcome. Historically, relapse (i.e., a return to heavy use following a period of abstinence or moderate use) has been construed by treatment providers as an end state—a treatment failure. One is either abstinent or relapsed. Conversely, in the Relapse Prevention Model (Marlatt & Donovan, 2005; Marlatt & Gordon, 1985), relapse is conceptualized as a transitional process that unfolds over time; the process of relapse begins before one returns to using, and it continues after one has once again initiated use.

The determinants of relapse find their genesis in Bandura's (1977) classic model on self-efficacy and behavior change. He noted that "cognitive processes mediate change but ... cognitive events are induced and altered most readily by experience of mastery arising from effective performance" (p. 191). In other words, the cognitive processes that lead up to cessation are important, but more important is the cessation itself, and the increasing confidence in one's ability to continue cessation. The Relapse Prevention Model suggests that both immediate and long-term determinants contribute to relapse. Immediate determinants include vulnerability in high-risk situations, one's choice of coping skills and outcome expectancies, and abstinence violation. Long-term determinants include lifestyle factors as well as urges and cravings. Specific interventions to deter relapse include identifying high-risk situations and enhancing related coping skills, increasing self-efficacy (i.e., confidence in one's ability to be successful), managing lapses, and restructuring the perception of relapse. Long-term strategies include helping the client find a healthy lifestyle balance, develop "positive" addictions, use effective cue reactivity and craving-management techniques, and develop relapse road maps (Larimer, Palmer, & Marlatt, 1999).

There are two broad-based determining factors of relapse—the intrapersonal and the interpersonal. Intrapersonal determining factors include one's relationship with self, personal self-assessment, self-concept, and self-esteem, along with environmental factors and physiological and psychological contributors such as levels of cognition, brain biology, and coping style. Interpersonal factors include relational or social variables such as support from or conflict with others (Blume & Garcia de la Cruz, 2005; Larimer et al., 1999). While Marlatt (1985) found that intrapersonal variables were more predictive of relapse than interpersonal variables, little is known about which determinants best predict relapse in African Americans because there are so many differences in worldview, family structure, and organizational patterns. As yet, it is undetermined whether the constructs of relapse prevention developed by the majority culture and conceptualized through the values of that culture (e.g., "self," "coping," and "skills") will translate to successful outcomes in minority cultures.

In the United States, people from ethnic minority cultures often live in and are affected by the expectations of more than one culture. In order to optimize coping, they must become competent in understanding the skills of the predominant culture as well as their culture of origin. This is referred to as "bicultural competence." People need different skills to successfully negotiate different cultures (LaFromboise & Rowe, 1983; Blume & Garcia de la Cruz, 2005). Many treatment programs have developed interventions that focus on enhancing cultural skills training in order to promote bicultural competence. However, the focus on this continues to be less than optimal.

While there have been successful prevention programs targeted at enhancing effective coping skills for minority youth (Botvin & Kantor; 2000; Botvin, Schinke, Epstein, Diaz, & Botvin, 1995; Litrownik et al., 2000), research is limited on whether teaching skills is effective for relapse prevention. Walton, Blow, and Booth (2001) found that African Americans reported significantly greater coping skills and higher self-efficacy in regard to using those skills than Whites, even though the African Americans had less postdischarge support.

As noted earlier, several factors are strong predictors of long-term behavioral cessation or relapse, transcending culture in many respects. The constructs of the Relapse Prevention Model certainly fall into this category. Even while cultural influences may impact one's response to the constructs of the Relapse Prevention Model to some degree, foundationally, these constructs subsume culture. Motivation and change, as discussed below, also lie at the heart of behavior change.

Motivation and Change

Why and how do people change? What is motivation? Can motivation be modified in order to change addictive behaviors? Unquestionably, motivation and change are inextricably bound. Addiction researchers have developed a better understanding of the many dimensions of motivation as well as the determinants of and processes involved in personal change. By developing a better understanding of how people change naturally, without professional help, researchers and clinicians alike now better understand these dynamics and have developed more effective interventions to help clients change unhealthy behaviors.

Change is a process, not an outcome (Sobell et al., 1996; Tucker, Vuchinich, & Gladsjo, 1994). Change occurs naturally for all people, relative to many behaviors—including addictive behaviors—and it frequently happens without professional help. This self-directed change is well documented in the literature (Blomqvist, 1996; Chen & Kandel, 1995; Orleans et al., 1991; Sobell & Sobell, 1998). One classic study of natural change and recovery focused on returning Vietnam War veterans ($N = 943$) across ethnicities who had become addicted to heroin while in Vietnam. Of these individuals, only 5% continued their addiction a year after returning home, and only 12% began to use heroin again within the first 3 years of their return, most for only a short time. The majority did not enter formal treatment programs; they recovered on their own (Robins, Davis, & Goodwin, 1974). Recognizing the processes involved in natural recovery and self-directed change helps illuminate how changes related to substance use can be precipitated and stimulated by enhancing motivation.

Stages of Change

The change process has been conceptualized as a biopsychosocial sequence of stages through which people typically progress as they think about, initiate, and maintain new behaviors. In their classic study on change, Prochaska and DiClemente (1984) developed a transtheoretical model (i.e., crossing biopsychosocial domains) of change that emerged from an examination of 18 psychological and behavioral theories about how change occurs, including a framework for understanding addiction. Importantly, the model also reflects how change occurs outside a therapeutic environment. Comparing *natural* self-change with *therapeutic intervention*, investigators noted similarities that led them to conclude that change occurs in stages. They observed that people who make behavioral changes, either on their own or with professional guidance, initially shift from a lack of awareness about the problem, or an unwillingness to do anything about the problem, to considering the possibility of change, to becoming determined and prepared to make the change, to finally taking action and sustaining that change over time (DiClemente, 2002). The stages of change are briefly described below.

Precontemplation

In the precontemplation stage, individuals are often partially or wholly unaware that a problem exists or that they have to make changes, and that they may need help in doing so. They may also be unwilling or too discouraged to initiate behavior change on their own at this point.

Contemplation

As individuals become aware that a problem exists, they may become concerned and see the necessity for change. At this point, they typically feel ambivalent about and resistant to change. Still using their drugs of choice, they may consider stopping or cutting back in the near future. They may seek out relevant information and reevaluate their behavior, or seek help to support the possibility of changing. Individuals often remain in this stage for extended periods of time—sometimes years—vacillating between wanting and not wanting to change.

Preparation

When people finally perceive that the advantages of change outweigh any positive features of their continued use, they begin to shift their attitudinal balance in favor of change. Once the decision has been well conceptualized, individuals enter the preparation stage, where they begin to strengthen their commitment to change. Preparation includes more specific planning for change as well as an examination of their level of self-efficacy for changing (Bandura, 1997). People continue to participate in using, but typically they intend to quit very soon. They have often already made at least one attempt to reduce or stop using on their own and may be experimenting now with ways to quit. They begin to set goals for themselves and make commitments to stop using, even telling select others about their plans.

Action

Individuals in the action stage choose strategies for change and begin to activate them. They now begin to actively modify both their habits and their environment. They are in the middle of making extreme lifestyle changes and are often faced with particularly challenging situations, which in some cases may include the physiological effects of withdrawal. They may begin to reevaluate their own self-image as they move from unhealthy to healthy behaviors. This stage typically lasts for 3 to 6 months following behavior cessation and is often called the honeymoon period. Individuals now face the daunting challenges of long-term cessation.

Maintenance

During maintenance, people work to sustain their behavior change and prevent recurrence (Marlatt & Donovan, 2005). They may have to be hypervigilant to keep from reverting back to comfortable old patterned behaviors. They learn how to detect and guard against high-risk situations and other triggers. In most cases, individuals at this stage will revert back to their unhealthy behaviors at least once, but learning from this reversion can and should be viewed as part of the educational process that eventuates in metamorphosis.

Motivation

Motivation, conceptualized as something one does, not something one has, has a great deal of cultural relevance; while it is unique to each individual, it results, in part, from the interactions between the individual and the people he or she encounters, as well as other environmental factors. Motivation to change is barometric—subject to the influence of family, friends, emotions, and self-appraisals. Furthermore, one's motivation can be deeply affected by a lack of community support, particularly barriers to health care and employment, as well as social isolation.

Internal factors are the *basis* for change, but external factors are the *conditions* of change (Miller & Rollnick, 2002). Motivation to change involves recognizing a problem, searching for a way to change, and then beginning and sticking with that change strategy. There are, it turns out, many ways to help people move toward such recognition and action (Miller, 1995).

As previously noted, however, there may well be a biological component to motivation that adds greater complexity to solving the behavior-change problem. Recall that researchers posit that the reward pathway in the brain system governs *motivated behavior*. The evidence suggests a cyclical phenomenon—that the long-lasting brain changes resulting from habitual drug use are responsible for the cognitive distortions and emotional functioning that characterize people with addictive disorders, particularly the compulsion to use drugs, which is the essence of addiction. It is as if drugs have highjacked the brain's natural *motivational* control circuits, resulting in drug use becoming the primary *motivational priority* for the individual.

Integrating the Foundational and Cultural Constructs of Treatment

While it is clear that many foundational elements of addictive behavior transcend culture, it can also be said that aspects of culture transcend the foundational elements. If there can be no individualizing of treatment in order to meet each person where he or she is right now, not only in the context of that person's culture but also in the person's evolution toward motivation and change, the potential for harm reduction will be greatly reduced (Marlatt & Witkiewitz, 2002).

The construct of self-efficacy may also be worth exploring from a cultural perspective. One of the primary goals of relapse prevention is to develop greater self-efficacy in order to better navigate through high-risk situations. Some research suggests that the construct of self-efficacy may be different among minority populations that hold a more collectivistic rather than individualistic worldview (Blume & Garcia de la Cruz, 2005). Collective efficacy can be conceptualized as a communal belief by a group of people in their ability to effectively organize and complete specific tasks in order to achieve particular goals (Bandura, 1997). Individuals with collectivistic worldviews have been shown to process *group*-efficacy feedback better than *self*-efficacy feedback (Earley, Gibson, & Chen, 1999) and have demonstrated increased self-efficacy to complete tasks better when exposed to group rather than *individual* training (Earley, 1994).

Prevention

Four decades of research into preventing substance abuse has demonstrated that it is not an easy thing to do. We know that prevention has to begin early. We also know that teaching children of any culture about drugs, engaging them in values clarification, teaching them to "just say no," and helping them understand about peer pressure and other risks, as well as protective factors, do not necessarily stop them from using.

Many approaches have been employed, some more effectively than others. As discussed throughout this chapter, some cultural differences do influence the effectiveness of prevention outcomes, yet some prevention concepts seem to be relevant across different groups. Most programs use a combination of the following strategies and approaches for drug prevention (Belgrave & Allison, 2006; Center for Substance Abuse Prevention, 1996):

Knowledge-based prevention programs are designed to teach children about alcohol and other drugs and the negative consequences of using them. Used alone, without a larger frame of reference, knowledge-based programs are not typically effective in changing behaviors.

Personal, interpersonal, and self-enhancement programs are designed to promote feelings of self-worth and competence, which in turn may minimize the likelihood that young people will use alcohol and other drugs.

Life skills training and *social skills programs* teach drug-refusing skills and infuse young people with more in-depth knowledge and awareness of the social context of drug use. They also attempt to instill in children the skills necessary for coping with anxiety and help them identify the types of social and interpersonal relationships that place them at higher risk for making unhealthy choices about alcohol and other drugs.

Family-based programs focus on improving parenting skills and fostering family cohesiveness. They help children build competence and healthy connections to better deter drug use.

Community-based programs target elements of the community that influence drug accessibility and attitudes. People involved in a community-based program may, for instance, petition for liquor stores to be removed from certain areas. These programs may also provide watchdog services, scrutinizing how law enforcement intervenes in drug trafficking. Community programs may confront advertisers that target vulnerable youthful populations with cigarette and alcohol ads, or other ads suggestive of a drug-using lifestyle.

Alternative programs provide young people with constructive and healthy activities that are appealing enough in and of themselves that they can offset the attractiveness of drugs. Typical activities include anything from athletic and popular recreational programs to tutoring and other educationally enhancing programs.

Cultural enhancement programs focus on the infusion of cultural values, attitudes, and behaviors that can also help children make healthy choices. These kinds of programs not only help children to better identify with and honor their own cultural identity, but also help them to contextualize their cultural identity within a worldview framework.

Conclusion

When there are so many differences and similarities between and across cultures, it becomes especially difficult to conceptualize any group of people in terms of the specific influences that shape their behaviors and attitudes and their unique risk factors for and protective factors from physiological, psychological, and social harm. African Americans are particularly vulnerable because of the atrocities of enslavement and racism that have been inflicted on them for centuries, and the effects of the never-ending racist and oppressive attitudes that continue to alter the way they conceptualize themselves and the world outside their culture. Alcohol and other drugs have had devastating consequences for African Americans, and tunneling through to the other side of this problem is difficult indeed. The research clearly shows that while young African Americans use fewer drugs than young Whites, the patterns of use change with age, with African Americans increasing their drug use as they age; this does not bode well for the resulting health consequences. Drug use for African Americans typically begins in adolescence and seems to co-occur with many other social and personal problems (Belgrave & Allison, 2006). As previously noted, while African Americans tend to use fewer drugs less frequently, they suffer greater negative health effects, and health-care costs are higher, if coverage exists at all. This dynamic serves to underscore the need for more and better treatment options that address the unique needs of African Americans.

Much, and yet little, has changed in the treatment of addiction in the past few decades. Despite the clear evidence of the relationship between brain chemistry and addiction, there remains a strong propensity to treat addiction using 12-step practices, which have not been demonstrated to be particularly effective over time (Florentine, 1999; Peele, Bufe, & Brodsky, 2000). In addition, little research has been done on how racism affects treatment.

What is clear is that individualizing treatment within a cultural context, as well as focusing on those interventions that transcend culture, will most likely optimize successful outcomes. Treatment and prevention programs that teach coping and motivational skills, mobilize community forces, and instill values favoring prosocial behavior have demonstrated the most success. The focus of successful treatment and prevention has to be on the *interaction* of self and the environment, helping people develop beliefs in both *self*-efficacy and *group*-efficacy, depending on their cultural perspective. Nonetheless, even treatment programs that have demonstrated success will always face limitations in their ability to address every individual's intentions and values, their community norms, and the environmental pressures and opportunities they experience. There is much to learn from those individuals who have given up addictive behaviors and made necessary changes *on their own*. As many researchers are now discovering, targeting treatment based on how change naturally occurs, understanding how to better help people activate a more natural change that comes from the inside out rather than the outside in, and finding the key that unlocks intrinsic motivation are the best hope for permanent change, regardless of culture.

References

Aharonovich, E., Nunes, E., & Hasin, D. (2003). Cognitive impairment, retention and abstinence among cocaine abusers in cognitive-behavioral treatment. *Drug and Alcohol Dependence, 71*(2), 207–211.

Ambler, C. (2003). Alcohol and the slave trade in West Africa, 1400–1850. In W. Jankowiak & D. Bjradburd (Eds.), *Drugs, labor, and colonial expansion* (pp. 73–87). Tucson: University of Arizona Press.

Anti-Drug Abuse Act of 1986, 21 U.S.C. § 801 (1986).

Bandura, A. (1977). Self-efficacy: Toward a unifying theory of behavioral change. *Psychological Review, 84*(2), 191–215.

Bandura, A. (1997). *Self-efficacy: The exercise of control.* New York: W. H. Freeman.

Barna Group. (2005). *African Americans.* Retrieved February 19, 2009, from http://www.barna.org/

Bates, M. E., Bowden, S. C., & Barry, D. (2002). Neurocognitive impairment associated with alcohol use disorders: Implications for treatment. *Experimental and Clinical Psychopharmacology, 10*(3), 193–212.

Belgrave, F. V., & Allison, K. W. (2006). *African American psychology: From Africa to America.* Thousand Oaks, CA: Sage.

Benowitz, N. L., Herrera, B., & Jacob, P. (2004). Mentholated cigarette smoking inhibits nicotine metabolism. *The Journal of Pharmacology, 310*(3), 1208–1215.

Blomqvist, J. (1996). Paths to recovery from substance misuse: Change of lifestyle and the role of treatment. *Substance Use and Misuse, 31*(13), 1807–1852.

Blume, A. W., & Garcia de la Cruz, B. (2005). Relapse prevention among diverse populations. In G. A. Marlatt & J. R. Gordon (Eds.), *Relapse prevention* (pp. 45–64). New York. Guilford Press.

Botvin, G. J., & Kantor, L. W. (2000). Preventing alcohol and tobacco use through life skills training. *Alcohol, Health, and Research World, 24,* 250–257.

Botvin, G. J., Schinke, S. P., Epstein, J. A., Diaz, T., & Botvin, E. M. (1995). Effectiveness of culturally focused and generic skills training approaches to alcohol and drug abuse prevention among minority adolescents: Two-year follow-up results. *Psychology of Addictive Behavior, 9,* 183–194.

Bowman, P. J., & Forman, T. A. (1997). Instrumental and expressive family roles among African American fathers. In R. J. Taylor, J. S. Jackson, & L. M. Chatters (Eds.), *Family life in black America* (pp. 248–261). Thousand Oaks, CA: Sage.

Bramlett, M. D., & Mosher, W. D. (2002). Cohabitation, marriage, divorce, and remarriage in the United States. *Vital Health Statistics, 23*(22), 1–93.

Brewer, D. D., Catalano, R. F., Haggerty, K., Gainey, R. R., & Fleming, C. B. (1998). A meta-analysis of predictors of continued drug use during and after treatment for opiate addiction. *Addiction, 93,* 73–92.

Carter, J. H. (1994). Racism's impact on mental health. *Journal of the American Medical Association, 86,* 543–547.

Center for Substance Abuse Prevention. (1996). *Training evaluation: Lessons learned by the CSAP training team.* Retrieved February 12, 2010, from http://preventiontraining.samhsa.gov/LESSONSL/PRAC/introduction.htm

Center on Alcohol, Marketing, and Youth. (n.d.). *Exposure of African American youth to alcohol advertising, 2003–2004* (Executive summary). Retrieved February 12, 2010, from http://www.camy.org/research/afam0606/

Chen, K., & Kandel, D. B. (1995). The natural history of drug use from adolescence to mid-30s in a general population sample. *American Journal of Public Health, 85*(1), 41–47.

Civil Rights Act of 1964, 42 U.S.C., chap. 21.

Dei, K. A. (2002). Ties that bind: Youth and drugs in a black community. Prospect Heights, IL: Waveland Press.

Di Chiara, G., & Imperato, A. (1988). Drugs abused by humans preferentially increase synaptic dopamine concentrations in the mesolimbic system of freely moving rats. *Proceedings of the National Academy of Sciences of the United States of America, 85*(14), 5274–5278.

Earley, P. C. (1994). Self or group? Cultural effects of training on self-efficacy and performance. *Administrative Science Quarterly, 39,* 89–117.

Earley, P. C., Gibson, C. B., & Chen, C. C. (1999). "How did I do?" versus "how did we do?" Cultural contrasts of performance feedback use and self-efficacy. *Journal of Cross-Cultural Psychology, 30,* 594–619.

Fetal alcohol syndrome. (n.d.). Retrieved January 8, 2009, from http://www.mayoclinic.com/health/fetal-alcohol-syndrome/DS00184/DSECTION=symptoms

Fields, J. (2003). *Children's living arrangements and characteristics: March 2002* (U.S. Bureau of the Census, Current Population Report, pp. 20–547). Washington, DC: U.S. Government Printing Office.

Florentine, R. (1999). After drug treatment: Are 12-step programs effective in maintaining abstinence? *The American Journal of Drug and Alcohol Abuse, 25*(1), 93–116.

Freid, V. M., Prager, K., MacKay, A. P., & Xia, H. (2003). *Health, United States, 2003.* Hyattsville, MD: National Center for Health Statistics.

Gaines, S. O., Jr., Marelich, W. D., Bledsoe, K. L., Steers, W. N., Henderson, M. C., Granrose, C. S., Barajas, L., Hicks, D., Lyde, M., Takahashi, Y., Yum, N., Rios, D. I., Garcia, B. F., Farris, K. R., & Page, M. S. (1997). Links between race/ethnicity and cultural values as mediated by race/ethnic identity and moderated by gender. *Journal of Personality and Social Psychology, 72,* 1460–1476.

Goldman, M. S. (1990). Experience-dependent neuropsychological recovery and the treatment of chronic alcoholism. *Neuropsychology Review, 1*(1), 75–101.

Goldman, M. S. (1995). Recovery of cognitive functioning in alcoholics: The relationship to treatment. *Alcohol, Health and Research World, 19*(2), 148–154.

Gordon, R. (2003). Inside the Wind hoek: Liquor and lust in Namibia. In W. Jankowiak & D. Bjradburd (Eds.), *Drugs, labor, and colonial expansion* (pp. 117–134). Tucson: University of Arizona Press.

Griesler, P. C., Kandel, D. B., & Davies, M. (2002). Ethnic differences in predictors of initiation and persistence of adolescent cigarette smoking in the National Longitudinal Survey of Youth. *Nicotine and Tobacco Research, 4*(1). Retrieved January 7, 2009, from http://www.informaworld.com/smpp/content~content=a713688228~db=all

Guntheroth, P. S., & Spiers, P. S. (2006). Sudden infant death syndrome. *Medlink Neurology.* Retrieved February 21, 2009, from http://www.medlink.com/medlinkcontent.asp

Gushue, G. V., & Sciarra, D. T. (1995). Culture and families: A multidimensional approach. In J. G. Ponterotto, J. M. Casas, L. A. Suzuki, & C. M. Alexander (Eds.), *Handbook of multicultural counseling* (pp. 586–606). Thousand Oaks, CA: Sage.

Haiman, C. A., Stram, D. O., Wilkens, L. R., Pike, M. C., Kolonel, L. N., Henderson, B. E., & Le Marchand, L. (2006). Ethnic and racial differences in the smoking-related risk of lung cancer. *New England Journal of Medicine, 354*(4), 333–342.

Hecker, L. L., Mims, G. A., & Boughner, S. R. (2003). General systems theory, cybernetics, and family therapy. In L. L. Hecker & J. L. Wetchler (Eds.), *An introduction to marriage and family therapy* (pp. 39–58). Philadelphia: Haworth Press.

Hill, R. B. (1998). Understanding black family functioning: A holistic perspective. *Journal of Comparative Family Studies, 29*(1), 15–25.

Hogan, D. P., & Lichter, D. T. (1995). Children and youth: Living arrangements and welfare. In R. Farley (Ed.), *State of the union: America in the 1990s: Vol. 2. Social trends* (pp. 93–139). New York: Russell Sage.

Huffman, K. (2004). *Psychology in action.* Hoboken, NJ: Wiley.

James, A. D. (1998). What's love got to do with it? Economic viability and the likelihood of marriage among African American men. *Journal of Comparative Family Studies, 29*(2), 373–386.

James, W. H., & Johnson, S. L. (1996). *Doin' drugs: Patterns of African American addiction.* Austin: University of Texas Press.

Kaiser Permanente National Diversity Council. (2003). *A provider's handbook on culturally competent care: African American population* (2nd ed.). New York: Routledge.

Kantor, D., & Lehr, W. (1976). *Inside the family.* San Francisco: Jossey Bass.

Kessler, R. C., McGonagle, K. A., Zhao, S., Nelson, C. B., Hughes, M., Eshleman, S., et al. (1994). Lifetime and 12-month prevalence of DSM-III-R psychiatric disorders in the United States: Results from the National Comorbidity Study. *Archives of General Psychiatry, 51*(1), 8–19.

Kinney, J., & Leaton, G. (1978). *Loosening the grip: A handbook of alcohol information.* St. Louis, MO: Mosby.

Kochanek K. D., Murphy S. L., Anderson, R. N., & Scott, C. (2004). Deaths: Final Data for 2002. *National Vital Statistics Reports 2004, 5* (5). Retrieved January 27, 2010, from http://mchb.hrsa.gov/mchirc/chusa_04/pages/0800graphsources.htm

Koob, G. F., & Bloom, F. E. (1988). Cellular and molecular mechanisms of drug dependence. *Science, 242,* 715–723.

Kreider, R. M., & Simmons, T. (2003). *Marital status: 2000* (U.S. Census Bureau, Census 2000 Special Tabulation). Washington, DC: Government Printing Office.

LaFromboise, T. D., & Rowe, W. (1983). Skills training for bicultural competence: Rationale and application. *Journal of Counseling Psychology, 30,* 589–595.

Larimer, M. E., Palmer, R. S., & Marlatt, G. A. (1999). Relapse prevention: An overview of Marlatt's cognitive-behavioral model. *Alcohol, Health and Research World, 23,* 151–160.

Lawson, S. R. (1991). Freedom then, freedom now: The historiography of the Civil Rights. *The American Historical Review, 96*(2), 456–471.

Leshner, A. I. (1997). Addiction is a brain disease, and it matters, *Science, 278,* 45–47.

Leshner, A. I. (2001). Addiction is a brain disease. *Issues in Science and Technology Online.* Retrieved January 28, 2009, from http://www.issues.org/17.3/leshner.htm

Lincoln, C. E., & Mamiya, L. H. (1990). *The black church in the African American experience.* Durham, NC: Duke University Press.

Litrownik, A. J., Elder, J. P., Campbell, N. R., Ayala, G. X., Slymen, D. J., Parra-Medina, D., Zavala, F. B., & Lovato, C. Y. (2000). Evaluation of a tobacco and alcohol use prevention program for Hispanic migrant adolescents: Promoting the protective factors of parent-child communication. *Preventative Medicine, 31,* 124–133.

Littlejohn, S. W. (1978). *Theories of human communication.* Columbus, OH: Charles Merrill.

Maffly-Kipp, L. (2001). *The church in the Southern Black community.* Retrieved February 12, 2010, from http://docsouth.unc.edu/church/intro.html

Marlatt, G. A. (1985). Situational determinants of relapse and skills-training interventions. In G. A. Marlatt & J. R. Gordon (Eds.), *Relapse prevention: Maintenance strategies in the treatment of addictive behaviors.* New York: Guilford Press.

Marlatt, G. A., & Donovan, D. M. (Eds.). (2005). *Relapse prevention: Maintenance strategies in the treatment of addictive behaviors* (2nd ed.). New York: Guilford Press.

Marlatt, G. A., & Gordon, J. R. (Eds.). (1985). *Relapse prevention: Maintenance strategies in the treatment of addictive behaviors.* New York: Guilford Press.

Marlatt, G. A., & Witkiewitz, K. (2002). Harm reduction approaches to alcohol use: Health promotion, prevention, and treatment. *Addictive Behaviors, 27*(6), 867–886.

Mattis, J. S. (2000). African American women's definitions of spirituality and religiosity. *Journal of Black Psychology, 26*(1), 101–122.

Mauro, T. (n.d.). *Fetal alcohol effects.* Retrieved January 9, 2009, from http://specialchildren.about.com/od/gettingadiagnosis/g/FAE.htm

McAdoo, H. P. (1998). African American families: Strengths and realities. In H. I. McCubbin, E. A. Thompson, A. I. Thompson, & J. A. Futrell (Eds.), *Resiliency in African American families* (pp. 17–30). Thousand Oaks, CA: Sage.

Mental Health Center of Dane County. (2003). *2003 annual report.* Retrieved February 12, 2010, from http://namidanecounty.org/annualreport03.pdf

Miller, W. R. (1995). Increasing motivation for change. In R. K. Hester & W. R. Miller (Eds.), *Handbook of alcoholism treatment approaches: Effective alternatives* (pp. 89–104). Boston: Allyn & Bacon.

Miller, W. R., & Rollnick, S. R. (2002). *Motivational interviewing: Preparing people to change addictive behaviors.* New York: Guilford Press.

Musto, D. (2001). *The history of legislative control over opium, cocaine and their derivatives.* Retrieved January 23, 2009, from http://www.druglibrary.org/schaffer/History/ophs.htm

Mustonen, T. K., Spencer, S. M., Hoskinson, R. A., Sachs, D. L., & Garvey, A. J. (2005). The influence of gender, race, and menthol content on tobacco exposure measures. *Nicotine and Tobacco Research, 7*(4), 581–590.

Neighbors, H. W., & Jackson, J. S. (Eds.). (1996). *Mental health in black America.* Thousand Oaks, CA: Sage.

Nunn, K. B. (2002). Race, crime, and the pool of surplus criminality: Or why the "war on drugs" was a "war on blacks." *Journal of Gender, Race and Justice, 6,* 381–445.

Orleans, C. T., Schoenbach, V. J., Wagner, E. H., Quade, D, Salmon, M. A., Pearson, D. C., et al. (1991). Self-help quit smoking interventions: Effects of self-help materials, social support instructions, and telephone counseling. *Journal of Consulting and Clinical Psychology, 59*(3), 439–448.

Partnership Attitude Tracking Study. (2003). *Teens study: Survey of teens' attitudes and behaviors toward marijuana.* Retrieved February 12, 2010, from http://www.whitehousedrugpolicy.gov/publications/pats/final_rpt.pdf

Peele, S., Bufe, C., & Brodsky, A. (2000). *Resisting 12-step coercion: How to fight forced participation in AA, NA, or 12-step treatment.* Tucson, AZ: Sharp Press.

Pérez-Stable, J., Herrera, B., Jacob, P., & Benowitz, N. (1998). Nicotine metabolism and intake in Black and White smokers. *Journal of the American Medical Association, 280,* 152–156.

Powledge, T. M. (1999). Addiction and the brain. *BioScience, 49*(7), 513–519. Retrieved January 28, 2009, from http://caliber.ucpress.net/doi/abs/10.1525/bisi.1999.49.7.513

Prochaska, J. O., & DiClemente, C. C. (1984). *The transtheoretical approach: Crossing traditional boundaries of therapy.* Homewood, IL: Dorsey Press.

Rhodes, R., & Johnson, A. (1997). A feminist approach to treating alcohol and drug addicted African American women. *Women and Therapy, 20,* 23–37.

Robins, L. N., Davis, D. H., & Goodwin, D. W. (1974). Drug use by U.S. Army enlisted men in Vietnam: A follow-up on their return home. *American Journal of Epidemiology, 99,* 235–249.

Robins, L. N., Helzer, J. E., Weissman, M. M., Oraschel, H., Gruenberg, E., Burke, J. D., et al., (1984). Lifetime prevalence of specific psychiatric disorders in three sites. *Archives of General Psychiatry, 41,* 949–958.

Schmidt, L., Greenfield, T., & Mulia, N. (2001). *Unequal treatment: Racial and Ethnic Disparities in Alcoholism Treatment Services.* Retrieved February 12, 2010, from http://pubs.niaaa.nih.gov/publications/arh291/49-54.htm

Scott, J. W., & Black, A. W. (1989). Deep structures of African American family life: Female and male kin networks. *The Western Journal of Black Studies, 13*(1), 17–24.

Sobell, L. C., Cunningham, J. A., Sobell, M. B., Agrawal, S., Gavin, D. R., Leo, G. I., & Singh, K. N. (1996). Fostering self-change among problem drinkers: A proactive community intervention. *Addictive Behaviors, 21*(6), 817–833.

Sobell, L. C., & Sobell, J. A. (1998). Guiding self change. In W. R. Miller & N. Heather (Eds.), *Treating addictive behaviors.* New York: Springer.

Stellman, S. D., Chen, Y., Muscat, J. E., Djordjevic, M. V., Richie, J. P., Jr., Lazarus, P., et al. (2003). Lung cancer risk in white and black Americans. *Annals of Epidemiology, 13*(4), 294–302.

Substance Abuse and Mental Health Services Administration. (2002). *2002 National survey on drug use and health.* Rockville, MD: U.S. Department of Health and Human Services. Retrieved February 18, 2009, from http://www.oas.samhsa.gov/nhsda/2k2nsduh/Results/apph.htm#tabh.10

Substance Abuse and Mental Health Services Administration. (2004). *National survey on drug use and health.* Retrieved February 12, 2010, from: http://www.oas.samhsa.gov/nsduh.htm

Sue, D. W., & Sue, D. (2003a). Barriers to effective multicultural counseling/therapy. In D. W. Sue & D. Sue (Eds.), *Counseling the culturally diverse: Theory and practice* (pp. 95–121). New York: Wiley.

Sue, D. W., & Sue, D. (2003b). Counseling and therapy with racial/ethnic minority populations. In D. W. Sue & D. Sue (Eds.), *Counseling the culturally diverse: Theory and practice* (pp. 291–376). New York: Wiley.

Sue, D. W., & Sue, D. (2003c). Multicultural family counseling and therapy. In D. W. Sue & D. Sue (Eds.), *Counseling the culturally diverse: Theory and practice* (pp. 151–176). New York: Wiley.

Suggs, D. N., & Lewis, S. A. (2003). Alcohol as a direct and indirect labor enhancer in the mixed economy of the Batswana, 1800–1900. In W. Jankowiak & D. Bjradburd (Eds.), *Drugs, labor, and colonial expansion* (pp. 135–148). Tucson: University of Arizona Press.

Taylor, R. J., & Johnson, W. E. (1997). Family roles and family satisfaction among black men. In R. J. Taylor, J. S. Jackson, & L. M. Chatters (Eds.), *Family life in black America* (pp. 248–261). Thousand Oaks, CA: Sage.

Taylor, R. J., Leashore, B. R., & Toliver, S. (1988). An assessment of the provider role as perceived by black males. *Family Relations, 37,* 426–431.

Tucker, J. A., Vuchinich, R. E., & Gladsjo, J. A. (1994). Environmental events surrounding natural recovery from alcohol-related problems. *Journal of Studies on Alcohol, 55,* 401–411.

U.S. Census Bureau. (2004). Special tabulation. Retrieved February 19, 2009, from http://www.census.gov/prod/2004pubs/censr-14.pdf

U.S. Census Bureau. (2004–2005). *Statistical abstracts of the United States.* Retrieved December 16, 2008, from www.census.gov/prod/2004pubs/04statab/health.pdf

U.S. Sentencing Commission (2002). Retrieved on January 27, 2010, from http://www.ussc.gov/ANNRPT/2002/SBTOC02.htm

Volkow, N. D., Wang, G., Telang, F., Fowler, J. S., Logan, J., Childress, A., et al. (2006). Cocaine cues and dopamine in dorsal striatum: Mechanism of craving in cocaine addiction. *Journal of Neuroscience, 26*(24), 6583–6588. Retrieved January 27, 2009, from http://www.jneurosci.org/cgi/content/full/26/24/6583?maxtoshow=&HITS=10&hits=10&RESULTFORMAT=1&author1=volkow&andorexacttitle=and&andorexacttitleabs=and&andorexactfulltext=and&searchid=1&FIRSTINDEX=0&sortspec=relevance&resourcetype=HWCIT

Veroff, J., Douvan, E., & Hatchett, S. J. (1995). *Marital instability: A social and behavioral study of the early years.* Westport, CT: Praeger.

Walton, M. A., Blow, F. C., & Booth, B. M. (2001). Diversity in relapse prevention needs: Gender and race comparisons among substance abuse treatment patients. *American Journal of Drug and Alcohol Abuse, 27,* 225–240.

Weil, A., & Rosen, W. (2004). *From chocolate to morphine: Everything you need to know about mind-altering drugs.* New York: Houghton Mifflin.

Williams, J. M., Gandhi, K. K., Steinberg, M. L., Foulds, J., Ziedonis, D. M., & Benowitz, N. L. (2007). Higher nicotine and carbon monoxide levels in cigarette smokers with and without schizophrenia. *Nicotine and Tobacco Research, 9*(8), 873–881.

Wilson, M. N., Green-Bates, C., McCoy, L., Simons, F., Askew, T., Curry-El, J., et al. (1995). African American family life: The dynamics of interactions, relationships, and roles. In M. Wilson (Ed.), *African American family life: Its structural and ecological aspects* (pp. 5–21). San Francisco: Jossey Bass.

Wingo, L. K. (2001). Substance abuse in African American women. *Journal of Cultural Diversity, 20,* 23–37.

World War I and postwar society. (n.d.). Retrieved January 23, 2009, from the Library of Congress Web site: http://memory.loc.gov/ammem/aaohtml/exhibit/aopa

CHAPTER 7

Substance Abuse and the Physician

Arthur J. Farkas, Duane E. Rogers, and Gary R. Lewis

Since the 1960s, there has been an enormous growth in substance abuse awareness, education, treatment, and research. The *Diagnostic and Statistical Manual of Mental Disorders–Fourth Edition–Text Revision* (DSM-IV-TR; American Psychiatric Association, 2000) recognizes that everything from tobacco and caffeine to heroin can be addictive and that the addiction can be treated. One segment of society in which substance abuse is still somewhat in the closet, at least as far as the general population is concerned, is the substance-abusing physician.

There has always been a certain mystique surrounding those people that society thinks of as "professionals." Physicians, especially, are endowed with almost godlike powers because the knowledge and expertise they have is to a great extent outside the knowledge and experience of the general public and because they have traditionally been accorded high status. Compounding this protection against critical scrutiny is that physicians have created a rather closed fraternity. When they become stressed, ill, or otherwise impaired, their fellow professionals form a tight circle around them to protect them and keep their impairment from the general public—as well as from licensing boards. This cocoon places the impaired professional in a difficult position when it comes to seeking the help he or she may need.

The problem of physician substance abuse has not gone unnoticed by the medical community. In 1958, the Federation of State Medical Boards concluded that physician impairment due to substance abuse was a serious disciplinary problem that state boards needed to address ("Impaired Physicians Get More Attention," 2004). In 1973, the American Medical Association's (AMA) Council on Mental Health issued two recommendations concerning physicians impaired by psychiatric disorders, including alcoholism and drug dependence. First, the council recommended that state medical societies create programs to identify and assist impaired physicians. Second, it recommended that the American Medical Association (AMA) create model legislation so that the laws governing medical practice would emphasize treatment rather than punitive forms of discipline (AMA, 1973). Prior to the council's report, only seven states had impaired physician programs, but by 1983 such programs were in place in all 50 states (Gallegos & Talbott, 1997; Stimson, 1985).

Prevalence

The methodological limitations of published studies on medical students, residents, and physicians make it difficult to estimate the true prevalence of substance abuse among physicians (O'Connor & Spickard, 1997). A comprehensive review of the literature published in 1986 indicated that the rate of substance abuse among physicians could not be determined (Brewster, 1986). Flaherty and Richman (1993) noted that close scrutiny of the research on prevalence was necessary because of the use of varying definitions of abuse and dependence, the overreliance on data from treatment populations, and statistical limitations due to sampling and cohort effects.

As noted by Centrella (1994), the AMA, based on data from P. H. Hughes, Brandenburg, et al. (1992), currently accepts 8% as the lifetime prevalence for substance abuse among physicians. Further, physicians were more likely than their age and gender nonphysician counterparts to drink and use prescription drugs, particularly minor opiates and benzodiazepine tranquilizers; 11.4% of the physicians had used benzodiazepines and 17.6% had used opioids in an unsupervised fashion in the previous year (Centrella, 1994). Physicians were five times more likely than controls to take sedatives and tranquillizers without medical supervision (Valliant, 1992). Also, in contrast with the general population, where women are less likely to drink or use drugs than men, male and female physicians were equally likely to drink and use drugs. In addition, P. H. Hughes, Brandenburg, et al. (1992) found that 10% of the physicians were daily drinkers, and 9.3% reported having five or more drinks a day, a common definition of binge drinking (Grant & Dawson, 1999), at least once in the previous month.

The studies reviewed above indicate that the lifetime rate of substance abuse among physicians is higher than the 8% rate accepted by the AMA. Since the data show that female medical students, residents, and physicians use and abuse alcohol and drugs at rates similar to those of their male colleagues (Baldwin, Hughes, Conrad, Storr, & Sheehan, 1991; P. H. Hughes et al., 1991; P. H. Hughes, Brandenburg, et al., 1992), the rates observed for men in the general population may provide a better estimate for the rates of alcohol and drug abuse and dependence expected for physicians. Based on DSM-IV criteria (American Psychiatric Association, 1994), men in the general population are more likely to experience lifetime and past-year alcohol use disorders, which includes both abuse and dependence (25.5% and 11%, respectively) and are more likely to experience lifetime and past-year drug use disorders (8.1% and 2.2%, respectively) (Grant & Dawson, 1999).

Richman, Flaherty, and Pyskoty (1992) used the Michigan Alcohol Screening Test (MAST; Selzer, 1971) to assess alcohol abuse in cohort of students entering a state college of medicine. The MAST is a self-report instrument with high reliability and validity that has been validated on a broad range of American drinkers (Favazza & Cannell,

1977; Selzer, 1971). In screening for alcoholism, a score of 4+ on the MAST strongly suggests the presence of an alcohol use disorder. Using this cut score, 26.3% of the cohort of students upon entrance to medical training had already experienced problems due to their alcohol use, and more than 7% of the men had already gotten into trouble at work or school due to drinking (Richman & Flaherty, 1990). Another survey of medical students using the Alcohol Use Disorders Identification Test (AUDIT; Babor, Higgins-Biddle, Saunders, & Monteiro, 2001) questionnaire indicated that a significant proportion (33%) drank more than the recommended safe limit and screened positive at the AUDIT cutoff score of 11 (Varga & Buris, 1994). During the first year of medical school, a sizable proportion of the medical students who had been problem drinkers prior to entrance "matured out" (19.4%) and experienced no problems due to their use of alcohol, whereas 6.9% continued to have alcohol-related problems, and 6.3% of the students who had entered medical school with no history of alcohol-related problems became problem drinkers. By the end of their first year, 13.2% of the students were problem drinkers (Richman et al., 1992). A similar pattern of abuse prior to entrance, as well as remission and new onset, was also observed in another medical student cohort (Clark, Eckenfels, Daugherty, & Fawcett, 1987). Richman and Rospenda (1992) found that there was an increase in problem drinking after the start of clinical training among the members of her medical student cohort. Since drinking behavior is generally stabilized by the college years, problematic drinking during medical training is likely to progress to alcohol dependence later in life (Donovan, Jessor, & Jessor, 1983).

By the time medical students complete their residency training, a high percentage have already experimented with alcohol (97.3%), marijuana (65.1%), tobacco (51.5%), cocaine (29.2%), benzodiazepines (22.7%), and amphetamines (20.8%), with over 70% of the initial use occurring in college, high school, or earlier (P. H. Hughes, Conrad, Baldwin, Storr, & Sheehan, 1991). Nevertheless, among the resident physicians who used prescription drugs, a significant minority initiated their use of benzodiazepines (31.4%) and opiates (23.1%) during their residency training, the period in their training when they first receive prescribing privileges. The residents used these drugs for self-treatment that was not under the supervision of another physician (P. H. Hughes et al., 1991). In addition, 5% of the residents reported daily drinking and daily cigarette smoking.

A conservative estimate is that rates of physician use of, abuse of, and dependence on alcohol and other substances are at least equal to those observed in the general population. The Epidemiologic Catchment Area Study (Robins, Locke, & Regier, 1990), using DSM-III-R (American Psychiatric Association, 1987) criteria, indicated that 3.5% of United States adults had abused alcohol and 7.9% had been alcohol dependent at sometime during their lifetime. The National Comorbidity Study (Kessler, McGonagle, & Shanyang, 1994), also based on DSM III-R criteria, indicated that 2.5% of United States adults had abused alcohol and 7.2% were alcohol dependent during the previous 12 months. Based on DSM-IV criteria (American Psychiatric Association, 1994), the rate for an alcohol use disorder during the past year is 7.4% and during one's lifetime is 18.2%. More respondents were diagnosed with dependence than abuse (4.4% during the past year and 13.3% during their lifetime) (Grant & Dawson, 1999). The rates for DSM-IV drug use disorders are lower than those observed for alcohol use disorders (1.5% and 6.1%, respectively, for past year and lifetime). In line with their higher rates of use, men are more likely to experience lifetime and past-year alcohol use disorders, which includes both abuse and dependence (25.5% and 11.0%, respectively) and are more likely to experience lifetime and past-year drug use disorders (8.1% and 2.2%, respectively). Since female medical students, residents, and physicians use and abuse alcohol and drugs at rates similar to their male colleagues' (Baldwin et al., 1991; P. H. Hughes et al., 1991; P. H. Hughes, Baldwin, Sheehan, Conrad, & Storr, 1992), the higher rates observed for males in the general population are the best estimate for substance use disorders for all physicians, regardless of gender.

Etiology

According to Coombs (1997),

> Professionals—especially health professionals—are particularly vulnerable to drug abuse. They attend colleges where recreational drug use—especially alcohol—is the norm and matriculate to professional schools that promote a view of drugs as a way to solve human problems. Open-ended careers, those with no established starting and quitting times, encourage overwork, unbalanced lifestyles, and self-neglect. Some professionals, coming from emotionally abusive families, select professional careers for the status and approval they never received at home. When their careers fail to meet emotional and spiritual needs, these high achieving, perfectionist caretakers, like so many of their parents, turn to alcohol and other drugs. These risk factors—together with the tendency of professionals to feel immune to addiction—greatly increase their chances of drug involvement. (pp. 101–102)

Nace (1995) concludes,

> Why a given physician becomes drug or alcohol dependent cannot be known with certainty. Several factors are well recognized as contributing: availability of drugs, stress of practice, personality factors, and genetics. In the literature, one can find advocates for each as the predominant contributing variable. Similarly, discussion with informed colleagues will reveal strong opinions as to the "primary" cause. Perhaps we desire to find simple, straightforward explanations. Yet, to do justice to physician impairment and professional impairment in general, we must tolerate complexity and inconsistency. On a case-by-case basis, any given factor may seem to stand out, but most often an amalgam of the above factors are present. (p. 63)

Taken together, the quotes from Coombs (1997) and Nace (1995) nicely summarize what we know, or think we know, about the etiology of substance use disorders in physicians. Other researchers have proposed overlapping multifactor explanations for physician impairment (McAuliffe et al., 1987; Moore et al., 1990; Talbott, Gallegos, Wilson, & Porter, 1987; Wright, 1990). Talbott et al. (1987) noted that the following factors play a role in physician impairment due to substance abuse: genetic predisposition and environmental exposure, stress and poor coping skills, lack of education about impairment, the absence of effective prevention and control strategies, drug availability in the context of a permissive professional and social environment, and denial. McAuliffe et al. (1987) concluded that the following factors were important correlates of substance abuse in medical students and physicians, and that these factors were more likely causes than effects: access to pharmaceuticals, family history of chemical dependency, emotional problems, stress at home or work, sensation seeking, chronic fatigue, and self-treatment of pain and emotional problems. According to Moore et al. (1990), the youthful precursors associated with subsequent alcohol abuse in physicians included lack of religious affiliation, regular use of alcohol, past history of alcohol-related difficulties, non-Jewish ancestry, cigarette use of half a pack or more per day, maternal alcoholism or mental illness, anxiety or anger as reactions to stress, and frequent use of alcohol in nonsocial settings. Wright (1990) listed the following in his summary of the risk factors for substance abuse in physicians: history of illicit drug use, membership in a high-risk specialty (e.g., anesthesiology), a pattern of overprescribing, and a pattern of academic success or habitual overwork accompanied by a combination of grandiosity and excessive guilt. Alcoholism and other forms of substance abuse have a multifactorial etiology to which genetics, opportunity, and social patterns all contribute (Vaillant, 1995).

Family History

Findings from family, twin, and adoption studies strongly suggest that genetics are an important etiologic determinant of alcohol use disorders in both men and women (Anthenelli & Schuckit, 1997). For a variety of reasons, there is less research on the relationship between genetic susceptibility and substance use disorders for substances other than alcohol and nicotine (Anthenelli & Schuckit, 1997; Carmelli, Swan, Robinette, & Fabitz, 1992; J. R. Hughes, 1986; Swan, Carmelli, Rosenman, Fabsitz, & Christian, 1990), but the available research does suggest that family history of substance abuse is one of the strongest risk factors for all of the substance use disorders and that familial transmission has a significant genetic component (Merikangas et al., 1998). There appears to be a general vulnerability to substance abuse consisting of genetic, family, and nonfamily environmental factors that are common to all drugs of abuse, as well as unique genetic and environmental factors for each particular class of drugs (Tsuang et al., 1998). Siblings of alcoholic probands were not only more likely to have a lifetime alcohol use disorder, but were also at risk for cannabis, cocaine, and nicotine dependence (Bierut et al., 1998).

Individuals with a positive family history for alcoholism are three to seven times more likely to develop an alcohol use disorder, and those with a positive family history for substance abuse are eight times more likely to develop a substance use disorder (Cotton, 1979; Merikangas, 1990; Merikangas et al., 1998; Schuckit, 1987). The methodological limitations that make it difficult to estimate the true prevalence of substance abuse among physicians also make it difficult to estimate the true prevalence of positive family history. Available data indicate that upon entrance to medical school, between 14% and 27% of the students have a positive family history for alcoholism (Clark et al., 1987; Forney, Ripley, & Forney, 1988; Lutsky et al., 1994; McAuliffe et al., 1987; Richman et al., 1992). Again, the conservative assumption is that rate of exposure to familial alcohol abuse or dependence in physicians is at least equal to that observed in the general population. Data derived from population-based surveys indicate that approximately 18% to 25% of children younger than 18 years in the United States are exposed to alcohol abuse or dependence in the family (Grant, 2000; Schoenborn, 1991).

Future physicians with a positive family history for substance abuse, besides having a potential genetic predisposition, are also likely to grow up in families that are dysfunctional due to a parent's active substance abuse. The family dysfunction associated with the parent's active substance abuse increases the child's risk for antisocial or undercontrolled behaviors, depressive symptoms, anxiety disorders, low self-esteem, and difficulties in intimate relationships, as well as generalized distress and maladjustment as an adult. However, none of these outcomes are uniformly observed and none are specific to adult offspring of substance abusers. Comorbid parental pathology, childhood abuse, family dysfunction due to reasons other than substance abuse, and other childhood stressors may contribute to or produce similar outcomes (Harter, 2000). The presence of one or more of these negative outcomes also increases the future physician's risk of developing a substance use disorder. Some studies suggest that individuals from dysfunctional families may be overrepresented among health-care professionals due to self-selection (Coombs, 1997; Vaillant, Sobowale, & McArthur, 1972).

Normative Support for Recreational Drug Use

Normative support for recreational drug use refers to social tolerance and encouragement of alcohol use and, to a lesser extent, cannabis and cocaine use. Exposure to alcohol among future physicians is almost universal; exposure to other drugs by the time they get to college is substantial. On most college campuses, the normative pressure to use and abuse alcohol and other drugs is intense. At heavy-drinking campuses, about half the freshmen "get smashed" in the first week and most regard drunkenness as an integral part of college life (Wechsler, Davenport, Dowdall, Moeykens, & Castillo, 1994). A recent study indicated that nearly 45% of students on American college campuses engage in binge drinking at least once every 2 weeks (Wechsler et al., 2002).

Vaillant (1995) defined the incubation period for substance use disorders as the time from first use of a substance until the person first seeks treatment. For future physicians with a positive family history of substance abuse, an active social life in college is guaranteed to initiate the incubation period in previously abstinent students and to sustain it in those who have already started to use substances. Recreational use of alcohol continues into professional school, where incoming students are often welcomed by the preceding class with a party where alcohol is served (Coombs, 1997). The incubation period for alcohol dependence, the major drug of abuse among physicians, typically lasts from 5 to 30 years; the premedical college student is thus likely to become a practicing physician before showing significant impairment due to alcohol abuse (Mansky, 1999).

Availability

The lifetime exposure to alcohol and other drugs for medical students is, with the exception of tobacco, similar to that of college-educated adults of similar age. During medical training, the pattern of use shifts from illicit to prescription drugs. Future physicians are more likely than their college-educated peers to use benzodiazepines and opiates, and those with a history of alcohol or drug abuse throughout college, medical school, and residency are more likely to avail themselves of pharmaceutical agents that are readily accessible via prescription and free samples. With the possible exception of anesthesiologists, addressed below, availability, especially in the workplace, does not appear to cause abuse per se but it does have a strong influence on the choice of drugs abused (Nace, 1995). While alcoholic beverages and street drugs are readily accessible to most people, physicians have much easier access to controlled substances (Coombs, 1997). After alcohol, prescription drugs, especially opiates and benzodiazepines, are the substances most frequently abused by chemically dependent physicians prior to treatment (Mansky, 1999; Talbott et al., 1987).

Stress

In a national survey, physicians' stress scores were above those for all other occupations in the areas of "work overload" and "too much responsibility for people" (Caplan, Cobb, French, Van Harrison, & Pinneau, 1975). McCue (1982) identified several intrinsic stressors associated with the practice of medicine, including patient fear, suffering, sexuality, and death; patient noncompliance and malingering; and clinical uncertainty. Other commonly described sources of stress include fatigue, not having enough personal time, being on call and receiving phone calls at night, time pressure, heavy workload (including fears of not keeping up with new knowledge), interpersonal conflicts with nurses and consultants, fear of malpractice and the need to practice defensive medicine, excessive paperwork, peer review, and managed care (Krakowski, 1982; Mawardi, 1979; Nace, 1995). The most stressful aspects of medical practice appear to be factors extrinsic to medicine, rather than clinical aspects of medicine: government regulations, insurance companies, malpractice suits, and defensive practice style (J. M. Lewis, Barnhardt, Howard, Carson, & Nace, 1993a). Work satisfaction may buffer the effects of work stress, given that only 15% of physicians with high work satisfaction versus 43% with low work satisfaction reported that their work was very stressful (J. M. Lewis, Barnhardt, Howard, Carson, & Nace, 1993b).

Several studies suggest a link between stress and alcohol and drug use among medical students, residents, and physicians. Medical students who abused alcohol, particularly when the onset of abuse occurred after entrance into medical school, reported significantly higher levels of technological knowledge and status, as well as lower interpersonal concerns, than non-abusers (Richman & Pyskoty, 1991). It was hypothesized that the reported low interpersonal concerns might indicate deficits in the social skills and empathy needed to relate successfully to patients, physician educators, and other health professionals; in time, these deficits could manifest as a stressor that is alleviated through the use and abuse of alcohol. Moore et al. (1990) reported that medical students who responded with excessive anxiety or anger to stressful events were more likely to abuse alcohol in midlife than were students who were less reactive. Stout-Wiegand and Trent (1981) found that only 3% of low-stress physicians reported using drugs (i.e., narcotics, barbiturates, amphetamines, and cocaine) in the previous month, compared to 23% of those who reported high stress in their work. Krakowski (1984) concluded that personal and professional stressors increased the rates of smoking and drinking in physicians. McAuliffe et al. (1987) reported that among medical students and physicians, life stress and emotional problems were the strongest predictors of the number of recreational drug use episodes, while chronic pain and emotional problems were the strongest predictors of the number of episodes of self-treatments. Jex et al. (1992) differentiated between "stressors" (stressful job conditions) and "strains" (reactions to stressors), observing that strains rather than stressors were more strongly correlated with substance use in resident physicians. This was especially true for the use of benzodiazepines, which suggested that this class of drug was being used for self-treatment.

Personality

In a 30-year follow-up of a cohort of physicians and socioeconomically matched controls, Vaillant et al. (1972) found that the physicians who abused alcohol and drugs were more likely to have experienced childhood instability and adolescent adjustment problems. Nearly three quarters (72%) of the physicians undergoing treatment for addiction in one study reported that they had experienced parental deprivation as children (Johnson & Connelly, 1981), and between 14% and 27% of medical students come from families that were dysfunctional due to a positive family history for substance use (Clark et al., 1987; Forney, Ripley, & Forney, 1988; Lutsky et al., 1994; McAuliffe et al., 1987; Richman et al., 1992). Vaillant et al. (1972) reported that the physicians in their study were also more likely than the controls to show traits of dependency, pessimism, passivity, and self-doubt. Physicians, due to a high level of compulsivity, often have difficulty relaxing, fail to take vacations, neglect their families, and chronically feel they are not doing enough (Gabbard, 1985). The high level of compulsivity in physicians leads to higher rates of marital discord as well (Gabbard & Menninger, 1989).

Khantzian (1985) described addicted physicians in treatment as being deficient in ego functions such as regulation of feelings, self-care skills, and maintenance of self-esteem. These physicians engaged in an attempt at self-repair by caring for patients; but when this failed, they resorted to the restorative properties of alcohol and other drugs. In more recent samples of physicians in treatment for chemical dependency, 26% had a personality disorder and a majority of those (57%) received a diagnosis of narcissistic personality disorder (Angres, Talbott, & Bettinardi-Angres, 1998). McGovern, Angres, and Leon (2000) found that among physicians with substance abuse problems assessed at a behavioral health center, nearly 29% had an Axis II disorder, with narcissistic (50%) and antisocial (27%) being the most frequently observed disorders. Richman (1992) found that the major predictors of alcohol abuse among medical students during clinical training were social-relational skill deficits and a narcissistic personality style.

Ignorance and Misinformation

In 1987, D. C. Lewis, Niven, Czechowicz, and Trumble noted that substance abuse was largely ignored by medical educators. A few years later, Paton (1991) noted that little had changed in Great Britain and the United States. A decade later, Miller, Sheppard, Colenda, and Magen (2001) reported that the typical 4-year medical school devoted less than 12 hours of curricular time to alcohol- and comorbid drug-related disorders. Even as recently as 2004, the Office of National Drug Control Policy—backed by the U.S. Surgeon General, the Center for Substance Abuse Treatment, the National Institute on Drug Abuse, the National Institute on Alcohol Abuse and Alcoholism, and the National Highway Traffic Safety Administration—requested improvement in physician education on this health problem (Wyatt, Vilensky, Manlandro, & Dekker, 2005). In a 2006 study of 52 physicians and other medical professionals in a multiyear state diversion program, 34.6% of the participants reported having had no substance abuse education, 69.9% had had a range of 1 day to 1 week, and only 15.4% (8 participants) had had more than a week (Rogers, 2006).

Given this small amount of curricular time spent on addiction, it should not be surprising that few physicians understand its dynamics; this naiveté may be a contributing factor to the addiction of some physicians (Coombs, 1997). Undereducated physicians are likely to fail to recognize the early signs and symptoms of addiction in themselves or others. We have mistakenly expected physicians to be better informed about addiction than they are and to use their knowledge to assist their patients and themselves.

Medical Specialty

Rates of substance use disorders vary across medical specialties. The specialties with higher rates include anesthesiology (P. H. Hughes et al., 1999; McAuliffe et al., 1986; Myers & Weiss, 1987; Storr, Trinkoff, & Hughes, 2000; Talbott et al., 1987), emergency medicine (P. H. Hughes, Baldwin, et al., 1992; P. H. Hughes et al., 1999; Shore, 1982; Storr et al., 2000), family practice (Bissell & Jones, 1976; Morse, Martin, Swenson, & Niven, 1984; Myers & Weiss, 1987; Storr et al., 2000; Talbott et al., 1987), and psychiatry (Bissell & Skorina, 1987; P. H. Hughes, Baldwin, et al., 1992; P. H. Hughes et al., 1999; Maddux, Tinnerman, & Costello 1987; McAuliffe et al., 1986; Myers & Weiss, 1987; Shore, 1982; Storr et al., 2000). The higher rates of substance use disorders among physicians in certain specialties may in part be due to self-selection on the part of medical students with a history of alcohol abuse (Richman & Pyskoty, 1991).

Among the medical specialties, anesthesiologists appear to have the highest risk for substance use disorders. Ward, Ward, and Saidman (1983) surveyed the chairmen of 247 anesthesia training programs. Over a 10-year period between 1970 and 1980, they found a total of 334 confirmed cases of dependence, including a substantial number of instructors, and 30 deaths due to overdose. Ikeda and Pelton (1990) reported that while anesthesiologists represent only about 5% of the licensed physicians in California, nearly 18% of the physicians enrolled in the California Physician Diversion Program were anesthesiologists. The risk of chemical dependency was 3.5 times greater for anesthesiologists than for the average physician in California. These figures are similar to those reported in other studies (Gold, Byars, & Frost-Pineda, 2004; Gold, Dennis, Morey, & Melker, 2004; Talbott et al., 1987).

The traditional explanation for the high rate of substance use disorders observed among anesthesiologists is that they have ready access to potent drugs that require only small amounts for a full therapeutic effect, small quantities are easy to divert without detection, and the drugs produce addiction quickly (Gallegos, Browne, Veit, & Talbott, 1988). According to Gold and associates (Gold, Byars, & Frost-Pineda, 2004; Gold, Dennis, et al., 2004; Gold et al., 2006), stress and access may have less of a role in explaining the risk of addiction in anesthesiologists than unintentional exposure to very low doses of opiate drugs in the operating room. Secondhand exposure to fentanyl can induce sensitization. Once the anesthesiologist's brain is sensitized, drug-seeking and drug-related behavior can occur without a conscious craving or conscious drive for the drug (Elster, 1999).

Identification

Talbott and Benson (1980) concluded that the development of addiction-related problems appears to follow a predictable course. The chemically dependent physician usually experiences problems in the following order: first with family life, then with community involvement, followed by erratic employment, deteriorating health, inappropriate conduct at the office, and finally inability to perform hospital duties. The detection of substance abuse in physicians is often delayed because they invariably protect job performance at the expense of every other aspect of their lives (Talbott & Wilson, 2005). By the time a significant deterioration in clinical skills becomes apparent, the physician's substance use disorder is usually severe and long-standing (Boisaubin & Levine, 2001). One study indicated that alcoholic physicians were able to continue practicing on average for 6 years after the onset of dependency (Brooke, Edwards, & Taylor, 1991).

The identification of physicians who are impaired due to substance abuse is mainly hindered by two factors: the conspiracy of silence and self-deception (Talbott & Benson, 1980). Boisaubin and Levine (2001) noted that physicians are accorded wider latitude for eccentric behavior than are the members of other occupations. Combining the wide latitude for eccentric behavior with self-deception on the part of the impaired physician, his or her professional colleagues, and the members of the physician's immediate family creates the "conspiracy of silence" that leads everyone involved to rationalize, minimize, and even deny the possibility that the physician may be suffering from a substance use disorder (Boisaubin & Levine, 2001). Fellow physicians often fail to confront an impaired colleague, even when the presence of a substance use disorder is undeniable (Blondell, 1993). Their hesitancy is due to fears about being wrong and facing retaliation for making false accusations; they also delay confronting impaired colleagues out of a misguided attempt to protect the impaired physician from shame, social stigmatization, and loss of income, as well as the loss of the license to practice medicine (Nelson, Matthews, Girard, & Bloom, 1996). Family members and colleagues often falsely assume that the impaired physician will resolve the problem without assistance or that the problem will disappear on its own (Boisaubin & Levine, 2001).

Treatment

Several methodological limitations make a formal meta-analysis of treatment outcomes difficult (Gallegos, 1987). These limitations include the following factors: patient selection bias, significant difference in treatment parameters, overreliance on patient self-reports, use of inadequate or incomplete diagnostic criteria, improper accounting for treatment dropouts, inadequate follow-up duration, inability of chemical assessments to detect all drug use, and the frequent failure to provide multidimensional treatment outcome measures. However, a growing body of literature indicates that substance abuse treatment for physicians is at least as effective as for members of the general population.

Vogtsberger (1984) reviewed articles published between 1950 and 1982 on the effectiveness of substance abuse treatment for physicians. Of the 15 studies conducted on United States physicians, positive outcomes ranged from a low of 27% to a high of 94%. Because these studies used small samples of physicians and showed considerable variation as to type and intensity of treatment, duration of follow-up, and the measures used to define a successful outcome, Vogtsberger decided that valid conclusions about the effectiveness of treatment were not possible. Only 3 of the 15 articles reviewed by Vogtsberger (Kliner, Spicer, & Barnett, 1980; Johnson & Connelly, 1981; Herrington, Benzer, Jacobson, & Hawkins, 1982) had a sample size of at least 30 physicians, used abstinence as the measure of treatment effectiveness, provided information about the duration of follow-up, and used chemical screening or information from collaterals to validate the physicians' self-reports. In Table 7.1, these three quality studies have been combined with eight additional studies that were published subsequently to those included in Vogtsberger's review.

Kliner et al. (1980) studied treatment outcomes for 85 alcoholic physicians treated at the Hazelden inpatient facility in Minnesota. The physicians were discharged between 1973 and 1976, after an average stay of 33 days, and were surveyed by questionnaire 1 year after discharge. In the year following discharge, 10 (12%) of the physicians died. The study failed to identify the causes of these deaths, which could have been alcohol related. Four of the respondents did not return the questionnaire, 3 refused to allow contact, and 1 could not be located. Kliner et al. reported a very impressive continuous abstinence rate of 76% that was based on the physicians who completed questionnaires. As shown in Table 7.1, a still respectable but more conservative estimate of 60% is obtained when the 18 physicians lost to follow-up are accounted for. The adjusted figure may still overestimate the effectiveness of the program, since the initial sample included only those patients who completed treatment; the study did not provide data on the number of physicians who dropped out before treatment completion.

Johnson and Connelly (1981) reported the outcomes for a sample of 50 chemically dependent patients that included 43 physicians and 7 dentists treated at Menninger Memorial Hospital in a short-term psychiatrically oriented addiction program. The members of the sample were discharged between 1974 and 1979 after a normal stay of 6 weeks. Seven patients (14%) who did not complete the program were included in the evaluation. The criteria for a successful treatment outcome were more stringent than in most studies, requiring both abstinence and a return to effective job functioning; however, this stringency may be more apparent than real, since 38 (76%) of the patients were still practicing at the time of admission. Patients were followed for varying periods, ranging from 9 to 54 months. Since a "brief relapse" was not considered a treatment failure in this study, it is not clear from the report how long each patient was continuously abstinent, but 32 (64%) of the study population were sober and practicing medicine at the time of follow-up. As in the study by Kliner et al. (1980), some of the patients (4, or

Table 7.1
Comparison of Impaired Physician Treatment Outcomes

Study	Program	*N*	Study characteristics	Outcome	Follow-up (in years)
Kliner et al. (1980)	Hazelden (Minnesota)	85[a]	Inpatient with average stay of 33 days; 1973–1976; survey 1 year after discharge	60% abstinent for 1 year at follow-up[b]	1.0
Johnson and Connelly (1981)	Menninger Memorial Hospital (Kansas)	50[c]	Inpatient for 6 weeks; 1974–1979; record review	64% abstinent at follow-up[b]	0.75–4.5
Herrington et al. (1982)	De Paul Rehabilitation Hospital (Wisconsin)	40[c]	Inpatient for 30 days; out-patient with monitoring for 2 years; 1979–80; record review	68% continuously abstinent; 15% abstinent after lapse[d]	0.08–2.0
Morse et al. (1984)	Minnesota Mayo Clinic	73	Inpatient, with average stay of 4 weeks; 1974–1978; survey	42% continuously abstinent; 18% abstinent after lapse[b]	3.1[e]
Shore (1987)	Oregon Board of Medical Examiners Rehabilitation Program	39	Individualized treatment plans and monitoring; on probation; 1977–1985; record review	51% continuously abstinent; 23% abstinent after lapse[b,d]	6.0[e]
Ikeda and Pelton (1990)	California Physician Diversion Program	371[f]	Individualized treatment plans; usually inpatient for 1 month; outpatient 3–5 years; monitoring; 1980–1989; record review	66% continuously abstinent for at least 2 years[d]	3.0–5.0
Reading (1992)	New Jersey Physicians' Health Program	308[c]	Individualized treatment plans and monitoring; 1982–1990; survey	74% continuously abstinent for an average of 4 years[b,d]	0.75–9.0

Table 7.1 (*continued*)

Study	Program	*N*	Study characteristics	Outcome	Follow-up (in years)
Gallegos et al. (1992)	Georgia Impaired Physicians Program	100	20-month continuing care contract plus monitoring; 1982–1987; survey	77% continuously abstinent for an average of 7.5 years; 17% continuously abstinent for at least 2 years after lapse[b,d]	7.5[e]
Lloyd (2002)	North West Doctors and Dentists Group	100	Self-help group for at least 6 months; 1980–1988; surveyed in 2001	51% abstinent, 19% died abstinent, 24% died from alcoholism; average duration of abstinence 17.3 years[b]	13.0–21.0
Domino et al. (2005)	Washington Physicians Health Program	292[c]	5 years of posttreatment monitoring; 1991–2001; record review	75% continuously abstinent for at least 5 years[b,d]	0.0–10.0
Ganley et al. (2005)	North Carolina Physicians Health Program	251	Individualized treatment plan, usually self-help groups and and monitoring for 5 years; 1995–2000; record review	60% continuously abstinent for 1 to 5 years; 24% continuously abstinent for 1–5 years after lapse[d]	1.0–5.0

[a] Treatment completers.
[b] Confirmation by collaterals.
[c] Included other health professionals (e.g., dentists, veterinarians, podiatrists, nurses, pharmacists, and physician assistants).
[d] Confirmed by random biological screening tests.
[e] Mean.
[f] Not currently enrolled.

8%) died between discharge and follow-up, and for some of these, the cause of death was documented as substance related.

Herrington, Benzer, Jacobson, and Hawkins (1982) reported the outcome of 40 chemically dependent patients (36 physicians, 3 dentists, and 1 nurse-anesthetist) treated through the Impaired Physicians Treatment Program at De Paul Rehabilitation Hospital. The members of the sample entered treatment during 1979–80. The program was designed to last 2 years and consisted of inpatient treatment for an average of 30 days followed by nearly 2 years of at least weekly random urine screening tests and weekly self-help meetings for the patients and their spouses (i.e., sample members in Alcoholics Anonymous, Narcotics Anonymous, and sample members' spouses in Al-Anon groups). Patients were followed for varying periods, ranging from 1 to 23 months. As in Johnson and Connelly (1981), a brief relapse, which Herrington et al. defined as resumption of alcohol or drug use for less than a month without associated life problems, was not considered a treatment failure. At follow-up, 27 (68%) had experienced no relapse, 6 (15%) had had a brief relapse but continued in treatment, and 7 (18%) had relapsed and dropped out of the program.

Morse et al. (1984) compared the outcomes of 73 chemically dependent physicians and 185 general patients who completed inpatient treatment at the Mayo Clinic, with an average stay of 4 weeks. The physicians were contacted in 1978, an average of 37 months after the completion of treatment, and the general patients were contacted in 1975, 1 year after treatment. Morse et al. defined a successful outcome as continuous abstinence since discharge or current abstinence after a brief lapse (a week or less). The entire series of patients was evaluated, and general patients were compared with physicians. Two percent of general patients versus 12% of physicians had died; 20% of general patients versus 10% of physicians failed to complete treatment; and 2% of general patients versus 5% of physicians were lost to follow-up. Sixty percent of the physicians and 47% of the general patients had a favorable outcome, with 42% continuously abstinent and 18% abstinent with a brief lapse.

Shore (1987) reported on an 8-year follow-up of 49 chemically dependent physicians who had been on probation for an average of 6 years with the Oregon Board of Medical Examiners between 1977 and 1985. The rehabilitation program developed individualized treatment plans for each impaired physician, but all plans involved long-term monitoring. Among the 39 physicians who abused alcohol or drugs, but not both, 51% were continuously abstinent at follow-up and 23% were abstinent after a lapse. The mean time to relapse was 22 months after the start of probation. About half of these physicians were monitored long-term using random weekly urine screenings. The physicians who were monitored had a 94% improvement rate, while those who were not monitored had an improvement rate of only 64%.

Ikeda and Pelton (1990) reported the outcomes for 371 physicians who were enrolled in the California Physician Diversion Program for impaired physicians between 1980 and 1989. Similar to the Oregon program, the California Physician Diversion Program developed an individualized treatment plan for each physician that usually included 1 month of inpatient treatment. Some were treated with mandatory naltrexone or disulfiram. Inpatient treatment was followed by 3 to 5 years of outpatient treatment that involved two diversion program group meetings per week, two to four 12-step group meetings per week, and weekly chemical monitoring. Two factors defined a successful outcome: 2 years of continuous abstinence and an assessment by the five-member Diversion Evaluation Committee that the physician had developed a lifestyle that would support abstinence for the rest of the physician's life. As of 1989, 66% of the 371 physicians had successfully completed the program. A subsequent analysis (Pelton & Ikeda, 1991) on a subsample of 51 anesthesiologists enrolled in the program between 1980 and 1990 indicated that 69% had successfully completed the program. Pelton, Lang, Nye, and Jara (1993) found that the rate of license complaints filed against physicians who had successfully completed the California Physician Diversion Program between 1980 and 1990 was lower than that for the rest of the licensed physician population in California. Thus, the available research on the California Physician Diversion Program indicates that physician treatment and rehabilitation is effective.

Reading (1992) reported the outcomes for 308 chemically dependent physicians treated by the New Jersey Physicians' Health Program (PHP) between 1982 and 1990. Only physicians who did not have a significant dual diagnosis were included in this analysis. The program developed an individualized treatment plan for each physician, and if a relapse occurred, a more intensive level of treatment was prescribed. The program included formal, structured outpatient aftercare counseling that continued for 1 to 2 years, a highly structured urine monitoring program, and personal, face-to-face contact with PHP staff that gradually decreased from monthly in the first year to annually in the sixth year and beyond. Seventy-four percent of the physicians were continuously abstinent for an average of 4 years, and 13% relapsed only once. Those physicians with two or more relapses were confronted about their relapse and had their treatment reinstated or intensified; all returned to practice.

Gallegos et al. (1992) reported the outcomes for 100 physicians who entered a 20-month continuing care contract with the Georgia Impaired Physicians Program between 1982 and 1987. The continuing care contract required the physicians to have a primary care physician, a monitoring physician who would serve as a recovery mentor, and a 12-step sponsor. The physicians were also required to undergo frequent random urine drug screens; attend a minimum of five 12-step meetings and one Caduceus Club (a self-help group for physicians) meeting per week; participate in individual or marriage and family therapy, as indicated; and create their own spiritual, physical fitness, and leisure activity programs. Seventy-seven physicians maintained documented continuous abstinence from all mood-altering substances from the initiation of their continuing care contract to between 3 and 10 years of follow-up. One physician was lost to follow-up, and of the 22 remaining physicians who had a documented relapse, 18% underwent another round of treatment for their chemical dependence. One of these physicians became a chronic relapse, while the remaining 17 had at least 2 years, continuous sobriety after their relapse. Overall, 94% of the physicians in this study were able to maintain documented, continuous abstinence for at least 2 years.

Lloyd (2002) reported the results of a 21-year follow-up of the first 100 doctors to join the North West Doctors and Dentists Group (NWDDG). To be included in the study, the physician had to have attended this self-help group for at least 6 months between 1980 and 1988. In comparison with the other studies reviewed, this study was of low intensity, as the only treatment was attendance at NWDDG meetings (held monthly) and at local 12-step groups (held weekly). Lloyd (2002) combined prospective data obtained from each physician at the time of first contact with the results of questionnaires distributed in 1988 (Lloyd, 1990) and 2001 as well as continuing prospective reporting of mortality by relatives. Based on reported mortality over the study period, 24% of the physicians died directly of their alcoholism, and 19% died while abstinent. Of the remaining physicians, 3% appeared to have returned to normal drinking and 73% achieved recovery, with an average duration of 17 years. Of the 51 physicians who were alive and abstinent in 2001, 12 had had a relapse but at the time of the survey had at least 4.5 years of continuous abstinence.

Domino et al. (2005) reported the results of a retrospective cohort study of 292 health-care professionals enrolled in the Washington Physicians Health Program, a posttreatment monitoring program, between 1991 and 2001. The sample consisted of physicians (82%); physician assistants (11%); veterinarians (5%); and dentists, podiatrists, and pharmacists (2%). Seventy-five percent of the health-care professionals in this study were continuously abstinent for at least 5 years. Twenty-five percent had at least one relapse during the monitoring period. Most of the relapses were detected by way of chemical or workplace monitoring; 58% occurred within the first 2 years in the program. Having one relapse increased the risk of subsequent relapses (hazard ratio [HR] = 1.7; 95% confidence interval [CI] = 1.1–2.5). A family history of a substance use disorder more than doubled the risk of relapse (HR = 2.3; 95% CI = 1.4–3.6). The use of a major opioid increased the risk of relapse more than fivefold in the presence of a co-occurring psychiatric disorder (HR = 5.8; 95% CI = 2.9–11.4) but not in the absence of a co-occurring disorder (HR = 0.9; 95% CI = 0.3–2.2). Health-care professionals with all three risk factors—major opioid use, co-occurring disorder, and family history—were at the highest risk for relapse (HR = 13.3; 95% CI = 5.2–33.6). The risk factors for relapse among alcohol users who did not use opioids were family history (HR = 2.3; 95% CI = 1.0–5.3) and a co-occurring disorder (HR = 2.4; 95% CI = 1.3–4.6). Of the health-care professionals tracked for at least 5 years who did not relapse, 100% successfully returned to the practice of medicine; among those who did relapse, only 61% were able to return to the practice of medicine.

Ganley, Pendergast, Wilkerson, and Mattingly (2005) reported the outcomes for 251 physicians under contract with the North Carolina Physicians Health Program between 1995 and 2000. As in other state PHPs, participants signed a multiyear monitoring contract whose length depended on the individual's condition, typically 1 to 2 years for substance abuse and 5 years for substance dependence. For cases of chemical dependence, these contracts included random drug screening; meetings with a voluntary monitor; and participation in Alcoholics Anonymous, Caduceus Club, and other self-help group meetings; as well as other terms relevant to the individual case. During this 6-year retrospective study, 60% of the participants were continuously abstinent for 1 to 5 years and 24% were continuously abstinent for 1 to 5 years after a relapse.

The available data support several conclusions regarding the treatment of physicians with chemical dependency problems (see also Gallegos & Talbott, 1997). First, chemical dependency treatment for physicians does work. The research reviewed here also suggests that treatment may even be more effective for physicians than for members of the general public (e.g., Morse et al., 1984). Second, strict, long-term aftercare monitoring enhances abstinence and well-being among chemically dependent physicians. Morse et al. noted that structured aftercare monitoring is probably the reason for the higher rate of treatment success observed among physicians when compared with socioeconomically similar patients from the general population. They further noted that airline pilots who receive similar monitoring also show higher rates of recovery. Third, the existing evidence supports the theory that physicians are responsive to structured, long-term treatment and monitoring, which includes body fluid testing (Brewster, 1986; Flaherty & Richman, 1993; Morse et al., 1984; Shore, 1987). In an 8-year follow-up of 63 impaired or addicted physicians on probation with the Oregon Board of Medical Examiners, Shore (1987) found that the most successful treatment outcomes occurred with addicted physicians who were subjected to random urine monitoring to detect repetitive drug abuse. Shore compared outpatient supervision of monitored and unmonitored subgroups. A significant difference in the improvement rate was observed for physicians monitored by random urine screens (96%) versus those who were unmonitored (64%). Shore concluded that there is increasing evidence that random urine monitoring during a 2- to 4-year posttreatment period is positively correlated with treatment outcome, whether the treatment program is sponsored by a state medical board, a medical society, or a regional referral program. The combination of urine monitoring, contingency contracting, and a medically oriented addiction treatment philosophy has become more widely accepted in the treatment of addicted physicians. Fourth, death is more prevalent among physicians who drop out of treatment or relapse. The long-term death rate from alcoholism in the minimal treatment intervention reported by Lloyd (2002) was very high (24% of the sample died from alcoholism and 8% died after extended periods of abstinence from alcohol-linked diseases, such as esophagopharyngeal cancer). Later studies of programs using strict, long-term aftercare monitoring showed reduced mortality rates. More intensive treatment coupled with long-term monitoring does appear to significantly reduce the death rate from substance use disorders observed among physicians. Fifth, the majority of physicians who complete treatment and participate in aftercare monitoring do return to the practice of medicine. The recent study by Domino et al. (2005) reported a return-to-practice rate of 100% among physicians who completed 5 years of aftercare monitoring without a lapse and a rate of 61% for those who relapsed during the 5 years of monitoring, for an overall return-to-practice rate of 88%.

Summary

Physicians appear to have a similar lifetime risk of experiencing a substance use disorder as members of the general population. Alcohol is the primary substance abused by physicians, but because of their unique access, physicians are much more likely than the general population to abuse prescription drugs and are much less likely to abuse "street" drugs. In general, the same factors that increase the risk of substance abuse disorders in the general population also apply to physicians (e.g., a family history of substance abuse, family-of-origin dysfunction, and certain personality patterns). There are also some unique factors that apply specifically to physicians (e.g., high levels of compulsivity and perfectionism, which lead to overwork, unbalanced lifestyles, and self-neglect; high levels of stress associated with the practice of medicine, and choice of medical specialty). The pattern of deterioration observed in physicians follows a course similar to that observed in the general population. Certain work-related indicators (e.g., conducting rounds at odd hours, overprescribing) are unique to physicians. The wide latitude for eccentric behavior accorded physicians, coupled with self-deception on the part of the impaired physician, his or her professional colleagues, and the members of the physician's immediate family, creates the "conspiracy of silence" that impedes early intervention for physicians with substance use disorders. The research reviewed herein indicates that chemical dependency treatment is effective for physicians. The research also suggests that abstinence and well-being are enhanced by strict, long-term aftercare monitoring combined with random body fluid testing. Finally, the studies reviewed show that a large percentage of physicians who complete treatment and participate in aftercare monitoring return to the practice of medicine.

References

American Medical Association. (1973). The sick physician: Impairment by psychiatric disorders, including alcoholism and drug dependence. *Journal of the American Medical Association, 232,* 684–687.

American Psychiatric Association. (1987). *Diagnostic and statistical manual of mental disorders* (3rd ed., Rev. ed.). Washington, DC: Author.

American Psychiatric Association. (1994). *Diagnostic and statistical manual of mental disorders* (4th ed.). Washington, DC: Author.

American Psychiatric Association. (2000). *Diagnostic and statistical manual of mental disorders* (4th ed., text rev.). Washington, DC: Author.

Angres, D. H., Talbott, G. D., & Bettinardi-Angres, K. (1998). *Healing the healer: The addicted physician.* Madison, CT: Psychosocial Press.

Anthenelli, R. M., & Schuckit, M. A. (1997). Genetics. In J. H. Lowinson, P. Ruiz, R. B. Millman, & J. G. Langrod (Eds.), *Substance abuse: A comprehensive textbook* (pp. 41–51). Baltimore: Williams & Wilkins.

Babor, T. F., Higgins-Biddle, J. C., Saunders, J. B., & Monteiro, M. G. (2001). *Alcohol use disorders identification test: Guidelines for use in primary care* (2nd ed.). Geneva: World Health Organization.

Baldwin, D. C., Hughes, P. H., Conrad, S. E., Storr, C. L., & Sheehan, D. V. (1991). Substance use among senior medical students: A survey of 23 medical schools. *Journal of the American Medical Association, 265,* 2074–2078.

Bierut, L. J., Dinwiddie, S. H., Begleiter, H., Crowe, R. R., Hesselbrock, V., & Nurnberger, J. I. (1998). Familial transmission of substance dependence: Alcohol, marijuana, cocaine, and habitual smoking. *Archives of General Psychiatry, 55,* 982–988.

Bissell, L., & Jones, R. W. (1976). The alcoholic physician: A survey. *American Journal of Psychiatry, 133,* 1142–1146.

Bissell, L., & Skorina, J. K. (1987). One hundred alcoholic women in medicine: An interview study. *Journal of the American Medical Association, 257,* 2939–2944.

Blondell, R. D. (1993). Impaired physicians. *Primary Care, 20,* 209–219.

Boisaubin, E. V., & Levine, R. E. (2001). Identifying and assisting the impaired physician. *American Journal of Medical Sciences, 322,* 31–36.

Brewster, J. M. (1986). Prevalence of alcohol and other drug problems among physicians. *Journal of the American Medical Association, 255,* 1913–1920.

Brooke, D., Edwards, G., & Taylor, C. (1991). Addiction as an occupational hazard: 144 doctors with drug and alcohol problems. *British Journal of Addiction, 86,* 1011–1016.

Caplan, R. D., Cobb, S., French, J. R. P., Jr., Van Harrison, R., & Pinneau, S. R., Jr. (1975). *Job demands and worker health.* Washington, DC: U.S. Department of Health, Education, and Welfare.

Carmelli, D., Swan, G. E., Robinette, D., & Fabitz, R. (1992). Genetic influence on smoking—A study of male twins. *New England Journal of Medicine, 327,* 829–833.

Centrella, M. (1994). Physician addiction and impairment—Current thinking: A review. *Journal of Addictive Diseases, 13,* 91–105.

Clark, D. C., Eckenfels, E. J., Daugherty, S. R., & Fawcett, J. (1987). Alcohol-use patterns through medical school: A longitudinal study of one class. *Journal of the American Medical Association, 257,* 2921–2926.

Coombs, R. H. (1997). *Drug-impaired professionals.* Cambridge, MA: Harvard University Press.

Cotton, N. (1979). The familial incidence of alcoholism. *Journal of Studies on Alcohol, 40,* 89–116.

Domino, K. B., Hornbein, T. F., Polissar, N. L., Renner, G., Johnson, J., Alberti, S., & Hankes, L. (2005). Risk factors for relapse in health care professionals with substance use disorders. *Journal of the American Medical Association, 293,* 1453–1460.

Donovan, J., Jessor, R., & Jessor, L. (1983). Problem drinking in adolescence and young adulthood: A follow-up study. *Journal of Studies on Alcohol, 44,* 109–137.

Elster, J. (1999). *Strong feelings: Emotion, addiction, and human behavior.* Cambridge, MA: MIT Press.

Favazza, A., & Cannell, B. (1977). Screening for alcoholism among college students. *American Journal of Psychiatry, 134,* 1414–1416.

Flaherty, J. A., & Richman, J. A. (1993). Substance use and addiction among medical students, residents, and physicians. *Psychiatric Clinics of North America, 16,* 189–197.

Forney, M. A., Ripley, W. K., & Forney, P. D. (1988). A profile and prediction study of problem drinking among first-year medical students. *International Journal of the Addictions, 23,* 767–779.

Gabbard, G. O. (1985). The role of compulsiveness in the normal physician. *Journal of the American Medical Association, 254,* 2926–2929.

Gabbard, G. O., & Menninger, R. W. (1989). The psychology of postponement in the medical marriage. *Journal of the American Medical Association, 261,* 2378–2381.

Gallegos, K. V. (1987). The pilot impaired physicians epidemiological surveillance system (PIPESS). *Maryland Medical Journal, 36,* 264–266.

Gallegos, K. V., Browne, C. H., Veit, F. W., & Talbott, G. D. (1988). Addiction in anesthesiologists: Drug access and patterns of substance abuse. *Quality Review Bulletin, 14,* 116–122.

Gallegos, K. V., Lubin, B. H., Bowers, C., Blevins, J. W., Talbott, G. D., & Wilson, P. O. (1992). Relapse and recovery: Five to ten year follow-up study of chemically dependent physicians—The Georgia experience. *Maryland Medical Journal, 41,* 315–319.

Gallegos, K. V., & Talbott, G. D. (1997). Physicians and other health professionals. In J. H. Lowinson, P. Ruiz, R. B. Millman, & J. G. Langrod (Eds.), *Substance abuse: A comprehensive textbook* (3rd ed., pp. 744–754). Baltimore: Williams & Wilkins.

Ganley, O. H., Pendergast, W. J., Wilkerson, M. W., & Mattingly, D. E. (2005). Outcome study of substance impaired physicians and physician assistants under contract with North Carolina Physicians Health Program for the period 1995–2000. *Journal of Addictive Diseases, 24,* 1–23.

Gold, M. S., Byars, J. A., & Frost-Pineda, K. (2004). Occupational exposure and addictions for physicians: Case studies and theoretical implications. *Psychiatric Clinics of North America, 27,* 745–753.

Gold, M. S., Dennis, D. M., Morey, T. E., & Melker, R. (2004). Exposure to narcotics in the operating room poses occupational hazard for anesthesiologists. *Psychiatric Annals, 34,* 794–797.

Gold, M. S., Melker, R. J., Dennis, D. M., Morey, T. E., Bajpai, L. K., Pomm, R., & Frost-Pineda, K. (2006). Fentanyl abuse and dependence: Further evidence for second hand exposure hypothesis. *Journal of Addictive Diseases, 25,* 15–21.

Grant, B. F. (2000). Estimates of US children exposed to alcohol abuse and dependence in the family. *American Journal of Public Health, 90,* 112–115.

Grant, B. F., & Dawson, D. A. (1999). Alcohol and drug use, abuse and dependence: Classification, prevalence and comorbidity. In B. S. McCrady & E. E. Epstein (Eds.), *Addictions: A comprehensive guidebook* (pp. 9–29). New York: Oxford University Press.

Harter, S. L. (2000). Psychosocial adjustment of adult children of alcoholics: A review of the recent empirical literature. *Clinical Psychology Review, 20,* 311–337.

Herrington, R. D., Benzer, D. C., Jacobson, G. R., & Hawkins, M. K. (1982). Treating substance abuse disorders among physicians. *Journal of the American Medical Association, 247,* 2253–2257.

Hughes, J. R. (1986). Genetics of smoking: A brief review. *Behavior Therapy, 17,* 335–345.

Hughes, P. H., Baldwin, D. C., Jr., Sheehan, D. V., Conrad, S., & Storr, C. L. (1992). Resident physician substance use, by specialty. *American Journal of Psychiatry, 149,* 1348–1354.

Hughes, P. H., Brandenburg, N., Baldwin, D. C., Storr, C. L., Williams, K. M., Anthony, J. C., & Sheehan, D. V. (1992). Prevalence of substance use among U.S. physicians. *Journal of the American Medical Association, 267,* 2333–2339.

Hughes, P. H., Conrad, S. E., Baldwin, D. C., Storr, C. L., & Sheehan, D. V. (1991). Resident physician substance use in the United States. *Journal of the American Medical Association, 265,* 2069–2073.

Hughes, P. H., Storr, C. L., Brandenburg, N. A., Baldwin, D. C., Anthony, J. C., & Sheehan, D. V. (1999). Physician substance use by medical specialty. *Journal of Addictive Diseases, 18,* 23–37.

Ikeda, R., & Pelton, C. (1990). Diversion programs for impaired physicians. *Western Journal of Medicine, 152,* 617–621.

Impaired physicians get more attention. (2004.) *Psychiatric News, 39,* 11a.

Jex, S. M., Hughes, P., Storr, C., Conrad, S., Baldwin, D. C., Jr., & Sheehan, D. V. (1992). Relations among stressors, strains, and substance use among resident physicians. *International Journal of the Addictions, 27,* 979–994.

Johnson, R. P., & Connelly, J. C. (1981). Addicted physicians: A closer look. *Journal of the American Medical Association, 245,* 253–257.

Kessler, R. C., McGonagle, K. A., & Shanyang, Z. (1994). Lifetime and 12-month prevalence of DSM-III-R psychiatric disorders in the United States: Results from the National Comorbidity Study. *Archives of General Psychiatry, 51,* 8–19.

Khantzian, E. J. (1985). The injured self, addiction, and our call to medicine: Understanding and managing addicted physicians. *Journal of the American Medical Association, 254,* 249–252.

Kliner, D. J., Spicer, J., & Barnett, P. (1980). Treatment outcome of alcoholic physicians. *Journal of Studies on Alcohol, 41,* 1217–1220.

Krakowski, A. J. (1982). Stress and the practice of medicine. II: Stressors, stresses, and strains. *Psychotherapy and Psychosomatics, 38,* 11–23.

Krakowski, A. J. (1984). Stress and the practice of medicine. III: Physicians compared with lawyers. *Psychotherapy and Psychosomatics, 42,* 143–151.

Lewis, D. C., Niven, R. G., Czechowicz, D., & Trumble, J. G. (1987). A review of medical education in alcohol and other drug abuse. *Journal of the American Medical Association, 257,* 2945–2948.

Lewis, J. M., Barnhardt, F. D., Howard, B. L., Carson, D. I., & Nace, E. P. (1993a). Work stress in the lives of physicians. *Journal of Texas Medicine, 89,* 62–67.

Lewis, J. M., Barnhardt, F. D., Howard, B. L., Carson, D. I., & Nace, E. P. (1993b). Work satisfaction in the lives of physicians. *Journal of Texas Medicine, 89,* 54–61.

Lloyd, G. (1990). Alcoholic doctors can recover. *British Medical Journal, 300,* 728–730.

Lloyd, G. (2002). One hundred alcoholics: A 21-year follow-up. *Alcohol and Alcoholism, 37,* 370–374.

Lutsky, I., Hopwood, M., Abram, S. E., Cerletty, J. M., Hoffman, R. G., & Kampine, J. P. (1994). Use of psychoactive substances in three medical specialties: Anaesthesia, medicine and surgery. *Canadian Journal of Anaesthesia, 41,* 561–567.

Maddux, J. F., Tinnerman, I. M., & Costello, R. M. (1987). Use of psychoactive substances by residents. *Journal of Medical Education, 62,* 852–854.

Mansky, P. A. (1999). Issues in the recovery of physicians from addictive diseases. *Psychiatric Quarterly, 70,* 107–122.

Mawardi, B. H. (1979). Satisfaction, dissatisfaction, and causes of stress in medical practice. *Journal of the American Medical Association, 241,* 1483–1486.

McAuliffe, W. E., Rohman, M., Breer, P., Wyshak, G., Santangelo, S., & Manguson, E. (1991). Alcohol use and abuse in random samples of physicians and medical students. *American Journal of Public Health, 81,* 177–182.

McAuliffe, W. E., Rohman, M., Santangelo, S., Feldman, B., Manguson, E., Sobol, A., & Weissman, J. (1986). Psychoactive drug use among practicing physicians and medical students. *New England Journal of Medicine, 315,* 805–810.

McAuliffe, W. E., Santangelo, S., Manguson, E., Sobol, A., Rohman, M., & Weissman, J. (1987). Risk factors of drug impairment in random samples of physicians and medical students. *International Journal of the Addictions, 22,* 825–841.

McCue, J. D. (1982). The effects of stress on physicians and their medical practice. *New England Journal of Medicine, 306,* 458–463.

McGovern, M. P., Angres, D. H., & Leon, S. (2000). Characteristics of physicians presenting for assessment at a behavioral health center. *Journal of Addictive Diseases, 19,* 59–73.

Medical Board of California. (2006). *Physician Diversion Program* (Program Brochure). Sacramento: State of California.

Merikangas, K. R. (1990). The genetic epidemiology of alcoholism. *Psychological Medicine, 20,* 11–22.

Merikangas, K. R., Stolar, M., Stevens, D. E., Goulet, J., Preisig, M. A., Fenton, B., Zhang, H., O'Malley, S. S., & Rounsaville, B. J. (1998). Familial transmission of substance use disorders. *Archives of General Psychiatry, 55,* 973–979.

Miller, N. S., Sheppard, L. M., Colenda, C. C., & Magen, J. (2001). Why physicians are unprepared to treat patients who have alcohol- and drug-related disorders. *Academic Medicine, 76,* 410–418.

Moore, R. D., Mead, L., & Pearson, T. A. (1990). Youthful precursors of alcohol abuse in physicians. *American Journal of Medicine, 88,* 332–336.

Morse, R. M., Martin, M. A., Swenson, W. M., & Niven, R. G. (1984). Prognosis of physicians treated for alcoholism and drug dependence. *Journal of the American Medical Association, 251,* 743–746.

Myers, T., & Weiss, E. (1987). Substance use by interns and residents: An analysis of personal, social and professional differences. *British Journal of Addiction, 82,* 1091–1099.

Nace, E. P. (1995). *Achievement and addiction: A guide to the treatment of professionals.* New York: Brunner/Mazel.

Nelson, H. D., Matthews, A. M., Girard, D. E., & Bloom, J. D. (1996). Substance-impaired physicians: Probationary and voluntary treatment programs compared. *Western Journal of Medicine, 165,* 31–36.

O'Connor, P. G., & Spickard, A., Jr. (1997). Physician impairment by substance abuse. *Medical Clinics of North America, 81,* 1037–1052.

Paton, A. (1991). Barriers to education about alcohol. *Journal of the Royal Society of Medicine, 85,* 476–478.

Pelton, C., & Ikeda, R. M. (1991). The California Physicians Diversion Program's experience with recovering anesthesiologists. *Journal of Psychoactive Drugs, 23,* 427–431.

Pelton, C., Lang, D. A., Nye, G. S., & Jara, G. (1993). Physician diversion program experience with successful graduates. *Journal of Psychoactive Drugs, 25,* 159–164.

Reading, E. (1992). Nine years experience with chemically dependent physicians: The New Jersey experience. *Maryland Medical Journal, 41,* 325–329.

Richman, J. A. (1992). Occupational stress, psychological vulnerability and alcohol-related problems over time in future physicians. *Alcoholism: Clinical and Experimental Research, 16,* 166–171.

Richman, J. A., & Flaherty, J. A. (1990). Alcohol-related problems of future physicians prior to medical training. *Journal of Studies on Alcohol, 51,* 296–300.

Richman, J. A., Flaherty, J. A., & Pyskoty, C. E. (1992). Shifts in problem drinking during a life transition: Adaptation to medical school training. *Journal of Studies on Alcohol, 53,* 17–24.

Richman, J. A., & Pyskoty, C. E. (1991). Interpersonal versus technological orientations and alcohol abuse in future physicians. *British Journal of Addiction, 86,* 1133–1138.

Richman, J. A., & Rospenda, K. M. (1992). Gender roles and alcohol abuse: Cost of noncaring for future physicians. *Journal of Nervous and Mental Disease, 180,* 619–626.

Robins, L. N., Locke, B. Z., & Regier, D. A. (1990). An overview of psychiatric disorders in America. In L. N. Robins & D. A. Regier (Eds.), *Psychiatric disorders in America: The Epidemiological Catchment Area Study* (pp. 328–366). New York: Free Press.

Rogers, D. (2006). *Perceptions of family environment by licensed health professionals in a multi-year state diversion program.* Unpublished doctoral dissertation, Alliant International University, San Diego, CA.

Schoenborn, C. A. (1991). *Exposure to alcoholism in the family: United States, 1988* (PHS Report No. 91-1250). Rockville, MD: U.S. Department of Health and Human Services, Public Health Service.

Schuckit, M. A. (1987). Biological vulnerability to alcoholism. *Journal of Consulting and Clinical Psychology, 55,* 301–310.

Selzer, M. L. (1971). The Michigan Alcoholism Screening Test (MAST): The quest for a new diagnostic instrument. *American Journal of Psychiatry, 127,* 1653–1658.

Shore, J. H. (1982). The impaired physician: Four years after probation. *Journal of the American Medical Association, 248,* 3127–3130.

Shore, J. H. (1987). The Oregon experience with impaired physicians on probation: An 8-year follow-up. *Journal of the American Medical Association, 257,* 2931–2934.

Stimson, G. V. (1985). Recent developments in professional control: The impaired physician movement in the USA. *Sociology of Health and Illness, 7,* 141–166.

Storr, C. L., Trinkoff, A. M., & Hughes, P. (2000). Similarities of substance use between medical and nursing specialties. *Substance Use and Misuse, 35,* 1443–1469.

Stout-Wiegand, N., & Trent, R. B. (1981). Physician drug use: Availability or occupational stress. *International Journal of the Addictions, 16,* 317–330.

Swan, G. E., Carmelli, D., Rosenman, R. H., Fabsitz, R. R., & Christian, J. C. (1990). Smoking and alcohol consumption in adult male twins: Genetic heritability and shared environmental influences. *Journal of Substance Abuse, 2,* 39–50.

Talbott, G. D., & Benson, E. B. (1980). Impaired physicians: The dilemma of identification. *Postgraduate Medicine,* 68, 56, 58–59, 62–64.

Talbott, G. D., Gallegos, K. V., Wilson, P. O., & Porter, T. L. (1987). The medical association of Georgia's impaired physician program. *Journal of the American Medical Association, 257,* 2927–2930.

Talbott, G. D., & Wilson, P. O. (2005). Physicians and other health professionals. In J. H. Lowinson, P. Ruiz, R. B. Millman, & J. G. Langrod (Eds.), *Substance abuse: A comprehensive textbook* (4th ed., pp. 1187–1202). Baltimore: Williams & Wilkins.

Tsuang, M. T., Lyons, M. J., Meyer, J. M., Doyle, T., Eisen, S. A., Goldberg, J., True, W., Lin, N., Toomey, R., & Eaves, L. (1998). Co-occurrence of abuse of different drugs in men: The role of drug-specific and shared vulnerabilities. *Archives of General Psychiatry, 55,* 967–972.

Vaillant, G. E. (1992). Physician, cherish thyself: The hazards of self prescribing. *Journal of the American Medical Association, 267,* 2373–2374.

Vaillant, G. E. (1995). *The natural history of alcoholism revisited.* Cambridge, MA: Harvard University Press.

Vaillant, G. E., Sobowale, N. C., & McArthur, C. (1972). Some psychological vulnerabilities of physicians. *New England Journal of Medicine, 287,* 372–375.

Varga, M., & Buris, L. (1994). Drinking habits of medical students call for better integration of teaching about alcohol into the medical curriculum. *Alcohol and Alcoholism, 29,* 591–596.

Vogtsberger, K. N. (1984). Treatment outcomes of substance-abusing physicians. *American Journal of Drug and Alcohol Abuse, 10,* 23–37.

Ward, C. F., Ward, G. C., & Saidman, L. J. (1983). Drug abuse in anesthesia training programs. A survey: 1970 through 1980. *Journal of the American Medical Association, 250,* 922–925.

Wechsler, H., Davenport, A., Dowdall, G., Moeykens, B., & Castillo, S. (1994). Health and behavioral consequences of binge drinking in college: A national survey of students at 140 campuses. *Journal of the American Medical Association, 272,* 1672–1677.

Wechsler, H., Lee, J. E., Kuo, M., Seibring, M., Nelson, T. F., & Lee, H. (2002). Trends in college binge drinking during a period of increased prevention efforts. Findings from four Harvard School of Public Health College alcohol study surveys: 1993–2001. *Journal of American College Health, 50,* 203–217.

Wright, C. (1990). Physician addiction to pharmaceuticals: Personal history, practice setting, access to drugs, and recovery. *Maryland Medical Journal, 39,* 1021–1025.

Wyatt, S. A., Vilensky, W., Manlandro, J. J., & Dekker, M. A. (2005). Medical education in substance abuse: From student to practicing osteopathic physician. *Journal of the American Osteopathic Association, 105*(Suppl. 3), S18–S25.

CHAPTER 8

Children of Alcoholics and Adult Children of Alcoholics

Ann W. Lawson

Life with a parent who is alcoholic or with a family where alcohol abuse is a central dynamic can be damaging to children. Children of alcoholics (COAs) have been ignored by alcohol treatment agencies in favor of working with the alcoholic individually or working with the alcoholic and his or her spouse. Clinicians who treat children are often unaware of possible alcohol abuse in the family, or they believe that only people with special information or training can treat alcohol problems. They typically refer such families to alcohol treatment agencies as soon as alcohol becomes an issue in treatment. This would seem logical if treating the alcoholic would produce positive change in the children. However, in a study of alcoholic families in Pennsylvania, Booz-Allen and Hamilton, Inc. (1974) found that "the treatment and recovery of the alcoholic parent does not appear to reduce the problems experienced by the children" (p. 63).

The family system was out of balance before the alcoholic parent was treated; it tends to remain unbalanced after treatment. Children do not give up their coping roles. Cork (1969) did a study of 115 children between the ages of 10 and 16 who lived in alcoholic homes. She found that the home situations of the abstainers were not much different from the home situations of those who continued to drink. These children did not report that family life became significantly better when drinking stopped. One child described the impact of his father's sobriety in this way:

> Dad's changed now that he's not drinking. He's friendlier, and he talks more. Sometimes he even tries to act like a father and makes some rules, but he never sticks to what he says. I think he's afraid we won't love him if he does. My parents don't fight quite as much now but they're not really happy. Mom never lets Dad forget about his drinking days. She's still the one who runs things. Dad seems more like one of us kids. (Cork, 1969, p. 53)

This family continued to operate with a poor marital subsystem and a parent who crossed generational boundaries. The child who spoke these words is still affected by the marital fighting and a lack of consistent parenting.

Children living in homes where alcohol abuse is occurring or has occurred in the past total 28 million, and nearly 11 million are under the age of 18; countless others are affected by parents impaired by other psychoactive drugs (National Association for Children of Alcoholics, 2006). A national longitudinal epidemiologic survey reported that one in four children under the age of 18 are exposed to alcohol abuse or alcohol dependence (Grant, 2000). Children of addicted parents constitute the highest risk group both genetically and environmentally to become alcohol and drug abusers (Kumpfer, 1999). These children are at high risk for developing social and emotional problems, and they are twice as likely to develop alcohol-related problems as children of non-alcoholics (Bosma, 1975; Goodwin, Schulsinger, Hermansen, Gruze, & Winokur, 1973). Sons of alcoholic fathers are at fourfold risk of developing alcoholism compared to sons whose fathers were not alcoholic (Goodwin, 1985). Fifty-two percent of the alcoholic parents raising children came from homes where one or both parents had a drinking problem (Fox, 1968). In light of this information, it does not seem appropriate to exclude children from the treatment process. Children need to develop new channels of communication within the family, and they should have an opportunity to explain their perspective of the family process.

Problems of the Children

Many studies and reports have documented various problems in children who live with alcoholics (Christensen & Bilenberg, 2000; Eiden, Leonard, & Morrisey, 2001). Sloboda (1974) found that parents often do not live by society's rules; discipline is inconsistent, and the children become confused and unable to predict parental behavior. Chafetz, Blane, and Hill (1977) compared 100 alcoholic families with 100 non-alcoholic families that were seen at a child guidance center. They found that marital instability, poor marital relationships, prolonged separations, and divorce were considerably more prevalent in the alcoholic families (41% vs. 11%). Their observation regarding marital discord is supported by family theory, which views marital disruption as a major contributor to children's symptoms. Additionally, Chafetz et al. discovered a greater number of serious illnesses and accidents (possibly as a result of neglect) as well as more school problems in alcoholic families versus non-alcoholic families. Children from alcoholic homes more frequently externalized conflict and were more often involved with police or the courts. According to Chafetz et al., "This suggests that children of alcoholics have a difficult time becoming socially mature and responsible adults" (p. 696).

With regard to mental health, children of addicted parents show more signs of depression and depressive symptoms than do children with non-addicted parents (Fitzgerald et al., 1993). They are also more likely to have anxiety disorders and exhibit anxiety symptoms (Earls, Reich, Jung, & Cloniger, 1998). Elevated rates of psychiatric and psychosocial dysfunction, as well as alcoholism, were found in children of addicted parents compared with those who did not have addicted parents (West & Printz 1987). Children with addicted parents were also 24% more likely to be admitted to an inpatient treatment program, and 29% had higher average treatment lengths than children who did not have addicted parents (Children of Alcoholics Foundation, 1990). Fifty percent of hospitalized children with psychiatric disorders were found to have addicted parents (Rivinus, Levoy, Matzko, & Cloninger, 1998). Mylant, Ide, Cuevas, and Meehan (2002), after studying adolescent COAs, concluded that they were at risk for depression, suicide, eating disorders, chemical dependency, and teen pregnancy. When compared to adolescents who did not identify themselves as COAs, these adolescents were lower on all psychosocial measures of family and personal strengths, as well as school bonding. They also scored higher on at-risk measures of temperament, feelings, thoughts, and behaviors. Finally, COAs ages 6 through 17 exhibited elevated rates of attention-deficit disorder (ADD) and oppositional defiant disorder (ODD) (Earls et al., 1998).

Tobacco use and nicotine dependence were also found to be strongly related to having an alcoholic parent (Cuijpers & Smit, 2002). COAs were found to be at higher risk of developing dependence and using nicotine at an earlier age. The mean age for COAs was 16.77 years if the father was alcoholic, 15.89 if the mother was alcoholic, and 16.24 if both parents were alcoholic, as opposed to 18.22 if there was no parental alcoholism. COAs also have telescoped trajectories (quicker progression) from the initiation of drinking to the development of an alcohol disorder (Hussong, Bauer, & Chassin, 2008). Ohannessian et al. (2004) found that adolescents progressed more quickly from initiating drinking to the onset of the disorder than did matched controls. Further, children whose parents were actively drinking or who had comorbid depression or antisocial personality disorder progressed more quickly than other children in the sample. In a sample of 13- to 17-year-old adolescents and their parents ($N = 665$), the adolescents whose parents had been diagnosed with alcohol dependence along with either drug dependence or depression were more likely to have higher levels of psychological symptoms than were those with parents diagnosed with alcohol dependence only. Adolescents who had parents with alcohol dependence, depression, and drug dependence were the most likely of all the subjects in the sample to have psychological problems (Ohannessian et al., 2004).

Childhood exposure to alcohol-abusing parents and family violence independently influence the development of problem behaviors in adolescents (Ritter, Stewart, Bernet, Coe, & Brown, 2002). Ritter et al. found that adolescent substance use was associated with an alcohol-abusing family environment, but not with exposure to family violence. The frequency of male adolescents' substance use was more closely related to parental abuse than was females' use. However, conduct disorders were more highly associated with alcohol-abusing and family violence environments in female than in male subjects. Parental alcohol abuse was related to poor self-esteem in females but not in males. However, both male and female adolescents' self-esteem was affected by exposure to family violence, which was defined by spouse abuse and child abuse.

Family Dynamics

Hindman (1975–76) noted that children experience alcoholic families as chaotic, confusing, and unpredictable. Children are often subjected to neglect, abuse, and inconsistent discipline, and they are rarely provided with structure. As a result, they become isolated, develop adjustment problems, and have difficulty with peer relationships. Ranganathan (2004) reported that drinking behavior interrupts family tasks and causes conflict, which demands adjustment and responses from family members who do not know how to respond. Ranganathan concluded, "In brief, alcoholism creates a series of escalating crises in family structure and function, which may bring the family to a system crisis" (p. 399). This leads to what Ranganathan called a "conformity orientation" in which children feel pressure not to talk about what is happening in the family, especially anything that might upset the alcoholic. The unpredictability of the parents' behavior is later manifested in adult children of alcoholics (ACAs) in the form of seeing the world as unpredictable, which in turn may increase the probability of ACAs using drugs and alcohol to cope (Ross & Hill, 2001).

One of the outcomes for children who live with alcoholic parents is *parentification,* where one of the children assumes the parent's caretaking role in relation to the other children in the family. Such role reversal robs the parentified child of his or her childhood. Burnett, Jones, Bliwise, and Ross (2006) concluded that unpredictability and parental alcoholism make independent contributions to parentification. In their study, female children were more likely to assume the caretaking role. In a study of 360 young adults, Chase, Deming, and Wells (2000) found that those who perceived themselves as having assumed a parentified role in their families of origin had lower academic status and higher scores on a parentification measure than did other children of problem drinkers and children of non-alcoholics.

In a study of a community sample, Keller, Cummings, and Davies (2005) concluded that parental problem drinking was related to reduced family functioning, increased marital conflict, ineffective parenting, and poor child adjustment. Mezzich et al. (2007) conducted a study of male children with neurobehavior disinhibition who had parents with substance use disorders. They found that the parents' discipline style increased the children's risk for substance use disorder. Their research called for family-based interventions to reduce the risk in these children.

In a study of 50 COAs and 50 matched comparisons aged 16 to 35, COAs reported weaker bonds between their parents and between themselves and the alcoholic parent, as well as less family cohesion as a whole (Orford, Krishnan, & Velleman, 2003). However, the more siblings there were in the family, the stronger family cohesion became, and this effect was even stronger with the comparison group.

In a study of the effects of drinking patterns of male alcoholics, Lease (2002) found that drinking did not have an effect on depression, but it did directly affect multigenerational family functioning and indirectly influence self-esteem in family members. The primary pattern of drinking-related behavior that influenced the family was loud, violent, or abusive behavior. This behavior was associated with decreased intimacy and personal authority, and increased intimidation. These family interactions indirectly influenced depression via the mediating variable of self-esteem. The "visibly present but quiet drinking pattern" had only a minimum effect. Lease suggested that not all ACAs are affected in the same way by their fathers' drinking behavior and should not be seen as a homogeneous group.

Booz-Allen and Hamilton, Inc. (1974) reported, "Having an alcoholic parent is an emotionally disturbing experience for children. If children do not resolve the problems created by parental alcoholism, they will carry them the rest of their lives" (p. 73). The most frequent disturbances they found (60%) were emotional neglect and family conflict, defined as violence, aggression, fighting, arguments within the home, and spouse abuse. Emotional neglect occurred when the alcoholic withdrew from the child, building a wall that did not provide the child with communication, affection, or parenting. These families also experienced the full range of other family problems, including nonfulfillment of parental responsibilities, instability, divorce, separation, death, physical abuse, and inappropriate physical behavior to meet the needs of the other parent.

The children in this study expressed strong feelings about living with an alcoholic parent (Booz-Allen & Hamilton, Inc., 1974). They frequently reported resenting their situation, particularly the parental duties they had to perform, and not having "normal" parents. Often they expressed embarrassment about their parents' inadequacies and lack of responsiveness. They did not bring their friends home because they did not want them to witness the chaos. They also expressed a full range of feelings, including love, admiration, respect, fear, anger, hate, guilt, and loneliness. The children loved their parents, but their ambivalent feelings caused confusion.

As the children grew up in these families, they experienced various problems (Booz-Allen & Hamilton, Inc., 1974). Young children developed school problems, delinquency, and fighting. A high percentage of the children had difficulties in developing relationships with peers. Less common problems included alcohol and drug abuse, depression and suicidal tendencies, repressed emotions, and a lack of self-confidence and direction.

Children were at a higher risk of developing problems when they (a) belonged to a lower socioeconomic group, (b) witnessed or experienced physical abuse, (c) were 6 years old or younger at the onset of the parental alcohol abuse, (d) were an only or oldest child, and (e) lived in a nonsupportive family situation. These are the children who most need to be included in a family treatment process. Booz-Allen and Hamilton, Inc. (1974) noted that although children's personalities, attributes, and personal internal resources determine the degree of difficulties they will have, "the nuclear and extended family had the greatest potential for positively affecting the child" (p. 76).

Hecht (1973) concluded that communication in the alcoholic family was often inconsistent and unclear, which led to the isolation of family members. Children observed their parents say one thing and do another and would not know which message to respond to. The children could not win with either choice. Spouses of alcoholics would often protect the child with half-truths about the alcoholic, but unfortunately the children came to believe that neither parent could not be trusted. To survive in this environment, the children learned to ignore verbal messages and to watch for actions and deeds. Similarly, the children imitated the parental communication style of fighting and hostile sarcasm, often acting out their impulses. Children living in these systems felt alone and had difficulty trusting others.

These families had further difficulties with role behavior (Hecht, 1973). The parents did not perform parental duties, and sex role models were distorted or non-existent.

Children also crossed generational boundaries and were functioning as parents in many areas. Family members took on survival role behaviors when the alcoholic was drinking.

Inconsistencies in discipline made it difficult for children to see a clear cause-and-effect structure in the world. Family rules were vague and changed frequently. It is generally axiomatic that when parents are overly involved with alcohol, it is difficult for them to understand their children's distress (Hecht, 1973).

Hecht (1973) reported that children had a great need to love their parents, but when their parents were abusing alcohol or neglecting their children, the children became angry. This anger was not directed at their parents, but was turned inward. The children were also afraid that matters would worsen and their home would disappear. If the children lived in a single-parent family, this fear often became reality if the parent entered inpatient treatment or was incapable of providing a home for the children. The children could be placed in a foster home or institution until the parent was capable of parenting again. This need to love a parent and have that love returned caused the children distress when the parent was drinking. The children then became ashamed of the parent. Their anger and resentment were translated into rebellious behavior. Ironically, this rebellious behavior may have been the very thing that led the children to be taken away from their parents. The child often became the "bad" person, while the alcoholic was hidden and protected by other family members.

Clinebell (1968) reported four factors that produce damage in the lives of COAs. The first factor is role reversal. Children may undertake parental duties because the parent is unable or because responsibilities are forced on the children. Also, the alcoholic may be treated as a child and, in return, act helpless. In incestuous families, the daughter and mother switch roles. Second, an inconsistent and unpredictable relationship with the alcoholic is emotionally depriving to the child. Third, the non-alcoholic parent is struggling with major problems, and because his or her own needs are unmet, he or she is unable to attend to the needs of the children. The fourth damaging factor is social isolation of the family as protection from further pain and suffering. Due to embarrassment, the family builds a wall of defenses around itself that leaves no room for social relationships or adequate peer relationships for the children. These conditions do not occur in all alcoholic families, but they are damaging when they do exist.

Cork (1969) interviewed 115 children who lived in alcoholic families, seeking to gain an understanding of the child's perspective. She found that children became so absorbed in family problems that they were unable to develop a sense of responsibility or an ability to solve problems. These children were dealing with adult problems and had not expressed their feelings about this with others. As Cork interviewed them, they enthusiastically talked about a subject that was ordinarily taboo.

The following is a list of some of the children's concerns:

1. They would not go to a friend's house because they would not dare reciprocate and invite friends to their home because of the unpredictable and embarrassing behaviors of their parents.
2. They were angry at everybody.
3. They were preoccupied at school with worry about what would happen when they returned home.

4. They envied children who seemed to have fun with their families.
5. If they were only children, they felt alone.
6. When both parents were drinking, the children felt neglected.
7. The children felt they had to be parent-like, especially if the mother was drinking.
8. If the parents were separated, the children worried about each parent's loneliness. They wished for their parents to reunite even if the home was calmer during the separation. The children seemed to feel an even deeper loss if the alcoholic parent moved out of the home.
9. Adolescents were unable to separate and individuate from their parents. They did not experience a sense of responsibility for or control over their lives. It was difficult to break away from somebody with whom they had no real ties. One child said poignantly, "I want to be somebody, but I feel like a nobody."
10. The children often excused the alcoholic for his or her behavior and condemned the non-alcoholics in the family for being hostile and angry. These children believed that love and caring could cure alcoholism. Unfortunately, research indicates that many ACAs marry alcoholics to prove this hypothesis.
11. The children experienced multiple separations and reunions of their parents and learned not to depend on any consistent state.
12. Even when the alcoholic stopped drinking, the children continued to have problems.

Additionally, the study surveyed (a) the children's focus of concern in their family life, (b) how the children felt they were affected by having an alcoholic parent, (c) the children's views about drinking, (d) problems the children identify as caused by drinking, and (e) the children's attitudes about their own future use of alcohol. Interestingly, the children's primary concern about their family was not alcohol consumption. The main concerns were parental fighting and quarreling, and a lack of interest in them on the part of both parents. Children felt affected in many ways by parental alcoholism, and approximately two thirds made a choice not to drink because they were afraid of being like their alcoholic parents; a third said they would drink in moderation. Five of the children were already drinking. Previous research indicates that 25% to 30% of COAs who decide not to drink or to drink moderately will become alcoholic. If this is the case, making a decision about drinking in and of itself, without further therapy to eliminate the child and family problems, is not enough to prevent alcoholism in these children. Cork noted that the children she had rated as "most disturbed" were the children who planned to drink moderately or were already drinking.

Cork (1969) also looked at the grandparents of these children and found that two thirds of the fathers of alcoholic parents were alcoholic and 10% of their mothers were alcoholic. Half of the fathers and 7% of the mothers of the non-alcoholic parents were alcoholic. This seems to substantiate theories of an intergenerational process and makes these third-generation children truly at high risk, even those who have decided not to drink.

Although this multigenerational component could point to a genetically inherited problem, there are many other characteristics of interpersonal relationships that may be contributors as well. Cork (1969) deduced from her work that "the key to alcoholism lies in the interpersonal relationships within the family" (p. 79). She believes that the major environmental stresses affecting the parents and grandparents in this study were difficulties in marriage and family life.

Studies of COAs have revealed a wide range of child and family problems that occur in alcoholic families, depending on the nature of the study and the questions asked. There appear to be two focuses: an individual focus on the problems of children and a second focus on family relationship problems. Table 8.1 lists problems reported by children living in an alcoholic family. These problems were reported by families who had been identified as having alcohol-related difficulties by either social services or self-referral to therapy, and do not necessarily represent all families with alcoholic family members. Not all COAs have these problems, and some children without alcoholic parents will exhibit these problems. The areas of difficulties are (a) physical neglect or abuse, (b) acting-out behaviors, (c) emotional reactions to alcoholism and chaotic family life, and (d) social and interpersonal difficulties. It is possible that all of these

Table 8.1
Problems of Children Who Live in Alcoholic Families

Physical Neglect or Abuse
Serious illness
Accidents
Acting-Out Behaviors
Involvement with police and courts
Aggression
Alcohol and drug abuse
Emotional Reactions to Alcoholism and Chaotic Family Life
Suicidal tendencies
Depression
Repressed emotions
Lack of self-confidence
Lack of life direction
Fear of life direction
Fear of abandonment
Fear of future
Social and Interpersonal Difficulties
Family relationship problems
Peer problems
Adjustment problems
Feeling of being different from norm
Embarrassment
Hyperresponsibility
Feeling of being unloved, inability to trust

individual problems are a result of living in a system that is not functioning in the best interests of its members.

In a community sample of 235 mothers and fathers of kindergarten children, Keller, Cummings, and Davies (2005) found that problem drinking led to greater marital conflict, which was in turn related to ineffective parenting and poorer child adjustment. These researchers found that "marital conflict is related to ineffective parenting, specifically inconsistent discipline and psychological control" (p. 948), which in turn are associated with internalizing and externalizing problems in children.

Wilens et al. (2002) studied three groups of children ages 6 to 18 years old. The groups consisted of children of opioid-dependent parents, children of parents with alcohol use disorders, and children of parents with no substance use disorder. Wilens et al. found that 59% of the children of the opioid-dependent parents had a least one major psychopathological problem compared to 41% of the alcohol use disorder group and 28% of the controls. The children from the opioid and alcohol problem groups had lower socioeconomic status and significantly more difficulties in academic, social, and family functioning than the controls. Opioid-dependent parents reported significantly less cohesion than the alcohol and control groups as measured by the *Moos Family Environment Scale–Third Edition* (Moos & Moos, 1994).

When the mother is alcoholic, children experience more of these problems than when the father is alcoholic. When both parents are alcoholic, the child is without a parental resource (Cork, 1969; Fox, 1968). Table 8.2 lists family problems by dyadic marital relationship, parental relationship, and triadic parent–child relationships. Family therapy treats dysfunctional family relationships, separates overinvolved coalitions and joins underinvolved members, reduces family tension, and creates a new family balance at a higher level of functioning. This allows for each member to feel more fully centered and self-determined. As a result, the adaptive consequences of alcoholism are reduced or eliminated, and problem symptomatology in the children and parents often disappears. Family conflicts produce persons with a high degree of inner tension who may reduce anxiety with alcohol consumption (McCord, McCord, & Gudeman, 1960). If this family conflict is reduced, the inner tension of the alcoholic and the drinking may also be reduced or eliminated. With a reduction of family tension, individual members are able to survive in the family without rigid role behavior and can pursue self-determination that is not dependent on another family member.

Role Behavior in Children of Alcoholics

Satir, a pioneer in family therapy, identified role behaviors that family members play when they are under stress (Bandler, Grender, & Satir, 1976). Family members work hard at these roles to save the family system at the expense of their own emotional and physical health. Satir described these roles as follows:

1. The *placater* agrees with everyone, appears helpless, and feels worthless.
2. The *blamer* disagrees and blames but feels lonely and unsuccessful.

Table 8.2
Problems of the Alcoholic Family That Affect More Than One Person

Marital
Marital instability and fighting
Prolonged marital separation
Divorce
Death of a spouse
Physical abuse of a spouse
Parental
Inadequate parenting
Lack of structure
Inconsistent behavior
Emotional neglect of children
Inability or unwillingness to perform parental duties
Parent–Child Relationships
Physical and sexual abuse of children
Parentification of a child
Role reversal
Family conflicts
Isolation of family from society
Isolation of individual family members
Incongruent communication
Lack of trust between family members
Family secrets

3. The *computer* is logical and computes in a calm way but feels vulnerable.
4. The *distractor* makes no sense, is obtuse and off the subject, and feels nobody cares.

These roles hide the true feelings of these people and interfere with clear communication. When these role behaviors fail and the stress continues, family members change roles in a desperate attempt to cope.

Wegscheider (1981a, 1981b), a student of Satir, identified six role behaviors specific to an alcoholic family. These role behaviors function as defenses that cover the true feelings of the person and make communication difficult. These role behaviors are as follows:

1. The *dependent* is angry, rigid, a perfectionist, charming, righteous, and grandiose, but feels guilt, hurt, shame, fear, and pain.
2. The *chief enabler* is a spouse, parent, or coworker who assumes disproportionate responsibility but feels hurt, angry, guilty, and afraid.

3. The *family hero,* usually the oldest child, provides self-worth for the family with hard work, achievement, and success, but feels lonely, hurt, and inadequate. The achievement is for others and the family; the hero him- or herself is not rewarded with self-worth.
4. The *scapegoat* is the child who acts out, abuses alcohol and drugs, and takes the focus off the seemingly unsolvable family problem of alcoholism. The scapegoat volunteers for this position but feels lonely, rejected, hurt, and angry.
5. The *lost child* offers relief by not being a problem. These children withdraw and are quiet and independent, but they feel lonely, hurt, and inadequate.
6. The *mascot,* often the youngest child, provides fun and humor and distracts family members. The mascot is protected from what is really happening but senses the family tension and feels insecure, frightened, and lonely.

In Wegscheider's years of work with alcoholics, she has observed many family members assume these roles as a means of survival. She uses a family approach to help all of the family members recover and reestablish a functional family system.

These role behavior descriptions have often been used almost as pathological diagnostic categories for COAs and ACAs. In fact, these role behaviors can be found in any family. When stress is high, family members revert to these behaviors to problem-solve. The difficulty comes when the stress is constant and the role behaviors become rigid. These behaviors have even been described by Wegscheider (1981a, 1981b) and others as survival roles. The important thing for therapists to know is that these roles can become more flexible. The goal of therapy with a "family hero," therefore, is not to make him or her a "scapegoat," but to broaden the repertoire of behaviors of the individual within his or her chosen role. Wegscheider (1981b) discussed what is likely to happen in adulthood to children who are inflexibly identified with a given role. Without help, family heroes may become workaholics, take responsibility for everything, and marry a dependent person. With help, they can learn to relax, accept failure, and only take responsibility for themselves. The scapegoat may develop delinquency, have trouble at school or work, or have an unplanned pregnancy. With help, scapegoats can accept responsibility for their behavior, have the ability to see reality more clearly, and may become good counselors. Lost children are likely to have little zest for life, develop sexual identity problems, suffer from bedwetting, have difficulty with long-term relationships, and suffer premature death. With help, they can learn to be independent, talented, creative, and imaginative. Family mascots may become compulsive clowns, have difficulty with stress, marry a hero, and be at risk for chemical dependency. With help, they can give up their clownishness, learn to handle stress, and cultivate their sense of humor in a more balanced way.

Black (1979, 1981a) distinguished two types of role behaviors in COAs: (a) the misbehaving, obviously troubled children, and (b) the mature, stable, overachieving, well-behaved children (the majority, Black believes). Well-behaved children develop survival roles to provide their own stability. They learn the family rule: Don't talk about what is happening. They detach from others, repress their feelings, and take care of other family members. In the alcoholic family, the children learn to trust only themselves, and in school they are self-reliant and set short-term goals that will lead to accomplishment. Consequently, these children develop a good self-image through their successes outside of the home. As long as COAs are getting some secondary gains for their role behaviors, they maintain a positive self-image. This process works well until long-term life decisions have to be made, and COAs often find themselves unable to cope with adulthood when they reach their mid-20s. Alcohol alleviates their loneliness and pain. They repeat the stress reduction process that worked in their family of origin. COAs may also marry an alcoholic, perpetuating their childhood role behavior in their own families.

In her research on ACAs, Brown (1979) found that they are often unable to trust their own feelings and are afraid of not being in control. They may have problems with intimacy, responsibility, identification, and expression of feelings. As children, these people learned to avoid upsetting their parents by holding in their feelings at all costs. Their parents were unpredictable, and the children never could be certain how their parents would react to their expression of feelings.

Black (1979) classified COAs into three types of role behavior. "Responsible" children are usually the oldest children, who feel responsible for everyone. They provide structure for the family and become angry at themselves if they cannot control the situation. These children are adultlike, serious, rigid, and inflexible. They have little time for play or fun. Their self-reliance leads to loneliness, and they often marry alcoholics. This role is very similar to Wegscheider's family hero. "Adjusters" follow directions and must be flexible to adjust to the fighting, separation, and multiple life changes of the alcoholic family. They feel they have no power over their own lives. "Placaters" are emotionally sensitive children. They take care of others first to reduce their own pain and make life easier. They believe they do not deserve to have their own needs met. They smooth over conflicts and are rewarded for their help. They work too hard at taking care of others and neglect their own feelings and needs. Placaters can become "empty-nest" alcoholics when their own children grow up and no longer need care.

An example of the adjuster role is illustrated in the following case study. An 11-year-old girl, an adjuster, lived with her alcoholic father, who was divorced from the girl's mother when the daughter was less than a year old. His transient lifestyle took the two of them throughout the country, and his daughter never went to the same school for an entire year until she was placed in a foster home, after it was discovered that she had been sexually abused by her father for 5 years. This child explained to a child protective services worker that she did not mind the lifestyle except for the sexual abuse. When her father was not making progress in treatment, she explained this by saying, "You can't expect a lot from him, or you'll be disappointed." Her acceptance and adjustment represented a desperate attempt to hold on to the only family member she had ever known. Adjusters work hard at taking care of others and deny any feelings of their own. They are adaptable and adjust to many situations, but they are often manipulated by others and have low self-esteem.

These role behaviors can be rewarding—responsible children are successful, adjusters are adaptable, and placaters are appreciated—but they also entail negative consequences. The children who are rigidly attached to these role behaviors have difficulty expressing feelings, especially feelings with a negative connotation. In their family of origin, anger and sadness went unnoticed or were punished.

These roles do not change when COAs leave the alcoholic family or when the alcoholic achieves sobriety unless there is a positive change in the family system. The children relate to the behavior and attitudes of their parents, not to their parents' drinking (Cork, 1969). The children learn to deny their feelings because they are unable to tolerate their strong reactions to chaotic family situations. They protect themselves with denial and will continue to do so even when the parent's drinking stops.

In their report, Booz-Allen and Hamilton, Inc. (1974) identified four coping mechanisms that parallel the above-mentioned role behaviors of children:

1. Flight—Children who engage in the flight coping mechanism avoid the alcoholic by not being at home, hiding in their rooms, running away, becoming involved in activities outside of the home, going to college, getting married, getting a job, emotionally withdrawing, blocking memory, or turning to religion.
2. Fight—Children who cope by fighting are the aggressive, rebellious, acting-out children that are typically seen as behavior problems. They sometimes end up in court or are placed out of the home.
3. Perfect child—Children who cope by striving for perfection never do anything wrong. They mind their parents and excel in school. Parents bring them out of the shadows to show them off as examples to the others.
4. Supercoper—Children who cope by being hyperresponsible are usually oldest children. They sometimes become confidantés of non-alcoholic spouses. They are parentified children who feel responsible for the other family members.

In practice, the role behaviors of COAs do not fall into discrete categories. Children typically have blends of several of these behaviors and use different ones at different times or switch to different roles. A family hero who goes off to college and is influenced by his peer group to drink abusively (and fails at school) can quickly become the scapegoat. If a scapegoat leaves home and the family is still in need of one, the next youngest may fill the scapegoat position.

Table 8.3 combines the child behavior roles of Black, Wegscheider, and Booz-Allen and Hamilton, Inc., to highlight the similarities of these role behaviors. The Satir role behaviors, which pertain to all of the family members, parallel the role behaviors outlined by the other researchers.

Veronie and Fruehstorfer (2001) attempted to determine the influence of family dynamics on role behaviors. In their study of child gender, alcoholic parent gender, and child birth order, they found significant gender differences for the mascot and lost child. Mascots were less likely in families with both a male and female alcoholic. Veronie and Fruehstorfer hypothesized that the mascot might be a luxury for an alcoholic family. The hero creates esteem for the family, and the scapegoat absorbs negative emotion, and they are thus more critical to the alcoholic family system.

Treatment to Help Children

Children who live in alcoholic families are sometimes identified as "the problem" and sometimes seem like perfect children. Both of these roles take the focus off the central problems of negative family dynamics, marital stress, and the tension around the abuse

Table 8.3
Child Behavior Roles of Black, Booz-Allen and Hamilton, Inc., Wegscheider, and Satir

Black (1981a)	Booz-Allen & Hamilton, Inc. (1974)	Wegscheider (1981a, 1981b)	Characteristic	Satir (Bandler et al., 1976)
Adjuster	Flight	Lost children	Loneliness, isolation Escapes, never complains Will not cause further problems	Irrelevant (no place for me)
(No roles)	Fight	Scapegoat	Hurt, anger, rejection Feelings are close to the surface Takes the focus off of the alcoholic	Blamer (lonely and unsuccessful)
Placater	Perfect child	Mascot	Provides relief Emotionally isolated Makes others feel good	Placater (feels worthless)
Responsible one	Supercoper	Family hero	Loneliness Overachiever Parentified	Super-responsible (vulnerable, no feeling)

of alcohol. The best way to help children who live in alcoholic families is to improve the functioning of the nuclear family. Improvement in family communication patterns, rebuilding of marital and parental relationships, reestablishment of trust and respect, and facilitation of emotional contact will improve the family environment.

If the alcoholic is still drinking, work with the non-alcoholic spouse could lead to identifying the non-alcoholic parent as the primary protector and caretaker for the children. The spouse must stop taking responsibility for the alcoholic's drinking or sobriety. It is difficult for anyone to solve a problem when someone else has taken responsibility for it. The spouse could then begin to take care of himself or herself and begin to structure the home environment, as well as consistently parent the children. Hecht (1973) stated, "The spouse, as much as possible, must avoid assigning tasks to the children that they are not ready to undertake, and avoid directing toward them the anger the nonalcoholic parent feels toward the alcoholic" (p. 1767).

In addition to the family work, children can benefit from group work with other children. The group provides them with a place where they can express feelings without fear of reprisal and where role behavior is not necessary. In this setting, children also realize that they are not alone and that they can establish relationships with peers. Ackerman (1978) noted, "Helping children of alcoholics to work through their feelings and establish effective relationships with others will be very helpful in overcoming the impact of an alcoholic parent" (p. 109). When children develop self-confidence, they feel they can control themselves and influence life outcomes. These feelings are preventative medicine for children who are at high risk for turning to alcohol as a problem solver.

Black (1981a) recommended using group work with children to let them know that they are not alone, that their parents' alcoholism is not their fault, that addiction is hard to stop but the parent can get help, and that the children need to take care of themselves. Black (1981a) also recommended using art therapy in her children's groups to help them talk about difficult subjects. Black (1981a) (quoted in Patterson, 1980) noted, "Asking youngsters to draw pictures of their family life and their views on alcoholism helps reverse a tendency in the children to deny the existence of a problem" (p. 18).

Treatment Outcome Research

Even when the children are not involved in therapy, they show improvement in psychosocial functioning when their substance-abusing fathers are treated with behavioral couples therapy (Kelly & Fals-Stewart, 2002). Kelly and Fals-Stewart compared three treatment modalities for alcohol- and drug-abusing men: couples-based treatment (CBT), individual-based treatment (IBT), and a couples-based psychoeducational attention control treatment (PACT). For both alcohol- and drug-abusing men, children's psychosocial functioning was higher in the CBT group both at the end of treatment and at 6- and 12-month follow-up than it was in the other two groups. The CBT group reported greater improvements in their marital relationships and in the fathers' substance abuse. From a family systems point of view, there was a second-order change that happened in these families, where a significant change in the marital relationship and in the identified patient yielded a change in the children.

In a recent study of the psychosocial adjustment of COAs, Andreas, O'Farrell, and Fals-Stewart (2006) measured the adjustment prior to and at three follow-up times in the 15 months after the alcoholic fathers' admission to treatment. Before treatment, the children had greater clinical-level symptomatology than the matched sample. They improved significantly after their fathers' treatment. The children whose fathers had a stable recovery were similar to the matched controls, with fewer adjustment problems than children whose fathers relapsed. The fathers' recovery was associated with significant reduction in the children's problems. An earlier study also indicated that COAs whose parents received treatment and remained sober for 2 years afterward had emotional functioning similar to that of the control group (Moos & Billings, 1982; Moos, Finney, & Cronkite, 1990) . It is very encouraging that a change in the fathers' drinking behavior, as a result of treatment and sustained recovery, could have a positive effect on the children. Several earlier studies, including DeLucia, Belz, and Chassin (2001), did not indicate a positive change in the children when fathers recovered, but we believe this finding might have been due to the fact that they studied adolescents, whereas Andreas et al. studied children ages 4 to 16. The length of time the children were exposed to the fathers' alcoholism may be a factor. Andreas et al.'s finding is consistent with family systems theory, which suggests that a change in any part of the system affects all of the other parts. Thus, the alcoholic parent's recovery has the potential to affect every part of the system. Family therapy posttreatment or during the individual treatment of the substance abuser would certainly enhance this possibility.

Kelly and Fals-Stewart (2007) examined the effect on preadolescent and adolescent children of a treatment model that combines behavioral couples therapy and individual counseling for alcoholic fathers and non-substance-abusing mothers. This model combines conjoint treatment, individual counseling, and group therapy (Learning Sobriety Together, or LST). Kelly and Fals-Stewart found that improvement in children's externalizing behaviors was stronger for preadolescents than for adolescents and that adolescents were generally more resistant to the effects of improvement in the couple's relationship after alcoholism treatment (see also DeLucia et al., 2001). More direct treatment may be needed for adolescents, who may have had longer exposure to the father's drinking and marital discord.

Positive effects were seen in several areas using a multifamily group therapy approach that involved several families over a period of 4 to 12 weeks, including the addicted member(s): participants' continued sobriety, increased knowledge and awareness of addiction issues, and increased closeness and better understanding among family members (Litzke & Glazer, 2004). This was a semistructured psychoeducational group based on a family systems approach. It was designed to intervene on an informational, attitudinal, and behavioral level. One of the components, Quality Time, included family mealtime and nutrition information. Genograms (family maps) were used to track multigenerational addictions and family relationships.

The school is also a setting for treatment and prevention for COAs. Lambie (2005) stated that many COAs remain unidentified in schools, calling for school counselors to identify these high-risk children and provide the counseling services they need. School provides an opportunity to intervene with children who may have generations of substance abuse in their families of origin. Intervention with these children has the potential to stop a multigenerational problem even if the parents aren't in treatment.

A Model Prevention Program

Treating the behavioral or emotional problems of children who have lived with an alcoholic parent is surely a major step in preventing these high-risk children from becoming alcoholics themselves. Such children have been overlooked in alcohol treatment in favor of working individually with the alcoholic or the marital couple, but they should become a target population for prevention efforts. In the 1980s, some treatment centers pioneered special group programs for children of their clients. These were support groups with structured activities. For example, Black (1979, 1981a) used art therapy with groups of children in a California treatment center. However, this direct treatment with young COAs diminished with the advent of the powerful ACA social movement, which put the focus on the problems these children have as adults.

The Children From Alcoholic Families Program provides a model of a prevention designed specifically for COAs. Developed in the early 1980s and still funded by the Nebraska Division on Alcohol and Drug Abuse, this program is based on the theory of prevention through reduction of risk in the physiological, sociological, and psychological areas. There is little that can be done to move children from high risk to low risk in the physiological area. Genetically, these children may be unable to drink without problems. However, children can be educated about this high-risk factor and can be taught warning signals if they should choose to drink. Changes can be made, though, in the sociological and psychological areas.

Sociologically, these children have lived in an environment where alcohol has been used abusively. People have modeled drinking to get drunk and to avoid reality. Often the other parent drank abusively, as well, or abstained and was morally critical of the spouse. Neither of these positions models a responsible approach to alcohol. In this program, parents become more aware of the model they are setting for their children, and they talk about appropriate and inappropriate drinking with their children. They can educate their children about alcohol and begin to open up communication processes in the family so that the children can come to the parents when they need answers to difficult questions. Parents are also taught new parenting strategies. Improvement in parenting skills can lower the risk factors of the children. Children who learn to make good choices, who feel responsible for their behavior, and who can control their environment will grow up with more self-assurance and tolerance for stress.

Ethnic factors are examined, and the family history of alcoholism is charted in a genogram over the course of three generations. Generally, an effort is made through education and family therapy to improve the family system, including communication patterns, parenting skills, and drinking-related values, all of which affect the children.

Psychologically, prevention of alcoholism in these children of alcoholic families involves improving self-esteem and allowing the children to feel they can make good decisions and be capable people. Chemically dependent persons have low self-esteem, are unable to cope, are unable to relate to others, and are lacking in decision-making ability. They also have unhealthy dependencies and a low tolerance for tension (Glenn, 1981).

To decrease these children's risk factors, work is done to promote a positive self-image and to teach them the life skills needed to create successful life experiences. Group work is used to improve their ability to relate to peers, enhance their ability to make decisions, increase their independence, and develop positive techniques to help them deal with stress (see also Albee, 1981, for a prevention model focused on problems that are multicausal).

Figure 8.1 is a schematic representation that can be viewed as a fraction. Prevention occurs when the numerator is reduced or the denominator is increased. COAs can do little about the organic factors related to an inherited genetic predisposition to alcoholism, and it is impossible to eliminate stress from the environment. It seems more possible to increase the denominator by teaching coping skills to the children and their families, increasing the competence and self-esteem of all of the individuals involved in

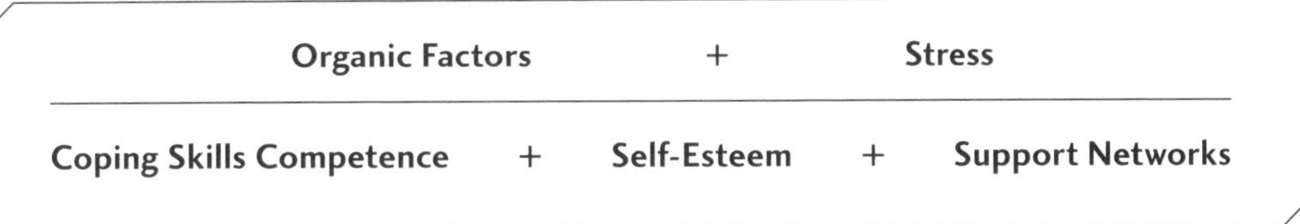

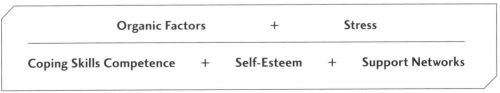

Figure 8.1. Prevention fraction.

the program, and connecting these people with support networks in the aftercare portion of the program.

The Children From Alcoholic Families Program works in three areas to increase the denominator of the prevention fraction. The children's groups increase their coping skills, build their competence, and improve their self-esteem. The family therapy component improves the children's communication skills, enhances family relationships, and increases problem-solving abilities. The aftercare component provides support groups and connects families and individuals with community agencies and resources that build support networks for these children and their families.

The Children From Alcoholic Families Program is housed in the Lincoln/Lancaster County Child Guidance Center and is not affiliated with any alcohol treatment program, nor does it support any one treatment philosophy for alcoholism. It was created to prevent alcoholism by interrupting the intergenerational processes of alcoholism. The focus is on the children.

The program has five components:

1. *Intake component.* The goal of the intake component is to screen and evaluate children and families to determine family goals, degree of risk, and areas in need of treatment. Families are eligible if at least one parent has had a drinking problem or currently is drinking abusively. These families may include a parent with long-term sobriety, a parent having recently entered or completed chemical dependency treatment, or a chemically dependent parent without sobriety. At intake, children are referred to an age-appropriate group; parents are placed in the parents' group; and a case manager/family therapist is assigned to the family. The groups are closed and time limited (6 weeks). Family therapy occurs once a week in addition to the groups.

2. *Parents' component.* The parents are offered a two-pronged approach: a psychoeducational group and individual treatment for stress management. The parents' group is a forum for discussion of prevention strategies, role behaviors, family systems, and parenting education. Individual treatment includes biofeedback to encourage increased control of the automatic functions that affect levels of bodily tension and relaxation. The client is taught how to obtain more complete relaxation in the bodily musculature most vulnerable to tension buildup. At least one parent is required to attend the parents' group. If the alcoholic will not attend, work is done with the spouse to improve the family environment and possibly change the family system.

3. *Children's component.* The children experience alcohol education, socialization, and treatment for emotional and behavioral problems through a peer group modality. Therapists attempt to induce a level of comfort conducive to the spontaneous expression of feeling. The intent of the group is to communicate that reasonable freedom of expression should exist without fear of reprisal and that inflexible role behavior should not be necessary.

The goals of these peer groups are to (a) let the children know they are not alone; (b) inform them that it is not their fault that their parents are alcoholics; (c) teach them about the nature of addictions and the difficulty their parents have in achieving and maintaining sobriety; (d) reassure them that alcoholism is treatable; (e) help them learn about themselves and take care of themselves; (f) allow for expression of positive and negative feelings; (g) foster improved peer relationship skills; (h) teach problem-solving techniques; and (i) evaluate the level of coping skills, social skills, and overall function in conjunction with the family. This diagnostic information is needed to determine a reasonable plan for aftercare or continued treatment involvement.

4. *Family component.* Each family has a family therapy session once a week for 6 weeks. Family therapy goals are unique to each family. The goal of this component is to allow the family to view the effects of alcoholism on each member and the system as a whole. The family can then view the problem as it exists within the family system and begin to move from an unhealthy system to a healthy system. That is, the family can move from being a family with secrets and limited intimacy, with hidden rules in which only performance has value, to a healthier family system. The healthy state allows open communication and can accept differences, negotiates rules openly, and values the feelings of its members. Because each family is unique, the type and degree of change needed to achieve a healthier system varies. However, the overall goal is movement toward a healthy system that produces children who are emotionally strong.

5. *Aftercare component.* When the family members have completed the 6-week group and family sessions, an aftercare assessment is conducted by gathering information from each counselor who is familiar with a family member, results of formal evaluations, and contacts with other sources in the community capable of providing a measure of social and emotional coping. The results of this assessment determine if the family member would benefit from further family therapy, inclusion in a long-term aftercare group, referral to self-help groups (i.e., Al-Anon, AA, Alateen, or Alakid), referral to the child guidance center's Children of Divorce Project, or a networking of family members to outside supports and recreation facilities. The long-term support groups are an extension of the children's groups, but with less intensity. Therapeutic camping experiences for these groups are being developed in conjunction with the YWCA. Further, many families who have participated in the Children From Alcoholic Families Program are working to establish an Adult Children From Alcoholic Families group to address the intergenerational issues of alcoholism.

Given the range of problems and coping skills across families, each family in the aftercare component of the Children From Alcoholic Families Program is assessed individually, and risk for the children is estimated. The aftercare plan reflects the needs of the family. Booz-Allen and Hamilton, Inc. (1974) underscored the need to recognize that families are different. They concluded that

> parental alcoholism is not equally disruptive in all families. In some cases, alcoholism is a relatively minor characteristic in the total fiber of family life; the family functions well with a basically positive atmosphere, whether in spite of or because of the alcoholism of a parent. If the situation is not seriously uncomfortable, the child need not take extreme measures to defend himself against it; he simply accommodates the alcoholism as a limited problem. (p. 41)

Focusing on the strengths of families disrupted by alcohol problems, the Children From Alcoholic Families Program gives them concrete methods for reducing their children's risk. Further, families are given realistic projections for the success of their family functioning and are encouraged to develop their own support networks after leaving the program.

In sum, COAs are at high risk for developing behavioral and emotional problems, as well as alcoholism. These problems can be seen in aggressive, acting-out behavior or can be hidden behind achieving, mature, perfect behavior. These seemingly perfect children can have difficulties in relationships as they grow older, and are at risk for abusing alcohol. Even children who make a decision to avoid alcohol may turn to alcohol when they can no longer cope. COAs often develop resiliencies and strengths as they learn to cope with destructive family environments. This topic will be covered more thoroughly in the next section.

Adult Children of Alcoholics

As alcoholism came to be seen as a problem that affects not just the individual but also family members and others around the alcoholic, the scope of treatment widened to include family members, including children. There was one affected group, however, that was ignored until the early 1980s, when it was recognized that adults who were raised in alcoholic families did not escape their families unharmed. They often brought a variety of problems with them into adulthood and played out in their own families what they learned or did not learn in their families of origin. Jacobson (1991) reported that the term *adult children of alcoholics* (ACAs) was first used in 1979, and this naming was pivotal to the rise of the powerful ACA movement. Black (1987) reported that

> the term "Adult Children of Alcoholics" was one that Stephanie Brown and I coined as we described our work to Newsweek magazine in 1979 ... We thought that within the adult today who was raised in an alcoholic home, there is a child that continues to need nurturing. That same child still needs to learn skills that many others learned in childhood. (p. xxvi)

A generation of self-help books aimed at ACAs followed. Claudia Black's (1981b) *It Will Never Happen to Me* and Janet Woititz's (1983) *Adult Children of Alcoholics* deeply affected many of the 21 million ACAs in the United States, many of whom began to seek help. The acknowledgment of the long-range consequences of living in a chaotic, alcoholic family began the drive to legitimate treatment for this population. This drive brought with it, however, a trend to pathologize all ACAs. The ACA label began to be seen as a diagnosis, even though there is no official psychiatric diagnosis for ACAs and it was never intended to function as such. Stephanie Brown (1983) pointed out, "Patients and therapists alike are using the term inappropriately as if there were an individual diagnosis" (p. 281).

As the popular literature grew concerning ACAs, a pathological profile developed with a long list of problems attributed to ACAs. Most of these problem lists came from therapists treating ACAs who actively sought therapy, but the problems were falsely generalized to the entire population of ACAs. The popular literature cites the following problems:

1. difficulty with intimate relationships
2. lack of trust in others
3. fear of loss of control
4. conflicts over personal responsibility characterized by super-responsible or super-irresponsible behavior
5. denial of feelings and of reality
6. harsh and relentless self-criticism
7. low self-esteem and lack of identity
8. denial of personal needs
9. black-and-white thinking
10. inability to relax or have fun
11. fear of abandonment

This is only a partial list of problems attributed to ACAs. Vannicelli (1989) listed 30 problems she found in the popular literature, but noted that many of these were problems that the general public also brings to therapy. They are not unique to ACAs. Vannicelli further pointed out that ACAs themselves are not all the same and don't all have the same profile of problems. Factors that differentiate the type and severity of problems ACAs bring into therapy include the following (Vannicelli, 1989):

1. whether one or both parents are alcoholics
2. the age of the child at the onset of the parent's alcoholism
3. the economic stability of the family
4. the availability and use of external support
5. the duration and severity of the alcoholism
6. the number of generations of addiction in the family
7. the successful recovery of the alcoholic
8. the presence of psychiatric illnesses in the family
9. the presence of physical or sexual abuse in the family
10. the abilities of the non-alcoholic spouse

Several studies have reported negative effects of parental alcoholism on adults who were raised in alcoholic families. For example, one study indicated that women were more pessimistic about the future, endured more emotional and physical hardship, and showed more impulsivity (Baker & Stephenson, 1995). In another study, women ACAs reported higher levels of depression and lower levels of self-esteem; lower levels of social support, family cohesion, and marital satisfaction and higher marital conflict; more parental role distress; more feelings of powerlessness; and more drinking to cope and relieve stress (Domenico & Windle, 1993). Women ACAs were also found to have a distinctive dysfunctional attachment profile as compared to men (El-Guebaly, West, Maticka-Tyndale, & Pool, 1993). Women with alcoholic parents had worse outcomes on social adjustment, alcohol problems, depressed mood, and life satisfaction. The effect of parental alcoholism was indirect and mediated by other stressors and resources (Griffin, Amodeo, Fassler, Ellis, & Clay, 2005).

In a sample of college students, parental alcoholism was positively related to psychological distress (Kashubeck, 1994). In families where family process was negatively affected by parental alcoholism, dating relationships were negatively affected, and parental divorce was directly related to this effect (Larson & Reedy, 2004). A study on attachment style and relationship satisfaction in college students indicated that ACAs had a significantly higher need for control and lower relationship satisfaction (Beesley, 2002). However, there was no significant difference between ACAs and non-ACAs on the measure of insecure attachment. Another study indicated that ACAs experienced less intimacy in their closest current relationship (Martin, 1995).

Jaeger, Hahn, and Weinraub (2000) used attachment theory to study female college students with alcoholic fathers. These ACAs were found to have less secure attachment organization than the matched comparison group, but did not have higher scores on compulsive caregiving. Not all of the ACAs had insecure attachments, which may be related to resilience in this population. There was considerable heterogeneity within the group. Jaeger et al. concluded that studying attachment issues may be helpful in understanding parenting problems in alcoholic families.

Jacob, Windle, Seilhamer, and Bost (1999) compared three groups of adults: 84 ACAs from intact families whose alcoholic parent did not have a diagnosed psychiatric disorder in addition to alcoholism, 111 adult offspring of normal controls (CONs), and 102 adult offspring of a non-alcoholic parent with depression (CODs). They found that the ACAs had more problems with drinking, drug use, behavioral control, and educational achievement than the CONs or the CODs. Specifically, ACAs were more likely to be diagnosed with alcoholism (21.1%) than CONs (9.2%) or CODs (6.9%). ACAs were also more likely to use drugs (13.1%) than CONs (2.7%) or CODs (10.7%). Further, the ACAs had more externalizing behavior and exhibited more undercontrolled behavior. Lower socioeconomic status of the ACA families increased risk. An interesting finding was the difference in the amount of alcoholism in female subjects. Seventeen percent of daughters of alcoholics became alcoholics, in contrast with 2% of CONs and 4.5% of CODs, whereas 27.3% of the sons became alcoholics. The authors hypothesized that the daughters might have been more sensitive to the family environment or experienced less cultural pressure to drink than the sons.

Zhou, King, and Chassin (2006) examined family harmony as a mediator of the effects of family alcoholism on the development of drug versus alcohol abuse in young ACAs. They also considered the density of family alcoholism, or the number of alcoholic relatives in the family. A higher density of family alcoholism was predictive of lower family harmony during adolescence. That high conflict, in turn, increased the likelihood of substance dependence in early adulthood for these adolescents. Zhou et al. distinguished between alcohol and drug disorders. They found that family harmony decreased the risk of drug use, with or without alcohol dependence, as compared to only alcohol dependence or adolescents with no diagnosis. Family harmony did not differentiate those with alcohol dependence from those with no diagnosis, however. The positive effects of family harmony varied when the density of family alcoholism rose. Family harmony was not effective in protecting against drug abuse in families with a high density of alcoholism.

Flora and Chassin (2005) found that parental alcoholism was associated with higher rates of drug use during the transition from emerging adulthood to young adulthood. The sample consisted of COAs who had at least one alcoholic biological parent who was also a custodial parent and a demographically matched group with no parental alcoholism (non-COAs). The non-COAs significantly decreased their drug use during the transition from emerging adulthood into young adulthood, but the COAs did not. Flora and Chassin also found that COAs were significantly less likely to be married, and that for the male subjects, marriage was associated with a decrease in drug use during the mid to late 20s. The non-abstaining COA men used drugs approximately weekly, whereas the non-abstaining non-COA men's use decreased from one to three times a month to slightly less than monthly. By the age of 25 to 30, the level of drug use by COAs was much higher than that of non-COAs, suggesting that COAs do not mature out of drug use before age 30.

King and Chassin (2004) tested the deviance proneness model of alcohol use (Sher, 1991) in a study of the relationship between parenting during adolescence and drug use during the transition to adulthood in a sample of COAs. The deviance proneness model proposes that parental alcoholism increases the risk of alcohol use problems in young adulthood. Behavioral undercontrol and poor parenting lead to conduct problems, emotional distress, school failure, and affiliation with a deviant peer network, resulting in elevated risk for alcohol use and associated problems. Behavioral undercontrol among alcoholic parents was strongly related to drug abuse and dependence in emerging adulthood. King and Chassin stated, "Adolescents who are impulsive and high in sensation seeking are likely to have difficulty in school, coping with emotional distress, and forming relationships with peers, thus raising the risk for affiliation with drug-using peers and subsequent drug abuse and dependence" (p. 245). Adolescents of non-alcoholics experienced more parental discipline and had reduced risk for drug use. These findings suggest that COAs are at a greater risk than non-COAs for developing drug problems due to their impulsiveness, high sensation seeking, and lack of parental discipline.

Research has also indicated a difference between ACAs who enter therapy and those who do not. Barnard and Spoentgen (1986) compared college-age ACAs who went to the campus clinic for therapy with ACAs at the same college who did not. They found that those who sought treatment had more parental loss, fewer financial resources, lower inner-directedness, lower self-regard, lower self-acceptance, lower capacity for intimate contact, and more reactivity. This finding is important because it indicates that research done with a clinical population cannot be generalized to the population as a whole. Barnard and Spoentgen also found that the 8-week group therapy for ACAs was effective in improving inner-directedness, self-regard, and capacity for intimate contact with others.

Noting that ACA researchers tend to study college students to the exclusion of other types of samples, Kashubeck and Christensen (1992) compared ACA 12-step support group members with ACA college students who were not attending these groups. They found that "support group members reported higher levels of psychological distress, lower levels of hardiness, and less satisfaction with perceived social support than did the college student ACAs" (p. 356). The support group members had more negative attitudes, feelings, and behaviors surrounding parental alcoholism. Subjects who reported hardiness and social support had less psychological distress. This study provides more evidence that ACAs are not a homogenous group.

More recent studies have suggested that in the early excitement of the ACA movement, the problems of ACAs may have been overstated (Hunt, 1997). Hunt did a secondary analysis of longitudinal data comparing COAs and non-COAs. Few differences were found between the two groups on family-of-origin factors. The parents in the COA group were less educated and from a lower socioeconomic class. The COAs did, however, report less supportiveness from mothers and more inconsistent parenting. They did not see their parents' marriage as something to emulate. Hunt concluded that the clinical literature on ACAs may have overgeneralized the experiences of COAs in treatment to the larger population.

Rodney (1996) reviewed 50 research literature entries concerning ACAs between 1981 and 1996. She found many inconsistencies, including varying definitions of ACAs and empirical findings about their characteristics, their roles, and how they differed from non-ACAs. She concluded, "Clinicians and those who develop alcohol prevention programs should stop believing that certain characteristics are typical of all adult children of alcoholics" (p. 19).

In an earlier study, Rodney (1994) found no significant differences between college-age African American ACAs and non-ACAs in terms of the amount of support they received as adolescents from their father, their closest friend, or a significant other (e.g., teacher, minister, coach). Rodney also found that health in the family of origin and availability of and use of mother support were related to lower levels of problem drinking. In addition, she reported a gender difference. For female ACAs, the level of health in the family of origin or other social support was not related to the mastery of developmental tasks in the ACA group. For the male ACAs, social support from a significant adult and felt support from their mothers were related to greater mastery of developmental tasks and a sense of purpose.

In a study that compared ACAs with adult children of divorced parents and controls, the authors found no group differences on current outcome measures when they controlled for stressors often associated with alcoholic families (parental depression and antisocial personality, maternal alcoholism, and low socioeconomic status) (Senchak, Leonard, Greene, & Carroll, 1995). The ACAs and children of divorced parents reported more conflict than controls, and the ACAs reported less warmth from their fathers. Senchak et al. concluded, "Our findings suggest that negative outcomes among adult children of alcoholics are neither pervasive nor specific to paternal alcoholism" (p. 152).

Assortative Mating

When ACAs are examined in the general (nonclinical) population, some of the problems they are believed to share as a group are not validated. Boye-Beaman, Leonard, and Senchak (1991), in a longitudinal research project examining alcohol use and marital functioning of newlywed couples, discovered an interesting pattern of assortative mating. They found that daughters of alcoholics, who have been thought to frequently marry alcoholics, were no more likely to marry heavy drinkers than were those not raised in an alcoholic home. The same was true of sons of alcoholics. They were no more likely to marry a woman who drinks heavily. The COAs were, however, twice as likely to marry each other as those not from alcoholic families. Heavy drinkers, as well, were more likely to marry other heavy drinkers than expected by chance. Another important point made by the research team was that many of the COAs did not marry spouses who were raised in alcoholic families. Nearly 70% of women from alcoholic families married men from non-alcoholic families, and 59% of men from alcoholic families married women from non-alcoholic families. It may be that at least some ACAs are deliberately selecting spouses from well-functioning non-alcoholic families. Bennett, Wolin, and Reiss (1988) reported that such deliberate mating choices reduce the transmission of alcoholism across generations. This research is discussed in the next section, on the intergenerational transmission of alcoholism.

A more recent study of assortative mating showed that non-alcoholic daughters of alcoholics were more than twice as likely to marry an alcoholic as non-alcoholic daughters of non-alcoholics, regardless of the gender of the alcoholic parent (Schuckit, Tipp, & Keiner, 1994). Sons of alcoholics, however, did not marry alcoholics more frequently than daughters of non-alcoholics.

A longitudinal study of a nonclinical, non-self-identified sample of 128 married and engaged young couples indicated that alcoholics tend to marry other alcoholics, with male ACAs more likely than females to be identified as "moderate-to-severe" and "severe only" (Olmstead, Crowell, & Waters, 2003). The authors noted, however, that females tend to develop alcohol problems later in life and progress more rapidly. Alcoholic subjects were more likely to be married to other alcoholics, regardless of the severity. Another finding was that both male and female ACAs were more likely to marry moderate-to-severe alcoholics, but not severe-only alcoholics. Olmstead et al. noted that therapists need to be aware that ACAs are at risk for alcoholism and that females are at risk for marrying an alcoholic, suggesting that ACAs and their partners who enter therapy should be screened for alcoholism.

A Developmental Model

In trying to understand the etiology of ACA problems, it is most useful to view them as developmental problems that are solvable. This does not eliminate the possibility that ACAs may also have severe mental illnesses that may require more treatment. A developmental view helps to clarify why some ACAs seem problem free, while others seem to struggle with life.

Depending on the time of onset and the severity of alcoholism in the family, COAs arrive at adulthood having missed out on normal childhood development. If the alcoholic parents are consumed by their illness early in the child's life, care may be inadequate, inconsistent, and rejecting. The infant learns that he or she cannot depend on his or her parents and does not develop the sense of trust that is necessary to move to the next step in healthy child development. This failure to develop a sense of trust interferes with adult interpersonal relationships and intimacy (Beletsis & Brown, 1981). As children move into their second and third years, they begin to explore their world more actively. In alcoholic families, children are often stifled in many ways so they won't upset the drinking or hungover parent. If this restriction is excessive, the child develops a sense of shame about his or her natural inquisitiveness. At this stage, the child may be overprotected from the negative environment and limited in a way that denies the child a sense of self-control. Adults who experience these restrictions as children feel a sense of shame and a lack of control. As the child becomes more involved with the environment, motor skills develop. In alcoholic families, curiosity is often treated as inappropriate. Feelings and play are shut down, and children are often blamed for their parents' problems. The child can develop a sense of guilt and blame that lasts throughout his or her life.

As the child goes off to school, he or she begins to separate from his or her parents. This developmental milestone is accomplished when the child knows that he or she can return to the nurturing home. The child of the alcoholic is often unequipped to navigate this separation. At the same time, the child may be pushed to take on adult responsibilities. In school, the child may become an excellent student, driven to perfection that is never achieved; alternatively, the child may give up before he or she even starts. The COA may reach adulthood with a sense of helplessness and inferiority.

Adolescent COAs find themselves trying to develop an identity and separate from their families. Children who have mastered earlier developmental tasks have developed the self-esteem and confidence required for these difficult tasks. In the alcoholic family, needs, feelings, and true identity are denied. Beletsis and Brown (1981) noted that "the driving need to deny feelings and needs is a denial of self" (p. 204).

The pull to remain in the alcoholic family system either doesn't allow the child to leave or pushes the child to rebel. The rebellion may turn into early marriage (sometimes to alcoholics or dependent spouses) or an exit from home under negative circumstances. The child may leave adolescence with only the facade of an identity that covers fear of autonomy and confusion about life direction.

Early adulthood for the ACA is a time of denial of personal problems, a denial of personal needs, and a feeling of having escaped the chaos of the alcoholic family. It is not until the late 20s, nearing Levinson's (1978) "Age-Thirty Transition," that children from alcoholic families begin to recognize their emotional attachment to the struggles of their childhood. People often find themselves approaching 30 alone, after several disastrous relationships, overly devoted to their career, unsure of their goals, unable to trust, obsessed with controlling everyone and everything, and terrified of intimacy yet desperately wanting it. This identity crisis may include the discovery that they have been acting all of their life, and they don't know who they are. This may lead them to seek therapy.

Those ACAs who do not respond at this age may find themselves at 40 still emotionally tied to their families of origin. They are still trying to fix things, but as they approach the mid-life transition of the 40s, they may be forced to look more closely at themselves. There is a strong possibility that they will find themselves repeating the patterns and dynamics of their families of origin. They may be alcoholic themselves, married to alcoholics or divorced from several, and they may be raising children in the same environment in which they were raised. This is the time when they can take some steps to break the intergenerational chain of alcoholism, or they can conclude that there is never going to be any hope for them as they slide into self-pity and stagnation. Many ACAs seek therapy at this time.

ACAs who miss this chance may find themselves in later years looking back on their lives as a series of missed opportunities and disastrous relationships; they feel a sense of despair. If the chain of alcoholism was not broken, they may experience a repetition of the same problems in their children and grandchildren.

Looking at ACA problems from a developmental perspective clarifies our understanding of the etiology of the common problems experienced by ACAs. The problems that exist for ACAs can be linked directly to the years of their lives that were disrupted by the alcoholism of their parents. For instance, ACAs with intimacy problems may have been deprived of a nurturing parental relationship early in life. Other problems that ACAs may experience are lack of trust, obsession with control, fear of intimacy, fear of feelings, lack of self-identity, fear of conflict, inability to relax, overresponsibility, and black-and-white thinking. Some of the research and popular literature on ACAs makes it seem like such problems are immutable. However, recasting such problems as developmental lags gives therapists a new perspective that has great potential for treatment.

Just as there are stages of development that children and adults pass through in life, so there are stages of recovery for ACAs. Gravitz and Bowden (1984, 1990) observed from a clinical perspective that ACAs present clearly delineated patterns of problems that develop and unfold sequentially. They grouped these into six developmental stages: the survival stage, the emergent awareness stage, the core issue stage, the transformation stage, the integration stage, and the genesis stage.

ACAs in the survival stage are still operating with the role behaviors they learned in their childhood to survive the turmoil of their alcoholic families. Although these behaviors may have been adaptive at one time, they limit choices and spontaneity in adulthood. ACAs in this stage experience a varying amount of psychological stress, but they do not connect it to their parents' alcoholism or the family disruption this caused. They often remain in this stage unless an event such as reading a newspaper story or attending a lecture on ACA issues breaks their denial, and they begin to make the connection between their present nonproductive behavior and their parents' alcoholism. Those ACAs who remain in this stage are at high risk for becoming alcoholic or marrying an alcoholic.

The denial-breaking event marks the beginning of the emergent awareness stage. These adult children begin to identify themselves as ACAs and become aware of their physiological and psychological vulnerabilities. They often seek education about the syndrome, attend lectures, and read incessantly. They discover that they are not alone and begin to see the connections between their past and present behavior. Along with the excitement of these new discoveries comes the guilt associated with breaking the long-standing family rule of silence.

Stephanie Brown (1986), who pioneered a program of long-term ACA groups at the Stanford Alcohol Clinic, described ACAs who decide to join their groups as being in this stage. The decision to participate in the group represents a conscious choice to break the denial, look at the myths, and tell the family secrets. People join the groups so they can separate from their families of origin by joining the substitute family of the group. The decision to join an ACA group poses a paradox. These ACAs are concerned about whether the decision to join will allow them to finally separate from their families of origin or only intensify their involvement. They see the joining process as admitting that their parents are alcoholic, which they usually see as the abandonment of a family in need. They have to work hard in group, which could mean working less on their family.

There is relief for ACAs in knowing that their current dilemmas have a legitimate and external reason for existing. In fact, they are not alone with these feelings. There are others with similar problems and there is hope for change. This emergent awareness stage is not complete until ACAs recognize that they have not been able to will themselves free of their families and the associated emotional baggage. They need to surrender to this recognition.

Although the identification of commonalities and understanding of the connection between past and present provide some relief for ACAs, this awareness does not yield deep changes in behavior, emotions, or relationships. Such change requires longer term, individualized therapy. "With the break in denial and acquisition of the label ACA, individuals begin a process of recovery that centers on a transformation in identity . . . The process of recovery is a process of new knowledge construction, including a revision of core beliefs about the self and the family leading to ultimate differentiation and emotional separation from parents and the family of origin" (Brown, 1986, p. 7).

During the emergent awareness stage, it may be beneficial for ACAs to attend a time-limited psychoeducational group that would help them identify their core issues and work through the feelings of guilt that are often associated with their new identity. It is important for therapists who are leading these groups or working individually with ACAs in this stage to avoid imposing core issues on them—issues that may be associated with ACAs, but that may not characterize a given individual. ACAs often have denied their sense of self and, in their rush to gain their own identity, may readily adopt the core issues they have read about in the ACA literature.

Once the process of recognizing the influence of the past on present thoughts, feelings, and behaviors is in progress, ACAs move into the core issues stage. In their work at the Stanford Alcohol Clinic, Cermak and Brown (1982) identified five core issues common to their ACA group members: control, trust, personal needs, responsibility, and feelings. Of the five issues, control was the most pervasive and involved in all of the other core issues. Group members feared either that they were trying to control the group too much or that someone else would control it and, thus, control them. Group members used silence as a form of passive resistance or as a roundabout means of controlling other group members: If group members didn't speak, they didn't give others the chance to critique, reject, or otherwise control them. The group process was filtered through the paradigm of control versus lack of control. They wanted to be "good" group members and speak when appropriate, yet they felt controlled and forced to do so. The expression of feelings was tightly controlled because such expression was, people felt, defined by group members as bad. They feared that if they ever began to express their anger, they would lose control. In their youth, denial, suppression, and repression of feelings allowed them to survive their chaotic families, and they built a dam to hold back the flood of emotions. Depression, loss, and joy were all seen as out-of-control states and were accompanied by anxiety and vulnerability. This intense need to control was tied to their desire to will themselves to be different from their alcoholic parents. These strong emotions were equated with out-of-control drunkenness and neediness.

For some ACAs, trust has been a problem since infancy. As adults, these ACA group members showed their distrust of others by controlling their emotions and not trusting the genuineness of others' expressions of feelings, assuming they were using this expression for the effect it had on others. If a group member trusted someone, it was the same as giving that person control.

This suppression of emotion was evaluated in a study of 55 ACAs who were in treatment and 52 individuals who were in treatment for non-ACA issues (Hart & McAleer, 1997). The authors found that ACAs had a unique style of coping with anger. When anger was experienced by the ACA subjects, they adopted an anger suppression (anger-in) coping style. Hart and McAleer suggested that future studies explore this coping style to see if it contributes to sociobehavioral, psychological, and medical problems.

In the ACA groups at the Child Guidance Center in Lincoln, Nebraska, modeled after the Stanford groups, I observed a confusion exhibited by group members with the concepts of control, trust, and understanding. Control was expressed as making people do what you want them to do. Trust was expecting people to do what you want them to do, and understanding meant knowing why people do what they do. These group members had spent a lifetime trying to find out why their parents acted the way they did. Unless they could answer the question "Why?" they could not trust, nor could they stop controlling. Their thinking went like this, "I can't trust them, because I can't control them, because I don't understand them." This kind of thinking leads to the desire to read everything written that might give them a clue to the puzzle. If they could just fix their parents, they believed, then they would be rewarded or loved or successful.

Group members also had difficulty expressing their personal needs. For many ACAs, their personal needs as a child had not been acknowledged or met by their parents. These needs were further suppressed to avoid embarrassing their parents and to avoid further hurt. As adults, acknowledging the existence of personal needs was equal to admitting vulnerability—which gives others control. It was also connected to being dependent on others—which gives others control. Acknowledging personal needs was also connected to feelings of guilt about imposing on others.

The feeling of responsibility for group members was also an echo of the past. Responsibility and blame are passed around like a hot potato in the alcoholic family. The alcoholic does not take responsibility for his or her drinking, and other family members are willing to accept blame for what is not their responsibility. The children are unable to control their environment and feel dependent on their parents; the acceptance of blame for the drinking of the alcoholic and other problems of the family gives them hope: If they can just change themselves, they can control or change their family. If they can just make better grades, clean their room, be less of a problem, or become the problem, then maybe the craziness will go away. Boundaries between children and parents are confused, which entails role reversals and a lost sense of self. ACAs spend much of their time "other focused," and it is easy for them to become preoccupied with another group member's problem, taking responsibility for it and avoiding the painful job of self-examination and responsibility for their own behavior.

The feelings that the group members were trying to control had many negative connotations. When they were able to squarely place the blame for their loss of childhood and the trauma that resulted from the alcoholism on their parents, they were overwhelmed with anger. Because feelings were seen as bad and potentially overwhelming, it was difficult for the group members to express them directly or respond to another's expression of feelings.

Gravitz and Bowden (1984) have identified another core issue that they find pervasive in their work with ACAs. This is the issue of "all-or-none" functioning that is characterized by black-and-white, or polarized, thinking. This is a prevalent thinking style of the alcoholic and is learned by family members. Children cope with their divided loyalties to their alcoholic parent by splitting them into the "good, sober parent" and the "bad, drunk parent." This helps them understand their continuing love for their parents in the face of drunken and often violent behavior. In their effort to control their family, children take on the family blame and only allow themselves to see bad qualities in themselves. As adults, they have difficulty acknowledging and using their resources and strengths. Although the role behaviors of the child often stifle adult growth, they can also become strengths and competencies. A participant in a Lincoln, Nebraska, group shifted her rescuing, "other-focused" behavior into seeing herself as being naturally therapeutic and able to help others help themselves.

The all-or-nothing stance retards progress in group therapy. Members feel they are either all wrong or all right. If they disagree with someone, especially the group leader, they must be all wrong. They see their mistakes as value laden. Therefore, if they are wrong, they are bad. Perfectionism has its roots in this thinking process. A group member in Nebraska explained her need for perfection in herself and her demand of perfection in others as her only option. For her, the only other choice was "averageness," a totally unacceptable state.

ACAs bounce back and forth between extremes, with little knowledge of the option in between. This is especially true in relationships, where they demand total, smothering loyalty, which often leads to rejection and abandonment, or they never ask for anything out of fear of rejection or dependence.

Another issue identified by Gravitz and Bowden (1984) is dissociation, the separation of emotion from awareness. Young COAs do not have words for their feelings, but can tell stories about emotional happenings. As adults they protect themselves from this flood of emotion by dissociating themselves from the pain. It is common for ACAs to have childhood memory losses, especially losses of painful events such as sexual abuse or a time of extreme fighting in the family.

As group members begin to confront their core issues, they can learn strategies that allow them to function in a better way, as they enter the transformation stage. Awareness of the connection between their present circumstances and the past gives ACAs energy to change. Gravitz and Bowden (1984) have devised a technique called "chunking it down" to attack the core issues that ACAs want to work on. This method foils the black-and-white thinking process that prevents ACAs from jumping from trusting no one to trusting everyone, or missing many of the choices that are available to them. This method allows ACAs to feel successes and rewards as they make small steps forward. Group members in this stage develop personal rights. This allows for boundary setting between themselves and others. This is especially important for those ACAs who have parents who are still drinking. A group member in Nebraska made a deal with his actively alcoholic father. He informed his father that their relationship was very important to him, but he was not willing to spend time with him when he was intoxicated. He let his father know that he would leave his father's house or ask him to leave his house if the father started to drink. This is a good option, especially for ACAs who have children of their own that they do not want to expose to the trauma of their alcoholic families of origin.

The integration stage is marked by a synthesis of thought, feelings, and behavior into a congruent identity. The byproducts of this integration are increased relaxation and joy. Growth is seen as a process of small changes, and mistakes are acceptable. These mistakes can even be viewed as part of the risk of learning. If people are making mistakes, they must be taking risks and thus making progress. Relationships are characterized by negotiation rather than control, with appropriate boundaries between people. Self-trust occurs at this stage and allows for trusting others, even at the cost of potential hurt. Life becomes more pleasurable, and setbacks are experienced with new skills and the confidence that they can be overcome. Black-and-white thinking has mellowed to allow for many possibilities and a new openness to ideas.

The final stage, genesis, is the process of transcending the recovery from past trauma to a sense of harmony and balance. It is not just the absence of dysfunction, but the presence of a new and varied responsiveness to life (Gravitz & Bowden, 1984). ACAs at this point have found their unique strengths that were developed in the trauma of the past, and have integrated them into their sense of self. They are able to access all of their resources and enjoy life. They are no longer ACAs. They are adults who belong to a larger world, who have learned from their pain how to be whole human beings. They achieve this not by denying their past or their problems, but by understanding them and using them for their benefit.

ACAs may enter group or individual therapy at any point on this continuum. Crawford and Phyfer (1988) have developed counseling strategies for each of these stages. For ACAs in the survival stage, public education can help to break their denial. Workshops and lectures to civic organizations, as well as writing stories for newspapers or newsletters, are appropriate interventions at this stage. Group and/or individual counseling sessions may be appropriate for ACAs in the emergent awareness or core issue stage. Gestalt techniques are recommended for exploring unfinished business and residue left over from the alcoholic family. The expression of feelings in therapy is painful but necessary, and should be encouraged. Cognitive restructuring and behavioral rehearsal are techniques recommended for ACAs in the transformation stage. These techniques examine self-defeating behaviors and beliefs. The integration stage requires recognizing that recovery is a continuing process and not an event. "Acquiring new, more functional living styles is a gradual process, a recovery continuum, rather than a unidimensional occurrence" (Crawford & Phyfer, 1988, p. 108). Plans for ongoing recovery and support are emphasized. The maintenance of gains made in counseling is the primary goal of this stage.

Group therapy with ACAs is a way of doing family-of-origin work without sending ACAs back home or having them bring the family in, which may be dangerous or counterproductive if there is active alcoholism or violence in the family of origin. Models for conducting group therapy with ACAs indicate that the healing process is rooted in the transference relationships between group members and group leaders (Vannicelli, 1989). The group becomes a surrogate family and the leaders substitute parents. In this safe environment, group members can explore painful issues and try new behaviors without fear of activating a drinking episode and instigating violence.

Since alcoholism in the family doesn't affect children equally, and 70% to 75% of COAs do not become alcoholic, researchers have been interested in how alcoholism is transmitted from generation to generation, who is at most risk, and why so many COAs seem immune. This is important for developing prevention strategies aimed at breaking the intergenerational pattern of alcoholism, where alcoholism and its effects are passed from generation to generation.

The Intergenerational Transmission of Alcoholism

A consistent finding in the field of families and addiction is that addictions and their effects tend to be intergenerational. The most important question for the field of addiction prevention is this: How do alcoholism and other addictions transmit from generation to generation or even jump generations in families? Further, it is important to study families that seem to function adequately in spite of addiction and that do not transmit these addictions to their offspring.

In an attempt to determine how the family environment may be a transmitter of alcoholism, several researchers investigated the importance of family rituals (Bennett, Wolin, Reiss, & Teitelbaum, 1987; Haugland, 2005; Steinglass, Bennett, Wolin, & Reiss, 1987; Wolin & Bennett, 1984). Wolin, Bennett, and Noonan (1979) studied a group of 25 families of middle- and upper-class background and European origin. All families included at least one parent who met Wolin et al.'s criteria for the identification of an alcoholic or problem drinker. Structured individual interviews that covered personal history of the interviewee and the continuity of family heritage from the grandparents' generation into the current nuclear family provided information on seven areas of family rituals: (a) dinnertime, (b) holidays, (c) evenings, (d) weekends, (e) vacations, (f) visitors in the home, and (g) discipline. These investigators defined family rituals as patterns of behavior that have meaning beyond their practical outcome or function. "Patterned behavior is behavior that is repetitive, stable with respect to roles, and continues over time" (Wolin et al., 1979, p. 590). They suggested that these rituals were important because they "stabilize ongoing family life by clarifying expectable roles, delineating boundaries within and without the family, and defining rules so that all family members know that 'this is the way our family is' " (Wolin et al., 1979, p. 590). Steinglass et al. (1987) stated that "family rituals are, in effect, condensed, prepackaged training modules intended to convey to all family members the important facts about family identity" (p. 309). They identified three types of families: *distinctive families,* in which rituals did not change during drinking episodes; *intermediate subsumptive families,* which rejected intoxicated behavior when it was present; and *subsumptive families,* in which drinking changed the "fabric of the family" and highly disrupted the family life. They found that families whose rituals were disrupted or changed during the period of heaviest drinking by the alcoholic parent were more likely to transmit alcoholism to the younger generation than were families whose rituals remained intact. The more that alcoholism became a central organizing force and a disruption to family rituals, the more the children were at risk for developing alcoholism. The nontransmitter families had one outstanding quality in common: "rejection of the intoxication of the alcoholic parent openly or privately, or talking about his or her behavior disapprovingly" (Wolin et al., 1979, p. 591).

To follow up this study, Bennett et al. (1987) interviewed 68 married COAs and their spouses regarding dinnertime and holiday rituals in their families of origin and in the couples' current families. They identified 14 predictor variables that contributed significantly ($p < .01$) to the couples' alcoholism outcomes. The COAs who remained non-alcoholic had limited attachments to their families of origin or selective disengagement, and the families of origin had been able to separate the rituals from the alcoholism. Specifically, they found that the couples who were most resistant to transmission lived at least 200 miles away from their families of origin and visited them two times per year.

In a summation of these studies on family ritual, Steinglass et al. (1987) said,

> We believe that the transmission of alcoholism from one generation to the next involves the whole family system over time. The context for transmission is the sum total of interactions, attitudes, and beliefs that define the family. The process is ongoing and dynamic and has no particular beginning, end, or pivotal event. And it often goes on outside the awareness of the participants involved, the "senders" as well as the "receivers." (p. 304)

Haugland (2005) conducted a study on daily or weekly disruptions in family rituals. She did semistructured family interviews with families who were in treatment and found that recurrent disruptions of rituals were often found with the fathers' participation in rituals and routines, role behavior, and responsibility. The study delineated four types of families:

1. *Protective families*—Low levels of change in family rituals, father maintaining his role, less severe drinking, children protected, low levels of psychological problems in family members
2. *Emotionally disruptive families*—Mothers maintaining structure and rituals, mothers' parenting affected negatively, children not protected from drinking, hangovers, fighting, and psychological problems in family members
3. *Exposing families*—Changes in rituals, routines, and annual celebrations; major changes in family atmosphere; children exposed to drinking; hangovers; serious and frequent fighting; and high levels of psychological problems in family members
4. *Chaotic families*—Considerable disruption in rituals and celebrations, lack of mothers' compensating for fathers' disruption, poor structure in routines and rituals during sobriety, children exposed to drinking and violence, destructive parentification of children, serious drinking problems, and psychological problems in fathers

Haugland (2005) further reported the importance of maternal compensation for the fathers' lack of responsibility in upholding family rituals. She suggested that the mothers' maintenance of rituals and routines may have a moderating effect. It was also important for the mother to be able to regulate her emotions and be available to the children. Further, the family needs to maintain the affect and meaning of the rituals for them to be protective. When the rituals are disrupted, children perceive their environment to be unpredictable, which may lead to confusion and a feeling of being unsafe. This disruption also undermines the rituals' meaning and symbolism, which weakens family cohesion. Children may then view the family as unpredictable or uncontrollable. Ross and Hill (2001) found parent unpredictability to be associated with alcohol abuse in COAs.

Another concept that Bennett et al. (1988) have proposed as a risk-reducing factor is "deliberateness." Families with serious problems such as parental alcoholism that can still maintain the family's identity communicate important messages to their children regarding their ability to take control of present and future life events. These messages, in turn, can play an important role in the extent to which the offspring are protected from developing problems in childhood or alcoholism in adolescence and adulthood.

Bennett et al. (1988) suggested several strategies for reducing the likelihood of intergenerational transmission of alcoholism: the deliberate selection of a nondrinking spouse, establishment by the couple of their own family rituals and heritage, participation in community institutions, and selective disengagement from the families of origin. This is important information for family therapists working with newly constituted families who are concerned about their own risk for addictive disorders and transmission of these disorders to their own children.

COAs who later become alcoholic report the absence of a "supportive other" or cohesion in the family of origin (Booz-Allen & Hamilton, Inc. 1974; Lawson, 1988; O'Sullivan, 1991; Simmons, 1991). Booz-Allen and Hamilton, Inc. (1974) listed "having a supportive person" in the family as a risk reducer for COAs. Lawson (1988) found that non-alcoholic ACAs perceived their families of origin as more cohesive and supportive than did alcoholic ACAs. In looking at these supportive others, O'Sullivan (1991) noted that the presence of a childhood mentoring relationship was related to resiliency in ACAs. Even in families with alcoholic fathers and families with psychiatrically disturbed fathers, the presence of a "healthy" mother was seen to have a mitigating influence; as young adults, the COAs appeared to be as well adjusted as the control group of young adults, whose parents had neither alcoholism nor psychiatric problems (Simmons, 1991). Healthy mothers were defined in this study as having no diagnosis of substance abuse or psychiatric disorder. The common message of these studies seems to be that children can emerge from dysfunctional, substance-abusing families with some degree of resilience if they receive some nurturing and guidance from someone in the family or even someone outside of the family system. From a prevention standpoint, this cohesion and support in families seems to provide a buffering effect against the damage done to children in dysfunctional families.

Another group of investigators (Jacob, Seilhamer, & Rushe, 1989) observed intact families under a broad range of conditions, including laboratory observations involving experimental drinking procedures and naturalistic home observations focused on dinnertime interactions. They were interested in the impact of alcoholism on the process and structure of family life, the degree to which varying patterns of family interactions served to potentiate or inhibit the development of alcoholism in COAs, and the degree to which patterns varied in relation to alcoholism versus depression. In observing episodic versus steady and in-home versus out-of-home drinking behaviors, they found that steady, in-home drinkers seemed to have a positive impact on family life. The steady, in-home drinkers and their wives engaged in more productive problem solving during the drink versus nondrink conditions. This is consistent with the "adaptive consequences" theory of alcoholism. Jacob et al. acknowledged that causality could not be determined, but the study did underscore how the interplay of familial stressors associated with alcohol abuse, parental psychiatric status, and the mother's ability to mediate negative effects affects the children.

In viewing ACAs' responses to parental drinking styles, Tarter (1991) found that the same drinking style that Jacob et al. (1989) found to be a productive problem-solving style for the alcoholic couple was the most problem-creating style for the ACA who had grown up in a family with this drinking style. As compared to ACAs from "binge drinker at home," "binge drinker away," and "daily away drinker" groups, families with daily at-home drinkers produced ACAs who rated their families of origin as the most unhealthy of the four groups (on the Family of Origin Scale; Hovestadt, 1985). These ACAs who had daily at-home drinking parents reported that they had more alcohol problems as measured by the Michigan Alcoholism Screening Test (Selzer, 1971) and more depression as measured by the Beck Depression Inventory (Beck, Ward, & Mendelson, 1961) than did members of the other three groups.

Family system studies have added another dimension to the nature versus nurture controversy in the etiology of alcoholism. It is quite possible that there is no single etiology for alcoholism. Genetics may play a major role in the father–son transmission of alcoholism, whereas family environment may have more of an impact on women's alcoholism. The importance of finding family environment patterns that predispose children for alcoholism is that it may be possible to prevent alcoholism in these children by changing the patterns through family therapy and parent training.

Resilient Children of Alcoholics

It is clear that all COAs are not the same. Some suffer greatly from living in substance-abusing families, and others from similar families appear to be much less negatively affected. As noted earlier, being a COA is not a diagnosis. Many COAs have high self-esteem, do not have problems with substance abuse, and are good at adapting to various environments (Walker & Lee, 1998).

Wolin and Wolin (1993) and Jacobs and Wolin (1991) characterized those children who appear to be less affected by family-of-origin alcoholism as "resilient children"—adults who are working well, playing well, and loving well. These researchers called their model of resiliency the Challenge Model because these children see the adversity of a troubled childhood as a challenge. This is in contrast to the Damage Model, so pervasive in the mental health field, which is based on the idea that a troubled family damages the child, who then has childhood pathologies and succumbs to pathology in adolescence and adulthood. The Challenge Model says that the troubled family creates damages and challenges that in turn create both pathologies and resiliencies in the child. The child both succumbs and rebounds.

The idea that some COAs are resilient is not new. In a longitudinal study, Werner (1986) focused on child characteristics and the qualities of the caregiving environment that differentiated COAs who developed serious problems by the age of 18 and those who did not. The study consisted of 49 subjects of multiracial backgrounds, born in 1955 on the island of Kauai, Hawaii. They were evaluated at ages 1, 2, 10, and 18. Werner found that males and offspring of alcoholic mothers had higher rates of psychosocial problems in childhood and adolescence than females and the offspring of alcoholic fathers. COAs who did not develop serious deficits in coping skills were different from those who did in terms of the characteristics of temperament, communication skills, self-concept, and locus of control. These resilient children also experienced fewer stressful life events that disrupted the family unit in the first 2 years of their lives.

Wolin and Wolin (1993) developed a list of seven resiliencies that they believe develop out of the challenge to maintain self-esteem in the face of the troubled family's neglect, criticism, physical abuse, denial, and pull to engulf its members in its emotional turmoil. These resiliencies may be innate. "Early signs of these resiliencies can be found in the first memories of successful survivors and can be traced in progressive stages through their childhood, adolescence, and adulthood" (Jacobs & Wolin, 1991, p. 9). These seven resiliencies are insight, independence, relationships, initiative, creativity, humor, and morality. Each resiliency has a child, adolescent, and adult manifestation.

Insight refers to a psychological sophistication, an early sensing that something is wrong with the troubled parent(s). By adolescence, this sensing becomes a knowing. The adolescent understands the family dynamics and attributes the family's problems to factors outside of him- or herself. In adulthood the knowing becomes understanding about self and others.

Independence refers to the ability to live apart yet relate to others without pressures or demands. An early sign of independence is straying away from the family. Adolescents realize that distance feels better than closeness, and they move from straying to disengaging emotionally from their families. As adults, they have separated from their families in a freely chosen, rational way. This is reminiscent of Bowen's notion of a healthy differentiation from the family of origin.

Relationships refers to a connecting, a selective process whereby children can bond with parents or others. Early in life, children with this resiliency begin interacting with the healthier parts of their families. As they get older, they begin connecting with neighbors, teachers, coaches, and other substitutes for parents. As adults, they bond with friends, spouses, children, and siblings. The two resiliencies of independence and relationships can be seen as a common goal of all of the family therapy theories. Family therapists try to help families develop a sense of belonging or cohesion, while at the same time allowing for the independence and individuality of their members.

Initiative refers to the ability to recover from adversity, a deep sense of self-trust and personal control—survivor's pride. Individuals with initiative love a challenge. They have the inner confidence to explore their world and test their limits.

Creativity and *humor* are linked together and share common processes. Creativity refers to the ability to express and resolve inner conflicts in a symbolic form through the arts. Humor refers to the ability to laugh at oneself and use play as an emotional healer. Young children use their imagination to protect themselves from the trauma of their family life. *Shaping* refers to the refinement of play. It adds the elements of discipline and effort to the production of art. The adult version of creativity is composing, and the adult version of humor is laughing. Wolin and Wolin (1993) described creativity as making nothing into something, and humor as something into nothing. Children with this type of resilience could greatly benefit from creative art therapy.

Morality refers to the activity of an informed conscience. Young children want to know why and begin judging the rights and wrongs of daily life and their parents. In adolescence, this changes into valuing decency, compassion, honesty, and fair play. In adulthood, these survivors serve others even though they did not receive what they deserved in their families. They restore themselves by helping others.

In keeping with the idea of resiliency, Wolin (1993) outlined Challenge Model Therapy. The goal of this therapy is to change a survivor's view of him- or herself from damaged goods to one who prevails. Challenge Model Therapy involves a five-step process:

> *Step 1: Begin with the damage story.* This stage begins with building trust and empathy and allowing the damage to be discussed and felt. The therapist takes a complete history of the damage story and helps the survivor see how the consequences are experienced in adulthood.
>
> *Step 2: Select one resiliency.* The therapist identifies the most easily accepted resilience, returns to the history of damage, and questions the resilient behavior in detail, acknowledging both the damage and the strength. The therapist should expect resistance to acceptance of the resilience and should compliment appropriate behavior.
>
> *Step 3: Explore remaining resiliencies.* The therapist should know all three stages of each resilience and try to reframe all seven to fit with the survivor's story. The therapist should work with the resistances and accept areas of moderate to little resilience.
>
> *Step 4: Build a new narrative.* At this stage, the therapist offers explanations of the resiliences and the damage. The therapist teaches the survivor that he or she had a false mirroring of blame from his or her family, yet somehow he or she has avoided contracting all the family's problems. Therapists need to foster the survivor's pride and observe the shifting balance between damage and resilience.
>
> *Step 5: Apply resiliencies to current problems.* The therapist can use the "chunking down" technique of Gravitz and Bowden (1984) to break problems into smaller components. Therapists at this stage apply insight to the weakest areas of resilience; they help survivors to attempt more or less independence (as appropriate), to create healthy relationships, and to initiate and maintain family rituals.

Alvord and Grados (2005) developed a group process that teaches children to be resilient. They have a systems model that involves the family, the school, and the community. It is referred to as the Alvord-Baker Social Skills Group Model. The group has a resiliency-based curriculum that uses a proactive orientation and cognitive behavior strategies. The model has five structural components: (a) an interactive component to teach children new skills and ideas, (b) a free-play component to encourage negotiation and interaction, (c) a stress-reduction/self-regulation component to show children how to practice relaxation and self-regulation, (d) a generalization component to teach children how to practice what they learn outside of the group, and (e) a family component to encourage the inclusion of the parents in the lessons and to encourage them to do homework with their children.

References

Ackerman, R. J. (1978). *Children of alcoholics: A guide book for educators, therapists and parents.* Holmes Beach, FL: Learning Publications.

Albee, G. (1981, October). *Primary prevention.* Workshop presented at Kellogg Center, Lincoln, NE.

Alvord, M. K., & Grados, J. J. (2005). Enhancing resilience in children: A proactive approach. *Professional Psychology Research and Practice, 36*(3), 238–245.

Andreas, J. B., O'Farrell, T. J., & Fals-Stewart, W. (2006). Does individual treatment for alcoholic fathers benefit their children? A longitudinal assessment. *Journal of Consulting and Clinical Psychology, 74*(1), 191–198.

Baker, D. E., & Stephenson, L. A. (1995). Personality characteristics of adult children of alcoholics. *Journal of Clinical Psychology, 51*(5), 694–702.

Bandler, R., Grender, G., & Satir, V. (1976). *Changing with families.* Palo Alto, CA: Science and Behavior Books.

Barnard, C. P., & Spoentgen, P. A. (1986). Children of alcoholics: Characteristics and treatment. *Alcoholism Treatment Quarterly, 3,* 47–65.

Beck, A. T., Ward, C., & Mendelson, M. (1961). Beck Depression Inventory (BDI). *Archives of General Psychiatry, 4,* 561–571.

Beesley, D. (2002). Control, attachment style, and relationship satisfaction among adult children of alcoholics. *Journal of Mental Health Counseling, 24*(4), 281–298.

Beletsis, S., & Brown, S. (1981). A developmental framework for understanding the adult children of alcoholics. *Focus on Women: Journal of the Addictions and Health, 2,* 187–203.

Bennett, L. A., Wolin, S. J., & Reiss, D. (1988). Deliberate family process: A strategy for protecting children of alcoholics. *British Journal of Addiction, 83,* 821–829.

Bennett, L. A., Wolin, S. J., Reiss, D., & Teitelbaum, M. A. (1987). Couples at risk for transmission of alcoholism: Protective influences. *Family Process, 26,* 111–129.

Black, C. (1979, Fall). Children of alcoholics. *Alcohol Health and Research World,* pp. 23–27.

Black, C. (1981a). Innocent bystanders at risk: The children of alcoholics. *Alcoholism, 1*(13), 22–25.

Black, C. (1981b). *It will never happen to me.* Denver: MAC.

Black, C. (1987). Introduction. In V. Rachel (Ed.), *Family secrets* (pp. xxvi–xxxviii). San Francisco: Harper & Row.

Booz-Allen & Hamilton, Inc. (1974). *An assessment of the needs of and resources for children of alcoholic parents* (Unpublished report prepared for National Institute on Alcohol Abuse and Alcoholism).

Bosma, W. (1975). Alcoholism and teenagers. *Maryland State Medical Journal, 24*(6), 62–68.

Boye-Beaman, J., Leonard, K. E., & Senchak, M. (1991). Assortative mating, relationship development, and intimacy among offspring of alcoholics. *Family Dynamics of Addiction Quarterly, 1*(2), 20–33.

Brown, S. (1979, May 28). Kids of alcoholics. *Newsweek,* p. 82.

Brown, S. (1983). Adult children of alcoholics: The history of a social movement and its impact on clinical theory and practice. *Recent Developments in Alcoholism: Children of Alcoholics, 9,* 267–285.

Brown, S. (1986). *Treating adult children of alcoholics: A developmental perspective.* New York: Wiley.

Burnett, G., Jones R. A., Bliwise, N. G., & Ross, L. T. (2006). Family unpredictability, parental alcoholism, and the development of parentification. *American Journal of Family Therapy, 34,* 181–189.

Cermak, T., & Brown, S. (1982). Group therapy with adult children of alcoholics. *International Journal of Group Psychotherapy, 32*(3), 375–389.

Chafetz, M., Blane, H., & Hill, M. (1977). Children of alcoholics: Observations in a child guidance clinic. *Quarterly Journal of Studies of Alcoholism, 32,* 687–698.

Chase, N. D., Deming, M. P., & Wells, M. C. (2000). Parentification, parental alcoholism, and academic status among young adults. *American Journal of Family Therapy, 26,* 105–114.

Children of Alcoholics Foundation. (1990). *Children of alcoholics in the medical system: Hidden problem, hidden costs.* New York: Author.

Christensen, H. B., & Bilenberg, N. (2000). Behavioral and emotional problems in children of alcoholic mothers and fathers. *European Child and Adolescent Psychiatry, 9*(3), 219–226.

Clinebell, N. J. (1968). Pastoral counseling of the alcoholic and his family. In R. Catanzaro (Ed.), *Alcoholism: The total treatment approach.* Springfield, IL: Thomas.

Cork, M. (1969). *The forgotten children.* Toronto: Alcoholism and Drug Addiction Research Foundation.

Crawford, R., & Phyfer, A. (1988). Adult children of alcoholics: A counseling model. *Journal of College Student Development, 29,* 105–111.

Cuijpers, P., & Smit, F. (2002). Nicotine dependence and regular nicotine use in adult children of alcoholics. *Addiction Research and Theory, 10*(1), 69–81.

DeLucia, C., Belz, A., & Chassin, L. (2001). Do adolescent symptomatology and family environment vary over time with fluctuations in parental alcohol improvement? *Developmental Psychology, 37,* 207–216.

Domenico, D., & Windle, M. (1993). Intrapersonal and interpersonal functioning among middle-aged female adult children of alcoholics. *Journal of Consulting and Clinical Psychology, 61*(4), 659–666.

Earls, F., Reich, W., Jung, K. G., & Cloninger, C. R. (1998). Psychopathology in children of alcoholics and antisocial parents. *Alcoholism: Clinical and Experimental Research, 12,* 481–487.

Eiden, R. D., Leonard, K. E., & Morrisey, S. (2001). Parental alcoholism and toddler noncompliance. *Alcoholism: Clinical and Experimental Research, 25,* 1621–1633.

El-Guebaly, N., West, M., Maticka-Tyndale, E., & Pool, M. (1993). Attachment among adult children of alcoholics. *Addiction, 88,* 1405–1411.

Fitzgerald, H. E., Sullivan, L. A., Ham, H. P., Zucker, R. A., Bruckel, S., Schneider, A. M., et al. (1993). Predictors of behavior problems in 3-year-old sons of alcoholics: Early evidence for the onset of risk. *Child Development, 64,* 110–123.

Flora, D. B., & Chassin, L. (2005). Changes in drug use during young adulthood: The effects of parent alcoholism and transition into marriage. *Psychology of Addictive Behaviors, 19*(4), 352–362.

Fox, R. (1968). Treating the alcoholic's family. In R. J. Catanzaro (Ed.), *Alcoholism: The total treatment approach.* Springfield, IL: Thomas.

Glenn, S. (1981, April). *Steven Glenn on prevention.* Seminar on drug and alcohol abuse prevention, Omaha, NE.

Goodwin, D. W. (1985). Alcoholism and genetics. *Archives of General Psychiatry, 42,* 171–174.

Goodwin, D. W., Schulsinger, F., Hermansen, L., Gruze, S. B., & Winokur, G. (1973). Alcohol problems in adoptees raised apart from biological parents. *Archives of General Psychiatry, 28,* 238–243.

Grant, G. F. (2000). Estimates of US children exposed to alcohol abuse and dependence in the family. *American Journal of Public Health, 90*(1), 112–116.

Gravitz, H. L., & Bowden, J. D. (1984, Spring). Therapeutic issues of alcoholic children of alcoholics. *Alcohol Health and Research World,* 25–36.

Gravitz, H. L., & Bowden J. D. (1990). Therapeutic issues of adult children of alcoholics. In D. A. Ward (Ed.), *Alcoholism: Introduction to theory and treatment.* Dubuque, IA: Kendall/Hunt.

Griffin, M. L., Amodeo, M., Fassler, I., Ellis, M. A., & Clay, C. (2005). Mediating factors for the long-term effects of parental alcoholism in women: The contribution of other childhood stresses and resources. *American Journal on Addictions, 14,* 18–34.

Hart, K. E., & McAleer, M. (1997). Anger coping style in adult children of alcoholics. *Addiction Research, 5*(6), 473–486.

Haugland, B. S. M. (2005, April). Recurrent disruptions of rituals and routines in families with paternal alcohol abuse. *Family Relations, 54,* 225–241.

Hecht, M. (1973). Children of alcoholics. *American Journal of Nursing, 73*(10), 1764–1767.

Hindman, M. (1975–76, Winter). Children of alcoholic parents. *Alcohol Health and Research World,* pp. 2–6.

Hovestadt, A. (1985). A family of origin scale. *Journal of Marriage and Family Therapy, 11*(3), 287–297.

Hunt, M. E. (1997). A comparison of family of origin factors between children of alcoholics and children of non-alcoholics in a longitudinal panel. *American Journal of Drug and Alcohol Abuse, 23*(4), 597–613.

Hussong, A., Bauer, D., & Chassin, L. (2008). Telescoped trajectories from alcohol initiation to disorder in children of alcoholic parents. *Journal of Abnormal Psychology, 117*(1), 63–78.

Jacob, T., Seilhamer, R. A., & Rushe, R. H. (1989). Alcoholism and family interactions: An experimental paradigm. *American Journal of Drug and Alcohol Abuse, 5*(1), 73–91.

Jacob, T., Windle, M., Seilhamer, R. A., & Bost, J. (1999). Adult children of alcoholics: Drinking, psychiatric, and psychosocial status. *Psychology of Addictive Behaviors, 13*(1), 3–21.

Jacobs, J., & Wolin, S. J. (1991, October). *Resilient children growing up in alcoholic families.* Paper presented at the National Consensus Symposium on Children of Alcoholics and Co-Dependence, Warrenton, VA.

Jacobson, S. B. (1991, October). *The recovery movement: From children of alcoholics to codependency.* Paper presented at the National Consensus Symposium on Children of Alcoholics and Co-Dependence, Warrenton, VA.

Jaeger, E., Hahn, N. B., & Weinraub, M. (2000). Attachment in adult daughters of alcoholic fathers. *Addiction, 95*(2), 267–276.

Kashubeck, S. (1994). Adult children of alcoholics and psychological distress. *Journal of Counseling and Development, 72,* 538–543.

Kashubeck, S., & Christensen, S. A. (1992). Differences in distress among adult children of alcoholics. *Journal of Counseling Psychology, 39*(3), 356–362.

Keller, P. B., Cummings, E. M., & Davies, P. T. (2005). The role of marital discord and parenting in relations between parental problem drinking and child adjustment. *Journal of Child Psychology and Psychiatry, 46*(9), 943–951.

Kelly, M. L., & Fals-Stewart, W. (2002). Couples- versus individual-based therapy for alcohol and drug abuse effects on children's psychosocial functioning. *Journal of Consulting and Clinical Psychology, 70*(2), 417–427.

Kelly, M. L., & Fals-Stewart, W. (2007). Treating parental alcoholism with learning sobriety together: Effects on adolescents versus preadolescents. *Journal of Family Psychology, 21*(3), 435–444.

King, K. M., & Chassin, L. (2004). Mediating and moderated effects of adolescent behavioral undercontrol and parenting in the prediction of drug use disorders in emerging adulthood. *Psychology of Addictive Behaviors, 18*(3), 239–249.

Kumpfer, K. L. (1999). Outcome measures of interventions in the study of children of substance-abusing parents. *Pediatrics, 103*(Suppl. 5), 1128–1144.

Lambie, G. W. (2005). Children of alcoholics: Implications for professional school counseling. *Professional School Counseling, 8*(3), 266–273.

Larson, J. H., & Reedy, B. M. (2004). Family process as a mediator of the negative effects of parental alcoholism on young adult dating relationships. *American Journal of Family Therapy, 32,* 289–304.

Lawson, A. W. (1988). *The relationship of past and present family environments of adult children of alcoholics.* Unpublished doctoral dissertation, United States International University.

Lease, S. H. (2002). A model of depression in adult children of alcoholics and nonalcoholics. *Journal of Counseling and Development, 80,* 441–451.

Levinson, D. (1978). *Seasons of a man's life.* New York: Ballantine Books.

Litzke, C. H., & Glazer, E. (2004, March/April). "Quality time" serves families with a parent in recovery. *Holistic Nursing Practice, 18*(2), 82–86.

Martin, J. I. (1995). Intimacy, loneliness, and openness to feelings in adult children of alcoholics. *Health and Social Work, 20*(1), 52–59.

McCord, W., McCord, J., & Gudeman, J. (1960). *Origins of alcoholism.* Palo Alto, CA: Stanford University Press.

Mezzich, A. C., Tarter, R. E., Kirisci, L., Feske, U., Day, B. S., & Gao, Z. (2007). Reciprocal influence of parent discipline and child's behavior on risk for substance use disorder: A 9-year prospective study. American *Journal of Drug and Alcohol Abuse, 33,* 851–867.

Moos, R. H., & Billings, A. G. (1982). Children of alcoholics during the recovery process: Alcoholics and matched control families. *Addictive Behaviors, 7,* 155–163.

Moos, R. H., Finney, J. W., & Cronkite, R. C. (1990). *Alcoholism treatment: Context, process and outcome.* New York: Oxford University Press.

Moos, R. H., & Moos, B. (1994). *Family environment scale* (3rd ed.). Palo Alto, CA: Consulting Psychologist Press.

Mylant, M., Ide, B., Cuevas, E., & Meehan, M. (2002). Adolescent children of alcoholics: Vulnerable or resilient? *Journal of the American Psychiatric Nurses Association, 8,* 57–64.

National Association for Children of Alcoholics. (2006). *Children of addicted parents: Important facts.* Retrieved August 26, 2006, from http://www.aacp.org/page.ww?section=Factstfor+Families&name=Children=Of+Alcoholics.html

Ohannessian, C. M., Hesselbrock, V. M., Kramer, J., Kuperman, S., Bucholz, K. K., Schuckit, M. A., & Nurnberger, J. I. (2004). The relationship between parental alcoholism and adolescent psychopathology: A systemic examination of parental comorbid psychopathology. *Journal of Abnormal Child Psychology, 32*(5), 519–533.

Olmsted, M. E., Crowell, J. A., & Waters, E. (2003). Assortative mating among adult children of alcoholics and alcoholics. *Family Relations, 52,* 64–71.

Orford, J., Krishnan, M., & Velleman, R. (2003). Young adult offspring of parents with drinking problems: A study of childhood family cohesion using simple family diagrams. *Journal of Substance Use, 3*(3), 139–149.

O'Sullivan, C. (1991). Making a difference: The relationship between childhood mentors and resiliency in adult children of alcoholics. *Family Dynamics of Addiction Quarterly, 1*(4), 13–15.

Patterson, R. (1980, March). Children of alcoholics: Focus for social worker. *The Oregonian.*

Ranganathan, S. (2004). Families in transition: Victims of alcoholism and new challenges ahead. *International Journal for the Advancement of Counseling, 26*(4), 399–405.

Ritter, J., Stewart, M., Bernet, C., Coe, M., & Brown, S. A. (2002). Effects of childhood exposure to familial alcoholism and family violence on adolescent substance use, conduct problems, and self-esteem. *Journal of Traumatic Stress, 15*(2), 113–122.

Rivinus, T. M., Levoy, D., Matzko, M., & Cloninger, C. R. (1998). Hospitalized children of substance-abusing parents and sexually abused children: A comparison. *Journal of the American Academy of Children and Adolescent Psychiatry, 31*(6), 1019–1923.

Rodney, H. E. (1994). What differentiates ACOAs and non-ACOAs on a Black college campus. *Journal of American College Health, 43*(2), 57–62.

Rodney, H. E. (1996). Inconsistencies in the literature on collegiate adult children of alcoholics: Factors to consider for African Americans. *Journal of American College Health, 45*(1), 19–25.

Ross, L. T., & Hill, E. M. (2001). Drinking and parental unpredictability among adult children of alcoholics: A pilot study. *Substance Use and Misuse, 36*(5), 609–638.

Schuckit, M. A., Tipp, J. E., & Keiner, E. (1994). Are daughters of alcoholics more likely to marry alcoholics? *American Journal of Drug and Alcohol Abuse, 20*(2), 237–245.

Selzer, M. L. (1971). The Michigan alcoholism screening test: The quest for a new diagnostic instrument. *American Journal of Psychiatry, 127*(12), 1653–1658.

Senchak, M., Leonard, K. E., Greene, B. W., & Carroll, A. (1995). Comparisons of adult children of alcoholic, divorced, and control parents in four outcome domains. *Psychology of Addictive Behaviors, 9*(3), 147–156.

Sher, K. J. (1991). *Children of alcoholics: A critical appraisal of theory and research.* Chicago: University of Chicago Press.

Simmons, G. M. (1991). *Interpersonal trust and perceived locus of control in the adjustment of adult children of alcoholics.* Unpublished doctoral dissertation, United States International University, San Diego, CA.

Sloboda, S. (1974). The children of alcoholics: A neglected problem. *Hospital and Community Psychiatry, 25*(9), 605–606.

Steinglass, P., Bennett, L. A., Wolin, S. J., & Reiss, D. (1987). *The alcoholic family.* New York: Basic Books.

Tarter, R. E. (1991). *The effects of parental alcohol drinking patterns of adult children of alcoholics.* Unpublished doctoral dissertation, United States International University, San Diego, CA.

Vannicelli, M. (1989). *Group psychotherapy with adult children of alcoholics.* New York: Guilford Press.

Veronie, L., & Fruehstorfer, D. B. (2001). Gender, birth order and family role identification among adult children of alcoholics. *Current Psychology: Developmental, Learning, Personality, Social, 20*(1), 53–67.

Walker, J. P., & Lee, R. E. (1998). Uncovering strengths of children of alcoholic parents. *Contemporary Family Therapy, 20*(4), 521–538.

Wegscheider, S. (1981a, January/February). From the family trap to family freedom. *Alcoholism,* pp. 36–39.

Wegscheider, S. (1981b). *Another chance: Hope and health for the alcoholic family.* Palo Alto, CA: Science and Behavior Books.

Werner, E. E. (1986). Resilient offspring of alcoholics: A longitudinal study. *Journal of Studies on Alcohol, 47*(1), 34–40.

West, M. O., & Printz, R. J. (1987). Parental alcoholism and childhood psychopathology. *Psychological Bulletin, 102,* 204–218.

Wilens, T. E., Biederman, J., Bredin, E., Hahesy, B. A., Abranntes, A., Neft, D., et al. (2002). A family study of the high-risk children of opioid- and alcohol-dependent parents. *American Journal of Addictions, 11,* 41–51.

Woititz, J. (1983). *Adult children of alcoholics.* Hollywood, CA: Hollywood Communications.

Wolin, S. J. (1993, January). *The resilient self.* Workshop presented at United States International University, San Diego, CA.

Wolin, S. J., & Bennett, L. A. (1984). Family rituals. *Family Process, 23,* 401–420.

Wolin, S. J., Bennett, L. A., & Noonan, D. L. (1979). Family rituals and recurrence of alcoholism over generations. *American Journal of Psychiatry, 136,* 589–593.

Wolin, S. J., & Wolin, S. J. (1993). *The resilient self: How survivors of troubled families rise above adversity.* New York: Villard Books.

Zhou, Q., King K. M., & Chassin, L. (2006). The roles of familial alcoholism and adolescent family harmony in young adults' substance dependence disorders: Mediated and moderated relations. *Journal of Abnormal Psychology, 115*(2), 320–331.

Resources

Adult Children of Alcoholics
www.adultchildren.org
(includes ACA world meetings list)

The National Association of Children of Alcoholics
11426 Rockville Pike, Suite 100
Rockville, MD 20852
888-554-2627
nacoa@nacoa.org

CHAPTER 9

Working With Gay Men and Lesbian Women With Addiction Concerns

Martin Adam and Veronica Gutierrez

This chapter addresses some of the specific issues that may arise when a gay man or lesbian woman addicted to drugs or alcohol attends therapy. Topics covered include an overview of specific drug and alcohol cultures in the gay community, gay identity development, unique characteristics in gay men and lesbian women, and therapist training. While many of these topics apply to other sexual minorities (e.g., people in bisexual and transgender communities), this chapter focuses on gay men and lesbian women.

No one stereotype fits all gay men and lesbian women with substance abuse problems. Clients may present with various concerns, with different addictions, and with widely varying social circumstances:

- Mike is a 65-year-old veteran living in low-income housing in a metropolitan area. Divorced and cut off from his Italian family, he is alcoholic, occasionally saving enough money to meet with a male prostitute.
- Celeste is a 33-year-old Latina who has been in an abusive romantic relationship for 3 years and has recently begun using alcohol as a coping mechanism. She realizes that she has a lot to lose if she leaves the relationship and has no other support networks; she has not had any contact with her family of origin for the past 5 years, and they do not know about her sexual orientation.
- Alan is a 32-year-old psychiatrist who spends much of his free time either at the gym or partying. He is self-identified as gay and in an open relationship; his family of origin is supportive and attends PFLAG (Parents, Families and Friends of Lesbians and Gays) meetings. Alan is worried because his weekend crystal methamphetamine use is expanding into his workweek.
- Maggie is a 25-year-old woman who wants to keep her sexual orientation a secret. She has repeatedly been told by her girlfriend that she has a drug problem, and her girlfriend has threatened to leave the relationship if she does not get some help.

- For over a year, Larry has been surreptitiously visiting the local gay and lesbian youth center. Larry is African American and aged 17. His parents bring him to therapy because his grades are slipping and he has been smoking marijuana. They know nothing about his sexual identity.

Mike, Celeste, Alan, Maggie, and Larry may have different reasons and etiologies for their drug and alcohol use, may require different therapeutic modalities, and may see different mental health providers. Regardless, the therapist working with them must respond to the issue of gay identity when raised and have a certain knowledge base and comfort level with this client group to be therapeutically effective.

Drug and Alcohol Culture in the Gay Community

It is useful to know a little about the more common drugs that gay men and lesbian women are exposed to in the club scene. Gay men and lesbian women are overrepresented in rates of substance abuse when compared to the non-gay community. In a review of the literature, Cabaj (2000) suggested a substance abuse incidence of approximately 30% for gay men and lesbian women, in comparison to 10% to 12% in the general population. These figures are hard to verify given the difficulty in determining the number of gay people in the general population. Many gay people are not "out," and only a subsection of them frequent clubs and bars. People who do not experience problems with addiction (and perhaps are not involved in the gay scene) tend to remain invisible to research investigators. According to a study by Cochran, Ackerman, Mays, and Ross (2004), both lesbian and gay participants reported more problems with drug use across all classes of drugs than did heterosexual participants. Specifically, more gay men reported use of marijuana, heroin, and cocaine than heterosexual men did. Lesbian women were more likely than heterosexual women to use marijuana and analgesics. Hallucinogen use was also significantly higher for lesbian women than heterosexual women. Marijuana was the most commonly used drug for both gay and lesbian participants. The homosexual participants were more likely to meet the criteria for dependence (i.e., a need so strong for a substance that individuals must have this substance to function properly) on marijuana than were heterosexual participants.

Adolescent Population

Gay adolescents are also identified at a high level of risk for substance abuse (Olson, 2000). The feeling of same-sex attraction generally runs counter to familial and societal expectations. This is a particular problem for adolescents who are simultaneously trying to establish a sense of self while running the risk of peer and family rejection. Olson stated: "Substance use can emerge both in the context of self medication, and in relation to self marginalization" (p. 71). Recent research has found that gay adolescents are more likely to abuse hard drugs than marijuana or alcohol (Orenstein, 2001).

Social Places and Drugs of Choice

For decades much of the gay social life has revolved around bars and drinking. Clubs, raves, and circuit parties are now common meeting places for the younger gay set (McDowell, 2000). Circuit parties are large-scale events that take place over a number of days in different parts of the United States and beyond. They were originally fund-raising parties for HIV/AIDS charities and are associated in the popular press with illicit drug use.

While alcohol continues to be widely available in most gay venues, drugs have also become popular, though they are by no means limited to use by gay men and lesbian women. These club drugs are generally known to therapists who work with gay clients. They include ecstasy, which can induce depression and panic; Ketamine, or "Special K," a dissociative anesthetic that can cause feelings of unreality—not to mention catatonia; Gamma Hydroxybutyrate (GBH), a drug with effects similar to alcohol and potentially resulting in sleep or coma; LSD; crystal methamphetamine; and smoked cocaine or crack (Guss, 2000). Some gay individuals associate an "out" gay lifestyle with bar and club nightlife. Friends and acquaintances established in this context can become a surrogate family. Drugs and alcohol help to lower sexual inhibitions but are correlated with unsafe sexual practices (Halkitis, Parsons, & Stirrit, 2001). In their research, Kalichman, Tannenbaum, and Nachimson (1998) described the "sensation seeking personality" as a precursor to sexual risk-taking behavior and drug and alcohol abuse. The development of such a personality may have its roots in self-hatred or dissociation from reality. Greenan and Tunnell (2003) believed that recreational drug use is meeting a need for connectedness, "a need that is only heightened in gay men by their feeling so disconnected to the majority culture" (p. 197).

Over time, an increasing number of alternatives to the gay scene have been developed; however, they are generally limited to the larger urban areas. Places that offer the chance to meet others outside of pubs and clubs include gay community centers; outdoor groups; sports teams; religious groups (Catholics, Muslims, Mormons, Jews, and Protestants are all represented); university lesbian, gay, bisexual, and transgender (LGBT) societies; book clubs; senior groups; and gay online chat rooms. Some services specifically recognize the problems of addiction within the LGBT community and provide social activities that are drug and alcohol free. In New York City's LGBT Community Center, for example, a monthly dance is held that excludes alcohol and drugs.

Gay Identity

Drug and alcohol use may be tightly bound to the gay man's or lesbian woman's sense of self. In therapy, careful assessment should include an evaluation of internalized homophobia and identity development. For some gay men and lesbian women, sustained abstinence is only achievable if they experience a change in the sense of gay identity. Gay social networks may be implicated in the required change, along with the psychological sense of gay expression and freedom. Changes may be required in family, social, and occupational systems in order to maintain abstinence. This change may involve a sense of loss and grieving.

Cass (1979) proposed a model that helps to explain the process of gay or lesbian identity development. The six stages can be traversed in order or may be regressed to in cases of relapse. Not everyone chooses to move through all the steps, and some steps may be missed; some people may prioritize other elements of their identity, such as culture or religion, before sexual orientation.

1. Identity confusion: Becoming conscious of being different; experiencing feelings of alienation and incongruence. Prior to this stage, individuals assumed they were heterosexual.
2. Identity comparison: Questioning previously held convictions; trying on the label "gay" to see if it fits. The person may ask himself or herself, "What are all the implications of being gay?"
3. Identity tolerance: Having an "I am probably gay" phase. Increased contact with other gay individuals and an investigation of the subculture occur.
4. Identity acceptance: Forming supportive friendships and making choices regarding coming out to family and friends.
5. Identity pride: Reacting to society's rejection, feeling angry at injustices, and having willingness to act. Not everyone goes through this stage.
6. Identity synthesis: Seeing sexuality as part of a total identity.

It is important to prepare clients in the process of coming out to family and friends so that they allow time for the information receivers to integrate the new understanding of their loved one before they are able to respond. One goal of therapy is to help the client form a positive gay identity, as Allen and Oleson (1999) described: "A positive gay identity is seen as a psychological process of development contingent upon a commitment and opportunity for growth and not simply resulting from self-labeling as homosexual" (p. 41).

Unique Characteristics of Gay Men

The issue of HIV/AIDS is never far away when working with gay men. A person's judgment is affected by drug and alcohol use, and the issue of safe sex should be stressed in recovery. The gay man may never have had sex without being under the influence, so discussion concerning intimacy and self-acceptance is necessary. Such a discussion should include male cultural stereotypes and the types of pressures that may exist within each family and community concerning the meaning of being male. The image of "maleness" varies among different cultures and families; some attribute great stigma to perceived signs of weakness and anything "feminine" in a male. Effeminate and therefore more visibly gay men experience the prejudice associated with not being "man enough." Within the gay community itself, there is increasing pressure to be more "butch," which can add to stress for some men. As Cabaj (2000) noted, "The desire to be masculine also contributes to the great focus on looks and body image for many gay men" (p. 17). Certain drugs play a role in enhancing sexual performance; indeed, the act of risk taking may be viewed as a masculine trait and therefore encouraged. Some gay men link self-acceptance to the perfect body image, denying the reality of aging and attaching their self-confidence to physical appearance (Peters, Copeland, & Dillon, 1999). For the therapist, a focus on underlying fears and self-image surrounding masculinity and internalized homophobia is pertinent.

For some gay men, sexual compulsivity is a problem. This condition may or may not be associated with addiction. Amphetamines, poppers (the street term for various alkyl nitrates taken for recreational purposes through direct inhalation), and cocaine are sometimes used to prolong sexual experiences, improve stamina, and heighten orgasms.

Avoidance of intimacy and relationships is etiologically diverse. Certainly shame and guilt about being gay can contribute to the problem. The laws of many states continue to discriminate against gay men, while religious institutions have moralized and campaigned against the "sin of Sodom." Inhibitions concerning gay sex and same-sex affection are often desensitized through the use of alcohol and drugs. Family-of-origin issues and a societal lack of recognition for gay couples are areas worth exploring in therapy.

Unique Characteristics of Lesbian Women

Given the differences between them and gay men, lesbian women may present in therapy with different manifestations of their addictions and reasons for these addictions. For example, lesbian women are more likely to use communication and openness in their relationships than are gay men (V. Gutierrez, 2004; Huston & Schwartz, 1995; Rutter & Schwartz, 1996), who are typically raised to be competitive and value power (Brown, 1995). These differences may exist as a result of different norms and values in the communities of lesbian women and gay men, rather than gender role socialization (V. Gutierrez, 2004). Regardless, the unique characteristics of lesbian women include being communicative (Bryant & Demian, 1994; Haas & Stafford, 1998; Huston & Schwartz, 1995; Ossana, 2000), embracing equality (Klinger, 1996; Weeks, Heaphy, & Donovan, 2001), sharing tasks (Kurdek, 1995; Ossana, 2000), being family-oriented (Bryant & Demian, 1994; Mendola, 1980), and, overall, centering on emotional connectedness (Brown, 1995; Kurdek, 1998; Ossana, 2000; Peplau, Cochran, & Mays, 1997; Rutter & Schwartz, 1996). Thus, when lesbian women present for therapy, someone close to them is likely to be concerned for their well-being, or they may be attempting to get some help for someone they care about (McCabe, Boyd, Hughes, & d'Arcy, 2003). They may also have increased responsibility in their roles of caretakers and family members, suggesting that more individuals for whom they care are involved in their lives.

Other factors to consider in the assessment of substance use with lesbian women include a history of sexual abuse, relationship violence, level of stress, job-related concerns (e.g., being underpaid), and depression (Hughes & Eliason, 2002). For example, research has shown that females are more likely to have a history of sexual abuse than are males, and having two females in a romantic relationship increases the chances of this occurring (Brown, 1995). This is not to suggest that sexual abuse does not occur in gay men, but the pressure to experiment sexually may preclude men from making such an incident known (Gutierrez, 1992). Lesbian women have the same likelihood as heterosexual women of experiencing relationship violence, a high level of stress, job-related concerns, and depression (Hughes & Eliason, 2002). However, researchers have yet to determine how these factors are triggered or manifested specifically in lesbian women with addiction.

Lesbian women have been compared to gay men and heterosexual women in their rates of using alcohol and experiencing problems arising from such use, and it appears that (a) gay men tend to use alcohol more than lesbian women do, though they do not significantly differ in the problems that arise from using alcohol (Amadio, 2002), and (b) lesbian women are no more likely than heterosexual women to use alcohol, but they are at greater risk of using other drugs, such as ecstasy and marijuana (McCabe et al., 2003), and having alcohol-related problems (Hughes & Eliason, 2002). Thus, considering differences between gay men and lesbian women is essential when providing treatment to them.

Therapeutic Considerations

A Safe Place

Every client deserves a safe place where he or she can express and explore new aspects of the self. Gay men and lesbian women often have had to segregate aspects of their lives and perhaps have never told anyone about their sexual identity. Professional psychological associations have established guidelines for mental health providers to use when working with sexual minorities. The American Association for Marriage and Family Therapy (AAMFT) Code of Ethics (2001) Section 1.1 states: "Marriage and family therapists provide professional assistance to persons without discrimination on the basis of race, age, ethnicity, socioeconomic status, disability, gender, health status, religion, national origin, or sexual orientation." The American Psychological Association holds a similar view and has established the Division 44/Committee on Lesbian, Gay, and Bisexual Concerns Joint Task Force, which has set forth guidelines to help psychologists understand their duties and roles in working with sexual minorities (2000). If a client has a history of substance use, psychologists are strongly encouraged to keep that information in mind when they work with the client since it tends to present challenges for LGBT individuals.

The amount of training available concerning sexual orientation at master's and doctoral levels appears to vary. A survey of doctoral psychology courses by Wiederman and Sansone (1999) found that "19–21% of programs in the U.S. did not offer any training with regard to sexual dysfunction, therapy with gay clients and HIV/AIDS" (p. 312). Training in gay and lesbian issues should ideally cover the issue on two fronts. First, therapists in training should be able to confront their own and society's homophobia

(LGBT therapists can also be homophobic), on both professional and personal levels, because many stereotypes of gay people exist and need to be acknowledged and challenged. Second, training should acknowledge a myriad of gay lifestyles and therapeutic approaches, and it should consider what constitutes "family" in the gay community. Each client brings a unique family, cultural, and religious background that affects assessment and treatment.

Given the high numbers of gay individuals purportedly addicted to substances, it is surprising that only 1% of clients in mainstream addiction programs self-identify as gay or bisexual (Niesen, 1996). This statistic could be attributed to one or more of the following reasons: (a) Gay clients do not enter addiction programs; (b) gay factors are not mentioned because they have little bearing on the recovery process; or (c) gay men and lesbian women are not inclined to talk about the issue within the program. Therapists can adopt a number of approaches to make disclosure easier for gay clients.

Adopting a neutral or objective stance can sometimes prove counter-therapeutic (Palma & Stanley, 2002). The term *marriage and family therapist,* for example, lends itself to notions of heterosexual exclusivity. Perhaps the term *couple and family therapist* might signify a more accepting and inclusive title. A recent article published in the *Journal of Marital and Family Therapy* suggests the use of conversion therapy to help LGBT persons remove unwanted same-sex physical attraction (Rosik, 2003). Such approaches continue to pathologize homosexuality. Furthermore, they have been shown to be unworkable and unethical (Haldeman, 1994). Articles such as these serve to alienate gay clients at all stages of self-acceptance. The controversy created by the publication of Rosik's article resulted in the AAMFT (American Association for Marriage and Family) Board of Directors issuing a statement reaffirming its central commitment to "openness and inclusion, and the freedom of our clients to hold their own moral perspectives" (AAMFT, 2002). An alternative approach is to encourage self-acceptance and the "coming out" process in therapy; strengths and resiliencies can become the focus, leading ultimately to solutions. For a gay addict, recovery is often linked to self-acceptance, which is a lifelong process (Cabaj, 2000; Niesen, 1996; Palma & Stanley, 2002). According to Cabaj (2000), a gay man in recovery is almost certain to relapse if he cannot acknowledge his sexual orientation in a safe environment.

As Niesen (1996) noted, a number of simple yet sensitive touches can lighten the fear of coming out to a therapist. These include having gay publications and posters in the waiting area, including sexual orientation in affirmative action statements, and designing forms to take into account gay lifestyles. For example, many forms continue to ask the question, "Are you married/divorced/separated/single?"

The therapist working with sexual minority individuals requires a relevant knowledge base and practice on how to introduce sex and sexuality in a conversation. This requirement holds true for gay and non-gay therapists. For example, appropriate terms should be used; use of the term *homosexual* is often linked to a pathologizing stance, while the term *sexual identity* includes both a behavioral predisposition and an affectional orientation. In a qualitative study, Conley, Calhoun, Evitt, and Devine (2001) asked lesbian, gay, and bisexual clients how therapists *should not* respond to their coming-out process. These clients said that therapists should not exhibit the following responses:

- stating that they know another gay person
- relying on stereotypes
- being overcautious or asking too many questions
- using subtly prejudicial language

The authors acknowledged "how heterosexuals may feel that they are between a rock and a hard place as they attempt to negotiate pleasant interactions" (p. 41). With improved training, however, the therapist will feel more comfortable and, consequently, the client will be at greater ease.

Davies (1996) suggested that a gay affirmative model be adopted. The main tenets of gay affirmative practice outline the challenges that LGBT youth face and delineate the environmental and individual strengths that can be enhanced to promote well-being. This approach can be incorporated into a systemic framework that regards homophobia, not the gay person, as the major pathological variable, which may contribute to symptoms, such as drug and alcohol abuse and difficulty in identity formation.

Factors Related to Substance Use

Many books and articles provide helpful suggestions for therapists working with sexual minority individuals (Davies & Neal, 2000; Greenan & Tunnell, 2003; Hicks, 2000; Palma & Stanley, 2002). First and foremost, each client is different, and the issues addressed in therapy depend on, among other factors, the (a) clinical assessment, (b) life-cycle phase, (c) gay identity phase, (d) present and past relationships, (e) social life, (f) alcohol or drug of choice, (g) family-of-origin relationships, (h) experience of hate crimes, (i) domestic violence, and (j) internalized homophobia. Second, stressors need to be identified. These stressors can include visibility issues, family conflict, discrimination at work, general discrimination, violence and harassment, HIV/AIDS, and isolation (Lewis, Derlega, Berndt, Morris, & Rose, 2001). Some authors suggest that heterosexism and homophobia may be at fault for the high degree of substance use among lesbian women and gay men (e.g., Cabaj, 2000).

Not all gay substance abusers need to focus on homophobia and gay identity issues in therapy. Family-of-origin work can indicate a strong biological predisposition to addiction. Assessment, therefore, becomes crucially important. It is as much of an error to over-focus on issues related to gay identity as it is to avoid or negate those issues. Gay identity may be used as an excuse to avoid the issue of substance abuse, and a "poor me" syndrome can develop that is counter-therapeutic.

Recovery

The stage of recovery from addiction is important, and referral may be necessary for detoxification or treatment programs. Ideally these programs will be at least gay accepting if not affirming, such as those at the Lambda Center in Washington, DC (Hicks, 2000). The therapist might need to make contact with the various programs in his or her area for referral purposes and, where there is a lack of knowledgeable professionals, choose to provide or arrange training on LGBT issues in recovery. Some areas have LGBT Alcoholics Anonymous (AA) groups or other community-run living sober groups that may be useful. Many gay individuals avoid AA groups because of AA's perceived spiritual base, though many of the attendees have variously interpreted the notion of a "higher power." Previous experience with organized religion may have been negative for some people; however, many gay individuals have a strong spirituality (Olson, 2000).

Confidentiality

The issues of confidentiality and secure record keeping are worth verbalizing in the first session. Homophobic attacks and social and legal discrimination and insurance problems related to HIV infection have all served to highlight the dangers of inappropriate disclosures.

Social Support Networks

It may be particularly difficult for gay individuals to avoid certain friends and social arenas. Bars and clubs constitute the available gay social life in some areas. Because of shame or internalized homophobia, the gay individual may have been able to express his or her sexuality only when under the influence of alcohol or drugs. Helping a client find alternative and drug- and alcohol-free social venues and activities is beneficial for the client. The therapist should have a list of resources or offer suggestions about how to find the necessary resources involving recovery. Some therapists, for instance, may want to facilitate coming-out groups, gay-living groups, or living sober groups, which serve as additional support.

Family Systems Therapy

The therapist who works from a family systems approach has a lot to offer in the recovery process when systemic problems are evident. Lawson and Lawson (1998) suggest a progression of different models for use with alcoholic families depending on the chronicity of the alcohol abuse. These models include Berenson's treatment approach for families with a chronic using alcoholic, Haley's solution-focused approach, couple therapy, and family-of-origin work.

For instance, when working with adolescents' coming-out process, the family therapist can help to avoid cutoff from the family and focus the family on resilience. Drug and alcohol experimentation is already common in adolescence without the added stressors associated with coming out. Education about addiction and referral to supportive local networks can help reduce the risk for addiction.

For same-sex couples, the user and partner (and other significant members) may be seen in family therapy once recovery is under way. Couples therapy for gay individuals tends to follow many of the traditional family systemic techniques: The family system becomes the client while the purpose and role of addiction within the family system are investigated. Feedback loops and homeostasis help to keep the family stuck in familiar patterns. Some particular problems for same-sex couples include male-role perceptions, competition for status and power, a lack of role models for gay long-term intimacy, stigma, homophobia, and lack of social support (many gay events have a singles outlook). As with heterosexual couples, some homosexual couples are not sexually exclusive, often by agreement, and so a nonjudgmental attitude is necessary (Brown, 1995).

Family-of-origin issues are of special concern. The gay-identified individual may be cut off from the family of origin, or the gay man may be leading a double life, keeping his sexual identity hidden from the family. Addiction and couple relationship problems often stem from these unresolved dilemmas. Intergenerational approaches are especially useful in tackling family-of-origin issues. A Bowen therapist, for example, might coach the lesbian woman to reconnect with family members, or, if that is not possible, to find some other means to lower reactivity and increase differentiation. This strategy may involve differentiating family of origin from family of choice, the substitute family many gay individuals formulate for themselves. The therapist should remain aware of triangles and how internalized homophobia and drugs and alcohol can be viewed as opposing corners of a triangle with the gay man caught in the middle.

Framo's (1991) model of group therapy in preparation for family-of-origin sessions might be adapted for either single gay individuals or gay couples by bringing together several couples or individuals to help articulate family-of-origin issues and to prepare an agenda for their family-of-origin sessions. The family-of-origin session's goals are to create more adult-to-adult relationships, reduce misunderstandings, and debunk mythology. The purpose of the sessions is not to change the parents or siblings, and Framo would not allow the adult child to reprimand his or her parents. If issues are resolved in the family of origin, they are less likely to be projected onto a partner where they do not belong.

When parents and siblings refuse to maintain contact with the gay-identified individual, the therapist can apply Boszormenyi-Nagy's concepts found in contextual therapy. Rejunctive efforts are methods used to address relational inequalities and provide self-validation. The client can work in therapy on exonerating and forgiving parents and siblings by understanding their respective upbringing and influences. This process serves to humanize the family of origin and remove destructive entitlement, which is a form of ethical credit based on actual past injustices. Rejunctive efforts can include finding ways to contribute to the gay community or present family and friends in nondestructive and self-affirming ways. Loyalty issues must also be addressed; the gay client is sometimes caught between loyalty to the family of origin and loyalty to a gay identity. The family of origin may pressure the gay-identified individual to choose between the two, or the individual may imagine having to make such a choice if he or she were to self-disclose his or her sexual orientation to the family.

Conclusion

The literature concerning both gay men and lesbian women and their resilience suggests adaptive and innovative methods for coping (Oswald, 2002). It is with tremendous courage and trust that a gay man reveals or starts to explore his sexual identity and addiction within the safety of the therapeutic relationship. It is inadvisable to treat the addicted lesbian woman without sensitivity to the myriad contributing factors that may underpin her presenting problem. The least a therapist can do is learn how to be gay affirming and to have some understanding of the strengths and problems of the gay lifestyle that may or may not contribute to drug and alcohol addiction.

References

Allen, D. J., & Oleson, T. (1999). *Journal of Homosexuality, 37*(3), 33–43.

Amadio, D. M. (2002). Internalized homophobia, alcohol use, and alcohol-related problems among lesbians and gay men [Abstract]. *Dissertation Abstracts International, 63,* 5503.

American Association for Marriage and Family Therapy. (2001). *AAMFT code of ethics.* Washington DC: Author. Retrieved July 10, 2007, from http://www.aamft.org/about/ethic.htm

American Association for Marriage and Family Therapy. (2002). *Board of directors statement.* Washington, DC: Author. Retrieved July 10, 2007, from http//www.aamft.org/about/boardletter.asp

Brown, L. S. (1995). Therapy with same-sex couples: An introduction. In N. S. Jacobson & A. S. Gurman (Eds.), *Clinical handbook of couple therapy* (pp. 137–153). New York: Guilford Press.

Bryant, A. S., & Demian, R. (1994). Relationship characteristics of American gay and lesbian couples: Findings from a national survey. *Journal of Gay and Lesbian Social Services, 1*(2), 101–117.

Cabaj, R. P. (2000). Substance abuse, internalized homophobia, and gay men and lesbians: Psychodynamic issues and clinical implications. *Journal of Gay and Lesbian Psychotherapy, 3*(3), 5–24.

Cass, V. C. (1979). Homosexual identity formation: A theoretical model. *Journal of Homosexuality, 4*(3), 219–235.

Cochran, S. D., Ackerman, D., Mays, V. M., & Ross, M. W. (2004). Prevalence of drug use and dependence among homosexually active men and women in the U.S. population. *Addiction, 99,* 989–998.

Conley, T. D., Calhoun, C., Evitt, S. R., & Devine, P. G. (2001). Mistakes that heterosexual people make when trying to appear non-prejudiced: The view from LGB people. *Journal of Homosexuality, 42*(2), 21–43.

Davies, D. (1996). Towards a model of gay affirmative therapy. In D. Davies & C. Neal (Eds.), *Pink therapy: A guide for counselors and therapists working with lesbian, gay and bisexual clients* (pp. 107–117). Philadelphia: Open University Press.

Davies, D., & Neil, C. (2000). *Therapeutic perspectives on working with lesbian, gay, and bisexual clients.* Philadelphia: Open University Press.

Division 44/Committee on Lesbian, Gay, and Bisexual Concerns, Joint Task Force on Guidelines for Psychotherapy with Lesbian, Gay, and Bisexual Clients. (2000). Guidelines for psychotherapy with lesbian, gay, and bisexual clients. *American Psychologist, 55,* 1440–1451.

Framo, J. (1991). *Family of origin therapy: An intergenerational approach.* New York: Brunner/Mazel.

Greenan, D. E., & Tunnell, G. (2003). *Couple therapy with gay men.* New York: Guilford Press.

Guss, J. R. (2000). Sex like you can't even imagine: "Crystal," crack and gay men. *Journal of Gay and Lesbian Psychotherapy, 3*(3), 105–122.

Gutierrez, F. J. (1992). Gay and bisexual male incest survivors. In S. H. Dworkin & F. J. Gutierrez (Eds.), *Counseling gay men and lesbians: Journal to the end of the rainbow* (pp. 191–201). Alexandria, VA: American Counseling Association.

Gutierrez, V. (2004). Maintenance behaviors and conflict level, areas, and resolution strategies in same-sex couples. *Dissertation Abstracts International, 65,* 4896.

Haas, S. M., & Stafford, L. (1998). An initial examination of maintenance behaviors in gay and lesbian relationships. *Journal of Social and Personal Relationships, 15*(6), 846–855.

Haldeman, D. C. (1994). The practice and ethics of sexual orientation conversion therapy. *Journal of Consulting and Clinical Psychology, 62*(2), 221–227.

Halkitis, P. N., Parsons, J. T., & Stirrat, M. J. (2001). A double epidemic: Crystal methamphetamine drug use in relation to HIV transmission among gay men. *Journal of Homosexuality, 41*(2), 17–35.

Hicks, D. (2000). The importance of specialized treatment programs for lesbian and gay patients. *Journal of Gay and Lesbian Psychotherapy, 3*(3), 81–94.

Hughes, T. L., & Eliason, M. (2002). Substance use and abuse in lesbian, gay, bisexual and transgender populations. *Journal of Primary Prevention, 22*(3), 263–298.

Huston, M., & Schwartz, P. (1995). The relationships of lesbians and of gay men. In J. T. Wood & S. Duck (Eds.), *Under-studied relationships: Off the beaten track* (pp. 89–121). Thousand Oaks, CA: Sage.

Kalichman, S. C., Tannenbaum, L., & Nachimson, D. (1998). Personality and cognitive factors influencing substance use and sexual risk for HIV infection among gay and bisexual men. *Psychology of Addictive Behaviors, 12*(4), 262–271.

Klinger, R. L. (1996). Lesbian couples. In R. P. Cabaj & T. S. Stein (Eds.), *Textbook of homosexuality and mental health* (pp. 339–352). Washington, DC: American Psychiatric Press.

Kurdek, L. A. (1995). Lesbian and gay couples. In A. R. D'Augelli & C. J. Patterson (Eds.), *Lesbian, gay, and bisexual identities over the lifespan: Psychological perspectives* (pp. 243–261). New York: Oxford University Press.

Kurdek, L. A. (1998). Relationship outcomes and their predictors: Longitudinal evidence from heterosexual married, gay cohabiting, and lesbian cohabiting couples. *Journal of Marriage and the Family, 60,* 553–568.

Lawson, A. W., & Lawson, G. W. (1998). *Alcoholism and the family: A guide to treatment and prevention* (2nd ed.). Austin, TX: PRO-ED.

Lewis, R. J., Derlega, V. J., Berndt, A., Morris, L. M., & Rose, S. (2001). An empirical analysis of stressors for gay men and lesbians. *Journal of Homosexuality, 42*(1), 63–88.

McCabe, S. E., Boyd, C., Hughes, T. L., & d'Arcy, H. (2003). Sexual identity and substance use among undergraduate students. *Substance Abuse, 24*(2), 77–91.

McDowell, D. (2000). Gay men, lesbians and substances of abuse and the "club and circuit party scene": What clinicians should know. Journal of *Gay and Lesbian Psychotherapy, 3*(3), 37–57.

Mendola, M. (1980). *The Mendola report: A new look at gay couples.* New York: Crown.

Niesen, J. H. (1996). If your clients are gay or bisexual can they tell you so? *Addiction Letter, 12*(2), 1–2.

Olson, E. D. (2000). Gay teens and substance use disorders: Assessment and treatment. *Journal of gay and lesbian psychotherapy, 3*(3), 69–80.

Orenstein, A. (2001). Substance use among gay and lesbian adolescents. *Journal of Homosexuality, 41*(2), 1–15.

Ossana, S. M. (2000). Relationship and couples counseling. In R. M. Perez, K. A. DeBord, & K. J. Bieschke (Eds.), *Handbook of counseling and psychotherapy with lesbian, gay, and bisexual clients* (pp. 275–302). Washington, DC: American Psychological Association.

Oswald, R. F. (2002). Resilience within the family networks of lesbians and gay men: Intentionality and redefinition. *Journal of Marriage and Family Therapy, 64,* 374–383.

Palma, T. V., & Stanley, J. L. (2002). Effective counseling with lesbian, gay and bisexual clients. *Journal of College Counseling, 5*(1), 74–89.

Peplau, L. A., Cochran, S. D., & Mays, V. M. (1997). A national survey of the intimate relationships of African American lesbians and gay men: A look at commitment, satisfaction, sexual behavior, and HIV disease. In B. Greene (Ed.), *Ethnic and cultural diversity among lesbians and gay men* (pp. 11–38). Thousand Oaks, CA: Sage.

Peters, R., Copeland, J., & Dillon, P. (1999). Ambolic-andronergic steroids: User characteristics, motivations and deterrents. *Psychology of Addictive Behaviors, 13*(3), 232–242.

Rosik, C. H. (2003). Motivational, ethical, and epistemological foundations in the treatment of unwanted homoerotic attraction. *Journal of Marital and Family Therapy, 29*(1), 13–38.

Rutter, V., & Schwartz, P. (1996). Same-sex couples: Courtship, commitment, context. In A. E. Auhagen & M. von Salisch (Eds.), *The diversity of human relationships* (pp. 197–226). Cambridge, England: Cambridge University Press.

Weeks, J., Heaphy, B., & Donovan, C. (2001). *Same-sex intimacies: Families of choice and other life experiments.* London: Routledge.
Wiederman, M. W., & Sansone, R. A. (1999). Sexuality training for professional psychologists: A material survey of training directors of doctoral programs and predoctoral internships. *Professional Psychology: Research and Practice, 30*(3), 312–317.

Resources

American Educational Gender Information Service
(resources for transgender individuals)
http//www.gender.org/aegis/body/body.html

BiNet USA
http://www.binetusa.org/

The Human Rights Campaign
(the largest national lesbian and gay political organization for equal rights, with more than 360,000 members, both homosexual and heterosexual)
http://www.hrc.org/

PFLAG
(Parents, Families and Friends of Lesbians and Gays)
http://www.pflag.org/

Queer Resources Directory
http://www.qrd.org/qrd/

The Renaissance Transgender Association
(a monthly magazine on transgender topics)
http://www.ren.org/maininfo.html

CHAPTER 10

Chemical Dependency Within the Hispanic Population

Considerations for Diagnosis and Treatment

Jodi Bunting Stanley

There are approximately 42.7 million people in the United States who are of Hispanic (or Latino) descent, making the Hispanic population the nation's largest ethnic minority (U.S. Census Bureau, 2006). As a group, Hispanics constitute 14% of the nation's total population and are the youngest and fastest growing minority in North America. Specifically, the median age of the Hispanic population is 27.2 years, compared with 36.2 years for the population as a whole (U.S. Census Bureau, 2006). In addition, approximately 22% of the total U.S. Hispanic population is under the age of 5. It is projected that by 2050, the Hispanic population will represent 102.6 million, or 24%, of the nation's total population (U.S. Census Bureau, 2006). This demographic transformation of the U.S. population and the composition of its minority populations underscores the importance of studying drug abuse trends and associated risk factors in the Hispanic population.

The Hispanic population is composed of individuals from many national backgrounds, including Mexican (64%), Puerto Rican (10%), Cuban (3%), Salvadoran (3%), and Dominican (3%) (U.S. Census Bureau, 2000). Racially, Hispanics are White, Black, Indian, or some combination thereof.

Approximately 10 million foreign-born people in the United States were born in Mexico, which is by far more than any other Latin American country—or any other country in the world (U.S. Census Bureau, 2000). Other countries of birth that largely contribute to the U.S. Hispanic population are El Salvador (937,000), Cuba (925,000), the Dominican Republic (688,000), Guatemala (590,000), and Colombia (500,000). It is estimated that 49% of the Hispanic-origin population resides in California (12.4 million) or Texas (7.8 million). Additionally, 43% of New Mexico's total population is Hispanic, which is the highest percentage of any state. It is estimated that in the United States, Spanish is either the primary or preferred language spoken in more than 1 in 10 households (U.S. Census Bureau, 2000).

In 2004, the real median income of Hispanic households was approximately $34,241, or 69% of the median for non-Hispanic White households ($48,977) (U.S. Census Bureau, 2004). Further, the income of approximately 22% of Hispanic Americans is below the poverty level, compared with about 11% for non-Hispanics.

Group Characteristics

Educational Attainment

The educational attainment of Hispanics is well below that of the rest of the population despite significant progress. One of the most notable improvements in educational achievement is the reduction in the proportion of Hispanics with very little formal education. The proportion of Hispanics 25 years old and over with less than a ninth-grade education decreased from 29% in 1998 to 25% in 2004 (U.S. Census Bureau, 2004). Despite that improvement, the proportion of Hispanics with low educational attainment, or less than a ninth-grade education, in 2004 was more than 7 times greater than that of non-Hispanic Whites (3.3%).

Of additional interest, the proportion of Hispanics 25 years old and over with high school diplomas increased from 27% in 1998 to 58% in 2004, with 12%, or 2.7 million, advancing to earn a bachelor's degree or higher (U.S. Census Bureau, 2004). Despite that significant improvement, in 2004 Hispanics were still much less likely to be high school graduates or to earn a bachelor's degree or more (30%) than were non-Hispanic Whites (90%).

Educational attainment levels also differ substantially across Hispanic subgroups. For example, in 1998, Mexican Americans age 25 years old or older were the most likely to have completed less than a ninth-grade education (18%), while Cuban Americans were more likely to have bachelor's degrees (22%) than the other Hispanic groups (U.S. Census Bureau, 2004).

Employment

Census figures indicate that Hispanics in general have employment rates that are similar to the national average. Specifically, it was estimated in 2004 that 68% of Hispanic Americans age 16 and older belong to the civilian labor force, which is slightly higher than the 66% of non-Hispanic Whites that are in the labor force (U.S. Census Bureau, 2004). However, unemployment rates within the Hispanic population at that time were also slightly higher (8%) than in the non-Hispanic White population (5%). In addition, higher paying managerial and professional occupations were held by 18% of Hispanics, which is at one fourth the rate at which the larger U.S. population held them. Moreover, nearly 16% of Hispanics work in construction, extraction, and maintenance jobs, and 19% in production, transportation, and material-moving occupations (U.S. Census Bureau, 2004). These employment figures suggest that Hispanic substance-using clients may be experiencing problems related to employment as well as difficulties stemming from low income or poverty.

Families and Children

In 2004, approximately twice as many Hispanic families had five or more members (28.4%) as the non-Hispanic White population (11.3%) (U.S. Census Bureau, 2004). About 21% of all Hispanic American families with children under the age of 18 years were below the poverty level, compared with 6% of non-Hispanic White American families. Thirty-seven percent of these families were headed by women, with no husband living in the household.

Alcohol and Drug Use

Hispanics have the third highest percentage of illicit drug use and the second highest percentage of heavy alcohol consumption when compared to the total U.S. population (National Institute on Drug Abuse; NIDA; 2000). Specifically, research on substance abuse among Hispanics indicates that alcohol is the most frequently abused intoxicant, with more than 45% of the population reporting its usage. Tobacco cigarettes appear to be the second most used drug (25.8%), with marijuana being third (4.5%). Low educational attainment, unemployment, poverty, and acculturation stresses have been identified as significant contributors associated with the risk of drug and alcohol abuse within the Hispanic community.

Of additional importance, more than 14.9% of all incarcerated individuals in the United States are of Hispanic origin, and 23% of these Hispanics are being detained for drug-related offenses (U.S. Department of Justice, 2000). It is estimated that approximately 50% of Hispanic inmates will be released and placed on probation within 2 years of their sentence. Thus, it is likely that clinicians treating the Hispanic population will find some kind of drug problem among their clients or their clients' families.

The most recent prevalence estimates of drug and alcohol abuse suggest that drug and alcohol consumption patterns of Hispanic Americans largely reflect those of the broader U.S. population (Treno, Alaniz, & Gruenewald, 1999). For example, it was found that males generally consume more across all consumption measures, younger adults consume more than either youth or older adults, and economic and lifestyle factors such as income and the presence of children in the household impact consumption rates. In particular, it has commonly been found that those with the highest income level, who are often the most highly educated and the most integrated into mainstream society, also exhibit higher rates of alcoholism (Treno et al., 1999).

However, several differences distinguish Hispanic drinking behaviors. Treno et al. (1999) and Corbett, Mora, and Ames (1991) found that with regard to marital status, alcohol consumption among Hispanics increased with separation or divorce as opposed to being single, which also holds true in the general U.S. population. Additionally, consistent findings have indicated that high-risk drinking is the most prominent among

Hispanic males in their 30s as opposed to those in their 20s (Caetano, 1991; Treno et al., 1999).

Studies on Hispanics have also consistently shown that higher rates of acculturation are correlated with higher drinking levels (Burnam, Telles, Karno, & Hough, 1987; Cherpitel, 1992; Dawson, 1998; Fisher et al., 2004; Kail, Zayas, & Malgady, 2000; Treno et al., 1999). Specifically, it has been found that with greater acculturation, drinking levels among Hispanic Americans more closely resemble those of the mainstream culture. Moreover, U.S.-born individuals have been found to be more likely to consume alcohol on a daily basis than their immigrant counterparts (Canino, Burnam, & Caetano, 1992; Dawson, 1998). It may be that increased assimilation among Hispanic Americans results in greater exposure to the drinking styles of the dominant society and culture, in which alcohol is an integral part of after-hours socializing and camaraderie. An alternative explanation for this trend may involve stress-inducing factors that increase an individual's vulnerability to problem behaviors such as binge drinking (Guilamo-Ramos, Jaccard, Johansson, & Turrisi, 2004). For example, recent immigrants to the United States may experience problems associated with moving to a new country, such as language barriers and inadequate financial resources. They may also experience difficulties related to intergenerational differences of acculturation level in their families.

Recent research has also indicated subculture variations in drinking patterns among Hispanic men (NIDA, 2000). Both Mexican American and Puerto Rican men report greater levels of drug and alcohol use, alcohol-related health and marital problems, and impaired ability to control their drinking, compared to Cuban and Central and South American men. Additionally, Kail et al. (2000) found that the most acculturated Puerto Rican men reported drinking to relieve emotional distress; these authors concluded that it was this kind of drinking rather than the amount of drinking that predicts alcohol-related problems.

Reliable data showing the usage rate of heroin among Hispanics are difficult to obtain. However, Fisher et al. (2004) report that in Southern California, Hispanics, as compared to non-Hispanics, are more likely to be injection drug users, and heroin is the most commonly injected drug. In addition, those identifying as Mexican American reported greater numbers of overall injections and greater mean times sharing injection paraphernalia than Mexican drug users. This is consistent with previous findings suggesting that higher levels of acculturation may lead to greater drug and alcohol usage.

Data from the NIDA (2000) study indicate that the rate of heavy drinking among Hispanic women (2%) is significantly lower than that of Hispanic men (10.3%). Additionally, although Hispanic women report lower rates of alcohol consumption than non-Hispanic White women, they report similar rates of cocaine use and higher rates of crack use than non-Hispanic White women. Black and Markides (1993) found a positive association between acculturation and alcohol consumption in Mexican American, Puerto Rican, and Cuban American women, providing support for the acculturation theory of substance abuse. Higher levels of acculturation were consistently related to higher proportions of drinkers and greater frequency of consumption among women in all three groups. A possible explanation for these findings is that Hispanic women are in general more influenced by traditional values that do not sanction alcohol consumption among women; however, with increasing acculturation into the dominant U.S. society,

Hispanic American women appear to adopt the norms, practices, and values of the larger population (Black & Markides, 1993).

For Hispanic American adolescents, one of the largest and fastest growing population groups in the country, drug use may be magnified by difficulties associated with cultural, socioeconomic, and linguistic pressures (Ramirez et al., 2004). However, contrary to popular preconceptions, the latest data from the Monitoring the Future (MTF) study indicate that substance use by Hispanic American adolescents is not significantly greater than that of youth from other ethnicities (Johnston, O'Malley, & Bachman, 2001). Specifically, MTF results indicate that 20.9% of Hispanic youth in the United States are current users of at least one illicit substance, whereas 19.9% of the non-Hispanic White youth population and 15.3% of African American adolescents report similar usage. Nonetheless, despite comparable substance use rates among these groups, considerable differences exist with regard to patterns of usage and the variables that influence initiation and continuance of drug use. For example, it is estimated that Hispanic Americans engage in the use of illicit substances at earlier ages than do adolescents from other ethnic backgrounds. Specifically, Hispanic American eighth graders reported 10% more lifetime use of at least one illicit drug than non-Hispanic White eighth graders (Johnston et al., 2001). Additionally, in lower grades, Hispanic youth have higher rates of cocaine, crack, and marijuana use than other groups (NIDA, 2000).

Certain socioeconomic and demographic factors may place drug-using Hispanic youth at greater risk than youth from other backgrounds, including less educational attainment, greater population percentages below the poverty level, and social adaptational stressors. In particular, Hispanic youth are often confronted with having to accommodate to both the cultural milieu of mainstream America and that of the traditional, native culture of their country of origin (Guilamo-Ramos et al., 2004). In addition, deviant peer influence has been shown to be the strongest proximal predictor of Hispanic adolescent problem behavior for tobacco, alcohol, and marijuana use (Beauvais, Wayman, Jumper-Thurman, Plested, & Helm, 2002; Frauenglass, Routh, Pantin, & Mason, 1997).

Given that about one third of Hispanic Americans are under the age of 15, compared with one fifth for the rest of the population, it is clear that substance use problems within the young Hispanic population may eventually have a greater proportional impact on the nation as a whole. For this reason, it is imperative that future research expand knowledge related to patterns, trends, and sociodemographic correlates of Hispanic American adolescent drug use.

Diagnostic Considerations

The etiology of Hispanic clients' substance abuse problems should be examined in relation to sociological, psychological, and physiological factors. Sociological factors are relatively more easily identifiable as etiological determinants in the development of substance abuse among Hispanics. Such sociological risks include low family cohesion, a cultural acceptance of alcohol consumption as part of social interaction, low socioeconomic status, acculturation stress, and negative peer modeling. These risks may also place Hispanic clients at higher psychological and physiological risk. The therapist must recognize that sociological, psychological, and physiological risk factors are interrelated. A significant risk factor in one area may well impact one or both of the other areas.

Sociological Risk Factors

It should be noted that some of the sociological risk factors discussed here can be found both in the general U.S. population and in other ethnic groups (e.g., higher divorce rates are associated with higher levels of alcohol consumption). The point is not to associate risk factors with the Hispanic population, but rather to alert the therapist as to potential sociological risks that may be affecting the client's situation. The more the therapist knows, the more he or she can help the client. Differences in alcohol consumption patterns and problematic consequences may reflect variations in motivations for drinking. Social motivations, in particular, are based on expectations surrounding drinking and its perceived effects on social interactions, such as easing social situations and enhancing sexuality (Cantor, Markus, Niedenthal, & Nurius, 1986). Cervantes, Gilbert, Salgado de Snyder, and Padilla (1991) suggest that the strongest predictor of drinking level is the expected social benefit of alcohol consumption among both U.S.-born and immigrant Hispanics.

Often, sociological factors that tend to heighten the chemical dependency risk level of Hispanic clients are associated with positive cultural values regarding alcohol. For example, the consumption of large amounts of alcohol on special occasions is common among Mexican Americans and may be openly accepted and relied upon as a social bonding behavior. Some Hispanic clients may not perceive the relationship between their alcohol or drug dependency and the use of these substances as social enhancers during interactions with friends and family.

Several aspects of family structure and functioning can also pose significant sociological risks. Specifically, with regard to marital status, Treno et al. (1999) report that Hispanic clients who are separated or divorced appear to have higher rates of drinking than single persons. Additionally, research on the positive and negative influences that adolescents encounter in families, in schools, in communities, and among peers consistently identifies the family environment as an important component in the social etiology of adolescent substance use problems. For example, several studies have identified family modeling of drinking (Brooks, Stuewig, & LeCroy, 1998), permissive parental attitudes toward alcohol and drug use (Gfroerer & De La Rosa, 1993), and minimal familial cohesion (Brook, Brook, De La Rosa, Whiteman, Johnson, & Montoya, 2001) as strong predictors of adolescent substance use across ethnic groups. A study by Delva et al. (2005) indicates that the likelihood of drug use is significantly higher among Hispanic adolescents not living with their parents than among adolescents living with both parents. Thus, Hispanic youth residing with relatives or who are in foster care are likely to have a higher risk of developing a substance use problem.

Friends' influence on drug use has also received considerable attention in the literature and has been shown to be among the strongest sociological risk factors in adolescent substance use. Specifically, the use of tobacco, alcohol, and marijuana among

Hispanic youth has been found to be highly associated with deviant peer modeling (Beauvais et al., 2002; Frauenglass et al., 1997). High availability of drugs within specific communities is also an important sociological antecedent of drug use for Hispanics (Felix-Ortiz & Newcomb, 1992).

Acculturation to American society entails adaptation to new social values that may contribute to chemical dependency problems in Hispanic clients and their families. Differences in educational and accultural levels between family members of multiple generations may result in feelings of betrayal and familial distancing. If the changes in social and cultural values cause extreme emotional distress in a particular family member, alcohol or drugs may be used to alleviate these feelings. For example, Hispanic adolescents may adopt American cultural and social values instead of those of their parents. Difficulties can arise as parents and children attempt to adjust to the cultural differences that appear to be separating them. Additionally, in Hispanic American families that include adolescents, there may exist great differences in education, language, and social values between parent and child. The stress these differences cause may lead various family members to begin to rely on alcohol or drugs in order to cope.

Hispanics may also encounter difficulty obtaining and maintaining employment because of language differences and a lack of vocational and educational training. This problem tends to place Hispanic clients at increased sociological risk for substance abuse. Gainful employment has long been correlated with one's sense of self-esteem, and Hispanic clients may utilize alcohol or drugs as a means of managing feelings of low self-worth associated with unemployment. Further, although low socioeconomic status and poverty among Hispanic Americans may contribute to the sociological etiology of chemical dependency, it has also been found that those with the highest income level demonstrate higher levels of drinking (Treno et al., 1999). Thus, each risk factor may impact different clients to varying degrees.

Taken as a whole, these sociological factors can potentially position Hispanic clients at particularly high risk for developing a substance abuse problem. Any one variable or a combination of all of these variables may also contribute to increased psychological and physiological risk levels for chemical dependency in Hispanic clients.

Psychological Risk Factors

Psychological factors such as poor self-concept and low self-esteem, anxiety, or other depressed emotional states may act as internal motivations affecting the frequency and intensity of alcohol or drug consumption (Raynor & McFarlin, 1986). Hispanic clients who are experiencing acculturation, as with any person or group of persons attempting to overcome cultural and social differences between themselves and others, may experience feelings of rejection by the mainstream society and in turn may experience low self-esteem. Especially among newly immigrated Hispanics, feelings of rejection and low self-esteem can perpetuate and often increase the psychological risk for substance abuse.

The literature consistently documents a correlation between depression, heavy drinking, and drinking-related problems among Hispanic Americans (Golding, Burnam, Benjamin, & Wells, 1992; Johnson & Gurin, 1994; Kail et al., 2000). For example, research indicates that Mexican Americans who experience alcohol-related problems have twice the rate of depression of those who do not experience such problems (Golding et al., 1992). Johnson and Gurin (1994) report that depression and drinking problems are related among mainland Puerto Rican males and that this relationship is strongly mediated by the belief that alcohol will alleviate the depression. People who do not demonstrate this expectation have been found to not drink as much or experience as many alcohol-related problems (Johnson & Gurin, 1994). In a study including Hispanic women, Amaro, Nieves, Johannes, and Cabeza (1999) found that women are much more likely than men to have comorbid psychiatric conditions of anxiety disorders and affective disorders. Moreover, depression and anxiety disorders, which are known to be more prevalent among women, have also been found to heighten the risk of alcohol and nonprescription drug abuse. In addition, individuals with comorbidity have higher levels of impairment, underscoring the importance of including a thorough assessment in the treatment of women who are presenting symptoms of substance abuse or psychiatric disorders.

Chemically dependent Hispanic clients may also develop increased feelings of inadequacy as a result of the real or perceived loss of control over social, cultural, and economic situations, especially if they have little to no opportunity to implement change in these areas due to a lack of education or training. The feeling of being in control of oneself socially, and of being in control of one's environment, may depend a great deal on the degree of acculturation that a client has acquired. The strong links between substance abuse and depression may underscore the stresses of poverty and cultural distance from the host society as well as the strains of acculturation (Kail et al., 2000). For example, if a particular Hispanic client must live in a vastly different culture that he or she has difficulty adapting to, this dissonance and the stress it creates can exacerbate the psychological problems that he or she experiences. Thus, due to the social and cultural differences between themselves and the larger American society, Hispanic clients may feel a sense of social isolation that may lead them to use substances in order to boost, if only temporarily, their feelings of self-confidence and self-worth. In other words, substance abuse may serve as a temporary coping mechanism to help reduce anxiety, depression, or other pathological symptoms.

The significant relationship between depression and alcohol or drug use highlights the importance of awareness in the clinician of both social psychological problems, such as poor self-image, and the more personal psychological difficulties unique to each individual.

Physiological Risk Factors

Stress of any kind can alter human physiology (Allen, 1990); the sociological stressors to which Hispanics are often exposed, such as low income, unemployment, acculturation difficulties, discrimination, and language barriers, can intensify the physiological risk for developing chemical dependency. In addition, children of alcoholic parents are at higher risk for developing alcoholism; this predisposition may have a genetic component and/or a socialization component (Lawson & Lawson, 1998). In a review of family studies of alcoholism, Goodwin (1981) found that relatives of alcoholics had higher rates of alcoholism than rates found in the general population across all countries of origin. In light of the sociological stressors discussed in the previous section, it is imperative for the clinician to recognize the added risk when Hispanic clients experience alcoholism in their family of origin.

Genetic predisposition does not provide a complete explanation for alcoholism, but it is clearly one of the many contributing variables. Just as people inherit traits such as eye color from their parents, so they may inherit the manner in which their body responds physically to alcohol and other substances (Lawson & Lawson, 1998). Genetic predisposition does not necessarily lead to substance abuse, however. A person's response to such predisposition will depend on a complex interaction with social and psychological factors. The more the clinician knows about the client's family history, the sooner the clinician can make predictions regarding the possibility of alcohol and drug dependence, which in turns provide greater opportunity for effective treatment and prevention (Lawson & Lawson, 1998).

Treatment Considerations

The decision to obtain treatment for substance abuse and receptiveness to interventions and prevention efforts are profoundly influenced by the beliefs and values of one's culture. It is important to recognize that some Hispanic groups have a tolerant stance on the use of illicit substances for medicinal purposes, resulting in unclear definitions of substance abuse (Santisteban & Szapocznik, 1982). A more tolerant view toward substance use may result in avoidance of necessary treatment for abuse and may also produce a negative response to traditional treatment approaches that identify substance abuse as a disease. On the other hand, strong cultural beliefs against substance use for Hispanic women, as well as beliefs against sharing their personal problems with strangers, may also impose a barrier to treatment because of the stigma associated with violating cultural sanctions (Terrell, 1993).

When Hispanic clients do seek treatment, a lack of sensitivity to cultural beliefs, norms, and practices in regard to substance use may result in poor treatment outcomes. It is essential for clinicians to understand when working with Hispanic clients that people are culturally bound (Torres-Rivera, Wilbur, Phan, Maddux, & Roberts-Wilbur, 2004). In order for therapeutic interventions to be effective, they must reflect and include the client's cultural foundation. Traditional, normative approaches to substance abuse treatment often devalue individual differences and experiences, instead focusing on intrapsychic dysfunction. In addition, these conventional approaches generally focus on assisting Hispanic clients in adjusting more successfully to the dominant society by directing attention toward problems such as unemployment, poverty, family problems, and low educational attainment. Substance abuse problems among Hispanic Americans, however, are a multidimensional, complex problem that requires a bilingual, family-oriented perspective and a multimodal, culture-specific counseling method that looks beyond the symptoms (Torres-Rivera et al., 2004).

It is not surprising that Hispanics underutilize substance abuse services, considering that therapy involves having to ask for help, which automatically places clients in a one-down position in relation to the therapist (Lappin & Hardy, 1997). Hispanic clients may also feel that cultural and language barriers make it unlikely that they will be understood and accepted. In addition, chemical addiction may often be experienced by Hispanics as a moral weakness or failure, thereby engendering feelings of guilt and avoidance. It is possible, therefore, that Hispanic substance abusers have learned to medicate their problems through the use of alcohol and drugs.

Treatment Modalities

This section covers various treatment modalities used to treat Hispanic clients, including group therapy, Alcoholics Anonymous (AA), family therapy, inpatient care, and individual therapy.

Group Therapy

Martinez (1994) has asserted that no one counseling method is more effective than others in working with chemically dependent Hispanic clients, but Delgado (1997) suggests that bilingual, group-oriented approaches may be more effective because they are sensitive to cultural dynamics and provide an extended support network to the client. In order for any modality to be effective, it is imperative that abstention be achieved for a period of time to separate the physical from the psychological effects of drug use (Torres-Rivera et al., 2004).

Torres-Rivera et al. (2004) propose the process of group therapy through the psychoeducational modality as a productive method for assisting Hispanic clients to identify unmet psychological needs and drives. Such an approach is thought to present clients with alternatives and provide the opportunity to examine attitudes, values, and beliefs. The group format may also serve as a forum for Hispanics to become honest with themselves about their substance abuse.

However, the limitations of group therapy approaches must also be acknowledged. For example, it should be noted that the degree of a Hispanic client's acculturation and possible language barriers may present difficulties that should be taken into consideration before he or she is encouraged to participate in a group situation. Moreover, if a Hispanic client's level of acculturation and social adaptation is minimal, he or she may remain guarded within a heterogeneous group environment. If the social and cultural background of other group members is significantly different from that of the client, the desired effects of group therapy, such as a sense of cohesiveness, interpersonal learning, and universality, may not occur. Thus, the more difficult it is for Hispanic clients to feel a part of the group process, the less effective the therapeutic interventions will be. In particular, it has been found that Hispanics interact verbally at lower rates when placed in groups that include members of different cultural and ethnic origins (Shera, Sanchez, & Huang, 1984). For some chemically dependent Hispanic clients, thus, a more culturally homogenous group may be more effective for treatment. Additionally, proficiency in Spanish is necessary among treatment providers in order to successfully facilitate the group process.

Utilization of the therapeutic group process in the treatment of Hispanic adolescent substance abusers has been investigated by Santisteban et al. (2003), who found that there is a high possibility for reinforcement rather than reduction of delinquent behavior. Group therapy provides a cost-effective approach to alcohol and drug treatment, but it may have the potential of producing therapeutic deterioration among the members. Thus, in evaluating the various treatment options, it may be more efficacious to encourage youth to interact with a more positive peer group rather than with others struggling with similar substance use problems.

Alcoholics Anonymous

AA is based on a mutual-help 12-step program that is widely applied across diverse cultures. Epidemiological analyses of the general U.S. population suggest that AA is well known among Hispanic Americans and that a vast majority of this group would recommend AA to others for alcohol-related problems (Caetano, 1993). Tonigan, Connors, and Miller (1998) present findings from Project MATCH, a multisite research study aimed at developing guidelines for assigning alcoholics to appropriate treatment approaches. Specifically, they found that compared with non-Hispanic Whites, Hispanic clients reported higher levels of commitment to AA-related practices despite lower attendance. These results indicate that for those Hispanics who consistently attend AA, the practices of the program may be readily accepted and beneficial in assisting them with sobriety (Tonigan et al., 1998).

Although AA is a viable treatment modality for alcohol abuse among Hispanics, the cultural concept of machismo should be taken into account. Many Hispanic men may resist admitting that they are dependent on a substance, and this admission of dependency, as well as the notion of turning one's problem over to a higher power, is a required condition of treatment in AA programs. This requirement may cause many Hispanic men to feel guilt, shame, or a loss of control, and as a result, to reject AA as a form of treatment. When appropriate, Hispanic clients should be referred to Spanish-speaking and culturally sensitive AA organizations to help reduce the effects of cultural differences.

Family Therapy

Most Hispanics identify the family as their primary source of self-definition and self-esteem (Torres-Rivera et al., 2004). Especially in more traditional Hispanic cultures, the family plays an especially important and valuable role in lives of its members. Consequently, the therapist must gain the Hispanic client's trust and loyalty, as if he or she were a compadre, or coparent, of the client (Torres-Rivera et al., 2004). Additionally, both the nuclear and extended families of the Hispanic client should be included in the treatment process, which may mean that therapists must work with a large number of people (Terrell, 1993). Other prominent people in the community may also be involved in interventions with Hispanics, such as religious figures. Further ways in which clinicians may become a member of the family include interacting in community activities, such as *quinceñeras*, weddings, religious ceremonies, and community celebrations; demonstrating *respeto*, or knowledge and wisdom of cultural matters; and acknowledging the significance of familism, which refers to the central importance of family relationships and commitment (Terrell, 1993).

The initial purpose of using family therapy with Hispanic substance abusers is to evaluate the family's influence on the formation of the client's chemical dependency problem. Both the family of origin and the nuclear family should be utilized in gaining a clear and thorough understanding of the recursive, dysfunctional behaviors and interactions that may exist. Thus, a comprehensive assessment of the family structure, including hierarchies, alliances, and cutoffs, is critical during the working stage of the therapy process.

Of additional significance, when acculturation to American society occurs in the Hispanic family, traditional roles can deteriorate, causing further complications within family interactions. The use of alcohol or drugs can quickly become a method for reducing increased stress levels. Thus, family therapy is of vital importance in the treatment of substance abuse, especially within a newly acculturated Hispanic family.

Inpatient Care

Many Hispanic clients may not regard inpatient substance abuse care as a preferred treatment modality because most available facilities are non-Hispanic, which entails language and culture barriers. Some Hispanics, for cultural or personal reasons, may desire to have their chemical dependency issues treated by a family physician, and others may prefer spiritual and herbal treatment by an indigenous healer (Torres-Rivera et al., 2004). For these and other reasons, inpatient treatment has not been widely accepted by the Hispanic community (Alcocer, 1975; Karno & Edgerton, 1969).

In physically dependent Hispanic clients, however, it may be necessary to use inpatient treatment to ensure safe detoxification. For example, drug aversion therapy employing ipecac for alcoholism can be administered only on an inpatient basis. Barbiturate addiction frequently requires hospitalization in order to achieve medically safe and effective results. Inpatient treatment may also be needed for cocaine- and heroin-dependent Hispanic clients in order to remove them from easy access to the particular drug being used.

If a Hispanic client needs but resists institutionalized care, and hospitalized detoxification is not absolutely necessary, then outpatient treatment can be recommended at halfway house facilities, which may be more culturally and personally suited to the client's needs. Such services should support appropriate family reunification; allow family members to live in the program, especially children with their mothers; provide child care; and include parenting education and training (Amaro et al., 1999). These services acknowledge the centrality of family in Hispanic cultures.

Individual Therapy

Individual therapy may be a useful approach in treating chemical dependency in Hispanic clients; however, it is highly recommended that individual therapy be combined with family therapy when possible (Lawson & Lawson, 1998). This is particularly important in view of the meaning and value that Hispanic culture places on the family unit. In many cases involving addiction, the family is typically a part of the problem, and the family as a whole needs to be part of the solution. If there are cultural differences between the therapist and client, cultural flexibility and sensitivity are essential. With Hispanic clients who are seen by non-Hispanic therapists, language comprehension and fluency will have a great impact on the therapeutic process. If barriers are present, they must be dealt with before any therapy can begin. If the language barrier is insurmountable, the client may have to be referred to a therapist who is better able to serve the client's needs.

While the therapist should obtain as much information as possible regarding the client's Hispanic culture, the therapist should not focus exclusively on Hispanicity or treat it as a monolithic category. There are many subtle social and cultural differences among the diverse Hispanic groups, so the therapist should not make assumptions across subgroups. Further, the client is a unique individual who is personally influenced by contextual dynamics such as family, gender, race, socioeconomic status, education, and culture. Thus, substance abuse problems of Hispanics need to be examined, understood, and treated from the perception of the client's experience, as well as from the perspective of his or her culture (Torres-Rivera et al., 2004).

Therapists should also evaluate Hispanic clients' self-perceptions in order to determine the degree to which the client identifies with his or her ethnic background. The clinician will gain a better awareness of how cultural aspects may affect the therapeutic situation and can then structure the therapeutic process so as to maximize treatment.

Torres-Rivera et al. (2004) recommend that the essential first step in all interventions with drug users is abstention for a period of time in order to ascertain, assess, and disconnect the psychological and physiological components of dependency and coping. Once this has been accomplished, further interventions often require high levels of therapeutic skill in supportive confrontation, immediacy, and application of specific cultural principles (Torres-Rivera et al., 2004). Through abstention, therapists will have a better opportunity to influence clients' behavior and to begin addressing repressed psychological needs (Torres-Rivera et al., 2004). Additionally, therapists should focus on providing chemically dependent clients with a healthy role model through the honest expression of their own perceptions and life experiences. Clinicians should also provide Hispanic clients with direct feedback and openness, while also responding to increased levels of fear, hurt, and anger with expressions of warmth, empathy, positive regard, and support (Torres-Rivera et al., 2004). Including a spiritual component may also be an important variable in the substance abuse treatment of Hispanics, because spirituality is an essential part of identity for many Hispanics.

Prevention

Preventive interventions among Hispanic adolescents, adults, and their families may offer the best method of deterring first use or continuance of drug dependence. More school, community, and primary care programs for early intervention are needed, especially during the primary and middle school years. Whether substance abuse prevention programs are aimed at primary, secondary, or tertiary stages, or at the interplay of host, agent, and environment, as in the community health model, the application of prevention efforts will have the most success if bilingual communication methods are employed for presenting substance abuse information.

Building self-esteem is a widely recognized preventative intervention in substance abuse treatment, and it may be particularly effective for minority groups, many of whom must endure discrimination and negative stereotyping (Terrell, 1993). In addition, many intervention models propose increasing the social support network of ethnocultural groups struggling with substance use. This is especially true for Hispanic youth (Delva et al., 2005).

The family environment has consistently been identified as having significant protective influence against adolescent substance use (Frauenglass et al., 1997; Ramirez et al., 2004; Sale et al., 2005; Terrell, 1993; Vega, Sribney, & Achara-Abrahams, 2003). Specifically, it is suggested that clinicians provide family members of chemically dependent youth with culturally sensitive drug education in order to support prevention efforts (Terrell, 1993). Additionally, Sale et al. (2005) recommend that prevention programs in Hispanic communities focus on strengthening families by stressing family connectedness, family supervision, and parental disapproval of substance use as key protective factors against alcohol use in youth. Parental monitoring and strong familistic values have also been identified as serving important and unique roles in adolescent drug prevention (Frauenglass et al., 1997; Ramirez et al., 2004). Specifically, for both of these factors, it has been shown that strong family involvement reduces the influence of deviant peers on tobacco and marijuana use. Overall, interventions that impart knowledge and promote family cohesion offer the greatest hope of preventing the development of severe and long-lasting chemical dependency among Hispanic Americans.

References

Alcocer, A. M. (1975). *Chicano alcoholism.* Paper presented at the First Regional Conference of the Coalition of Spanish Speaking Mental Health Organizations, Los Angeles.

Allen, R. (1990). *Psychophysiology of the human stress response.* College Park: University of Maryland.

Amaro, H., Nieves, R., Johannes, S. W., & Cabeza, N. M. L. (1999). Substance abuse treatment: Critical issues and challenges in the treatment of Latina women. *Hispanic Journal of Behavioral Sciences, 21*(3), 266–282.

Beauvais, F., Wayman, J. C., Jumper-Thurman, P., Plested, B., & Helm, H. (2002). Inhalant abuse among American-Indian, Mexican American, and non-Latino White adolescents. *American Journal of Drug and Alcohol Abuse, 28*(1), 171–187.

Black, S. A., & Markides, K. S. (1993). Acculturation and alcohol consumption in Puerto Rican, Cuban-American, and Mexican-American women in the United States. *American Journal of Public Health, 83*(6), 890–893.

Brook, J. S., Brook, D. W., De La Rosa, M., Whiteman, M., Johnson, E., & Montoya, I. (2001). Adolescent illegal drug use: The impact of personality, family, and environmental factors. *Journal of Behavioral Medicine, 24,* 183–203.

Brooks, A., Stuewig, J., & LeCroy, C. (1998). A family based model of Hispanic adolescent substance use. *Journal of Drug Education, 28*(1), 65–86.

Burnam, M. A., Telles, C. A., Karno, M., & Hough, R. L. (1987). Measurement of acculturation in a community population of Mexican Americans. *Hispanic Journal of Behavioral Sciences, 9*(2), 105–130.

Caetano, R. (1991). Findings from the 1984 national survey of alcohol use among U.S. Hispanics. In W. B. Clark & M. E. Hilton (Eds.), *Alcohol in America: Drinking practices and problems* (pp. 293–309). Albany: State University of New York Press.

Caetano, R. (1993). Ethnic minority groups and Alcoholics Anonymous: A review. In B. S. McCrady & W. R. Miller (Eds.), *Research on Alcoholics Anonymous: Opportunities and alternatives* (pp. 209–232). New Brunswick, NJ: Rutgers Center of Alcohol Studies.

Canino, G., Burnam, M. A., & Caetano, R. (1992). The prevalence of alcohol abuse and/or dependence in two Hispanic communities. In J. Helzer & G. Canino (Eds.), *Alcoholism in North America, Europe, and Asia: A coordinated analysis of population data from 10 regions* (pp. 131–158). New York: Oxford University Press.

Cantor, N., Markus, H., Niedenthal, P., & Nurius, P. (1986). On motivation and self-concept. In R. M. Sorrentino & E. T. Higgins (Eds.), *Handbook of motivation and cognition: Foundations of social behavior* (pp. 96–121). New York: Guilford Press.

Cervantes, R. C., Gilbert, M. J., Salgado de Snyder, N., & Padilla, A. M. (1991). Psychosocial and cognitive correlates of alcohol use in younger adult immigrants and U.S.-born Hispanics. *International Journal of the Addictions, 25,* 687–708.

Cherpitel, C. J. (1992). Acculturation, alcohol consumption, and casualties among United States Hispanics in the emergency room. *International Journal of the Addictions, 27*(9), 1067–1077.

Corbett, K., Mora, J., & Ames, G. (1991). Drinking patterns and drinking-related problems of Mexican-American husbands and wives. *Journal of Studies on Alcohol, 52,* 215–233.

Dawson, D. A. (1998). Beyond black, white, and Hispanic: Race, ethnic origin, and drinking patterns in the United States. *Journal of Substance Abuse, 10,* 321–339.

Delgado, M. (1997). Hispanics/Latinos. In J. Philleo & L. Brisbane (Eds.), *Cultural competence in substance abuse prevention* (pp. 33–54). Washington, DC: National Association of Social Workers Press.

Delva, J., Wallace, J. M., O'Malley, P. M., Bachman, J. G., Johnston, L. D., & Schulenberg, J. E. (2005). The epidemiology of alcohol, marijuana, and cocaine use among Mexican American, Puerto Rican, Cuban American, and other Latin American eighth-grade students in the United States: 1991–2002. *American Journal of Public Health, 95*(4), 696–702.

Felix-Ortiz, M., & Newcomb, M. D. (1992). Risk and protective factors for drug use among Latino and White adolescents. *Hispanic Journal of Behavioral Sciences, 14,* 291–309.

Fisher, D. G., Reynolds, G. L., Moreno-Branson, C. M., Jaffe, A., Wood, M. M., Klahn, J. A., & Muniz, J. F. (2004). Drug treatment needs of Hispanic drug users in Long Beach, California. *Journal of Drug Issues, 34*(4), 879–894.

Frauenglass, S., Routh, D. K., Pantin, H. M., & Mason, C. A. (1997). Family support decreases influence of deviant peers on Hispanic adolescents' substance use. *Journal of Clinical Child Psychology, 26*(1), 15–23.

Gfroerer, J., & De La Rosa, M. (1993). Protective and risk factors associated with drug use among Hispanic youth. *Journal of Addictive Diseases, 12,* 87–107.

Golding, J. M., Burnam, M. A., Benjamin, B., & Wells, K. B. (1992). Reasons for drinking, alcohol use, and alcoholism among Mexican Americans and non-Hispanic Whites. *Psychology of Addictive Behavior, 6,* 155–157.

Goodwin, D. W. (1981). Genetic component of alcoholism. *Annual Review of Medicine, 32,* 93–99.

Guilamo-Ramos, V., Jaccard, J., Johansson, M., & Turrisi, R. (2004). Binge drinking among Latino youth: Role of acculturation-related variables. *Psychology of Addictive Behaviors, 18*(2), 135–142.

Johnson, P. B., & Gurin, G. (1994). Negative affect, alcohol expectancies and alcohol-related problems. *Addiction, 89,* 581–586.

Johnston, L. D., O'Malley, P. M., & Bachman, J. G. (2001). *Monitoring the Future national survey results on drug use, 1975–2000: Vol. 1. Secondary school students* (NIH Publication No. 011-4924). Bethesda, MD: National Institute on Drug Abuse.

Kail, B., Zayas, L. H., & Malgady, R. G. (2000). Depression, acculturation, and motivations for alcohol use among young Columbian, Dominican, and Puerto Rican men. *Hispanic Journal of Behavioral Sciences, 22*(1), 64–77.

Karno, M., & Edgerton, R. B. (1969). Perception of mental illness in a Mexican American community. *Archives of General Psychiatry, 20*, 233–238.

Lappin, J., & Hardy, K. V. (1997). Keeping context in view: The heart of supervision. In T. C. Todd & C. L. Storm (Eds.), *The complete systemic supervisor: Context, philosophy, and pragmatics* (pp. 41–58). Boston: Allyn & Bacon.

Lawson, A. W., & Lawson, G. W. (1998). *Alcoholism and the family.* Austin, TX: PRO-ED.

Martinez, C. (1994). Psychiatric treatment of Mexican-Americans: A review. In C. Telles & M. Karno (Eds.), *Latino mental health: Current research and policy perspectives* (NIMH Publication No. 94MF04837-24D, pp. 227–340). Los Angeles: National Institute of Mental Health and University of California, Los Angeles, Neuropsychiatric Institute.

National Institute on Drug Abuse. (2000). *Drug use among racial/ethnic minorities: Revised.* Retrieved August 1, 2006, from http://www.drugabuse.gov/pdf/minorities03.pdf

Ramirez, J. R., Crano, W. D., Quist, R., Burgoon, M., Alvaro, E. M., & Grandpre, J. (2004). Acculturation, familism, parental monitoring, and knowledge as predictors of marijuana and inhalant use in adolescents. *Psychology of Addictive Behaviors, 18*(1), 3–11.

Raynor, J. O., & McFarlin, D. B. (1986). Motivation and the self-system. In R. M. Sorrentino & E. T. Higgens (Eds.), *Handbook of motivation and cognition: Foundations of social behavior* (pp. 315–349). New York: Guilford Press.

Sale, E., Sambrano, S., Springer, J. F., Pena, C., Pan, W., & Kasim, R. (2005). Family protection and prevention of alcohol use among Hispanic youth at high risk. *American Journal of Community Psychology, 36*(3/4), 195–205.

Santisteban, D. A., Coatsworth, J. D., Perez-Vidal, A., Kurtines, W. M., Schwartz, S. J., LaPerriere, A., & Szapocznik, J. (2003). Efficacy of brief strategic family therapy in modifying Hispanic adolescent behavior problems and substance use. *Journal of Family Psychology, 17*(1), 121–133.

Santisteban, D. A., & Szapocznik, J. (1982). Substance abuse disorders among Hispanics: A focus on prevention. In D. A. Santisteban & J. Szapocznik (Eds.), *The Hispanic substance abuser: The search for prevention strategies* (pp. 83–100). New York: Grune & Stratton.

Shera, W., Sanchez, A., & Huang, T. (1984). Verbal participation in group therapy: A comparative study on New Mexico ethnic groups. *Hispanic Journal of Behavioral Sciences, 6*, 277–284.

Terrell, M. D. (1993). Ethnocultural factors and substance abuse: Toward culturally sensitive treatment models. *Psychology of Addictive Behaviors, 7*(3), 162–167.

Tonigan, J. S., Connors, G. J., & Miller, W. R. (1998). Special populations in Alcoholics Anonymous. *Alcohol Health and Research World, 22*(4), 281–285.

Torres-Rivera, E., Wilbur, M. P., Phan, L. T., Maddux, C. D., & Roberts-Wilbur, J. (2004). Counseling Latinos with substance abuse problems. *Journal of Addictions and Offender Counseling, 25*, 26–42.

Treno, A. J., Alaniz, M. L., & Gruenewald, P. J. (1999). Drinking among U.S. Hispanics: A multivariate analysis of alcohol consumption patterns. *Hispanic Journal of Behavioral Sciences, 21*(4), 405–419.

U.S. Census Bureau. (2000). *Summary File 2 and Summary File 4: American FactFinder.* Retrieved August 1, 2006, from http://factfinder.census.gov

U.S. Census Bureau. (2004). *Current population survey (CPS).* Retrieved August 1, 2006, from http://www.census.gov/population/www/socdemo/hispanic/cps2004.html

U.S. Census Bureau. (2006). *Press Releases: Facts for features: Hispanic heritage month, September 15–October 15, 2006.* Retrieved August 1, 2006, from http://www.census.gov/Press release/www/releases/archives/facts_for_features_special_editions/007173.html

U.S. Department of Justice. (2000). *Correction statistics* (Bureau of Justice Statistics). Retrieved August 1, 2006, from http://www.ojp.usdoj.gov/bjs/correct.htm

Vega, W. A., Sribney, W. M., & Achara-Abrahams, I. (2003). Co-occurring alcohol, drug, and other psychiatric disorders among Mexican-origin people in the United States. *American Journal of Public Health, 93*(7), 1057–1064.

CHAPTER

A Model for Treating Adolescent Substance Abuse

Matthew Berlin and Ann W. Lawson

Adolescence is a socially, emotionally, and psychologically challenging period. Unfortunately, adolescence has become all the more challenging and hazardous over the last few decades due to widespread adolescent use of licit and illicit substances. In spite of empirical evidence, parents' admonitions, and the obvious consequences of substance abuse, American teenagers are using and often abusing these substances. As evidence has shown, this use/abuse has often compromised these adolescents' entire futures and prospects for long-term happiness as adults.

Unfortunately, a large percentage of adolescents have used two of the most commonly used drugs, alcohol and marijuana. A 1997 study sponsored by the National Institute on Drug Abuse (NIDA) (D. Anderson, 1998) showed that in 1996, 82% of all high school seniors polled had tried alcohol at least once in their lifetime, and 50% of the seniors reported having tried marijuana at least once. And, both of these numbers were up, albeit incrementally, from the previous 2 years (D. Anderson, 1998). A more current NIDA-sponsored study of alcohol and other drug use indicated that alcohol use in the previous 30 days was 17% for 8th graders, 22% for 10th graders, and 47% for 12th graders (O'Malley, Bachman, & Schulenberg, 2006). The report also indicated use rates for illicit drugs other than marijuana at 8%, 13%, and 20%, respectively. Lifetime illicit drug use was 21%, 38%, and 50%, and for use in the current year 16%, 30%, and 38% in the three age groups (O'Malley et al., 2006).

African American female adolescents are at greater risk for smoking, particularly marijuana, than individuals from other minority groups (Nasim, Corona, Belgrave, Utsey, & Fallah, 2007). However, traditional religious beliefs and practices have been associated with decreased tobacco use, and supportive exchanges with friends, consultation and sharing with parents, and traditional religious beliefs and practices were found to be protective factors for marijuana use.

In another study, Johnston, O'Malley, and Bachman (1993) found that almost a third of high school seniors had consumed five or more drinks on at least one occasion within the 2 weeks prior to the study. The severity of this statistic is even more striking given that for adolescents who have experienced some type of recovery treatment, alcohol, although the most used substance, is rarely their reported drug of choice (Tapert, Stewart, & Brown, 1999). Rather, adolescents who have been admitted to treatment programs as a result of their substance abuse typically report regular use of at least three different substances at the time of treatment entry (Brown, Tapert, Tate, & Abrantes, 2000). Equally if not more worrisome is the bleak prospect of substance abuse recovery for adolescents, as evidenced by their dire relapse rates. These relapse rates have reportedly been extremely high (Brown, Vik, & Creamer, 1989; Brown et al., 2000), ranging from 35% to 70% (Newcomb & Bentler, 1989), and even as high as 90% (Todd & Selekman, 1991).

Despite these troubling statistics, research and an effective treatment approach designed specifically for adolescents are lacking (Blume, Green, Joanning, & Quinn, 1994; Brown, Myers, Mott, & Vik, 1994; Bukstein, 1994; Fromme & Brown, 2000; Liddle, Dakof, & Diamond, 1991; Norbert & McMenamy, 1996; Thomas & Corcoran, 2001). Liddle et al. (1991) attributed the lack of research and treatment designs to the fact that adolescents are generally considered "experimental users" who for the most part haven't established clear patterns of habitual, entrenched abuse. This perception has led to the substance abuse treatment community's unwillingness to devote the necessary research and treatment support that the problem clearly demands. As a result, the adolescent substance abuse treatment approaches offered in the United States today are a haphazard, disjointed collection of theories, ideas, and experiments with limited proven efficacy.

Although adolescent substance abuse in America didn't really become a recognized phenomenon until the 1960s (Blume et al., 1994), studies published as recently as 2001 indicate that for the substance-abusing adolescent there is a severe lack of treatment approaches, as well as outcome studies for those approaches (Brown, D'Amico, McCarthy, & Tapert, 2001; Hser, Grella, Hubbard, & Hsieh, 2001; Muck et al., 2001). However, some advances in treatment have been made since the mid-1960s (S. Kim, Crutchfield, Williams, & Hepler, 1998), and the decade of the 1990s witnessed a more concerted effort to develop and empirically evaluate treatment approaches for adolescent substance abusers (Winters et al., 2000). The literature does offer some positive results. Clearly, a small but dedicated cadre of bright individuals has accomplished some good work over the years. Unfortunately, however, a concrete, replicable, and reliable set of specific treatment techniques designed specifically for the adolescent substance abuser cannot be found within any one particular framework. One approach may address some of the adolescent's needs, but other salient points are left out—and might or might not be found in a different approach.

Controversy surrounds adolescent substance abuse and treatment, generating questions such as the following: Is it healthy and empowering to impose the disease concept of addiction on an adolescent? Can and should the 12-step approach be applied to the adolescent and his or her still-gestating life? Should an adolescent even be considered an addict, despite his or her current level of use, or should he or she be considered to be in an "experimental phase" of some sort until adulthood? And finally, should family therapy be an integral element of every adolescent substance abuse treatment program? As previously stated, various approaches to treating the adolescent may address one or more of these essential variables while leaving others out. In response to this, it is suggested that an in-depth examination of the nature of adolescence, as well as a variety of specific techniques taken from an array of sources, might be the key to formulating a specific, replicable, and effective adolescent substance abuse treatment program.

The stakes are high. Adolescent substance abuse not only has potentially catastrophic effects on the adolescent, but also has a negative impact upon society. As demonstrated by Newcomb and Bentler (1988), abuse of various types of substances, especially cigarettes and hard drugs, can harm the adolescent's mental health, social connectedness, dating and marriage, work stability, and educational aspirations (Newcomb & Bentler, 1988). Such harmful effects result from a "pattern of relatively heavy use during early and late adolescence" and not from infrequent experimental use (Newcomb & Bentler, 1988, p. 74).

Newcomb and Bentler (1988) also postulated that the adolescent's drug use may be linked to the bypassing of the maturational sequence as typically experienced in the school, work, and family formation domains; the drug-using adolescent may be pushed prematurely into more adult roles than he or she should be experiencing at that time. As a result, an illusory "pseudomaturity" occurs that reduces the likelihood that the individual will be able to successfully meet the responsibilities of adult life (Newcomb & Bentler, 1988).

In addition to the projected problems clearly foreseeable in the adolescent's burgeoning adult life, there are the glaringly obvious effects demonstrated in the present—namely, the high rate of adolescent fatalities resulting from drug and alcohol abuse. As U.S. Census Bureau (2001) statistics indicate, the leading causes of death in 1998 for individuals in the 15- to 24-year-old age range were accidents (13,349), homicides (5,506), and suicides (4,135). These three main causes of death are all strongly correlated with drug and alcohol use (MacDonald, 1989). Archambault (1992) reported that teenage drivers cause 44% of all alcohol-related automobile accidents at night. And, frighteningly enough, "drunk driving accidents are the leading cause of death in people aged 16 to 24" (p. 17). Regarding adolescent suicides, arguably the most destructive consequence of adolescent substance abuse, Morrison (1985) stated that 88% of all such suicides are the result of drug overdoses. Finally, Morrison offered the discouraging conclusion that more adolescents die in drug- or alcohol-related accidents than from any type of disease. In a more recent study, Windle (2004) concluded that binge drinking predicted suicide attempts significantly more frequently than did depression or stressful events.

The ultimate effect upon the society in which substance-abusing adolescents grow up is potentially devastating. As Archambault (1992) asserted, "Drug abuse is considered a threat to the healthy development of youth and, therefore, a threat to society" (p. 15). Consider the tasks that the adolescent must work through and complete: develop an individual identity, separate from the family of origin, establish social relationships, experiment with different values to discover his or her own, come to grips with the practical realities of life, create financial self-reliance, go to school, secure adequate employment, and learn to relate to an intimate partner (Archambault, 1992). These tasks would overwhelm most mature adults, let alone adolescents.

Adolescent substance abuse is not a harmless, fleeting activity that affects only the adolescent and his or her limited sphere of influence, and the need for adequate and effective adolescent substance abuse treatment approaches has never been more pressing.

Unfortunately, adolescent substance abuse treatment has been sorely neglected. A 1991 survey indicated that all of the adolescents in drug and alcohol abuse treatment units comprised a mere 6% of the total recovering population, and that adolescents have generally been treated with modalities designed for adults (Bukstein, 1994). Clearly, a great deal of work needs to be done for the adolescent.

Understanding the Adolescent

Archambault (1992) quite accurately characterized adolescence as a "physiological, cultural, and psychological no-man's land" (p. 11). Lawson (1992) added, "Along with the freedom of adolescence comes the responsibility of adulthood" (p. 3). The adolescent is clearly too old to be treated like a child and would rebel against anyone attempting to do so. On the other hand, the adolescent is too young to be treated as a fully responsible adult, and as a result, American society places limitations on the adolescent's full range of freedoms, such as age limits on legal drinking.

Similarly, it is difficult to pinpoint where the adolescent falls along the spectrum of addiction. As T. E. Smith and Springer (1998) pointed out, it is not clear whether "most drug-using ... adolescents meet diagnostic criteria to justify diagnoses of ... drug dependency" (p. 213). The definition of substance abuse used for adults may not be appropriate for adolescents. Lawson (1992) noted that an adult substance abuser has been defined as "an individual whose use of a chemical substance ... causes continuing difficulties of any kind in that person's life" (p. 4). Most adult substance abuse programs adhere to this definition. Adolescents who have been merely experimenting with substances could easily end up in the same type of treatment, regardless of the effects of their substance use. And although there is no "typical" adolescent substance abuser, programs typically try to squeeze the adolescent into an adult framework (Lawson, 1992; T. E. Smith & Springer, 1998).

It is difficult to determine what drug abuse is transitional and what is an addiction that needs intervention. Jessor and Jessor (1977), articulating a widely held view, argued that most drug use by adolescents can best be understood as transitional behavior that occurs within normal development from adolescence to adulthood. In another longitudinal study, Shedler and Block (1990) even reported that adolescents who had engaged in some drug experimentation (primarily with marijuana) were better adjusted in adulthood than adolescents who used drugs frequently or who had never used drugs.

In any case, the adolescent substance user perceives drugs differently from the adult user and has different motivations for drug use, and these differences are salient for treatment. Chambers (1999) identified four main differences between adolescent and adult substance use/abuse based on therapeutic interviews conducted with substance-abusing adolescents:

1. Adolescent substance use progresses much faster than adult use does.
2. By adult standards, some of Chambers's adolescent clients would be considered both psychologically and physically dependent.

3. Youth often have a particular drug of choice, but they also tend to take a "smorgasbord" of substances, whereas adults usually maintain a single drug of choice.
4. Adolescents tend to glorify their substance abuse, imbuing it with heroic qualities, while adults are more inclined to minimize their substance use/abuse.

Winters et al. (2000) reported that adolescents tend to have shorter histories of substance use, more usage of alcohol and marijuana, less use of opiates, more binge drinking, and a greater tendency toward polysubstance abuse.

Adolescent motivation is also different from that of the adult. As previously discussed, the tasks, challenges, and obstacles adolescents are expected to overcome are numerous and understandably overwhelming. Before the adolescent is aware of it, he or she is pulled out of the relative safety of childhood and expected to cope with the new complexities and expectations of the adult world (Archambault, 1992). It is no wonder that between juggling environmental expectations (family, school, and peer group pressures), physiological changes (body shape, size, skin, facial hair), and psychological stressors (intimate relationships, separation from the family of origin), many adolescents turn to substances because they are unwilling or unable to cope with the stresses of adolescence (Archambault, 1992). Unfortunately, adult substance abuse treatment approaches fail to address this developmental aspect of the adolescent's life. Adults, it is assumed, have already passed through these stages and are engaged with more adult-oriented issues, such as the threat of job loss, business failure, loss of spouse, and so forth.

Recognizing Adolescent Conflict in Treatment

These aspects of adolescent conflict should be recognized in substance abuse treatment. Concretely describing, highlighting, and acknowledging these conflicts to the adolescent in treatment will serve many purposes. For one, it will create a higher level of trust in and respect from the adolescent. The treatment provider who appears to grasp the often unspoken and infrequently understood conflicts of adolescence will no longer seem "out of it" or irrelevant. Instead, the treatment provider is likely to be trusted and admired. Another benefit is that the subtle, often unconscious guilt that the adolescent is harboring will be assuaged. Once the etiology of the adolescent's undefined yet persistent negative emotions can be defined and brought to the surface, the adolescent feels better about him- or herself through having identified and normalized the conflict, and the adolescent's desire to escape from these negative emotions through further drug use will also likely decrease. Finally, once trust and respect have been established, the treatment setting can be used as an alternative forum for adolescents to objectively explore and examine their feelings and ideas about their future, away from the pressure of parents. In a setting free from the goals established by parents, the adolescent can experience the positive emotions and excitement associated with exploring the possibilities surrounding career, family, and social goals in a nonthreatening, nonjudgmental manner.

Thus, any treatment approach that aims to successfully treat adolescent substance abuse must incorporate a recognition of the role that stress and conflict play in the adolescent's experience. Specifically, it is essential to understand the particular stressors, concerns, and conflicts that consume much of an adolescent's focus and awareness on a daily basis. During adolescence, conflict is inevitable and unavoidable (White, 1989). Many adolescents experience conflict within the self (contradictory ideals, values, experiences), conflict with others (parents, peers, authority figures), or conflict with society (mixed messages about drug use, sexuality, standards of conduct). The degree to which the adolescent successfully copes with this barrage of conflicts will affect his or her quality of life, or lack thereof, throughout adulthood. Any treatment approach that neglects to recognize and communicate about these realities is bound to be ineffective because it will fail to address what an adolescent desperately needs: an explanation for why he or she is feeling as confused, hurt, misunderstood, aloof, and torn as he or she does. When the treatment provider recognizes and articulates the very real conflicts and stressors underlying the adolescent client's feelings, the adolescent not only will breathe a sigh of relief, but also will likely be much more open to the further treatment modalities the treatment provider has to offer.

Types of Adolescent Substance Abusers

Recognizing and understanding the essential significance of the roles of stress and conflict in the adolescent's life, and the successful resolution of these conflicts, should be the firm foundation on which any successful treatment approach is built. A dilemma remains, however, regarding how to classify adolescent substance use/abuse. At least 90% of all adolescents have experimented with alcohol; thus, substance use has become a "rite of passage" for most adolescents (Bukstein, 1994). But should an adolescent who is caught smoking marijuana be labeled as an "addict" at 13 or 14 years old? Should a 15-year-old caught drunk at school be branded as having an "incurable disease"? Should that adolescent be sent to a 30-day rehab center where treatment is designed for adults? To start, we can distinguish between drug use and drug abuse, as well as between different kinds of adolescent substance abusers.

Beschner (1986) divided adolescent substance abusers into three groups: (a) experimenters; (b) compulsive users; and (c) "floaters," those who shift or "float" between experimental and compulsive use. Adolescents in the experimenter group can be said to use, as opposed to abuse, drugs, whereas compulsive users can be said to abuse drugs.

The first group, the *experimenters,* most often begin using drugs for reasons such as peer pressure, curiosity, boredom, or a new way to have fun. According to Beschner (1986), experimenters tend to use substances only on rare occasions and in small quantities, usually only experiment with alcohol and marijuana, and have a clear understanding of the difference between taking harmless risks and taking dangerous risks and between using drugs to have fun and using drugs to avoid reality.

The second group, the *compulsive users,* are much more dependent on drugs, have health problems as a result of using drugs, and have personal or social functioning problems due to their use of drugs. According to Beschner (1986), these individuals spend most of their time obtaining and taking drugs, talk about drugs constantly, and are quite savvy about drugs. In addition, the compulsive user usually has numerous personal problems and uses/abuses substances in order to cope with these problems.

The third group, the *floaters,* float or move between the experimental and compulsive groups. The rate of use/abuse for these adolescents alters depending on changes in the adolescent's environment and his or her varying abilities to cope with different problems. Beschner (1986) noted that floaters run the risk of becoming compulsive users.

Five Motivational Patterns of Use/Abuse

Rice (1984) proposed that substance use and substance abuse can be distinguished on the basis of where the substance usage falls along a continuum of five motivational patterns: (a) experimental, (b) social–recreational, (c) circumstantial–situational, (d) intensified, and (e) compulsive.

Rice's (1984) first motivational pattern, *experimental,* falls on the mild level of the continuum and refers to use motivated by curiosity, adventure, thrill seeking, and the desire to try something new. Most adolescents initially try drugs from the experimental motivational base. The second motivational pattern, *social–recreational,* is also considered mild on the continuum. Social–recreational usage is involved when an adolescent desires to use substances in order to share fun, pleasurable experiences with others or to fit in with the crowd. The third motivational pattern, *circumstantial–situational,* falls on the moderate level along the continuum. Here, the adolescent uses a substance in order to alter or achieve a specific mood or mental effect for a specific situation, such as using uppers to stay awake for finals, using downers to go to sleep, or using psychedelics to have fun at a party. The fourth motivational pattern, *intensified substance use,* falls on the severe end of the continuum. Intensified use denotes the habitual, long-term use of substances in order to escape from one's problems and the challenges of daily living. The fifth and last motivational pattern, also on the severe end of the continuum, is *compulsive substance use.* Here, the adolescent's substance use involves high frequency and high intensity. The adolescent at this end of the continuum uses substances continuously, with the goal of maintaining a particular drug high or the drug's particular psychological effects. The adolescent's life is completely engrossed with using, talking about, and thinking about using the drug. It is also at this stage that withdrawal symptoms occur with cessation of use.

The issue of how and where to divide the line between substance use and abuse for adolescents has been a constant challenge for treatment providers. According to White (1989), the best gauges are the frequency, intensity, and quantity of drugs consumed, the degree to which the adolescent is preoccupied with the substance, and the negative consequences the adolescent has experienced as a result of the substance use/abuse. The continuum offered by Rice (1984) can easily be utilized in conjunction with a questionnaire in order to assess the severity of an adolescent's substance usage. Although there is no universally agreed-upon definition of substance dependency (White, 1989), it can nonetheless be concluded that the closer an adolescent falls toward the intensified or compulsive motivational patterns at the severe end of the continuum, the more probable it is that the adolescent should be considered as having a chemical dependency issue.

The reasons why an adolescent chooses to experiment with, use, or abuse drugs are numerous and varied (McNeece & DiNitto, 1998). One thing we do know, however, is that the trials, tasks, and responsibilities of adolescence differ significantly from those of adulthood, as noted above, and these differences must be considered in treatment. Adolescents should not be treated like adults. The adolescent faces stressors and conflicts that are unique to adolescence. An adolescent most likely will not contend with issues such as marrying, having children, raising and supporting a family, or buying a house. Instead, the adolescent is still contending with separating from his or her family of origin, developing independent relationships, learning to relate to a romantic partner, and maintaining good grades in school. One might argue that these tasks aren't as significant as raising a family or securing a good job, but their importance should not be minimized; as a result of successfully meeting the challenges of adolescence, people experience critical psychological growth and learn basic, lifelong coping skills. When a treatment approach neglects these essential aspects of an adolescent's life, it is virtually guaranteed to fail. The adolescent needs concrete answers and directions regarding his or her frustrations, as well as recognition and identification of the various conflicts and stressors in life. An approach that includes these elements will likely result in much more effective and successful treatment outcomes. A psychoeducational approach that highlights all these aspects of adolescence is an important piece of the treatment puzzle. By itself, however, a psychoeducational approach isn't enough. There is one more essential factor: the adolescent's family.

Family Therapy

Numerous studies conducted in the last decade indicate that including the adolescent's family in the treatment process, that is, facilitating family therapy in conjunction with individual treatment, will likely yield a greater chance for successful treatment (e.g., Liddle & Dakof, 1995; Stanton & Shadish, 1997). Some of the positive outcomes include (a) a more thorough assessment of the various functional domains of the adolescent, as opposed to assessing just one or two (Liddle, 1999); (b) a greater assurance that the adolescent will remain in and complete treatment (Dakof, Tejeda, & Liddle, 2001); (c) a more direct assessment of the etiology of the adolescent's substance use/abuse (i.e., dysfunctional family, parent who uses, etc.) (Spooner, 1999); (d) improvement of the youth's relationship with his or her parents (Azrin, Donohue, Besalel, Kogan, & Acierno, 1994); (e) a reduction of the negative impact of the adolescent's addictive behavior on other family members (Thomas & Corcoran, 2001); and (f) a better treatment outcome overall compared to individual substance abuse treatment (Stanton & Shadish, 1997). According to these studies, including a family therapy component in the treatment of adolescents yields wide-ranging benefits and effectiveness. The positive influence that family therapy has had on the entire practice of adolescent substance abuse treatment has only begun to be recognized over the past decade or so. The beneficial and therapeutic contributions of family therapy to adolescent substance abuse recovery are likely to be even more widely recognized in the years to come.

In a systematic review of family-based interventions for adolescent substance abuse, Austin, Macgowan, and Wagner (2005) applied guidelines for effective treatment and a methodological review for each treatment. Brief Strategic Family Therapy (BSFT), Family Behavior Therapy, Functional Family Therapy, Multidimensional Family Therapy (MDFT), and Multisystemic Treatment were consistent with effective treatment. Some exceptions noted were no aftercare and poor retention of patients. MDFT and BSFT met the criteria for efficacious treatment. Additionally, MDFT was associated with clinically significant changes in substance use at posttreatment and follow-up.

In a broad-based study conducted by Williams, Chang, and the Addiction Centre Adolescent Research Group (2000), out of the 53 adolescent substance abuse treatment approach studies examined, they found that for the most part there was insufficient evidence to compare the effectiveness of different treatment types except for family therapy. Williams et al. stated, "The exception to [the inconclusiveness due to lack of evidence] is that outpatient family therapy appears superior to other forms of outpatient treatment" (p. 159; see also Stanton & Shadish, 1997).

Treatment setting doesn't seem to hinder its effectiveness. Hser et al. (2001) found that family therapy was an integral component in all three treatment approaches examined: residential inpatient, outpatient drug-free, and short-term inpatient programs. The particular family therapy approach adopted and utilized doesn't necessarily seem to be a factor, either. Williams et al. (2000) stated that "there is no evidence to date that one type of family therapy is superior to other types of family therapy" (p. 156). And there certainly is no shortage of family therapy approaches, including the structural-strategic, cognitive-behavioral, solution-focused, multidimensional, multisystemic, and cybernetic family therapy, to name just a few.

Probably the most basic idea behind family therapy for adolescent substance abusers is that the adolescent's family system significantly affects the development and subsequent maintenance of the adolescent's substance abuse (Muck et al., 2001). Reviewing over 20 studies, Spooner (1999) identified several factors that can influence whether an adolescent will begin experimenting with substances: (a) lack of or inconsistent parental discipline, (b) negative communication patterns such as severe criticism and blaming, (c) poor or negative family interactions, (d) low bonding with family members, (e) lack of sharing of affection and communication with children, (f) lack of parental interest in children's activities, (g) parental criminality/antisocial behavior, (h) positive parental attitudes toward drugs, and (i) parental drug use as a coping mechanism.

A significant body of research supports family. Stanton and Shadish (1997) found that family therapy was effective for both adults and adolescents, while Liddle (1999) noted that empirical support exists for the effectiveness of family therapy. Waldron et al. (2001) found that more substance-abusing adolescents enter and remain in family therapy than any other kind of therapy, and S. C. Anderson (1995) bluntly stated that family therapy is the most effective approach for substance-abusing adolescents. Thomas and Corcoran (2001) stressed the importance of including the family in any kind of substance abuse treatment, while Azrin et al. (1994) found a significant reduction in substance abuse after their subjects completed treatment incorporating family therapy. Both Cunningham and Henggeler (1999) and Liddle and Dakof (1995) reported that including family therapy in treatment seems to promise more engagement and treatment retention with the adolescent and his or her family.

In fact, family therapy approaches for adolescent substance abusers seem to be more fully developed at the present time than family therapy approaches for adult substance abusers (Liddle & Dakof, 1995) and have empirical support (Liddle, 1999; Muck et al., 2001; Thomas & Corcoran, 2001; Waldron, Slesnik, Brody, Turner, & Peterson, 2001). This body of evidence is largely due to several National Institute on Drug Abuse grants that funded treatment outcome studies for adolescent substance abuse. In one of these studies, Joanning, Quinn, Thomas, and Mullen (1992) found that family therapy was superior to the other two treatments—group therapy and family education—in reducing adolescent substance abuse. At posttest, 54% of the family systems therapy subjects were not using drugs compared with 28% in the family drug education model and 16% in the group therapy model. Despite these positive outcomes, there still remains a shortage of evidence to make any absolute statements about family therapy. To quote Liddle and Dakof (1995), the efficacy of family therapy for treating substance abuse is "promising, but not definitive" (p. 511).

A Multidimensional Approach to Treatment

Treating adolescents either with approaches designed for adults or with a myopic focus on the substance abuse behavior itself is outdated and inadequate. Rather, a more multidimensional approach is called for (Liddle, 1999; Spooner, 1999; Tarter, 1990) that incorporates sensitivity to the adolescent's social, psychological, emotional, and physical needs. Some specific areas of concern that have been noted in the literature are (a) stress management, social skills, behavioral self-control, and motivational training (Brown et al., 1994; Spooner, 1999); (b) development of coping skills and problem-solving abilities (Tapert, Brown, Myers, & Granholm, 1999); and (c) youth empowerment and self-esteem building (Kim et al., 1998; Richter, Brown, & Mott, 1991). Addressing these issues will help to equip the adolescent with the skills to not only resist substance abuse but, even more importantly, learn how to love and accept him- or herself in a culture that exerts increasing pressure (Selekman & King, 2001).

Because no two adolescents are exactly the same, treatment for the adolescent should be as personalized as possible. There are, however, recurring issues that seem to surround the experience of the substance-abusing adolescent. Semlitz (1996) listed the following considerations: (a) the adolescent's pattern(s) of substance abuse; (b) behavior problems such as running away, delinquency, school avoidance, and legal problems; (c) medical issues, including pregnancy and HIV; (d) comorbid psychiatric disorders; (e) developmental issues; (f) learning disabilities; (g) social skills levels; (h) the status of the adolescent's family system, including pathology and substance abuse; (i) peer relationships; (j) vocational skills and future opportunities; and (k) leisure and recreational interests. Few, if any, adolescents will ever present with difficulties in all of these areas. Treatment should be specialized and targeted in order to address the specific areas of need for a given adolescent.

It is especially important to assess for dual diagnosis. Adolescent substance abusers often suffer from additional disorders, such as attention-deficit/hyperactivity disorder (ADHD) (Wilson & Levin, 2005). Although there has been some concern that treating ADHD with stimulant drugs promotes illicit drug use in adolescents, Wilens, Faraone, Biderman, and Gunawardend (2003) found that stimulant therapy was actually associated with a reduction in risk for drug and alcohol use disorders. It is possible that those who are not given stimulant therapy may be using illicit drugs to self-medicate. Similarly, Whalen, Jamner, Henker, Gehricke, and King (2003) reported that the unmedicated adolescents in their study smoked cigarettes more frequently than those who were taking medication over 2 years of high school. These students may have been using nicotine to improve attentional and self-regulatory competence. These comorbid problems have a negative impact on treatment outcome (Shane, Jasiukaitis, & Green, 2003). In a study of comorbid mental disorders in relation to posttreatment outcome, Shane et al. found that adolescents with mental disorders had higher levels of substance-related problems and polydrug use at entry to treatment as well as poorer treatment outcomes, including relapse.

Bukstein (1994) offered the following treatment suggestions:

1. Treatment should be intensive and of a sufficient duration to effect change.
2. Treatment should be comprehensive and address multiple domains in the adolescents' lives.
3. Treatment must be sensitive to the cultural and socioeconomic milieu in which the adolescent resides.
4. Treatment needs to incorporate a wide variety of social services, including child welfare, juvenile justice, community outreach, recreational programs, and mentoring programs for youth, when applicable.
5. Treatment should encourage and facilitate family involvement and enhance communication among family members.

Hser et al. (2001) noted that because adolescents go through developmental stages that are specific to adolescence, they have unique treatment needs. In a study examining the effects of treatment on 1,167 adolescents from four major U.S. cities, Hser et al. reported that the subjects suffered from multiple problems, including poly-drug use, criminal behavior, mental disorders, family drug use, deviant reference groups, and academic failure.

Hser et al. (2001) also noted that limited retention is one of the major obstacles that needs to be overcome for successful treatment (Szapocznik et al., 1988; Thomas & Corcoran, 2001); in their study, 58.4% of the residential programs sample and 27.1% of the outpatient drug-free programs sample stayed in treatment for at least 90 days, the predetermined threshold, and 63.7% of the short-term inpatient sample stayed in treatment past the 21-day predetermined minimum. Regarding recovery, Hser et al. found that less than half of all participants (43.8%) reported weekly marijuana use during the year following treatment, a decrease from the reported 80.4% in the year before admission. Also, reported heavy drinking dropped from 33.8% to 20.3%, use of other illicit drugs dropped from 48.0% to 42.2%, and reported criminal involvement dropped from 75.6% to 52.8%. Hser et al. emphasized the subjects' length of stay, asserting that it positively affected the results.

Hser et al. (2001) also emphasized the importance of family therapy in all three therapeutic modalities. They reported that half of the residential programs placed great emphasis on family therapy; all but one of the outpatient drug-free programs emphasized family therapy; and all of the short-term inpatient programs placed a strong emphasis on family therapy, though they did not assess for differences concerning this variable.

A Unified Model for Adolescent Substance Abuse Treatment

A review of the available research yields the following two conclusions regarding treating adolescent substance abuse: (a) Some kind of treatment is better than no treatment at all (Catalano, Hawkins, Wells, & Miller, 1990; Williams et al., 2000), and (b) adolescent substance abusers as a whole have been severely underserved (Bukstein, 2000; Etheridge, Smith, Rounds-Bryant, & Hubbard, 2001). To date, researchers have agreed that no single, unified, replicable model for treating the adolescent substance abuser exists (Blume et al., 1994; Lewis, Piercy, Sprenkle, & Trepper, 1990; Muck et al., 2001). We offer a unified treatment model here that incorporates family therapy and a recognition of the developmental needs of adolescents.

Adolescent Needs

The substance-abusing adolescent's primary need, of course, is the cessation of his or her substance use/abuse. But as Winters et al. (2000), Liddle (1999), and Bukstein (1994), among other researchers, have pointed out, many important elements surround and affect adolescents' substance use/abuse. Semlitz (1996) listed the following areas:

1. the adolescent's pattern(s) of substance abuse
2. the adolescent's behavior problems (e.g., running away, delinquency, school avoidance, arrests)
3. the adolescent's medical issues (e.g., pregnancy, HIV)
4. the adolescent's developmental issues
5. the adolescent's social skills levels
6. the adolescent's family system
7. the adolescent's peer relationships
8. the adolescent's vocational skills and future employment opportunities
9. the adolescent's leisure and recreational interests

Bukstein (1994), a strong advocate for the need to design substance abuse treatment for the adolescent, also noted that treatment should address needs beyond abstinence, although that is the primary goal. Bukstein believes that truly effective treatment should help improve the adolescent's overall psychosocial functioning (e.g., family, educational), as well as specific problem areas (e.g., problem-solving or anger management skills) that will help the adolescent avoid relapse. In order to achieve these ends, Bukstein asserted that substance abuse treatment for adolescents should

1. be comprehensive, addressing multiple domains in the adolescents' lives;
2. be intensive and of sufficient duration to create change;
3. incorporate a wide variety of social services (e.g., child welfare, juvenile justice, community outreach, mentoring programs);
4. facilitate family involvement and communication; and
5. offer follow-up care or aftercare treatment.

Williams et al. (2000), who emphasized the need to include family therapy, offered the following general guidelines:

1. Treatment programs need to be readily accessible to the masses, given the large number of adolescent substance abusers seeking out treatment.
2. Programs should be designed in such a way as to minimize treatment dropout and encourage treatment completion.
3. Treatment must include after-care.
4. Programs need to provide comprehensive services besides substance abuse treatment, such as school assistance, psychological counseling, vocational training, and recreational opportunities.
5. Treatment must include some kind of family therapy.
6. Programs need to develop and facilitate parent and peer support, especially concerning abstinence from substances. (pp. 159–160)

Other researchers have noted the importance of teaching stress management, behavioral self-control, and motivation (Brown et al., 1994; Spooner, 1999); developing coping skills and problem-solving abilities (Bukstein, 1994; Tapert, Brown, et al., 1999); and building youth empowerment and self-esteem (Kim et al., 1998; Richter et al., 1991).

Gender is another important variable in treatment. Ellis, O'Hara, and Sowers (2000) advocate segregation between males and females in the treatment milieu both because their treatment needs are different and because females' treatment might be hindered or sabotaged by males in certain situations. According to Ellis et al. (2000), adolescent males, in comparison to females,

1. tend to have a greater tolerance for deviance;
2. expect more immediate gratification;
3. experience sexual intercourse at an earlier age;
4. shoplift, damage property, and sell drugs;

5. receive more positive reinforcement for participating in school;
6. are more often referred for treatment by the courts;
7. experiment with a wider array of substances;
8. attempt suicide more often; and
9. are more likely to develop antisocial personality disorder or substance abuse disorder.

And, according to Ellis et al. (2000), adolescent females, in comparison to males,

1. tend to have lower levels of self-esteem and perceived personal competence;
2. are more likely to suffer from depression, specific phobias, and eating disorders;
3. are more fully socialized into family-oriented activities;
4. first use amphetamines at an earlier age;
5. tend to use fewer substances; and
6. have a higher probability of having been either physically or sexually abused during their lifetime.

These distinctions between adolescent males and females support the argument that males and females should be treated separately, at least to some degree. In summary, the existing literature suggests four general principles in relation to the treatment needs of adolescents:

1. Treatment must be multidimensional and as comprehensive as possible, addressing the various domains affecting the adolescent's life (i.e., social, psychological, physical, and emotional needs). Treatment should focus on issues such as interpersonal functioning, problem solving, anger management, birth control needs, and HIV education (Brown et al., 1994; Bukstein, 1994; Semlitz, 1996; Williams et al., 2000).
2. Treatment must include either provision of or access to comprehensive services that address the multiple domains in the adolescent's life (i.e., educational assistance, vocational training, psychotherapy/therapeutic counseling, health/medical information) (Bukstein, 1994; Semlitz, 1996; Williams et al., 2000).
3. Treatment must also include some kind of family therapy in order to improve communication among family members and improve parenting skills (Bukstein, 1994; Liddle, 1999; Muck et al., 2001; Williams et al., 2000).
4. Treatment should also include aftercare to prevent relapse (Brown et al., 1994; Bukstein, 1994; Williams et al., 2000).

Treatment Length and Accessibility

Research also suggests that treatment should be of a sufficient duration (Bukstein, 1994) and be readily accessible to as many people as possible (Williams et al., 2000). However, researchers have come to different conclusions regarding these two treatment variables. For instance, Williams et al. examined duration in 53 different treatment approaches and concluded that treatment length did not affect success of treatment. Treatment length, especially in the therapeutic communities (TCs), which are typically of longer duration, was actually found to be a hindrance to treatment completion, with dropout rates ranging from 39% to 90% (Williams et al., 2000). Also, Muck et al. (2001), who examined six TC programs across nine sites, found that only 44% completed the program. On the other hand, Hser et al. claimed that length of stay positively affected abstinence rates. Finally, Ralph and McMenamy (1996) investigated a 45-day inpatient program that culminated in a 56.5% abstinence rate in the subjects who completed treatment. However, there did seem to be an increase in usage over time. Given these contradictory findings, no firm conclusions regarding treatment length should be offered. We can conclude only that length of treatment will depend on the model used, especially whether it is inpatient or outpatient specifically, a point to which we return later.

Treatment should be readily available and accessible to as many people as possible (Williams et al., 2000). Accessibility, however, involves several problems, as is illustrated by findings related to Henggeler, Pickrel, Brondino, and Crouch's (1996) multisystemic therapy (MST) model. The MST model contains some special and unique features, some of which are (a) having a therapist available 24 hours a day, 7 days a week; (b) conducting therapy in the home; (c) having low caseloads for the therapists; and (d) providing services that can be utilized by the families virtually any time that is convenient for them, including evenings and weekends. The provision of this type and amount of "custom-made" service for a large number of clients is impractical. The resources simply aren't there to have the number of therapists that would be required for such an undertaking. However, the model is proving to be effective with certain populations that require this very intense approach. Although MST is expensive, it is less expensive than housing or incarcerating serious juvenile offenders (Henggeler et al., 1991; Henggeler, Clingempeel, Brondino, & Pickrel, 2002). The goal is to reduce out-of-home placements. MST has also recently been used in conjunction with the juvenile drug courts (Henggeler et al., 2006).

Another area that is important to adolescent treatment is engagement. In order for treatment services to be utilized, the treatment approach must be able to engage the adolescent to begin with, especially given the fact that most adolescents are compelled to enter treatment (Dakof et al., 2001; Ellis et al., 2000).

Treatment Engagement

Many adolescents who enter treatment terminate prematurely (Dakof et al., 2001). The results of several studies shed some light on the reasons for high attrition among adolescents. In their review of the literature on dropout, Dakof et al. concluded that psychotherapy treatment dropout was greater among adolescents from lower income, minority, single-parent families and also among adolescents from families with low support and high conflict. Other researchers have found that treatment dropout is more likely when the adolescents' parents have serious psychological or social problems (Feigelman, 1987; Kazdin, 1990; Kazdin & Mazurick, 1994). Finally, Dakof et al. cited a study by Pelkonen, Marttunen, Laippale, and Loennquist (2000) indicating that premature terminations were more frequent for adolescents with a substance abuse disorder than for those with mood disorder or suicidal ideation. Dakof et al. identified the following predictors of engagement: (a) the parents' recognition that their adolescent has a serious problem,

(b) the parents' expectations about the adolescent's educational attainment potential, and (c) the adolescent's recognition of a serious problem.

Szapocznik et al. (1988) and Cunningham and Henggeler (1999) both identified family therapy as a key component in treatment engagement. Szapocznik et al. found that the strategic-structural family therapy approach successfully engaged and retained families in treatment. This approach, according to Szapocznik et al., focuses on engaging the family at the very first session. These authors reported that only 7.1% of those receiving the strategic-structural approach failed to come in for the initial session, and 77% of those strategic-structural families who attended the first session completed the treatment.

Cunningham and Henggeler (1999) also strongly recommend the inclusion of the family right away to ensure treatment engagement and subsequent retention. In MST, the adolescent's family or caregiver is considered integral to successful treatment, and treatment goals are actually prescribed by family members/caregivers. MST therapists work on their engagement with the family from the initial session, with immediate engagement being a primary goal. MST has been shown to be quite effective at engaging and retaining adolescents and their families in treatment (Cunningham & Henggeler, 1999; Schoenwald, Brown, & Henggeler, 2000). Cunningham and Henggeler noted four indicators of treatment engagement:

1. high rates of attendance at sessions
2. completion of homework assignments
3. emotional involvement in sessions
4. progress toward meeting therapy goals

Cunningham and Henggeler (1999) also noted several indicators of possible engagement problems:

1. difficulty scheduling appointments
2. missed appointments
3. failure to follow intervention plans
4. weak/insubstantial goals
5. uneven treatment progress
6. lying about important issues

Cunningham and Henggeler (1999) delineated several specific ways to enhance engagement. The therapist should be empathetic and should provide direct and immediate benefits to the adolescent and the family during the initial session. A benefit might be as simple as convincing the adolescent's parents to stop nagging him or her. Further, the therapist should demonstrate credibility to the family in order to gain their confidence. Finally, the therapist should demonstrate "scientific mindedness," which refers to the process whereby therapists formulate and test hypotheses regarding client behavior. (For further, more specific techniques, see Cunningham and Henggeler, 1999.)

Liddle et al. (1991) outlined techniques derived from the MDFT approach. The MDFT approach diverges from MST and Szapocznik et al.'s (1988) strategic-structural approach in that engagement is often pursued with the adolescent alone in the belief that this will create stronger rapport and engagement with the adolescent. Liddle et al. illustrate the six themes of this approach via vignettes; these concepts can be summed up in the following empathetic statements:

1. "I am interested in you." The expression of genuine interest in the adolescent often constitutes a new experience for the adolescent. What he or she says and thinks is given a forum to be expressed and appreciated.
2. "There is something in this for you." The promise of benefit motivates the adolescent to persevere with treatment.
3. "I know you are hurting." Acknowledgment of the adolescent's pain gives him or her an opening to let down his or her guard, express his or her emotions, and learn new coping skills and ways of managing his or her feelings.
4. "I think you can do this." The expression of faith in the adolescent's ability encourages him or her to go beyond the apathy and mental laziness inherent in substance abuse and affords him or her the opportunity to discover what he or she is truly capable of.
5. "This may seem strange to you." Acknowledgment of how strange the therapeutic process must seem to the adolescent creates an opening for trust.
6. "Let's see how it goes." An expression of the willingness to allow the adolescent to just see how the process develops can help the disengaged adolescent begin to participate in the process without pushing him or her too much.

The Assessment Process

As Semlitz (1996) stated, "Effective interventions are predicated upon a valid and clinically relevant assessment" (p. 227). Introducing the adolescent and his or her family to the treatment process by way of an orientation meeting is the first step of assessment. The orientation meeting can take place at the treatment facility and provides a comprehensive overview of the treatment process to the adolescent and his or her family. The orientation can be conducted in a lecture-type format, with the director or some other representative introducing the program as well as all relevant staff members. The presentation can also include a video of some kind that adds visual clarity to the actual components and setting of the program.

It is also recommended that the engagement techniques described by Cunningham and Henggeler (1999) and Liddle et al. (1991) be utilized—expressing empathy, performing gift-giving, establishing credibility, and practicing scientific mindedness. Further, the family's commitment to the treatment process should be secured immediately. The orientation process should convey to family members that their participation is essential; they must be committed to attending all of the scheduled family therapy sessions. If they aren't, it must be communicated to them that the adolescent will not be eligible for treatment until the family has committed to the program.

The next phase of the assessment process involves the utilization of formal assessment instruments. Fortunately, a number of assessment measures that were developed in the 1990s can be used to identify adolescent substance abuse (Brown et al., 1994). The wide variety of assessment options available is of inestimable value to the treatment process, for a thorough assessment is the prerequisite to effective treatment. Several popular and valid substance abuse assessment tools that address multiple life domains are currently in use. The adolescent form of the Substance Abuse Subtle Screening Inventory (SASSI; Miller, 1985) is a two-part questionnaire that has been shown to have validity in identifying substance-abusing adolescents even if they are in denial or are concealing their substance abuse (Miller, 1985). Another widely utilized questionnaire is the Positive and Negative Consequences Experienced (PNCE) questionnaire (D'Amico & Fromme, 1997). The PNCE has questions about consequences of choices and behaviors, listing consequences that adolescents have reported that they might suffer from as a result of participating in various risky activities (Fromme & Brown, 2000).

Still another measure that has been used with increasing frequency is the Customary Drinking and Drug Use Record (CDDR) developed by Brown et al. (1998). According to Brown et al. (2001), the CDDR is used to assess alcohol or drug use, the problems resulting from such use, withdrawal symptomatology, and substance dependence as defined by criteria drawn from the *Diagnostic and Statistical Manual of Mental Disorders* (DSM-III-R and DSM-IV; American Psychiatric Association, 1987, 1994, respectively). The CDDR is considered a valid assessment measure with good internal consistency and test–retest and interrater reliability, as well as convergent and discriminant validity for the adolescent population (Brown et al., 2001). Waldron et al. (2001) performed a study to assess, among other variables, the validity of the Timeline Follow-Back Interview (TLFB), an assessment measure devised by Sobell et al. (1980). The TLFB was designed to obtain information about substance use and is considered to be especially sensitive to assessing adolescent substance use (Waldron et al., 2001). The TLFB is also uniquely valuable in that it can interpret its findings regarding the time period in question into number of drinking days, number of standard drinks consumed, and number of drinks per drinking day (Waldron et al., 2001). The TLFB can be used to assess drug use as well. Waldron et al. found evidence for the convergent validity of the TLFB measures of percentage of days with any drug or alcohol use, percentage of days where marijuana was used, and number of drugs used.

Another valuable assessment model is the Drug Use Screening Inventory in combination with the Decision Tree method (Tarter, 1990). This three-phase model strongly ties assessment and intervention together, facilitating both a thorough evaluation and an accurate monitoring of treatment progress (Semlitz, 1996). Phase 1 consists of utilizing the Drug Use Screening Inventory (DUSI; Tarter & Hegedus, 1991), which screens for the effects of drug use in 10 domains of the adolescent's life: (a) substance use, (b) behavior patterns, (c) health status, (d) psychiatric disorders, (e) social skills, (f) family system, (g) school adjustment, (h) work, (i) peer relationships, and (j) leisure/recreation (Tarter, 1990). The DUSI consists of 149 yes/no questions and three questions that ask for specific substance usage. Scores on the DUSI indicate the density or severity of the problems in each domain resulting from substance use/abuse. For a complete listing of all 149 questions, the reader is referred to either Tarter (1990) or Tarter and Hegedus (1991). The following sample of DUSI questions illustrates the comprehensiveness and specificity of this instrument:

Domain I: Substance Use (18 questions). Have you ever missed out on activities because you spent too much money on drugs or alcohol? Have you ever had to use more and more drugs or alcohol to get the effect you want? Have you ever had trouble getting along with any of your friends because of alcohol or drug use?

Domain II: Behavior Patterns (20 questions). Do you argue a lot? Do you brag a lot? Do you do things a lot without first thinking about the consequences? Do you do dangerous or risky things a lot?

Domain III: Health Status (10 questions). Do you sleep too much or too little? Do you have less energy than you think you should have? Do you have trouble with your breathing or with coughing?

Domain IV: Psychiatric Disorder (20 questions). Do you get frustrated easily? Do you feel sad a lot? Do you have trouble getting your mind off things? Do you hear things that no one else around you hears?

Domain V: Social Competency (14 questions). Is it difficult to make friends in a new group? Do people take advantage of you? Do you have trouble saying "no" to people?

Domain VI: Family System (14 questions). Has a member of your family used alcohol to the point of causing problems at home, at work, or with friends? Does your family hardly ever do things together? Are there no clear rules about what you can and cannot do?

Domain VII: School Performance/Adjustment (20 questions). Are your grades below average? Do you cut school more than 2 days a month? Have alcohol or drugs ever interfered with your homework or school assignments?

Domain VIII: Work Adjustment (10 questions). Have you ever had a paying job that you were fired from? Have you ever used alcohol or drugs while working on a job? Do you mostly work so that you can get money to buy drugs?

Domain IX: Peer Relationships (14 questions). Do any of your friends regularly use alcohol or drugs? Have any of your friends ever been in trouble with the law? Do your friends cut school a lot?

Domain X: Leisure/Recreation (12 questions). Do you go out for fun on school nights without permission? Is your free time spent just hanging out with friends? Are you bored most of the time?

As this small sample of questions suggests, the DUSI is a comprehensive questionnaire that inquires deeply about many aspects of the adolescent's life. The DUSI addresses the essential developmental and contextual factors of adolescent substance abuse highlighted by T. E. Smith and Springer (1998). The DUSI covers the medical and psychiatric contexts (Domains III and IV), the legal context (Domains I, VI, VIII, and IX), the social context (Domains II, V, and IX), and the educational context (Domain VII). Domain I is comprehensive and sensitive enough to be able to establish which type of substance abuser the adolescent is according to Beschner's (1986) classification—experimenter, compulsive user, or floater. Also, the DUSI would be effective for identifying Rice's (1984) five motivational patterns of adolescent substance abuse: (a) experimental, (b) social-recreational, (c) circumstantial-situational, (d) intensified, or (e) compulsive.

The DUSI has also been shown to have good reliability and validity (Kirisci, Mezzich, & Tarter, 1995; Tarter, Laird, Bukstein, & Kaminer, 1992; Tarter, Mezzich, Kirisci, & Kaczynski, 1994) and to be a sensitive self-rating method for evaluating the severity of substance use/abuse disorders as defined by DSM criteria (Tarter et al., 1992). Kirisci et al. (1995) also noted the following positive aspects of the DUSI: (a) It only takes about 20 minutes to complete; (b) the format allows for a ranking of problem severity from *most severe to least severe;* (c) it can be utilized to mark treatment progress and can easily be administered at regular intervals; and (d) it can be used for tracking adolescents' progress in aftercare treatment.

Kirisci et al. (1995) have suggested that the DUSI should be supplemented by other measures (e.g., urinalysis) in order to reduce the likelihood of the results being confounded by false self-reports. To address this potential confound, the DUSI-R (Tarter, 1990), designed for adolescents and including a "lie scale," has been developed, but no outcome studies are available. The outcome studies performed on the original DUSI have yielded positive results (Kirisci et al., 1995; Tarter et al., 1992; Tarter et al., 1994). As noted, the DUSI has demonstrated good reliability and validity (Kirisci et al., 1995; Martin & Winters, 1998; Tarter et al., 1992), and the self-report method of administration has tended to be reliable and valid for the most part (Adair, Craddock, Miller, & Turner, 1996; G. T. Smith, McCarthy, & Goldman, 1995; Williams et al., 2000).

Phase 2 consists of the comprehensive diagnostic evaluation (Tarter, 1990). The comprehensive evaluation focuses on the 10 domains of the DUSI, but utilizes 10 different diagnostic tools for each domain. Although a comprehensive enumeration of each of the 10 diagnostic tools is beyond the scope of this chapter, the particular diagnostic tools utilized will be mentioned here, and the reader is referred to Tarter (1990) for a more in-depth examination of the tools themselves, their established validity, and the rationale for their use. The diagnostic tools used for each domain are as follows:

Domain I: Substance Use. The Chemical Dependency Assessment Scale (CDAS; Oetting et al., 1984)

Domain II: Behavior Patterns. The Child Behavior Checklist (CBCL; Achenbach, Edelbrock, & Howell, 1987) or the Youth Self-Report (YSR; Ivarsson, Gillberg, Arvidsson, & Broberg, 2002)

Domain III: Health Status. A comprehensive medical history and physical examination (see Tarter, 1990)

Domain IV: Psychiatric Disorder. Kiddie–Schedule for Affective Disorders and Schizophrenia (K-SADS; Kim et al., 2004) and Symptom Checklist–90 (SC-90; Lipman, Covi, & Shapiro, 1977)

Domain V: Social Competency. Constructive Thinking Inventory (CTI; Epstein & Meier, 1989); direct clinician observation

Domain VI: Family System. Family Assessment Measure (FAM; Skinner, Steinhauer, & Santa-Barbara, 1983)

Domain VII: School Performance/Adjustment. Wide Range Achievement Test–Fourth Edition (WRAT-4; Wilkinson, 2006); tests such as the California Achievement Test (CAT; Minehan, Newcomb, & Galaif, 2000), the Iowa Tests of Educational Development (ITED; Block & Ghoneim, 1993), or the Metropolitan Achievement Tests–Eighth Edition (MAT-8; Pearson, 2000)

Domain VIII: Work Adjustment. Generalizable Skills Curriculum (Green, 1986)

Domain IX: Peer Relationships. Problem Situation Inventory for Young Adults/Adolescent Problem Situation Inventory (Hollin & Palmer, 2006)

Domain X: Leisure/Recreation. Physical examination/health tests; *Individual and Group Counseling Step by Step* (a manual describing approximately 400 specific leisure/recreational activities; see Tarter, 1990)

After the comprehensive assessment has been completed, the treatment process can move on to Phase 3, which involves formulating the treatment plan (Tarter, 1990). Once the adolescent's problem domains have been determined and ranked in order of severity, the treatment plan can be tailored to his or her needs. Tarter and Hegedus (1991) noted, however, that no arbitrary threshold score has been recommended for treatment. Rather, they insist that the ultimate determination regarding treatment is the responsibility of the treatment provider, given the DUSI scores and other pertinent information.

Tarter's (1990) three-phase approach is consistent with the notion of a unified model of treatment. The protocol will be the same for every adolescent, male or female; each individual will be administered the DUSI and a corroborative test such as urinalysis, and then will undergo the comprehensive assessment. The individual will then move on to the treatment program, which will offer continuous, concurrent treatment for all 10 domains.

Treatment Setting

The findings on treatment setting are equivocal. Hser et al. (2001) found significant reductions in alcohol and marijuana for the whole subject pool they studied, regardless of whether the individuals were inpatient residential, outpatient, or short-term inpatient. The 45-day inpatient program investigated by Ralph and McMenamy (1996) indicated that over 50% of the patients had been completely abstinent since discharge. Winters et al. (2000) found no difference in treatment outcomes between the inpatient residential and outpatient participants. And Williams et al.'s (2000) comprehensive study of 53 different treatment approaches encompassing samples of residential, inpatient, and outpatient programs revealed no evidence to support the variables of treatment setting or length for adolescent substance abuse treatment. Further, Szapocznik et al. (1988) showed a high rate of engagement and retention with an outpatient approach to treatment, as did Henggeler et al. (1996). In fact, several researchers have reported that longer treatment durations, especially for 6 months or beyond, yield dropout rates between

39% and 90% (Muck et al., 2001; Williams et al., 2000), as was seen in the case of the therapeutic communities.

Still, it is unclear whether an outpatient setting would allow for the consideration of all 10 life domains. Henggeler et al. (1996) reported the effective utilization of family therapy in an outpatient setting with good treatment follow-through and completion, but this does not account for the other nine domains. It is possible that addressing all 10 domains of the adolescent's life demands a more focused and concentrated effort.

The approach described by Ralph and McMenamy (1996) may strike the right balance. It was inpatient residential, yet lasted for only 45 days, well below the 6-month mark of the high-attrition therapeutic communities (Muck et al., 2001). The treatment utilized an intensive milieu program with a token economy, daily therapeutic groups, chemical dependency education groups, family therapy, and an aftercare program.

The Model

Our proposed model resembles that of Ralph and McMenamy (1996); it consists of a highly structured 45-day program featuring recovery-oriented tasks, activities, and classes. However, we propose an outpatient day treatment program as opposed to inpatient approach. To begin with, an outpatient setting increases accessibility because its cost is lower. Further, adolescents would be returning home in the evenings, which would enhance the family therapy component. The family would have numerous opportunities to incorporate the various interventions and homework exercises recommended in therapy. Finally, having the adolescents back at home in the evenings would likely reduce the incidence of sexual acting out that sometimes occurs in residential settings (Ralph & McMenamy, 1996).

Treatment would involve a combination of (a) elements that would apply to all of the adolescents and (b) elements specifically tailored to the individual. For example, of the 10 adolescent life domains (substance use, behavior patterns, health status, psychiatric disorder, social competency, family system, school performance/adjustment, work adjustment, peer relationships, and leisure/recreation), the following should be addressed with every adolescent:

Domain I: Substance Use

Domain II: Behavior Patterns

Domain IV: Family Systems

Some (e.g., Bukstein, 1994) might argue that Domains VII and VIII, addressing school and work, respectively, should be included in order to ensure the adolescents' success in adult life. However, a given adolescent might not be having problems in these domains. If these domains are included for all program participants, they might be treated as optional, something like elective classes offered in high school that are meant to address adolescents' specific interests. Another important reason to include these domains as options is to enhance participants' sense of autonomy by giving them some freedom of choice, which in itself is a desired feature of the treatment model. One of the main tasks of adolescence is individuation, which entails a desire to be respected and treated as an individual young adult (Archambault, 1992; White, 1989). Treatment can be structured, be uniform, and address the essential needs of the adolescent while also assisting adolescents with their individuation, self-esteem, and confidence. Allowing adolescents some input into their treatment plan is likely to increase interest and excitement in the treatment and thus ensure both greater engagement and retention in treatment.

As in Ralph and McMenamy's (1996) approach, the program would be based on a token economy. This has a dual purpose: giving the adolescents incentives and providing opportunities for enhancing their self-esteem through accomplishment. For example, adolescents might receive daily points for attending each domain class and counseling session, completing assignments, and following through on daily chores. The points might be accrued for various privileges, such as being able to watch specific movies, play video games, use the telephone, or perhaps go out into the community to eat at a restaurant.

On a daily basis, treatment would address the different domains, probably in the form of some kind of psychoeducational classes that would (a) inform the adolescents about positive and negative (adaptive and maladaptive) behaviors in the domains; (b) help the adolescents identify their own negative/maladaptive behaviors in those domains; (c) offer the adolescents new frameworks, perspectives, and solutions to help them move toward more positive and beneficial behaviors for each domain; (d) provide opportunities for group discussion for each domain; (e) include daily assignments; and (f) provide plenty of positive feedback, reinforcement, and rewards for work completed and progress made, as described by Ralph and McMenamy (1996). Some hypothesized specifics for the facilitation of each domain's psychoeducation classes are as follows:

Domain I: Substance Use. This component would address the dangers of substance use/abuse, the dangers of each particular substance, individual and group counseling to discuss and process the adolescent's previous substance use/abuse, and possibly an introduction to available substance abuse treatment approaches (i.e., 12-step, cognitive behavioral, family therapy, and therapeutic communities; Muck et al., 2001).

Domain II: Behavior Patterns. This component would consist of individual and group counseling to discuss and process issues, anger management classes if indicated, stress management skills training, coping skills, self-control and self-empowerment training, and psychoeducation in the form of modeling appropriate behaviors, including role plays with acted-out vignettes.

Domain III: Health Status. This component would address health issues such as the negative effects of substances on the brain and body, the importance of exercise and proper nutrition, the formulation of an exercise regime and diet plan if desired by the adolescent, and other health issues.

Domain IV: Psychiatric Disorder. This component would include the prescription of medication if indicated (Bukstein, 1994) and individual and group counseling to address psychological issues/disorders besides substance abuse.

Domain V: Social Competency. This component would focus on modeling social skills training, appropriate interactions with people in the adolescent's realm of experience (parents, peers, teachers, siblings), role playing, self-assertiveness skills training and practice, and group counseling.

Domain VI: Family System. This component would consist of family therapy, an integral part of treatment (Williams et al., 2000). The family therapist should tailor the specific approach to the family. For instance, if the family hierarchy is out of line, then structural family therapy would be appropriate. If the substance abuse seems to be a function of the symptom in the family, then strategic family therapy should be pursued. Or, if it seems that the substance abuse is simply a maladaptive behavior that, once changed, will lead to a better functioning for everybody, then a behavioral family approach should be used. In terms of frequency, family therapy should take place two or three times per week, which over the 45-day period would be up to 18 family therapy sessions. In addition, the family sessions could be scheduled toward the end of the day, thus making it convenient for the family members to come for therapy right before bringing the adolescent home for the night.

Domain VII: School Performance/Adjustment. This component would consist of an on-site school program with daily instruction so that the adolescents wouldn't lose any credits while they are in treatment. The on-site school program could be taught by a roving schoolteacher who could work with the adolescents to create an Individualized Education Program to guide instruction. The adolescents could also be taught how to more efficiently approach school, including learning or memorizing techniques such as mnemonics; how to take notes more efficiently in class; and how to set and meet short- and long-term goals in school. Possible enhancement classes could also be included, such as speed reading or memory improvement courses, to excite and motivate the adolescents as they try to learn a new skill that will make them feel special and unique. If learning disabilities or related problems such as visual, auditory, or other issues that interfere with learning are suspected, referrals to a specialist would be made.

Domain VIII: Work Adjustment. This component would consist of career assessment, information about how to secure employment and employer expectations, resume workshops, the concept of starting on the bottom and working up to better positions, and referrals for vocational training programs available in the adolescent's particular community. In addition, daily milieu cleaning chores and tasks would be required of each adolescent in order to maintain productivity, foster a sense of accomplishment, and create or maintain a good work ethic.

Domain IX: Peer Relationships. This component would focus on the adolescents' appropriate interactions with their peers. Adolescent-related scenarios concerning issues such as fights between friends, jealousies, interactions with the opposite sex, one's role in a group of friends, and so forth, would be addressed and acted out to rehearse appropriate interactions with other peers.

Domain X: Leisure/Recreation. This component would consist of familiarizing/refamiliarizing adolescents with the virtually endless world of nondrug activities that are open to them, emphasizing "natural highs" from various activities such as sports, intellectual pursuits, or games.

Many of these classes could be conducted in a co-ed setting, with both male and female adolescents. As noted, Ellis et al. (2000) argued compellingly in favor of segregation. We would suggest an approach that is sensitive both to the treatment topic and to the individual. The DUSI, in combination with the comprehensive assessment, should be able to detect the kinds of volatile issues that might be better dealt with in a protected setting, such as physical and sexual abuse, depression, social problems, family problems, self-harm, and harm to others. As Ellis et al. noted, integration with males during treatment could be counterproductive for some females. Yet complete segregation of the two would be prohibitively expensive, demanding the utilization of two separate facilities. Further, given the goals of Domains V (Social Competency) and IX (Peer Relationships), some interaction with the opposite sex would be preferable. Female participants with a history of molestation or physical assault could discuss those issues through individual or female-only group counseling early in treatment, and then be integrated into more co-ed groups once they felt more comfortable.

Relapse/Aftercare

As previously discussed, aftercare is a highly recommended and essential component of treatment (Brown et al., 1994; Bukstein, 1994; Williams et al., 2000), in part because of the high rate of relapse for adolescent substance abusers, which ranges from 35% to 70% (Newcomb & Bentler, 1989) and even to 90% (Todd & Selekman, 1991). Although it is not entirely clear why relapse occurs at such a high rate, it has been established that relapse rates are high among both adults and adolescents (Brown et al., 2000). Brown et al. (1989) described the cognitive behavioral model of relapse, which predicts that relapse is more likely when people with poor coping skills find themselves in a high-risk situation, such as social pressure to consume alcohol. According to a study by Brown et al. (2000), alcohol was involved in 46% of initial posttreatment relapse episodes. Brown et al. (1989) recommended that treatment include self-monitoring training, behavioral training, and coping skills training to prevent posttreatment relapse.

The domain classes described above address several of the relapse concerns raised by the Brown et al. studies. Specifically, the concerns about the adolescents' coping skills, behavioral training, and self-monitoring would be addressed in the Domain I and II classes (Substance Use and Behavior Patterns). The skills training could be reinforced in Domain V and Domain IX classes (Social Competency and Peer Relationships), where adolescents can participate in role plays of highly stressful and tempting situations.

Aftercare is another important aspect of treatment because it addresses the problem of relapse. The literature on aftercare is, however, scarce. Williams et al. (2000) noted that aftercare is an important posttreatment variable and included it in their six principles for successful treatment. The only aspect of aftercare that Williams et al. mentioned, though, was regular attendance at Alcoholics Anonymous (AA) or Narcotics Anonymous (NA) meetings. McKay (2001), who analyzed the only 15 controlled studies of continuing care for alcohol or drug abuse published since 1988, found AA to be a key aftercare component in many of the studies, although the studies themselves were methodologically weak in terms of establishing efficacy (McKay, 2001).

If AA and NA are going to be a major component of aftercare, they should be a part of the treatment program. We recommend that AA/NA meetings be held at the facility rather than having the adolescents attend meetings in the community. The transportation would be time-consuming and costly. Further, on-site meetings could be tailored to the needs of adolescents, with the steps altered as appropriate. The meetings should be open to both program participants and graduates. Availability to program graduates would likely help foster the graduates' commitment to their sobriety through continued interactions with the treatment staff and the continued exposure to the treatment milieu. The meetings could alternate between having only the current adolescents at the meetings and including program graduates. For instance, Monday, Wednesday, and Friday meetings could be for the adolescents currently in the program, and Tuesday, Thursday, and Saturday meetings could be "alumni"-type meetings that were open to anybody who chose to attend. Some meetings might include the adolescents' parents. There might also be a multifamily processing group once or twice a week.

To avoid promoting the disease model associated with AA/NA, the 12 steps might be altered, as in the Minnesota model described by Winters et al. (2000). In that approach, only the first five steps were used, and the wording of each step was changed in order to increase the adolescent's reaching out while minimizing the imposition of a permanent label (i.e., having a lifelong "disease") (Winters et al., 2000). The goal here is for adolescents to have a positive experience with self-help groups that they can utilize their entire life. Then, once the initial 45 days are completed, the adolescents will be encouraged to attend meetings on their own to continue with their recovery. Program graduates could be provided with a comprehensive list of community resources.

Summary

Adolescent drug use/abuse is a serious problem. In many adolescents, use of alcohol and drugs is a transitory, experimental activity. For many others, however, drug use/abuse results in devastating consequences, including fatality. In the present chapter, we have sought to provide a unified adolescent substance abuse treatment model that addresses many of the problems that have been inherent in treatment approaches of the past. Some of these problems have been (a) attempting to apply adult-designed treatment to adolescents; (b) focusing solely on the adolescent's substance abuse while ignoring a whole host of other aspects of the adolescent's life, such as family, school, and peer group interaction; (c) failing to assist the adolescent in achieving a sense of independence and confidence; and (d) failing to help the adolescent develop appropriate coping and social skills for adult life. The model attempts to incorporate some of the empirically established elements of effective treatment for adolescents, including (a) approaching adolescent substance abuse treatment through a multimodal, comprehensive approach that treats the multiple domains of the adolescent's life; (b) incorporating family therapy; (c) separating adolescent males and females during some of the treatment; and (d) addressing the issue of relapse. The proposed model is not a panacea for adolescent substance abusers. However, we believe that this model has the potential to yield positive abstinence outcomes at discharge and beyond.

References

Achenbach, T. M., Edelbrock, C., & Howell, C. (1987). Empirically-based assessment of the behavioral/emotional assessment of the behavioral/emotional problems of 2–3 year old children. *Journal of Abnormal Psychology, 15,* 629–650.

Adair, E. B. G., Craddock, S. G., Miller, H. G., & Turner, C. F. (1996). Quality of treatment data: Reliability over time of self-reports given by clients in treatment for substance abuse. *Journal of Substance Abuse Treatment, 13,* 145–149.

American Psychiatric Association. (1987). *Diagnostic and statistical manual of mental disorders* (3rd ed., rev.). Washington, DC: Author.

American Psychiatric Association. (1994). *Diagnostic and statistical manual of mental disorders* (4th ed.). Washington, DC: Author.

Anderson, D. (1998). Teen drug use among 8th, 10th, and 12th graders. *NIDA Notes, 13*(2), n.p.

Anderson, S. C. (1995). Education for family-centered practice. *Families in Society, 76*(3), 173–182.

Archambault, D. (1992). Adolescence: A physiological, cultural, and psychological no man's land. In G. W. Lawson & A. W. Lawson (Eds.), *Adolescent substance abuse: Etiology, treatment, and prevention* (pp. 11–28). Gaithersburg, MD: Aspen.

Austin, A., Macgowan, M. J., & Wagner, E. F. (2005). Effective family-based interventions for adolescents with substance use problems: A systemic review. *Research on Social Work Practice, 15*(2), 67–83.

Azrin, N. H., Donohue, B., Besalel, V. A., Kogan, E. S., & Acierno, R. (1994). Youth drug abuse treatment: A controlled outcome study. *Journal of Child and Adolescent Substance Abuse, 3*(3), 1–16.

Beschner, G. (1986). Understanding teenage drug use. In G. Beschner & A. S. Friedman (Eds.), *Teen drug use* (pp. 1–17). Lexington, MA: Lexington Books.

Block, R. I., & Ghoneim, M. (1993). Effects of chronic marijuana use on human cognition. *Psychopharmacology, 110*(1/2), 219–228.

Blume, T. W., Green, S., Joanning, H., & Quinn, W. S. (1994). Social role negotiation skills for substance-abusing adolescents: A group model. *Journal of Substance Abuse Treatment, 11*(3), 197–204.

Brown, S. A., D'Amico, E. J., McCarthy, D. M., & Tapert, S. F. (2001). Four-year outcomes from adolescent alcohol and drug treatment. *Journal of Studies on Alcohol, 62*(3), 381–388.

Brown, S. A., Myers, M. G., Lippke, L., Tapert, S. F., Stewart, D. G., & Vik, P. W. (1998). Psychometric evaluation of the Customary Drinking and Drug Use Record (CDDR): A measure of adolescent alcohol and drug involvement. *Journal of Studies on Alcohol, 59*(4), 427–438.

Brown, S. A., Myers, M. G., Mott, M. A., & Vik, P. W. (1994). Correlates of success following treatment for adolescent substance abuse. *Applied and Preventive Psychology, 3*(2), 61–73.

Brown, S. A., Tapert, S. F., Tate, S. R., & Abrantes, A. M. (2000). The role of alcohol in adolescent relapse and outcomes. *Journal of Psychoactive Drugs, 32*(1), 107–116.

Brown, S. A., Vik, P. W., & Creamer, V. A. (1989). Characteristics of relapse following adolescent substance abuse treatment. *Addictive Behaviors, 14*(3), 291–300.

Bukstein, O. G. (1994). Treatment of adolescent alcohol abuse and dependence. *Alcohol Health and Research World, 18*(4), 296–302.

Bukstein, O. G. (2000). Disruptive behavior disorders and substance use disorders in adolescents. *Journal of Psychoactive Drugs, 32*(1), 67–80.

Catalano, R. F., Hawkins, J. D., Wells, E. A., & Miller, J. (1990). Evaluation of the effectiveness of adolescent drug abuse treatment, assessment of the risks for relapse, and promising approaches for relapse prevention. *The International Journal of the Addictions, 25*(9A & 10A), 1085–1140.

Chambers, J. C. (1999). Youth caught in the enchanting web of chemicals. *Reclaiming Children and Youth, 8*(1), 34–39.

Cunningham, P. B., & Henggeler, S. W. (1999). Engaging multiproblem families in treatment: Lessons learned throughout the development of multisystemic therapy. *Family Process, 38*(3), 265–281.

Dakof, G. A., Tejeda, M., & Liddle, H. A. (2001). Predictors of engagement in adolescent drug abuse treatment. *Journal of the American Academy of Child and Adolescent Psychiatry, 40*(3), 274–281.

D'Amico, E., & Fromme, K. (1997). Health risk behaviors of adolescent and young adult siblings. *Health Psychology, 16*(5), 426–432.

Ellis, R. A., O'Hara, M., & Sowers, K. M. (2000). Profile-based intervention: Developing gender-sensitive treatment for adolescent substance abusers. *Research on Social Work Practice, 10*(3), 327–347.

Epstein, S., & Meier, P. (1989). Constructive thinking: A broad concept variable with specific components. *Journal of Personality and Social Psychology, 57*(2), 332–350.

Etheridge, R. M., Smith, J. C., Rounds-Bryant, J. L., & Hubbard, R. L. (2001). Drug abuse treatment and comprehensive services for adolescents. *Journal of Adolescent Research, 16*(6), 563–589.

Feigelman, W. (1987). Day-care treatment for multiple drug abusing adolescents: Social factors linked with completing treatment. *Journal of Psychoactive Drugs, 19*, 335–344.

Fromme, K., & Brown, S. A. (2000). Special series: Empirically based prevention and treatment approaches for adolescent and young adult substance use [Introduction]. *Cognitive and Behavioral Practice, 7*(1), 61–64.

Green, J. (1986). Curriculum and assessment in generalizable skills instruction. *Journal for Vocational Special Needs Education, 9*(1), 3–10.

Henggeler, S. W., Borduin, C. M., Melton, G. B., Mann, B. J., Smith, L. A., Hall, J. A., Cone, L., & Fucci, B. R. (1991). Effects of multisystemic therapy on drug use and abuse in serious juvenile offenders: A progress report from two outcome studies. *Family Dynamics of Addiction Quarterly, 1*(3), 40–51.

Henggeler, S. W., Clingempeel, W. G., Brondino, M. J., & Pickrel, S. G. (2002). Four-year follow-up of multisystemic therapy with substance abusing and dependent juvenile offenders. *Journal of the American Academy of Child and Adolescent Psychiatry, 41*, 868–874.

Henggeler, S. W., Halliday-Boykins, C. A., Cunningham, P. B., Randall, J., Shapiro, S. B., & Chapman, J. E. (2006). Juvenile drug court: Enhancing outcomes by integrating evidence-based treatments. *Journal of Consulting and Clinical Psychology, 74*(1), 41–54.

Henggeler, S. W., Pickrel, S. G., Brondino, S. J., & Crouch, J. L. (1996). Eliminating (almost) treatment dropout of substance abusing or dependent delinquents through home-based multisystemic therapy. *The American Journal of Psychiatry, 153*(3), 427–428.

Hollin, C. R., & Palmer, E. J. (2006). The Adolescent Problems Inventory: A profile of incarcerated English male young offenders. *Personality and Individual Differences, 40*(7), 1485–1495.

Hser, Y. I., Grella, C. E., Hubbard, R. L., & Hsieh, S. C. (2001). An evaluation of drug treatment for adolescents in four U.S. cities. *Archives of General Psychiatry, 58*(7), 689–695.

Ivarsson, T., Gillberg, C., Arvidsson, T., & Broberg, A. G. (2002). The Youth Self-Report (YSR) and the Depression Self-Rating Scale (DSRS) as measures of depression and suicidality among adolescents. *European Child and Adolescent Psychiatry, 11*, 31–37.

Jessor, R., & Jessor, S. L. (1977). *Problem behavior and psychosocial development: A longitudinal study of youth.* New York: Academic Press.

Joanning, H., Quinn, W., Thomas, F., & Mullen, R. (1992). Treating adolescent drug abuse: A comparison of family systems therapy, group therapy, and family drug education. *Journal of Marital and Family Therapy, 18*(4), 345–356.

Johnston, L. D., O'Malley, P. M., & Bachman, J. G. (1993). *National survey results on drug use from monitoring the future study: Vol. 1.* Rockville, MD: National Institute on Drug Abuse.

Kazdin, A. E. (1990). Premature termination from treatment among children referred for antisocial behavior. *Journal of Child Psychology and Psychiatry, 31,* 415–425.

Kazdin, A. E., & Mazurick, J. L. (1994). Dropping out of child psychotherapy: Distinguishing early and late dropouts over the course of treatment. *Journal of Consulting and Clinical Psychology, 62,* 1069–1074.

Kim, S., Crutchfield, C., Williams, C., & Hepler, N. (1998). Toward a new paradigm in substance abuse and other problem behavior prevention for youth: Youth development and empowerment approach. *Journal of Drug Education, 28*(1), 1–17.

Kim, Y. S., Choon, K. A., Kim, B. N., Chang, S. A., Yoo, H. J., Kim, J. W., et al. 2004. The reliability and validity of Kiddie-Schedule for Affective Disorders and Schizophrenia—Present and lifetime version. *Yonsei Medical Journal, 45,* 81–89.

Kirisci, L., Mezzich, A., & Tarter, R. (1995). Norms and sensitivity of the adolescent version of the drug use screening inventory. *Addictive Behaviors, 20*(2), 149–157.

Lawson, G. W. (1992). Twelve-step programs and the treatment of adolescent substance abuse. In G. W. Lawson & A. W. Lawson (Eds.), *Adolescent substance abuse: Etiology, treatment, and prevention* (pp. 219–229). Gaithersburg, MD: Aspen.

Lewis, R. A., Piercy, F. P., Sprenkle, D. H., & Trepper, T. S. (1990). Family-based interventions for helping drug-abusing adolescents. *Journal of Adolescent Research, 5*(1), 82–95.

Liddle, H. (1999). Theory development in a family-based therapy for adolescent drug abuse. *Journal of Clinical Child Psychology, 28*(4), 521–532.

Liddle, H. A., & Dakof, G. A. (1995). Efficacy of family therapy for drug abuse: Promising but not definitive. *Journal of Marital and Family Therapy, 21*(4), 511–543.

Liddle, H. A., Dakof, G. A., & Diamond, G. (1991). Adolescent substance abuse: Multidimensional family therapy in action. In E. Kaufman & P. Kaufman (Eds.), *Family therapy of drug and alcohol abuse* (pp. 120–171). Boston: Allyn & Bacon.

Lipman, R. S., Covi, L., & Shapiro, A. K. (1977). The Hopkins Symptom Checklist: Factors derived from the HSCL-90. *Journal of Affective Disorders, 1,* 9–24.

MacDonald, D. I. (1989). *Drugs, drinking and adolescents* (2nd ed.). Chicago: Year Book Medical Publishers.

Martin, C. S., & Winters, K. C. (1998). Diagnosis and assessment of alcohol use disorders among adolescents. *Alcohol Health and Research World, 22*(2), 95–105.

McKay, J. R. (2001). Effectiveness of continuing-care interventions for substance abusers: Implications for the study of long-term treatment effects. *Evaluation Review, 25*(2), 211–232.

McNeece, C. A., & DiNitto, D. M. (Eds.). (1998). *Chemical dependency: A systems approach* (2nd ed.). Needham Heights, MA: Allyn & Bacon.

Miller, G. (1985). *Addiction research and consultation.* Spencer, IN: Spencer Evening World.

Minehan, J. A., Newcomb, M. D., & Galaif, E. R. (2000). Predictions of adolescent drug use: Cognitive abilities, coping strategies, and purpose in life. *Journal of Child and Adolescent Substance Abuse, 10*(2), 33–52.

Morrison, M. A. (1985). *Adolescence and vulnerability to chemical dependence.* Atlanta: Ridgeview Institute.

Muck, R., Zempolich, K. A., Titus, J. C., Fishman, M., Godley, M. D., & Schwebel, R. (2001). Adolescent substance abuse disorders: From acute treatment to recovery management. *Youth and Society, 33*(2), 143–168.

Nasim, A., Corona, R., Belgrave, F., Utsey, S., & Fallah, N. (2007). Cultural orientation as a protective factor against tobacco and marijuana smoking for African American youth women. *Journal of Youth Adolescence, 36,* 503–516.

Newcomb, M. D., & Bentler, P. M. (1988). Impact of adolescent drug use and social support on problems of young adults: A longitudinal study. *Journal of Abnormal Psychology, 97*(1), 64–75.

Newcomb, M. D., & Bentler, P. M. (1989). Substance use and abuse among children and teenagers. *American Psychologist, 44*(2), 242–248.

Norbert, R., & McMenamy, C. (1996). Treatment outcomes in an adolescent chemical dependency program. *Adolescence, 31*(121), 91–118.

Oetting, E., Beauvais, F., Edwards, R., et al. (1984). *The drug and alcohol assessment system.* Fort Collins, CO: Mountain Behavioral Sciences Institute.

O'Malley, P. M., Bachman, J. G., & Schulenberg, J. E. (2006). *Monitoring the future national results on adolescent drug use: Overview of key findings* (NIH Publication). Bethesda, MD: National Institute on Drug Abuse.

Pearson Education. (2000). *Metropolitan achievement tests.* Upper Saddle River, NJ: Author.

Ralph, N., & McMenamy, C. (1996). Treatment outcomes in an adolescent chemical dependency program. *Adolescence, 31*(121), 91–118.

Rice, F. P. (1984). *The adolescent: Development, relationships, and culture* (4th ed.). Boston: Allyn & Bacon.

Richter, S. S., Brown, S. A., & Mott, M. A. (1991). The impact of social support and self-esteem on adolescent substance abuse treatment outcome. *Journal of Substance Abuse, 3*(4), 371–385.

Schoenwald, S. K., Brown, T. L., & Henggeler, S. W. (2000). Inside multi-systemic therapy: Therapist, supervisory, and program practices. *Journal of Emotional and Behavioral Disorders, 8*(2), 113–127.

Selekman, M. D., & King, S. (2001). "It's my drug": Solution-oriented brief therapy with self-harming adolescents. *Journal of Systemic Therapies, 20*(2), 88–105.

Semlitz, L. (1996). Adolescent substance abuse treatment and managed care. *Child and Adolescent Psychiatric Clinics of North America, 5*(1), 221–241.

Shane, P. A., Jasiukaitis, & Green, R. S. (2003). Treatment outcomes among adolescents with substance abuse problems: The relationship between comorbidities and post-treatment substance involvement. *Evaluation and Program Planning, 26*(4), 393–402.

Shedler, J., & Block, J. (1990). Adolescent drug use and psychological health: A longitudinal inquiry. *American Psychologist, 45*(5), 612–630.

Skinner, H. A., Steinhauer, P. D., & Santa-Barbara, J. (1983). The family assessment measure. *Canadian Journal of Community Mental Health, 2*(2), 91–103.

Smith, G. T., McCarthy, D. M., & Goldman, M. S. (1995). Self-reported drinking and alcohol-related problems among early adolescents: Dimensionality and validity over 24 months. *Journal of Studies on Alcohol, 56*, 383–394.

Smith, T. E., & Springer, D. W. (1998). Treating chemically dependent children and adolescents. In C. A. McNeece & D. M. DiNitto (Eds.), *Chemical dependency: A systems approach* (2nd ed, pp. 213–228). Needham Heights, MA: Allyn & Bacon.

Sobell, M. B., Maisto, S. A., Sobell, L. C., Cooper, A. M., Cooper, T., & Sanders, B. (1980). Developing a prototype for evaluating alcohol treatment effectiveness. In L. C. Sobell, M. B. Sobell, & E. Ward (Eds.), *Evaluating alcohol and drug abuse treatment effectiveness: Recent advances* (pp. 129–150). New York: Pergamon.

Spooner, C. (1999). Causes and correlates of adolescent drug abuse and implications for treatment. *Drug and Alcohol Review, 18*(4), 453–476.

Stanton, M. D., & Shadish, W. R. (1997). Outcome, attrition, and family-couples treatment for drug abuse: A meta-analysis and review of the controlled, comparative studies. *Psychological Bulletin, 122*(2), 170–191.

Szapocznik, J., Perez-Vidal, A., Brickman, A. L., Foote, F. H., Santisteban, D., Hervis, O., & Kurtines, W. M. (1988). Engaging adolescent drug abusers and their families in treatment: A strategic structural systems approach. *Journal of Consulting and Clinical Psychology, 56*(4), 552–557.

Tapert, S. F., Brown, S. A., Myers, M. G., & Granholm, E. (1999). The role of neurocognitive abilities in coping with adolescent relapse to alcohol and drug use. *Journal of Studies on Alcohol, 60*(4), 500–508.

Tapert, S. F., Stewart, D. G., & Brown, S. A. (1999). Drug abuse in adolescence. In A. J. Goreczny & M. Hersen (Eds.), *Handbook of pediatric and adolescent health psychology* (pp. 161–178). Needham Heights, MA: Allyn & Bacon.

Tarter, R. E. (1990). Evaluation and treatment of adolescent substance abuse: A decision tree method. *American Journal of Drug and Alcohol Abuse, 16*(1), 1–46.

Tarter, R. E., & Hegedus, A. M. (1991). The Drug Use Screening Inventory: Its applications in the evaluation and treatment of alcohol and other drug abuse. *Alcohol Heath and Research World, 15*(1), 65–75.

Tarter, R. E., Laird, S. B., Bukstein, O., & Kaminer, Y. (1992). Validation of the adolescent Drug Use Screening Inventory: Preliminary findings. *Psychology of Addictive Behaviors, 6*(4), 233–236.

Tarter, R. E., Mezzich, A. C., Kirisci, L., & Kaczynski, N. (1994). Reliability of the Drug Use Screening Inventory among adolescent alcoholics. *Journal of Child and Adolescent Substance Abuse, 3*(1), 25–36.

Thomas, C., & Corcoran, J. (2001). Empirically based marital and family interventions for alcohol abuse: A review. *Research on Social Work Practice, 11*(5), 549–575.

Todd, T. C., & Selekman, M. D. (1991). Crucial issues in the treatment of adolescent substance abusers and their families. In T. C. Todd & M. D. Selekman (Eds.), *Family therapy approaches with adolescent substance abusers* (pp. 3–28). Boston: Allyn & Bacon.

U.S. Census Bureau. (2001). *Statistical abstract of the United States: 2001* (121st ed.). Washington, DC: Author.

Substance Abuse and Mental Health Services Administration. (1998). *Substance abuse and mental health statistics sourcebook.* Washington, DC: U.S. Government Printing Office.

Vaughn, C., & Long, W. (1999). Surrender to win: How adolescent drug and alcohol users change their lives. *Adolescence, 34*(133), 9–24.

Waldron, H. B., Slesnick, N., Brody, J. L., Turner, C. W., & Peterson, T. R. (2001). Treatment outcomes for adolescent substance abuse at 4- and 7-month assessments. *Journal of Consulting and Clinical Psychology, 69*(5), 802–813.

Whalen, C. K., Jamner, L. D., Henker, B., Gehricke, J. G., & King, P. S. (2003). Is there a link between adolescent cigarette smoking and pharmacotherapy for ADHD? *Psychology of Addictive Behaviors, 17*(4), 332–335.

White, J. L. (1989). *The troubled adolescent.* New York: Pergamon Press.

Wilens, T. E., Faraone, S. V., Biederman, J., & Gunawardend, S. (2003). Does stimulant therapy of attention-deficit/hyperactivity disorder beget later substance abuse? A meta-analytic review of the literature. *Pediatrics, 111*(1), 179–185.

Wilkinson, G. W. (2006). *Wide range achievement test* (4th ed.). Austin, TX: PRO-ED.

Williams, R. J., Chang, S. Y., & the Addiction Centre Adolescent Research Group. (2000). A comprehensive and comparative review of adolescent substance abuse treatment outcome. *Clinical Psychology: Science and Practice, 7*(2), 138–166.

Wilson, J. J., & Levin, F. R. (2005). Attention-deficit/hyperactivity disorder and early-onset of substance use disorders. *Journal of Child and Adolescent Psychopharmacology, 15*(5), 751–763.

Windle, M. (2004). Suicidal behaviors and alcohol use among adolescents: A developmental psychopathology perspective. *Alcoholism: Clinical and Experimental Research, 28,* 29S–37S.

Winters, K. C., Stinchfield, R. D., Opland, E. O., Weller, C., & Latimer, W. W. (2000). The effectiveness of the Minnesota model approach in the treatment of adolescent drug abusers. *Addiction, 95*(4), 601–612.

Resources

Brown, S. A., Vik, P. W., Patterson, T. L., Grant, I., & Schuckit, M. A. (1995). Stress, vulnerability and adult alcohol relapse. *Journal of Studies on Alcohol, 56*(5), 538–545.

Cox, R. B., Jr., & Ray, W. A. (1994). The role of theory in treating adolescent substance abuse. *Contemporary Family Therapy: An International Journal, 16*(2), 131–144.

Diamond, G. M., Diamond, G. S., & Liddle, H. A. (2000). The therapist-parent alliance in family-based therapy for adolescents. *Journal of Clinical Psychology, 56*(8), 1037–1050.

Diamond, G., & Liddle, H. A. (1996). Resolving a therapeutic impasse between parents and adolescents in multidimensional family therapy. *Journal of Consulting and Clinical Psychology, 64*(3), 481–488.

Frances, R. J., & Franklin, J. E. (1989). *Treatment of alcoholism and addictions.* Washington, DC: American Psychiatric Press.

Friedman, A. S., & Granick, S. (Eds.). (1990). *Family therapy for adolescent drug abuse.* Lexington, MA: Lexington Books.

Gilvany, E. (2000). Substance abuse in young people. *Journal of Child Psychology and Psychiatry and Allied Disciplines, 41*(1), 55–80.

Jainchill, N., & Margolis, R. (2000). Editor's introduction: Issues in adolescent abuse treatment: Perspectives, approaches and solutions. *Journal of Psychoactive Drugs, 32*(1), 1–3.

Kaufman, E. (1985). *Substance abuse and family therapy.* New York: Grune & Stratton.

Kaufman E., & Kaufman P. (Eds.). (1992). *Family therapy of drug and alcohol abuse* (2nd ed.). Boston: Allyn & Bacon.

Lang, A. R. (1985). *Alcohol: Teenage drinking.* New York: Chelsea House.

Littrell, J. (1991). *Understanding and treating alcoholism* (Vol. 2). Hillsdale, NJ: Erlbaum.

Margolis, R., Kilpatrick, A., & Mooney, B. (2000). A retrospective look at long-term adolescent recovery: Clinicians talk to researchers. *Journal of Psychoactive Drugs, 32*(1), 117–126.

Meyers, M. G., Stewart, D. G., & Brown, S. A. (1998). Progression from conduct disorder to antisocial personality disorder following treatment for adolescent substance abuse. *American Journal of Psychiatry, 155*(4), 479–485.

Milkman, H. B., & Sederer, L. I. (1990). *Treatment choices for alcoholism and substance abuse.* New York: Lexington Books.

Myers, M. G., & Brown, S. A. (1996). The adolescent relapse coping questionnaire: Psychometric validation. *Journal of Studies on Alcohol, 57*(1), 40–46.

Nasim, A., Corona, R., Belgrave, F., Utsey, S. O., & Fallah, N. (2007). The moderating effects of culture on peer deviance and alcohol use among high-risk African-American adolescents. *Journal of Youth and Adolescence, 36,* 503–516.

O'Malley, P. M., Bachman, J. G., & Schulenberg, J. E. (2006). *Monitoring the future national results on adolescent drug use: Overview of key findings* (NIH Publication). Bethesda, MD: National Institute on Drug Abuse.

Porterfield, K. M. (1992). *Focus on addictions.* Santa Barbara: ABC-CLIO.

Santisteban, D. A., & Szapocznik, J. (1994). Bridging theory, research and practice to more successfully engage substance abusing youth and their families into therapy. *Journal of Child and Adolescent Substance Abuse, 3*(2), 9–24.

Segal, S., & Fairchild, H. H. (1996). Polysubstance abuse—A case study. *Adolescence, 31*(124), 797–805.

Stephenson, A. L., Henry, C. S., & Robinson, L. C. (1996). Family characteristics and adolescent substance use. *Adolescence, 31*(121), 59–78.

Storti, E., & Keller, J. (1988). *Crisis intervention: Acting against addiction.* New York: Crown.

Szapocznik, J., Kurtines, W. M., Foote, F., Perez-Vidal, A., & Hervis, O. (1986). Conjoint versus one-person family therapy: Further evidence for the effectiveness of conducting family therapy through one person with drug-abusing adolescents. *Journal of Consulting and Clinical Psychology, 54*(3), 395–397.

Tarter, R. E., & Kirisci, L. (1997). The Drug Use Screening Inventory for Adults: Psychometric structure and discriminative sensitivity. *American Journal of Drug and Alcohol Abuse, 23*(2), 207–219.

U.S. Department of Health and Human Services. (1983). *Data from the national drug and alcoholism treatment units* (DHHS Publication No. ADM 83-1284). Washington, DC: Author.

Vogler, R. E., & Bartz, W. R. (1992). *Teenagers and alcohol.* Philadelphia: Charles Press.

Wexler, D. B. (1991). *The adolescent self.* New York: Norton.

CHAPTER 12

Treatment and Prevention of Addiction Among Native Americans

Ron J. Llewelyn and Gary W. Lawson

Addiction of all forms impacts the Native American people, but most prominent is the addiction to alcohol, which is without a doubt one of the greatest problems affecting this population today. The effects are spiritually, physically, mentally, and emotionally tragic, and the consequences are found in the increasing rates of suicide, accidental deaths, criminal arrests, family violence, family breakdown, birth defects, and a multitude of medical problems. In the Native American population, the four leading causes of death are accidents, cirrhosis of the liver, suicide, and homicide (French, 2004). The Native American death rate is 300% higher than the average death rate of the United States as a whole, and the rate of alcohol-related deaths is 770% higher (Gone, 2004; Gordis, 1994). Drinking patterns and behaviors vary widely across tribes (Levy & Kunitz, 1974; Stratton, Zeiner, & Pardes, 1978), but where heavy drinking patterns exist, the effects on the family are devastating. We must ask: Why has the Native American population suffered such devastating consequences as a result of addiction? This chapter examines the research on this question as well as numerous variables that affect treatment outcomes in the Native American population.

According to recent studies, Native Americans have the highest addiction rates of any cultural group in the United States (French, 2004). Native American youth use nearly every type of substance at a significantly greater rate of frequency than their non-native counterparts, and most start using at a much earlier age (Thurman, Plested, Edwards, Chen, & Swaim, 2000). A new type of addiction is currently creeping onto the native reservations—the gambling addiction. The Indian Gaming Regulatory Act, which was passed in 1988, authorized Native American tribes to build and operate casinos on their reservation lands. Both U.S. government and Native American officials believed that gaming would help spur Native American economic growth, stability, and independence (Zitzow, 2003). It is unclear whether the act has resulted in stability and economic gain, but what is clear is the pathology that has developed due to the availability of gambling. It is possible that gaming has been adopted as another coping tool, similar to substance use, to deal with the economic and social hardships that have stricken this population for many years.

Research indicates that pathological gambling is higher in both Native American adults and adolescents than in Whites (Volberg & Abbott, 1997). Natives are 2 to 15 times more likely to have a pathological gambling problem than are non-natives (Wardman, Khan, & El-Guebaly, 2001). Elia and Jacobs (1993) found that 41% of Native Americans, compared to 21% of Whites, in their study admitted to having a problem with gambling. Among adolescents, the discrepancy can be explained by differences in socioeconomic status, culture issues, vicarious exposure, and availability of gaming (Zitzow, 1996a). Among adults, gambling addiction may be related to low socioeconomic status, high rates of unemployment, high alcohol and drug use, historical trauma, and a lack of other social events (Zitzow, 1996b). Substance abuse and depression can aggravate problematic or pathological gambling behaviors (French, 2000).

Numerous authors have identified risk factors related to addiction in the Native American population, which include poor family bonding, poor parenting skills, poverty, poor social conditions, positive attitudes toward substance use, loss of cultural identity, negative modeling, and historical trauma (Beauvais & LaBoueff, 1985; Christensen & Manson, 2001; French, 2004; Swaim, Oetting, Thurman, Beauvais, & Edwards, 1993; White, 2004). These variables, each of which has its own role in the overall pathology of addiction, create a very complex picture for the treatment provider.

Another important variable is the poor state of mental health centers and providers available to Native Americans. Centers and providers currently working with this population are drastically understaffed and underfunded. According to Gone (2004), the United States Congress has allocated only enough federal funds to satisfy approximately 52% of the needs of the Native American people. Of those funds, only 7% goes toward behavioral health and substance abuse treatment. In 2001, there were approximately 20 psychiatrists, 60 psychologists, and 110 social workers working under the Indian Health Services Contract; these needed to provide 208,000 client contacts. Clearly, the Native American population is drastically underserved, and those serving are drastically overburdened.

A Brief Summary of Native American History

Any therapist offering treatment to individuals who belong to a particular culture should have a working knowledge of that culture in order to better understand his or her clients. In fact, it would be unethical to lack the cultural understanding needed for appropriate care. In the case of Native Americans, it is imperative to have a clear understanding of their history.

There are four distinct eras in Native American history: (a) precontact, (b) Manifest Destiny, (c) assimilation, and (d) self-determination (Paniagua, 1998). The precontact period (–1492) refers to the era before colonization by European settlers, when Native

Americans developed traditions such as the Survival Pact. The Survival Pact is a manifesto holding that Native American people should live in harmony with all living things. Manifest Destiny refers to the period from 1493 to 1889 and corresponds to European settlement and westward expansion. The settlers believed that colonization was ordained by God. During this time, European settlers took the land from Native Americans and forced them to relocate and assimilate to European cultural beliefs. Institutionalizing Native American children in boarding schools was one of the many practices used by the settlers to forcibly instill European social structure, values, and religious beliefs. At the outset of European colonization, it is believed that there were 5 million Native Americans; by 1970, estimates indicate that only 250,000 Native Americans remained (Paniagua, 1998). During the assimilation period (1890–1969), Native Americans were forced to adapt their beliefs, government, and cultural structure to those of the European settlers. If Native Americans tried to engage in traditional practices, they were harshly punished or murdered. The Dawes Act, initiated in 1887, reflected a new policy focused specifically on dissolving reservations by granting land allotments to individual Native Americans. The U.S. government reasoned that if Native Americans owned their own land, wore White clothing, and practiced American ways, they would gradually drop their traditional ways and be assimilated into the population. Taxes on this land forced Native Americans to farm, which resulted in a significant change in Native American social structure and government. In 1954, the Western Oregon Indian Termination Act, or Public Law 588, was adopted; this law forced Native Americans to find new areas in which to live. In traditional Native American thought, the land belonged to everybody and would be respectfully utilized to benefit the whole tribe. Native American social structure adhered to a collectivistic way of life, not the individualistic social structure of the Europeans. During the assimilation period, U.S. policies were aimed at dissolving what was left of Native American social and political organization.

The self-determination period (1970–present) refers to the current period, when attempts have been made to restore Native American culture to its former state. With the prolonged assault on Native American culture and the dominance of Euro-American culture, however, a full-fledged, pure rejuvenation of Native American ways may not be possible. Forced boarding school and forced relocation, in particular, continue to have devastating effects on the Native American population (French, 2004; White, 2004). The boarding school experience not only forced Native Americans to adopt the culture, beliefs, and religious values of Euro-America, but also took young children away from their parents, causing irreparable damage to the Native American family. Forced relocation removed Native Americans from their land and the connection that the land held both to the past and to their shared value of collective land use. It also decimated the Native American governing structure. Moreover, Native Americans were forced to live in less productive areas, where they struggled to survive.

As horrifying as the idea may be to the psyche of all Americans, we must face the dismal fact that what Native Americans have experienced at the hands of both early and contemporary American government and citizens hauntingly resembles the genocide the Jewish people faced at the hands of the Nazis during the Holocaust. The eradication of a race and culture, whether by physical termination or psychosocial means, was the intent, and hundreds of thousands were simply killed. To this day, the Jewish people still bear the scars of the Holocaust, and people find it easy to understand why the culture still mourns. Many people lack that same empathetic understanding regarding Native American people, however. If we stand back and take an objective look, we can clearly see that the societal defense of denial is still alive and well. Our society finds it easy to point the finger at the Nazi agenda as evil, but when the blood is on our own hands, we find it easy to rationalize away. At the hands of the new dominant culture, Native Americans have faced over 500 years of trauma; between the years 1840 and 1850 alone, the Native American population dwindled from 600,000 to only 250,000. Three hundred fifty thousand Native Americans were slaughtered—through warfare with colonists, forced relocation into rival native territory, starvation, diseases brought by the Europeans, and murder.

Myths Concerning Native American Alcohol Consumption

Before we turn to patterns of Native American alcohol consumption, let us dispel some common myths concerning the drinking habits of Native Americans. Thatcher (2004), in his research on Canadian tribes, determined that the following nine stereotypes of Native American drinking are without empirical merit:

1. Native Americans have a greater-than-average attraction to alcoholic beverages.
2. Native Americans have, as a whole, a biological predisposition for alcohol dependency.
3. Native American drinking patterns are only a result of social and psychological predispositions.
4. Native Americans are out-of-control drinkers who are prone to violence when inebriated.
5. Native American drinking behaviors are different from White drinking behaviors.
6. Native Americans need to maintain abstinence and cannot use alcohol at a moderate or social level.
7. Native American treatment should be conducted in an intensive 4- to 6-week in-patient treatment setting that promotes abstinence.
8. If the Native American relapses after treatment, treatment needs to start again from the beginning.
9. Native American alcohol abuse is purely dysfunctional.

The therapist should avoid bringing such stereotypical notions to the treatment setting. Knowledge of a client's cultural background is crucial to effective treatment; stereotypes should not be mistaken for such knowledge. The common stereotype is that all Native Americans drink and cannot handle their liquor due to a metabolic dysfunction. Many people don't consider that there are numerous tribes in America and each has unique characteristics. As noted above, not all Native Americans consume alcohol or other addictive substances. Caution must be utilized, and the therapist must not automatically assume that an addictive disorder exists based on the person's Native American status.

The therapist should, however, be mindful of some basic differences between Native American and Euro-American cultures. Table 12.1 lists some dichotomies that may be relevant to treatment planning. For example, values about harmony and sharing are very different between the two cultures. This may have a negative effect on treatment, particularly regarding goals and outcomes that are expected by the client versus those of the therapist.

In the following sections, we examine specific physiological, sociocultural, and psychological factors that are relevant to the diagnosis and treatment of Native Americans who present with substance abuse problems.

Physiological Factors

We reviewed research conducted from 1978 to 2005 on ethnic differences in the physiological response to alcohol, specifically, consumption rate, absorption rate, metabolism rate, alcohol dehydrogenase, acetaldehyde dehydrogenase, alcohol sensitivity (facial flushing and dysphoria), cardiovascular changes, psychological alterations, and alcohol abuse. These findings are discussed in the following sections. We did not find support for a genetic etiology for alcoholism and other addictions among Native Americans (Garrett & Carroll, 2000). Currently, genetic predisposition to heavy drinking is not supported by the research (Weaver, 2003).

Consumption Rate

Native Americans vary greatly in alcohol consumption rates. Reed (1985) reported that the percentages of Utes and Ojibwas who drink heavily exceeded the total U.S. percentage; other tribes, such as the Standing Rock Sioux, had similar rates of alcohol use, and

Table 12.1
Dichotomies Between Native American Culture and the Dominant Euro-American Culture

Cultural concept	Native American perspective	Euro-American perspective
Nature	Harmony	Control
Society	Community based	Individual based
Family	Extended communities	Nuclear
Possessions	Sharing	Amassing
Time	Cyclical	Linear
Body/mind	Holistic	Dualistic
Disease	Imbalance of mind/body/spirit	Biological pathology
Treatment	Toward wellness	Away from illness

the Navajo had lower rates than the total U.S. rate of consumption. The majority (62.4%) of Native American women from Southwestern tribes did not consume alcohol, whereas 30% of Southwestern and Northern Plains men met the criteria for lifetime alcohol dependence. Risk factors for both Southwestern and Northern Plains tribes include being male and being part of an older cohort (DATA, 2004; Spicer et al., 2003). Research currently shows that Native Americans may actually have a higher rate of abstinence than the general population. When surveyed, 70% of Americans indicated that they drink alcohol, compared to 40% of Native Americans (Nofz, 1988).

Ethnic Differences in Metabolism

The skin response to alcohol referred to as "flushing" has been researched to determine the associated degree of blood alcohol concentration and rate of alcohol metabolism. Flushing generally indicates a slower oxidation of acetaldehyde, which increases the amount of acetaldehyde levels in the blood when alcohol is consumed (Chao, 1995). The principle markers of flushing include increased blood flow to the face; flushing may also be accompanied by rapid heartbeat, headache, nausea, and drowsiness (Thomasson & Li, 1993). Research shows that ethnic differences do exist in the rate and degree of skin flushing as a response to alcohol (Thomasson & Li, 1993; Reed, 1985). Although flushing has commonly been used as an indicator of alcohol metabolism, several concerns about this method have been expressed. Chao recommends a reassessment of research methods using flushing to examine genetic etiology of drinking behaviors because it may lead researchers to draw false conclusions. Asians, for example, generally have a low rate of alcoholism—as well as the flushing reaction. With this in mind, we review some of the research on the flushing response in Native American and other cultures.

Reed (1985) compared the average time to reach peak blood alcohol concentration or peak earlobe flushing in different ethnic groups after the consumption of a test drink. Subjects were compared after fasting, and clear differences were found: Native Americans showed the fastest rate of absorption. Faster rates usually produce a higher blood alcohol concentration than do slower rates of absorption (Reed, 1985).

On the other hand, Gill, Eagle Elk, Liu, and Dietrich (1999) reported that flushing among Native American populations was less severe than flushing responses found among Asians. Notably, the authors stated that there were no differences in the rate of alcohol metabolism among Whites, Native American flushers, and Native American nonflushers.

Native Americans' metabolism rate of ethanol to acetaldehyde, measured as the rate of disappearance from the blood after a test dose, indicated a high average among the four tribes studied. Native Americans were found to have a higher alcohol metabolism rate, indicating a physiological difference. Although the data were based on the study of a small sample (four tribes) of the total Native American population, they do suggest the need for further exploration for a possible genetic factor (Reed, 1985).

Metabolism of alcohol is a function of the liver, where alcohol is changed to acetaldehyde by alcohol dehydrogenase. Acetaldehyde is very toxic to the human body; therefore, continued metabolism is needed. The aldehyde dehydrogenase 2 (ALDH2) enzyme changes the acetaldehyde into acetic acid, also known as vinegar. Further oxidation turns the acetic acid into CO2 and water (Thomasson & Li, 1993).

Genetic Predisposition

Alcohol dehydrogenase (ALDH) is the enzyme that catalyzes the metabolism of alcohol, producing acetaldehyde. Douglas, Bosron, Smialek, and Lie (1985) determined that Native Americans and Whites have similar ADH and ALDH phenotypes. There were no mutations detected in the ALDH2 genes among Native American flushers and Native American nonflushers (Gill et al., 1999). Those Native Americans who were diagnosed as alcohol dependent had the ADH2*1 allele on chromosome 4, and Native Americans who were not alcohol dependent had an ADH2*3 allele. The Native Americans with the ADH2*3 allele reported a significantly lower number of maximum drinks ever imbibed within a 24-hour period. An earlier study indicated that there was a mutant variance in the structural gene for the enzyme, which has major consequences for alcohol use and abuse; such ability to metabolize alcohol may lead to rapid drinking to avoid the effect of the flushing reaction experienced because of the enzyme (Ricciardo, Saunders, Williams, & Hopkins, 1983).

Physical Alterations

Cardiovascular responses such as heart rate, systolic blood pressure, and diastolic blood pressure following the consumption of alcohol have been extensively studied. Reed (1985) examined the responses to alcohol of individuals in three ethnic groups. Native Americans were not included; however, the responses of Asians to alcohol appeared to be largely due to the deficiency in the ALDH-l isozyme. Since Native Americans were found to have similarly deficient levels of ALDH-1, research in the area of alcohol response among Native Americans is warranted.

Farris and Jones (1978) studied the effects of alcohol on memory. A comparison of 15 White and 15 Native American women revealed that both groups were equally affected. Kaemingk, Mulvaney, and Halverson (2003) found that children with fetal alcohol syndrome (FAS) and fetal alcohol effect (FAE) were significantly less capable of recalling visual and verbal memory stimuli on the Wide Range Assessment of Memory and Learning (WRAML; Adams & Sheslow, 1990). Because of the greater incidence of FAS and FAE in the Native American population (Ma, Toubeh, Cline, & Chisholm 1998), it is possible that alcohol abuse will lead to an increase in cognitive problems such as memory impairment among the Native American population with FAS and FAE.

Alcohol Abuse

Reed (1985) also examined alcohol abuse and alcoholism, finding that it was difficult to compare ethnic groups due to the variations in definitions of alcohol abuse, the lack of reliable data, and the unclear diagnostic criteria used to define alcoholism. However, the relative frequencies of alcohol-related problems among Native Americans were used to compare this ethnic group to the total U.S. population. It was found that Native Americans had much higher rates of motor vehicle deaths (50% to 60% alcohol related), other accidental deaths (15% to 50% alcohol related), cirrhosis of the liver (85% alcohol related), and arrests for intoxication, which were extremely high by comparison (DATA, 2004). A similar disparity was found among Canadian native people. For example, in the province of Ontario in 1977, 26.4% of the offenses related to alcohol were committed by Canadian native people, who constitute 2.1% of the total population, according to Irvine (cited in Reed, 1985).

These high rates of alcohol abuse and the problems associated with them have long been recognized. The variations from tribe to tribe require acknowledgment. It is important to note that a high level of alcohol abuse and alcohol-related problems are experienced by both U.S. and Canadian native peoples; however, there is a variation within this population that seems to have some physiological basis, particularly in the area of alcohol response. Reed's (1985) study indicates that Native Americans are at a particularly high risk for alcohol abuse and alcoholism; however, further research is necessary, as most of the information was gleaned from a small sample of the native population and from a comparison with the alcohol responses of Asians. The identification of physiological differences within the Native American population seems to be necessary in order to determine possible variations in alcohol response.

The possibility of differences in alcohol response based on a genetic predisposition has important implications for determining the level of risk for a particular family, tribe, or native community, as it appears that alcohol responses vary across tribes. Tribal differences in alcohol responses require further examination.

Determining Risk Level

The following questions, developed by Lawson, Peterson, and Lawson (1983) to determine high and low risk for alcoholism based on physiological factors, can be used in the assessment of Native Americans who present with an alcohol- or other substance-related problem:

1. Do you have a parent or grandparent who was, or is, alcoholic?
2. When you started drinking, were you, or are you, able to drink more than your friends with fewer physical consequences (e.g., nausea, hangover)?
3. Did you consume large amounts of alcohol from the first time you drank?

Age and medical condition are the only two of many physiological variables that are likely to affect physiological risk (Lawson et al., 1983). For example, physical risk is greater with increasing age because the body is not able to metabolize alcohol as efficiently as it could in earlier years. Younger people can consume large amounts without the same physical effects the same amount would have for an older individual (Lawson et al., 1983). A high-risk person would answer "yes" to any one of the questions, whereas a low-risk person would answer "no" to all three questions (Lawson et al., 1983).

In sum, the results of the research on the physiological factors that are particularly relevant to the Native American population are mixed, but they generally indicate a higher rate of alcohol abuse in this group. The therapist should consider the possible role of metabolic factors while recognizing that each individual is unique. Knowledge of possible underlying physiological factors should be brought to bear on helping, rather than stereotyping, Native American individuals.

Sociocultural Factors

Sociocultural factors play a particularly important part in Native American patterns of alcohol and other substance issues. First, Native American culture is quite varied across tribes; but as a whole, it differs starkly from the Euro-American culture in which treatment is generally conducted (see Table 12.1). Further, as noted earlier in this chapter, Native American history is characterized by horrific patterns of oppression and even genocide; this history continues to leave its mark on Native Americans. In a review of the literature, Mail (1985) found that 295 studies supported the premise that Native American addiction was influenced by sociocultural factors. The following specific factors tend to dominate the research: acculturation, anomie, recreation, deprivation, celebration, early exposure, gregariousness, affluence, poverty, role models, unemployment, learned behavior, and a lack of social norms. Overall, two major factors have been defined in the research: (a) loss of culture and (b) acculturation strain (French, 2004; Lewis, 1982).

French (2004) suggests that Native American alcohol dependence was a social phenomenon brought about by Native American modeling of European drinking behavior. Before European influence, it is believed, Native Americans used psychoactive substances purely for ceremonial and ritual purposes. Of course, this is only one of the major transformations that Native Americans experienced under the pressure from European settlers. As discussed earlier in this chapter, Native Americans were forced to change their religion, values, beliefs, government, education system, home settlements, and family structure. These changes caused the loss of culture. Drugs, even to this day, are being used to escape the torture and trauma that constitute Native American history (Kawamoto, 2001). This trauma, referred to as "historical trauma," continues to have a devastating effect. Native Americans have a strong connection to the people of both their past and their present. Because of their strong connection to the past, they continue to experience the violence that was perpetrated on their ancestors. And, of course, the trauma of the past can still be seen in the contemporary economic and social oppression of this group of people.

Research supports the theory that addictive behaviors such as drinking are a direct result of cultural marginalization and loss of culture (Weaver, 2003). Tribes that relied on agricultural means have suffered to a lesser degree than those tribes that relied on hunting and gathering, because the farming groups were better suited to the agricultural lifestyle of the Europeans. Research has indicated that alcoholism is lower among these agriculturally based tribes (Weaver, 2003).

Loss of culture is only one of the significant variables that influence the substance abuse problems faced by these people. The need to escape trauma through substance use was brought about by the loss of their culture, and it was maintained by the strain of acculturation. Even to this day, Native American people struggle to acculturate to the dominant Euro-American culture. This is due to psychocultural marginalization, or the process of having one's culture forcefully taken but not being adequately socialized into the new culture (Erickson, 1950; French, 2004). Belonging to a culture gives a person the skills and knowledge needed to function within that culture. Some Native

Americans, being ill acculturated and still suffering from the loss of their own culture, lack the ability to function in either culture. This means they lack the ability, know-how, education, and network connections to get adequate employment, connect with social service agencies, and navigate the many obstacles present in the dominant culture. This can often lead to unemployment, low education levels, and economic difficulties, which are commonly faced by Native American people (Gone, 2004). The prejudice faced by Native Americans, coupled with the lack of access to social services, has a dramatic impact on the rate of substance abuse in this population (Thurman et al., 2000). Due to acculturation strain and loss of culture, Native American people have developed a number of maladaptive survival skills that help them cope with the atrocities of their past and the hardships of the present. These include learned helplessness, manipulative behavior, passive-aggressive behavior, alcohol/drug abuse, compulsive gambling, denial, suicide, and resentment of successful Native Americans (N. Tafoya & Del Vecchio, 1996).

Negative social stereotypes have had a significant impact upon the way other cultures view and treat Native Americans. Because Native Americans have largely been tucked away on reservations, the mainstream Euro-American understanding of them is often derived from media and Hollywood. Misperception is a better way to describe a typical Euro-American person's understanding of this culture. For many years, Hollywood and the media have portrayed Native Americans as lazy drunkards who cannot hold their alcohol (Garrett & Carroll, 2000).

The Family System

The family system, the most intimate of social venues, has a dramatic impact upon the addictive behavior of its members, especially among cultures that adhere to a collectivistic mentality. The family and tribe are of primary concern and the individual is secondary among Native American people, influencing their members to adhere to the structural and functional characteristics of the family (Paniagua, 1998). Research indicates that the attitudes, beliefs, and behaviors toward alcohol use are influenced by the family and maintained within the sociocultural context where the drinking behavior occurs. The use of alcohol by youth is greatly influenced by family dynamics such as weak family bonds, positive parental views of alcohol, and weak sanctions against drugs (Swaim et al., 1993).

According to Christensen and Manson (2001), three main factors have contributed to the deterioration of the Native American family structure: (a) the forced education of Native American children in boarding schools, (b) placement of Native American children in foster homes, and (c) substance abuse. Recall that the assimilation period did not end until 1970, meaning that many people are still alive who were raised in the boarding schools. The impact of family separation and attempted assimilation still impact the structuring and functioning of the family, which means that many parents and children still suffer from the violent impact that separation and re-education has had upon the family. As previously discussed, many Native Americans are turning to drinking alcohol or other addictive behaviors to cope with the historical trauma. Native American children continue to be taken from their families, but now they are being placed in foster homes. Native American children are being placed in foster homes at a significantly higher rate than children in other cultures—approximately 50 to 60 times more often than children of other cultures. Research indicates that Native American children placed in foster homes have a significantly higher rate of substance abuse compared to children who have not been placed (Westermeyer, 1977).

Toward a Bicultural Family System

To determine an individual's risk of developing alcoholism, the therapist must examine the family life cycle in terms of age, sex role expectations, value orientations, cultural traditions, and rituals in relation to expectable life cycle events, from courtship to later life experiences (Kalicov & Karrer; cited in McGoldrick, Pierce, & Giordano, 1982). The effects of acculturation, history, and change must be considered for their implications on the family life cycle within the cultural context. From a family systems perspective, each developmental stage requires an internal reorganization and elicits a different response from individual family members. Treatment approaches must take into account the family's experience of acculturation, traditional cultural values, and the present cultural context. According to Weisner, Weibel-Orlando, and Long (1984), drinking levels vary across cultural areas; this finding has important implications for Native American tribes. Levy and Kunitz (1974) found that tribes vary in their response to acculturation, which in turn would affect drinking patterns.

Drinking style is maintained by entire families, not by individuals, and, in a sociocultural context, drinking is viewed as a social response that is culturally relative. Cultural affiliation and perceived psychological stress, both of which are influenced by the relationship between the tribe and the dominant society, appear to be the most important predictors of alcohol consumption. Native families with a higher degree of traditionalism and traditional cultural knowledge tend to experience lower levels of alcoholism (Weisner et al., 1984).

Determining Risk Level

Five fundamental questions can be posed to determine the risk level of alcohol dependence from a sociocultural perspective. Each question that is answered affirmatively is worth 1 point. A score of 0 indicates a low risk, a score of 1 or 2 indicates moderate risk, and a score of 3 or higher indicates high risk.

1. *Do/did one or both of your parents have strong religious or moral views against drinking alcohol?* The answer to this question, by itself, does not indicate a predisposition to alcoholism; however, it does recognize the eight characteristics of low rates of family alcoholism identified by O'Connor in 1975 (cited in Lawson et al., 1983). The question also taps into the individual's early environment, where most behaviors and values are learned.
2. *Is either of your parents alcoholic?* An individual growing up in an alcoholic home experiences an alcoholic role model.
3. *Do you come from a tribe or native community that has a high rate of alcoholism?* The reliability of this question will depend on the definition of alcoholism that is used by the individual. It will also depend on the perception that the tribe or native community has concerning alcoholism.
4. *Do you consider your friends or extended family members to be heavy drinkers?* Heavy drinking is a relative concept and can be perceived differently

by different people and cultures, depending upon their experience and perceptions about alcohol. The context and temporal characteristics of the drinking should also be considered here; for example, is the individual drinking heavily alone or at a social function that promotes drinking behavior? Does heavy drinking occur every day or once a year? A clear understanding of the expectations of drinking behavior during specific social functions such as ceremonies or celebrations is needed.

5. *Does your social role and self-identity match your concept of what you should be doing and where you feel you should be within your family and native group?* For Euro-Americans, this question is more focused on achievement; for the Native American population, the question has been adjusted slightly to account for the native cultural value celebrating equality. If the individual is aware of his or her cultural heritage and has been socialized in the traditional customs, values, and beliefs of the tribe, he or she will have some knowledge of his or her native identity and role in the family and community; if not, this individual would be at high risk. Cultural awareness by the individual does not necessarily eliminate the risk for alcohol abuse or alcoholism, but the native individual who has no knowledge of cultural identity and native family roles is at particularly high risk. Of course, one must also assess the degree of acculturation and the development of an identity and role outside the native cultural context and extended family unit.

Psychological Factors

Psychological factors such as depression, posttraumatic stress disorder (PTSD), an external locus of control, coping problems, and cognitive deficits have all played a role in addiction in the Native American population (Weaver, 2003). Strong empirical evidence supports the notion that mood and anxiety disorders are comorbid with substance abuse disorders (Kessler, Sonnega, Bromet, Hughes, & Nelson, 1995; McNally, 1999; Zoltnick, Zimmerman, Wolfsdorf, & Mattia, 2001). A strong case has already been made supporting the premise that historical trauma has led to a long-standing traumatic reaction in the Native American population. Cognitive theories of trauma suggest that a person's fundamental understanding about him- or herself and the world has been altered by the traumatic event. Three fundamental cognitions are altered: We are not vulnerable, the world is predictable and controllable, and we merit self-worth (Epstein, 1990; Janoff-Bullman, 1985). Clearly, murder, forced assimilation, and the boarding school experience would negatively affect these fundamental cognitions. History has shown that Native Americans have been vulnerable, that the world has not been safe for them, and that they have not been encouraged to believe they merit self-worth. Compare these fundamental cognitions to the cognitive triad of depression (Beck, Rush, Shaw, & Emery, 1987). There is not only an alteration concerning perceptions of safety, but also a change in the understanding of self and world.

Native Americans generally have not been afforded control over their environment. This, in turn, can lead to feelings of helplessness, which can easily descend into hopelessness. Regardless of culture, when people lack control over their external reality, they attempt to gain control through manipulation of their internal reality. They may try to accomplish this through defense mechanisms, such as denial, regression, and sublimation, or through other external coping mechanisms, such as substance abuse. Self-medication through the use of substances to cope with the difficulties of depression, PTSD anxiety, and social strain is very common among various cultures.

Jones-Saumty, Hochhaus, Dru, and Zeiner (1983) suggest that Native American substance use is escapist in nature and seems to stem from people's attempts to deal with the dilemma of acculturation to the dominant society while retaining their own cultural identity. These researchers identified psychological stresses of acculturation, the retaining of cultural identity, and the alcoholic environment as potent forces predisposing Native Americans toward alcoholic drinking. The Native Americans in that study also viewed external causes (stressful events, environmental situation, etc.) as the most important influences on alcoholic drinking.

Psychological Assessment of Native Americans

Very little research has been conducted to determine the validity of widely used psychological tests with Native Americans who are less acculturated to the dominant Euro-American culture. Of the available tests, only a handful yield specific information concerning substance use and abuse. Although psychological testing can offer significant information concerning the personality structure of the individual and how it might contribute to substance abuse, this information is secondary to developing a solid diagnosis of substance dependence through valid measures. Psychological measures rarely have a significant population of Native Americans in their standardization sample, making the use of such tests inappropriate. Although projective tests are generally interpreted using a psychoanalytic framework, which allows for greater generalization, they still remain inappropriate for the assessment of Native Americans (Dana, 1986).

Standardized tests such as the Minnesota Multiphasic Personality Inventory-2 (MMPI-2; NCS Pearson, 2001) and the Substance Abuse Subtle Screening Inventory (SASSI; Miller, 1999) are regularly used to assess for addiction and addictive behaviors in both the general and the Native American populations. A search revealed no research that looks at the SASSI's validity with the Native American population. Robin, Greene, Albaugh, Caldwell, and Goldman (2003) determined that Native Americans from two different tribes had elevated MMPI-2 *t* scores on five validity and clinical scales (L, F, 4, 8, 9), six content scales (DEP, HEA, ASP, CYN, BIZ, TRT), and two supplementary scales (MAC-R and AAS) compared to the MMPI-2 standardization sample. There were no statistical differences between the two Native American tribes. Of particular interest is the elevation on the MacAndrews Scale (MAC-R; Lachar, Berman, Grisell, & Schoof, 1976) and the Addiction Acknowledgment Scale (AAS; Butcher et al., 1992), both of which are used to assess substance abuse. The authors suggest that the historical trauma that Native Americans have endured may play a significant role in these elevations; further, they report that the results are due to a realistic difference between the

Native American and normative groups, and not test bias. Test administrators should be aware that these elevations are most likely valid and accurate reflections of behaviors and symptoms of the Native American being tested (Greene, Robin, Albaugh, Caldwell, & Goldman, 2003).

Scant research exists to verify the validity and reliability of the currently available assessment instruments in the Native American population. Until research is published that supports the use of these tests, caution should be used.

Implications for Treatment and Prevention

Information regarding treatment of Native Americans is insufficient, especially when compared to the literature for other cultures (Garrett & Carroll, 2000). Delgado-Romero, Galvan, Maschino, and Rowland (2005) note that the Native American is underrepresented in the research literature, comprising only .9% of all the sampled populations over a 10-year period in three prominent journals. These statistics strongly suggest that there is still much to be learned about treating Native Americans with substance abuse problems. Here, the treatment of Native Americans will be looked at from different modalities, given the information that is currently available.

The examination of physiological, sociocultural, and psychological factors is essential in identifying not only risk for addiction but also phenomena that may be perpetuating the addictive behavior. Physiological, sociocultural, and psychological aspects, for the most part, influence each type of addiction, from alcohol to gambling. As noted, the physiological realm offers information on the genetic predisposition for addiction, the sociological realm offers information regarding aspects of the person's early learning and current environment that might influence addiction, and the psychological realm offers insight into the coping deficits and other mental aspects of the person that perpetuate the addiction (A. W. Lawson & Lawson, 1998).

Clinicians need to be aware of six key variables when treating Native Americans: (a) acculturation level, (b) the effects of historical trauma and current socioeconomic deprivation, (c) the importance of tribal-centric treatment, (d) the vast diversity across tribes, (e) common expectations of treatment, and (f) type of residence (e.g., reservation vs. nonreservation). French (2004) identifies three major barriers to successful treatment with Native Americans: (a) mistrust of outsiders, (b) language, and (c) geography. By having a full understanding of these six key variables and finding means to minimize their impact, the clinician should be able to offer viable treatment to the Native American population and offer an environment where the Native American client can feel safe. This cultural sensitivity is one of the most important characteristics a clinician can have (Bichsel & Mallinckrodt, 2001)

Acculturation Level

Acculturation level is an extremely important area for the clinician to assess when treating anyone who is not from the dominant culture. *Acculturation level* refers to the degree to which a person has adopted the values, beliefs, traditions, and ways of living of the dominant culture. Native Americans are different from most other culturally diverse groups in the United States in that they did not migrate here; they were migrated upon and forced to take on new values and ways of living.

Assessment of acculturation is essential in part because not all Native American individuals hold to traditional beliefs. Utilizing a treatment that enhances cultural identity with a person who never knew his or her culture will have little chance of success (Weaver, 2003). Acculturation is not an all-or-nothing phenomenon. The clinician should view acculturation on a continuum from unacculturated to acculturated, using an assessment instrument to determine where on the continuum the person lies. Individuals who are more acculturated will benefit from Westernized therapeutic methods, whereas individuals who are less acculturated will benefit more from treatment methods that take traditional views and values into account.

However, the concept of two opposing endpoints is too simplistic for the complexities involved in acculturation. For some individuals, a bicultural emphasis, or mastery of both cultures, is necessary for optimal mental health. Renfrey (1992) indicates the need to assess the client for acculturation, deculturation (the degree to which a person has been stripped of his or her native culture), and bicultural competency. The treatment methods presented here will benefit those Native American people who have neither a close connection with their own culture nor a mastery of the dominant culture. For the treatment of well-acculturated Native Americans, the clinician should turn to more Westernized methods. Attneave (1982) notes that families who are both willing to learn about and interested in maintaining their native identity seem to benefit from Westernized treatment approaches. Eurocentric treatments do not work for Native Americans who are not acculturated, which in turn is likely related to the astonishing rate of treatment failure (French, 2004; White, 2004).

Historical Trauma

The effects of historical trauma and the current socioeconomic status of the Native American population on the development of mental illness have been substantially detailed previously in this chapter. Clearly, Native Americans are still suffering significant hardships because of past and current government policies. Mistrust of other cultures, especially Euro-American culture, is a by-product of these harsh sociopolitical realities. Beyond this distrust, historical trauma has also caused the multigenerational destruction of many Native American families. Given the lack of mental health and financial resources, family turmoil and its attendant difficulties may continue for many more generations.

Incarceration has been the long-standing treatment used with the Native American population (French, 2004). Only recently have research and understanding developed about the appropriate ways to treat Native American mental illness.

Tribal-Centric Treatment

The low rate of treatment success can be offset by the utilization of tribal-centric treatment if the person wants to remain connected with his or her native culture. The use of a tribal-centric approach can improve treatment effectiveness and outcome (French, 2004). *Tribal-centric treatment* refers to methods that incorporate aspects of the traditional Native American tribe to which the person belongs. Such treatments may consist of sweat lodges, the Ghost Dance, the Sun Dance, and story circles that include local myth and legend. Such approaches may also use the local shaman as a cotherapist or as the sole therapist. Imagery such as the circle of life and the broken circle (Garrett & Carroll, 2000) can be used and discussed in stories and narratives. One would need to have a firm understanding of the local myths, legends, healing practices, and ceremonies of the tribe to be able to adequately initiate such treatment methods.

Garrett and Carroll (2000) offer brilliant insight into treating Native Americans using native symbolism and philosophies. They state that the concept of the circle of life is a universal concept across all the Native American tribes, although not all tribes express the concepts and philosophies in exactly the same way. For the clinician, it is imperative to understand and make use of these concepts. The following discussion is summarized from Garrett (1998) and Garrett and Carroll (2000).

Circles, life energy, harmony/balance, and spiritual practices are among some of the most important concepts of Native American people, with each making its own unique contribution to the ideology of wellness and illness. The concepts of wellness and illness are holistic, taking into consideration the importance of the roles that body, mind, and spirit play in illness. Illness, including mental illness, is the result of disharmony among mind, body, and spirit, and to achieve wellness, harmony needs to be restored within oneself, between self and others, and with one's environment.

The circle, according to Native American tradition, is a symbol of power, peace, and unity in relationships with all things. Each individual is part of the circle of life and therefore contributes to its flow of energy. It is the individual's responsibility to live in harmony and balance in all relationships in order to keep the flow of energy positive and pure. Life energy is seen as a series of four circles, each of varying size inside the next larger circle, much like the "rippling of water" (Garrett & Carroll, 2000, p. 381). The smallest, innermost circle is a representation of entities inside of us, such as our spirit, experiences, and power. The next larger circle represents the social environment, such as family, tribe, and peers, and the individual's acceptance and belonging in these arenas. Mother Earth is represented by the third largest circle, while the fourth circle, the largest one, represents the all-encompassing spirit world. Thus, the circle of life deals with everything from the person's interactions with self to the person's interactions with the external and spiritual worlds.

Emanating from the center of these four concentric circles are four arrows pointing in the opposing directions of east, west, north, and south, which are used to represent the individual's inner power, or medicine. The arrow pointing north represents the individual's mind, south the natural environment, east the spirit, and west the body. Wellness is found when these areas are in complete balance with each other. When a person is addicted, these aspects become unbalanced; spirit and mind are damaged. Spirit and mind start to introduce negative energies into the circle of life, which influences everything from self and the natural environment to other people. Many tribes refer to addiction as a "broken circle."

Brendtro, Brokenleg, and Van Bocker (1990) describe four other related meanings for the directional arrows: East is belonging, south is mastery, west is independence, and north is generosity. Native Americans strive to balance each of these aspects in relation to the others. *Belonging* is finding one's place in the universe, *mastery* is determining one's strengths. *Independence* is defining one's strengths and limitations, and *generosity* is one's willingness to offer strengths to the environment. This concept lends itself well to treatment of addiction, in that addiction affects the environment, often inhibits that which we had once mastered, causes limitations, and reduces generosity. The focus on knowing one's strengths can be effectively used in a treatment plan.

Tribal Diversity

Across the different tribes, there are many different beliefs, values, ceremonies, and healing practices, as well varying degrees of illnesses and pathologies, such as substance addiction, abuse, depression, PTSD, and impulse control disorders. The therapist should become familiar with the particular tribe in which he or she is working. If the therapist is not working within a particular tribe, he or she should learn as much as possible about the tribe of the person he or she is treating.

Treatment Expectations

Native Americans generally hold a characteristic set of behavioral expectations for the treatment environment and the therapist. Although these expectations may not be found in all Native Americans, they do apply to most. According to Sutton and Broken Nose (1996), Native Americans have a unique perception of time. They see time as cyclical and always present, whereas the dominant culture sees time as linear and always running out. Thus, a Native American may show up to the scheduled appointment late and not understand why the therapist is upset. Thus tardiness should not necessarily be considered a sign of resistance to treatment. A handshake is seen as aggressive or competitive, especially a firm handshake. Such an act may damage rapport and any future treatment efforts. One of the best ways to start to develop rapport is to introduce yourself—say who you are and where you are from, and then, as a sign of respect, ask the person the same. Because Native Americans value listening over speaking, be prepared for long periods of silence during the session. Silence is often seen as a sign of respect; it may also be the result of the client wanting to form his or her thoughts, wanting to experience the environment, or being unsure that it is the correct time to speak. Bringing family members or respected community figures for support is not uncommon. This practice, however, does cause ethical concerns and should be discussed early on in treatment. Family members and respected others can become very powerful tools in treatment.

Type of Residence

Research indicates that Native Americans who reside on reservations suffer greater hardship and often experience more pathology than those who have relocated to a setting off the reservation. This may seem counterintuitive, given the research suggesting that addiction and other pathologies are the result of cultural loss. However, the therapist must consider the possibility that those who have moved away from the reservation are more willing and possibly better able to acculturate to the dominant culture. Of course, the situation is not black and white; Native Americans living away from the reservation can also suffer from addiction and pathology (Beauvais, 1992).

Treatment Methods

As mentioned previously, the nature of treatment will depend on a number of variables, with the type of disorder and level of acculturation being of extreme importance. Depending on the acculturation of the individual, the therapist can determine if traditional, Euro-American, or a combination of the two forms of treatment methods would be best suited for a given individual. Of course, the etiology of the disorder plays a significant role in the selection of a treatment method. If the pathology is a result of family discourse, then family therapy is most likely indicated, but if the pathology seems to come from a lack of cultural identity or the presence of cultural distress from the dominant society, then a bicultural skills method that incorporates both Westernized and tribal-centric features would be most appropriate. The therapist should not assume that the treatment of a pathology is as simple as prescribing a few practices that will reduce symptoms. The dynamics of pathology, especially for the Native American client, should be treated using clinical, spiritual, cultural, economic, community/social, and political methods (Weaver, 2003). Clinical, spiritual, and community/social methods seem to be more aligned with the training of mental health professionals. When working in these domains, the therapist should apply methods that utilize metaphor, storytelling, paradoxical interventions, rituals, and concrete practical advice; these practices have demonstrated ability to aid in treatment (Sutton & Broken Nose, 1996).

Family Therapy

Family therapy seems to be compatible with the Native American philosophy of community and family interconnectedness, especially since substance abuse is generally learned by modeling family members (Kawamoto, 2001; Sutton & Broken Nose, 1996). The Native American way is generally one of families working together for the common good.

The therapist must be alert to the differences in cultural expectations between Native American families and Euro-American families. The Native American family often designates the grandparents as head of the household, and a stronger relationship often exists between grandparents and grandchildren than between parents and children. In some tribes, uncles are the head of the household (Sutton & Broken Nose, 1996). Community members and extended family members are often considered as integral parts of the nuclear family (T. Tafoya, 1989). It would be ill-advised for a therapist to assume that a Native American family would fit the structure of the Westernized family.

Cognitive Behavioral Therapy

In many ways, Cognitive Behavioral Therapy (CBT) fits the general Native American expectation of therapy (Renfrey, 1992). T. Tafoya (1989) suggests that treatments focusing on altering specific behaviors, focusing on the here and now, using experiential exercises, and focusing on altering behavior to influence emotional states work best with the Native American population. Identifying skill deficits that are keeping the client from meeting the goals of the dominant culture and the goals of the client's own culture, as well as exploring the client's bicultural identity, will help the clinician define specific behaviors that are amenable to treatment. Once areas of deficit or pathology are determined, it is important to thoroughly assess whether the problem involves a biological etiology, or physical addiction (Renfrey, 1992). A medical evaluation may be necessary.

Research indicates that using CBT in conjunction with bicultural skill development has had a positive impact on the Native American substance-abusing population (Hawkins, Cummins, & Marlatt, 2001; LaFromboise, Coleman, & Gerton, 1993; LaFromboise & Rowe, 1983; Schinke et al., 1988; Schinke, Tepavac, & Cole, 2000). Bicultural competence is the ability to effectively interact with people of the dominant culture as well as your own and to have a mastery of the behaviors and expectations of both groups (LaFromboise & Rowe, 1983). The development of bicultural skills has helped to reduce substance abuse in the Native American population; these skills include problem solving, coping skills, communication techniques, discrimination skills, positive cultural identity, and role definition (Schinke et al., 1988; Schinke et al., 2000).

Community Interventions and Prevention

Community intervention can take many forms, including public education, support groups, and school prevention programs, among others. Community intervention should play an integral role in the treatment of substance abuse among tribal members (N. Tafoya & Del Vecchio, 1996).

Community treatment enhances the ideology of social connectedness that is held by many tribes (Hawkins et al., 2001). Due to historical trauma and current social hardship, community interventions should have an effect on more than just the substance-abusing client. The importance of including the whole community in treatment interventions cannot be understated. In some cases, the Native American client may protest the treatment proposed by a White therapist; many Native Americans still feel great animosity against the White race because of the early historical trauma and continuing hardships (Weaver, 2003). This resistance to treatment can be averted by having the community play an active role in the treatment program. Strengthening a community will help build social networks and support, which in and of itself is a healing tool. The therapist can engage the participation of groups such as the Native American Church, the Indian Shaker Church, the Native American Christian sects, and the Native American version of Alcoholics Anonymous.

Religious groups such as the Native American Church are revitalizing early native traditions and have a strict code of abstinence. The Native American Church prohibits the use of all substances except peyote, which is used only for ceremonial purposes. The United States government initially banned the use of peyote in the Native American Church, but the American Indian Religious Freedom Coalition was able to promote the American Indian Religious Freedom Act Amendments of 1994 (Public Law 103-344, or the "Peyote Law," as it is sometimes called), which allowed the Native American Church to use peyote in ceremonial rituals (French, 2004).

The Native American form of Alcoholics Anonymous utilizes non-Western concepts such as circular group methods, the medicine wheel, purification ceremonies such as sweat lodges, and pipe healing. Table 12.2 illustrates some of the key differences between Native American AA and Euro-American AA.

Tribal-Centric Approaches

As noted, the use of tribal ceremonial methods of healing can enhance treatment and substantially increase positive results for Native Americans struggling with substance abuse. Unless the therapist is well versed in tribal forms of treatment, it may be best to utilize the knowledge of the local shaman or an elder in the community. Shamans can serve as cotherapists, lead therapists, or consultants.

Some of the more universal tribal-centric treatments include sweat lodges, the Sun Dance, use of story circles, narratives, images, local myths, ghost dances, the sacred pipe, and vision quest (French, 2000; Hawkins et al., 2001; Weaver, 2003). Some of these ceremonies are extremely complex, such as the Sun Dance, which is a 12-day event full of purification exercises and dances. Due to the complexity of these treatments, they cannot be adequately described within the confines of these pages. The interested clinician should seek the guidance of a tribal leader or shaman.

Treatment Goals

One of the most fundamental differences between Native American and Euro-American medicine is that the former conceives of treatment as a movement toward health, whereas the latter conceives of treatment as a movement away from illness. The Native American emphasis on moving toward health can play a key role in treatment. Utilization of cultural strengths will yield a treatment plan based on healthy traditional values that can help the client discharge the feelings of anger, shame, and fear that are associated with the many years of historical trauma (N. Tafoya & Del Vecchio, 1996). Those wishing to gain skills of the dominant culture while at the same time maintaining their own cultural identity will benefit from bicultural skills training (Hawkins et al., 2001). Hawkins recommends using (a) a continuum framework for gauging prevention and behavioral change; (b) a stepped approach, starting with self-motivated abstinence; (c) brief peer intervention, group therapy, and intensive outpatient therapy; (d) a focus on bicultural life skills, and (e) community involvement.

Table 12.2
Contrasting Cultural Perspectives of Native American AA and Euro-American AA

Native American AA	Euro-American AA
Values	
Noncritical attitude	Critical attitude
Cooperation	Competitiveness
Sharing of problem	Ownership of problem
Humble presentation	Outgoing/self-righteous presentation
Focus on happiness	Focus on success
Desire to honor elders	Desire to honor self
Silence	Communication
Tribal values	Individual values
Simplicity	Complexity
Tradition	Innovation
Spiritual values	Material values
Learning from elders	Formal education
Few rules	Many rules
Mysticism	Empiricism
Smallness	Bigness
Natural medicine	Synthetic drugs
Unity with nature	Separation from nature
Acceptance of others for who they are	Desire to change others
Belief Statements	
We come to believe that the power of the pipe is greater than ourselves and can restore us to our culture and heritage.	We come to believe that a power greater than ourselves can restore us to sanity.
We acknowledge to the Great Spirit, to ourselves, and to the Native American Brotherhood our struggles against the tide and its manifest destiny.	We admit to God, to ourselves, and to another human being the exact nature of our wrongs.
Be entirely ready for the Great Spirit to remove all the defects of an alien culture.	We are entirely ready to have God remove all these defects of character.
Make a list of all the harm that comes to our people from demon alcohol, and become willing to make amends to them all.	Make a list of all persons we have harmed and become willing to make amends to them all.
Seek through prayer and meditation to improve our conscious contact with the equality and brotherhood of all Mother Earth's children and the Great Balancing Harmony to the Total Universe.	Seek through prayer and meditation to improve our conscious contact with God, as we understand him, praying only for knowledge of His will for us and the power to carry that out.

Note. Adapted from "Alcohol and Other Drug Addictions Among Native Americans: The Movement Towards Tribal Centric Treatment Programs," by L. A. French, 2004, *Alcohol Treatment Quarterly, 22*(1), p. 86.

Conclusion

For Native Americans, historical trauma has resulted in cultural, political, and economic marginalization. Native Americans have limited access to social services and a high rate of unemployment. In the name of assimilation, they have had their culture stripped away by a culture that doesn't want them, leaving them without an identity, a way of being, or a place to call home. Given these atrocities, it is not difficult to understand the numerous pathologies that plague this population. Fortunately, Native Americans have demonstrated a striking resilience in the face of the historical trauma that has confronted them. Euro-American substance abuse professionals need to cultivate an awareness of the history behind the current plight of Native Americans; they also need to learn about the myriad cultural expressions of Native American culture so that they are able to offer culturally sensitive treatment. "Psychological treatment" is a Western concept, alien to native cultures. If the Euro-American therapist takes the time to immerse him- or herself in Native American cultural concepts such as the Harmony Ethos and the framing of treatment as a movement toward health, he or she will be better able to adapt Westernized treatment approaches so that they are more amenable to collectivist thought. By so adapting our current views of pathology, illness, and health, we can start to build culturally appropriate treatment—and begin to redefine the limited constructs in which psychology is currently based.

References

Adams, W., & Sheslow, D. (1990). *Wide range assessment of memory and learning.* Wilmington, DE: Wide Range.

American Indian Religious Freedom Act Amendments of 1994, 42 U.S.C., sec. 3.

Attneave, C. (1982). American Indians and Alaska Native families: Emigrants in their own homeland. In M. McGoldrick, J. K. Pearce, & J. Giordana (Eds.), *Ethnicity and family therapy* (pp. 167–189). New York: Guilford Press.

Beauvais, F. (1992). Comparison of drug use rates for reservation Indian, non-reservation Indian and Anglo youth. *American Indian and Alaska Native Mental Health Research, 5*(1), 13–31.

Beauvais, F., & LaBoueff, W. (1985). Drug and alcohol abuse intervention in American Indian communities. *International Journal of the Addictions, 20,* 139–171.

Beck, A. T., Rush, A. J., Shaw, B. F., & Emery, G. (1987). *Cognitive therapy of depression.* New York: Guilford Press.

Bichsel, R. J., & Mallinckrodt, B. (2001). Cultural commitment and the counseling preferences and counselor perceptions of Native American women. *Counseling Psychologist, 29*(6), 858–881.

Brendtro, L. K., Brokenleg, M., & Van Bocker, S. (1990). *Reclaiming youth at risk: Our hope for the future.* Bloomington, IN: National Education Services.

Butcher, J. N., Williams, C. L., Archer, R. P., Tellegen, A., Ben-Porath, Y. S., & Kaemmer, B. (1992). *MMPI-A: Minnesota Multiphasic Personality Inventory–A: A manual for administration, scoring, and interpretation.* Minneapolis: University of Minnesota Press.

Chao, H. M. (1995). Alcohol and the mystique of flushing. *Alcoholism: Clinical and Experimental Research, 19*(1), 104–109.

Christensen, M., & Manson, S. (2001). Adult attachment as a framework for understanding mental health and American Indian families. *American Behavioral Scientist, 44*(9), 1447–1465.

Dana, R. H. (1986). Personality assessment and Native Americans. *Journal of Personality Assessment, 50*(3), 480–500.

DATA. (2004). Alcohol dependence higher in specific Native American groups. *Brown University Digest of Addiction Theory and Application, 23*(2), 1.

Dawes Act. An Act to Provide for the Allotment of Lands in Severalty to Indians on the Various Reservations (General Allotment Act or Dawes Act), Statutes at Large 24, 388-91, NADP Document A1887.

Delgado-Romero, E. A., Galvan, N., Maschino, P., & Rowland, M. (2005). Race and ethnicity in empirical counseling and counseling psychology research: A 10-year review. *Counseling Psychologist, 33*(4), 419–448.

Douglas, R. K., Bosron, W. F., Smialek, J. E., & Lie, T. (1985). Alcohol and aldehyde dehydrogenase isoenzymes in North American Indians. *Alcohol: Clinical and Experimental Research, 9*(2), 147–152.

Elia, C., & Jacobs, D. G. (1993). The incidence of pathological gambling among Native Americans treated for alcohol dependence. *International Journal of Addictions, 28*(7), 659–666.

Epstein, S. (1990). Beliefs and symptoms in maladaptive resolutions of traumatic neurosis. In D. Ozer, J. M. Healy, & A. J. Stewart (Eds.), *Perspectives on personality* (Vol. 3, pp. 323–347). London: Jessica Kingsley.

Erickson, E. (1950). *Childhood and society.* New York: Norton.

Farris, J., & Jones, B. M. (1978). Ethanol metabolism in male American Indians and whites. *Alcoholism: Clinical Experience, 2,* 77–81.

French, L. A. (2000). *Addictions and Native Americans.* London: Praeger.

French, L. A. (2004). Alcohol and other drug addictions among Native Americans: The movement towards tribal centric treatment programs. *Alcohol Treatment Quarterly, 22*(1), 81–91.

Garrett, M. T. (1998). *Walking on the wind: Cherokee teachings for harmony and balance.* Santa Fe, NM: Bear.

Garrett, M. T., & Carroll, J. J. (2000). Mending the broken circle: Treating substance dependence among Native Americans. *Journal of Counseling and Development, 78*(4), 379–389.

Gill, K., Eagle Elk, M., Liu, Y., & Dietrich, R. A. (1999). An examination of ALDH2 genotypes, alcohol metabolism and the flushing response in Native Americans. *Journal of Studies on Alcohol, 60*(2), 149–158.

Gone, J. P. (2004). Mental health services for Native Americans in the 21st century United States. *Professional Psychology: Research and Practice, 35*(1), 10–18.

Gordis, E. (1994, January). *Alcohol and minorities* (Alcohol Alert No. 23). Rockville MD: National Institute on Alcohol Abuse and Alcoholism.

Greene, R. L., Robin, R. W., Albaugh, B., Caldwell, A., & Goldman, D. (2003). Use of the MMPI-2 in American Indians: II. Empirical correlates. *Psychological Assessment, 15*(3), 360–369.

Hawkins, E. H., Cummins, L. H., & Marlatt, G. A. (2001). Preventing substance abuse in American Indian and Alaska Native youth: Promising strategies for healthier communities. *Psychological Bulletin, 130*(2), 304–323.

Indian Gaming Regulatory Act of 1988. 25 U.S.C. § 2701 *et seq.*

Janoff-Bullman, R. (1985). The aftermath of victimization: Rebuilding shattered assumptions. In C. R. Figley (Ed.), *Trauma and its wake: The study and treatment of post-traumatic stress disorder* (pp. 147–163). New York: Brunner/ Mazel.

Jones-Saumty, D., Hochhaus, L., Drug, R., & Zeiner, A. (1983). Psychological factors in familial alcoholism in American Indians and Caucasians. *Journal of Clinical Psychology, 39,* 783–790.

Kaemingk, K. L., Mulvaney, S., & Halverson, P. T. (2003). Learning following parental alcohol exposure: Performance on verbal and visual multitrial tasks. *Archives of Clinical Neuropsychology, 18*(1), 33–47.

Kawamoto, W. T. (2001). Community mental health and family issues in sociohistorical context: The confederate tribes of Coos Lower Umpqua and Siuslaw Indians. *American Behavioral Scientist, 44*(9), 1482–1491.

Kessler, R. C., Sonnega, A., Bromet, E., Hughes, M., & Nelson, C. B. (1995). Post-traumatic stress disorder in the National Comorbidity Survey. *Archives of General Psychiatry, 52,* 1048–1060.

Lachar, D., Berman, W., Grisell, J., & Schoof, K. (1976). The MacAndrews Alcoholism Scale as a general measure of substance misuse. *Journal of Studies on Alcohol, 24,* 23–38.

LaFromboise, T. D., Coleman, H. L. K., & Gerton, J. (1993). Psychological impact of biculturalism: Evidence and theory. *Psychological Bulletin, 114*(3), 395–412.

LaFromboise, T. D., & Rowe, W. (1983). Skills training for bicultural competence: Rationale and application. *Journal of Counseling Psychology, 30,* 589–595.

Lawson, A. W., & Lawson, G. W. (1998). *Alcoholism and the family: A guide to treatment and prevention* (2nd ed.). Austin, TX: PRO-ED.

Lawson, G. W., Peterson, J., & Lawson, A. W. (1983). *Alcoholism and the family: A guide to treatment and prevention.* Rockville, MD: Aspen.

Levy, J. E., & Kunitz, S. J. (Eds.). (1974). *Indian drinking: Navajo practices and Anglo American theories.* New York: Wiley.

Lewis, R. (1982). Alcoholism and the Native Americans: A review. In *National Institute on Alcohol Abuse and Alcoholism: Special Population Issues.* (Alcohol and Health Monograph No. 4, DHHS Pub. No. ADM 82-1193). Washington, DC: U.S. Government Printing Office.

Ma, G. X., Toubeh, J., Cline, J., & Chisholm, A. (1998). Fetal alcohol syndrome among native American adolescents: A model prevention program. *Journal of Primary Prevention, 19*(1), 43–55.

Mail, P. (1985). Alcohol and Native Americans. *Alcohol Topics: Research Review,* pp. 1–8.

McGoldrick, M., Pearce, J. K., & Giordana, J. (Eds.). (1982). *Ethnicity and family therapy.* New York: Guilford Press.

McNally, R. J. (1999). Posttraumatic stress disorder. In T. Millon, P. H. Blaney, & R. D. Davis (Eds.), *Oxford textbook of psychopathology* (pp. 237–260). New York: Oxford University Press.

Miller, G. A. (1999). *The substance abuse subtle screening inventory (SASSI) manual* (2nd ed.). Springville, IN: SASSI Institute.

NCS Pearson (2001). *Minnesota multiphasic personality inventory* (2nd ed.). Minnetonka, MN: Author.

Nofz, M. P. (1988). Alcohol abuse and culturally marginal American Indians. *Social Casework, 69*(2), 67–73.

Paniagua, G. A., (1998). *Assessing and treating culturally diverse clients: A practical guide* (2nd ed.). Thousand Oaks, CA: Sage.

Reed, T. E. (1985). Ethnic differences in alcohol use. *Social Biology, 32*(3–4), 195–209.

Renfrey, G. S. (1992). Cognitive-behavior therapy and the Native American client. *Behavior Therapy, 23,* 321–340.

Ricciardo, B. R., Saunders, J. B., Williams, R., & Hopkins, D. A. (1983). Hepatic ADH and ALDH isoenzymes in different racial groups and in chronic alcoholics. *Pharmacology, Biochemistry and Behavior, 18*(Suppl.), 61–65.

Robin, R. W., Greene, R. L., Albaugh, B., Caldwell, A., & Goldman, D. (2003). Use of the MMPI-2 in American Indians: Comparability of the MMPI-2 between two tribes and with the MMPI-2 normative group. *Psychological Assessment, 15*(3), 351–359.

Schinke, S. P., Botvin, G. J., Trimble, J. E., Orlandi, M. A., Gilchrist, L. D., & Locklear, V. S. (1988). Preventing substance abuse among American Indian adolescents: A bicultural competence skills approach. *Journal of Counseling Psychology, 35,* 87–90.

Schinke, S. P., Tepavac, L., & Cole, K. C. (2000). Preventing substance use among Native American youth: Three-year results. *Addictive Behaviors, 25,* 387–397.

Spicer, P., Beals, J., Croy, C. D., & American Indian Service Utilization, Psychiatric Epidemiology, Risk, and Protective Factors Project Team. (2003). The prevalence of DSM-III-R alcohol dependence in two American Indian populations. *Alcoholism: Clinical and Experimental Research, 27*(11), 1785–1797.

Stratton, R., Zeiner, A., & Pardes, A. (1978). Tribal affiliation and prevalence of alcohol problems. *Journal of Studies on Alcoholism, 39,* 1166–1177.

Sutton, C. T., & Broken Nose, M. A. (1996). American Indian families: An overview. In M. McGoldrick, J. Giordano, & J. K. Pearce (Eds.), *Ethnicity and family therapy* (2nd ed., pp. 126–135). New York: Guilford Press.

Swaim, R. C., Oetting, E. R., Thurman, P. J., Beauvais, F., & Edwards, R. W. (1993). American Indian adolescent drug use and socialization characteristics: A cross-cultural comparison. *Journal of Cross Cultural Psychology, 24*, 53–70.

Tafoya, N., & Del Vecchio, A. (1996). Back to the future: An examination of the Native American holocaust experience. In M. McGoldrick, J. Giordano, & J. K. Pearce (Eds.), *Ethnicity and family therapy* (2nd ed., pp. 136–147). New York: Guilford Press.

Tafoya, T. (1989). Coyote's eyes: Native cognition styles. *Journal of American Indian Education* [Special issue], pp. 29–40.

Thatcher, R. W. (2004). *Fighting firewater fictions: Moving beyond the disease model of alcoholism in first nations.* London: University of Toronto Press.

Thomasson, H. R., & Li, T. (1993). How alcohol aldehyde dehydrogenase genes modify alcohol drinking, alcohol flushing, and the risk for alcoholism. *Alcohol Health and Research World, 17*(2), 167–172.

Thurman, P. J., Plested, B., Edwards, R. W., Chen, J., & Swaim, R. (2000). Intervention and treatment with ethnic minority substance abusers. In J. F. Aponte & J. Wohl (Eds.), *Psychological intervention and cultural diversity* (2nd ed., pp. 98–109). Needham Heights, MA: Allyn & Bacon.

Volberg, R. A., & Abbott, M. W. (1997). Gambling and problem gambling among indigenous peoples. *Substance Use and Misuse, 32*(11), 1525–1538.

Wardman, D., Khan, N., & El-Guebaly, N. (2001). Problem and pathological gambling in North American aboriginal populations: A review of the empirical literature. *Journal of Gambling Studies, 17*(2), 81–100.

Weaver, H. N. (2003). Native Americans and substance abuse. In S. L. A. Straussner (Ed.), *Ethnocultural factors in substance abuse treatment* (pp. 136–157). New York: Guilford Press.

Weisner, T. S., Weibel-Orlando, J. C., & Long, J. (1984). "Serious drinking," "white man's drinking" and "teetotaling": Drinking levels and styles in an urban Indian population. *Journal of Studies on Alcohol, 45*, 237–249.

Westermeyer, J. (1977). Cross-racial foster home placement among Native American psychiatric patients. *Journal of the National Medical Association, 69*, 231–236.

Western Oregon Indian Termination Act. (1954, August 13). *Indian affairs: Laws and treaties* (Vol. 6). Washington, DC: Government Printing Office.

White, W. L. (2004). Native American addiction: A response to French. *Alcoholism Treatment Quarterly, 22*(1), 93–99.

Zitzow, D. (1996a). Comparative study of problematic gambling behaviors between American Indian and non-Indian adolescents within and near a Northern Plains reservation. *American Indian and Alaska Native Mental Health Research, 7*(2), 14–26.

Zitzow, D. (1996b). Comparative study of problematic gambling behaviors between American Indian and non-Indian adults in a Northern Plains reservation. *American Indian and Alaska Native Mental Health Research, 7*(2), 27–41.

Zitzow, D. (2003). American Indian gaming. In H. J. Shaffer & M. N. Hall (Eds.), *Futures at stake: Youth, gambling and society* (pp. 23–51). Reno: University of Nevada Press.

Zoltnick, C., Zimmerman, M., Wolfsdorf, B. A., & Mattia, J. I. (2001). Gender differences in patients with posttraumatic stress disorder in a general psychiatric practice. *American Journal of Psychiatry, 158*(11), 1923–1925.

Resources

http://ezinearticles.com/

http://www.come-over.to/FAS/NAFAS.htm

http://www.peele.net/faq/indians.html

http://findarticles.com/p/articles/mi_m0QTQ/

CHAPTER 13

A Family Systems Treatment for the Impaired Physician

Barbara R. Cunningham

Researchers in the field of alcoholism and addiction have criticized the disease model of treatment, with its narrow focus on the individual instead of the family system (Bowen, 1978; Kerr & Bowen, 1988; Lawson & Lawson, 1998; Morgan, 1981; Wallack, 1981). Such criticism is especially applicable to the treatment of impaired physicians and their families.

Recent research supports the notion that adults who have grown up in families with addiction have a tendency to choose careers in the health-care professions (Mansky, 1999). Vaillant, Sobowale, and McArthur (1972) reported that physician vulnerability to addiction correlates with unmet personal needs. According to their prospective study, doctors were more likely to experience problems with drugs and alcohol, require psychotherapy, and have marital problems than were matched non–health professional controls. In fact, Vaillant et al. noted that some doctors choose a medical career to help themselves by helping others. Vaillant et al. concluded that these doctors, dogged by their perfectionism, were dedicated in the extreme to the well-being of their patients, to their own detriment and often that of their families.

Gabbard and Menninger (1989) further concluded that physicians tend to be less happy in their marriages than those in many other professions. Physicians' long hours are not the *cause* of their marital problems, these researchers found, but rather, doctors' excessive work was often a result of their desire to run away from facing marital tensions. Emotional remoteness and withholding of anger are two of seven attributes of physicians identified by Ellis and Inbody (1988). In an early study, Martin and Bird (1959) characterized the troubled medical marriage as the "love-sick wife" and "cold-sick" husband. The notion that relationship difficulties underlie chemical dependency in physicians is additionally supported by the findings of Angres, McGovern, Rawal, and Shaw (2002), who found the percentage of physicians suffering from comorbid psychiatric disorders or marital discord to be 60.3%.

In his review of the psychosocial factors contributing to physician addiction, Coombs (1996) found that physicians were generally ignorant of the developmental and interpersonal dynamics of addiction. More severe marital difficulties have also been found to be highly correlated with physician addiction (McGovern, Angres, & Leon, 1998). Robb (1998) noted that medical schools typically do not include training in alcoholism and addiction. It is alarming that physicians are not trained to recognize or treat signs and symptoms in their patients or in themselves.

This chapter presents a family systems treatment for the impaired physician based upon Bowen Family Systems Theory (BFST). Conceptualizing treatment of the impaired physician from a perspective that includes the partner shifts the focus from the individual perspective characterized by the disease model of treatment to a systems focus that addresses the multiple variables within the physician family that can contribute to addiction and keep it alive. Addiction is seen not as an individual deficiency (Wallack, 1981), but as the result of multiple influences. Lawson and Lawson (1998) concur with the need to conceptualize addiction as a problem in relationship systems. They cite Morgan (1981), who theorizes that the disease model "provides an out for society in dealing with serious social problems by creating a need to treat the individual and thereby legitimizes the problem as based in the individual rather than in the larger system of social relations (the family, the school system, the church, the community)" (p. 360). Thus, in lieu of a reductionistic focus, treatment should identify the systemic and maladaptive family patterns that are transmitted through multiple generations.

A broader, family-oriented approach is especially important for impaired physicians because they tend to have detached interpersonal styles (Sotile & Sotile, 2000), avoidance of intense emotions (Meyers, 1994), a stressful practice (Talbott & Gallegos, 1990), and easy access to narcotics. Clinicians are encouraged to conceptualize chemical dependence as a likely reflection of serious relationship issues in the doctor's nuclear and extended families, between and within generations (Bowen, 1978). Conversely, using an individual treatment approach with the impaired physician is like throwing him or her out of a whitewater current, resuscitating him or her, and then throwing him or her right back into the torrential waters.

To underline the veracity of this metaphor, Talbott (1987) found in an analysis of 500 physicians, followed for 4 years subsequent to treatment, that the relapse rate was dramatically higher when the spouse was uninvolved and untreated. Similarly, a recent study of adult opiate users indicated better outcomes for those receiving family treatment than for those receiving two individually based interventions, particularly for those living with a partner (Yandoli, Eisler, Robbins, Mulleady, & Dare, 2002). In fact, impaired physicians and their families, like any other family suffering with chemical dependence, cannot be treated effectively without a thorough assessment and treatment of dysfunctional dynamics within the family. A paradigm shift from individual treatments typified by the disease model to a family systems treatment as typified by BFST offers an opportunity for lasting change that goes deeper than placing a Band-Aid on a gaping wound.

BFST, with its set of interlocking principles, provides a road map for systemic treatment. Treatment shifts from focusing on the patient to discoveries regarding what part each family member plays in maintaining the problem (Papero, 1990). The patient helps to create a family diagram covering three or more generations as part of a cognitively focused effort to view the family's emotional process across time (Kerr & Bowen, 1988). After an organized effort to collect facts and identify patterns of family functioning, the client (or clients) in treatment is asked to identify and take responsibility for his or her part in the maintenance of the symptom.

An important part of treatment involves bridging the distance between family members and repairing the emotional cutoff between generations (Bowen, 1978). Treatment involves active efforts by the family to discover how relationships functioned in previous generations, in order to understand how past relationships influence current relationships. Particular attention is paid to identifying the overfunctioning of one member in relation to the underfunctioning of another (Bowen, 1978; Gilbert, 1994). With the family diagram as a blueprint to guide further discovery, therapy is conceptualized as the beginning of a lifelong journey toward increased awareness of how emotional forces and anxiety are transmitted across generations (Kerr & Bowen, 1988).

The Promise of Bowen Family Systems Therapy

In the late 1950s, Dr. Murray Bowen observed that seemingly cured schizophrenic patients relapsed upon returning home to their families soon after they were discharged from inpatient treatment programs (Bowen, 1978). After observing this phenomenon, Dr. Bowen decided to try hospitalizing the schizophrenic along with his or her entire family. Obtaining more favorable results, Bowen came to conclude that the family, rather than the individual, was the proper unit of treatment. His unique approach assumed that all families operated from a highly emotionally interdependent position (Kerr & Bowen, 1988), meaning that the more interdependent the family members are, the more highly fused each individual is with the other (Kerr & Bowen, 1988). Fused family members have little autonomy from one another. In extremely fused families, members are overly involved with one another. If one family member has an itch, for example, everyone else in the family scratches.

Bowen posited that the more highly fused the family system is, the more vulnerable the entire family is to developing symptoms that often are carried by only one family member for the whole system. Bowen (1978) characterized this highly fused family unit as an "undifferentiated ego mass." Families could increase the level of their collective health, Bowen hypothesized, by increasing the level of individuality of each member (Kerr & Bowen, 1988). In essence, individuals could choose when to be separate and when to remain connected (Kerr & Bowen, 1988). If family members are viewed as highly interdependent, then identifying multiple variables to account for symptoms will be more likely to effect real change.

This chapter hypothesizes that when a treatment protocol aims to change the *structure of a system* instead of aiming to change the *behaviors of an individual,* a positive treatment outcome is more likely to be long term. This second-order change means that the game itself has been altered rather than only the rules (Harper & Capdevila, 1990). Within the worldview of BFST, therapists are offered a distinctly different and promising approach to treating emotional problems such as chemical abuse and dependence.

Bowen (1978) posits that "therapists with the motivation and discipline to work towards systems thinking can reasonably expect a different order of therapeutic results as they are more successful in shifting to systems thinking" (p. 262). This change in approach reflects a paradigm shift in the field of alcoholism and addiction.

Research by Talbott and Martin (1986) corroborates Bowen's (1978) theoretical assumptions. They cited family problems as the single most important factor leading to relapse in chemically dependent physicians. Similarly, research conducted by Nyman and Cocores (1991) supports the assumptions of BFST. They found that addicts whose families participate in treatment have better outcomes than do those addicts who are treated alone. Similarly, Mann (1991) asserts that treating the patient as an isolated entity almost guarantees a poor outcome. Thus, research findings underline the notion that without considering the family as the unit of treatment, achieving more than temporary symptom relief may not be possible. Lawson and Lawson (1998), experts in the field of chemical dependency, also emphasize that successful treatment of the impaired family system must maintain a focus on the relationship processes between and within the generations. This focus makes it possible to interrupt multigenerational patterns of chemical dependency, shifting the legacy for future generations.

Unfortunately, in many treatment programs for the impaired physician, family members are virtually ignored, or at best, viewed as support systems cheering on the patient from the sidelines (A. Lawson, personal communication, spring, 2001). Family members are not treated, but are merely provided with psychoeducation to aid them in supporting the identified patient's recovery. Rehabilitation facilities that direct family members to attend Al-Anon or psychoeducational support groups proudly, but erroneously, label such rehabilitation efforts as "family-centered" treatment. As we will see, BFST goes much further in its conceptualization of a family-systems-based approach.

A treatment and relapse prevention protocol for impaired physicians and their families informed by BFST, a family systems model, offers great promise for achieving long-term positive results. Impairment cannot be understood apart from the multigenerational context in which it occurs. Broad application of Dr. Bowen's ideas regarding this symptom and how to effect treatment are outlined below.

Underlying Philosophy and Theoretical Concepts

Bowen (1978) characterized chemical dependence as one of the more prevalent human dysfunctions. Like all dysfunctional patterns in a family, one cannot conceptualize this behavior without viewing it in the broader context of an imbalance in functioning in the whole family system (Bowen, 1978). Treatment is aimed at raising each family member's awareness of the part he or she plays in maintaining the symptom. The treatment is initiated with the family member who has the greatest motivation and ability to modify his or her functioning in the system. Often this is the family member who overfunctions and is in the greatest pain (Bowen, 1978). Pain that is not so overwhelming as to paralyze efforts to move forward but that provides enough discomfort that family members welcome the idea of change may turn out to be the gateway to resourcefulness. Bowen offered the unique insight that "when it is possible to modify the family relationship system, the alcoholic [or drug addicted] dysfunction is alleviated, even though the dysfunctional one may not have been part of the therapy" (p. 262).

BFST is comprised of eight interlocking concepts. Although it is difficult to conceptualize them apart from one another, key concepts will be reviewed briefly to underline how chemical dependency dysfunction fits into the theory.

Chronic Anxiety Versus Acute Anxiety

Bowen (1978) noted that human beings share more similarities than differences with other forms of life. Perhaps the most salient shared feature is that the organism will react defensively to a real or imagined threat to survival. This survival reaction may be physical, emotional, or a combination of both. The clinician will observe that in some people, anxiety is so continuously present that this heightened reactivity need not necessarily be stimulated by real or imagined threat (Gilbert, 1992). Instead, the anxiety is chronic, an anxiety that has likely been passed along in a family system over many generations.

Whereas chronic anxiety strains or exceeds people's ability to adapt, acute anxiety is a response to a real threat. The reaction to a real threat is of limited duration, and people can usually adjust. Acute anxiety is rooted in fear of what is, while chronic anxiety is rooted in fear of what *might be* (Kerr & Bowen, 1988).

People who exhibit high levels of emotional reactivity in response to minor or even imagined stresses tend to act and react without thinking. One goal in BFST is to move families toward decreasing their reactivity to one another while increasing their ability to respond more thoughtfully (Bowen, 1978).

BFST focuses on the emotional system's struggle with two opposing instinctual life forces: those forces that keep family members connected and the contrary forces that compel people toward individuality (Bowen, 1978). One force is oriented toward togetherness, and the other force is oriented toward separateness. From the perspective of BFST, the two vectors within the familial environment that influence chronic anxiety are people's reactivity to their personal space being intruded upon and their complementary need for connection (Kerr & Bowen, 1988). The cliché "Can't live with them, can't live without them" describes this common dilemma. Patterns of emotional functioning are all related to the ways a family deals with its members' impinging upon one another or, in reaction to impingement, disengaging from one another (Kerr & Bowen, 1988).

When anxiety escalates in a system, the forces for togetherness increase. One can recall how people came together in the United States after 9/11. Over time, the togetherness forces threaten group members' sense of individuality. Family roles and family rules become inflexible, and normal developmental life cycle changes are perceived as upsetting. A defensive measure in the face of such a perceived emotional threat is to distance oneself from the forces of togetherness in order to achieve some separateness and avoid feeling "swallowed up whole." In families with a high degree of fusion, there is an increased risk that one or more members will cut off from their parents in a move to preserve what little is left of "self." This reactive cutoff is not helpful and can lead to symptoms such as substance abuse (Bowen, 1978).

Two Opposing Life Forces: Can't Live With Them and Can't Live Without Them

Intrapsychic fusion describes a lack of differentiation and clarity between cognitive and affective functioning. Bowen (1978) explains, "The capacity to differentiate between thoughts and emotions allows some choice over being directed by one's 'head' or by one's 'gut'" (p. 62). He notes that what sets humans apart from other species is their ability to think and their ability to be aware of the difference between their thoughts and emotions. However, if the human organism becomes overwhelmed with anxiety, cognitive ability may become compromised or may even shut down. If the cognitive ability shuts down, the human species operates just as reactively and instinctually as other species that do not have the advantage of a highly evolved intellect.

Interpersonal fusion describes a lack of differentiation between oneself and others. It manifests itself in a way that disallows a person from knowing where he/she stops and another begins. When fusion is intense, family members seem to have no separate identities. Intense fusion results in family members making "we" rather than "I" statements. Husbands and wives who complain that they cannot live with their spouse or without them are describing an inability to manage effectively the universal conflict of these opposing life forces.

It has been suggested that a disowning of the need for family ties may be a motivating factor for some people who choose a medical career (Twerski, 1982). The intensity of the hospital environment and long work hours may fulfill a person's wish to feel needed and emotionally connected while at the same time safely distanced from his or her important family relationships. It may be true, as the conventional wisdom goes, that the hallmark of addiction is denial; yet if we look beneath the surface, we can see that it is within the denial of needing others that chemical dependency thrives. Thus, the problem of addiction may be viewed as an outcome of avoiding the task of resolving attachment issues in the relationship system.

The smoothest period between partners is during courtship (Kerr & Bowen, 1988). Predictably, however, relationship tension may escalate to problematic proportions over time. Typically, when two people marry, the emotional patterns that first attracted them to one another may intensify. As the relationship develops and as day-to-day stressors remind them of their heightened emotional interdependence upon one another, each partner may become reactive and even disgusted by the personality characteristics that initially attracted them to one another. McKnight (1998) observed that "the more intensely a person seeks to fill the emotional deficits of the other or to have another shore up his or her life, the more fused the marriage relationship becomes" (p. 272). When people with high levels of need for togetherness marry, each partner invests heightening levels of "self" in the other. This fusion becomes more binding as the sharing of daily living duties heightens their need for one another.

Unlike during courtship, when they experienced more freedom to be themselves, the spouses begin to assume that they can read the mind of the other and begin to behave as if they know how the other will react. The couple becomes like two cells that have merged and now have one nucleus. Neither individual can chart independent goals. One spouse feels swallowed up in the relationship while the other spouse becomes drained from being hypervigilant lest he or she be abandoned. A heightened sense of dependence on another can raise anxiety levels. Heightened anxiety may result in increased efforts to cope by creating distance. Drinking and/or drug abuse is one way to achieve this distance in the short term, but in the long term, the heightened anxiety that the abuse causes in the individuals who depend on the abuser creates increasingly complex problems in the family system.

The relationship system in each spouse's family of origin influences the degree of the desire for emotional closeness in the marriage. If individuals have emotionally cut themselves off from their respective families of origin, there is enormous pressure upon the nuclear family to be everything to one another. The high degree of investment in their spouses and children is based in a wish to compensate for the emotional deficits from their own families. Disappointingly, the pressure has a deleterious effect on the union, and anxiety rises within such a context.

People may find that they married someone with a similar degree of neediness. As the disappointment, depression, and loneliness mounts, these people experience conflict with their spouses and may look to their children to fill the void of connection with their spouses. The parents then project their inability to deal with relational closeness/distance management in themselves onto their children, and the children become caught in the crossfire of unresolved emotional attachment.

Bowen (1978) noted that when "two pseudo-selves 'fuse' into the emotional 'weness' of marriage, [there is also] a high potential for impairing the functioning of one spouse" (p. 263). The discomfort of this fusion may be handled in various ways. However, almost all fused marriages involve adaptive efforts to create some degree of emotional distance between partners. It is a reactive move based in the survival instinct to preserve selfness.

One way emotional distance is increased is through marital conflict. During the making-up phase, the couple may experience the togetherness that they missed during the distancing period. After tiring of holding onto one's own position and not "giving in," a partner may move back toward the other. And so it goes, in a continuing cycle of tension building, conflict, and making up.

Bowen (1978) believed that the most common pattern for dealing with emotional fusion is an underfunctioning/overfunctioning reciprocity. One spouse assumes a dominant role and the other spouse assumes an adaptive role. The adaptive spouse becomes "wired" to support the more dominant, decision-making spouse. In most respects, the adaptive spouse becomes a functional "no self" (Bowen, 1978). The one who accommodates the most gives up the most self to the other. This adaptive person is more vulnerable to some type of chronic dysfunction.

Bowen (1978) believed dysfunctions expressing systemic chronic anxiety might include one or more of several patterns. Heightened chronic anxiety in the family system may emerge in an individual as physical illness, emotional illness, or a social dysfunction, such as alcoholism or drug addiction. The other common pattern is one in which parents project their immaturity onto one or more of their children. A combination of all of these patterns may be present.

Bowen (1978) noted that when things are calm within a family, these adaptive patterns function to maintain homeostasis in the system without serious symptoms arising in a family member. However, when anxiety escalates, the adaptive patterns lose flexibility. The patterns rigidify until symptoms erupt. Because patterns are multigenerationally transmitted, they are programmed into the nuclear family from the respective families of origin. This means that the family has no conscious choice about the selection of adaptive patterns. Bowen (1978) emphasized that there is greater flexibility in a family with a spectrum of such transmitted patterns than in a family using only one or two patterns.

The quality and degree to which each spouse is in emotional contact with his or her family of origin is the other key variable in assessing the adaptability in a family system. The geographical distance between them and the quality of their relationship interactions can determine emotional distance or closeness to the family of origin. It is assumed that the greater the degree of emotional cutoff from the family of origin, the more likely it is that the nuclear family will be symptomatic (Bowen, 1978).

Differentiation of Self

Differentiation of self is inversely related to chronic levels of anxiety and may be conceptualized as emotional maturity (Kerr & Bowen, 1988). The concept of differentiation of self is core to BFST, and working to increase differentiation of self is a lifelong process (Papero, 1990). The ability to choose between thinking and feeling, along with the ability to differentiate oneself from another person (i.e., knowing where one stops and the other begins) are the basic characteristics of the emotionally mature or differentiated individual (Bowen, 1978).

It is erroneous to equate differentiation with autonomy, individuation, or independence. Kerr and Bowen (1988) emphasize that differentiation describes the *process* by which individuality and togetherness are managed within a relationship system. One's level of differentiation of self is determined by three factors: the level of differentiation of one's parents, the quality of relationship one has with one's parents, and the manner in which one handles unresolved attachment to parents in adulthood (Bowen, 1978).

Levels of differentiation may vary between siblings and between generations. A sibling who receives more of the parents' anxious focus will be less free to grow and develop, because this individual is more fused with one or both parents. From this evolutionary perspective, one can understand how it is that siblings turn out so differently. Sibling variability accounts for one line moving slightly upward with each succeeding generation and another line moving slightly downward with each succeeding generation (Kerr, 2008).

Gilbert (1992) points out that variation in the tendency toward fusion exists in other mammalian species as well, citing Jane Goodall's observations of chimpanzees at Gombe, where Goodall saw a wide range of differentiation. Gilbert (1992) provides the example of one chimp, Flint, and his mother, Flo. They were so emotionally attached that Flint's infancy was prolonged. He would always stay close to his mother, never venturing very far away. As Gilbert explains, "When his mother became old and died, Flint, although he was eight and a half years old (an age of independence for most chimps), fell into a state of grief and depression. He died three and a half weeks after her death in the same spot where she had died" (pp. 19–20).

The intensity of fusion with the parents will replicate in the marital relationship. Undifferentiated spouses tend to have an external locus of control and measure their worth through the eyes of others. Inside of their "we-ness," there is little solid self. Instead, two pseudoselves marry and have few principles that cannot be co-opted by a pressure to conform to the needs and wishes of the other.

The higher the level of fusion within the marital couple, the greater the risk for impairment in one or both spouses. The lower the level of the differentiation, the more each spouse operates within a reactive, feeling state and the less each spouse is able to call upon cognitive functions or adapt smoothly to change. Instead of thinking through responses to stress, the person with a low level of differentiation or immaturity will blame others for his or her unhappiness. Additionally, at the lower levels of differentiation, a person will look to fuse into an emotional symbiosis with another or, in reaction to the symbiosis, cut off, much as he or she merged with and/or cut off from his or her parents. Relational life takes on the quality of being reactive rather than reflective or proactive. Individuals with low differentiation have little ability to be selves independent of their reactions to what others say, do, or demand. "No-selves" are defined by others and have no internal compass with which to navigate along their life journeys (Bowen, 1978). Bowen believed that people with similar levels of differentiation marry one another.

In assessing the ability of an impaired family to tolerate difference among its members, Gilbert (1992) suggests questioning along the following lines: In what ways can individuals become freer to live their own lives, without instinctively repeating the emotional processes of past generations? Can people think in opposites and tolerate ambivalence arising from internal conflicts? Can people think clearly even amidst the roiling emotional forces that affect the core of their being? Can people react less automatically and more thoughtfully inside of their attachments? Can they tolerate being separate people yet remain connected to other family members, or do they rush to cut themselves off from uncomfortable relationships? Do individuals have the ability to be an "I" when the group is screaming to be a "We"?

The differentiated person has an abiding awareness that no person can change another (Kerr & Bowen, 1988). One cannot regulate another person's life. Taking responsibility for self means that one learns to define self, develops a sense of one's boundaries, and has a clear idea of one's core beliefs and values. Differentiated people realize that charting a course for responsible functioning in a family requires a lifetime of work, trial and error, and trouble shooting (Kerr & Bowen, 1988). One cannot significantly raise one's level of differentiation in a few therapeutic sessions, or even within a few years. However, one can be helped to embrace the course of such a journey and learn to make one's own life a research project. By being responsible for self, the entire family, of which the differentiating member is a part, is affected in a positive way. Differentiating members model their efforts to develop in ways they may not have thought possible prior to treatment.

When one does not experience a sense of self and a separate identity of one's own, defense mechanisms aimed at survival will emerge. People may cut off emotionally from those who threaten their sense of individuality. Substance abuse is one way that threatened people emotionally cut off from important others, and it is a pattern that is multigenerationally transmitted.

In BFST, the differentiating journey involves finding ways to honor one's own separateness in intense relationships and to become freer of automatic reactions to others. Paradoxically, the extent to which one can honor one's own separateness is also the extent to which one can remain viably connected to the others in the family. To accomplish this goal, the clinician guides family members to become more cognizant of their reactions to the family. If a family member is constantly responding to others' needs, this person is directed to look at internal anxiety not being addressed and to consider the overhelpfulness as a red flag. It is important for family members to understand the systemic concept that one person may carry the anxiety for the system, and that person is most vulnerable to developing symptoms.

Adults are directed to look at patterns and triangles in which they are caught so that they can develop a plan to increase differentiation. The therapist coaches clients to return to their families of origin in a quest to gather new facts about family roles and functioning. The client and therapist may brainstorm a list of questions to ask family members. Clients are coached to engage in one-on-one conversations to gain contextual facts about each parent's family-of-origin experiences. They are educated about detriangling moves and directed to look for key triangles through the generations. Additionally, assertiveness training, practice making "I" statements, empty chair work, and mailed or unmailed letters written by the differentiating members (especially to parents) may be helpful. The emphasis is upon taking responsibility for moving differently in one's key triangles. Taking the focus off another and keeping the focus on oneself requires increasing discipline as anxiety rises.

The effort to define a self is full of twists, turns, and detours. As a person learns new ways to manage in emotionally intense relationships, a stronger sense of identity emerges that allows for clearer life direction. To increase one's functional level of differentiation, the work must be done within a person's own family, whether one suffers from chemical dependency or any other category of human difficulties. The thrust of BFST is to become clearer about one's part in a family system and then to learn new ways of being in relationship that assume increasingly higher levels of self-responsibility.

The goal of becoming more objective when observing one's part in family dynamics may have particular appeal to the scientist-physician. BFST might be defined as a "thinking person's therapy" that is not so much for those who are "broken" as it is for those who wish to become more whole. Clients are taught systemic ideas, and, like Bowen-trained therapists, take on the posture of researchers in their own families. The therapy requires experiential work outside of session, in that clients are called upon to apply new concepts as they explore their family systems.

Bowen (1978) believed that it is possible to move toward a science of human behavior, and his positivist view clearly reflected his assumption that a real world exists that is independent of an observer's subjective perceptions of it (Papero, 1990). This worldview may be attractive to the physician, who is trained to be objective and detached from emotional processes. However, it is important to remember that within the effort to increase one's objectivity by collecting facts of family functioning, one also is increasing one's ability to be in anxious emotional fields without losing the ability to think and make good decisions. It is in managing this balance of distance and togetherness for oneself while at the same time honoring a significant other's differing closeness/distance needs that one achieves a heightened level of differentiation of self.

Solid Self Versus Pseudo-self

The solid self consists of a person's core, non-negotiable, clearly defined values and beliefs. These are formed gradually and are not easily coerced or changed from outside forces (Kerr & Bowen, 1988). Building or developing a solid self is an important goal in BFST. In contrast, the pseudo-self can be defined as a "pretend" or false self that is acquired by emotional pressure and that can also be changed by emotional pressure (Kerr & Bowen, 1988). It is made up of random, discrepant beliefs and principles, acquired because these ideas were considered "right" by the group. The pseudo-self is a self with an external locus of control that conforms to the environment in order to feel a sense of belonging.

Codependency Versus Fusion

During the 1980s, the field of chemical dependency extended its focus to include the family members of chemically dependent persons, generating a separate body of clinical theory and treatment for codependency. As Lawson and Lawson (1998) explain, "With the broadening of the context of understanding of alcoholism from the alcoholic to the alcoholic family, many nonsystemic ideas became popular in the field" (p. 317). Gierymski and Williams (1986) noted that the term *codependency* originally designated the spouse of the alcoholic, but that it came to be generalized to all family members and the chemical dependent's close social network. Pathologizing labels such as *enabler, codependent,* and *coalcoholic* blamed family members for the alcoholic's or addict's problems (Lawson & Lawson, 1998). The popular literature on codependency offers a plethora of definitions, ranging from "a disease" to "immaturity" to "toxic brain syndrome" (Lawson & Lawson, 1998). There were even efforts in the chemical dependence field to make codependency a diagnostic entity, even though the concept was not supported empirically (Babcock & McKay, 1995).

The codependency movement has been viewed by many, especially feminists, as an attempt to stigmatize and pathologize women (Babcock & McKay, 1995). Feminists have characterized the codependency movement as dangerous in that it revictimizes victims (Lawson & Lawson, 1998). Babcock and McKay allowed that women living with alcoholics did, in fact, suffer and that they often engaged in self-blame, but these researchers took issue with the notion that their behavior constituted a disease (Lawson & Lawson, 1998). Lawson and Lawson describe the codependency movement as one of hysteria, noting that the myriad definitions floating around in popular culture ultimately rendered the term meaningless. They emphasize that blame and pathologizing labels are not congruent with systems theory.

Many in the codependency movement believe that marital therapy may threaten the recovery of the chemically dependent person. Brown (1985) found marital therapy to be contraindicated for the alcoholic in early recovery, a nebulous time period, while Stanton and colleagues (1982) considered the wife to be secondary in importance to the family of origin for the addict's treatment. Such practices may well have been the death knell for many marriages in which the symptom was alleviated. Unfortunately, for the addict and his spouse, these practices did not address the avoidance of the relationship tension giving rise to the symptom. Marriages may become unbalanced and break apart when the homeostatic balance of the family has been disturbed by a significant change in the functioning of the alcoholic.

Codependency is often confused with fusion, a central concept used in BFST. Fusion is consistent with a systemic view. It is a concept that does not assign blame. The symptom is not viewed as the "problem," but rather is viewed as an attempt at adaptation to relationship tensions. In the closeness of an intense relationship, the emotional selves of each individual blend or fuse together in a common self, a kind of "we-ness" (Papero, 1990). Fusion refers to each partner trying to deal with the intensity of this common self by using mechanisms similar to those he or she used in relationship to his or her parents (Papero, 1990). Conversely, those in the codependency movement believe that the "problem" is rooted in the person or in the substance. This is not a systemic conceptualization. From the perspective of BFST, the problem is not in the person or dyad, but in the multigenerational system, each generation of which has passed on ways to behave in relationship with regard to closeness and distance. The difference between codependency and fusion is very important. To reiterate, alcohol or drugs are not viewed as "the problem," from a systemic perspective. Instead, alcohol or drugs are viewed as one of many possible ways to bind anxiety in response to tension in the relationship system (Bowen, 1978).

Triangles

The triangle is a basic unit of analysis in BFST. It refers to a three-cornered relationship system. Bowen (1978) observed that when tension arises within an unstable two-person relationship system (the dyad), there is a tendency to recruit a third person into the system in order to reduce tension and to reestablish stability. To *detriangle* means to redirect the energy of the triangle back to the dyad that was originally involved in the conflict or tension. Functional triangles are composed of person-to-person relationships among all people involved in the triangle. Interlocking triangles refer to a system consisting of four or more people who share more than one triangle (Kerr & Bowen, 1988).

Some children may occupy a position in a parental triangle wherein the youngster is pivotal to the stability of the parents' relationship. This child may function as a kind of diplomatic messenger or negotiator for the disagreements between the parents. Each parent depends on the child to manage the tension experienced with the other parent. For example, a child may align with a parent who is suffering from the effects of the other parent's substance abuse or dependence. The other parent is shoved to the outside position and feels alone and isolated. The person in the outside position of the triangle may experience increased anxiety as a result of feeling "left out" and disconnected from important others.

Family systems theory posits that the triangle is the basis of all relationships. There are many triangles within a given family. As tension escalates in a family, predictable patterns emerge. Anxiety in a parental dyad, for example, may be rerouted through one or more children. To manage anxiety in a dyad, one partner may turn to substance abuse and or dependence. In a physician's family, triangles can include relationships in the medical workplace as a third leg in a triangle. Anxiety is spread among three instead of being managed between two, decreasing the intensity and making it more tolerable. For this reason, triangles are more stable than dyads and the basic building blocks of relationship systems (Bowen, 1978). Triangles are used to manage closeness/distance forces. When tension is high enough in a triangle, the outside position may be more favorable as the bonds between two become overwhelming (Kerr & Bowen, 1988).

Medical couples have a ready-made diversion from working out their relationship problems (Meyers, 1994). Work pressures can both cause relationship distress and simultaneously offer escape from facing up to being a self in the context of the relationship distress. Excessive involvement in work is one way to avoid resolving marital conflicts, with avoidance being a multigenerationally transmitted pattern of functioning in close relationships. Work relationship demands thus become a convenient third leg of a triangle. However, as anxiety in the system increases, formerly adaptive patterns will become maladaptive. It is at this point that a person who avoids marital conflict may abuse and come to depend upon substances as a maladaptive way to work out tension in the relationship. In the words of one physician, "I really think the reason I worked so hard at my practice, working to be special and needed, was so that I felt I wasn't alone" (Gerber, 1983).

The Family Projection Process

The *family projection process* refers to the tendency of parents to defuse stress or anxiety by projecting their own problems onto their children. The child most attached to the parents will have the lowest level of self-differentiation and have the most difficulty separating from the parents. The greater the level of the parents' undifferentiation (defined as immaturity), the more they will rely on the projection process to stabilize their relationship with one another and within the system (Kerr & Bowen, 1988).

Multigenerational Transmission Process

From Bowen's (1978) perspective, people have much less emotional autonomy than they think they do. The concept of the *multigenerational transmission process* describes the inheritance of the family emotional field through the succeeding generations (Kerr & Bowen, 1988). Physical, emotional, and interactional patterns are passed down through the generations via this process (Kerr & Bowen, 1988).

The multigenerational transmission process can illustrate how relatively small differences in the levels of differentiation between parents and their offspring, and between members of a sibling group, can lead over several generations to more significant variances in differentiation among diverse lines of the family system (Kerr, 2008). Children develop levels of differentiation of self similar to their parents' levels as a result of parents' actively shaping their children's development and children innately responding to their parents' moods, attitudes, and actions (Kerr, 2008). Different siblings will likely develop varying levels of differentiation, and the child receiving the greatest degree of anxious focus from the parents will be most vulnerable to symptoms (Kerr, 2008). In fact, the multigenerational transmission process programs the ways in which people interact with others and factors into the level of "self" an individual may develop.

Essentially, the multigenerational transmission process includes two critical concepts. First, people tend to select spouses who have a similar level of differentiation as their own (Bowen, 1978). Second, through the dynamics of the family projection process, there tends to be a focus on the child who is the most vulnerable or the most emotionally connected to the parents (Bowen, 1978). Thus, through the family projection process, certain children will have slightly lower levels of differentiation than others in their sibling group. Over several generations, significant dysfunction will unfold. One possible outcome, for example, might be severe problems with chemical dependency emerging in one generation and becoming increasingly intense in future generations.

The therapist's focus on helping the client to identify and interrupt multigenerational patterns of dysfunction should be balanced with a focus on the identification and building upon of multigenerational resiliencies or strengths. In this way, the therapist scaffolds the client coming from an intense system, so that he or she does not feel doomed to repeat the severity of dysfunction discovered within many previous generations (Cunningham, 2006). Both individual resiliencies and family process resiliencies may be identified (see Wolin & Wolin, 1993, for a list of individual resiliencies and Walsh, 1998, for a list of family resiliencies).

Sibling Position

Bowen (1978) believed that the family birth order, referred to as *sibling position*, contributes significantly to the development of personality. Because of this phenomenon, he paid close attention to each parent's sibling position. Bowen's theory was expanded on in research completed by Toman (1993). Toman concluded that children take on different characteristics, in part because of their sibling position in terms of birth order. Gender has influence as well. He noted that children who grew up to marry people who were compatible with the rank and gender they experienced in their families of origin had a better chance at success in their marriage. For example, an oldest sister of brothers would be most compatible with a younger brother who had older sisters. Both partners would feel comfortable with familiar roles. Toman (1993) described characteristics of each birth position. First-born children, for example, might become leaders, accomplished, and highly responsible members of society. At the other extreme, they might become such perfectionists that they find it impossible to meet their own expectations. As such, a first-born may become an overfunctioner in a reciprocal relationship with a substance-dependent partner.

Emotional Cutoff

Emotional cutoff refers to the process of running away or denying the emotional ties to the family of origin (Bowen, 1978). Emotional cutoff and distancing can be confused with actions of differentiation. Instead, emotional cutoff–behaviors are merely pseudo-moves that do not change the intensity of emotional attachments. In fact, one may assume that to the extent that one tries to cutoff is the extent to which he or she is fused into his or her family system. Emotional cutoff is a fear-based response or an apprehension that one has lost self in the face of intense fusion. The clinician needs to assess for the extent of cutoff, as this pattern is highly associated with severe symptomology (Kerr & Bowen, 1988).

The Role of the Therapist in Bowen Family Systems

BFST is unique in its emphasis upon the self-development of the therapist. Therapists must continually do their own work on increasing their separation from their families of origin while still retaining good emotional connections with their extended and nuclear family systems. Friedman (1991) points out that "Bowen has consistently maintained that it is hard for the patient to mature beyond the maturity level of the therapist, no matter how good his or her technique" (p. 138). In fact, as Friedman explains, "In Bowen theory, the differentiation of the therapist *is* the technique" (p. 138). In order to maintain a non-anxious presence in the presence of the anxiety of a family suffering with an impaired physician, one must have personal boundaries strong enough to resist fusing into the intense emotional environment.

Bowen (1978) saw himself as an objective researcher who helped his clients become researchers into their own ways of functioning. A goal of this therapy is to help the client make a research project out of a life as lived within a multigenerational family system. The focus is on learning more about the family rather than fixing the family problem. Therapists who become too eager to "fix it" reflect their own reactivity and undifferentiation. As a coach, the therapist asks questions that facilitate the client's thinking process. Therapy sessions are controlled and cerebral. Family members talk through the therapist, and direct confrontations are avoided to minimize tension and emotional reactivity. Throughout treatment, the therapist maintains an emotionally neutral position.

The therapist generally works with the marital dyad, even when the presenting problem involves a child. The belief is that the addition of the therapist to the two-person emotional system creates a therapeutic triangle, which will result in changes in family relationships. A Bowen-trained therapist may also choose to work individually with the more motivated partner for a period of time. The assumption is that when this individual speaks from an "I" position, other family members will follow with the same responsible position. A Bowen therapist may also choose to see spouses individually in cases where the couple presents with a level of emotional reactivity high enough to preclude the conducting of a productive dialogue.

The overarching goal of a Bowen therapist is to remain in good emotional contact with the clients while resisting the pressure to be triangled into their conflict. The therapist's stance is objective and neutral, which serves to stabilize the dyad. The therapist insists that each person focus on the part he or she plays in family problems. The Bowen therapist's demeanor should not be misconstrued as passive. The therapist is respectful and curious. Thought-provoking questions are asked. Bowen-trained therapists frequently call upon clients to think about what their part has been in the family's relational conflicts, and they request that members of the couple speak directly to the therapist in order to prevent heightened emotional exchanges. It is assumed that escalating anxiety expressed in emotional exchanges between family members interferes with the ability to call upon cognitive resources. An emphasis upon increasing one's cognitive, objective capacity when in the midst of intense emotional environments may have particular appeal to the impaired physician-scientist.

Use of the Family Diagram as a Major Tool of Assessment

The use of the family diagram, a graphic representation of the functioning patterns of at least three generations, is used in the beginning sessions of treatment (Kerr & Bowen, 1988; Papero, 1990). It is a tool that helps the clinician work with a client to identify multigenerational patterns that may be playing out in the current system. Additionally, the family diagram functions to calm people. Knowing facts, identifying patterns of multigenerational emotional process, and acknowledging the universality of these mechanisms leads to more objectivity about one's family. The search for patterns includes looking for triangles that block growth, emotional cutoff, fusion, overfunctioning/underfunctioning reciprocity, substance abuse, divorce, and other ways to avoid managing the self in regard to closeness/distance needs. The clinician tries to establish a broadening context to clarify details of the functioning of the nuclear and extended family systems. Inquiries as to the quality of marriages during times of tranquility and times of distress are useful. Occupational changes and geographical moves may be understood in the context of what else was going on in the family at the time. A client's perceptions of family and individual strengths may be noted.

Assessment is ongoing and is a part of treatment (Kerr & Bowen, 1988). The rigorous and methodical search for patterns may resonate with the impaired physician-patient, who has also been trained to search for underlying causes. Illness may be an expression of increased emotional intensity occurring in the system and may be a ripple effect, for example, of the death of an important family member. Such events are viewed as nodal events, often marking a turning point in the family (Papero, 1990). Marriages, births, deaths, divorces, moves, and problems with substance abuse and dependency may be closely related to events in the nuclear family (Papero, 1990). Emotional shock waves (Bowen, 1978) from the death of an important family member, for example, may create a cascading chain of events in nuclear families. Such ripple effects underline the interdependent nature of family systems (Bowen, 1978).

In constructing the family diagram, it is important to ascertain the members of the family who greatly influence others as well as those members who are peripheral. All triangles are assessed carefully, as they are the basic units of the system (Bowen, 1978).

Assessing for emotional cutoffs in the family of origin is a crucial piece of diagnostic information. Cutoffs from each partner's family of origin increase the pressure for togetherness in the nuclear family. Cutting off a relationship by physical or emotional distance does not end a fused emotional process. To the contrary, it intensifies it.

Therapists explore the context into which each child is born. What was going on during the pregnancy, as well as immediately before conception and after birth? What is the relative position of each child in relation to each parent? The overarching concept behind family diagram construction is that events and changes in a family do not occur in a vacuum (Papero, 1990). It is important to learn about the frequency and nature of contact that the nuclear family has with the extended family (Papero, 1990).

The clinician's effort in collaboratively creating the family diagram is to embody the attitude of a warm, respectful, and objective researcher (Papero, 1990). The point of creating the diagram is not to "do something" with any bit of information. Instead, each fact leads to further inquiry and a clearer view of how each person fits into the patterns and events of the family. The goal is not to find answers, but to keep asking questions that invite other questions (Papero, 1990). In the creation of the family diagram, the clinician models an attitude of curiosity. Together, the client and therapist put together an ever-broadening picture of how the family has evolved over time. Clients are honored as experts on their own family systems, and the emphasis is upon asking *who, what, where, when,* and *how* questions. There is an avoidance of *why* questions, as such questions imply blame.

For examples of family diagrams with the appropriate symbols explained, see *Family Evaluation* (Kerr & Bowen, 1988, pp. 307–312). Readers may also peruse family diagrams of famous people in *You Can Go Home Again* (McGoldrick, 1995) to increase their understanding of how to properly use this valuable assessment tool.

Broadness of Perspective in Bowen Family Systems Theory: Universalist Concepts

It is not possible to explain the multilayered complexities of Bowen theory within the framework of an entire volume, let alone a single chapter (Friedman, 1991). Diverse populations all share the reality of multigenerational emotional processes that involve the struggle to manage the forces of togetherness and separateness. Thus, whatever the differences among cultures, diverse populations may be considered as different spices in the soup of life. Bowen emphasized the idea that humans are more like than unlike nonhuman life forms (Friedman, 1991). Other theories tend to focus upon differences. A perspective highlighting differences, according to Bowen (1978), decreases objectivity about, and even increases denial of, what really drives human behavior and motivations.

Bowen theory is rooted in the assumption that the human species is part of a stream of evolutionary emotional processes that can be traced back to the beginning of life. When a clinician views a family, he or she must consider the fact that the opposing forces for togetherness and separateness reflect the degree of reactivity in the evolving system. The more reactive a family is to forces of closeness and separateness, the more likely that symptoms will appear in one or more individuals in the system. Also, one may assume that a family that has a high degree of emotional cutoff is most vulnerable to serious problems such as chemical dependence. Finally, if it is assumed that emotional process is evolutionary, families that contain high degrees of emotional cutoff may be further along in an emotional regression that is generations deep—a regression caused by reaction to intolerable degrees of fusion or togetherness passed on from previous generations. The work in the differentiation process is to help clients become more objective in an effort to get a bit more outside the emotional forces dominating the family. Increased differentiation, as explained earlier, involves being able to remain connected as much as it involves being a separate self.

Bowen (1978) once said,

> There is nothing in schizophrenia that is not also present in all of us. Schizophrenia is made up of the essence of human experience many times distilled. With our incapacity to look at ourselves, we have much to learn about ourselves from studying the least mature of us. (p. 89)

This comment epitomizes Bowen's consistent effort to make continuous what other theories tend to dichotomize (Friedman, 1991). Bowen's idea that the family is the preferred unit of treatment places emphasis upon the emotional forces shared by all families. Similarly, it significantly decreases the focus on which family member is the symptom bearer. Friedman explained, "The unity of perspective turns the therapeutic endeavor of promoting differentiation into a broad-spectrum antibiotic that may be applied to any family no matter what its nature or the nature of the 'dis-ease'" (p. 137). Thus, from Bowen's perspective, asking what unit of treatment a clinician is treating has no meaning. Similarly, whether one sees couples, individuals, or families is irrelevant. The focus is always on universal, systemic factors rather than on specific problems. The clinician's approach is informed less by his or her formal technique than it is by the rigor with which the clinician consistently works on increasing his or her own level of differentiation over the life course.

Common Patterns in Families With an Impaired Physician

Physicians who experience chemical dependency likely handled the emotional attachment to their parents, and especially to their mothers, by a denial of the attachment and by a pseudo-independence or false bravado (Bowen, 1978). This child would insist that he did not need the parent. "I can do it myself," might be this youngster's rallying cry. During the adolescent years, for example, such children would be more defiant than children less fused with their parents (Bowen, 1978). In more differentiated families, parents and teenagers are calmer as the adolescents work toward separation. In fact, in the more differentiated family, there is greater flexibility and adaptation to change as members pass through the various developmental stages in the individual and family life cycles (Bowen, 1978). Families on the higher end of differentiation may tolerate and even honor differences in individual members.

Bowen posited that all people have a fairly intense level of attachment to their parents. It is not the *level* of intensity that is salient in the case of impairment. Instead, it is the *manner* in which the attachment is handled that is important.

The posture of physicians who spend a lot of their life energy denying this attachment to their parents (and later to their spouses) may be able to function quite well for a long time. Such doctors' functional level of differentiation may appear to be quite high, as they excel in medical school and later, in their profession. These physicians are overly responsible to others and, in many respects, have such high standards that they are impossible to maintain over time. They continue to assume the pseudo-independent posture in their nuclear families. Spouses, children, and society participate in reinforcing this posture by developing the expectation that the physician upon whom they depend will continue to function at an impossibly high level. Sadly, unrealistic self-expectations and an extreme sense of responsibility seriously compromise the overfunctioning doctor's quality of life. In denying their need for others and keeping up a pseudo-independent posture, they become increasingly isolated from their family. The children and the spouse play a part in maintaining the physician's distance in the family system. As the physician feels increasingly burdened, the loneliness and isolation intensify. It is at this point that such individuals may become most vulnerable to developing a relationship with alcohol or drugs, especially if this pattern has been prevalent in past generations.

At the opposite end of the spectrum of attachment patterns are the physicians who are symbiotically attached to their parents, and especially to their mothers. These individuals are so merged with their parents that they are unable to function independently in the world. In their emotional fusion with mothers who had a low level of differentiation of self, these doctors were de-selfed. They used the defense of denial to avoid facing the depth of their need for the mother. This intensity of denial of need replicates in the subsequent marriage(s). As Bowen (1978) explained, this type of individual "collapses into drinking early in life, while loudly affirming his independence and his continuing 'I can do it myself' posture" (p. 265). Bowen identified these individuals as having the poorest prognosis for permanent recovery from substance abuse. He characterized them as social outcasts whose need for emotional closeness is so overpowering that they must go to extremes to deny it, referring to them as "dysfunctional refugees from the family relationship system" (p. 265). Because they run from their families of origin, they will continue to run from their spouses. The spouses, who are similar to the impaired member in their level of differentiation, can predictably be expected to play a reciprocal role in the alcoholic- or drug-addicted dysfunction.

As noted earlier, Bowen (1978) postulated that people marry people with similar levels of differentiation of self. While each partner may present as having opposite ways of dealing with stress, each maintains the stability of the relationship by playing out both sides of the coin of togetherness/distance forces. Conflict, overfunctioning/underfunctioning reciprocity, and a degree of projecting their problems onto their children are patterns usually used in some combination by the medical couple who is threatened with attachment fears. The pattern of one partner adapting or giving in to the other spouse is the salient pattern in problems with alcohol or drug dependence (Bowen, 1978). Both spouses usually believe that they are the ones who are giving in to the other the most. But it is the one who is, in fact, most accommodating that loses an increasing level of self and then becomes most vulnerable to the development of a problem with chemical dependence. In the recovery process, the de-selfed spouse will regain more functioning self.

It is important for the clinician to alert the family to the probability of increasing anxiety in the face of change. As the accommodating member realizes that in "thinking alike," they have relinquished their ability to think for themselves, there will be a significant amount of intensity in the family system's adjustment to the impaired family member's shift in perception. There will be pressure from other family members to "change back" as the impaired family member progresses in treatment. The whole of a family system is greater than the sum of its parts. This means that the ferocity of systemic forces will challenge the individual to maintain the positive change. The Bowen therapist will predict this challenge to clients and coach them to just "hold on."

A Family Systems Therapy Approach With the Impaired Physician Family

BFST offers the impaired physician family a set of principles for understanding the underlying connections among people that create predictable patterns of interaction in the family's emotional process. BFST pushes the distressed medical family to broaden its lens from seeing only a particular symptom such as alcoholism. Instead, the family is called upon to view the symptom in the context of multigenerational problems within the wider relationship system and in the context of the natural world of emotional patterns of which humans are a part.

From the perspective of this theory, no matter what symptom appears in the family system, the treatment is always the same. The family is directed to look at the ways in which tension in relationships has been avoided and coached to begin to confront the tension. The family learns that if avoidance of relationship pressure continues across the generations, the risk and severity of symptoms intensifies with each generation to come. The emphasis is upon *process* rather than upon *content* or the nature of the symptom.

From the perspective of BFST, alcoholism and addiction are viewed as a human condition that is an outcome of family relationship processes across generations. In this sense, the drinking or drug problem is not viewed as a disease residing in the individual who is impaired, or in his overfunctioning partner. Instead, the anxiety-binding mechanism of chemical dependence is explored for how it functions in a misguided attempt to manage relationship tension. The therapy, in fact, becomes a motivational force that calls upon family members to research the emotional system from which they emerged. When the symptom of alcoholism or drug addiction is seen as one of many ways in which people bind anxiety, the focus upon one person and the tendency to blame diminish. The anxiety of the system is bound in the symptom, and coaching people to let go of the symptom pushes them to redirect the anxiety where it belongs: inside the relationship system. If only one person in the system functions differently, the entire system can be rearranged. The family is coached to develop greater strength in their collective "emotional muscle." Clients' work of going home again may be compared with achieving greater fitness from a workout in a gym, where *fitness* is defined as tolerance to stay the course in relationships without rushing to cut off or deny the fact of one's own interdependence. It is also defined as the ability to be a self with a core set of non-negotiable principles, even in the face of pressure from a loved one to conform.

Like all families, families with an impaired physician struggle with underlying relationship issues. The problem is not the substance, but rather how severe tensions go unaddressed. When family members relate through drinking or through drug abuse, they are attempting to regulate emotionality and attachment to important others in the family. The medical family's handling of neediness through dependency and caretaking, through cycles of distance and closeness, and/or through overinvestment in the needs of others, such as children, need to be explored in treatment. Alternative ways of handling interdependency needs should be identified and considered.

Information Is Power: Suggested Questions for the Impaired Physician Family

Calling upon impaired physicians and their families to think about the relationship system rather than the defined problem of chemical dependence opens up the possibility of increased freedom to explore the complexity and richness of a family's emotional process (McKnight, 1998). Treatment should pose questions for family members to explore on their own between sessions.

McKnight (1998) suggests questioning along the following lines:

- Can the family shift from viewing the alcohol or drug impairment as an individual problem to viewing the impairment as a family problem?
- Can the family come to view the impairment as a disguised opportunity to allow members to understand their relationship system rather than as a disease to be cured in an individual?
- How do people in the family hold on to their personal boundaries?
- How do family members manage to stay connected?
- How do people play out underfunctioning and overfunctioning reciprocal positions in the family?
- What is the maturity level of each person? Of the system?
- What new directions might people take in an attempt to make more thoughtful and less reactive decisions in a family?
- What patterns can each member of the marital unit identify as coming from their respective families of origin, and how do they think about these patterns?
- How are these family-of-origin patterns being replicated or reacted to in the nuclear family?
- In what other ways do people in the family system bind anxiety, in addition to substance abuse?

- How do people think about their sibling roles and position in their primary triangle with their parents in their families of origin, and how are these roles related to thoughts, beliefs, and behaviors in the nuclear family?

McGoldrick (1995) also suggests myriad questions that may aid the client-researcher (see her *You Can Go Home Again: Reconnecting With Your Family,* which contains useful lists of such questions at the end of each chapter). The idea is to learn wherever and whatever you can, because it may become apparent that a certain piece of information will help you connect pieces of the jigsaw puzzle in a way that creates a clearer picture.

Opening up the family's communication system strengthens the family (Bowen, 1978; Walsh, 1998). Guiding clients in their efforts to gather collateral information from various family members builds an individual's identity within the system. Also, it reduces polarizations, eliminating the notion that people must be assigned labels of "saint" or "sinner." In family systems thinking, there are no saints or sinners; instead, there are reciprocal family processes that serve a function to maintain the stability of the system.

Conclusion

In other theoretical orientations, chemical dependence is typically defined as a problem that resides in the individual. In place of the disease model of alcoholism and addiction, a broader, contextual interpretation of this pattern of binding anxiety is offered here. A significant number of studies have tested the validity of BFST and provide empirical support for the relationship between differentiation of self and chronic anxiety, marital difficulties, and psychological distress (Miller, Anderson, & Keala, 2004).

In treating the medical family suffering from substance-related impairment, the Bowen-trained clinician coaches the motivated family members to explore their roles and multigenerational family patterns rather than keeping the primary focus upon changing the alcoholic or addict. The BFST clinician realizes that a push to change the impaired physician may exacerbate the problem and deny the family a remarkable opportunity to grow and develop in a more functional way.

Therapy based on the set of interlocking concepts and principles developed by Bowen (1978) guides the family with an impaired physician to move into increasingly anxious environments, trying to assume greater responsibility and make more meaningful connections while at the same time holding on to individuality in the face of group pressure to conform.

By embarking upon this journey across time, impaired physicians and their families can triumph in the face of tragedy. They can begin to define a responsible direction in their lives as they learn to think differently about human relationships (Gilbert, 1992). Such an effort insures that if people struggling with adversity remain true to the course of exploration and fact-finding, they can replace shame with "survivor's pride" (Wolin & Wolin, 1993).

Medical students should be taught from the very beginning of their careers that they have as much responsibility for their own mental health and physical well-being as they do for those of their patients. They must realize that it is crucial to pay attention to their connections with their own families even as they attend to their patients. Fulfilling their family responsibilities and nurturing their own relationships not only helps physicians to more successfully navigate the ever-present struggle between the forces of connectedness and those of individuality, but also protects the public from lapses in medical judgment. The development of a sound, systemic view of their own lives as doctors and family members cannot help but to enhance overall functioning, both at home and in the workplace. If clinicians look for patterns instead of causes, see solutions and problems as being inextricably codetermined, and develop the ability to think and apply "systems," medical doctors and their families may come to appreciate the abiding wisdom underlying the injunction, "Physician, heal thyself."

References

Angres, D. H., McGovern, M. P., Rawal, P., & Shaw, M. (2002). Psychiatric comorbidity and physicians with substance use disorders: Clinical characteristics, treatment experiences, and post-treatment functioning. *Addictive Disorders and Their Treatment, 1*(3), 89–98.

Babcock, M., & McKay, C. (Eds.). (1995). *Challenging codependency: Feminist critiques.* Toronto: University of Toronto Press.

Bowen, M. (1978). *Family therapy in clinical practice.* Northvale, NJ: Jason Aronson.

Brown, S. (1985). *Treating the alcoholic: A developmental model of recovery.* New York: Wiley.

Coombs, R. H. (1996). Addicted health professionals. *Journal of Substance Misuse, 1,* 187–194.

Cunningham, B. R. (2006). *A resiliency-based, Bowen family systems approach to treating a sibling survivor of homicide: A case study.* Doctoral dissertation, Alliant International University, San Diego, CA.

Ellis, J. J., & Inbody, D. R. (1988). Psychotherapy with physician's families: When attributes in medical practice become liabilities in family life. *American Journal of Psychotherapy, 42,* 380–388.

Friedman, E. H. (1991). Bowen theory and therapy. In A. S. Gurman & D. P. Kniskern (Eds.), *Handbook of family therapy* (Vol. 2, pp. 134–170). New York: Brunner/Mazel.

Gabbard, G. O., & Menninger, R. W. (1989). The psychology of postponement in the medical marriage. *Journal of the American Medical Association, 261,* 2378–2381.

Gerber, L. A. (1983). *Married to their careers: Family dilemmas in doctors' lives.* New York: Tavistock.

Gierymski, T., & Williams, T. (1986). Codependency. *Journal of Psychoactive Drugs,* 18, 7–13.

Gilbert, R. M. (1992). *Extraordinary relationships: A new way to think about human interactions.* New York: Wiley.

Gilbert, R. M. (1994). Addiction to prescribed medications. *Family Systems: A Journal of Natural Systems Thinking in Psychiatry and the Sciences, 1,* 57–66.

Harper, J., & Capdevila, C. (1990). Codependency: A critique. *Journal of Psychoactive Drugs, 22,* 285–292.

Kerr, M. E. (2008). Why do siblings turn out differently? In A. Fogel, B. J. King, & S. Shanker (Eds.), *Human development in the 21st century: Visionary ideas from systems scientists* (pp. 206–215). New York: Cambridge University Press.

Kerr, M. E., & Bowen, M. (1988). *Family evaluation.* New York: Norton.

Lawson, A. W., & Lawson, G. W. (1998). *Alcoholism and the family: A guide to treatment and prevention* (2nd ed.). Austin, TX: PRO-ED.

Mann, G. A. (1991). History and theory of treatment for drug and alcohol addiction. In N. S. Miller (Ed.), *Comprehensive handbook of drug and alcohol addiction* (pp. 1201–1212). New York: Marcel Dekker.

Mansky, P. A. (1999). Issues in the recovery of physicians from addictive illnesses. *Psychiatric Quarterly, 70,* 107–122.

Martin, P. A., & Bird, H. W. (1959). The "love-sick" wife and the "cold-sick" husband. *Psychiatry, 22,* 245–249.

McGoldrick, M. (1995). *You can go home again: Reconnecting with your family.* New York: Norton.

McGovern, M. P., Angres, D. H., & Leon, S. (1998). Differential therapeutics and the impaired physician: Patient-treatment matching by specificity and intensity. *Journal of Addictive Diseases, 17*(2), 93–107.

McKnight, A. S. (1998). Family systems with alcoholism: A case study. In P. Titelman (Ed.), *Clinical applications of Bowen family systems theory* (pp. 263–298). New York: Haworth Press.

Meyers, M. F. (1994). *Doctors' marriages.* London: Plenum Press.

Miller, R. B., Anderson, S., & Keala, D. K. (2004). Is Bowen theory valid? A review of basic research. *Journal of Marital and Family Therapy, 30,* 453–466.

Morgan, P. (1981). *Alcohol, disinhibition, and domination: A conceptual analysis.* Paper presented at the Conference on Alcohol and Disinhibition, University of California, Berkeley.

Nyman, D. J., & Cocores, J. (1991). Co-addiction: Treatment of the family member. In N. S. Miller (Ed.), *Comprehensive handbook of drug and alcohol addiction* (pp. 877–888). New York: Marcel Dekker.

Papero, D. V. (1990). *Bowen family systems theory.* Boston: Allyn & Bacon.

Robb, N. (1998). Teaching on addiction issues lacking in medical school, specialists told. *Canadian Medical Association Journal, 158,* 640–642.

Sotile, W. M., & Sotile, M. O. (2000). *The medical marriage: Sustaining healthy relationships for physicians and their families.* Chicago: American Medical Association.

Stanton, D. M., Todd, T., & Associates (1982). *The family therapy of drug abuse and addiction.* New York: Guilford Press.

Talbott, G. D. (1987). The impaired physician: The role of the spouse in recovery. *Journal of the Medical Association of Georgia, 76,* 190–192.

Talbott, G. D., & Gallegos, K. V. (1990, September). Intervention with health professionals. *Addiction and Recovery,* pp. 13–16.

Talbott, G. D., & Martin, C. A. (1986, February). Treating impaired physicians: Fourteen keys to success. *Virginia Medical, 113,* 95–99.

Toman, W. (1993). *Family constellation.* Northvale, NJ: Jason Aronson.

Twerski, A. J. (1982). *It happens to doctors, too.* Center City, MN: Hazelden.

Vaillant, G. E., Sobowale, N. C., & McArthur, C. (1972). Some psychological vulnerabilities of physicians. *New England Journal of Medicine, 287,* 372–375.

Wallack, L. M. (1981, April). *The problems of preventing problems.* Paper presented at the Conference on Developing Prevention Programs, Nebraska Division of Alcoholism and Drug Abuse, Lincoln, NE.

Walsh, F. (1998). *Strengthening family resilience.* New York: Guilford Press.

Wolin, S. J., & Wolin, S. (1993). *The resilient self: How survivors of troubled families rise above adversity.* New York: Villard.

Yandoli, D., Eisler, I., Robbins, C., Mulleady, G., & Dare, C. (2002). A comparative study of family therapy in the treatment of opiate users in a London abuse clinic. *Journal of Family Therapy, 24,* 402–422.

CHAPTER 14

Substance Abuse and Homelessness

Susanne Friedrich

This chapter examines substance abuse within the homeless, or indigent, population in the United States. Homelessness has always existed in the United States, with incidence rising or falling depending on the prevailing social stress factors. In the past hundred years or so, the homeless population in the United States has become significantly more heterogeneous in terms of race, ethnicity, gender, veteran status, and age. Along with this demographic shift, there have been advances in the research techniques used to study the problem of homelessness, so we have an increasingly clear picture of the phenomenon. In this chapter, social and personal causes of homelessness are outlined, and substance use, as well as its physical and mental consequences among homeless subgroups, is examined. Further, an overview of treatment approaches is presented.

Homelessness in the United States

Prior to the Great Depression era of the 1930s, there were few studies that addressed homelessness and substance abuse. The available studies suggest that between 9.75% and 48% of homeless men in different U.S. cities experienced alcohol abuse or alcoholism (Stark, 1987). Most early research findings supported the idea that homelessness in the early 20th century resulted primarily from the dislocation associated with industrialization. A large number of men without shelter were laborers who had to move from one urban area to another in order to have continuing employment; these were mostly unskilled workers who had previously been working. Many even carried good references from former employers (Stark, 1987).

There was a dramatic increase in the homeless population during the Great Depression. We do not have definitive counts, but estimates range from 200,000 to 1.5 million, mostly young men who were searching for work across the country (Rossi, 1990). Study outcomes from the 1930s estimated alcohol abuse and alcoholism rates at between 7% and 30% (Stark, 1987).

With the entry of the United States in World War II, the homeless population decreased significantly in the face of the growing need for war technologies, supplies, and personnel. The unemployment rate likewise decreased dramatically. The postwar decades continued to provide steady employment for most workers; homelessness kept declining, and there was great optimism among social scientists that homelessness would soon belong to the past.

Up until the late 1970s, the term *homelessness* had a different meaning from that of today. A homeless person was somebody who lived outside of a family unit. Nevertheless, most of them did have a steady shelter, such as rooms or beds in cheap hotels or mission dormitories.

A study by Bogue (1963) of Chicago's homeless population, then known as "Skid Row" people, in the late 1950s described the following composition: The median age was about 50 years old, 90% were White, 25% were Social Security pensioners, another 25% were chronic alcoholics, 20% were physically disabled, another 20% were mentally ill, and the remaining 10% were socially maladjusted.

In the postwar period, Bogue (1963) found that the average homeless individual was living in social isolation; the majority were never married and did not have close bonds to their family of origin. Also noteworthy is that the number of homeless women and minority groups was low until the 1980s; or at least, studies usually did not refer to them. Homelessness was considered to be a male problem.

By the end of the 1970s and during the early 1980s, despite the predictions about the disappearance of homelessness, a new type of homelessness was emerging. As Young (1989) stated, three factors contributed to this change in demographics: an economic recession, the return of Vietnam veterans, and the deinstitutionalization of patients with mental illness. An increasing number of young people filled the streets. A study of homelessness in Chicago by Rossi, Fisher, and Willis (1986) indicated that the average homeless age was 37 years. This finding is in contrast to Bogue's (1963) finding that the average age was 50 years. A second emergent phenomenon was the large number of women, often with small children. Rossi et al.'s study indicated that 25% of Chicago's homeless population were women. Another difference between the "old" and the "new" homeless population was the increasing overrepresentation of racial and ethnic minorities. For instance, in the Rossi et al. Chicago study, 54% were Black, and this proportion has continued to increase. It is not known whether this means that there were more women and minorities, or more reporting of women and minorities.

Compared to the homeless population of the 1950s, today's homeless population faces more severe conditions: These individuals have proportionally less income, a lot more of them are chronically unemployed, and many more are forced to sleep in the streets or in public places.

It has never been possible to say exactly how many homeless people there are at a given time. Hombs (1990) reported that estimates range from 250,000 to 3 million. Link et al. (1995) suggested that about 12 million adult people in the United States have been homeless at some point in their lives, even though the percentage for whom this is an ongoing lifestyle condition is probably less than 1%. Link et al. (1994) found that 8.5 million people were homeless between 1985 and 1990.

Both, the "old" and the "new" homeless populations share similar levels of disability, including chronic mental illness (33%), acute alcoholism (33%), serious physical disabilities (25%), and serious criminal records (20%). About 75% have one or more of these conditions (Rossi, 1990). Since the 1970s and 1980s, several social and structural changes have caused an increase in homelessness in the United States. The shortage of affordable housing, the increase in poverty for the working poor, and cuts in welfare and other safety net programs are probably the most important factors. Personal factors that interact with the social issues include mental illness, substance abuse, lack of income and family support, and negative childhood experiences, including lack of care, early disruption (e.g., family breakdown, frequent moves), physical and sexual abuse, and exposure to violence.

Social Factors

Income for the 20% of the population with the lowest income has dropped in the past several decades, while the stock of affordable rental housing has decreased. Poverty among the already underprivileged has deepened, the duration of episodes of poverty have increased, and spatial and social isolation have become more pronounced (J. D. Wright, Rubin, & Devine, 1998). According to T. Wright (2000), the number of those living in poverty increased from 29.2 million in 1980 to 36.5 million in 1996, an increase of 7.3%. Additionally, the poorest fifth of the population, which earned 5.4% of the total national income in 1970, experienced a decline in income to 4.2% of the total national income in 1996, while the most wealthy fifth of the country's population was able to massively increase its share of total national income. Increasingly, poor working people are threatened by homelessness because housing costs are rising beyond the reach of their income. The minimum wage, for instance, remained unchanged from 1981 until 1990, while inflation increased by 31% during the same period (Hombs, 1990). These economic conditions intensified the risk for homelessness for those making less than 50% of the poverty wage. Moreover, the availability of low-income housing simultaneously shrank, which created an "affordability gap" (Shinn & Gillespie, 1994). For example, while the number of renters making less than $10,000 a year increased from 7.3 million in 1970 to 9.6 million in 1989, the number of affordable housing units declined by 14%, generating a shortfall of 4.1 million units (Timmer, Eitzen, & Talley, 1994). The limited housing opportunities traditionally available to low-income populations, such as single-room occupancy hotels, have declined with the gentrification of urban areas. Increasingly, homeless shelters have replaced the housing options traditionally associated with homeless individuals (T. Wright, 2000).

Cutbacks in government cash and food assistance have worsened the already difficult situation for many low-income people, especially for single mothers on welfare. T. Wright (2000) points out that as welfare reform took hold in the mid-1990s and the number of people who received food stamps declined, the monthly income of the poorest 20% (2 million families, 6 million people) fell from almost $700 to an average of $580 per family from 1995 to 1997, although the average earnings of low-income female-headed families with children increased between 1993 and 1995 due to economic expansion. The cutbacks in welfare were supposed to reduce federal dependency. While the effort worked for some of low-income people, it increased the impoverishment of others (T. Wright, 2000). A number of mothers who were formerly dependent on welfare did find jobs, but these jobs were mostly low paid and with few benefits. Others could not manage to find any type of job and ended up homeless.

Another important factor in the increase of homelessness in the early 1980s is the deinstitutionalization of people with severe mental illness (Berlin & McAllister, 1992). Deinstitutionalization was meant to release inappropriately institutionalized people with mental illness from long-term hospital care. Even though the idea was a good one, the failure of state institutions to provide the community support facilities and services that would allow released patients to live securely in the community resulted in disaster.

Personal Factors

Social factors go a long way toward explaining the causes of homelessness, but proximate causes within the individual also contribute to the problem. Caton, Hasin, Shrout, and Opler (2000) tried to identify risk factors for homelessness among indigent urban adults without dependent children and with no history of psychotic illness. In a matched case control study with 200 newly homeless men and women and 200 indigent men and women with no history of homelessness, the authors found that the lifetime presence of a nonpsychotic psychiatric disorder, including antisocial personality disorder, is not a risk factor for homelessness when severe mental illness is not present. Alcohol or drug abuse/dependence was not a risk factor for homelessness among men, but it was among women. Lifetime heroin or cocaine abuse/dependence was more common among homeless women than among never-homeless women. Also, homeless women had received more treatment for substance use problems, which suggests that the substance use problems were severe and long-standing. Furthermore, symptoms were more severe in the homeless men than in the nonhomeless men. The authors suggested that either impairment precipitated homelessness or the increased hardship imposed by being homeless increased symptoms. Contrary to expectations, among women, symptoms were more severe than among the never-homeless samples. Possibly these higher symptom severity levels are due to greater stress or dissatisfaction associated with being indigent and housed. Family support in adulthood, especially economic support, seemed to be a good protective factor. For men, income support was most important; for women, both income and social support were found to be important. Further, more of the homeless lacked a high school diploma and had less income from all sources, including their families.

An important limitation of Caton et al.'s (2000) study is its cross-sectional nature, which makes it difficult to determine whether some variables were causes or consequences of homelessness. Nonetheless, their study does offer some evidence that personal factors contribute to homelessness. Substance abuse, lack of education, and absence of family support are likely contributing factors. Mental illness and a lack of sustained relationships are other factors that might explain homelessness (T. Wright, 2000).

Herman, Susser, Struening, and Link (1997) tested the hypothesis that adverse childhood experiences were risk factors for adult homelessness. They interviewed a representative sample of 92 formerly homeless individuals and a comparison group of 395 individuals without prior homelessness. They found that the combination of lack of care and either physical or sexual abuse during childhood was highly associated with adult homelessness. Lack of care and physical abuse contributed significantly to the risk of homelessness. Sexual abuse showed a nonsignificant trend in that direction. The authors concluded that adverse childhood experiences and adult homelessness are linked. A limitation of the study is recall bias; measures of risk factors and homelessness were collected retrospectively. The authors also noted that assessing abuse histories was difficult.

In a study of the life histories of crack-using African American homeless men, E. Cohen and Stahler (1998) interviewed 31 African American male crack cocaine users in Philadelphia. Their life histories revealed several common early experiences related to later residential instability and homelessness: serious disruptions in early life, often involving exposure to violence and loss of family members and friends; physical and emotional abuse; participation in gangs; and worsening of life functioning after exposure to crack cocaine. Street gang culture was identified as an important agent of socialization for many of the interviewees. One limitation of this study was that randomized sample strategies were not used. Furthermore, only African American crack-using men were interviewed, which limits the generalizability to other crack-using populations.

E. Cohen and Stahler's (1998) findings offer evidence that several personal risk factors may be related to homelessness. Physical or sexual abuse and a lack of family care in childhood, disruptions in early life, mental illness, substance abuse, a lack of education, and association with gang culture contribute to lower life functioning, which elevates the risk for homelessness. Although identifying social and personal causes is definitely an important step toward explaining homelessness, it should be recognized that there is a lot of interaction between the various causes and that every homeless individual has his or her own life story.

Diversity in the Homeless Population

Traditionally, the homeless individual was stereotyped as a drunken, White, middle-aged urban male who was responsible for the life he led. In fact, however, the homeless population is quite diverse. Further, blaming homeless individuals for their homelessness is an easy way to overlook society's responsibility to take care of those in need. The following profile of the homeless population in San Diego, California, illustrates the heterogeneity of today's homeless individuals.

San Diego's Homeless Population—An Example of Diversity

The San Diego Regional Task Force on the Homeless issued a report in August 1999 describing the homeless population in San Diego County. This report contains information that likely would be applicable to U.S. cities of similar size with two exceptions: First, San Diego is close to the Mexican border; this geographic characteristic involves factors that are specific to border cities. Second, San Diego is home to a large military presence, which is not characteristic of other U.S. cities. The homeless population in San Diego County can be divided into two general groups: (a) the urban homeless (b) and day labors/farmworkers. The latter are primarily found in the hillsides, canyons, and fields of the county. Combined, these two groups total at least 15,000 out of over 2 million in the county, but many undocumented workers are not included in this estimate. Here, the focus is on the urban homeless group because their situation is more representative of U.S. urban areas as a whole.

The majority of the urban homeless people in San Diego are single adults (64%), most between 27 and 40 years old; approximately 20% of these have been homeless for more than 4 years. Eight percent of the total are women, most of whom cite as reasons for their homelessness abandonment by spouse, male friends, or families; or flight from abusive situations. Half of the homeless women are believed to be victims of domestic violence.

Homeless families, the majority of which are led by single mothers, make up at least one quarter of the urban homeless population in San Diego County. A third of these women reported having been abused during childhood. Compared to women who are not homeless, these woman are more likely to have substance abuse problems or be involved with a man who has substance abuse problems. Homeless children often present with emotional, developmental, and behavioral problems. They tend to be anxious, depressed, aggressive, dependent, and demanding; they also tend to experience a variety of physical problems.

The number of teenage runaways on any given night is estimated to be between 1,500 and 2,000 in San Diego County. The problem of chronically homeless youth, about 800 at any given time, seems to be intractable in part because in urban areas they can easily merge with other youth. Drug and alcohol use among them is common, and a high proportion also sell drugs and/or sex in order to meet their basic needs.

Elderly homeless people represent a relatively small subgroup among the homeless population in San Diego County. The majority of them are poorly educated men in their 60s. They tend to be particularly vulnerable to illness, crime, exploitation, and abuse.

Homeless individuals with mental illness number about 1,900 in San Diego County. Seventy percent of them are male, most are single, more than half are White, and their mean age is 30. One third have no contact with medical professionals, nor do they receive prescribed medication. Up to half of them abuse alcohol and/or drugs.

Homeless veterans number about 2,000 in the county, which represents 40% of San Diego's urban single homeless men. This rate is higher than in other American cities because of the large military presence in San Diego. The average homeless veteran is 40 years old, ranging from 25 to 65, from at least five different wars. Many suffer from posttraumatic stress disorder (PTSD), and about 80% have drug and alcohol-related problems.

In summary, the homeless population in San Diego is much like homeless populations in other urban areas, with three possible exceptions: the larger number of veteran homeless, the larger number of migrant workers from just across the border, and the high cost of housing. San Diego is similar in that single men are the largest group among the homeless. Minorities and those with mental health and substance abuse problems represent a substantial proportion of the homeless. The following section focuses on the prevalence of homeless' substance use nationwide.

The Prevalence Alcohol and Drug Abuse in the Homeless Population

The most prevalent health problem among homeless men and women is alcohol abuse (Institute of Medicine, 1988). About 35% to 40% of the homeless people in the United States abuse alcohol—about half of the homeless men and a sixth of the homeless women (Regional Task Force on Homelessness, 1999). In an analysis of studies published since 1980, Fisher (1989) found that homeless men were more likely to report alcohol- and drug-related problems, whereas higher rates of mental illness were reported among women. He concluded that alcoholism could be as much as nine times more prevalent among the homeless population than in the general community.

J. D. Wright and Weber (1987) found the highest prevalence of alcohol among homeless men aged 30 to 49 years (40%) and 50 to 64 years (43%). Alcohol abuse within the whole homeless population is estimated to be about 30% to 40%, while drug abuse is common among 10% to 15% (McCarty, Argeriou, Huebner, & Lubran, 1991). Here, prevalence rates are highest among minority men, followed by African American women and White men (Regional Task Force on Homelessness, 1999). Some evidence suggests that younger homeless people are more likely to abuse drugs. J. D. Wright and Weber found the strongest correlate of drug use to be age. Rates of drug abuse decreased with advancing age and were greatest among younger homeless individuals.

Ethnicity has also been found to correlate with alcohol- and drug-related problems. J. D. Wright and Weber (1987) reported, in a sample of nearly 30,000, alcohol problems in 60% of homeless Native American men, 47% of homeless Latino men, and 17% of homeless Asian men. Alcohol problems were found among 38% of homeless African American men, and 35% of homeless White men. Among homeless women, the prevalence of alcohol-related problems was highest for Native Americans (36%), followed by African Americans (13%), Whites (12%), and Latinos (4%). The differences in drug abuse prevalence were less obvious in this study. African American (13%) and Latino (12%) homeless men had the highest rates.

D. C. Cohen and Krating (1993) studied the characteristics of substance abusers and non-abusers in a sample of homeless individuals participating in an outreach program (N = 1,166). Two thirds abused substances, had a mental illness, or both. As in other studies, Cohen and Krating found that significantly more men than women abused alcohol. Contrary to the findings of other studies, women were slightly but not significantly more likely to abuse drugs. More than one third of those who abused substances used both alcohol and drugs. More than 40% of the same group had some form of mental illness. Compared to the non-abusers, substance abusers were more often male, Black, and unmarried with no dependents, and had been homeless for a longer period of time. A larger proportion of the substance abusers, compared to the non-abusers, had

(a) relatively more severe impairment in functioning, (b) mental illness, (c) less access to the social service system, and (d) less income. Almost half of the drug abusers were female. This part of the sample had the highest proportion of people with children; Hispanics and younger people were overrepresented. The authors of the study listed several important limitations. The outreach program from which the sample was taken was not designed to facilitate the collection of research data. The data were not collected in a systematic way; outreach program staff had only brief contact with clients and might have been more likely to record information about problems for which they could make suitable referrals. Further, the sample was not necessarily representative of the general homeless population. A shelter sample might have yielded findings that were more representative.

E. Y. Lambert and Caces (1995), in a study of substance use among homeless and transient people in Washington, DC, found no sex differences in needle use, but men were significantly more likely than women to have used marijuana and cocaine in the past year. Differences related to race were found only among the users of cocaine, with homeless Whites nearly half as likely as homeless Blacks to have used cocaine in the past year. Also, the authors found correlations between age and the type of substance used. Individuals between 26 and 34 years of age were at greatest risk for marijuana and cocaine use, while past-year needle use was almost twice as likely among persons 35 and older than among those who were 26 to 34 years old and 10 times more likely than among those who were 18 to 25. The authors also noted that the average age of heroin users treated in hospital emergency rooms increased between 1990 and 1992, suggesting that there might be a downward trend in younger needle users. Lambert and Caces further reported that chronically homeless people were less likely to use cocaine than were those at risk for homelessness. And, needle use was less prevalent among newly or intermittently homeless individuals than among those at risk for homelessness. It is possible that those at risk for homelessness might have had greater access to financial resources and social networks, enabling them to obtain cocaine and needles. Homeless people who had been institutionalized in either correctional or noncorrectional facilities used more marijuana and cocaine than did those who had not been institutionalized. The authors also found that there were no significant differences in drug use on the basis of social achievement or socioeconomic status, including education, employment, and marital status.

These studies generally indicate a high rate of alcohol and drug abuse in the homeless population. Further, this research seems to indicate a relationship between alcohol and drug use and gender, age, race, ethnicity, and mental illness. Finally, there is some evidence of a correlation between age and the type of substance used.

Health Problems as a Consequence of Homelessness

People living on the streets must endure harsh conditions. Many lack personal hygiene, sound nutrition, sufficient clothing, and health care. The exposure to the elements and the absence of shelter contribute to a variety of health problems among homeless individuals. Psychiatric problems, substance abuse, and physical health problems are strongly correlated with homelessness, both contributing to the risk of homelessness and resulting from homelessness. J. D. Wright and Weber (1987) found that mental illness, alcohol abuse, and drug abuse all had a significant and independent effect on the increased rates of physical health problems and chronic diseases in homeless people.

General Health Problems

Harris, Mowbray, and Solarz (1994) examined the physical health, mental health, and substance abuse problems of 72 individuals who used four large Detroit homeless shelters. A majority of these people had at least one noticeable existing dental problem, more than 40% had vision problems, more than 40% experienced at least one measured irregularity in hearth rhythm, pulse, or both, and 40% had had at least one of the following problems in the past year: asthma, pneumonia, bronchitis, and cold. More than half of the participants had at least one dysfunctional symptom of the musculoskeletal system. Fifty percent of the women reported missed, irregular, or painful menstrual periods, and almost one third of the participants had had problems with headaches during the past year. Problems related to ear, skin, hair, and the immune system were also reported. Alcohol use was common among many of the participants; 60.8% reported drinking in the previous month. A large minority (30.6%) reported using marijuana within the past month. Drugs other than marijuana were used by 11%. About one quarter of the sample had a history of psychiatric hospitalization. Some gender differences were found. The mean age for men was 37.5 years. The men reported more vision problems than did the women. The mean age for women was 29.5 years. They reported more problems with anemia and headache than did the men.

Harris et al. (1994) noted several limitations of the study. The data was collected in only one geographical area, and the sample contained only sheltered homeless individuals. The authors suggested that those who were too dysfunctional to seek shelter might have had much more serious problems.

Sachs-Ericsson, Wise, Debrody, and Paniucki (1999) identified similar health problems and utilization patterns of 292 homeless individuals seeking medical services in a small southern community. The most prevalent symptoms reported by the participants were upper respiratory infections, colds, and flu. Other symptoms named were gastrointestinal problems, headaches, skin rash or irritation, and breaks or sprains. The most important finding of the study was the high rate of medical service utilization for recurring medical problems for which many had already received treatment. The authors suggested that this reoccurrence might reflect the chronic nature of the problem or possibly inadequate treatment, lack of follow-up, or patient noncompliance in relation to the prior treatment. It is likely that homeless individuals typically wait until the problem has become serious before seeking services. In addition, several barriers seem to prevent some homeless individuals from seeking treatment at outpatient facilities, such as poor accessibility of services, costliness of services, and disrespectful and uncaring treatment from health-care providers. Health-care facilities providing services to homeless individuals should be aware of such barriers and institute the measures necessary to address them.

HIV and Homelessness

The homeless population has a high risk for HIV infection. According to a survey of homeless adults entering a storefront medical clinic in the southern United States, 69% were at risk for HIV infection from (a) unprotected sex with multiple partners, (b) use of injectable drugs, (c) sex with a partner using injectable drugs, or (d) the exchange of unprotected sex for money or drugs (Lee, Ross, Mizwa, & Scott, 2000). Torres, Mani, Altholz, and Brickner (1990) found that 62% of injection drug users receiving services at a New York City homeless shelter were infected with HIV.

Several other studies support the finding of a high risk for HIV in the homeless population. The number of sex partners might be the most significant risk factor (Lee et al., 2000). Homosexual and bisexual males practicing unsafe sex are most likely to be affected, but the general homeless population is at risk, too. Homeless individuals typically have difficulty forming stable intimate relationships because of drug use, mental illness, violence, and transient living conditions (Lee et al., 2000). According Lee et al., "survival sex" is also a common practice, especially for homeless women and youth, who regularly exchange sex for housing, food, money, and drugs. Homeless women often experience sexual assault or rape, which increases their risk of HIV infection. Lee et al. also reported that compared to Whites, more African Americans and Hispanics die of AIDS.

Somlai, Kelley, Wagstaff, and Whitson (1998) investigated psychosocial, relationship, and situational factors associated with HIV risk in a sample of 152 inner-city homeless men and women. Homeless men were more likely than women to have multiple sex partners. Risk of AIDS for women was associated with the likelihood of their having a relatively exclusive relationship with a high-risk male partner. Somlai et al. also found that unprotected sex tended to be higher for homeless women than for homeless men. In men, high-risk patterns were associated with negative attitudes toward condom use, low levels of intention to use condoms, and an attitude of fatalism (high perceived risk of AIDS and low perceived ability to avoid that risk). Among women with high HIV risk, greater dissatisfaction with life was paramount: They were less optimistic, held negative attitudes toward condom use, perceived themselves to be at risk, and tended to use substances. The authors noted several limitations of this study. Its cross-sectionalism does not allow determining causal relationships, and the self-report nature of the data might compromise reliability. Additionally, shelter users in other areas of the country might yield different risk patterns.

Somlai et al. (1998) concluded that prevention activities must extend beyond the provision of educational information about AIDS. Instead, intervention with men should primarily focus on increasing positive attitudes toward condom use, strengthening plans and intentions to use condoms, and teaching the skills needed to avoid risk. Among homeless women, HIV prevention should integrate activities with both substance abuse treatment programs and social service programs intended to improve self-esteem, self-sufficiency, and orientation toward the future.

In a study of rates of HIV in 839 alcohol-abusing veterans, Gordon et al. (2006) found that homelessness and alcohol were associated with a reduction in the rate of participants' utilization of health services. Homeless HIV-infected veterans reported alcohol consumption (36%), hazardous drinking (34%), binge drinking (46%), and a diagnosis of alcohol abuse (25%). The veterans who reported higher levels of illicit drug use, more hazardous drinking behaviors, and greater severity of HIV symptoms reported, on average, only a one-time use of outpatient clinics. This low rate of outpatient clinic use might be the result of a lack of financial resources, a lack of health insurance, or limited access to health-care facilities. Fear of stigma might also be a factor.

Homeless Subgroups and Methods of Treatment

As pointed out earlier in this chapter, the homeless population is quite heterogeneous. Four important subgroups are described here: dually diagnosed, street youth, women and families, and veterans. Information on the characteristics of each group is provided, and specific treatment needs and options are outlined.

Dual Diagnosis Prevalence, Etiology, and Subject Characteristics

Individuals with dual diagnosis, who form a heterogeneous subgroup within the homeless population, are those with severe mental illness and substance use disorders (Drake, Osher, & Wallach, 1991). As Drake et al. stated, few studies have thus far addressed the specific needs of this group because of problems with defining the term *dual diagnosis*, a lack of assessment instruments, and the extreme heterogeneity of this group. Those with mental illness make up approximately one third of the homeless population in the United States (Morrissey & Dennis, 1986; Morrisey & Levine, 1987). About 30% to 40% of them have alcohol problems (Fisher & Breakey, 1987), and 10% to 20% have problems with other drugs (Milburn, 1989). In a review of the literature between 1980 and 1990, Fisher (1990) identified 19 studies that differentiated between individuals with a single diagnosis of alcohol, drug, or mental health problems and those with dual or multiple diagnoses. The rate of mental disorders plus alcohol use disorders ranged from 3.6% to 26.0% in seven studies. The rate of mental disorders plus other drug use disorders ranged from 1.7% to 2.5% in three studies, and the rate of mental disorders ranged from 8.0% to 31.1%.

People referred to as "dually diagnosed" usually have several additional problems, including abuse of drugs other than alcohol, general medical illness, and legal problems (Drake & Mueser, 1996). Furthermore, this group is likely to also have histories of trauma and behavior disorders, deficits in social and vocational skills, and support networks that include people involved in alcohol and other drug abuse or other illegal behavior. As Fisher (1990) stated, individuals with dual diagnosis are more likely than other homeless groups to experience harsh living conditions, such as living on the streets rather than in shelters; to suffer from psychological distress; to trade sexual favors for money and food; to be picked up by the police; to become incarcerated; to be estranged from their families; and to be victimized. Fisher (1990) further noted that those with dual diagnosis were more likely to be older and male and were less likely to be working than homeless persons with no diagnosis or a single diagnosis. Also, along with alcoholics, those with dual diagnosis were more likely to be local residents and to have longer durations of homelessness than were other homeless subgroups. Several clinical studies suggest that dually diagnosed individuals are strongly predisposed to homelessness because their substance abuse and treatment noncompliance lead to disruptive behaviors, loss of social support, and housing instability (Drake et al., 1991).

In a study of gender differences across homeless individuals with co-occurring schizophrenia and substance abuse, Brunette and Drake (1998) found that women in this group had more children and were more socially connected than men. Women also had higher rates of sexual and physical victimization, comorbid anxiety and depression, and medical illness. The hypothesis that men and women would have a similar level of substance abuse was supported in this study. The authors concluded that homeless women with dual disorders, like women with substance use disorders in the general population, have distinct characteristics, vulnerabilities, and treatment needs compared with men.

A. Cohen and Koegel (1996) used ethnographic data from a lower income area of Los Angeles to study homeless substance users with mental illness. The authors found that the number of shelters available to dually diagnosed individuals was limited. Further, some of the individuals who were able to rent a room in a single-room occupancy hotel were threatened daily with theft, robbery, and assault. Options to fulfill other basic needs were not better: Food, clothing, and the means of maintaining personal hygiene were limited; danger was constantly present, as well as poverty, psychopathology, and substance use. Environmental factors usually contributed to recognizable behavior patterns. When the money was gone, the former hotel renters were forced to return to the streets, missions, or shelters. The individuals' attempts to adapt to the demands of survival were constrained by limited options as well as by both internal and external pressures. Substance use had a negative impact on the ability of the individuals in the sample to meet their basic needs, but the extent of that influence varied. Drugs and alcohol totally dominated the lives of some individuals, whereas subsistence activities and substance use were more balanced for other individuals, although this balance could be easily shifted. The individuals in this study could be divided into four groups: (1) those with low levels of psychopathology who were not substance users, (2) those with low levels of psychopathology who were substance users, (3) those with high levels of psychopathology who were not substance users, and (4) those with high levels of psychopathology who were substance users. Those in Groups 1 and 4 were opposite on the continuum, with those in Group 1 being the most successful in meeting their basic needs and those in Group 4 being the least successful. The two middle groups were not as clearly defined. Those in Group 3 experienced significant problems fulfilling their needs, whereas those in Group 2 displayed a variable profile, with only half experiencing difficulties meeting their basic needs. These findings indicate that severe psychopathology results in a decreased ability to meet basic needs, while substance use can but does not automatically overwhelm the ability to meet subsistence needs. This finding is in contrast to that of Koegel, Burnam, and Farr (1990), who suggested that substance use has a more potent effect than serious mental illness on people's ability to meet subsistence needs. Cohen and Koegel suggested the possibility that the most psychotic and functionally impaired homeless individuals might have selected themselves out of participating in a survey, which demands a degree of interaction with which they are not comfortable. In any case, it seems that substance use and psychopathology coexist in a complicated and intricate relationship in which neither functions exclusively as a cause or a consequence.

Research on mental health issues in substance-abusing or homeless populations indicates that PTSD coexists in some people who are struggling with substance abuse and dependence (Heilemann, Kury, & Lee, 2005; Poleshuck, Giles, & Tu, 2002). PTSD is also found to be comorbid with major depression, anxiety disorders, and other mental health diagnoses (Briere, 1992; Kilpatrick et al., 2003). Interpersonal violence has been linked to major depression and other mental health problems (Lown, Schmidt, & Wiley, 2006; Scott, London, & Myers, 2002). Drug use in those with PTSD may be an attempt to self-medicate in the absence of access to medical services. Unfortunately, self-medication with alcohol and street drugs is likely to exacerbate the mental illness, increasing anxiety and depression.

Treatment Possibilities

Treating homeless individuals with a dual diagnosis is extremely difficult. As Craig and Timms (2000) pointed out, homeless people with mental illness are far less likely than homeless people without mental illness to make use of general medical or psychiatric services. They tend to search for help only during a crisis. Craig and Timms also noted that because of their mental and physical illness, these individuals are particularly limited in their capacity to cope with many aspects of daily life. Many have lost their place of residence as a direct result of their illness, being evicted for failing to pay rent or neglecting or damaging property. The support provided by government assistance barely permits access to the absolute necessities of daily life.

There are also barriers within the social and health services systems. Physical health care is usually provided separately from mental health care, and substance abuse treatment, like basic housing and welfare support, is provided separately from either (Craig & Timms, 2000). The prejudice among service providers against homeless people is another barrier to treatment (Shiner & Leddington, 1991). Even if a homeless individual finds a receptive service provider, the emphasis on treatment does not address more immediate needs, such as food, shelter, and physical safety (Herman et al., 1993).

Drake et al. (1991) suggested that the following features are essential for successful treatment of the homeless individual with a dual diagnosis:

1. integrated treatment for substance abuse and mental illness
2. intensive case management
3. group treatment
4. inclusion of four phases of treatment: engagement, persuasion, active treatment, and relapse prevention
5. activities to enhance self-esteem, skill building, and group identity
6. cultural relevance to minorities, which are overrepresented in this group
7. longitudinal (rather than episodic) training
8. education for families regarding the individual's mental illness

There have been several recent studies on treatment outcomes. Despite the different efficacy rates of these studies, most seem to suggest that long-term care is more successful than short-term intervention and that providing continuing support is essential (Craig & Timms, 2000). In addition to duration of treatment, several other factors can contribute to a more successful treatment outcome. A study by Meisler, Blankertz, Santos, and McKay (1997) suggests that the severity of substance use is a stronger predictor of outcomes than the length of treatment. They evaluated the impact of an integrated assertive community treatment program, noting a high retention rate in treatment, housing stability, and community tenure for all but the most severe substance users. The intervention seemed to be effective in terms of treating and monitoring this dually diagnosed sample, but it did not yield high rates of abstinence and social benefits in severe users. The authors identified several limitations of the study. It was based upon case managers' ratings of substance abuse, some information might have been overlooked, and critical life events might have gone unrecorded.

Blankertz and Cnaan (1993) reported the outcomes of a 3-year federally funded demonstration project in which they compared the effectiveness of the experimental intervention with that of another program for dually diagnosed homeless individuals. The experimental program was found to be significantly more successful than the comparison program; in the experimental program, 15 out of 84 clients stayed 60 days or longer in treatment, thus graduating successfully from the program. This rate of graduation was four times higher than that of the comparison group. The authors found that client characteristics did not account for positive program outcomes as much as did key interventions such as establishing a trusting relationship; providing clients with warm, nurturing treatment; giving clients a set daily structure; setting limits; using positive reinforcement; developing self-esteem; using crisis prevention and intervention; and using a holistic orientation that deals with the client's whole person. The authors suggested that interventions with dually diagnosed homeless individuals should focus on a structured group residential environment based on a psychological rehabilitation model that encourages clients to develop the internal controls necessary for successful independent living.

Rahav, Nuttbrock, Rivera, and Ng-Mak (1997), in a study of treatment recruitment among 1,924 homeless, mentally ill, chemical-abusing men who looked for community-based treatment in New York City between 1991 and 1996, found that personality characteristics affected treatment recruitment, with staff favoring prospective clients who were more compliant. Of the total 1,924 men, 826 were recruited for treatment after completing a prescreening interview; for several reasons, the remaining 1,098 men were never interviewed. The authors found that men at high risk for rejection by the treatment programs tended to be older, White, not likely to have a mood disorder, likely to have a cognitive disorder, and likely to have a severe psychiatric impairment, along with alcohol abuse. Several other factors also seemed to appear frequently among the individuals who were rejected from the program: a low level of education; a diagnosis of schizophrenia; a history of disruptive, assaulting, violent behavior; a history of criminality; and no history of shelter use. Instead, the treatment staff were looking for outgoing clients who were likely to be compliant; frequently, these were depressed and suicidal clients with no violent personality background. The results showed that certain personality characteristics seem to contribute to the staff decision about treatment rejection or acceptance.

Street Youth and Substance Abuse

Homeless youth belong to a growing subgroup at high risk for medical problems. Substance abuse among them is likely to be comorbid with the HIV virus and other sexually transmitted diseases, psychotic behavior, depression, suicide attempts, prostitution, and trauma (Ringwalt, Greene, Robertson, & McPheeters, 1998). As Ringwalt et al. noted, many homeless youth have multiple problems and are struggling to meet basic needs because of a lack of appropriate services and limited access to housing, education, medical and mental health services, and social welfare programs.

Prevalence and Etiology

The incidence of homelessness among youth has been estimated to be as high as 2 million (Council on Scientific Affairs, 1989); estimates of how many street youth use substances are even more vague, but substance abuse is assumed to be widespread.

Ringwalt et al. (1998) examined the 12-month incidence of homelessness in a sample of 6,496 adolescents. Between 1992 and 1993, adolescents age 12 to 17 were interviewed within a representative household sample about whether they had spent the night in any of a variety of locations other than home during the previous 12 months. The results showed that about 7.6% of these individuals reported having spent at least one night away from home in that period of time: in a shelter, in a public place, in an abandoned building, outside in a park or on the street, under a bridge or similar, in a subway, with a stranger who gave them a place to stay overnight, or in a car or similar place. Boys were much more likely to report a homeless episode than girls. Otherwise, the prevalence of homelessness varied little on the basis of sociodemographic or geographical factors. The most frequently reported place to stay during the homeless episode was a youth or adolescent shelter. The authors limited their conclusions because they assumed that a proportion of the youth misunderstood the term *shelter*. Therefore, they changed their estimate to from 7.6% to 5%, which they still considered a surprisingly high number. Further weaknesses of the study, the authors pointed out, were the exclusion of youth staying in single-room occupancy hotels or other group quarters. This population is assumed to have more experience with homelessness. Currently homeless youth with longer periods of homelessness were also underrepresented.

Wyman (1997) discussed in a *NIDA Notes* article a study of 432 homeless youth in Los Angeles, 71% of whom had an alcohol or drug abuse disorder at the time of the survey. She also mentioned a nationwide study of 600 homeless youth in which 50% of those who had tried to kill themselves said that alcohol and drug use led them to their suicide attempt.

In an analysis of three national surveys, Greene, Ennett, and Ringwalt (1997) compared the prevalence of substance use by runaway and homeless youth between the ages of 12 and 21 years across settings (street vs. shelter) and with youth of the general population. They found that homeless and runaway youth used tobacco, alcohol, and especially illicit drugs to a much higher extent than the general population. The risk of substance use by the homeless youth varied depending on current living circumstances. Street youth had a higher prevalence than shelter youth and youth who were currently living at home. Street youth were also involved in more serious drug use than the other two groups. The drug abuse rates were higher among older than younger youth, among males than females, and among Whites than African Americans, in both the shelter and the street survey. About 75% of the street youth consumed marijuana; 33% used hallucinogens, analgesics, and stimulants; and 25% used crack or consumed other forms of cocaine, inhalants, and sedatives. One limitation of the study was the use of the different reference periods, which were much longer for the household surveys than for the street and shelter surveys. Additionally, the mode of administration differed across the surveys; shelter surveys were interviewer-administered, whereas household surveys were self-administered.

Ennett, Bailey, and Federman (1999) examined the social network characteristics associated with risky behavior among 166 runaway and homeless youth and found that most of the youths interviewed reported having current social relationships, but 26% did not. This significant minority was more likely to report illicit drug use, multiple sex partners, and survival sex. These results suggest that a lack of social relationships contributes to risky behavior such as substance abuse.

Communities with higher levels of homelessness have areas of high drug activity such as the sale and use of drugs and increased high school dropout rates (Freisthler, Lascala, Gruenewald, & Treno, 2005). Low school attendance and lack of academic success are frequent problems in communities with low-income areas and significant minority populations; these factors, in turn, contribute to homelessness in youth (Freisthler et al., 2005; Luthar & Ansary, 2005).

Baron (1999) identified several important factors that increase the risk of youth substance use:

1. Exposure to parental substance abuse is related to an increased risk of using hard drugs.
2. Physical abuse is related to later use of psychedelic drugs.
3. Long-term homelessness is likely to lead to the use of hard drugs.
4. The use of alcohol, marijuana, and psychedelic drugs is increased by exposure to alcohol- and drug-using peers.
5. Property crime history is related to the use of alcohol and hard drugs.
6. Drug distribution is associated with a higher rate of the use of soft drugs.
7. Job difficulties and depression are linked to the use of alcohol and hard drugs.
8. Alcohol use is associated with self-blame.

Consequences of Adolescent Homelessness and Treatment Requirements

For homeless youth, critical life events do not necessarily begin after the adolescent runs away or is pushed out of the home. In fact, an unpublished study by Robertson (cited in Sherman, 1992) conducted at the Alcoholic Research Group in Berkeley, California, in 1989, indicated that 39% of homeless adolescents had experienced sexual abuse, 44% had run away from another long-term crisis such as substance-abusing parents, and 20% had fled from short-term crisis (e.g., divorce, sickness, or school problems).

Once adolescents are on the street, victimization continues. As Kurtz, Jarvis, and Kurtz (1991) noted, depression, low self-esteem, alcohol/drug abuse, antisocial behavior, crime-related problems with law enforcement, survival sex, prostitution, pregnancy, and sexually transmitted diseases are only some of the consequences homeless adolescents face. Further, homeless children and adolescents are likely to drop out of school because of low achievement or because of the lack of acceptable clothing (Linehan, 1992). Reganick (1997) summarized factors that predispose children and adolescents to chronic homelessness as follows: (a) poor physical conditions, such as poor nutrition, hunger, and a lack of access to health care; (b) socially unacceptable behavioral characteristics developed in response to the demands of street survival; (c) inadequate social skills; (d) psychological devastation (e.g., anxiety, anger, depression, low self-esteem); and (e) delayed cognitive and motor skills due to environmental deprivation.

Unger, Kipke, Simon, Montgomery, and Johnson (1997) examined the prevalence of symptoms of depression, low self-esteem, attention-deficit/hyperactivity disorder, suicidal impulses, self-injurious behavior, and drug and alcohol use disorder in 432 homeless juveniles in Los Angeles between 12 and 23 years of age. They found extremely high rates of mental health problems that differed by age and ethnicity. African Americans were at lower risk for suicide. Depressive symptoms were more prevalent among older respondents and females, and younger homeless youth were at higher risk for self-injurious behavior. A previous history of sexual assault or abuse was associated with suicidal thoughts and self-injurious behavior. The authors mentioned several limitations of this study: Its cross-sectionalism did not allow establishing causal relationships between the factors. Also, the data were gathered by means of self-report, which may be subject to reporting bias. Finally, the Hollywood area, where the sample was from, is not necessarily representative of other areas of the United States.

Providing services for homeless adolescents is difficult in part because they often merge with other youth on the streets. They seem to be "invisible." Furthermore, in many cases their past living experiences have led to a basic distrust of and skepticism toward adults and society in general. Providing continuing assistance that is flexible enough to adapt to individual needs and that can offer understanding and forgiving support to the child or adolescent is essential (Reganick, 1997). At first, basic needs such as food, clothing, and shelter must be met; then, intensive home-based intervention, intermediate, or long-term residential care should be provided (Kurtz et al., 1991). Homeless youth are a heterogeneous group. Kipke, Unger, O'Conner, Palmer, and LaFrance (1997) identified several subgroups: "punks/skinheads," "gang members," "druggies," "loners," and "hustlers"; each subgroup has a different norm, value, and belief system.

As Kipke et al. suggested, the most important intervention might be to link homeless youth to needed services and nonstreet peer groups to enhance prosocial behavior and prevent them from becoming completely integrated into the street subculture.

Besides providing services that cover basic physical needs, it is necessary to address mental health problems in order to improve the homeless youth's ability to find permanent shelter, reconnect with school, find employment, or reestablish contact with family members. It is important to treat mental health problems because these are associated with (a) high-risk behavior such as unprotected sex, which in turn increases the risk of HIV infection, and (b) injectable drug use, drug dealing, and prostitution, which in turn increase the likelihood of violence, victimization, and criminal prosecution (Kipke et al., 1997). Treatment compliance is another big problem for this population. Nontraditional mental health service such as informal drop-in centers allow youth to make contact with youth mental health care staff without being stigmatized. Service providers should encourage these youth to express their emotions through art, drama, or poetry; training youth to be peer counselors might also result in more compliance than is seen with traditional therapy and medication (Kipke et al., 1997).

Because of the high risk of HIV infection, it is necessary to provide prevention education for runaway and homeless youth. In a study of a teen outreach program in which peer educators were matched with adult outreach staff, Podschun (1993) found that it is very useful to identify natural leaders with the same ethnic, cultural, and sexual backgrounds as their clients, and then provide education and skill development. By combining this outreach program with basic-needs service programs that offer food, clothing, and shelter, immediate and concrete support can be provided.

Homeless Women and Families

Since the rapid increase of homelessness in the 1980s, the number of homeless women and families has risen steadily, currently between 500,000 and 600,000. Women are much more likely than men to be accompanied by children, while men are more likely to be single.

Women, Family Dynamics, and Homelessness

The Interagency Council on the Homeless (1994) found that 80% of U.S. homeless households with children were headed by single mothers, whereas 98% to 99% of homeless males lived by themselves, although a majority of them had children. Metraux and Culhane (1999) observed that women are more likely than men to stay in emergency shelter facilities rather than on the street, in vacant buildings, or in encampments. On the street, women are more likely to be exposed to physical and sexual violence, and when they are accompanied by children, they have great difficulties caring for them under street conditions. However, when homeless mothers access services, they face the threat of losing their children to foster care placements. In general, three major types of programs are available for homeless families: emergency shelters designed to provide temporary shelter, facilities offering mental health services, and transitional living programs that provide housing for several months (McChesney, 1990).

In a large sample of homeless women from New York City, Metraux and Culhane (1999) identified three subgroups who were at especially high risk for extended periods of homelessness: (a) younger women who had recently given birth, (b) women who reported a history of domestic violence in their households, and (c) women whose children did not stay with them or who were taken from their mother's household during the time the women were in the shelter and placed in foster care or in informal placements. For the first and second groups, difficult financial and social conditions lead them into homelessness; for the third group, the reasons for homelessness are only poorly understood.

Wenzel, Koegel, and Gelberg (2000) found that compared to their housed counterparts, homeless women face much greater health risks, including physical and sexual victimization. Mental disorders, substance dependence, and engagement in high-risk economic survival strategies were the factors that most strongly predicted homeless women's victimization, especially sexual harassment. The authors suggested that alcohol- and drug-dependent homeless women are at high risk because they are exposed to dangerous environments that render them prone to assault. Further, a homeless woman is more likely to be assaulted by a person she knows than by a stranger. Wenzel et al. made several suggestions for ameliorating these conditions. Safer living conditions must be provided for homeless women in order to prevent victimization as much as possible. Furthermore, support must be given for establishing safe and permanent housing. Continuing assessment and ongoing intervention in order to treat mental health and substance abuse, including educational and vocational training, are necessary to protect homeless women from victimization and to end their homelessness.

Treatment Outcomes for Substance-Abusing Homeless Mothers

Research on treatment outcomes for substance-abusing men far exceeds the available research on women. Hardly anything is known about the effectiveness of programs that address substance abuse in women. Research on treatment in other fields suggests that women's treatment needs differ from those of their male counterparts.

In one of the few studies that address this issue, Smith, North, and Fox (1995) conducted an 18-month follow-up on 149 homeless substance-abusing mothers and children who had participated in a treatment program. They were divided in two groups—a residential group (women who lived at the center) and a nonresidential group (women who attended the center only during the day). The effectiveness of these groups was compared. The most significant finding was the low participation and retention rates: 15% did not show up for treatment at all, and 85% of those who started treatment dropped put. The authors, though, did not find this outcome remarkable; it just confirms the rates of other studies. Nevertheless, there were also some encouraging results: Women in the residential as well as in the nonresidential treatment program improved in drug use and housing stability in spite of their length of stay in the program. The fact that these women were actively seeking help, the authors noted, in itself may have contributed to recovery, regardless of any formal treatment. It is also possible that the women reduced their drug use and increased their functioning after just brief exposure to the treatment. Another interesting finding was that the residential group had a lower dropout rate than the nonresidential group, suggesting that women whose need for housing is met during substance abuse treatment may experience better outcomes.

One limitation of the study is that all the participants were African American, which might affect generalizability to other groups. Additionally, the high no-show and dropout rates resulted in a small number of participating individuals. Outcomes might have been substantially different with a larger sample.

Comfort, Shipley, White, and Shandler (1990) described a pilot study in which the characteristics, attitudes, and treatment of a sample of substance-abusing women were examined. The study was set up by the Diagnostic and Rehabilitation Center (DRC) with the main goal of providing services for substance abuse recovery. The DRC first focused on meeting the basic needs of the clients, such as food, clothing, and medical care. The DRC then began substance abuse therapy with an emphasis on achieving and maintaining sobriety. Data was collected from 66 homeless poly-drug-addicted women that were enrolled in various DRC programs. The most frequently used substances among these women, who were mostly Black and unmarried, were alcohol, marijuana, and cocaine. For many of the clients, negative affective reactions were associated with drug and alcohol use. The majority reported abuse during childhood. Despite their current situation, most clients reported strong support from relatives, such as their mother, siblings, or children. However, the authors suggested that this finding could be the result of idealization as opposed to being a realistic assessment of family support. According to DRC staff, the cocaine-addicted clients had less stable living situations and were more likely to drop out of treatment than the clients who abused alcohol. The center seemed to frighten them, and they experienced uneasiness in dealing with their children in that setting. In general, the women reported two primary family concerns: the need for a safe place to live independently with their children and the need to develop close relationships with their children.

These studies on substance-abusing homeless women indicate that they need a transitional residence where they can feel safe with their children before substance abuse is addressed. Treatment of homeless women with chemical dependency is complex.

Tucker et al. (2005) surveyed 402 women living in temporary shelters in Los Angeles. They found that these women had multiple problems, including depression, high-risk sexual behavior (and thus high risk for HIV), alcohol abuse, and use of marijuana and crack. Further, the authors observed that the women had low social support, low self-esteem, poor coping skills, and avoidant behavior. Tucker et al. suggested that treatment should focus on multiple psychological, relational, and social issues. The goals of treatment should include decreasing risky behavior, substance abuse, and unemployment.

Homeless Veterans

According to a national survey of homeless individuals (Interagency Council on the Homeless and the Urban Institute, 1999), homeless military veterans comprise about

23% of the homeless population in the United States. A large proportion of them belongs to the group of Vietnam veterans who are now in their 50s and 60s.

Special Problems of Homeless Veterans

Many combat veterans suffer from PTSD, schizophrenia, affective disorders, and substance abuse disorders. Compared to the general homeless population, more homeless veterans tend to be White and non-Hispanic, with a better education, and with higher premorbid functioning levels (Douyon, Guzman, Romain, & Ireland, 1998). The relationship between military service and homelessness is clear. Possible reasons include physical injury, mental illness caused by war-related trauma, and substance abuse that was exacerbated during combat exposure. Douyon et al. (1998) observed that programs targeting this population have had low success rates; a majority of homeless veterans remain on the street.

A U.S. Department of Health and Human Services study conducted by Winkleby and Fleshin (1993) compared the prevalence of physical, addictive, and psychiatric disorders between homeless veterans and nonveterans. These authors did not find significant differences for adverse childhood events between these two groups, but the prevalence of physical and mental disorders combined with alcohol use was higher among the veterans, especially among combat veterans. In general, more veterans than nonveterans reported excessive alcohol consumption before they became homeless. The combat veterans' prevalence for psychiatric hospitalizations and physical injuries was higher than among noncombat veterans and nonveterans. Lower education level was not a factor; the combat veterans were actually the most highly educated group. The nonveterans reported more use of illegal drugs than the veterans, but this finding was not significant. The authors also found that 76% of the combat veterans and 50% of the noncombat veterans lost their home more than a decade after leaving military service. Given the time lag, it might be the case that their homelessness and physical, mental, and substance-related problems are not related to their military service. However, as the authors noted, studies of Vietnam veterans indicate that posttraumatic stress can have a delayed onset and might not lead to homelessness until it becomes serious enough to affect the individual's functioning within the family and at work. The onset of (or increase in) posttraumatic stress might also lead to an increased intake of substances, which further increases the risk of homelessness.

Winkleby and Fleshin (1993) noted several limitations to their study. The cross-sectional design of the study did not allow for a conclusion about the possible causality between military service and medical disorders. Additionally, the sample included only homeless men who sought shelter at armories during the winter; the findings might have been different if the study had included individuals from other settings. Another important limitation was that the assessment of psychiatric hospitalization did not distinguish between hospitalization for substance-related problems and psychiatric problems. Nevertheless, the analysis did show important differences between homeless veterans and the nonmilitary homeless population.

A number of other studies have indicated special problems among homeless veterans. For example, Douyon et al. (1998) found higher levels of hostility, prior criminal activity, and a family history of psychiatric illness in homeless veterans than in nonhomeless veterans. The authors also discovered more neurological impairments among acutely and chronically homeless veterans than among their nonhomeless counterparts. It is likely that these neurological deficits predated the veterans' homelessness and might have caused the homelessness in the first place. M. T. Lambert and Fowler (1997) reported an increased risk for suicide among homeless veterans, citing various contributing factors such as the presence of mental illness, poor physical health, substance abuse, and poor social/psychological support (e.g., absence of family and marital support or a stable shelter).

These studies all offer evidence of the severe problems that homeless veterans face. To the present day, efforts to alleviate homelessness have been shown to have only limited success. The following sections discuss possible treatment options.

Treatment Requirements

What better way to find out about treatment requirements than to ask the homeless veterans themselves about their needs? Applewhite (1997) analyzed the nature and scope of homelessness and the issue of service use by interviewing 60 male veterans between 25 and 68 years of age regarding what they consider to be the major problems and barriers homeless veterans have to confront when seeking social services. The veterans reported among other things a lack of respect by service personnel, service-based labeling, degrading comments, and put-downs. The veterans also reported negative policies. For example, the bureaucratic procedures of the service delivery system seemed to be designed to delay or even prevent veterans from obtaining help. Instead of meeting the needs of its clients, the system was designed to support its own bureaucratic requirements. The system offered complicated programs with limited resources, had inadequate staffing, and had inadequate funding. Applewhite made the following suggestions for improving the service delivery system:

- Provide programs that deal with the specific problems that veterans have, such as war-related PTSD, readjustment problems, feelings of victimization, and unmet expectations about war service recognition by the public.
- Provide community-based services as a primary resource in order to reintegrate veterans into society. A comprehensive multidisciplinary network service system combined with public entitlements, along with coordinated case management, has been shown to be effective, as well as on-site shelter services that work with individuals and families to secure long- and short-term services.
- Provide mental health intervention through the Veterans Administration (VA). VA medical centers and mental health programs have been shown to be a good way to end homelessness.
- Provide social service systems that are not overly bureaucratic but that focus on clients' basic needs, stabilization needs, emergency needs, change-oriented needs, economic needs, and educational needs. A special issue to be addressed is the feeling of powerlessness often experienced by homeless veterans. Empowerment-centered practice can be an effective way to develop personal and interpersonal power within the individual.

A comprehensive program network that addresses issues specific to homeless veterans is needed in order to break the cycle of homelessness in that population. The small sample size and the fact that only males were interviewed might limit the generalization of Applewhite's (1997) study for all homeless veterans. However, the study's interview approach yields important insight into the needs and concerns of this population.

General Treatment Efficacy for Substance Abuse in the Homeless Population

Substance abuse treatment is particularly difficult with homeless individuals because before they can even think about alcohol or drug treatment, they face a more basic need: housing. It is, therefore, hard to recruit substance-abusing homeless individuals into treatment in the first place and then to prevent them from dropping out once they are in treatment. Long-term success is even more difficult to achieve. Some treatment approaches have been shown to be more effective than others, especially those that address basic needs such as shelter, safety, food, medical care, and clothing.

Sosin, Bruni, and Reidy (1995) examined the effectiveness of the Progressive Independence Model, which focuses on offering immediate resources as well as providing additional treatment for abuse and other relevant personal and situational problems of the homeless client. The results showed both a reduction in substance abuse and an increase in housing stability. The authors concluded that providing tangible resources, as well as providing further treatment for abuse, other personal problems, and long-term financial needs, accounted for the positive outcomes.

Braucht et al. (1995) looked at the effectiveness of comprehensive services, including residential treatment and addiction counseling. The participants made significant improvement not only in regard to their alcohol and drug intake but also in regard to their housing status, physical and mental health, employment rate, and quality of life. These positive results, however, diminished over time, which suggests that continuing care is critical.

Schumacher et al. (1995) noted the importance of comprehensiveness and intensiveness of outpatient programs, observing that treatment of addictions, especially crack cocaine addictions, should be multifaceted. Psychoeducation, urine testing, and relapse prevention, as well as individual, family, and group counseling, should be included. The authors found that reduction of substance abuse and homelessness was more likely to occur in individuals who received intensive treatment (4.1 days per week) than in clients who attended treatment for less than 1 day a week. More attendance yielded a better long-term outcome. Schumacher et al. noted several limitations to their study. Since subjects were not randomly assigned to the two treatment groups, there was possible selection bias. Also, the study was driven by a post hoc hypothesis, which further limited the conclusions. Still, this study provides additional support for comprehensive and intensive treatment programs.

Milby et al. (2004) compared treatment models for cocaine-abusing homeless persons in a large health-care agency that serves homeless individuals in Birmingham,

Alabama. The participants were in a day treatment program. Milby et al. compared day treatment only (DT; $n = 69$) with day treatment plus abstinence-contingent housing and work (DT+; $n = 72$). Participants in the DT+ group "established abstinence, maintained abstinence for longer duration, were marginally significantly more likely to lapse, and significantly less likely to relapse" (p. 250). The DT+ participants relapsed later and were more like to reestablish abstinence than those who relapsed in the DT group.

Stahler (1995) noted that the following points should be considered in the treatment of substance-abusing homeless individuals:

- Treatment needs to address the basic needs of the client and should not focus exclusively on addiction.
- Dropout, often caused by low client motivation, might be reduced by providing low-demand interventions.
- Because treatment success seems to diminish over time, long-term, continuous care focused not only on relapse prevention but also on food, clothing, housing, employment, and other needs should be considered as a treatment component.
- Certain subgroups among homeless substance abusers seem to have better outcomes than others. The higher the education, the less severe the substance use, the less criminal involvement, and the less socially isolated the individual, the better the treatment prognosis.

Conclusion

Homelessness is a complex and challenging problem. A way to end or even to reduce this problem has yet to be found. The rate of substance abuse among the homeless population is high, and treatment effectiveness is limited due to the presence of other problems, mainly, the lack of shelter, food, and clothing. Additionally, the high prevalence of mental illness, lack of physical health, unemployment, legal problems, victimization, social isolation, and chronic poverty limits the chance of long-term treatment success. Service providers also have to consider the heterogeneity of the homeless population and to address the multiplicity of factors that aggravate and interact with substance abuse in order to assist these individuals in breaking the cycle of homelessness and substance abuse.

References

Applewhite, S. L. (1997). Homeless veterans: Perspectives on social service use. *Social Work, 42*(1), 19–30.

Baron, S. W. (1999). Street youth and substance abuse. *Youth and Society, 31*(1), 3–26.

Berlin, G., & McAllister, W. (1992). Homelessness: Why nothing has worked—and what will. *The Brookings Review, 10*(4), 12.

Blankertz, L. E., & Cnaan, R. A. (1993). Serving the dually diagnosed homeless: Program development and interventions. *Journal of Mental Health Administration, 20*(2), 100.

Bogue, D. (1963). *Skid row in American cities*. Chicago: University of Chicago Press.

Braucht, G. N., Reichardt, C. S., Geissler, L. J., Bormann, C. A., Kwiatkowski, C. F., & Kirby, M. W., Jr. (1995). Effective services for homeless substance abusers. *Journal of Addictive Diseases, 14*(4), 87–109.

Briere, J. N. (1992). *Child abuse trauma*. Newbury Park, CA: Sage.

Brunette, M., & Drake, R. E. (1998). Gender differences in homeless persons with schizophrenia and substance abuse. *Community Mental Health Journal, 34*(6), 627–642.

Caton, C. L. M., Hasin, D., Shrout, P. E., & Opler, L. A. (2000). Risk factors for homelessness among indigent urban adults with no history of psychotic illness: A case-control study. *American Journal of Public Health, 90*(2), 258–263.

Cohen, A., & Koegel, P. (1996). The influence of alcohol and drug use on the subsistence adaptation of homeless mentally ill persons. *Journal of Drug Issues, 26*, 219–243.

Cohen, D. C., & Krating, M. A. (1993). Characteristics of homeless alcohol and drug abusers identified through an assertive outreach program. *Journal of Social Distress and the Homeless, 2*(3), 193–205.

Cohen, E., & Stahler, G. J. (1998). Life histories of crack-using African-American homeless men: Salient themes. *Contemporary Drug Problems, 25*(2), 373–397.

Comfort, M., Shipley, T. E., Jr., White, K., Griffith, E. M., & Shandler, I. W. (1990). Family treatment for homeless alcohol/drug-addicted women and their preschool children. *Alcoholism and drug abuse among the homeless men and women* (pp. 129–147). New York: Haworth Press.

Council on Scientific Affairs. (1989). Health care needs of homeless and runaway youth. *Journal of the American Medical Association, 262*, 1358–1361.

Craig, T., & Timms, P. (2000). Facing up to social exclusion: Services for homeless mentally ill people. *International Review of Psychiatry, 12*(3), 206–211.

Douyon, R., Guzman, P., Romain, G., & Ireland, S. J. (1998). Subtle neurological deficits and psychopathological findings in substance-abusing homeless and nonhomeless veterans. *Journal of Neuropsychiatry and Clinical Neuroscience, 10*(2), 210.

Drake, R. E., & Mueser, K. T. (1996). Homelessness and dual diagnosis. *Alcohol Health and Research World, 20*(2), 90–91.

Drake, R. E., Osher, F. C., & Wallach, M. A. (1991). Homelessness and dual diagnosis. *American Psychologist, 46*(11), 1149–1175.

Ennett, S. T., Bailey, S. L., & Federman, E. B. (1999). Social network characteristics associated with risky behaviors among runaway and homeless youth. *Journal of Health and Social Behavior, 40*(1), 63–78.

Fisher, P. J. (1989). Estimating the prevalence of alcohol, drug, and mental health problems in the contemporary homeless population. *Contemporary Drug Problems, 16*, 333–389.

Fisher, P. J. (1990). *Alcohol and drug abuse and mental health problems among homeless persons: A review of literature, 1980–1990*. Rockville, MD: National Institute on Alcohol Abuse and Alcoholism and National Institute of Mental Health.

Fisher, P. J., & Breakey, W. J. (1987). Profile of the Baltimore homeless with alcohol problems. *Alcohol Health Research World, 11*, 36–37.

Freisthler, B., Lascala, E. A., Gruenewald, P. J., & Treno, A. J. (2005). An examination of drug activity: Effects of neighborhood social organizations on the development of drug distribution systems. *Substance Use and Misuse, 40*, 671–686.

Gordon, A. J., McGinnis, K. A., Conigliaro, J., Rodriguez-Barradas, M. C., Rabeneck, L., & Justice, A. C. (2006). Associations between alcohol use and homelessness with healthcare utilization among human immunodeficiency virus-infected veterans. *Medical Care, 44*(8), 37–43.

Greene, J. M., Ennett, S. T., & Ringwalt, C. L. (1997). Substance use among runaway and homeless youth in three national samples. *American Journal of Public Health, 87*(2), 229–235.

Harris, S. N., Mowbray, C. T., & Solarz, A. (1994). Physical health, mental health, and substance abuse problems of shelter users. *Health and Social Work, 19*(1), 37.

Heilemann, M. V., Kury, F. S., & Lee, K. A. (2005). Trauma and posttraumatic stress disorder symptoms among low income women of Mexican decent in the United States. *Journal of Nervous and Mental Disease, 193*(10), 665–672.

Herman, D. B., Struening, E. L., et al. (1993). Self-assessed need for mental health services among homeless adults. *Hospital and Community Psychiatry, 44,* 1181–1183.

Herman, D. B., Susser, E. S., Struening, E. L., & Link, B. L. (1997). Adverse childhood experiences: Are they risk factors for adult homelessness? *American Journal of Public Health, 87*(2), 249–255.

Hombs, M. E. (1990). *Contemporary world issues: American homelessness.* Santa Barbara, CA: ABC-CLIO.

Institute of Medicine. (1988). *Homelessness, health and human needs.* Washington, DC: National Academy Press.

Interagency Council on the Homeless. (1994). *Priority home: The federal plan to break the cycle of homelessness.* Washington, DC: U.S. Department of Housing and Urban Development.

Interagency Council on the Homeless and the Urban Institute. (1999). *Homelessness: Programs and the people they serve.* Office of Policy Development and Research, U.S. Department of Housing and Development. Retrieved February 8, 2010, from http://www.huduser.org/portal/publications/homeless/homelessness/contents.html

Kilpatrick, D. G., Ruggiero, K. J., Acierno, R., Saunders, B. E., Resnick, H. S., & Best, C. L. (2003). Violence and risk of PTSD, major depression, substance abuse/dependence, and comorbidity: Results from the National Survey of Adolescents. *Journal of Consulting and Clinical Psychology, 71*(4), 692–700.

Kipke, M. D., Unger, J. B., O'Conner, S., Palmer, R. F., & LaFrance, S. R. (1997). Street youth, their peer group affiliation and differences according to residential status, subsistence patterns, and use of services. *Adolescence, 32*(127), 655–669.

Koegel, P., Burnam, M. A., & Farr, R. K. (1990). Subsistence adaptation among homeless adults in the inner-city of Los Angeles. *Journal of Social Issues, 46,* 83–107.

Kurtz, D. P., Jarvis, S. V., & Kurtz, G. L. (1991). Problems of homeless youths: Empirical findings and human services issues. *Social Work, 36*(4), 309–314.

Lambert, E. Y., & Caces, M. F. (1995). Correlates of drug abuse among homeless and transient people in Washington, DC, metropolitan area in 1991. *Public Health Reports, 110*(4), 455.

Lambert, M. T., & Fowler, D. R. (1997). Suicide risk factors among veterans: Risk management in the changing culture of the Department of Veteran Affairs. *Journal of Mental Health Administration, 24*(3), 350–358.

Lee, D., Ross, M. W., Mizwa, M., & Scott, D. P. (2000). HIV risk in a homeless population. *International Journal of STD and AIDS, 11*(8), 509.

Linehan, M. F. (1992). Children who are homeless. Educational strategies for school personnel. *Phi Delta Kappan, 74,* 61–66.

Link, B., Phelen, J., Bresnahan, M., Steuve, A., Moore, R., & Susser, E. (1995). Lifetime and 5-year prevalence of homelessness in the United States: New evidence on an old debate. *American Journal of Orthopsychiatry, 65*(3), 347–354.

Link, B., Susser, E., Stueve, A., Phelan, J., Moore, R., & Stuening, E. (1994). Lifetime and 5-year prevalence of homelessness in the United States. *American Journal of Public Health, 84,* 1907–1912.

Lown, E. A., Schmidt, L. A., & Wiley, J. (2006). Interpersonal violence among women seeking welfare: Unraveling lives. *American Journal of Public Heath, 96*(8), 1409–1415.

Luthar, S. S., & Ansary, N. S. (2005). Dimensions of adolescent rebellion: Risks for academic failure among high- and low-income youth. *Development and Psychopathology, 17*(1), 231–250.

McCarty, D., Argeriou, M., Huebner, R. B., & Lubran, B. (1991). Alcoholism, drug abuse, and the homeless. *American Psychologist, 46*(11), 1139–1148.

McChesney, K. Y. (1990). Family homelessness: A systemic problem. *Journal of Social Issues, 46*(4), 191–205.

Meisler, N., Blankertz, L., Santos, A. B., & McKay, C. (1997). Impact of assertive community treatment on homeless persons with co-occurring severe psychiatric and substance use disorders. *Community Mental Health Journal, 33*(2), 113–122.

Metraux, S., & Culhane, D. P. (1999). Family dynamics, housing, and recurring homelessness among women in New York City homeless shelters. *Journal of Family Issues, 20*(3), 371–396.

Milburn, N. (1989). Drug abuse among the homeless. In J. Morneni (Ed.), *Homeless in the United States* (Vol. 2). Westport, CT: Greenwood Press.

Milby, J. B., Schumacher, J. E., Vuchinich, R. E., Wallace, D., Plant, M. A. Freedman, M. J., McNamara, C., & Ward, C. L. (2004). *Psychology of Addictive Behaviors, 18*(3), 250–256.

Morrissey, J. P., & Dennis, D. L. (1986). *NIMH-funded research concerning homeless mentally ill persons: Implications for policy and practice.* Washington, DC: U.S. Department of Health and Human Services.

Morrissey, J. P., & Levine, I. S. (1987). Researchers discuss latest findings, examine needs of homeless mentally ill persons. *Hospital and Community Psychiatry, 38,* 811–812.

Podschun, G. D. (1993). Teen peer outreach-street work project: HIV prevention education for runaway and homeless youth. *Public Health Report, 108,* 150–155.

Poleshuck, E. L., Giles, D. E., & Tu, X. (2006). Pain and depressive symptoms among financially disadvantaged women's health patients. *Journal of Women's Health, 15*(2), 182–193.

Rahav, M., Nuttbrock, C., Rivera, J. J., & Ng-Mak, D. (1997). Recruitment into treatment of homeless, mentally ill, chemical abusing men. *Journal of Drug Issues, 27*(2), 315–328.

Reganick, K. A. (1997). Prognosis for homeless children and adolescents. *Childhood Education, 73*(3), 133–135.

Regional Task Force on Homelessness. (1999, August). San Diego County's homeless profile. Retrieved July 7, 2008, from http://www.co.san-diego.ca.us/rtfh/profile.html

Ringwalt, C. L., Greene, J. M., Robertson, M., & McPheeters, M. (1998). The prevalence of homelessness among adolescents in the United States. *American Journal of Public Health, 88*(9), 1325–1329.

Rossi, P. H. (1990). The old homeless and the new homeless in historical perspective. *American Psychologist, 45*(8), 954–959.

Rossi, P. H., Fisher, G. A., & Willis, G. (1986). *The condition of the homeless of Chicago.* Amherst: University of Massachusetts Press.

Sachs-Ericsson, N., Wise, E., Debrody, C. P., & Paniucki, H. B. (1999). Health problems and service utilization in the homeless. *Journal of Health Care for the Poor and Undeserved, 10*(4), 443–452.

Schumacher, J. E., Milby, J B., Caldwell, E., Raczynski, J., Engle, M., Michael, M., & Carr, J. (1995). Treatment outcome as a function of treatment attendance with homeless persons abusing cocaine. In G. J. Stahler & B. Stimmel (Eds.), *The effectiveness of social interventions for homeless substance abusers* (pp. 73–85). New York: Haworth Press.

Scott, E. K., London, A. S., & Myers, N. A. (2002). Dangerous dependencies: The intersection of welfare reform and domestic violence. *Gender and Society, 16*(6), 878–897.

Sherman, D. J. (1992). The neglected health care needs of street youth. *Public Health Reports, 107,* 443–440.

Shiner, P., & Leddington, D. (1991, November 7). Sometimes it makes you frightened to go to hospital ... they treat you like dirt. *Health Service Journal,* pp. 21–24.

Shinn, M. B., & Gillespie, C. (1994). The role of housing and poverty in the origins of homelessness. *American Behavioral Scientist, 37,* 505–521.

Smith, E. M., North, C. S., & Fox, L. F. (1995). Eighteen-month follow-up data on a treatment program for homeless substance abusing mothers. In G. H. Stahler & B. Stimmel (Eds.), *The effectiveness of social interventions for homeless substance abusers* (pp. 57–72). New York: Haworth Press.

Somlai, A. M., Kelly, J. A., Wagstaff, D. A., & Whitson, D. P. (1998). Patterns, predictors, and situational contexts of HIV risk behaviors among homeless men and women. *Social Work, 43*(1), 7–20.

Sosin, M. R., Bruni, M., & Reidy, M. (1995). Paths and impacts in the progressive independence model: A homelessness and substance abuse intervention in Chicago. *Journal of Addictive Diseases, 14*(4), 1–20.

Stahler, O. J. (1995). Social interventions for homeless substance abusers: Evaluating treatment outcomes. In G. H. Stahler & B. Stimmel (Eds.), *The effectiveness of social interventions for homeless substance abusers* (pp. 174–198). New York: Haworth Press.

Stark, L. (1987, Spring). A century of alcohol and homelessness: Demographics and stereotypes. *Alcohol Health and Research World,* pp. 8–13.

Timmer, D. A., Eitzen, D. S., & Talley, K. D. (1994). *Paths to homelessness: Extreme poverty and the urban housing crisis.* Boulder, CO: Westview Press.

Torres, R. A., Mani, S., Altholz, J., & Brickner, R. W. (1990). Human immunodeficiency virus infection among homeless men in a New York City shelter. *Archives of Internal Medicine, 150,* 2030–2036.

Tucker, J. S., D'Amico, E. J., Wenzel, S. L., Golinelli, D., Elliott, M. N., & Williamson, S. (2005). A prospective study of risk and protective factors for substance use among impoverished women living in temporary shelter settings in Los Angeles County. *Drug and Alcohol Dependence, 80*(1), 35–43.

Unger, J. B., Kipke, M. D., Simon, T. R., Montgomery, S. B., & Johnson, C. J. (1997). Homeless youth and young adults in Los Angeles: Prevalence of mental health problems and the relationship between mental health and substance abuse disorders. *American Journal of Community Psychology, 25*(3), 371–394.

Wenzel, S. L., Koegel, P., & Gelberg, L. (2000). Antecedents of physical and sexual victimization among homeless women: A comparison to homeless men. *American Journal of Community Psychology, 28*(3), 367–390.

Winkleby, M. A., & Fleshin, D. (1993). Physical, addictive, and psychiatric disorders among homeless veterans and nonveterans. *Public Health Report, 108,* 30–36.

Wright, J. D., Rubin, B. A., & Devine, J. A. (1998). *Besides the golden door: Policy, politics and the homeless.* Hawthorne, NY: Aldine de Gruyter.

Wright, J. D., & Weber, E. (1987). *Homelessness and health.* New York: McGraw-Hill.

Wright, T. (2000). Resisting homelessness: Global, national, and local solutions. *Contemporary Sociology, 29*(1), 27–43.

Wyman, J. R. (1997). Drug abuse among homeless youth calls for focused outreach solutions. *NIDA Notes, 12*(3). Retrieved July 7, 2008, from http://www.drugabuse.gov/NIDA_Notes/NN97index.htmal

Young, T. (1989). Indigent alcoholics on skid row. In G. W. Lawson & A. W. Lawson (Eds.), *Alcoholism and substance abuse in special populations* (pp. 305–313). Austin, TX: PRO-ED.

CHAPTER 15

Chemical Dependency and Treatment With Professional Male Athletes

J. D. Friedman and Gary W. Lawson

It is no secret that some professional male athletes have substance abuse problems. No sport seems to be immune. Baseball, basketball, football, soccer, track, swimming, tennis, and even cycling and golf each has its share of individuals that have made headlines for some sort of substance abuse or related issue. But behind the stories reported in the media are the tragic lives of individuals and their families—and often teammates as well—suffering from the waste of potential and in some cases the loss of life resulting from the choices some professional athletes make in their use and abuse of mind- and body-altering substances. What makes this substance abuse behavior a mystery of interest to the public and the media is the large amounts money, power, and respect that are involved in decisions that seem to be so senseless. Why would an athlete risk millions of dollars and his career to use marijuana when he knows in advance he will be subject to a random urine screening?

Just as with other substance abusers, athletes have individual reasons and personal and family dynamics that propel them to self-destruct in such a manner. However, as a group, this population has some things that make it stand out from others. Athletes' talents, potential, and resources, as well as the public nature of their problems, all complicate the issue. It should be acknowledged here that women athletes also have problems with drugs. Although some of the issues are the same, there are major differences, primarily the much larger number of males in professional sports. As the chapter's title indicates, the present discussion focuses on male athletes. This chapter examines some of the factors involved, including the consequences for both individuals and society when much-admired athletes become substance abusers.

Drug use in professional sports is a problem that will not soon fade away; with this in mind, sports or clinical psychologists must have at least a rudimentary understanding of the subject from both a clinical and sociocultural perspective. Ultimately, what is typical for the icons of the sports culture may influence adolescent athletes who aspire to reach the same heights, and families everywhere can feel that impact. Research indicates that anabolic steroid use among adolescents and preteens has been on the rise (National Institute on Drug Abuse [NIDA], 2000), which is less surprising when seen in light of a separate finding that for 73% of boys, a career in professional sports was their most popular occupational choice (Stiles et al., 1999). A recent survey estimated that 219,500 teens use steroids annually, including a popular 17-year old whose suicide was linked with steroid abuse ("Designer Steroids," 2004).

The effects of drug abuse by professional athletes, like anyone else, also can damage athletes' families by fostering cycles of addiction. Research supports the contention that individuals raised in homes and families in which there is substance abuse or alcoholism are at higher risk for developing a substance abuse disorder. In a sad twist to his most recent arrest, a famous baseball player found himself in jail alongside his 19-year-old son, who was being held at the same facility following a probation violation stemming from a 2004 crack cocaine offense.

This chapter provides an overview of the drugs used, reasons for their use, and psycho-physiological effects these drugs produce. The etiology of drug abuse in professional sports is explored from a psychosocial perspective, and examples of modern professional athletes from the major sports—baseball, football, and basketball—are presented. Existing treatment and prevention models also are discussed.

Athletes from the major sports tend to dominate the interest of the American public, and focusing on this very public and increasingly influential demographic may shed light on a variety of concerns among athletes in general. Of course, the concerns of male athletes in the three major U.S. professional sports cannot be generalized to other populations. However, as Congress recognized, women in sports, student-athletes, and professionals in other sports (e.g., cyclists, weightlifters) unquestionably have specific issues related to substance abuse, an example being that steroid use among female athletes doubled from 1991 to 1996 (Melia, Pipe, & Greenberg, 1996). These areas are ripe for future research and elaboration.

Performance-Enhancing Drugs

Media interest about steroids and other performance-enhancing drugs, simmering throughout the 1990s, reached a tipping point in the spring of 2005, driving the issue all the way to the halls of the United States Congress on March 17. That day, the House Government Reform Committee conducted live televised hearings during which they queried baseball's top executives and players about the dangers of steroid use, Major League baseball's drug testing policies, and the negative psychosocial ramifications of steroid use among teens. Before the 109th Congress recessed, both the National Football League and the National Basketball Association came before the congressional panel, and a fourth hearing examined the use of steroids by female athletes (House Committee on Government Reform, 2005).

Issues of chemical abuse and dependency, and their consequences, are neither new nor disappearing from the lives of professional athletes, who reveal no specific genetic or biological predisposition to substance abuse. In ancient Greece, athletes were known to consume hallucinogenic mushrooms in attempts to improve their performance ("Use of Performance-Enhancing Drugs," n.d.), and in modern times it is easy to find similarly unbounded yearnings among athletes seeking success. The current era provides star professional athletes gargantuan salaries and nearly unlimited financial, political, and social opportunities. A top example is a New York Yankees All-Star player who earned a $25,705,118 salary in 2005, amounting to an average of $158,673 per game (New York Yankees, n.d.). The median income reported for professional athletes in 2004 was approximately $2.9 million, with minimum salaries of $300,000 and higher ("Major Professional Sports Leagues," n.d.). This income does not include the endorsements and the access afforded to people, places, and high-flying lifestyles well beyond the reach and scope of non-celebrities.

Male athletes typically enter professional sports via college, although exceptional baseball and more recently basketball players may begin their career immediately after high school. Most of these people have spent their entire lives involved in organized athletics and may have few life experiences outside the athletic playing fields. Their average career span is 3 to 4 years, with baseball being the exception at 4 to 5 years, and even a career of this length is akin to winning the lottery. "The reality is that fewer than one in 10,000 American boys become professional athletes" (Simons & Butow, 1997). Perhaps more telling, college basketball players participating in the final four of the NCAA annual tournament—who are often the very best collegiate athletes—still face odds of 250:1 against ever donning a professional uniform (Simons & Butow, 1997).

Given this context, the allure of finding a competitive edge—legal or otherwise—may be more seductive than ever. One study found that for adolescent boys dreaming of future athletic stardom, it is not the appeal of playing a sport for a living but instead the idea of its associated rewards—"money, enhancement of status, adoration, independence, and the admiration of women"—that grips them (Stiles, Gibbons, Sebben, & Wiley, 1999).

Anabolic Steroids

Anabolic steroids are derivatives of testosterone and were developed in the early part of the 20th century in an attempt to isolate the sex hormone's anabolic effects (tissue and muscle building) from its androgenic (masculinizing) effects (Goodman & Gilman, 1975). These steroids have been used in medicine beneficially to treat certain types of anemia and some neurodegenerative diseases like multiple sclerosis, and as a stimulating agent for sexual development in hypogonadal men (Goodman & Gilman, 1975). However, their medical benefit easily can be overshadowed by their abuse and dangers as performance-enhancing agents.

Anabolic steroids reportedly were bastardized during World War II by the Nazi Wehrmacht armies in order to increase aggressiveness (Wade, 1972). In the aftermath of that war, European athletes from Soviet-dominated East Germany began to use testosterone to boost strength and performance, catching the attention of Dr. John Ziegler in the 1950s. As the physician for the American national weightlifting team, Dr. Ziegler teamed with Ciba Pharmaceutical Company in 1958 to bring testosterone-enhancing steroids to the United States in the form of methandrostenolone (brand name, Dianabol). Drug testing was first introduced in Mexico City at the 1968 Olympic

Games, although steroids remained legal until 1990. That year, the United States Congress passed the Anabolic Steroid Control Act, which classified anabolic-androgenic steroids as Schedule III controlled substances, requiring a doctor's prescription for their use (Millman & Ross, 2003).

As a number of athletes have attested, the new law did not eradicate steroids from sports. While estimates of steroid use vary and research has not presented clear quantitative data about prevalence, many professional sports insiders believe the use of performance enhancing drugs is epidemic (Bahrke & Yesalis, 2002). This problem undoubtedly has been exacerbated by athletes' intense motivation to maintain or improve performance, increase their bodies' ability to rebound from fatigue and injury, and establish or prolong professional careers (Taylor, 1985). According to the National Collegiate Athletic Association (1997), approximately 17% of all athletes have used steroids, and among male football players the rate climbs to 30%.

Studies with animals show that use of anabolic steroids results in an increase in both total and lean body mass; their methods of effectiveness in humans continues to be researched. Haupt and Rovere (1984) reported in a review of the literature that using anabolic steroids results in increased strength when athletes engage in intensive weight training prior to a steroid regimen and then continue to lift weights while taking steroids.

Some athletes reportedly use another illegal substance, known as human growth hormone (HGH), to strengthen their bodies' supporting structure (e.g., bones, tendons, joints, ligaments) in response to steroid-induced weight gain. HGH is thought to strengthen joints and is legally prescribed by doctors to treat dwarfism. Untoward effects include changes in body structure, most typically in the form of protruding bone alignment and growth in the head, brow, and jaws.

Anabolic steroids can produce potentially harmful side effects, including liver cancer and hepatic peliosis (bleeding cysts), decreased libido, acne, salt retention, and elevated cholesterol levels; they can also stunt bone growth in children. Many steroid users prefer injection to oral intake because the former bypasses metabolic processes in the liver and diminishes risks of hepatic failures. In recent years, some athletes have begun to use scientifically advanced patches and gels to administer testosterone. Along with reduced risks for contracting HIV and hepatitis from shared needles, steroidal creams have an additional advantage of being harder to detect on drug tests. This is the case because they provide more stable levels of blood testosterone levels rather than a spike that typically follows injections (Bahrke & Yesalis, 2002).

When taken in large doses and with prolonged use, anabolic steroids can produce scarring acne and puffiness in the face and trunk, not to mention a heightened risk for cardiovascular disease. Major endocrine abnormalities can occur, such as decreased plasma testosterone, decreased luteinizing hormone, atrophy of the testes, and gynecomastia (growth of breasts in men). In addition, the androgenic effects of steroids can contribute to aggressive behavior by the individual, yielding in extreme cases bouts of explosiveness, colloquially known as "roid rage" (Pope & Katz, 1994). Users may experience significant mood swings, increased energy, sexual arousal, a lack of frustration tolerance, and paranoid ideation, and they also may manifest classic psychological withdrawal symptoms, such as major depression and even psychosis (Williamson & Young, 1992).

It is significant to note that most research on steroid use has focused on clinically and ethically acceptable doses, but in the athletic world outside the laboratory, users tend to ingest amounts between 10 and 100 times more than those prescribed for medical conditions (NIDA, 2000). Furthermore, many athletes do not take just one of the over 100 kinds of steroidal substances but instead engage in a practice known as "stacking." This process involves mixing various kinds of testosterone derivatives, sometimes combining both oral and injectable types, in the belief that stacking will produce greater effects than any one drug by itself. This theory has yet to be tested scientifically; however, it is safe to assume that this form of home chemistry involves health risks.

Allegations of an exponential increase in steroid use among professional athletes have been linked informally and anecdotally with an increase in major sports injuries, many of which previously were relegated to contact sports alone. From 1991 to 2001, the average weight of an all-star baseball player rose from 199 to 211 pounds, and at the same time incidences of Achilles tendon ruptures, hamstring tears, quadriceps tears, tearing of biceps at the elbow joints, and massive rotator cuff tears also increased in frequency and severity. During the 2001 season, Major League baseball players made 467 trips to the (inactive) disabled list and remained there for an average of 59 days, a 20% increase, or 10 days longer than the average from a prior injury report for the 1997 season (Verducci, 2002). It is logical to associate steroid use with an increase in significant injuries: When an athlete rapidly increases his muscle mass (weight), he places a heightened and unnatural strain upon his underlying body structure, which can prove either too rigid or too weak to provide adequate support for the added weight. While a direct causal link between the two is not yet substantiated by research, available statistics, anecdotal reports, and current information about steroids' effects on the body make these trends seem implausibly coincidental.

During that same period (1991 to 2001) the industry-wide cost in wasted salaries and for insuring players skyrocketed. In 2001, Major League baseball teams spent $317 million on players physically unable to play, for whom the cost of salary insurance rose more than 200% from 2000 to 2002 (Verducci, 2002).

Professional athletes—and those hoping to become professionals—use steroids and HGH because they believe they will yield a cyclic increase in muscle size and strength, improved performance, and in turn ever larger contracts and job security. These hopes can outweigh all contrary evidence of the dangers of steroids, and they make using steroids especially tempting in contact sports, where increased aggression is viewed as beneficial to performance and entertainment value. Informal estimates in the mid-1980s suggesting that 95% of professional football players took steroids may have seemed high at the time (Johnson, 1985), but the fact remains that players then and now, across the major sports, used and continue to abuse steroids.

Nutritional and Dietary Supplements

In 1998, a massive first baseman from the St. Louis Cardinals methodically and relentlessly bested one of Major League baseball's most cherished records. Mark McGwire smashed 70 home runs, easily outdistancing the late New York Yankees legend Roger Maris, who hit 61 in 1961. Throughout the summer and fall of 1998, reporters crowded around McGwire's locker, wanting to learn about his amazing feats. They also were quite curious to learn about a remarkable nutritional supplement he had been using.

He reluctantly admitted to using androstenedione, which at that time remained legal and available over the counter. "Andro," as it is known, is a naturally occurring hormone that is synthesized in the sexual and adrenal glands of both men and women, and it is considered a precursor agent for the production of testosterone. In short, androstenedione is a self-reinforcing substance that is thought to stimulate an increase in testosterone production, which in turn increases androstenedione levels, which stimulates more testosterone, and so on.

Several variations of androstenedione are found in supplements, including norandrostenedione. These variations can convert into nortestosterone, otherwise known as nandrolone, which is an illegal steroid when synthesized commercially (Zorpette, 1998). However, the effectiveness of androstenedione as a muscle builder analogous to steroids remains unclear, and further research is needed to clarify the risks and results of long-term use. Regardless of future findings, androstenedione and related agents like norandrostenedione are no longer available without medical prescriptions. In 2004, the United States Senate unanimously passed Senate Bill 2195, allowing the Drug Enforcement Agency the authority to reclassify testosterone precursors as Schedule III controlled substances, like anabolic steroids (Hatch, 2004).

Another popular supplement among athletes is creatine, a combination of three amino acids that is stored in muscles as a precursor for increased production of adenesinetriphosphate (ATP), which is the immediate source of energy for muscle contractions. By stimulating ATP synthesis, creatine helps athletes intensify and increase the frequency of their workouts (Millman & Ross, 2003). It seems to be especially useful for sports that consist of multiple sprint activities or necessitate weight training, such as basketball and football (Parish & Peterson, 1998). Side effects of extensive creatine use have not yet been fully studied, although theoretical models propose a risk of elevated strain on kidney and liver functioning. One study indicated a risk for severe diarrhea (Bahrke, 1994). Whatever the ultimate costs versus benefits, efforts already are under way to curb the use of creatine by reclassifying it as a performance-enhancing supplement (Bahrke & Yesalis, 2002).

A final supplement— ephedrine—was reportedly used by athletes during the 1990s. Ephedrine is a stimulant extracted from a Chinese herb called Má Huáng (which belongs to the genus Ephedra) and is used to facilitate weight loss, mask fatigue, and help athletes endure longer, more intensive workouts. However, use of the supplement may entail serious side effects, including high blood pressure, increased heart rate, seizures, strokes, heart attack, and death. In February 2003, 23-year-old Baltimore Orioles pitching prospect Steve Bechler collapsed and died while working out with teammates. The official cause of death was a heatstroke that sent his body temperature soaring to 108 degrees, but the report of the medical examiner indicated that ephedrine played a "significant role" in his death (Bodley, 2003).

While both androstenedione and ephedrine have been banned since McGwire and Bechler made them famous and infamous, respectively, new dietary supplements continue to flood the market. Athletes' drive to gain the upper hand in pursuit of competitive excellence, and money ensures there will be takers for these largely unregulated, as yet understudied, and potentially dangerous substances.

Amphetamines

Amphetamines are central nervous system (CNS) and cardiovascular stimulants that are classified as sympathomimetic amines, which cause the release of excitatory neurotransmitters. Trade names for amphetamines include Benzedrine, Dexedrine, and Methedrine, which are known in slang as "bennies" or "black beauties." First synthesized in 1887, they were initially used as an over-the-counter nasal decongestant before finding their way into warfare and then athletic competition.

Amphetamines are chemically related to epinephrine or ephedrine but are even more intensive CNS stimulants. Amphetamines stimulate activity of the postganglionic and synaptic nerves and possibly stimulate and facilitate synaptic transmission in the spinal cord (Kallant, 1968). As a CNS stimulant, amphetamines increase alertness, respiration rate, blood pressure, muscle tension, heart rate, and blood sugar and often induce an overall sense of physical well-being. These drugs also increase the production and release of dopamine and noradrenaline in the limbic system, which is considered the seat of neuro-emotional processes in the brain. Amphetamines can increase emotional arousal, especially feelings of euphoric well-being, and they also increase the release of neurotransmitters in the part of the brain that initiates movement, thereby increasing motor activity.

Symptoms of large doses of amphetamines may include restlessness, agitation, nausea, rapid pulse, dilation of the pupils, cardiac arrhythmia, anxiety, and mood swings that mimic the rapid cycling seen in bipolar disorder. In addition, large doses of amphetamines have been reported to produce symptoms similar to those seen in paranoid schizophrenic populations. Toxic symptoms, which are not necessarily related to overdose, include dizziness, headaches, confusion, and hormonal reactions resulting in the loss of libido and impotence. Amphetamines are highly addictive, and users are apt to develop a rapid tolerance to them. Unfortunately, this addictive nature leads to withdrawal and may contribute to periods of severe depression. In acute cases of amphetamine abuse, death can occur due to ruptured blood vessels in the brain or to heart attack.

Except for amphetamines' role in masking fatigue, results from research into the effects of amphetamine use on athletic performance have been inconsistent. Beecher and Smith established the benchmark for the field in 1959 with a study suggesting that the administration of small doses of amphetamines to athletes delays fatigue and improves performance. They found that this effect occurred when brief and explosive responses were needed, and they concluded that although these improvements were minimal, athletes found them beneficial. In another study, Clark (1970) found that amphetamines may improve performance but only under special circumstances and not without risks. More specifically, he found that use of amphetamines sustains attention and that, in order to improve performance reliably using amphetamines, three elements are necessary: (a) a sustained attention to the task, (b) habituation to the task, and (c) habituation to the drug. His findings revealed that athletes must accurately estimate the timing and dosage necessary for the desired performance effects, which suggests that a poorly timed or measured dose could effectively *impair* performance.

In contrast to these findings, several studies suggested that the use of amphetamines provided little if any improvement in athletic performance. Golding's extensive study in 1963 on the use of amphetamines and athletic performance found no significant differences between athletes' mean and placebo times on all-out treadmill runs. He tested fatigued as well as rested athletes to assess the alleged increase in endurance gained through the use of dextroamphetamine (a common form of the drug). During recovery following rested athletes' runs, d-amphetamine significantly retarded recovery for blood pressure but had no significant effect on heart rate. During the recovery period following the fatigued athletes' runs, d-amphetamine significantly retarded heart rate recovery and blood pressure recovery. Thus, administration of the drug had no significant effect on the all-out treadmill runs of either the conditioned or unconditioned athlete.

Wyndham (1971), however, found that an athlete could exercise for an extended time by using as little as 10 mg of methamphetamine (Desoxyn). He found that the amphetamines did not increase the athlete's capacity for aerobic exercise. He instead proposed that the drug's action enables athletes to tolerate acute discomfort, possibly resulting in a delayed awareness of the pain (not to mention accumulated injuries). Chandler and Blair (1980) found that administering small doses of Dexedrine to athletes yielded improvement in terms of endurance, knee strength, and acceleration. Although endurance was increased, no difference in sprinting speed was observed.

In all sports, amphetamine use is illegal and punishable by suspension or banishment, a fact that speaks to the health dangers, potential for unfair advantage, and sordid history associated with these drugs. *The Nightmare Season,* Dr. Arnold Mandell's (1976) controversial exposé, provides an inside look into widespread amphetamine abuse within the National Football League. *The Nightmare Season* came on the heels of Jim Bouton's *Ball Four* (1970), in which the former New York Yankee detailed the widespread use among Major League baseball players of "greenies" to help them cope with the rigors of a 162-game season schedule.

As team psychiatrist for the San Diego Chargers, Mandel was responsible for prescribing drugs to players for pain and injury. He was fired after allegedly overprescribing stimulants 3 years after NFL Commissioner Pete Rozell imposed a ban against amphetamines. Although Mandel admitted writing large prescriptions, he claimed he was treating athletes with long-term addictions. He argued that these addictions occurred primarily because team trainers routinely handed out amphetamines before games. He felt that by writing prescriptions he could protect athletes from turning to the black market sources to which they had easy access, notably in border towns like Tijuana, and could win their cooperation in a program of self-reform (Donohoe & Johnson, 1986).

In a later paper, entitled "The Sunday Syndrome," Mandell (1978) stated that amphetamines had been used by players in three ways: (a) only on game days, for the induction of analgesia and rage (30 to 150 mg or more); (b) only on game days, to increase speed and combat pain (5 to 30 mg), and (c) on a daily basis, to aid speed (15 mg). He revealed that the drugs were typically used more by older players and those in defensive positions. As with steroid use, he reported that players were more likely to use the drug because they believed that opponents may have done so.

Nevertheless, players continue to use black market sources—widespread throughout Latin America—to assist their efforts to gain a competitive edge. There even is a catch-phrase among professional baseball players about playing games without the use of stimulants. They call this presumably unusual phenomenon "playing naked" (Verducci, 2002).

Pain Killers

In many ways the phrase "no pain, no gain" symbolizes the experiences and expectations of today's professional athletes. This saying holds particularly true now, when the lure of potential contracts and endorsements is strong, players are more competitive, and their training regimens are more demanding. Although their cases are more extreme than most, a few players have been known to play an entire game with a broken bone in a hand, leg, or arm.

What can a player do when pain and injury becomes so severe that he is unable to continue? Many simply ask the trainer or team physician for a painkiller or analgesic to alleviate the discomfort, which can become even more serious when that athlete takes things into his own hands. A case in point is a star quarterback who spent several months of 1996 in the Menninger Clinic to treat an addiction to painkillers. He realized the depth of his addiction only after suffering a seizure following unrelated surgery, and in that sense he can be considered fortunate that his situation was not any worse (Carter, 2003).

In order to understand how players like this easily can become dependent on these drugs, it is helpful to examine some of the common painkillers used, how and when they are used, and their specific effects. Local anesthetics such as Novocain, Xylocaine, and Marcaine are often used just prior to the start of the game. These drugs are generally ingested and have prolonged effects that numb preexisting injuries during competition. However, they have also been reported to cause cardiac disorders and should be used minimally during competition. In fact, large doses of these drugs have been reported to cause overstimulation of the CNS, convulsions, and even death ("Xylocaine," n.d.).

Another group of substances, known as anti-inflammatory drugs, reduce the aches, pains, and inflammation associated with tissue damage. These drugs include Vioxx, Indocin, Naprosyn, Tandearil, Butazolidin ("bute"), and the most commonly used anti-inflammatory agent: aspirin. Bute is the most commonly abused drug by athletes in this category. Side effects of the prolonged use of these drugs (with the exception of aspirin) are gastrointestinal problems including ulceration of the intestine and stomach, diarrhea, headaches, dizziness, and disorientation, as well as risk of pronounced kidney damage with extensive use. Drugs that act by suppressing the inflammatory response to tissue injury are corticosteroids. These drugs are typically delivered directly to the injured area by injection into a joint with a local anesthetic. Corticosteroids (cortisone) can produce feelings of well-being and euphoria in addition to relief of pain. However, prolonged use of these drugs can result in serious side effects, including cardiovascular problems, infections, and even psychotic reactions (Cole & Schumacher, 2005).

Years of pounding on knees and joints tend to make regular ingestion and sometimes misuse of anti-inflammatory medications fairly common in sports like football and basketball, where star players have been forced to retire due to kidney disease and related kidney transplants. In the wake of these retirements, many players have begun to recognize and address the risks inherent in long-term abuse of anti-inflammatory medications. A former Los Angeles Lakers star launched an awareness campaign on his personal Web site, imploring his fellow professional basketballers to consider that they might be risking their kidneys and general health in exchange for their pursuit of championships.

It appears that professional athletes use performance-enhancing drugs, including painkillers, for a variety of reasons, perhaps oblivious or simply unconcerned with their risks. To complicate matters, players can have difficulty establishing boundaries between use for performance enhancement and use due to dependence. For example, a player may begin using amphetamines to help fight fatigue before or during a game. He may add painkillers to dull the pain from overextension and accumulating injuries that occur on account of masked fatigue. Next, he may increase his dose of both in order to "get up" for the following game, after which he returns to analgesics to soothe increasingly painful muscles and joints. Before long, the player may not be able to function at home or on the field without these drugs. After the season concludes, he lives with a body that no longer recovers as quickly or as fully as before and he may then turn to steroids to prolong his career. "Citius, altus, fortius" is the official motto of the Olympics, which translated means "swifter, higher, stronger." The use of steroids, dietary supplements, amphetamines, and painkillers in stark defiance of their dangers and often harmful consequences typifies the lengths to which some will go to achieve this ancient Athenian ideal ("Use of Performance-Enhancing Drugs," n.d.).

Lifestyle-Related Drugs and Substances

For all its luxuries, the life of a professional athlete has its drawbacks. The physiological and psychological demands placed on these men are enormous. Constant pressure to compete and achieve despite adversity often results in extreme anxiety for the athlete, who may live his life under the microscope of intense media scrutiny, idolatrous if not downright invasive fans, and unrealistic expectations of perfection. The lifestyle itself can be disorienting, as teams may spend weeks on end traveling from city to city, hotel to hotel, detached from friends, family, and the comforts of home. All the while, players' children grow up missing a father who can only rarely attend their musical recitals, Little League games, and so forth. Thousands of miles away from home, boredom, agitation, loneliness, and even despair can slowly but surely creep up on even the heartiest souls.

Alcohol

To handle the isolation and pressure, athletes must learn to relax and fill their downtime. For many, however, this includes resorting to drugs. The most accessible and commonly used drug is alcohol. Alcohol is a central nervous system depressant that may be also used to counteract the effects of other drugs. In moderation, alcohol can be used to diminish fatigue or worry and generally has a sedating effect. Some of the physiological effects of excessive alcohol intake include nausea, dehydration, headaches, amnesia, impotence, and depression. Alcohol can be highly addictive, and as tolerance develops, the user may become both physically and psychologically dependent (Donohoe & Johnson, 1986).

The effects of alcohol on performance reveal that drinking impairs reaction time, fine-motor judgments, hand–eye coordination, and general physiological coordination and balance. Excessive intake can have especially deleterious effects on athletes who participate in the major sports, all of which require precise and quick body movements. Despite these well-known consequences, alcohol remains closely associated with sports. Witness the countless athletes who serve as commercial spokesmen for beer advertisements, not to mention the inevitable champagne baths in locker rooms following every major playoff achievement.

Cocaine

If amphetamine use in professional sports was the shock of the 1970s, cocaine use was the scourge of the 1980s. Countless articles appeared detailing cocaine's widespread use among professional athletes, and the sudden deaths of athletes like Len Bias stunned even the most unflappable cynics. In 1985, several star baseball players testified in a highly publicized cocaine-trafficking trial. One report estimated that perhaps 40% of Major League baseball players were using cocaine at the peak of its use (Peele, 1985).

Considerable attention has since focused on understanding the nature of cocaine, its effects on the body, and the reasons for the widespread use by professional athletes. Cocaine is an alkaloid derived from a deciduous shrub found in the Peruvian Andes, Bolivia, and Colombia. Each shrub is steeped in kerosene, sulfuric acid, and alkali to produce a coca paste. The paste is 20% to 85% cocaine sulfate, which becomes powdery flakes or rocks of nearly pure cocaine hydrochloride when mixed with hydrochloric acid. At that point, cocaine becomes the white, odorless crystalline powder people recognize.

Pharmacologically, the drug acts as an anesthetic that blocks nerve conduction at the cellular membrane. It is a very powerful, short-acting stimulant with a low margin of safety. The actions of this drug are related to the administration route (snorting, eating, shooting, and freebasing) as well as to the set and setting. Cocaine can be absorbed through any mucous membrane and is carried by the blood to the heart, lungs, and rest of the body. Cocaine is metabolized quickly by the blood and the lungs. Its chemical action on the sympathetic nervous system minimizes the body's fight-or-flight response to fear or challenge. CNS effects include dilation of pupils; elevation of pulse, blood pressure, temperature, and blood sugar; digestive slowing; and hypothalamic stimulation (e.g., thirst, hunger, sexual arousal). Psychophysiological effects can include symptoms of euphoria, agitation, restlessness, pacing, teeth grinding, sweating, and vomiting. Disturbance of the heart regulatory center can cause fever and seizures and can be fatal (NIDA, 2004).

Cocaine users experience a sequence of effects that are very similar to those of amphetamines. Their "high" is often characterized by a spike of euphoria that quickly tapers off, followed in short order by a nadir of depression and irritability. Chronic cocaine use (as little as 3 gm weekly via nasal inhalation) can induce blackouts and damage to the liver, and also can lead to severely high blood pressure that can cause blood vessels in the brain to rupture and catalyze strokes. Heavy use can also cause angina, irregular heartbeats, and scarring of heart tissue. It can worsen preexisting heart disease and trigger a heart attack.

Psychologically, cocaine users may be plagued by an inability to concentrate, insomnia, fatigue, lack of sexual interest, and impotence. Some individuals experience panic attacks and become aggressive. Weight loss is common and can lead to malnutrition, a corollary to neglecting personal needs and hygiene. Chronic abuse can lower immune defenses and make the user susceptible to fungal disease, tuberculosis, and infections. These problems are often compounded by the lack of sleep and neglect of personal hygiene to form a downward, interdependent, destructive spiral.

Furthermore, the longer use continues, the higher the risk becomes for uncontrolled use. One animal research study showed that monkeys given a choice between food and cocaine preferred cocaine and might have died without investigator intervention. Such research suggests that a physiological basis for cocaine dependence may be rooted in its strength as a reinforcer. It may explain why some people, especially those with constant access and money to purchase the drug, may become compulsive users despite its adverse consequences (Dunham, n.d.).

Regular users of cocaine are almost certain to develop a psychological dependency. Direct methods of use, such as freebasing (smoking) and intravenous injection, are strongly linked with obsessive behaviors commonly associated with psychological addiction. Habitual users also are certain to develop a physical tolerance for the drug. Therefore, users often increase the dose or frequency in order to obtain a more intense high, although it has been reported that the individual can never obtain a high like the first one. While users may develop a tolerance for the cocaine high, they do not develop a tolerance for the cardiovascular actions of the drug. The overstimulation of the cardiovascular system can cause sudden death from cardiac standstill, and CNS overstimulation can lead to violent and even fatal seizures.

The effects of cocaine on performance are very similar to those of amphetamines: feelings of intense well-being, sharper and quicker reflexes (particularly during exhaustive events), increased endurance, and an alteration in perceived reality (NIDA, 2004). An extreme increase in confidence and the resulting belief that performance can undoubtedly be improved by using the drug are among cocaine's most striking characteristics. In contrast to amphetamines, however, cocaine's addictive qualities may result in such a total absorption in obtaining the drug that athletes may lose interest in the sport, ironically becoming less competitive and motivated. As mentioned, chronic users may neglect their physical health and hygiene, and this can be especially damaging for professional athletes, who may experience a substantial drop in physical fitness. Best put by a player, "To me the party did not begin until I got there and it ended when I left … my way did not work" (Foster, 2005).

A Sociological Perspective

For many professional athletes, *sports* and *life* are synonymous. From the first time a professional athlete participates in organized sports as a young boy until long after he retires, much of his identity revolves around his sense of himself as a successful athlete. While the old saying that "great athletes are born and not made" may be true with respect to genetic endowments, it neglects important developmental and environmental influences. It generally takes considerable time, training, and preparation to become a successful professional athlete, not to mention an exquisite combination of immense talent, opportunity, and good fortune.

A player's self-esteem, degree of identity development, and feelings of adequacy and self-worth may be tied inextricably to his successes and failures on the playing field—and why not? From day one, players who excel in sports are applauded by peers and validated by respected elders, often for the first time. Along the way, many players hear confusing and often contradictory messages from coaches, teachers, and parents about so-called acceptable forms of violence and aggression, and they may easily personalize slogans such as "there are no alternatives to winning" and "a good loser is a loser."

During the impressionable adolescent years spanning high school and college, athletics provide acceptance; group affiliation and group identity; leadership opportunities; a sense of meaning, purpose, and control; and adoration both on campus and in the larger community. In a culture that rewards individualism, sports stardom provides a rare opportunity to stand apart and atop one's social world. After the player turns professional, fans and admirers—sometimes romantic, other times offering business opportunities, endorsements, and so on—multiply and continue to offer unsolicited reinforcement, validation, and respect. Unfortunately, their adulation may have little to do with that player's character or level of integrity. This state of affairs is easily overlooked by many athletes, who mistake this unreserved and nondiscretionary positive attention for a carte blanche to disregard rules both on and off the field.

As one of the most highly visible groups in American life, professional athletes are alternately scrutinized, idealized, and subjected to unrealistic expectations. They are vilified and publicly shamed at the same time they are expected to be societal role models, which can result in their increasing alienation from the wider society; it is not uncommon to observe professional athletes band together as reciprocal sources of support. This segregation can create a self-reinforcing cycle of increasing isolation, not only from the public's often insatiable demands but also from potential sources of grounding, perspective, and support. Further complicating matters, athletes face frequent occupational uncertainties about being traded—and having to uproot themselves and their families—to another organization or city, or being demoted to the minor leagues, which can present additional obstacles against developing reliable, trusted, and consistent relationships.

The chance to bask in the adoring cries of cheering thousands surely is an unparalleled experience, one that few others will ever know. Not surprisingly, career termination represents a traumatic moment for many professional athletes. Retirement, whether voluntary or imposed by age, injury, or management, yields a swift decline in status, social contact, and income. Its arrival can leave many players without a clear sense of self or direction and may lead to (or exacerbate) depression, anxiety, grief, or substance abuse. These problems can be compounded by inadequate educational or vocational training and a lack of marketable skills in an increasingly technology-driven world, not to mention potentially limited psychological resources and coping skills, fostered by players' aforementioned cloistered, sometimes depersonalized, existence.

Given this backdrop, many athletes learn to view their athletic skills as their primary if not sole personal asset, which can intensify the importance of winning at any cost. Such a focus can increase the odds that athletes may turn to drugs for relief or performance enhancement, because failure on the playing field, injury, or retirement often results in a perceived obliteration of their identity, both in the sports world and in private. This pattern of events may be particularly true for athletes from disadvantaged socioeconomic backgrounds, who often feel a heightened sense of responsibility toward their families.

For many individuals, finding a balance between meeting their own needs and meeting the needs of others can create additional pressures, stress, and demands for continued if not greater achievement. For others, feelings of inferiority and inadequacy are recapitulated and reinforced as the result of lingering racism in sports. This point is exemplified in the experience of many African American athletes, who are confronted routinely with derogatory and limiting stereotypes that prejudicially equate Black athletic achievement with intellectual inferiority. It is difficult to overstate the importance of this issue. However, it is not the intent of this chapter to delve into this very complicated societal matter.

In sum, an athlete's perspective and reaction to the world are mediated by psychological dynamics specific to him and to a life of exclusivity within professional sports. The same lifestyle that affords him great opportunities and potential riches also is rife with psychosocial stressors that may leave him vulnerable to substance use, addiction, and worse. Clinicians, mentors, coaches, and others who are not mindful of this idiosyncratic state of affairs may jeopardize their effectiveness.

Treatment Overview

Drug abuse among athletes is clearly a serious and complicated matter. It may be argued that some of the same factors that advance and exacerbate drug abuse in athletes also provide formidable obstacles to prevention and treatment. Intense physical demands, long hours of rigorous training, extensive traveling, and pressure to perform provide an ideal situation for drug use while making standard treatment efforts difficult if not impossible.

More traditional treatment methods such as inpatient hospitalization, psychotherapy, and self-help groups can cause major career disruptions and are not compatible with the scheduling demands and public profile of professional athletes. The idealization of athletes as wholly self-sufficient gladiators can result in elevated self-esteem, sometimes to narcissistic proportions. This inflated self-esteem can contribute to a strong reluctance to seek treatment because it is an inherent contradiction to think or be told that one is a "superman" who also needs external help for drug problems. Not surprisingly, a stigma in professional sports exists against receiving psychiatric treatment (Ritvo & Glick, 2005).

Athletes often receive insidious encouragement for drug abuse in the sports environment itself. Peer pressure to use drugs makes it harder to confront the negative aspects of drug use, and when team physicians prescribe drugs for the purpose of maintaining performance despite pain and injury, they implicitly legitimize a role for substance use in competition. Also, issues of privacy and confidentiality are magnified as players seeking rehabilitation face strong public and peer reactions in addition to potentially massive financial losses. They also may face atypical psychosocial treatment complications. For example, when a star athlete requires inpatient hospitalization, he must deal with not only media attention but also unpredictable responses from fellow patients.

Historically, some professional sports management maintained a hands-off approach to drug use among athletes; that is, unless a player was unable to perform, drug abuse was not the organization's concern. In addition, attempts to regulate and screen for drug use have been plagued by inconsistencies. For example, prior to congressional involvement, Major League baseball and the Major League Baseball Players Association had not agreed upon testing or penalties for steroid use beyond a loophole-infested program targeting offenders solely in the minor leagues (Verducci, 2002). Furthermore, different sports and the franchises within them have differing policies and procedures designed to combat drug abuse. Consequences vary from mild to severe, depending on the league in question, ownership of the player's team, and perhaps even the perceived value of the individual player.

In the event that a player overcomes these systemic obstacles and seeks help, his treatment often is conceptualized at the levels of primary, secondary, and tertiary prevention. Primary prevention paints broad brushstrokes aimed at preventing drug use perceived as harmful to the individual or society. Generally, primary prevention models focus on providing information to players about the dangers of substance use from an educational or moral perspective. These models are implemented prior to abuse, and they typically explore alternative activities to drug use and available resources. Individuals at highest risk are identified, as are contributing risk factors (Jacob & Johnson, 1997), which may include any of the physiological, sociological, and psychological concerns discussed earlier. However, generalized drug education does not address the perceived benefits and negative consequences of drugs on sport performance, which is the core of the matter for athletes. As discussed, myriad factors can predispose athletes to drug abuse, and these factors also require attention as prevention issues.

Secondary prevention involves the early identification of substance use and a provision of intervention designed to prevent more serious addictive processes from flourishing. As a result of controversy over what constitutes use versus abuse (especially regarding alcohol), there is considerable blurring between primary and secondary prevention. However, tertiary prevention is more clear-cut and involves the treatment of more serious cases with hospitalization or detoxification. Successful efforts at combating drug use in the world of professional sports must include provisions for all three levels of prevention. Be that as it may, current policies for drug testing, treatment, and prevention among the three major professional sports leagues differ widely both in scope and in their historical record.

The National Basketball Association

The National Basketball Association's (NBA) treatment and penalties policy dates to 1983 and was updated during subsequent collective bargaining negotiations with the National Basketball Players Association. The prevention component consists of requiring all players to attend two specific drug seminars throughout the year. Rookies must attend an additional preseason seminar dealing with the potential problems facing professional athletes. The rationale for this seminar is that issues of lifestyle and competition (e.g., travel, losing games) may lead to drug abuse. The NBA program also includes treatment modules. Whenever a player first voluntarily requests help, he is referred for treatment at team expense, no penalty is imposed, and he continues to receive his paycheck. Treatment consists of referral and involvement in a hospital program with specified aftercare conditions. The second time a player voluntarily seeks help, the provisions are the same, but pay is suspended. Any subsequent illegal drug use, even if voluntarily disclosed, results in immediate dismissal from the league, after which the player must wait 2 years before appealing for reinstatement.

Beginning with the 1999–2000 season, the league adopted provisions for drug testing under certain conditions with predetermined penalties for drug use (Stern, 2005). Under the new arrangements, all players are tested during preseason training camp. Whereas treatment for players originally focused solely on eradicating so-called recreational drugs like cocaine and heroin, it has since added steroid and performance-enhancing agents to its testing regimens. Initially, the updated agreement penalized 5, 10, and 25 games (out of a possible 82 per season, pre-playoffs) for first, second, and future steroidal offenses, respectively. Subsequent negotiations between management and players yielded an agreement to double the penalty for first offenses (Associated Press, 2005).

The NBA program model has some advantages, including the written league-wide policy agreement between the association and players.

The National Football League Policy and Program for Substance Abuse

The National Football League (NFL) and the NFL Players Association have maintained a formal policy since 1993 that applies to all active players in the league. This policy specifically prohibits players from the use and possession of all illegal substances. The abuse of prescription drugs and the use of alcohol can be prohibited. Players are tested, evaluated, and monitored for substances and can be subject to discipline if they violate the policy. Testing of all players is administered during pre-season training camps, but all players remain eligible for random weekly testing throughout the 16-week regular season (NFL Players Association, n.d.).

Major League Baseball

Of the major sports, professional baseball appears to have been the slowest to respond to the growing wave of performance-enhancing drugs over the past 20 years. Prior to 2002 the league and its politically and financially powerful players' union had not agreed to any steroid testing procedures; as late as March 2005, a player could test positive for steroids and receive a minimum of a $10,000 fine without any suspension. New testing and penalties have since been agreed upon, and they also include a focus on ridding the sport of amphetamine use.

Under the new rules, positive steroid tests yield an automatic 50-game suspension, followed by a 100-game ban for a second offense, and a lifetime ban for a third. A three-time offender may appeal for reinstatement after 2 seasons. In the case of a player convicted for distributing steroids, a first offense triggers an automatic 60–80 game penalty with a second offense leading to a lifetime ban. As for amphetamines, a first offense leads to mandatory future testing, followed by 25 and 80 game and discretionary suspensions for subsequent positive tests (Associated Press, 2005).

Players are tested during preseason physicals and at least once during the regular season, although it will be interesting to see if this policy effectively curbs commonplace practices designed to circumvent testing mechanisms. Many minor leaguers have acknowledged using steroids during the off-season months and then stopping with enough time to spare before preseason tests commence (Verducci, 2002).

Concluding Thoughts

Before dying in 1992 from an aggressive brain tumor that he attributed to steroid abuse, a star football player spoke out against steroids. However, the pressures and predicaments of the current era make it difficult when the player next to you, who is after your job, is using, and if you do not use, he may take your job.

For better and worse, professional sports in this country embody some of the most cherished of American ideals as well as a share of America's darkest shadows. At their best, professional athletes display ancient virtues of courage and tenacious fortitude in defiance of great pressures in order to surmount complex obstacles. They can remind an increasingly individualistic culture of the transcendent possibilities inherent in teamwork and fellowship while linking generations both within the games themselves (e.g., coaches and players) and among their fans (e.g., parents and children). As a sociological phenomenon, professional sports also may provide a common bonding language, opportunities for communal pride, and enduring traditions that can be a unifying force for shared experiences that provide meaning and purpose.

However, they also mirror the tensions, anxieties, and problems of this society and the current era. Fractious interpersonal relationships, senseless violence and untamed aggression, and a win-at-any-cost attitude, as well as a creeping fiduciary nihilism and narcissism, reflect the unseemly aspects of the American cauldron. Questions abound for athletes and fans alike. Do limits exist for the importance of winning, or is it indeed the only thing that matters? At what point do the costs and risks of a fast-paced, drug-infused lifestyle outweigh the perceived benefits? What role should money play in the pursuit of athletic achievement? What does it mean to be a professional athlete (or even a fan, for that matter)? And just how important are championships relative to the potentially devastating physical, familial, and social costs of using drugs in order to proclaim oneself a winner?

As technology continues to advance, these issues will not likely fade but instead grow increasingly pronounced. For example, advances in genetic engineering may make the recent attention given to steroid use seem quaint by comparison. Gene transfer therapies, stem cell transplantation, muscle fiber phenotype transformation, red blood cell substitutes, and other advances loom large and will become factors in athletics in the not-too-distant future (Bahrke & Yesalis, 2002). If the past has any bearing upon that future, professional sports will likely remain a central part of America's moral and cultural evolution. However, without introspection and intelligent, principled leadership, it seems likely that they will not set new trends but merely follow into ever more difficult and confusing ethical terrains, with more lives ruined in the process.

References

Anabolic Steroid Control Act of 1990, 21 U.S.C. § 801 *et seq.* (1990).

Associated Press. (2005). *Steroid use penalties much tougher with agreement.* Retrieved January 3, 2006, from http://sports.espn.go.com/mlb/news/story?id=2224832

Bahrke, M. (1994). Weight training: A potential confounding factor. *Sports Medicine, 18,* 309–318.

Bahrke, M., & Yesalis, C. (2002). The future of performance-enhancing substances in sport. *The Physician and Sportsmedicine, 30*(11), 51–54.

Beecher, H., & Smith, G. (1959). Amphetamine sulfate and athletic performance. *Journal of the American Medical Association, 170,* 542–547.

Bodley, H. (2003, March 13). Medical examiner: Ephedra a factor in Bechler death. *USA Today.* Retrieved January 3, 2006, from http://www.usatoday.com/sports/baseball/al/orioles/2003-03-13-bechler-exam_x.htm

Bouton, J. (1970). *Ball four.* New York: Simon & Schuster.

Carter, B. (2003). Fearless Favre's a gameday gambler. Special to ESPN.com. Retrieved January 3, 2006, from http://espn.go.com/classic/biography/s/Favre_Brett.html

Chandler, J., & Blair, S. (1980). The effect of amphetamines on selected physiological components related to athletic success. *Medical Sciences in Sports, 12,* 65.

Clark, K. (1970). Drugs, sports and doping. *Journal of the Maine Medical Association, 1*(3), 55–58.

Cole, B. J., & Schumacher, H. R. (2005). Injectable corticosteroids in modern practice. *American Academy of Orthopedic Surgery,* 13, 133–140.

Designer steroids, by the numbers. (2004, February). *Popular Science, 264*(2), p. 41.

Donohoe, T., & Johnson, N. (1986). *Foul play: Drug abuse in sports.* New York: Blackwell.

Dunham, W. (n.d.). *Monkey cocaine study sheds light on addiction.* Retrieved February 8, 2010, from http://www.mail-archive.com/tips@acsun.frostburg.edu/msg01955.html

Foster, T. (2005, December 11). Roy Tarpley's long road back. *The Detroit News.* Retrieved January 3, 2006, from http://www.detnews.com/apps/pbcs.dll/article?AID=/20051211/SPORTS08/512110343/1131/SPORTS0201

Golding, L. (1963). The effects of I-amphetamine sulfate on physical performance. *Journal of Sports Medicine, 3,* 221–224.

Goodman, L. S., & Gilman, A. (1975). *The pharmacological basis of therapeutics.* New York: Macmillan.

Hatch, O. (2004). Senate passes Biden-Hatch bill to ban designer steroids. Press release. Retrieved on January 3, 2006, from http://hatch.senate.gov/index.cfm?FuseAction=PressReleases.View&PressRelease_id=1228

Haupt, H., & Rovere, G. D. (1984). Anabolic steroids: A review of the literature. *American Journal of Sports Medicine, 12,* 479–483.

House Committee on Government Reform Committee Hearings, 109th Congress. Retrieved January 3, 2006, from http://www.access.gpo.gov/congress/house/house07ch109.html

Jacob, T., & Johnson, S. (1997). Parenting influences on the development of alcohol abuse and dependence. *Alcohol, Health, and Research World, 21*(3), 204–209.

Johnson, W. (1985, May 13). Steroid explosion. *Sports Illustrated,* pp. 38–51.

Kallant, O. (1968). The amphetamines: Toxicity and addiction. In *Behavioral pharmacology.* Englewood Cliffs, NJ: Prentice-Hall.

Major professional sports leagues of the United States and Canada. (n.d.). In *Wikipedia: The free encyclopedia.* Retrieved January 3, 2006, from http://en.wikipedia.org/wiki/Major_professional_sports_league

Mandell, A. (1976). *The nightmare season.* New York: Random House.

Mandell, A. (1978). The Sunday syndrome: A unique pattern of amphetamine abuse indigenous to professional football. *Pharmacological Newsletter, 7,* 8–11.

Melia, P., Pipe A., & Greenberg, L. (1996). The use of anabolic-androgenic steroids by Canadian students. *Clinical Journal of Sports Medicine, 6,* 9–14.

Millman, R., & Ross, E. (2003). Steroid and nutritional supplement use in professional athletes. *American Journal on Addictions, 12,* S48–S54.

National Collegiate Athletic Association. (1997, January). Steroid and nutritional use in professional athletes. *NCAA Newsletter.*

National Institute on Drug Abuse. (2000). *Anabolic steroid abuse.* Retrieved January 3, 2006, from http://www.nida.nih.gov/ResearchReports/Steroids/AnabolicSteroids.html

National Institute on Drug Abuse. (2004). *Cocaine: Abuse and addiction.* Retrieved January 3, 2006, from http://www.nida.nih.gov/ResearchReports/Cocaine/Cocaine.html

New York Yankees. (n.d.). *Alex Rodriguez #13.* Retrieved January 3, 2006, from http://sports.espn.go.com/mlb/players/profile?statsId=5275

NFL Players Association. (n.d.). *Drug policy NFL Players Association.* Retrieved July 7, 2008, from http://www.NFLPlayers.com/user/template.aspx/

Parish, D., & Peterson, B. (1998). Creatine monohydrate and performance: A brief review of the literature. *Journal of Sports Chiropractic and Rehabilitation, 12*(3), 118–119.

Peele, S. (1985, October 18). Ballplayers put a twist on drug "truths." *Los Angeles Times.* Retrieved January 3, 2006, from http://www.peele.net/lib/coketime.html

Pope, H., & Katz, D. (1994). Psychiatric and medical effects of anabolic-androgenic steroid use. *Journal of General Psychiatry, 51,* 375–382.

Ritvo, E., & Glick, I. (2005). Family problems and sports performance. *The Physician and Sportsmedicine, 33*(9), 37–41.

Simons, J., & Butow, D. (1997). Improbable dreams: African Americans are a dominant presence in professional sports: Do Blacks suffer as a result? *U.S. News and World Report, 122*(11), 46–53.

Stern, D. (2005). David Stern's written testimony on steroids to U.S. House of Representatives. Retrieved January 3, 2006, from http://www.insidehoops.com/stern-steroids-house-reps-051805.shtml

Stiles, D., Gibbons, J., Sebben D., & Wiley, D. (1999). Why adolescent boys dream of becoming professional athletes. *Psychological Reports, 84,* 1075–1085.

Taylor, W. N. (1985). *Hormonal manipulation: A new era of monstrous athletes.* Jefferson, NC: McFarland.

Use of performance-enhancing drugs in Olympic Games. (n.d.). In *Wikipedia: The free encyclopedia.* Retrieved February 8, 2010, from http://wikipedia.org/wlki/use_of_Performance_enhancing _drugs_in_the_Olympic_GamesVerducci, T. (2002, June 3). Totally juiced. *Sports Illustrated,* pp. 34–48.

Wade, N. (1972). Anabolic steroids: Doctors denounce them but athletes aren't listening. *Science, 176,* 1399–1403.

Williamson, D., & Young, A. (1992). Psychiatric effects of androgenic and anabolic-androgenic steroid abuse in men: A brief review of the literature. *Journal of Psychopharmacology, 6*(1), 20–26.

Wyndham, H. (1971). Physiological effects of the amphetamines during exercise. *South African Medical Journal, 45,* 247–252.

Xylocaine. (n.d.). Retrieved February 8, 2010, from http://www.rxlist.com/xylocaine-drug.htm

Zorpette, G. (1998). Andro angst. *Scientific American, 279*(6), 22

CHAPTER 16

Substance Abuse in the Military

Emily Naughton Lindley

In terms of incidence and causes, substance abuse among military personnel differs from that in the general population. This chapter discusses demographics and trends related to substance abuse in the military population, diagnostic considerations for clinicians working with military personnel, treatment considerations for individuals in each branch of the military, and current prevention efforts.

Demographics of the Population

For the purposes of this chapter, the U.S. military consists of the Marine Corps, the Army, the Navy, the Air Force, and veterans of military service. The 2002 U.S. Department of Defense (DOD) *Survey of Health Related Behaviors Among Military Personnel* (Bray et al., 2003), the most recent DOD survey available, indicates an overall decrease in the use of illicit drugs between 1980 and 2002 and no statistically significant change in the heavy use of alcohol between 1980 and 2002 (see Figure 16.1). The survey suggested that one in five military personnel met the criteria of being a heavy drinker (i.e., five or more drinks per occasion at least once a week; see also Ames, 2002). According to the DOD survey, the Marine Corps population was found to have the highest rate of heavy alcohol consumption, with the Air force having the lowest rate. For the purposes of this study, binge drinking rates were defined as consuming five or more drinks on the same occasion at least once during the past 30 days. Compared with the low binge drinking rates of the civilian population, the DOD survey suggested similarities between the high binge drinking rates of military personnel and college populations. The DOD survey indicated that binge drinking is a social occasion for most military personnel. In comparison to the civilian population and military personnel ages 26 to 55 years, the DOD survey indicated that military personnel ages 18 to 25 were significantly more likely to engage in binge drinking and heavy alcohol use. The DOD survey also suggested that the military personnel with that highest rates of heavy alcohol use were unmarried Caucasian males between the ages of 21 and 25 with a lower pay grade (E1-E3) and education consisting of high school or less (see Table 16.1). The DOD survey indicated that male military personnel used alcohol, in general, more frequently than did women. They also use it as a coping mechanism for feelings of stress and depression. The overall findings of the DOD survey indicate that although the military appears to have made progress in decreasing the use of illicit drugs by military personnel, a considerable need remains to address consistent heavy use of alcohol by military personnel. Other research studies examining substance use and young adults in the military support the finding in the DOD survey (Ames, Cunradi, & Moore, 2002).

Why Is the Military Different in Terms of Risk?

In comparison with the majority of the civilian population, the military population is at higher risk of developing a substance use disorder due to the increased exposure of

(*text continues on page 376*)

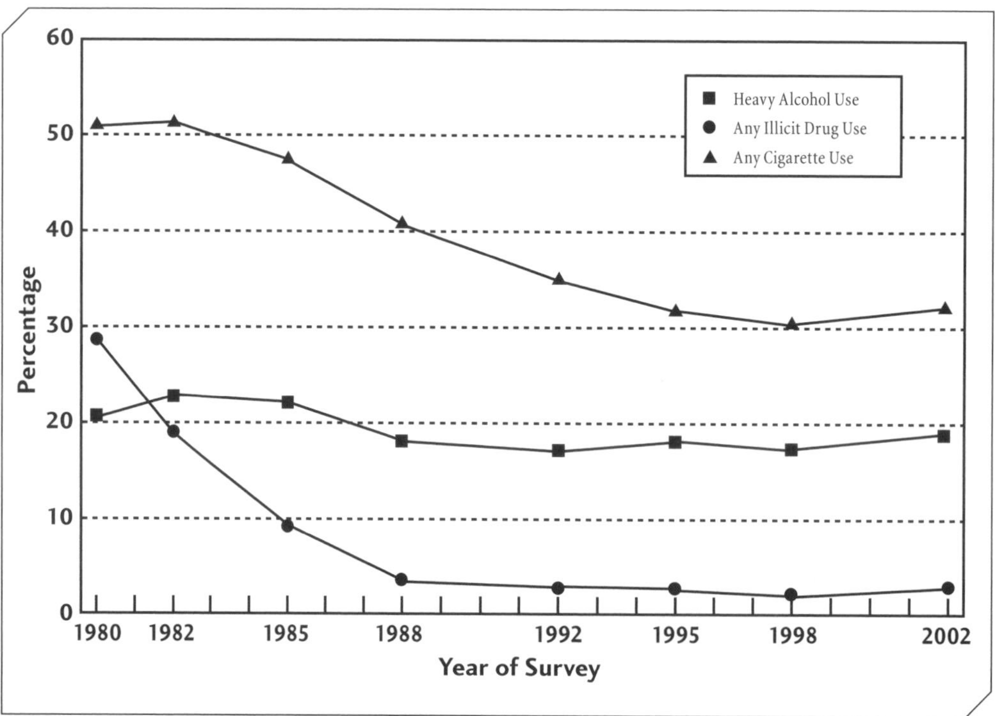

Figure 16.1. Trends in substance use during the 30-day period before the survey, total DOD, 1980–2002. *Note.* From *2002 Department of Defense Survey of Health Related Behaviors Among Military Personnel* (Report No. RTI/7841/006-FR), by R. M. Bray, L. L. Hourani, K. L. Rae, J. A. Dever, J. M. Brown, A. A. Vincus, M. R. Pemberton, M. E. Marsden, D. L. Faulkner, and R. Vandermaas-Peeler, 2003, Research Triangle Park, NC: Research Triangle Institute.

Table 16.1
Drinking Level (Percentages, With Standard Deviations in Parentheses), Total Department of Defense Survey Results, by Sociodemographic Characteristic

	Drinking level				
Sociodemographic characteristic	Abstainer	Infrequent/ light	Moderate	Moderate/ heavy	Heavy
Gender					
Male	21.2 (0.8)	16.6 (0.5)	17.6 (0.6)	24.2 (0.5)	20.3 (1.2)
Female	31.4 (1.2)	26.5 (1.0)	19.5 (0.6)	15.5 (0.6)	7.1 (0.8)
Race/Ethnicity					
White, non-Hispanic	19.6 (1.0)	17.7 (0.6)	19.0 (0.6)	24.1 (0.6)	19.6 (1.2)
African American, non-Hispanic	32.4 (1.3)	18.5 (0.9)	15.1 (1.0)	20.7 (0.8)	13.3 (1.4)
Other	25.2 (1.0)	21.0 (0.8)	17.1 (1.4)	18.7 (1.3)	18.0 (1.3)
Education					
High school or less	22.4 (0.9)	16.7 (0.9)	14.9 (0.5)	19.6 (0.7)	26.5 (1.5)
Some college	23.7 (1.0)	19.0 (0.8)	17.4 (0.7)	23.2 (0.8)	16.7 (0.8)
College graduate or higher	22.3 (1.2)	19.6 (1.1)	24.7 (1.1)	27.4 (1.0)	6.0 (0.7)
Age					
20 or younger	33.3 (2.3)	15.7 (1.0)	10.4 (1.4)	14.4 (1.4)	26.1 (2.4)
21–25	17.1 (1.0)	16.2 (0.8)	15.7 (0.6)	22.7 (0.7)	28.4 (1.1)
26–34	21.4 (0.9)	20.6 (1.0)	21.5 (0.8)	24.8 (0.7)	11.7 (0.9)
35 or older	26.8 (1.2)	19.8 (0.5)	21.2 (1.0)	25.1 (0.8)	7.1 (0.5)
Family Status					
Not married	20.6 (1.2)	15.5 (0.8)	15.1 (0.6)	23.0 (0.6)	25.8 (1.4)
Married, spouse not present	22.2 (1.5)	18.7 (1.7)	17.3 (1.2)	21.2 (1.9)	20.6 (1.4)
Married, spouse present	25.1 (0.7)	20.6 (0.6)	20.5 (0.7)	22.7 (0.6)	11.1 (0.8)
Pay Grade					
EI–E3	25.2 (1.6)	14.0 (1.1)	12.7 (1.1)	17.4 (0.9)	30.8 (1.9)
E4–E6	22.2 (0.7)	19.7 (0.7)	17.2 (0.5)	22.3 (0.6)	18.7 (0.8)
E7–E9	27.1 (1.3)	19.3 (0.7)	20.0 (1.1)	26.0 (1.0)	7.6 (0.5)
WI–W5	20.7 (1.7)	14.6 (1.2)	24.5 (3.4)	31.9 (1.5)	8.3 (1.4)
01–03	18.1 (1.3)	18.4 (1.5)	26.1 (1.6)	30.4 (2.0)	7.1 (1.0)
04–010	21.4 (1.9)	20.3 (1.7)	28.0 (2.0)	28.3 (2.0)	2.0 (0.5)
Region					
CONUS	24.2 (1.0)	18.6 (0.6)	17.9 (0.6)	22.5 (0.5)	16.9 (1.6)
OCONUS	20.2 (0.6)	17.6 (1.0)	18.1 (0.9)	23.4 (0.7)	20.7 (0.8)
Total	23.0 (0.7)	18.3 (0.5)	17.9 (0.5)	22.7 (0.4)	18.1 (1.1)

Note. From *2002 Department of Defense Survey of Health Related Behaviors Among Military Personnel* (Report No. RTI/7841/006-FR), Section 2.5.3, by R. M. Bray, L. L. Hourani, K. L. Rae, J. A. Dever, J. M. Brown, A. A. Vincus, M. R. Pemberton, M. E. Marsden, D. L. Faulkner, and R. Vandermaas-Peeler, 2003, Research Triangle Park, NC: Research Triangle Institute. Percentages in each row may not sum to 100 because of rounding. Alcohol use in the study was measured in terms of quantity of alcohol consumed and frequency of drinking. The quantity per typical drinking occasion and the frequency of drinking with the largest amount of alcohol per day were used to fit individuals into 1 of 10 categories. The resulting quantity/frequency categories were then collapsed into five drinking-level groups: abstainers, infrequent/light drinkers, moderate drinkers, moderate/heavy drinkers, and heavy drinkers. Heavy drinkers were defined as drinking five or more drinks per typical drinking occasion at least once a week in the 30 days before the survey.

chronic stress (Ames, 2002; Substance Abuse and Mental Health Services Administration [SAMHSA], 2006a). The history and culture in the military also may encourage heavy alcohol use and a predisposition for risk-taking behavior (Vaughan, 2006).

Research has indicated that exposure to stress and psychological distress may play a significant role in the development of substance use disorders (SAMHSA, 2006a). Military life can present special challenges to service members and their families, such as long separations, low wages among the lower ranking enlisted personnel, and frequent relocation (Ames, 2002). These factors all contribute to chronic stress and or psychological distress and may affect military personnel in the development of substance use disorders (Screening for Mental Health, 2006). Military life stress may also include exposure to trauma associated with combat, stress related to family responsibilities, and stress related to physical challenges (Ames, 2002). Research indicates that men may be prone to developing alcohol dependence when exposed to stressful events related to their jobs (SAMHSA, 2006a). Studies have also indicated that military members are more likely than civilians to describe their work responsibilities as more stressful than their family responsibilities (SAMHSA, 2006a). Compared to military men, military women describe being a woman in the military as the most frequent cause of work related stress (SAMHSA, 2006). Military personnel frequently describe deployment and separation from family as the most stressful work responsibility (Bray et al., 2003; SAMHSA, 2006a).

Military-related combat may contribute to the development of post-traumatic stress disorder (PTSD) in some military personnel (National Institute on Drug Abuse [NIDA], 2005). PTSD is a psychiatric disorder that may develop in individuals who are exposed to life-threatening events (NIDA, 2005). Research examining the effects of war on military personnel has indicated a high correlation between PTSD and substance use disorders, with 75% of combat veterans with PTSD meeting the criteria for a substance use disorder. Typically this disorder involves alcohol abuse or dependence (NIDA, 2005). In addition, research studies have shown that veterans and military personnel exhibiting symptoms of PTSD often turn to drug and alcohol use to help manage those symptoms (NIDA, 2005). Exposure to stress has been found to increase relapse in personnel with substance use disorders (NIDA, 2005).

The pressure to perform at the highest level, along with new responsibilities and rigid routines of military culture, may put military personnel at risk for developing a substance use disorder (White & Webber, 2003). Similar to new college students joining a fraternity, traditional rituals such as stopping at ports or getting tattoos may ultimately encourage heavy drinking and related activities (Ames, 2002). Historically, wartime conditions put military personnel at risk for increasing use of alcohol and drugs because substances often help to alleviate fear, pain, and boredom, and they increase confidence and energy in difficult situations (White & Webber, 2003). Studies have indicated that deployment is associated with increased substance use among military personnel (SAMHSA, 2006a). Increased use of alcohol and substances during deployment may be related to the absence of family-of-origin and community values that typically govern substance use (White & Webber, 2003).

Research has indicated a correlation between military personnel returning from deployment and increased heavy alcohol consumption, illicit drug use, and other dangerous risk-taking behavior (Vaughan, 2006). Studies show that some military personnel feel deprived of the stress, stimulation, and adrenaline they felt on a daily basis in the field of combat, and they attempt to decompress from their experience by replacing the high level of stimulation and adrenaline with risky behavior (e.g., heavy alcohol consumption, illicit drug use, reckless driving; Vaughan, 2006).

Alcohol and Drug Use: Diagnostic Considerations

Military personnel are exposed to conflict within their occupations (SAMHSA, 2006a). Recurrent exposure to stress and conflict may cause military members to develop anxiety disorders, mood disorders, or adjustment disorders, which in turn may cause military members to turn to unhealthy coping behaviors, including heavy use of drugs and alcohol (Cozza, et al., 2003). Research has indicated that military personnel frequently cite deployment as one of the most psychologically stressful military-related duties (SAMHSA, 2006a). Impending deployment may cause feelings of stress due to fear and uncertainty during times of war, which may cause military members to use substances to suppress uncomfortable emotions and feelings (SAMHSA, 2006a). Recurrent periods of deployment may cause increased stress due to pressure to manage family responsibilities during extended leaves of absence, harsh living conditions in the field, minimal communication with loved ones, and boredom (SAMHSA, 2006a; White & Webber, 2003). Thus, deployment may put some military personnel at increased risk of developing acute stress disorder or PTSD (NIDA, 2005). Substance abuse disorders are diagnosed separately from PTSD. However, consideration of both disorders is important in developing treatment plans and setting appropriate treatment goals.

Treatment Considerations

Research examining substance use in the military implies that comprehensive substance use treatment programs are necessary for military personnel and their families (Clay, 2006). Studies also show that military personnel and their families would benefit from programs providing psychoeducation on how to cope with stress (NIDA, 2005). Two barriers that may keep individuals from seeking treatment in the military may be the fear of losing clearance status and confidentiality for military personnel holding security clearances (SAMHSA, 2006a). Currently the DOD and the military branches are combating this psychological barrier to treatment by reassuring cleared personnel that their work status would not be affected if they voluntarily sought treatment for an alcohol-related problem (SAMHSA, 2006a). The DOD and the U.S. Department of Veterans Affairs (VA) guarantee confidentiality through policies and programs for military personnel seeking assistance for substance use disorders (SAMHSA, 2006a). The Marine Corps, Army, Navy, and Air Force all have individualized substance use treatment programs for their military personnel.

Marine Corps

Marine Corps Community Services (MCCS) is a substance abuse program Web site that provides information on family life and information downloads on alcohol and drugs, as well as related links to National Inhalant Prevention Coalition (Marine Corps Community Services Camp Pendleton [MCCSCP], 2006). The MCCS Web site provides links to SAMHSA's National Clearinghouse for Alcohol and Drug information, the NAVMC 2931, which outlines the Marine Corps program for drug and alcohol prevention and links to the American Society of Addiction Medicine. The Marine Corps Web site explains that the military substance use program treatment objective is to eliminate alcohol abuse through increased psychoeducation regarding risks and signs of substance use, increased training for leaders, and increased availability of substance abuse treatment programs for military personnel (MCCSCP, 2006).

The following statement comes from the Web site of the Marine Corps Community Services Camp Pendleton (2006):

> The Consolidated Substance Abuse Counseling Services (CSACC) at Camp Pendleton strives to: (1) "Mission: to provide a thorough and responsive substance abuse program aboard Camp Pendleton for prevention, education, and treatment of substance abuse, and to provide commanders with effective programs to establish an environment free of substance use; (2) Prevention: drug and alcohol abuse present a large and mounting concern for military leaders, CSACC is there to assist and provide active campaigning to help educate military personnel and their family members on the dangers of illegal drugs and alcohol abuse, as well as personal and professional consequences of their actions while under the influence of alcohol; (3) Treatment: CSACC offers outpatient programs free to all military personnel and family members, a residential program for dependency is available at the Naval Hospital; (4) Services: CSACC provides screening and assessments, a two-day course on alcohol impact, outpatient treatment, intensive outpatient treatment, residential treatment, training to commands, a one-day Marine alcohol awareness course, and a one-day Marine drug awareness course.

Navy

The Navy Personnel Command Web site links to Navy Alcohol and Drug Use Prevention (NADAP) page, which provides information and links to assistance resources to support individual and command alcohol abuse and drug abuse prevention efforts (Navy Personnel Command, Bureau of Naval Personnel, 2006). NADAP discusses the Navy's mission to "support fleet readiness by fighting alcohol abuse and drug use."

Army

The Army Center for Substance Abuse Programs (ACSAP, n.d.) provides information to Army personnel about substance abuse program services, including drug testing, drug and alcohol prevention and education, risk reduction programs, treatment and clinical programs, soldier risk assessment checklist, recent articles related to substance abuse, substance abuse testing for deployment, as well as training information for Army commanders (Army Substance Abuse Program [ASAP], n.d.). The ASAP and ACSAP Web sites also provide information about the health risks caused by substance abuse, reviewing the "no tolerance" policy of alcohol and drug abuse in the Army due to the impact on mission effectiveness. ACSAP and the Substance Abuse Rehabilitation Department (SARD) work together to provide military personnel with a staff of medical professionals trained in the biological, psychological, and sociological components of substance abuse (ACSAP, n.d.; ASAP, n.d.). The ACSAP Web site explains that military personnel on active duty, family members of personnel on active duty, civilian employees, military retirees, and family members of military retirees are all eligible for ACSAP services (ACSAP, n.d.; ASAP, n.d.). Services may include individual counseling, group counseling, family counseling, referrals for inpatient care, and coordination with self-help groups, including Alcoholics Anonymous, Al-Anon, and Alateen (ACSAP, n.d.; ASAP, n.d.).

Air Force

The Air Force Medical Service (AFMS) Web page contains information about the Air Force "zero tolerance" policy for drug use, as well as providing information about how military leaders should help fellow military personnel to address alcohol problems to increase productivity (AFMS, n.d.). The Air Force created a "Responsible Drinking Culture" program called the "0-0-1-3" in 2004 to help decrease alcohol-related problems on U.S. Air Force bases. The 0-0-1-3 stands for "zero drinks under age 21, zero DUI's, maximum one drink per hour, maximum 3 drinks in one night" (AFMS, n.d.). The Air Force medical Web site also contains links to the Alcohol and Drug Abuse Prevention and Treatment Program (ADAPT), which includes a checklist with objectives of the ADAPT program, including a list of early signs of problem drinking, roles and responsibilities of leaders, methods for identifying substance abusers, and the ADAPT referral and intervention process (AFMS, n.d.).

Veterans

The veteran military population consists of all military members who served in any of the U.S. Armed Forces in the past. The DOD does several thorough substance abuse screenings of personnel: before deployment, once a year during active duty, once at discharge, and again 3 to 6 months later to identify and assist those individuals who may be at increased risk of biological, psychological, and sociological problems (Clay, 2006). However, studies show that community mental health and primary care providers are critical in helping to identify veterans in need of treatment services for substance use disorders (Clay, 2006; SAMHSA, 2006a). SAMHSA's Web sites explain that veterans need to be aware that they aren't automatically eligible for VA care. In order to qualify, veterans must take the initiative to register in the VA system within 2 years of discharge. If veterans do not register within the allotted time, they risk losing their access to VA care in the future (Clay, 2006). To be eligible for most VA benefits, veterans must have participated in active military service and cannot have been dishonorably discharged. The VA defines active service as full-time service in the Marine Corps, Army, Navy, or Air Force; or full-time service as a commissioned officer of the Public Health Service, the Environmental Services Administration, or the National Oceanic and Atmospheric Administration (Military.com, n.d.).

The VA Web site provides veterans with detailed information regarding VA substance abuse and recovery Web sites as well as links to general mental health and recovery sites, peer support and education, veteran organizations and project sites, psychosocial rehabilitation sites, cultural diversity sites, work and vocational sites, Mental Illness Research, Education and Clinical Center (MIRECC) research, VA programs, and other support systems (Department of Veterans Affairs, 2006). Veterans who have incomes that exceed the threshold for free medical care (i.e., over $60,000 a year) may apply to enroll in VA substance abuse treatment programs and be asked to pay a co-payment for VA services (Clay, 2006; Military.com, n.d.). The VA created an initiative called the substance use disorder Quality Enhancement Research Initiative (QUERI) to provide better treatment for VA patients with substance use disorders (Clay, 2006); SAMHSA also sponsors the annual Recovery Month observance in September (SAMHSA, 2006b). Studies examining veteran resources have noted that the VA Veterans Health Administration (VHA) is one of the few programs in the world that provides funding for vocational rehabilitation services for individuals with substance use disorders (Kerrigan, Kaough, Wilson, Wilson, & Bostick, 2004). Further research is needed to determine the effectiveness of different programs treating substance use disorders in veterans (Kerrigan et. al., 2004).

Prevention Efforts

Currently, multiple Web sites provide helpful information about the effects of alcohol and drugs, along with links to resources for treatment programs across the United States. Military OneSource is a Web site with links to substance addiction and recovery resources for military personnel, as well as helpful information about smooth transition into civilian life, healthy habits, domestic violence prevention, and parenting advice (Ceridian Corporation, 2006). Military OneSource also provides military members with contact information for brief problem-focused in-person counseling sessions.

The U.S. Department of Defense Office of Health Affairs helped to create a Web site with the nonprofit organization Screening for Mental Health to provide an anonymous online mental health and alcohol self-assessment screening for military members and their families (Preidt, 2006). The screening service is free to military members and provides immediate screening results and referrals to military mental health services.

Summary

Overall the DOD and the VA are working hard to (a) assist military personnel in maintaining their health and well-being, (b) encourage a responsible drinking culture by providing psychoeducation, (c) create an environment where military members are encouraged to seek help for alcohol and drug problems without fear of negative consequences and before alcohol and drug-related incidents occur (AFMS, n.d.), (d) implement treatment confidentiality policies, (e) customize substance abuse treatment programs within each of the military branches, and (f) provide outreach and psychoeducation support to military members and their families to cope with stress and to increase quality of life.

References

Air Force Medical Service. (n.d.). *Alcohol and drug abuse: Leader's guide for managing personnel distress.* Retrieved August 11, 2006, from http://airforcemedicine.afms.mil/idc/groups/public/documents/webcontent/knowledgejunct

Ames, G. M. (2002). *Military work and drinking: Risks and prevention.* Retrieved June 28, 2006, from Prevention Research Center Web site: http://www.prev.org/prc/prc_summary_ames_mwdrp.html

Ames, G. M., Cunradi, C. B., & Moore, R. S. (2002). Alcohol, tobacco, and drug use among young adults prior to entering the military. *Prevention Science, 3*(2), 135–144.

Army Center for Substance Abuse Programs. (n.d.). Home page. Accessed June 28, 2006, https://acsap.army.mil/sso/pages/index.jsp

Army Substance Abuse Program. (n.d.). Home page. Accessed June 28, 2006: http://www.jackson.army.mil/Directorates/Asap.htm

Bray, R. M., Hourani, L. L., Rae, K. L., Dever, J. A., Brown, J. M., Vincus, A. A., et al. (2003). *2002 Department of Defense survey of health related behaviors among military personnel* (Report No. RTI/7841/006-FR). Research Triangle Park, NC: Research Triangle Institute.

Ceridian Corporation. (2006). *Military OneSource: We're available 24/7.* Retrieved June 29, 2006, from http://www.militaryonesource.com/skins/MOS/home.aspx

Clay, R. A. (May/June 2006). *A critical safety net: The Road Home National Conference on Returning Veterans and Their Families* (Part 2). (U.S. Department of Health and Human Services, Substance Abuse and Mental Health Services Administration report). Retrieved June 28, 2006, from http://www.samhsa.gov/SAMHSA_News/VolumeXIV_3.htm

Cozza, S. J., Benedek, D. M., Bradley, J. C. Grieger, T. A., Nam, T. S., & Waldrep, D. A. (2003). *Military personnel Iraq War clinician guide: Topics specific to the psychiatric treatment of military personnel.* Department of Veterans Affairs, National Center for Posttraumatic Stress Disorder. Retrieved August 8, 2006, from http://www.ncptsd.va.gov/war/iraq_clinician_guide_v2/iraq_clinician_guide_ch_2.pdf

Department of Veterans Affairs. (2006). *Veteran recovery.* Retrieved June 28, 2006, from http://www.veteranrecovery.med.va.gov/vettoc.htm

Kerrigan, A. J., Kaough, J. E., Wilson, B. L., Wilson, J. V., & Bostick, R. (2004). Vocational rehabilitation of participants with severe substance use disorders in a VA veterans industries program. *Substance Use and Misuse, 39*(13/14), 2513–2523.

Marine Corps Community Services. (2006). *Leaders guide for managing Marines in distress: Alcohol use.* Retrieved August 10, 2006, from http://www.usmc-mccs.org/leadersguide/SubstanceUse/Alcohol/generalinfo.cfm

Marine Corps Community Services Camp Pendleton. (2006). *Consolidated Substance Abuse Counseling Service.* Retrieved June 28, 2006, from http://www.mccscamppendleton.com/qol/csacc/csacc.html

Military.com. (n.d.). *Alcohol and substance abuse treatment.* Retrieved August 15, 2006, from http://www.military.com/benefits/veterans-health-care/alcohol-and-substance-abuse-treatment

National Institute on Drug Abuse. (2005). *Stress and substance abuse: A special report.* Retrieved August 11, 2006, from http://www.drugabuse.gov/stressanddrugabuse.html

Navy Personnel Command, Bureau of Naval Personnel. (2006). *Navy alcohol and drug abuse prevention (NADAP).* Retrieved June 28, 2006, from http://www.npc.navy.mil/commandsupport/NADAP

Preidt, R. (2006, March 29). *U.S. military has new online mental health resource: HealthDay News.* Retrieved June 28, 2006, from http://mentalhelp.net/poc/view_doc.php?type=news&id=92649&cn=74

Screening for Mental Health. (2006). *Feeling disconnected? Put the pieces together. The mental health self-assessment program.* Retrieved June 28, 2006, from http://www.militarymentalhealth.org/welcome.asp

Substance Abuse and Mental Heath Services Administration. (2006a). *Alcohol use and alcohol related risk behaviors among veterans.* Retrieved August 10, 2006, from http://www.oas.samhsa.gov/2k5/vetsAlc/vetsAlc.cfm

Substance Abuse and Mental Health Services Administration. (2006b). National Alcohol and Drug Addiction Recovery Month. Retrieved August 10, 2006, fromhttp://www.recoverymonth.gov/2006/kit/html/Targeted_Outreach/military.aspx

Vaughan, D. (2006, August). Risky business. *Today's Officer.* Retrieved August 11, 2006, from http://www.moaa.org/TodaysOfficer/HealthLiving/

White, W., & Webber, R. (2003, June). Drugs and war: Principles of addition and subtraction. *Counselor: The Magazine for Addiction Professionals.* Retrieved August 11, 2006, from http://www.stopalcoholabuse.gov/prevention.aspx

Resources

Army Center for Substance Abuse Programs
https://acsap.army.mil/sso/pages/index.jsp

Army Substance Abuse Program
http://www.jackson.army.mil/Directorates/Asap.htm

Department of Veterans Affairs, Veteran Recovery
http://www.veteranrecovery.med.va.gov

Marine Corps Community Services
http://www.usmc-mccs.org

MentalHelp.net
http://mentalhelp.net

Military.com
http://www.military.com

Military OneSource
www.militaryonesource.com

National Institute on Drug Abuse
http://www.drugabuse.gov/stressanddrugabuse.html

Navy Personnel Command, Bureau of Naval Personnel
http://www.npc.navy.mil/commandsupport/NADAP

Substance Abuse and Mental Health Services Administration
www.samhsa.gov

CHAPTER 17

Substance Abuse in the Criminal Population

Micah J. Mann and Gary W. Lawson

Drug and alcohol use within the United States has reached epidemic proportions. In 2008, 75 million Americans reported illicit drug use at least once in their lifetime; this represents a significant increase from years past (Substance Abuse and Mental Health Services Administration, 2009). By their senior year, 50% of adolescents report they have used illegal substances (National Institute on Drug Abuse, 2006). Concomitantly, our national levels of crime are also rising. During the 1990s we put more people behind bars than in any previous decade by a wide margin, and today, there are well over 2 million Americans incarcerated in the United States (Bureau of Justice Statistics, 2005). Are these alarming statistics related? Is the drug problem fueling our crime statistics, or vice versa? Is there a relationship between substance abuse and criminal behavior? The answer is undoubtedly yes.

One can observe the association between crime and substance abuse in every facet of society. Interpersonally, it can be seen in violence that ensues from alcohol- or substance-related domestic disputes. Locally, it manifests in property crimes such as theft, robbery, and burglary stemming from the abuse of illicit drugs. Nationally, it can be seen in the growing number of drug-related arrests engulfing our penal and judicial systems. Ultimately, the relationship between substance abuse and crime touches every level of our society, and impinges upon our governments, communities, and individual lives.

The connection between criminal behavior and substance use is intricate and sometimes inexplicable. For decades, the paths of crime and drugs have been intertwined. Given the complexity of the relationship, the various complicated and convoluted issues arising from it have been studied from different vantage points. Medical scientists and sociologists have investigated the etiology of addiction and crime, legislators have toiled over the policy aspects of drug control, and rehabilitation professionals have struggled with various treatment approaches. In the following chapter, each of these viewpoints will be addressed. First, the association between substance abuse and crime will be investigated by determining the prevalence of substance abuse in the criminal population. Next, a greater understanding of the causal relationship between drug and alcohol use and crime will be examined. Following that will be a historical perspective on past legislative approaches to substance abuse and crime. Finally, the treatment for the substance-abusing criminal will be discussed.

Prevalence of Substance Abuse Within the Criminal Population

The first step in investigating the relationship between drug use and crime entails determining the prevalence in which substance abuse occurs in the context of criminal behavior. Before public policy or treatment perspectives can be assessed, it is necessary to determine the extent of association between the two variables. The population that is appraised becomes an important and decisive factor in producing reliable information regarding prevalence. Specifically, three populations have been sampled extensively to determine whether there is a relationship between substance abuse and crime: non-arrested criminal offenders, arrestees, and inmate populations.

Non-Arrested Criminals

Within the population of non-arrested criminal offenders, a clear association between criminal behavior and drug abuse has been established. In a longitudinal study, Ball, Rosen, Flueck, and Nurco (1981) found that 97% of their sample of 243 male narcotic addicts reported committing crimes more days than not over an 11-year period. Furthermore, they found that criminality was directly affected by addiction, in that, during periods of narcotic addiction, the mean crime rates were 6 times higher than during periods of non-addiction (Ball, Rosen, Flueck, & Nurco, 1981; Nurco, 1998). Inciardi and Pottieger (1998) found similar results from a sample of 356 male and female heroin addicts who committed a total of 118,134 offenses in a 12-month period. He states, "Very few of these heroin addicts did no crime, and the great majority were involved in multiple types of crime" (Inciardi & Pottieger, 1998, p. 1846). Finally, an in-depth study on heroin addicts in the city of New York found that 96% of 201 heroin-abusing individuals admitted obtaining income from illegal activities over an average period of 57 days (Johnson et al., 1985).

Research has also demonstrated a clear association between alcohol abuse and criminal offending. In a study from New Zealand involving a birth cohort of over 1,000 participants, the association between alcohol and crime was unmistakable. In this research, the participants were assessed for a 6-year period (ages 15–21 years) on criminal activity and the corresponding extent (if any) of alcohol abuse/dependence. Through the use of a fixed regression analysis, the researchers found clear linkages between the extent of alcohol abuse and coinciding rates of offending behavior. Those individuals who had high rates of alcohol abuse also had high corresponding rates of involvement in violent crimes and property crimes. Conversely, those participants who had low rates of alcohol abuse also had lower rates of criminal behavior. The researchers concluded that alcohol abuse increases the likelihood of involvement in criminal behaviors (Furgusson & Horwood, 2000).

Arrestees

The Arrestee Drug Abuse Monitoring Program (ADAM) is a federally funded research project undertaken to monitor the substance abuse tendencies of recently arrested criminal offenders. This project, which began in 1987, uses self-report questionnaires and drug screens on individuals who have been recently arrested. The program collects data from 34 cities across the United States, and entails a sample size of over 45,000 participants (National Institute of Justice, 2003). For more than a decade, the ADAM program has shown that the majority of detained arrestees test positive for recent drug use within 48 hours of their arrest. Furthermore, in most cities, the drug use by detained arrestees has been rising at an alarming rate. For example, in Washington, DC, the percentage of arrestees testing positive for drug use was 55% in 1984, jumping to 75% by 1989 (Bureau of Justice Assistance, 2003). The current statistics from the ADAM program are equally as elevated. According to the 1997 Annual Report on Adult and Juvenile Arrestees from ADAM, more than 60% of the adult male arrestees tested positive for the presence of at least one drug, and for female arrestees the statistics were equally high (National Institute of Justice, 2003).

The types of drugs that were used by the participants within the ADAM project were vastly diversified. Marijuana was the most frequently detected drug in 24 of the 34 cities. However, in the other ten sites cocaine was found to be the most prevalent. In the southwestern section of the United States, methamphetamine was found to have extremely high rates. Opiate use was reported in lower rates relative to the other types of drugs that were tested. In fact, within the entire sample, only six sites reported opiate-positive rates of 10% or higher. The low reported use of opiates is an interesting finding given that much of the research conducted involving the association between crime and drug use has focused on heroin and other similar opiate-type drugs (Bureau Institute of Justice Assistance, 2003).

One type of drug that was not included in the ADAM project is alcohol. However, alcohol has been found to be an important factor in other research programs conducted on the recently arrested. According to the Bureau of Justice Assistance (2003), surveys conducted throughout the United States reveal that 30% to 40% of arrestees report having been under the influence of alcohol immediately prior to or during the commission of their offenses. In addition, research has shown that arrestees who have committed violent crimes are more likely to have reported recent use of alcohol than to test positive for use of an illegal substance (Bureau of Justice Assistance, 2003).

Inmates

Perhaps the most comprehensive and intriguing statistics regarding the prevalence of substance abuse within the criminal population stems from research conducted on the inmate population. A structured clinical interview conducted with 133 incarcerated men in a Massachusetts federal prison found that 95% were given the diagnosis of substance dependence. The specific types of dependence were varied, ranging from alcohol (the most prevalent) to hallucinogenic (the least prevalent). Moreover, "58% reported that they were acutely intoxicated with one or more substances at the time they committed the crime, and an additional 6% were withdrawing from a substance at the time of the crime" (Kouri, Pope, Powell, Olivia, & Campbell, 1997, p. 415). Given these findings, the authors conclude, "It seems clear that substance abuse and dependence are extraordinarily prevalent among men incarcerated for crimes in Massachusetts, and very likely elsewhere in the United States" (Kouri et al., 1997, p. 418).

This association between incarceration and substance abuse has been corroborated in recent government survey statistics. A 1991 survey of inmates in state and federal correctional facilities found that 60% of federal prisoners, and 79% of state prisoners, reported extensive prior drug use. Furthermore, these findings increased dramatically over the next several years, and in 1997 the percentage of state prisoners reporting extensive drug use was 83% compared with federal prisons at 73% (Mumola, 1999). In a study based on inmates held in local jails, 55% of those convicted reported they had used illegal drugs during the month before their offense. This percentage is an increase from 1989, when only 44% reported illegal drug use 1 month prior to the offense (Harlow, 1998). A similar study based on the specific drug involvement of jail inmates found that 64% had used drugs regularly, 42% had received treatment, 17% had used intravenous drugs, and 27% had a prior sentence of drug law violations (Wilson, 2000).

Extensive alcohol use is also found to be pervasive across federal, state, and local inmates. According to the U.S. government statistics, corrections authorities supervised an estimated 5.3 million convicted offenders on an average day in 1996. Of those offenders, nearly 2 million (36%) had been drinking alcohol when they committed their crime. Furthermore, 6 in 10 local jail inmates admitted to drinking on a regular basis a year before they committed their offense. The findings are similar for inmates held in state prisons: 50% admitted being daily drinkers at the time of their offense, and most of the 50% reported being extremely intoxicated at the time of their incarcerating offense (Greenfield, 1998).

Understanding the Causality of Criminal Behavior and Substance Abuse

The association between substance abuse and crime is unmistakable. The statistics highlight a clear correlation between arrest rates and addiction. Consequently, increasing arrest rates have led to a penal system teeming with addicts. The determination of a problem, however, does not necessarily yield a solution. To create meaningful public policy and treatment perspectives, a precise relationship of cause and effect must be established. As Walters (1998) suggested, "Demonstrating a relationship between drugs and crime is one thing; explaining this relationship is quite another" (p. 9). The difficulty in explaining the relationship between addiction and crime lies in the etiology. In other words, which comes first, the addiction or the crime? Although research on this topic is plentiful, a definitive answer has not been established. The four major hypotheses set forth by the literature include (Walters, 1998):

1. Substance abuse causes crime.
2. Crime causes substance abuse.
3. The causation between substance abuse and crime is reciprocal.
4. Crime and substance abuse are merely correlated, and no causal relationship exists.

Hypothesis 1: Substance Abuse Causes Crime

Many researchers suggest addiction causes one to engage in subsequent criminal behavior. This viewpoint contends that substance abuse acts as a catalyst, compelling an otherwise law-abiding citizen to resort to criminal behavior (Bean & Wilkinson, 1988).

This dynamic is often attributed to the pharmacological effects of the substances. Specifically, drug use impairs one's judgment, which might provide the impetus to engage in criminal behavior. The specific pharmacological effects experienced by an individual differ depending on the substance used and on the user's physiology, and may affect the type of crime committed. For example, alcohol has long been associated with high rates of aggression and violence, especially within cases of spousal abuse. Spouse- and/or child-abusing males are more likely than the general public to be addicted to alcohol. Furthermore, the highest rates of family violence are found in those households with moderate-to-heavy drinkers (Ross & Lightfoot, 1985). Ross and Lightfoot note that "drunkenness in one party appears to be the best predictor of family violence" (p. 11).

The pharmacological effects of many other substances are also conducive to catalyzing violent and illegal behavior. Stimulants such as cocaine and amphetamines may cause agitation, anger, and psychosis, while psychoactive drugs such as marijuana and phencyclidine (or PCP) are known to cause perceptual distortions and grandiosity (Sinha & Easton, 1999). Research has shown that the acute effects of all of these substances alter brain functioning with associated changes in personality, behavior, cognition, and emotionality (Sinha & Easton, 1999). Furthermore, frequent use of these substances can lead to increased tolerance, which in turn leads to increasing amounts of use, and ultimately to dependence. Consequently, using larger amounts for longer periods increases the probability that negative cognitive and behavioral consequences will occur, which in turn can lead to greater risk of participation in illegal behaviors (Sinha & Easton, 1999).

The economic impact of addiction is also an important consideration concerning etiology. This line of research implies that drug users (especially users of heroin and other opiates) engage in criminal behavior to finance their habits. Numerous researchers of the topic have concluded that there is a high prevalence of diversity of criminal activities on the part of narcotic addicts and that this involvement is largely for the purpose of supporting the use of drugs (Nurco, Ball, Shaffer, & Hanlon, 1985). This explanation is maintained by research that demonstrates that criminal behavior is increased during periods of addiction, and decreased during periods of non-addiction. It is thought that the reason for this correspondence between addiction and crime lies in addicts' need for money to buy their next fix.

The type of crime committed by substance abusers lends support to the notion that crime is motivated by monetary objectives. Specifically, in a study by Ball et al. (1981), it was established that the majority of crimes committed by narcotic addicts was theft and drug dealing. A number of other studies have found similar results (Nurco et al., 1985). Unlike violent or predatory crimes, the reasons for theft and drug dealing are monetary in nature. An in-depth study by Jarvis and Parker (1989) validated this assumption. Through interviews with 64 heroin users, Jarvis and Parker found that most of their sample depended on illegal activities to support their addiction. They found that most of the subjects were unable to support their expensive habits by legitimate means, and that "83% of the subjects admitted they made up this shortfall by resorting to various illegal activities" (Jarvis & Parker, 1989, p. 179).

Hypothesis 2: Crime Causes Substance Abuse

Another viewpoint concerning the relationship between substance abuse and crime holds that criminal behavior eventually leads to later substance abuse. This theory considers drug and alcohol abuse as an extension of a deviant lifestyle (Bean & Wilkinson, 1988). This theory is corroborated with research denoting that early antisocial behavior often precedes the use of drugs and alcohol (Walters, 1998). In a summary of past findings, Nathan (1988) notes that "research into links between personality and the etiology of alcohol and drug abuse has found, with considerable consistency, a relation between a range of childhood and adolescent behaviors associated with rejection of the rules of society and later alcoholism" (p. 185). These rejections of societal rules in childhood and early adolescence may be the beginning of a life of illegal acts and criminal behavior. Also lending itself to this hypothesis, researchers have concluded that at-risk adolescents can be distinguished by their early behavior before they begin to use addictive substances. These behavior patterns consist of valuing independence to the point of being a loner, failing to value conventional societal institutions, and holding critical views of society in general. Interestingly, these same behavior patterns are also frequently found in adult convicted criminals (Nathan, 1988).

Anglin and Speckart (1988) researched the temporal relationship between the onset of criminal behavior and substance abuse. They interviewed a sample of 671 self-reported heroin addicts. Through these interviews, the authors investigated the chronological time period in which substance abuse and criminal behavior occurred. Their results indicated that 60% to 75% of the participants were arrested before ever trying illicit narcotics. Furthermore, they found that theft was more likely to occur before addiction began.

In a similar study undertaken by Pettiway, Dolinsky, and Grigoryan (1994), a Markov chain analysis was used to assess the day-to-day activity patterns of 431 criminal offenders in Philadelphia. Through this method of investigation, the probabilities of sequential behaviors were assessed. Their results confirmed that substance use was more likely to occur after a criminal act than vice versa. They concluded, "Overall, crime-related ventures are more likely to lead to drug-related activities, whereas drug-related activities are less likely to give rise to criminal activity" (Pettiway et al., 1994, pp. 79–107). According to this research, addiction does not appear to provide the impetus for additional crime-related activity, supporting the viewpoint that crime causes drug abuse rather than the other way around.

Hypothesis 3: Causation Is Reciprocal

As noted by Walters (1998), the bi-directional theory of addiction and crime contends that the relationship is reciprocal. This theory rejects the notion of simplistic causality in favor of a more complex systemic loop, in which both substance abuse and crime feed off of each other. The reciprocal effect model is often used in parenting paradigms to explain parental socialization. According to this model, not only does parenting affect child behavior, but child behavior also affects parenting (Stice & Barrera, 1995). The same paradigm can be applied to the substance abuse and crime debate, in that not only can substance abuse affect criminal behavior, but criminal behavior can also affect substance abuse (Walters, 1998).

This theory was supported by a study undertaken by Hammersley, Forsyth, Morrison, and Davies (1989). These investigators conducted interviews with 151 Scottish prisoners and non-prisoners, all with varying levels of substance abuse. Their results indicated that the relationship between substance abuse and crime might be far more complex and dynamic than other researchers have suggested. Namely, they found that many factors, such as criminal history, type of drug used, and polydrug history, variably influenced those who engaged in criminal behavior and substance abuse. They stated, "Despite the essential simplicity of the idea that addiction causes crime because the addict is compelled to obtain drugs by any means, this idea was not supported by these data" (Hammersley et al., 1989, p. 1040). In a summary of their findings the authors concluded that the need for opioids and other drugs did not simply cause crime, but crime and drug use actually tended to influence each other (Hammersley et al., 1989).

An investigation by Faupel and Klockars (1987) regarding the life histories of 32 heroin addicts also lends support to the notion of reciprocal causality within the substance abuse and crime debate. In establishing the life histories of their participants, the authors found that virtually all respondents reported their criminal and drug careers began independently of one another, and it was only after a considerable time period that both activities became interconnected (Faupel & Klockars, 1987). Furthermore, the participants related that their addictive and criminal behaviors had developed slowly over long periods of time, and each had gone through differing established phases. Within each of these phases, the authors found that the relationship between heroin use and crime was not necessarily consistent. In other words, the causality between substance abuse and criminal behavior varied depending upon where the participant was in his or her developmental addiction process. The authors concluded, "While in any given instance, it may be possible to specify a causal sequence, our data suggests that any generalizations suggesting a simple cause–effect scheme fails to capture the complexity of the drug-crime connection throughout the addict's career" (Faupel & Klockars, 1987, p. 64).

Hypothesis 4: No Causal Relationship

The final hypothesis regarding the relationship between substance abuse and criminal behavior contends that the two variables are not causally related. This theory asserts that the relationship between substance abuse and crime is spurious and illusory (Walters, 1998). One example of this type of assumption maintains that the intoxication of the addict is used as an excuse to commit criminal acts (Walters, 1998). This argument contends that a cognitive decision is made by the substance user to intoxicate him- or herself in order to relieve any consequences that eventually may be incurred. For example, a study by Coleman and Strauss in 1979 found that abusive husbands sometimes drank alcohol so that they could blame drunkenness for their inclination to beat their wives (Ross & Lightfoot, 1985).

Another common argument maintains that substance abuse and crime are the result of common causes, but do not directly influence each other. This theory asserts that a common third variable is the explanation for the concurrent high rates of substance abuse in the criminal population. Although these theories all contend that common variables connect substance abuse and crime, they disagree as to the exact nature of what those common variables are. In a review of the literature, Fagen, Weiss, and Cheng (1990) found that "a variety of social, psychological, and economic factors have been found to be associated with both crime and drug use, and the overlap between joint behaviors may suggest common correlates and etiological paths" (p. 358). They stated that these common correlates can take many forms. For example, several studies have identified family history, religious ties, and school performance as being important variable correlates between substance abuse and criminal behavior.

In an empirical study of the relationship between drug abuse and delinquency among 2,022 adolescents, a group of common correlates were found (Lopez, Martin, Redondo, Carrillo, & Trinanes, 1994). Specifically, these researchers established that deviant behavior and substance abuse could best be predicted from the adolescent's primary social environment. This primary social environment was further broken down into the adolescent's family and peer network. The authors concluded that drug abuse and delinquency could be considered a single syndrome in which a single set of major causes is responsible for both aspects. They warned that future research in the area should abandon investigation of causal relationships, and instead concentrate on identifying the common variables affecting both phenomena (Lopez et al., 1994).

Summary of the Etiology

As previous research demonstrates, the relationship between substance abuse and crime is complicated. Though the causal relationship has been the subject of extensive research, the findings of these studies are generally not mutually exclusive (Lopez et al., 1994). Each of the four hypotheses may explain a portion of the variance shared by substance abuse and crime, however none of the interpretations are capable of completely accounting for the drug–crime relationship (Walters, 1998). For example, in one circumstance, the cause of criminality may be linked to substance abuse, in another it may be reciprocal, while in another it may be noncausal. The hypothetical situations are endless. Whereas one theory may account for a certain proportion of criminals, none of the hypotheses can account for all of them (Walters, 1998). Clearly, the substance-abusing criminal is a diversified population. Given this diversity, a single treatment approach is unlikely to be effective (Kinlock, Hanlon, & Nurco, 1999). However, before specific treatment approaches are considered, it is important to understand the legislative context in which the treatment occurs.

Historical Perspective on Legislative Approaches to Substance Abuse and Crime

The legislative response to crime and substance abuse in the United States has alternated between two opposing perspectives on correctional justice: the criminal model and the treatment model. Each model asserts conflicting values, which in turn affects their end goals. The goals of the criminal model include punishment and retribution in the form of incarceration. This model regards offenders as confirmed criminals who endanger society by their antisocial behavior, whether their crime might be attributable to an addiction or not. By contrast, the treatment model advocates for rehabilitation of and therapy for the offender, and attempting to restore the individual to a positive lifestyle (Kinlock et al., 1999). During the past 50 years, the correctional philosophy in the United States has vacillated between these perspectives (Gebelein, 2000).

During the 1950s, rehabilitation was widely accepted as the primary goal for correctional institutions. Numerous programs were implemented to provide the criminal offender with the tools necessary to put his or her life back together. The dominance of rehabilitation during this period also led to indeterminate sentencing in which the parole boards decided upon the offender's problem, treatment, and subsequent release date (Gebelein, 2000). If the parole board felt that a certain offender was rehabilitated, he or she was subsequently released. But such decision making was highly subjective. In theory, this method of sentencing ensured that the criminal had the capacity to change his or her life before reentering society. However, in reality, indeterminate sentencing ultimately led to the demise of the rehabilitation model's acceptance (Gebelein, 2000; Kinlock et al., 1999).

By the mid-1970s, the effectiveness of rehabilitation and indeterminate sentencing was beginning to be questioned. These philosophical shifts were brought about by several factors. First, the liberal-mindedness of the time brought into question the fairness of the policies. Specifically, the use of parole boards to determine the length of sentences was seen as unfair, as offenders would receive disparate sentences for similar crimes. Moreover, there was a concern that the parole boards were being unfair to minorities, as evidenced by jails and prisons that are mostly made up of African Americans

(Kinlock, et al., 1999). Finally, crime and recidivism rates were increasing, overwhelming many jurisdictions' financial ability to provide quality programs for incoming new and recidivist prisoners (Gebelein, 2000).

All of these factors led to a complete shift in philosophy as the ultra-punitive 1980s began. "Just say no!" became the slogan for the "War on Drugs" campaign instituted by the federal government during this era. The campaign touted retribution and punishment as the ultimate goals of corrections. As noted by Gebelein (2000), "Incapacitation became the primary goal and rehabilitation the last" (p. 2). Policies such as "mandatory minimums," "zero tolerance," and "three-strikes" guaranteed long sentences for any criminal offender, including the substance abuser. The war on drugs promised less crime, fewer drugs, and cleaner streets. However, by the end of the 1980s these promises were unfulfilled. Drug use and crime continued to rise. Offenders were being recycled in and out of the penal system; their underlying problems were left untreated. The emphasis on punishment had failed, and once again a philosophical shift began.

The lessons learned from previous decades facilitated the implementation of the latest model of criminal justice. The moderate approach of the 1990s was a balance between the leniency of the 1950s and the severity of the 1980s. In 1992, the Office of National Drug Control Policy summarized the new policy (Inciardi & Martin, 1993):

> Drug treatment and criminal justice are allies in the fight against drug use, and appropriate actions by the criminal justice system can foster treatment effectiveness. Researchers have found that the threat of criminal justice sanctions motivates the offenders to enter treatment and perhaps more important, to stay in treatment for a period of time sufficient for behavior change. The strategy supports the expansion and improvement of treatment for drug-dependent offenders, and the increased capability of the criminal justice system to identify, refer, and monitor offenders in treatment. (p. 4)

By combining the treatment and criminal models of correctional justice, both sides are encouraged to work in concert rather than against one another. The enmeshment of these two perspectives has led to a criminal justice system that maintains dual roles—incarceration and rehabilitation. In other words, the incarceration of the criminal offender is viewed as an opportunity to both punish and treat. Moreover, through these dual roles, the offender can have the opportunity to change his or her negative lifestyle and become a productive member of society.

Treatment for the Substance-Abusing Criminal

The goal of psychological treatment is behavioral change (Lawson, 1989). For substance-abusing criminals, this behavioral change is twofold. Not only must the individual break his or her addiction, but he or she must also resign from criminal behavior. As previously evidenced by the etiology of the drug–crime relationship, separating these behaviors can be a difficult task. The efficacy of treatment will be hampered if only a portion of the problem is solved. For example, if treatment only considers addiction, the client is likely to return to his or her criminal behavior upon release, which in turn may lead back to the addiction. In order to obtain complete change, the treatment must address the person as a *whole*. This includes treating the addiction, the criminality, and any other variables that contributed to the client's previous lifestyle (Walters, 1998).

Overall, criminal-based substance abuse treatment has shown promising results. Several studies have found that treatment within the penal system is effective in reducing rates of relapse, rearrests, convictions, and reincarcerations (Wald, Flaherty, & Pringle, 1999; Wexler, 1992; Wexler, Falkin, & Lipton, 1990). However, the treatment of this population has its difficulties. First, the judicial system is often not conducive to the therapeutic process. Wald et al. (1999) note, "Inmates find it difficult to attend treatment or counseling sessions where they are expected to address difficult personal issues, and then be returned to a jail cell with the general population" (p. 370). Additionally, within the prison system the access to drugs and alcohol is widespread, making it difficult for an addict to begin the recovery process (Wald et al., 1999). In fact, motivation is always an issue when dealing with coerced individuals. Most criminal offenders seek treatment as a part of their sentence because they were ordered by a judge to do so, or because they will receive leniency if they attend. Whatever the reasons, coercion creates low motivation and willingness to actively be involved in the therapeutic process.

Project REFORM, a federally funded technical assistance project, began in the late 1980s to assist correctional programs throughout the United States in implementing successful treatment interventions (Wexler & Lipton, 1993). The members of project REFORM believed that the primary goal for corrections is the reduction of recidivism in both substance abuse and criminal behavior. To attain this goal they were guided by seven intervention principles, which served as the hallmark for individual and group treatment. These seven principles were based on clinical experience and a review of the treatment literature. When working within the correctional setting, these principles become the basis for treatment efficacy and subsequent success. The REFORM project principles are (Wexler & Lipton, 1993):

- Self-Identification—Offenders often place the blame of their criminal behavior and substance abuse on external circumstances. Although the conditions of one's background are an important aspect of treatment, criminal offenders often need assistance identifying their own internal impediments to recovery.
- Motivation—Lack of motivation can be a difficult problem to overcome. However, through the use of incentives and positive feedback, participation can be significantly increased. Motivational techniques can become part of the therapeutic process and implemented within the client's treatment plan.
- Involvement—For treatment to be effective, offenders need to have some control regarding the therapeutic process. This can be accomplished by involving the offenders in their own program planning, and letting them decide what parts of their own lives need improvement.
- Reflection—This principle involves allowing clients to have contact with the general population, giving them an opportunity to test their progress in higher risk environments and see how much they have changed since inception of treatment.

- Reinforcement—Criminal offenders have often been acclimated to receiving punishment for their behaviors. This can potentially create mistrust within the treatment setting. Trust can be regained by the therapist through positive reinforcement of prosocial behaviors, rather than directly attempting to reduce the frequency of negative behaviors through punishment.
- Reward—Related to reinforcement, appropriate rewards for positive behavior and attitude are critical within the correctional setting. Such rewards may include increased privileges, early release, better housing, better clothes, better jobs, and more pay.
- Transition—Upon release, it is important to insure that there is a transition to a community-based treatment program, if necessary. Furthermore, the offender should have provisions for basic survival and security needs, such as housing, food, and employment.

Given the range of issues that must be addressed, not to mention the various difficulties that will consequently ensue, it is important to use a wide latitude of interventions when conducting treatment with substance-abusing offenders. Cognitive and behavioral therapies are commonly used to enhance the offenders' problem-solving skills and interpersonal-reasoning strategies. Life skills are essential for offenders who have deficits in such areas as managing finances or maintaining health and personal hygiene. Communication skill training is typically used when offenders have a history of interpersonal conflict. Finally, drug education and relapse prevention are implemented as key components within substance abuse treatment (Peters, 1993a). Most treatment models that address the criminal population use any number of the above modalities. However, the number and type of interventions often depend on the treatment model. The wider range of modalities that one model incorporates, the better the expected outcome.

Walters (1998) advocated the use of a lifestyle model of intervention with substance-abusing offenders. The lifestyle approach to intervention is an integrated model, combining many modalities within its structure. Psychoanalytic techniques are used to recognize underlying issues, behavioral and cognitive therapies are used for skill development, and social supports as promoted by 12-step programs are used for motivation and inspiration. By combining these modalities, the lifestyle model of intervention focuses the treatment upon the person as a whole, and not the individual's subparts. Walters's (1998) model of intervention consists of three phases of treatment. The first phase involves addressing the client's dysfunctional criminal and drug-using lifestyle, the second phase entails teaching the client basic social coping and thinking skills, and the third phase uses resocializing to facilitate a lifestyle for the client that is incompatible with substance abuse and crime (Walters, 1998).

The models of intervention currently used within the judicial system vary according to numerous factors. These factors include levels of funding, involvement of correctional staff, and philosophical values of the policy makers. Furthermore, most models of intervention are multimodal in that they incorporate a range of therapeutic modalities and techniques. Currently the most frequently used models are the therapeutic community, the Bureau of Prisons Substance Abuse Program, and drug courts.

Therapeutic Community

Extensively used within the jail and prison system, the therapeutic community operates a total treatment environment that is isolated from the rest of the prison population (Inciardi, 1996). Based on the traditions of self-help modalities, the therapeutic community is self-governed with day-to-day activities that are conducted by the residents themselves. Although, there is extensive group and individual counseling, the residents also benefit from feedback by peers, who model social responsibility and proper interpersonal behaviors. Strategies such as confrontation and peer pressure are also commonly used to encourage motivation and commitment to maintain a drug-free lifestyle (Peters, 1993b). Rules and regulations in the therapeutic community are numerous and strict. The staff, who are usually recovering addicts, give privileges to the residents only when they are earned, thus creating an environment of mutual responsibility (Inciardi, 1996).

Cornerstone Prison in Oregon operates a successful therapeutic community (Wald et al., 1999). It serves approximately 80 offenders each year, and provides treatment to individuals who have an extensive history of chronic addiction. In addition to the basic therapeutic community model, the Cornerstone program utilizes four phases of treatment. The orientation and intensive phases span a 5- to 9-month time span. During this period, cognitive and behavioral therapy, 12-step meetings, and psychoeducational classes are used to develop a recovery support system. In the transition and aftercare phase, the client is prepared for reentry into the community. The residents perform community volunteer work and secure employment. In addition, the program staff facilitates meetings with family members and parole officers in order to develop an aftercare plan (Wald et al., 1999). Cornerstone's outcome studies have yielded low recidivism rates as defined by arrest, convictions, and prison incarceration. These studies also reveal a direct positive correlation between the length of treatment and decreased reinvolvement in the criminal justice system. (Field, 1985; Wald et al., 1999).

There are several advantages to using therapeutic communities with criminal populations. First, the participants within the therapeutic community are isolated from the general population and this "tends to foster a sense of community identity and to reduce negative peer influence of inmates who are not involved in treatment" (Peters, 1993a, p. 56). Additionally, the therapeutic community is usually long-term and very intensive, which may be valuable for hardcore chronic addicts. Finally, the therapeutic community aims at making complex lifestyle changes instead of simple behavioral adjustments, which is critical given the complexity of the drug–crime relationship (Peters, 1993b).

The disadvantages of the therapeutic community model involve the uniformity of treatment approaches. Given the diversity of this population, matching of treatment modality to the needs of each individual is critical. This need for diverse modalities may be impossible in the self-help type of social structure inherent in this model. While, the use of confrontation and peer pressure may be appropriate for one type of substance abuser, it may not be appropriate for another. The overall lack of flexibility within the therapeutic community could be viewed as a significant shortcoming of this particular model.

Bureau of Prisons Substance Abuse Program

The drug and alcohol programs within the federal Bureau of Prisons (BOP) are an example of a flexible approach to substance abuse treatment in the offender population. The BOP model bases individualized treatment plans on comprehensive assessments. Through these individualized treatment plans each offender is given appropriate treatment based on their individual needs. These treatment plans are reviewed every 60 days to give additional flexibility over time. According to Murray (1996), the attention given to each individual helps the BOP programs avoid the uniformity that is common in other programs, including therapeutic communities.

In addition to comprehensive assessments and individualized treatment plans, the BOP model requires that each inmate participate in 500 hours of group and individual therapy. The group curriculum is structured, didactic, and experimental. The topics covered within the group setting include communication and interpersonal skills, wellness lifestyle training, criminal thinking confrontation, and relapse prevention. Individual sessions are used to update and work on each participant's treatment plan (Murray, 1996). Once the inmate has completed the required 500 hours of residential treatment, he or she moves on to the transitional phase of the model. In this phase the participant is released to a community treatment center with specialized therapeutic drug and alcohol programming provided by contracted professionals. During the aftercare phase of the model, additional treatment is coordinated with U.S. courts and federal probation (Murray, 1996).

The flexibility and individualized commitment to each participant is the obvious advantage of the BOP model of rehabilitation. The extensive lists of topics that are covered in the curriculum are diverse and comprehensive, not only addressing substance abuse, but also confronting the criminal lifestyle. However, there are potential weaknesses in this method of treatment. First, participants run the risk of negative peer influence while incarcerated by not being isolated from the rest of the general population. Second, the treatment methods used may not provide enough impetus for change in the long-term chronic addict.

Drug Court

A recent innovation of substance abuse treatment in the criminal justice system is the drug court. Drug courts offer judicially supervised treatment to nonviolent criminals with chronic drug and alcohol abuse problems in lieu of incarceration. Drug court programs usually entail intensive outpatient treatment with frequent urinalysis testing. However, sobriety is only the first step in completing the program. Typically, drug courts require meeting educational goals, such as obtaining a GED or high school diploma, and financial goals, such as paying off child support or other debts, and some drug courts also include mandated community service work (Belenko, 1998). Participants are required to appear in court once or twice a month on specified dates where a judge reviews the case and progression is assessed. Any deviation from the mandated treatment program results in immediate sanctions, varying from increased treatment protocols to short-term incarceration (Belenko, 1998; Substance Abuse and Mental Health Services Administration, 1997).

The foremost goal of the drug court model is to reduce drug use and the associated criminal behavior by engaging and retaining the offender in programmatic and treatment services (Belenko, 1998). The innovation of the drug court stems from the blending of judicial and treatment perspectives. In any courtroom, the judge is the central figure in handing down sanctions and allotting criminals due justice. However, within the drug court model a judge participates proactively in the participant's case, acting more as a reinforcer of positive behavior than a punishment-seeking authority figure. In fact, most drug courts utilize the entire staff, including the prosecutors, defense attorneys, and counselors working as a team to help the offender overcome his or her drug problems and resolve other issues related to work, finances, and family (Belenko, 1998).

Since its 1989 introduction in Dade County, Florida, the use of the drug court model has proliferated across the nation. In 48 of the 50 states, more than 320 drug courts are operating nationwide. Over 140,000 individuals have enrolled in the drug court program, with 98,000 graduates, most of whom were never previously exposed to any type of substance abuse treatment (Drug Court Clearinghouse and Technical Assistance Project, 1998).

According to research, drug courts have been extremely successful at engaging and retaining criminals who have substantial substance abuse and criminal histories, but little to no prior treatment. Data also suggest significantly reduced drug use and criminal behavior during the drug court process and that criminal behavior is significantly lower after program participation. Furthermore, according to cost-saving analyses, for every dollar spent in drug court, $10 is saved in reduced jail/prison use, reduced criminality, and lower criminal justice system costs (Drug Court Clearinghouse and Technical Assistance Project, 1998).

The benefits of the drug court model are numerous. With the judicial and treatment sectors working hand in hand, the supervision of offenders within the community is streamlined and therefore more effective. This also allows greater accountability to be placed on the clients in terms of compliance. Additionally, utilizing outpatient treatment reduces the overcrowding of jails and prisons, which in turn reduces cost (Belenko, 1998). However, what has made the drug court movement so powerful is its ability to humanely rehabilitate without resorting to incarceration. Ultimately, drug courts offer treatment that serves the public, the offender, and society as a whole.

Summary of Treatment

Flexible yet effective treatment programs are an indispensable weapon in the battle against substance abuse and criminal behavior. By providing offenders with the necessary education and prevention techniques, significant change can be achieved. As described previously, the method used to provide this treatment varies from one model to the next. However, the fundamental goal of treatment is clear—reduce the recidivism rates of substance abuse and criminal behavior. Several basic values are constant throughout all modalities of treatment. These values are the groundwork for the establishment of efficient and successful therapeutic models within the justice system. These values include (Peters, 1993b, p. 93):

- Development of individualized multidisciplinary treatment plans that address the full range of supervision, control, habilitation, and rehabilitation needs.
- Matching offenders with supervision, control, and treatment programs appropriate to their assessed needs and perceived risks.
- Providing a range of services, from drug education to intensive residential programs.
- Providing drug education to all offenders.
- Enhancing prerelease treatment programming.
- Using an integrated staffing approach to deliver treatment.
- Providing incentives and sanctions to increase offender motivation for treatment.
- Increasing the availability of self-help groups as an adjunct to treatment and as an integral part of aftercare.
- Providing targeted treatment programs for special populations.
- Providing education and treatment for relapse prevention.

Though these principles are not an exhaustive summary of the important facets within treatment, they provide the necessary groundwork if innovative models of intervention are to be introduced in the future.

Summary

The relationship between substance abuse and criminal behavior is a subject of many differing viewpoints and perspectives. Addiction and criminality are so tightly intertwined, it is almost impossible to tell where one stops and the other begins. This chapter has summarized the basic variables regarding this multifaceted topic. The etiology of criminal behavior and substance abuse, the history of legislation, and the various treatment perspectives are all important pieces to this seemingly endless puzzle. Through tireless efforts of researchers, legislators, and treatment providers, many obstacles have been overcome in reducing recidivism and providing effective treatment. However, continued effort is required to develop new and improved approaches of treatment and prevention. Through this continued effort the insidious cycle of crime and addiction may finally be halted.

References

Anglin, D. M., & Speckart, G. (1988). Narcotic use and crime: A multisample–multimethod analysis. *Criminology, 26,* 197–122.

Ball, J. C., Rosen, L., Flueck, J. A., & Nurco, D. N. (1981). The criminality of heroin addicts: When addicted and when off opiates. In J. A. Inciardi (Ed.), *The drugs-crime connection* (pp. 39–65). Thousand Oaks, CA: Sage

Bean, P. T., & Wilkinson, C. K. (1988). Drug taking and the illicit supply system. *British Journal of Addiction, 83,* 533–539.

Belenko, S. (1998). Research on drug courts: A critical review. *National Drug Court Institute Review, 1,* 1–24.

Bureau of Justice Assistance. (2000). Breaking the cycle of substance abuse and crime. In *FY 2000 program plan.* Retrieved May 5, 2007, from http://www.ojp.usdoj.gov/BJA/

Bureau of Justice Statistics. (2005). *Corrections statistics: Summary of findings.* Retrieved August 12, 2006, from http://www.ojp.usdoj.gov/bjs/prisons.htm

Drug Court Clearinghouse and Technical Assistance Project. (1998). *Looking at a decade of drug courts.* Washington, DC: U.S. Department of Justice.

Fagan, J., Weiss, J. G., & Cheng, Y. T. (1990). Delinquency and substance use among inner-city students. *Journal of Drug Issues, 20,* 351–402.

Faupel, C. E., & Klockars, C. B. (1987). Drugs-crime connections: Elaborations from the life histories of hard-core heroin addicts. *Social Problems, 34,* 54–68.

Field, G. (1985). The cornerstone program: A client outcome study. *Federal Probation, 48,* 50–55.

Furgusson, D. M., & Horwood, J. L. (2000). Alcohol abuse and crime: A fixed-effects regression analysis. *Addiction, 95,* 1525–1536.

Gebelein, R. S. (2000). The rebirth of rehabilitation: Promise and peril of drug courts. *Sentencing and Corrections: Issues for the 21st Century, 6,* 1–7.

Greenfield, L. A. (1998). *Alcohol and crime* (NCJ Publication No. 168632). Washington, DC: U.S. Department of Justice.

Hammersley, R., Forsyth, A., Morrison, V., & Davies, J. B. (1989). The relationship between crime and opioid use. *British Journal of Addiction, 84,* 1029–1043.

Harlow, C. W. (1998). *Profile of jail inmates: 1996* (NCJ Publication No. 164620). Washington, DC: U.S. Department of Justice.

Inciardi, J. A. (1996). The therapeutic community: An effective model for corrections-based drug abuse treatment. In K. E. Early (Ed.), Drug treatment behind bars: Prison-based strategies for change (pp. 65–74). Westport, CT: Praeger.

Inciardi, J. A., & Martin, S. S. (1993). Drug abuse treatment in criminal justice settings. *Journal of Drug Issues, 23,* 1–6.

Inciardi, J. A., & Pottieger, A. E. (1998). Drug use and street crime in Miami: An (almost) 20-year retrospective. *Substance Use and Misuse, 33,* 1839–1869.

Jarvis, G., & Parker, H. (1989). Young heroin users and crime. *British Journal of Criminology, 29,* 175–185.

Johnson, B. D., Goldstein, P. J., Preble, E., Schmeidler, J., Lipton, D. S., Spunt, B., & Miller, T. (1985). *Taking care of business: The economics of crime by heroin abusers.* Lexington, MA: Lexington Books.

Kinlock, T. W., Hanlon, T. E., & Nurco, D. N. (1999). Criminal justice responses of adult substance abuse. In R. E. Ammerman, P. T. Ott, & R. E. Tarter (Eds.), *Prevention and societal impact of drug and alcohol abuse* (pp. 201–220). Mahwah, NJ: Erlbaum.

Kouri, E. M., Pope, H. G., Powell, K. F., Olivia, P. S., & Campbell, C. (1997). Drug use history and criminal behavior among 133 incarcerated men. *American Journal of Drug and Alcohol Abuse, 23,* 413–419.

Lawson, G. W. (1989). A rationale for planning treatment and prevention of alcoholism and substance abuse for specific populations. In G. W. Lawson & A. W. Lawson (Eds.), *Alcoholism and substance abuse in special populations* (pp. 1–10). Austin, TX: PRO-ED.

Lopez, J. M., Martin, A. L., Redondo, L. M., Carillo, M. T., & Trinanes, E. R. (1994). An empirical study of the relations between drug abuse and delinquency among adolescents. *British Journal of Criminology, 34,* 459–478.

Mumola, C. J. (1999). *Substance abuse and treatment: State and federal prisoners,* 1997 (NCJ Publication No. 172871). Washington, DC: U.S. Department of Justice.

Murray, D. W. (1996). Drug abuse treatment in the federal bureau of prisons: A historical review and assessment of contemporary initiatives. In K. E. Early (Ed.), *Drug treatment behind bars: Prison-based strategies for change* (pp. 89–100). Westport, CT: Praeger.

Nathan, P. E. (1988). The addictive personality is the behavior of the addict. *Journal of Consulting and Clinical Psychology, 56,* 183–188.

National Institute of Justice. (2003). *2000 arrestee drug abuse monitoring: Annual report* (NJC Publication No. 193013). Washington DC: U.S. Department of Justice.

National Institute on Drug Abuse. (2006). *Monitoring the future: National results on adolescent drug use: Overview of key findings, 2005* (NIH Publication No. 06–5882). Bethesda, MD: Author.

Nurco, D. N. (1998). A long-term program of research on drug use and crime. *Substance Use and Misuse, 33,* 1817–1837.

Nurco, D. N., Ball, J. C., Shaffer, J. W., & Hanlon, T. E. (1985). The criminality of narcotic addicts. *Journal of Nervous and Mental Disease, 173,* 94–102.

Peters, R. H. (1993a). Drug treatment in jails and detention settings. In J. A. Inciardi (Ed.), *Drug treatment and criminal justice* (pp. 44–80). Newbury Park, CA: Sage.

Peters, R. H. (1993b). Substance abuse services in jails and prisons. *Law and Psychology Review, 17,* 86–116.

Pettiway, L. E., Dolinsky, S., & Grigoryan, A. (1994). The drug and criminal activity patterns of urban offenders: A Markov chain analysis. *Journal of Quantitative Criminology, 10,* 79–107.

Ross, R. R., & Lightfoot, L. O. (1985). *Treatment of the alcohol-abusing offender.* Springfield, IL: Thomas.

Sinha, R., & Easton, C. (1999). Substance abuse and criminality. *Journal of the American Academy of Psychiatry and Law, 27,* 513–526.

Stice, E., & Barrera, M. (1995). A longitudinal examination of the reciprocal relations between perceived parenting and adolescents' substance use and externalizing behaviors. *Developmental Psychology, 31,* 322–334.

Substance Abuse and Mental Health Services Administration. (1997). *Substance abuse treatment planning guide and checklist for treatment based drug courts* (DHHS Publication No. SMA 97-3136). Rockville, MD: U.S. Department of Heath and Human Services.

Substance Abuse and Mental Health Services Administration. (2009). *Results from the 2008 national survey on drug use and health: National findings* (DHHS Publication No. SMA 09-4434). Rockville, MD: U.S. Department of Heath and Human Services.

Wald, H. P., Flaherty, M. T., & Pringle, J. L. (1999). Prevention in prisons. In R. E. Ammerman, P. T. Ott, & R. E. Tarter (Eds.), *Prevention and societal impact of drug and alcohol abuse* (pp. 369–381). Mahwah, NJ: Erlbaum.

Walters, G. D. (1998). *Changing lives of crime and drugs: Intervening with substance abusing offenders.* New York: Wiley.

Wexler, H. K. (1992). Overview of correctional drug treatment evaluation research. *Psychotherapy Bulletin, 27,* 25–27.

Wexler, H. K., Falkin, G. P., & Lipton, D. S. (1990). Outcome evaluation of a prison therapeutic community for substance abuse treatment. *Criminal Justice and Behavior, 17,* 71–92.

Wexler, H. K., & Lipton, D. S. (1993). From reform to recovery: Advances in prison drug treatment. In J. A. Inciardi (Ed.), *Drug treatment and criminal justice* (pp. 209–227). Westport, CT: Praeger.

Wilson, D. J. (2000). *Drug use, testing, and treatment in jails* (NCJ Publication No. 179999). Washington, DC: U.S. Department of Justice.

CHAPTER 18

Substance Abuse Among Individuals With Disabilities

Thuy-Phuong Do

A vast segment of the U.S. population is underserved in the treatment of chemical dependency: According to the U.S. census of 2000, there are 48.9 million people who have a disability. Roughly, this equates to one out of five people in America possessing some form of disability (U.S. Census Bureau, 2000). Of this group, an estimated 20% suffer from substance abuse, a rate that is approximately double that of the general population (Krahn & Gabriel, n.d.; Li & Moore, 1998). Yet, Americans with disabilities use chemical dependency services at a rate much lower than that of the general population (Krahn & Gabriel, n.d.). This chapter explores some of the reasons why a disproportionate number of people with disabilities suffer from substance abuse, why they have been underserved, and what substance abuse professionals can do about it.

Central to an understanding of the issues facing individuals with disabilities is the notion of the *disability coculture*. A coculture is not the same as a subculture; a coculture is not "under" the mainstream culture; it is "with" the mainstream culture. People with disabilities comprise a unique coculture, as anyone can suddenly become a member of this group at any stage in life. Becoming a member of the disability coculture crosses the identification boundaries of a person's ethnicity, race, gender, age, sexual orientation, and economic status. As with any culture, the disability coculture has a set of shared beliefs, ideas, customs, and skills that are a result of the group's common embodiment within a mainstream culture. What people with disabilities face as members of the disability coculture is the reality that society may define them by their disability. For instance, a person may be a lawyer who happens to have a disability; from a mainstream viewpoint, the person is more often than not perceived as a "disabled lawyer." Although often subtle, the identification of a person as disabled usually carries a stigma. Assimilation into the disability coculture can be a beneficial counterbalance to mainstream attitudes. The primary benefit of the disability coculture is its celebration of the uniqueness of each individual and its reframing of disability as a positive aspect of that individual.

The disability coculture offers individuals with disabilities a group through which to gain the empowerment needed to overturn negative mainstream attitudes. People who have assimilated into the disability coculture learn how to more successfully navigate the hurdles of mainstream life. For example, a person with a disability may learn to use humor in order to communicate with people in a comfortable manner that can put them at ease about his or her disability and help him or her connect more successfully. Or, a person who acquires a disability through an injury may choose to celebrate the day she or he was injured as a rite of passage that represents a significant milestone in her or his journey. People who have assimilated into the disability coculture frequently believe that the growth they experienced helped promote their psychological development and thus improved their lives (Do, 1997a). However, difficult obstacles may stand in the way of reframing disability in a positive way.

One of these obstacles is substance abuse. As noted, the rate of substance abuse in individuals with disabilities is twice that of the general population. According to Hepner, Kirshbaum, and Landes (1980–81), "persons with disabilities run a high risk of developing alcohol and drug abuse" (p. 11). Several factors contribute to this high risk level. First, prescription drugs are easily accessible. In many cases, physicians liberally prescribe medications for pain or severe spasms. Second, people with disabilities often use drugs as a coping strategy to buffer their feelings of frustration and anxiety about being disabled and being thrust into an often disempowering situation (Hepner et al., 1980–81). People with disabilities are also uniquely defined by their physical embodiment (Do, 1997a). They face discrimination and stereotyping, which in turn can lead to feelings of low self-worth and helplessness. Alcohol and drug use may provide the illusory promise of relief by numbing these painful feelings (Hepner et al., 1980–81).

In spite of the high prevalence of substance abuse among people with disabilities, they use substance abuse treatment services at a rate lower than those with substance abuse problems who are not disabled. This statistic is often attributed to the absence of specialized services to fit the unique needs of individuals with disabilities. Statistics do show that once a person with a disability is in treatment, the rate of success is equal to that of the general population (Krahn & Gabriel, n.d.).

One of the main problems is that access to treatment centers is often difficult, and personnel are generally not trained to treat people with disabilities. In addition, individuals with disabilities are excluded from "professional substance abuse agencies by a wide variety of physical, cultural, attitudinal and communications barriers" (Hepner et al., 1980–81, p. 13).

For professionals treating chemical dependency, knowledge of the disability coculture can be of tremendous use in making programs more accessible. The following discussion (a) outlines four major categories of disability to expand and refine our cultural awareness as professionals, (b) presents six negative myths associated with mainstream attitudes toward disabilities in order to increase our sensitivity to their damaging effects, and (c) discusses treatment strategies that take into account the needs of people with various kinds of disabilities, specifically, deafness and hearing impairment, spinal cord injuries, blindness and visual impairment, and developmental disabilities. Having a professional that is sensitive to the issues a person with disabilities may face can make a crucial difference in that person's receptiveness to treatment.

Types of Disabilities

It would be impossible to classify every type of disability that exists. Generally, there are four major categories of disability: (a) mobility impairments, (b) sensory impairments, (c) cognitive impairments, (d) and multiple disabilities. The intention here is not to contribute to the already overdeveloped zeal to categorize but rather to utilize the structures that those in the disability field are using, with the ultimate goal of increasing the accessibility to and effectiveness of substance abuse treatment.

Mobility impairments are disabilities that impact one or more of an individual's basic physical activities. Some examples are spinal cord injuries, polio, cerebral palsy (CP), muscular dystrophy (MD), multiple sclerosis (MS), arthritis, osteogenesis imperfecta, and fibromyalgia. Examples of mobility devices and access aids people may use are wheelchairs, a cane or crutches, prosthetics, hand controls for driving, adaptive athletic equipment such as mono- and bi-skis, personal care attendants, and scooters or other motorized devices.

Sensory impairments are disabilities that affect a person's senses. Some examples are visual impairments, blindness, hearing impairments, deafness, and speech impairments. Examples of technology and mobility aids that people may use are white canes, guide dogs, hearing aids, telephone relay services, interpreters, sighted guides, modified magnifiers, readers, Braille, talking keypads, fonts that are easier to read, audio material, and speech or screen magnification software.

Cognitive impairments are disabilities that impact a person's mental functioning. Some examples are traumatic brain injury, mental health disorder, developmental disability, learning disability, Down syndrome, and autism. Examples of assistive technology and aids that help those with cognitive impairment are speech technology, care providers, tutors, and adaptive computer devices.

Multiple disabilities refers to more than one impairment. For instance, a person might have both a mental health disorder and a physical impairment. A person might also have dual impairments in a similar category, like being visually impaired and deaf. A person might also have a secondary disability that is a result of his or her primary disability. For instance, a person with CP might have a speech impairment due to the CP, or a person with MS might have a visual impairment due to the MS. Having multiple disabilities may require several forms of the technological devices listed above.

People with disabilities comprise a heterogeneous group consisting of many disability types. The heterogeneity of this group is increased exponentially when one considers that disability interacts with a host of other demographic characteristics, such as race, ethnicity, gender, sexual orientation, education level, and income level. Given this broad diversity, treating individuals with disabilities requires a unique set of approaches and strategies. Substance abuse professionals need to cultivate an in-depth understanding of the particular issues faced by members of this diverse community. Before we turn to treatment considerations for specific disability groups, we look at some fundamental attitudinal barriers to treatment, and then at six common myths about disability. Overcoming commonly held beliefs, attitudes, and myths about disability is a first and effective step toward improved treatment.

Attitudinal Barriers That Impact Treatment

Every human being has capabilities and limitations. Further, we all want to experience as much independence as we are capable of. How other people see us has an enormous impact on our own estimation of what we can and cannot do. This is why assimilation into the disability coculture is so important for individuals with disabilities. Assimilation into the disability coculture offers the person with disabilities a new language, a new self-image, and a new way of dealing with the negative stereotypes and myths that have traditionally permeated American society. An understanding of the disability coculture starts with a glimpse at a moment in cultural and political history.

The Americans With Disabilities Act (ADA), passed in 1990, was considered by people in the disability movement to be civil rights legislation. Before this law, there was no legislation to prevent discrimination against people with disabilities (Shapiro, 1993). In fact, many people with disabilities were kept out of view; they were considered an embarrassment, a curse, or a burden (Shapiro, 1993). The spirit of the ADA was to counter the discomfort people had with disability by integrating people with disabilities socially, economically, and politically. Integration of people with disabilities was conceived in the form of accessibility. Prior to the ADA, most people with disabilities had a limited role in society and limited independence, not having the freedom to access businesses without ramps, buses without lifts, or employment without reasonable accommodations (Shapiro, 1993). Even with this law, which has been in place for almost 2 decades, some negative stereotypes still permeate mainstream attitudes toward those with disabilities.

Negative stereotyping has the effect of delegitimizing the personhood of individuals with disabilities, which can lead to increased rates of depression, anger, and chemical abuse (Bombardier et al., 2004; Li, Ford, & Moore, 2000; Li & Moore, 2001; McAweeney, Forchheimer, Moore, & Tate, 2006; Morris, 1990; Shapiro, 1993). Through extensive research, Li and Moore (1998) found that the perceived discrimination and hostility that people with disabilities face can impede their acceptance of their disability and increase their risk of using substances.

Myths and Their Implications

As a service provider, understanding one's own notions of disability is essential. There are many myths about people with disabilities. Six of the most common myths are explored here. As you read, consider how the expressions of these myths in the form of negative comments or questions—or the lack of any communication at all—can be extremely damaging to the self-esteem of the individual with disabilities, who must defend him- or herself against a constant barrage of nonacceptance even now, almost 20 years after the passage of the ADA. For people with and without disabilities, there is a direct link between feelings of worthlessness and the use of substances. Reflecting upon your attitudes and responses to each myth can be a powerful way to enhance your ability as a professional to provide more effective substance abuse treatment to those with disabilities.

Myth #1: *People who are disabled are not complete and therefore are valueless.* A disability is often seen as a "fatal flaw" that makes it impossible for the affected individual to be seen as "normal." No matter how much skill the person has or how much effort is put forth, his or her work and achievements are seen as less worthy than those of a person without disabilities. Paul Davis shares his experience of this myth in his account of his first date:

> It got rougher in junior high school when dating became a big thing, because, you just didn't date a blind person. And even if you could get a girl to go out with you, she'd be ridiculed by all her girlfriends. Once, I got this girl to go out with me. The father informs me when I get into the house that "no daughter of [his] is going to date anyone who is less than a whole man." And he says to me, "You're not leaving the house with my daughter." And I said, "That's fine with me," and we sat down and watched TV all evening. He didn't like it. (quoted in Phillips, 1990, p. 852)

Davis's experience illustrates how his lack of sight—one part of the whole—is interpreted as making him less than human, "less than a whole man." Davis's response to the father is poignant; he doesn't leave the house with the man's daughter, but he doesn't retreat, either. At the same time, his account makes it clear that this instance was far from being an isolated experience.

Consider the implications of Myth #1. Imagine how a person with a disability that is devalued must see the world. The constant barrage deeply affects the person's self-esteem. The individual may begin to internalize the devaluation he or she keeps experiencing at the hands of others. The person may begin to expect that others will not respect what he or she does. This impedes progress and healing. A person who has a healthy view of his or her thoughts, opinions, feelings, work, and energy will be more likely to succeed.

Creating a perspective of value can be a challenge in the face of societal expectations that are still low (Do, 1997a). One way for people with disabilities to obtain a perspective of value is by seeking out a mentor who is able to model a healthy self-concept. Positive feedback is highly influential in boosting self esteem. A person with a disability who experiences positive feedback in social situations can interact more easily and build confidence.

For instance, in many rehabilitation facilities, when someone is newly injured, a mentor will be assigned to visit the patient within the first couple of weeks (personal communication, Melanie Benn, January 2007). The injured person takes a great deal of hope from talking with someone who has experienced what he or she is going through, and the patient is less likely to remain in a depressive state. The mentor can then begin to model habits and behaviors that will lead to self-care and positive social interaction. An attitude free of misconception or limits is the most important component of the first phase of mentoring.

The individual needs appropriately paced goals in order to experience a high-quality lifestyle that includes economic, social, and politic integration; many people with disabilities do not believe that they are able to live fully like they once have. In fact, many people with disabilities report having a better lifestyle *after* acquiring their disabilities because of their new attitudes and perspectives (Do, 1997a). For instance, a person who was unhappy or who did not value life before an injury may have a renewed perspective on what it means to live. Such a person may also take less for granted. The person may become more aware of how important his or her family and friends are. In the process of assimilating into the disability coculture, a person is likely to appreciate the family and friends that remain steadfast, to reevaluate lost friendships, and to have an enhanced, deep appreciation of bonds to new friends that are made in the process of acculturation (Do, 1997a). If clients feel they are unable to do anything of value, they have little hope that their lives will be meaningful and fulfilling. Yet there are many examples of those with slight to severe disabilities that demonstrate high satisfaction with life (Do, 1997a).

Myth #2: *People with disabilities are always mentally impaired.* People often view people with disabilities as automatically unintelligent due to their disabilities. This belief is especially prevalent for those with visible disabilities (Do, 1997a). Expressions of this belief are frustrating for the person with a disability and embarrassing for the person without. The following illustrates:

> I remember going to a boutique looking for a dress to wear for a friend's wedding. The salesperson came up to me. She must have been in her early twenties and asked, "What is wrong? Did you get into an accident?" My response was "No, I have polio." She replied, "Oh I am so sorry, what do you do with all your spare time?" I was sure she did not ask other customers the same question. The assumption was that without the ability to walk I had all of a sudden become unable to think and thus unable to do anything besides sit behind four walls and wait to die. My initial response was to be angry but I decided not to act on this. Instead I said, "Well I do a lot actually ..." I then proceeded to explain to her that I was in college getting a graduate degree and that I had a skiing trip planned and that I was socially active. In the end of that ten minutes I spent sharing what I did in my life I saw her blush. I left feeling confident that she would not ask the same question again. (Do, 1997a, p. 48)

It is frustrating to have to constantly be on guard and ready to prove oneself as intelligent. It becomes tiring. It wears on one's self-esteem.

Some examples of behaviors that go along with this assumption are as follows: a person speaking louder to someone who is blind, a person who speaks to an interpreter rather than to the deaf person, and someone asking the friend or family member information about the person with a disability while that person is present. This kind of condescension and prejudging can build frustration and damage the person's sense of self-worth.

Consider the implications of Myth #2. The insight gained here is invaluable; so many people with disabilities get so tired of being treated as if they were unintelligent or an object of pity. Treating people with the expectation that they have intelligence is a much more positive and realistic approach. The presence of disabilities does not mean that a person's intellectual abilities are compromised. Let the person who is disabled tell you what his or her limitations are rather than making unwarranted assumptions. A professional's curiosity can be useful. Be curious and ask about details that are unknown in a manner that allows the person to be the expert on his or her own life. For example, a person who is blind or visually impaired may be perceived as being unable to give the right amount of cash for an item because the size of a dollar bill is the same as the size of a hundred-dollar bill. It is much better for a professional to ask how the visually impaired person is able to make change rather than assuming that it cannot be done. The professional will learn that there are money-folding systems where a person can fold bills of varying denominations into different sizes.

Myth #3: *People with disabilities are fragile.* When people are young, they are taught to be polite toward those who are disabled by not talking about their disabilities. People are taught to believe that if they refer to a person's flaws, that person will become absolutely inconsolable. People without disabilities dare not say the wrong thing for fear of crushing the ego of a person with disabilities (Do, 1997b). Disability is often such an uncomfortable subject for those who are ablebodied that they will literally avoid the person with a disability in order to not say the wrong thing.

The large majority of people with disabilities would rather have a person communicate about the obvious than to avoid communication altogether, shutting off any contact (Do, 1997b; Morris, 1991). It is obvious to the person with a disability when a person is uncomfortable and wants to avoid him or her solely because of the presence of a disability.

Consider the implications of Myth #3. People with disabilities spend a lot of time talking about their disabilities and are usually quite open about what has happened to them. They often invite a person to talk to them directly (Thompson, 1983). The only solution to misunderstanding is exposure. Believing that people with disabilities cannot bear to talk about something that significantly impacts their lives is not the answer. Communicating about it is more respectful and promotes ultimate acceptance. Keeping a view of discomfort can continue to make a person with disabilities feel isolated.

The way to treat a person with a disability is to talk to that person in a comfortable manner, the way one would with a person without a disability. It is OK to say, "I see what you mean" around a person who is visually impaired or blind. A person who is mobility impaired will be comfortable with the words *walk, run,* and *dance.* A person who is hearing impaired or deaf will be fine with the words *hear* and *speak.* A person with a speech impairment who is difficult to understand is aware of the difficulty and will not be offended if you ask her or him to repeat the utterance. Your comfort will become infectious. Do not be dis-eased when using everyday language and idioms.

Myth #4: *People with disabilities are asexual.* People with disabilities may make great pals but they are not boyfriends or girlfriends or wives or husbands. This myth perpetuates the unobtainable body myth where people who are flawed will inevitably fall short. This myth can be very damaging to a person's self-esteem if they internalize the idea that they are not lovable. This area is where issues of low self-esteem are most explicit. It is painful to think that a disability makes one unattractive. Having no sexual identity in the eyes of society can be difficult to overcome. Further, the idea that a woman or man with a disability is not whole adds to the difficulty. Mike, who has cerebral palsy and uses crutches, illustrates:

> One reason why I don't get asked out a lot I think, is due to the discomfort ablebodied people experience when they think about dating a disabled person ... This guy asked me once, if you had a choice between a disabled and an ablebodied woman, you wouldn't pick the disabled woman, would you? And I said I don't know. It would depend on if I loved her or not. I didn't want to make a big scene but I really wish I would have. Because by implying that disabled women are inferior you are implying that I am inferior. (quoted in Do, 1997a, p. 63)

Amy, a wheelchair user who is a mother, had to overcome people's belief that motherhood would be impossible for her:

> Growing up I always wanted to get married and have children. I had doctors and others tell me that I can't or couldn't have children. Fortunately, the whole area of disabled women having children has opened up in the last fifteen years. Unfortunately, I think that disabled women are still being told that they can't have children. For example, my doctors wondered how I was going to take care of my newborn children. But I figured it out when it happened and I came up with my own methods of how to care for my children. (Do, 1997a, pp. 95–96)

The widespread myth that people with disabilities are asexual robs them of an important means of seeing themselves as sexual beings. Expressions of this myth can negatively impact self-esteem on a deep level.

Consider the implications of Myth #4. Amy's story illustrates that motherhood and sexuality are not excluded from the lives of people with disabilities. It also illustrates the degree to which she had to overcome people's beliefs to the contrary. Mike's story illustrates the societal belief that people with disabilities are "inferior" when it comes to relationships: the last to be picked. Mike's story also illustrates his frustration at the offhand and indirect insult he received. There are many people with disabilities who are able to form relationships. It is important for professionals to have a sense of the person's social skills. Social skills are key to finding a mate and being perceived as a fit partner.

The important insight here is to realize that people with disabilities should be accorded equality in the realm of sexuality and parenthood. Helping a person who has been isolated from the mainstream to develop strong social skills will vastly enhance his or her ability to have meaningful interpersonal connections. Many people with disabilities enhance their social skills by becoming involved in active recreation. Having access to group activities in many forms is helpful. Further, participation in groups that contain people with and without disabilities is vital.

Myth #5: *People with disabilities are not employable.* Employment is an important ingredient in the integration of people with disabilities. There are many barriers to the employment of people with disabilities, the main one being employer attitudes.

As noted, the myth that individuals with disabilities are subhuman devalues the work they perform. The devaluing myth is the reason why employability is so difficult for people with disabilities; work is a core value, and when it is devalued, the person's sense of self-worth suffers. The statistics illustrate the point: In 2004, approximately 70% of those with disabilities who wanted to work were not working. The unemployment rate for the general population, by contrast, was a mere 4.3% (U.S. Department of Education, 2005).

Consider the implications of Myth #5. The implications of the myth of unemployability are staggering, as the statistics suggest. For the professional, it is important to also understand another statistic: Ninety percent of employers who have employees with disabilities report experiencing satisfaction with their employees with disabilities (U.S. Department of Education, 2005). Employers also report that employees with disabilities are more reliable and miss fewer days of work (U.S. Department of Education, 2005). People with disabilities are good employees, and it is important that they be reminded of this.

Understanding how tough it must be for a person with any disability to get up every morning and handle details and obstacles that someone who is able-bodied never needs to think about is important to appreciating the strength and ability of people with disabilities. People who are disabled deserve respect from others and from themselves for how much energy it takes to manage their lives on a daily basis (Do, 1997b; Morris, 1991).

Moreover, it is precisely the creativity, grit, and skill involved in living with a disability that makes these individuals good workers. People with disabilities are good workers and are highly capable of finding meaningful work. Also, a lot of technology is available that can make jobs that were once impossible highly accessible. More employers need to be made aware of the reliability and productivity of individuals with disabilities. And people with disabilities need to know how to gain access to reasonable accommodations at work.

Myth #6: *People with disabilities need charity but not help.* Another word for charity is pity. One who is pitied is not seen as capable of anything. The myth of charity is subtle but powerful in its impact on the lives of people with disabilities. It is assumed that a person with a disability cannot function; the able-bodied automatically rush in to accomplish what they believe the person with a disability cannot. Help involves interdependence and respect; charity involves dependence and pity. For example, a woman with a visual impairment recounts a situation where help became charity:

> I remember when my friend and I were at a department store. We were coming out of the fitting rooms. My friend was in front of me and I was using my white cane. I have had extensive mobility training to use my cane when crossing streets and using escalators. I have traveled independently for two decades. I also have some usable sight though not much. Many people do not know the intense training you have to get before using a white cane or what the difference is between being visually impaired and blind. So as we left the fitting rooms another woman says to my friend with almost an angry tone, "Don't leave your friend behind! Help her!" Luckily my friend was pretty

> cool about it and just said, "She can do it on her own." But the lady seemed to be adamant about not letting me travel on my own. (Nikki Warren, personal communication, January 2007)

All too often, people rush to assist without asking and create a situation where the individual with a disability will be unable to reach her or his full independence. Such "help" often leaves the person who was not expecting charity feeling less independent or responsible.

Consider the implications of Myth #6. The key insight is to ask first. Both people who are disabled and people who are able-bodied need to know to communicate first. Asking is a sign of respect, and it allows the person with a disability to stay in control and direct the help he or she gets. Willingness to help is fine; charity is not.

As a professional, helping a person who is disabled know when and how to ask for help is important. It can be uncomfortable for a person with a disability to ask for help. It is equally uncomfortable for a person with a disability to be assertive and say "no" to help when someone is trying to be a Good Samaritan. It is nonetheless extremely important for a person who offers help to accept the person's "no, thank you." Such acceptance is a sign of support for a person's independence.

Treatment Strategies

The report of the Commission on California State Government Organization and Economy (1987), known as the "Little Hoover Commission," reported that between 10% and 18% of the state's population has some form of significant disability, and as many as 500,000 Californians with disabilities also have alcohol or drug problems. The commission cited a variety of barriers to effective treatment services as reported by the Darrell McDaniel Independent Living Center, which surveyed 27 treatment programs in Southern California:

- 25% of the facilities surveyed would not permit persons using prescription medication to enter their programs.
- Only 7% of the facilities surveyed accepted Medi-Cal or Medicare as payment for treatment.
- Only 59% of the programs would use a sliding scale according to the client's income.
- 40% of the treatment programs were not accessible to persons using wheelchairs.
- 30% of the treatment programs were in areas where there was no public transportation for persons in wheelchairs, even though all treatment programs receiving federal or California state funding are required by law to have facilities accessible to persons in wheelchairs.

In 99.7% of the treatment programs surveyed, American Sign Language interpreters for deaf persons were not available and would not be paid for by the treatment program or the person's insurance, even though 45% of the programs were required to provide such interpreters (Commission on California State Government Organization and Economy, 1987). The commission further reported that "the main issue is not new funding dedicated to special programs for the disabled, but rather to integrating the disabled community into existing substance abuse treatment facilities" (Commission on California State Government Organization and Economy, 1987, p. 5). Thus, accessibility is an important issue that needs to be addressed.

Another global treatment issue is the importance of integrating people with disabilities rather than segregating them. Depending on the specific disability, the person might need some accommodations as well as some individual tailoring of treatment; but these should be provided in the context of an integrated setting to the extent possible. The "one program fits all" approach is not good for anyone, but it is especially detrimental to people with disabilities. Individualizing treatment requires looking at the individual needs associated with each disability, and then looking at the individual needs of each person with a disability. Once the needs have been determined, an individualized treatment program can be developed.

The following sections give an idea of some of the specialized needs associated with specific disability areas, namely deafness and hearing impairment, spinal cord injuries, blindness and visual impairment, and developmental disabilities.

Deafness and Hearing Impairment

The deaf or hearing impaired person who is abusing alcohol should be treated in a mainstream setting; there are special needs of the deaf that need to be addressed. Some of these needs arise from social and political characteristics that are specific to the deaf community.

The deaf community is a closely knit culture that opposes characterization of deaf people as prone to substance abuse. The deaf have just recently overcome the stigma of "deaf and dumb." Attempts to start rehabilitation programs for the deaf people with substance abuse problems have met with massive denial by the organized deaf community; they refuse to accept the existence of the problem (Isaacs, Buckley, & Martin, 1979). They do not want the stigma of "deaf and drunk." The deaf community shows a great mistrust of the hearing community (Watson, Boros, & Zimrec, cited in Boros, 1980–81).

Problems the Deaf and Hearing Impaired Encounter in Treatment

The main factor inhibiting treatment and recovery for the deaf or hearing impaired person is that most substance abuse professionals do not sign. The care provider must determine, before treatment, the level and type of communication of the deaf person and the type of interpreters needed, if any. It is also important to determine the background of the deaf person. Most agencies surveyed by Isaacs et al. (1979) were at a loss regarding what to do if a deaf person should enter their treatment program. Once in treatment, the deaf person encounters many problems (Isaacs et al., 1979).

Another problem involved in the recovery of the deaf or hearing impaired person is the attitude of substance abuse professionals, who sometimes focus too much on the disability and its causes rather than on the deaf person's self-image and family structure. In addition, care providers may become "enablers" to the deaf person who is abusing alcohol in that they may patronize the patient, deciding what the patient does or does not need to do rather than making sure that the deaf patient utilizes the program to the greatest extent, much as a person without disabilities would. On the other hand, care providers can also be inflexible and negative. They may require the deaf person to attend meetings without an interpreter because that is what everyone is "supposed to do." The deaf or hearing impaired person should be treated as an equal with special needs that are accommodated within the program (Cleland, 1980–1981).

The professional should also recognize that the communication problem does not lie in simply being unable to hear and thus to speak clearly. Communication and language problems can lead to serious social and psychological problems. Feelings of low self-esteem, isolation, loneliness, and frustration contribute to the incidence of alcoholism among the deaf (Watson et al., cited in Boros, 1980–81). The language problem can cause serious gaps in education and social situations, which in turn can lead to a lack of understanding and comprehension of situations and reading materials. The subtle and inferred aspects of communication are often not learned by the deaf because abstract and inferred terms are difficult to sign.

Treatment: Deafness and Hearing Impairment

Treatment for deaf people with substance abuse problems has been slow in coming. A 1968 article in the Alcoholics Anonymous (AA) newsletter *Grapevine* written by a recovering deaf person helped raise awareness of the need for services. However, it was not until the mid-1970s that the Hearing Society in the San Francisco Bay Area developed one of the first programs designed specifically for the hearing impaired person. The program provided interpreters to deaf substance abusers, aided the police in understanding the unique communication problems of the deaf substance abuser, and operated a 24-hour telephone service to facilitate communication between the staff of community agencies and deaf clients. Although this group is no longer in existence, it paved the way for similar groups to be established (Boros, 1980–81).

Watson et al. (cited in Boros, 1980–81) discussed eight basic requirements for adapting a treatment program that would be responsive to the needs of the deaf patient:

1. Develop an outreach program whose main goal is to develop the trust of the hearing people within the deaf community. Without trust, education of the deaf community is impossible. The next step is to obtain support of the program among deaf leaders.

2. Identify an "influence leader who is a member of the hearing community, supportive, and communicative with the patient on the patient's level.... This person should be with the patient constantly to enhance effective communication with the communicatively impaired patient. The influence leader ensures that the patient understands all counseling sessions" (Watson et al., cited in Boros, 1980–81, p. 28).
3. Maintain therapy with a therapist who can communicate effectively with the patient at a level that is comfortable to the patient.
4. Establish counseling rapport. The counselor must have a thorough awareness of the other implications of deafness.
5. Integrate the deaf patient with hearing patients not only for socialization reasons but so that the deaf can realize that others have serious problems, too.
6. Place deaf patients in small groups in which they will discuss the aspects of lectures and didactic sessions to make sure that they understand the material covered.
7. Use visual aids to further understanding.
8. Develop an aftercare program in which interpreters are available (e.g., Substance and Alcohol Intervention Services for the Deaf [SAISD]).

Spinal Cord Injuries

"Alcohol and drugs appear to be a major, but seldom discussed, factor in spinal cord injuries" (O'Donnell, Cooper, Gesner, Shehan, & Ashley, 1981–82, p. 27). A study conducted at the Montebello Center Spinal Cord Unit in Baltimore indicated that of 47 patients, 62% were identified as having alcohol- or drug-related injuries. However, a search of the literature of the past 10 years revealed that "no studies linking alcoholism or drug abuse to spinal cord injuries have been published" (O'Donnell et al., 1981–82, p. 27).

In 1973, spinal cord injury service wards were raided by federal marshals, and the "quantity of drugs and alcohol confiscated from the patients brought the problem to the attention of the Veterans Administration and other officials in Washington, D.C." (Anderson, 1980–81, p. 37). This raid increased awareness of the extent of drug abuse among individuals with spinal cord injuries. The realization that drug abuse in this population was a nationwide problem led to the development of the Drug Dependency Treatment Program, which would serve as a model for other Veterans Administration (VA) centers.

The problems associated with drug and alcohol abuse in this population are not just a result of the disabling consequences of the injury; often, they were involved in causing the injury. In addition, prior to their injury, many spinal cord injury patients led a lifestyle fraught with great risk taking, including the use of alcohol or other substances. Such pre-injury use predisposes the individual to continued use of alcohol and drugs after the injury. Prescription drugs are often added to those previously used (O'Donnell et al., 1981–82).

Problems Individuals With Spinal Cord Injuries Encounter in Treatment

One of the major problems individuals with spinal cord injuries encounter in treatment is that many programs are not physically accessible due to the lack of wheelchair ramps, elevators, or accessible facilities. The ADA was passed almost 20 years ago, yet there are still many facets of the law that are misunderstood. Further, most patient treatment centers are not equipped to provide the physical maintenance needs of these patients (Anderson, 1980–81).

Physical maintenance problems seriously affect many areas of an inpatient program; one such area is scheduling. Most individuals with spinal cord injuries need more time to accomplish daily self-care chores and thus cannot attend scheduled sessions on time. In the morning, for example, a quadriplegic patient typically needs from 2 to 4 hours to get out of bed and complete morning grooming chores. The patient has to be lifted from the bed (sometimes by a lift device), accomplish bowel care, and shower and dress (with the help of two attendants) (O'Donnell et al., 1981–82).

The spinal cord injury patient who abuses alcohol often has additional physical problems that are due to overuse of alcohol and drugs. For instance, many clients have decubitus ulcers, or bedsores, due to sitting in their wheelchairs for days while they are drunk. Poor nutrition also plays a role, as the patient will neglect eating while she or he is using. In addition, a major complication occurs when bladder and kidney infections develop. Such infections may cause toxicity, further compromising health status.

Substance abuse treatment may be further complicated for those whose substance abuse was connected with or was a direct cause of their injury (Anderson, 1980–81):

> The battle wounded veteran often returns to the community after treatment somewhat intact, because prior to their injury they had their lives in pretty good order, and felt good about themselves. Others who became injured while under the influence of drugs and alcohol, were using alcohol and drugs before the injury to help themselves feel better about themselves, and this pattern has continued and possibly escalated after the injury. (Anderson, 1980–81, p. 38)

Clients in residential VA programs may have little incentive to leave and attend a substance abuse treatment program. The residential setting is a clean, comfortable, no-risk environment. In addition, there is a Catch-22 in that the paralyzed veteran is financially rewarded to remain institutionalized. A veteran with a service-connected injury who is a quadriplegic with loss of bowel and bladder function receives over $2,000 per month tax free; for many, there is little incentive to do anything but alcohol and drugs. Veterans with non-service-connected injury receive much less—$200 to $400 per month (Anderson, 1980–81).

In addition to the many physical problems of those with spinal cord injuries, their psychological problems present special barriers. "Not unexpectedly the paralyzed person will try to use his disability to manipulate the treatment program, as an excuse to escape responsibility for his or her actions" (Anderson, 1980–81, p. 38). An ambulatory addict goes into treatment to deal with his or her addiction, whereas "the spinal cord injured have come into treatment to deal with their addiction plus a physical disability that may well have been a result of their drug or alcoholic abuse" (Anderson, 1980–81, p. 38).

Finally, drug or alcohol abuse may interfere with motivation. Alcohol and marijuana, for example, are central nervous system depressants that interfere with motor activities, especially those that are learned. Because patients with spinal cord injury and substance problems are often hung over, they do not participate in a motivated manner in the physical rehabilitation program (O'Donnell et al., 1981). Such drug use is also likely to exacerbate the depression that often accompanies spinal cord injury, which in turn negatively affects motivation.

Medical Problems Due to the Mixing of Alcohol and Prescription Drugs

The use of alcohol and drugs interferes with prescribed medication, sometimes in dangerous ways. For example, the "patient who drinks while taking warfarin compounds to prevent blood clot formation risks life-threatening internal bleeding because alcohol's interaction with blood-clotting substances may further decrease clotting activity" (O'Donnell et al., 1981–82, p. 28).

The sheer volume of urine produced by heavy beer drinking can ruin an intermittent catheterization program. "Men and women who have attained a level of reasonable control due to regaining bladder reflexes may blow this by drinking which causes large volumes of urine to stretch the bladder so that useful reflexes are lost and chances of getting off constant drainage are ruined" (O'Donnell et al., 1981–82, p. 28). The distended bladder can trigger a reflex that causes blood vessels to constrict, resulting in excessive and in some cases life-threatening high blood pressure (O'Donnell et al., 1981–82).

Disulfiram (Antabuse) therapy must be either avoided or very carefully monitored because of the dangers of severe alcohol–disulfiram reactions in an individual who already has disabilities. Suicide by this means could also be viewed as a "way out" by a depressed patient with a drinking problem (O'Donnell et al., 1981–82).

It is important to provide constant nursing surveillance to avoid adverse interactions between alcohol or other substances and tranquilizers, sedatives, narcotics, antibiotics, or anticoagulants in patients who may have been given a drug or alcoholic beverage by a well-meaning friend, relative, or staff member. Sometimes people perceive giving alcohol as a way to provide their loved ones with some enjoyment and normalcy (O'Donnell et al., 1981–82).

Psychological and Social Concerns

Many patients were very active before their injury. They were risk-taking, daring individuals who often ignored possible consequences of their lifestyle. This attitude often prevails after the accident. Very often they continue to run the "tightrope" between life and death by not heeding restrictions on drug and alcohol use while using prescribed drugs (O'Donnell et al., 1981–82).

The devil-may-care outlook that led them to activities of high risk and high mobility, often causing injury, makes rehabilitation difficult, as they are often not interested in intellectual pursuits and miss their thrill-seeking adventures. This situation may cause greater depression, which can lead to greater alcohol and drug consumption (O'Donnell et al., 1981–82). The continued use of alcohol impairs the patient's capacity to adapt to limitations and to plan for a return to the community. Rather than using their energy to cope with reality, patients often invest it in maintaining defenses of fantasy, denial, and projection. For example, patients fantasize about walking or running again; they deny their own role in the accident or the grimness of the prognosis; and they shift the responsibility for their feelings onto others. For example, they feel helpless, and instead of acknowledging this feeling, they blame physicians for being unable to bring about recovery. The inadequacy of these defenses in warding off anxiety is often disguised by alcohol consumption (O'Donnell et al., 1981–82). Counseling is needed to address these concerns.

The patient's family also needs to adapt to both the physical and the psychological impact of the injury. Family members may feel guilty about not having taken better care of the injured person. They may be feeling anger and hostility toward the patient because the accident has seriously impacted their lives, too. Because of these feelings, family members may be supportive, or enabling, of the injured person's alcohol and drug consumption.

Hospital personnel may also fall into this trap. They too may have unresolved anger or guilt regarding people with disabilities. These issues may lead service providers to "overlook" the injured person's use of alcohol and drugs. At times, personnel may participate in helping the patient obtain or consume drugs and alcohol (O'Donnell et al., 1981–82).

O'Donnell et al. (1981–82) found in their study that the 32 patients (out of 42 subjects with spinal cord injury) who used alcohol and drugs before the accident that caused their severe disability continued to use and abuse alcohol after the study. The results clearly indicate that the majority of the patients had a common problem: alcohol and drug impairment (O'Donnell et al., 1981–82). The continued use of drugs or alcohol only compounds the trauma of the injury for the patient and the family. Education and preventative measures can be developed for patients and their families. And alcohol and drug education for care providers is a must.

Treatment: Spinal Cord Injuries

Care providers should locate the drug and alcohol treatment unit in the spinal cord injury rehabilitation center. In addition to the ongoing physical and occupational services provided for patients, they can receive drug and alcohol treatment. The treatment focuses on "community living and on encouraging patients to learn to assume responsibility for their behavior as well as educating them to the reasons they are relying on alcohol and drugs to cope" (Anderson, 1980–81, p. 39).

In such a setting, each day begins with a staff meeting in which those on turning shifts can touch base regarding how the patient has been progressing over the past 24 hours. Once a week the staff meets with the client to discuss his or her progress and to get input from the client as to his or her particular concerns. Treatment planning is done at this time. The staff also meets twice a month to make major decisions (Anderson, 1980–81). This meeting is much like a town hall meeting, where staff and patients discuss aspects of the program and its progress. At this time, short- as well as long-term plans are made. Topics of discussion range from promotions of patients from one phase to another to demoting patients for not complying with the rules of the community. Upcoming events are discussed and planned. In most meetings, staff and patients are afforded equal time to discuss and vote. In this way, the division between staff and patients is minimized. Patients are encouraged to plan and implement as many events as possible in order to encourage independence and to reduce feelings of hopelessness and powerlessness (Anderson, 1980–81).

In addition to the varied activities and physical rehabilitation, all patients receive counseling to help with psychological problems. Both support and crisis counseling are continued by the staff even after the patient has moved into the community.

Assertiveness training is incorporated into program activities. Group therapy using a Gestalt therapy model is also offered. Occupational therapy is provided that develops skills such as communication, assertiveness, manual dexterity, and a sense of responsibility and accomplishment. Patients are also encouraged to develop some kind of spiritual life. Spirituality is discussed from a universal perspective and is geared toward developing "good feeling" (Anderson, 1980–81).

Patients are required to keep a journal in which they write down their daily feelings and how these have affected their thinking and behavior. At times, these are shared with the group, and the group responds by helping the patient examine his or her coping mechanisms (Anderson, 1980–81).

Volunteers are a vital part of the program. They bring into the treatment community someone who can help establish contact with the community outside the hospital. Volunteers offer many kinds of activities, from information on finance to general education on anthropology, history, and psychology. Patients learn about establishing networks in the community. As part of this effort, they are encouraged to attend Narcotics Anonymous or AA meetings in the community (Anderson, 1980–81). More recently, alternatives to AA have become available, as noted in Chapter 4 of this text.

Blindness and Visual Impairment

As with other disabilities, one of the basic problems in the treatment of individuals with blindness or visual impairment is that care providers tend to focus too much on the disability and not enough on the substance abuse. With this focus, the clinician tends to overlook the long history of learning experiences and adaptive behaviors to life problems learned by the individual.

Glass (1980–81) discussed two types of problem drinkers with visual impairment: Type A, the person who drank prior to the onset of the visual disability, and Type B, the person who drank after the onset of the disability. The Type A individual is characterized by a history of life problems, anxiety, tension, depression, and stress, with which he or she has never been able to cope effectively. Type A's principal problem-solving technique is drinking. Because of the deficiency in problem-solving and coping skills, the onset of disability serves only to intensify and magnify the inability to cope effectively. The Type B person's problem drinking began after the onset of the visual disability. Although the Type B individual's coping and problem-solving skills may have been somewhat limited before the onset of the disability, the drinking had not become habitual. "Both Type A and Type B tend to share an absence of preparation for the stress experience that all will surely encounter during the process of adapting to the severe physical disability of blindness" (Glass, 1980–81, p. 20).

The disability of blindness impacts "the individual in terms of emotional feeling states, interpersonal social interactions, cognitive functioning in terms of thought structure, and its verbal expression and physical function in terms of performance of skills necessary to daily activity" (Glass, 1980–81, p. 20). The individual experiences stress as he or she learns to adapt to the disability. The feelings of powerlessness and frustration increase as one realizes that his or her independence has been significantly curtailed.

Individuals with visual impairment may develop anxiety related to the disability: They may worry that they will become a burden to others, that they are becoming less than a whole person, that they will be rejected by the opposite sex, that they will not be able to live up to expectations of others and themselves, or that they will not be able to participate in sports (Glass, 1980–81).

Individuals with visual impairment often engage in less and less activity, are exposed to less stimulation, experience increased social isolation, and sometimes go into depression. "If alcohol has been a part of their lifestyle, there is an increased likelihood of its becoming a more and more dominant part of their daily living" (Glass, 1980–81, p. 21).

Since the Type B person's drinking was not habitual prior to the onset of visual impairment, alleviating the underlying problems of stress related to the disability and developing concrete supportive coping skills may serve to stop the alcohol abuse. Type A individuals require treatment specifically designed for alcohol abuse (Glass, 1980–81).

Treatment: Blindness and Visual Impairment

VA medical centers throughout the United States send referral applications to VA rehabilitation centers specifically for veterans with blindness or visual impairment. These applications are sorted into Type A and Type B categories. The Type A individual is generally first referred to a psychiatric clinic, where underlying life problems and problem drinking are the focus of therapy. The psychiatric clinic also emphasizes the development of mobility and personal management (Glass, 1980–81). Further, this program emphasizes learning, lifestyle change, and relaxation strategies. Behavior change techniques include social skills training, assertiveness training, aversion therapy, and observation/concentration training. Before being transferred to the blind or low-vision rehabilitation unit, the Type A problem drinker must make some progress toward resolving the life problems that led to alcohol dependence (Glass, 1980–81, p. 22).

The Type B person is usually admitted directly to the rehabilitation center, with the understanding that his or her drinking problem can be managed through either total abstinence or controlled drinking (Glass, 1980–81). The rehabilitation process for Type B patients consists of developing survival skills to help them cope with the world without resorting to alcohol. The development of independence is a key focus of treatment. Patients are encouraged to be responsible for the upkeep of themselves and their lodgings. A program of physical conditioning begins after 2 weeks of evaluation. This program takes into account nutrition and excessive weight. With this program, patients with visual disabilities are taught to integrate recreational activities into their lives. Since alcohol has been such a significant part of their lifestyle, "there is an increased likelihood of its becoming a more and more dominant part of their daily living" (Glass, 1980–81, p. 21).

Developmental Disabilities

Some individuals with developmental disabilities use substances to "feel like everyone else," to "hang out at bars where people are friendly," "to overcome loneliness," and "to be liked" (Wenc, 1980–81). "As more states deinstitutionalize residence in public psychiatric hospitals and more developmentally disabled persons attempt to integrate into the community, it is expected that the incidence of problems with alcohol and other drugs among this special population will increase" (Wenc, 1980–81, p. 43). A person with developmental disabilities is someone with an IQ between 60 and 85. The disability is severe, chronic, and attributable to a mental or physical impairment, or to a combination of mental or physical impairments. Developmental disability is manifested before the person attains the age of 22. It is a disability that is likely to continue for the rest of the person's life. Individuals with developmental disabilities have substantial limitations in three or more areas of a major life activity, such as self-care, receptive and expressive language, learning mobility, self-direction, capacity for independent living, and economic self-sufficiency. Being developmentally disabled does not mean that the person cannot learn; it means that the person will need more time to learn and that learning will need to take place in concrete terms, as abstract learning is extremely difficult. Learning focuses on developing or modifying behavior.

Treatment: Developmental Disabilities

Individuals with developmental disabilities generally participate in drinking because it allows them to socialize in situations that would not otherwise be available to them. Service providers need to keep in mind that an individual with disabilities has a limited capacity to understand and then act on new information. When the detoxification facility becomes aware of the presence of a person with developmental disabilities, it needs to have a specific person who acts as a liaison to the disability community who will act as an advocate for the person. "There is a necessity for a team consisting of law enforcement, alcohol treatment, developmental disability advocacy, and medical personnel to develop a realistic, comprehensive treatment plan for the alcohol impaired person" (Wenc, 1980–81, p. 45). If the client is able, he or she should be allowed to participate in and contribute to the treatment plan. The advocate for the person with developmental disabilities should act as the coordinator of this team.

Often a referral to AA meetings is made. However, the "individual may lack the verbal and motivational skills needed to voluntarily attend a self-help meeting. It is better if the disabled person attends the meeting with a volunteer, and the two attend the self-help meetings, and not the testimonial. This provides an alternative to the social scene of the bars" (Wenc, 1980–81, p. 45).

Emotions Anonymous (EA) is a group that borrows heavily from AA but is primarily for individuals with developmental disabilities. The AA format is followed, and educational and relaxation techniques are incorporated into this format. James Voytilla founded this group with the goal of providing a range of services, within a group setting, for the substance abuser with mental retardation. EA is a long-term option that is sensitive to the "pervasive social isolation and high anxiety levels among this population" (Small, 1980–81, p. 46). "Emotions Anonymous uses the Twelve Steps of AA but substitutes the word 'emotions' for 'alcohol.' The emphasis on group problem solving techniques is maintained and group members are taught to listen closely to the stories of others. Basically, we try to boil down the Twelve Steps into practical, do-it-yourself exercises that people can do during the week" (Small, 1980–81, p. 46).

Every week, members set goals; the following week, they report on how they did. When they succeed, the group gives them a lot of social reinforcement. The social reinforcement is probably the most important part of the group process (Small, 1980–81). The goal of the group process is to teach participants to relax and reduce their anxiety. They are educated about the effects of alcohol abuse and what it means to be alcoholic. Relaxation techniques, group exercises, and movement with music are aspects of the development of relaxation. Voytilla says, "They hold a lot of tension in. We believe that by helping them learn to control this tension and anxiety we can help them control their drinking problems" (quoted in Small, 1980–81, p. 46).

Conclusion

A disproportionate number of Americans with disabilities have substance abuse problems, and these individuals use chemical dependency treatment programs at a rate that is much lower than in the general population. As we have seen, a variety of factors contribute to this situation. Individuals with disabilities face not only the limitations that inhere in their disability; they also must contend with societally imposed barriers and stigma. The stigma associated with disabilities can lead to damaged self-esteem and limited work opportunities. These, in turn, can be a factor in substance abuse, where the person tries to numb feelings of unworthiness and social isolation. As noted in this chapter, different disability groups have different types of etiology and treatment needs. A substance abuse professional who is sensitive to these phenomena will be better able to provide effective treatment.

It is important to emphasize integration and independence from the start in working with this population. Research shows that approaching the person in an integrated way is key to the success of the treatment program (Krahn & Gabriel, n.d.). Making sure that an individual with a disability has a balanced and diverse activity base is important; that may include active recreation, education, opportunities for social interaction, education of the family, opportunities for employment, and identification as a member of the disability coculture (Krahn & Gabriel, n.d.; Li & Moore, 1998). Identification with the disability coculture is important because it celebrates the uniqueness of each individual and reframes disability as a positive aspect of the individual. The disability coculture can be a powerful means of challenging negative mainstream stereotypes.

Finally, it is important for professionals in the field to see the total person and not just the disability. Although people with disabilities need specialized treatment within a program, they also need to be integrated into the mainstream during the treatment program, which can help them both to be accepted by others and to accept themselves. In other words, people can learn that their disability does not define them; rather, it is they who define their disability.

References

Americans With Disabilities Act of 1990, 42 U.S.C. § 12101 *et seq.* (1990).

Anderson, P. (1980–81). Alcoholism and the spinal cord disabled: A model program. *Alcohol Health ad Research World, 5*(2), 37–41.

Bombardier, C. H., Blake, K. D., Ehde, D. M., Gibbons, L. E., Moore, D., & Kraft, G. H. (2004). Alcohol and drug abuse among persons with multiple sclerosis. *Multiple Sclerosis, 10*, 35–40.

Boros, A. (1980–81). Alcoholism intervention for the deaf. *Alcohol Health and Research World, 5*(2), 26–30.

Cleland, M. (1980–1981). Perspectives: An AH & RW interview feature. *Alcohol Health and Research World, 5*(2), 57–63.

Commission on California State Government Organization and Economy. (1987). *The Little Hoover Commission report.* Retrieved January 15, 2010, from http://www.lhc.ca.gov/studies/079/report79.pdf

Do, T. P. (1997a). *How can you expect me to succeed if you keep telling me how to fail? Messages encouraging or limiting the transformation of persons with disabilities.* Unpublished master's thesis, San Diego State University, San Diego, CA.

Do, T. P. (1997b). In my shoes for life: A disabled woman's journey. In L. A. M. Perry & P. Geist (Eds.), *Courage of conviction: Women's words, women's wisdom* (pp. 129–143). Mountain View, CA: Mayfield.

Glass, E. J. (1980–81). Problem drinking among the blind and visually impaired. *Alcohol Health and Research World, 5*(2), 20–25.

Hepner, R., Kirshbaum, H., & Landes, D. (1980–81). Counseling substance abusers with additional disabilities: The Center for Independent Living. *Alcohol Health and Research World, 5*(2), 11–15.

Isaacs, M., Buckley, G., & Martin, D. (1979). Patterns of drinking among the deaf. *American Journal of Drug and Alcohol Abuse, 6*, 463–476.

Krahn, G., & Gabriel, R. (n.d.). Alcohol and drug treatment access project. Retrieved February 2, 2007, from http://www.healthwellnes.org/archive/research/study6.htm

Li, L., Ford, J., & Moore, D. (2000). An exploratory study of violence, substance abuse, disability, and gender. *Social Behavior and Personality, 28*(1), 61–71.

Li, L., & Moore, D. (1998, February). Acceptance of disability and its correlates. *Journal of Social Psychology, 138*(1), 13–25.

Li, L., & Moore, D. (2001). Disability and illicit drug use: An application of labeling theory: *Deviant Behavior, 22*(1), 1–21.

McAweeney, M., Forchheimer, M., Moore, D., & Tate, D. (2006). Psychosocial aspects related to dual diagnosis of substance use disorder and disability. In K. J. Haggland & A. W. Heinemann (Eds.), *Handbook of applied disability and rehabilitation research* (pp. 117–140). New York: Springer.

Morris, J. (1991). *Pride against prejudice: Transforming attitudes to disability.* Philadelphia: New Society Publishers.

O'Donnell, J. J., Cooper, J. E., Gesner, J. E., Shehan, I., & Ashley, J. (1981–82). Alcohol drugs and spinal cord injury. *Alcohol Health and Research World, 6*(2), 27–29.

Phillips, M. J. (1990). Damaged goods: Oral narratives of the experience of disability in American co-culture. *Social Science and Medicine, 30,* 849–856.

Shapiro, J. P. (1993). *No pity: People with disabilities forging a new civil rights movement.* New York: Random House.

Small, J. (1980–81). Emotions Anonymous: Counseling the mentally retarded substance abuser. *Alcohol Health and Research World, 5*(2), 46–47.

Thompson, T. L. (1983). Communication with the people with disabilities: A three year study of the effectiveness of mainstreaming. *Communication Education, 32,* 185–194.

U.S. Census Bureau. (2000, December). *Census 2000 operational plan.* Washington, DC: U.S. Department of Commerce.

U.S. Department of Education. (2005). *Disability employment 101.* Retrieved January 3, 2007, from http://www.ed.gov/about/offices/list/osers/products/employmentgude/index.htm/

Wenc, F. (1980–81). The developmentally disabled substance abuser. *Alcohol Health and Research World, 5*(2), 42–46.

APPENDIX

Further Resources on Cultural Competency, Culturally Adapted Interventions, and Evidence-Based Practices

Cultural Competency

Abe-Kim, J. S., & Takeuchi, D. T. (1996). Cultural competence and quality of care: Issues for mental health service delivery in managed care. *Clinical Psychology: Science and Practice, 3,* 273–295.

Abney, V. D. (1996). Cultural competency in the field of child maltreatment. In J. Briere, L. Berliner, J. A. Bulkley, C. Jenny, & T. Reid (Eds.), *The APSAC handbook on child maltreatment* (pp. 409–419). Thousand Oaks, CA: Sage.

Alladin, W. (1999). Models of counseling and psychotherapy for a multiethnic society. In S. Palmer & P. Laungani (Eds.), *Counseling in a multicultural society* (pp. 90–112). Thousand Oaks, CA: Sage.

Alvidrez, J., Azocar, F., & Miranda, J. (1996). Demystifying the concept of ethnicity for psychotherapy researchers. *Journal of Consulting and Clinical Psychology, 64,* 903–908.

Arredondo, P. (1999). Multicultural counseling competencies as tools to address oppression and racism. *Journal of Counseling and Development, 77,* 102–108.

Arthur, T. E. (2000). Issues in culturally competent mental health services for people of color. *Psychiatric Rehabilitation Skills, 4,* 426–447.

Arthur, T. E., Reeves, I., Morgan, O., Cornelius, L. J., Booker, N. C., Brathwaite, J., et al. (2005). Developing a cultural competence assessment tool for people in recovery from racial, ethnic and cultural backgrounds: The journey, challenges and lessons learned. *Psychiatric Rehabilitation Journal, 28,* 243–250.

Atkinson, D. R., Abreu, J., Ortiz-Bush, Y., & Brewer, S. (1994). Mexican American and European American ratings of four alcoholism treatment programs. *Hispanic Journal of Behavioral Sciences, 16,* 265–280.

Azocar, F., Miranda, J., & Dwyer, E. V. (1996). Treatment of depression in disadvantaged women. *Women and Therapy, 18,* 91–105.

Bernal, G., & Saez-Santiago, E. (2006). Culturally centered psychosocial interventions. *Journal of Community Psychology, 34,* 121–132.

Betancourt, J. B., Green, A. R., Carillo, J. E., & Park, E. R. (2005). From the field: Cultural competence and health care disparities: Key perspectives and trends. *Health Affairs, 24,* 499–505.

Beutler, L. E., Mohr, D. C., Grawe, K., Engle, D., & MacDonald, R. (1991). Looking for differential treatment effects: Cross-cultural predictors of differential psychotherapy efficacy. *Journal of Psychotherapy Integration, 1,* 121–141.

Beutler, L. E., Patterson, K. M., Jacob, T., Shoham, V., Yost, E., & Rohrbaugh, M. (1993). Matching treatment to alcoholism subtypes. *Psychotherapy: Theory, Research, Practice, Training, 30,* 463–472.

Bhugra, D., & Bhui, K. (1998). Psychotherapy for ethnic minorities: Issues, context and practice. *British Journal of Psychotherapy, 14,* 310–326.

Boyd-Franklin, N., & Garcia-Preto, N. (1994). Family therapy: The cases of African American and Hispanic women. In L. Comas-Diaz & B. Greene (Eds.), *Women of color: Integrating ethnic and gender identities in psychotherapy* (pp. 239–264). New York: Guilford Press.

Brach, C., & Fraserirector, I. (2000). Can cultural competency reduce racial and ethnic health disparities? A review and conceptual model. Medical *Care Research and Review, 57,* 181–217.

Bussema, E., & Nemec, P. (2006). Training to increase cultural competence. *Psychiatric Rehabilitation Journal, 30,* 71–73.

Campbell, C. I., & Alexander, J. A. (2002). Culturally competent treatment practices and ancillary service use in outpatient substance abuse treatment. *Journal of Substance Abuse Treatment, 22,* 109–119.

Castonguay, L. G., & Beutler, L. E. (2006). Principles of therapeutic change: A task force on participants, relationships, and techniques factors. *Journal of Clinical Psychology, 62,* 631–638.

Celano, M. P., & Kaslow, N. J. (2000). Culturally competent family interventions: Review and case illustrations. *American Journal of Family Therapy, 28,* 217–228.

Chin, J. L. (2002). Assessment of cultural competence in mental health systems of care for Asian Americans. In K. S. Kurasaki, S. Okazaki, & S. Sue (Eds.), *Asian American mental health: Assessment theories and methods* (pp. 301–314). New York: Kluwer Academic/Plenum.

Church, A. T. (1982). Sojourner adjustment. *Psychological Bulletin, 91,* 540–572.

Clinton, D., Gierlach, E., Zack, S. E., Beutler, L. E., & Castonguay, L. G. (2007). Toward the integration of technical interventions, relationship factors, and participants variables. In S. G. Hoffman & J. Weinberger (Eds.), *The art and science of psychotherapy* (pp. 131–153). New York: Routledge/ Taylor & Francis.

Coleman, H. L. K., Wampold, B. E., & Casali, S. L. (1995). Ethnic minorities' ratings of ethnically similar and European American counselors: A meta-analysis. *Journal of Counseling Psychology, 42,* 55–64.

Comas-Diaz, L. (2003). Review of cultural competency: A practical guide for mental health service providers. *Journal of Nervous and Mental Disease, 191,* 556.

Comas-Diaz, L. (2006). Cultural variation in the therapeutic relationship. In C. D. Goodheart, A. E. Kazdin, & R. J. Sternberg (Eds.), *Evidence-based psychotherapy: Where practice and research meet* (pp. 81–105). Washington, DC: American Psychological Association.

Comas-Diaz, L., & Jacobsen, F. M. (1991). Ethnocultural transference and countertransference in the therapeutic dyad. *American Journal of Orthopsychiatry, 61,* 392–402.

Cornelius, L. J., Booker, N. C., Arthur, T. E., Reeves, I., & Morgan, O. (2004). The validity and reliability testing of a consumer-based cultural competency inventory. *Research on Social Work Practice, 14,* 201–209.

Costantino, G., Dana, R. H., & Malgady, R. G. (2007). *TEMAS (Tell-Me-A-Story) assessment in multicultural societies.* Mahwah, NJ: Erlbaum.

Cunningham, P. B., Foster, S. L., & Henggeler, S. W. (2002). The elusive concept of cultural competence. *Children's Services: Social Policy, Research, and Practice, 5,* 231–243.

Dana, R. H. (2000). Psychological assessment in the diagnosis and treatment of ethnic group members. In J. F. Aponte & J. Wohl (Eds.), *Psychological intervention and cultural diversity* (2nd ed., pp. 59–74). Boston: Allyn & Bacon.

Danish, S. J., Forneris, T., & Schaaf, K. W. (2007). Counseling psychology and culturally competent health care: Limitations and challenges. *Counseling Psychologist, 35,* 716–725.

Davis, T. S. (2007). Mapping patterns of perceptions: A community-based approach to cultural competence assessment. Research on Social Work Practice, 17, 358–379.

DePalma, J. A. (2006). Evidence regarding cultural competency. *Home Health Care Management and Practice, 18,* 405–407.

Dillard, M., Andonian, L., Flores, O., Lai, L., MacRae, A., & Shakir, M. (1992). Culturally competent occupational therapy in a diversely populated mental health setting. *American Journal of Occupational Therapy, 46,* 721–726.

Duckworth, M. P. (2005). Behavioral health policy and eliminating disparities through cultural competency. In N. A. Cummings, W. T. O'Donohue, & M. A. Cucciare (Eds.), *Universal healthcare: Readings for mental health professionals* (pp. 151–162). Reno, NV: Context Press.

Ecklund, K., & Johnson, W. B. (2007a). The impact of a culture-sensitive intake assessment on the treatment of a depressed biracial child. *Clinical Case Studies, 6,* 468–482.

Ecklund, K., & Johnson, W. B. (2007b). Toward cultural competence in child intake assessments. *Professional Psychology: Research and Practice, 38,* 356–362.

Eiser, A. R., & Ellis, G. (2007). Cultural competence and the African American experience with health care: The case for specific content in cross-cultural education. *Academic Medicine, 82,* 176–183.

Eleftheriadou, Z. (1997). Cultural differences in the therapeutic process. In I. Horton & V. Varma (Eds.), *The needs of counselors and psychotherapists* (pp. 68–83). Thousand Oaks, CA: Sage.

Fenster, A. (1996). Group therapy as an effective treatment modality for people of color. *International Journal of Group Psychotherapy, 46,* 399–416.

Fierros, M., Smith, C., & Gillig, P. M. (2006). The relevance of Hispanic culture to the treatment of a patient with posttraumatic stress disorder (PTSD). *Psychiatry, 3,* 49–55.

Flaskerud, J. H. (2007a). Cultural competence: Acculturation. *Issues in Mental Health Nursing, 28,* 543–546.

Flaskerud, J. H. (2007b). Cultural competence: Can we achieve it? *Issues in Mental Health Nursing, 28,* 309–311.

Flaskerud, J. H. (2007c). Cultural competence: What else is necessary? *Issues in Mental Health Nursing, 28,* 219–222.

Flaskerud, J. H. (2007d). Cultural competence: What effect on reducing health disparities? *Issues in Mental Health Nursing, 28,* 431–434.

Flaskerud, J. H. (2007e). Cultural competence: What is it? *Issues in Mental Health Nursing, 28,* 121–123.

Flaskerud, J. H., & Nyamathi, A. M. (2000). Attaining gender and ethnic diversity in health intervention research: Cultural responsiveness versus resource provision. *Advances in Nursing Science, 22,* 1–15.

Forehand, R., & Kotchick, B. A. (1996). Cultural diversity: A wake-up call for parent training. *Behavior Therapy, 27,* 187–206.

Foulks, E. F., Bland, I. J., & Shervington, D. (1995). Psychotherapy across cultures. *American Psychiatric Press Review of Psychiatry, 14,* 511–528.

Groth-Marnat, G., Roberts, R. I., & Beutler, L. E. (2001). Client characteristics and psychotherapy: Perspectives, support, interactions, and implications for training. *Australian Psychologist, 36,* 115–121.

Guarnaccia, P. J. J., & Rodriguez, O. (1996). Concepts of culture and their role in the development of culturally competent mental health services. *Hispanic Journal of Behavioral Sciences, 18,* 419–443.

Han, A. L., & Vasquez, M. J. T. (2000). Group intervention and treatment with ethnic minorities. In J. F. Aponte & J. Wohl (Eds.), *Psychological intervention and cultural diversity* (2nd ed., pp. 110–130). Needham Heights, MA: Allyn & Bacon.

Hays, P. A. (2001). *Addressing cultural complexities in practice: A framework for clinicians and counselors.* Washington, DC: American Psychological Association.

Hays, P. A. (1996). Culturally responsive assessment with diverse older clients. Professional Psychology: Research and Practice, 27, 188–193.

Hemmelgarn, A. L., Glisson, C., & James, L. R. (2006). Organizational culture and climate: Implications for services and interventions research. *Clinical Psychology: Science and Practice, 13,* 73–89.

Holcomb-McCoy, C. C., & Myers, J. E. (1999). Multicultural competence and counselor training: A national survey. *Journal of Counseling and Development, 77,* 294–302.

Huang, L. (1994). An integrative approach to clinical assessment and intervention with Asian-American adolescents. *Journal of Clinical Child Psychology, 23,* 21–31.

Hwang, W.-C., & Wood, J. J. (2007). Being culturally sensitive is not the same as being culturally competent. *Pragmatic Case Studies in Psychotherapy, 3,* 44–50.

Ida, D. J. (2007). Cultural competency and recovery within diverse populations. *Psychiatric Rehabilitation Journal, 31,* 49–53.

Kirmayer, L. J. (2001). Cultural variations in the clinical presentation of depression and anxiety: Implications for diagnosis and treatment. *Journal of Clinical Psychiatry, 62,* 22–28.

Kurasaki, K. S., Okazaki, S., & Sue, S. (Eds.). (2002). *Asian American mental health: Assessment theories and methods.* New York: Kluwer Academic/Plenum.

Kwon, P. (1995). Application of social cognition principles to treatment recommendations for ethnic minority clients: The case of Asian Americans. *Clinical Psychology Review, 15*(7), 613–629.

Lee, R. M., & Darnell, A. J. (2002). Theory and method of multicultural counseling competency assessment. In K. S. Kurasaki, S. Okazaki, & S. Sue (Eds.), *Asian American mental health: Assessment theories and methods* (pp. 283–299). New York: Kluwer Academic/Plenum.

Lo, H.-T., & Fung, K. P. (2003). Culturally competent psychotherapy. *Canadian Journal of Psychiatry/La Revue canadienne de psychiatrie, 48,* 161–170.

Lopez, S. R. (1997). Cultural competence in psychotherapy: A guide for clinicians and their supervisors. In C. Watkins (Ed.), *Handbook of psychotherapy supervision* (pp. 570–588). Hoboken, NJ: Wiley.

Lopez, S. R., & Guarnaccia, P. J. J. (2000). Cultural psychopathology: Uncovering the social world of mental illness. *Annual Review of Psychology, 51,* 571–598.

Lung, A. Y., & Sue, S. (1997). Chinese American children. In G. Johnson-Powell, J. Yamamoto, G. E. Wyatt, & W. Arroyo (Eds.), *Transcultural child development: Psychological assessment and treatment* (pp. 208–236). Hoboken, NJ: Wiley.

Malgady, R. G., & Costantino, G. (1999). Ethnicity and culture: Hispanic youth. In W. K. Silverman & T. H. Ollendick (Eds.), *Developmental issues in the clinical treatment of children* (pp. 231–238). Needham Heights, MA: Allyn & Bacon.

Matthews, A. K., & Peterman, A. H. (1998). Improving provision of effective treatment for racial and cultural minorities. *Psychotherapy: Theory, Research, Practice, Training, 35,* 291–305.

McGoldrick, M. (1998). *Re-visioning family therapy: Race, culture, and gender in clinical practice.* New York: Guilford Press.

Mezzich, J. E., Kleinman, A., Fabrega, H., Jr., & Parron, D. L. (1996). *Culture and psychiatric diagnosis: A DSM-IV perspective.* Washington, DC: American Psychiatric Association.

Middleton, R. A., Stadler, H. A., Simpson, C., Guo, Y.-J., Brown, M. J., Crow, G., et al. (2005). Mental health practitioners: The relationship between White racial identity attitudes and self-reported multicultural counseling competencies. *Journal of Counseling and Development, 83,* 444–456.

Miranda, J., Bernal, G., Lau, A., Kohn, L., Hwang, W.-C., & LaFromboise, T. (2005). State of the science on psychosocial interventions for ethnic minorities. *Annual Review of Clinical Psychology, 1,* 113–142.

Mock, M. R. (2003). Cultural sensitivity, relevance, and competence in school mental health. In E. Weist & N. A. Lever (Ed.), *Handbook of school mental health: Advancing practice and research* (pp. 349–362). New York: Kluwer Academic/Plenum.

Moodley, R. (1998). "I say what I like": Frank talk(ing) in counseling and psychotherapy. *British Journal of Guidance and Counselling, 26,* 495–508.

Morales, P. (1999). The impact of cultural differences in psychotherapy with older clients: Sensitive issues and strategies. In M. Duffy (Ed.), *Handbook of counseling and psychotherapy with older adults* (pp. 132–153). Hoboken, NJ: Wiley.

Murphy-Shigematsu, S. (1999). Clinical work with minorities in Japan: Social and cultural context. *American Journal of Orthopsychiatry, 69,* 482–494.

Odell, M., Shelling, G., Young, K. S., Hewitt, D. H., & L'Abate, L. (1994). The skills of the marriage and family therapist in straddling multicultural issues. *American Journal of Family Therapy, 22,* 145–155.

Okazaki, S. (1998). Psychological assessment of Asian Americans: Research agenda for cultural competency. *Journal of Personality Assessment, 70,* 54–70.

Okazaki, S. (2000). Assessing and treating Asian Americans: Recent advances. In I. Cuellar & F. A. Paniagua (Eds.), *Handbook of multicultural mental health* (pp. 171–193). San Diego: Academic Press.

Parks, F. M. (2003). The role of African American folk beliefs in the modern therapeutic process. *Clinical Psychology: Science and Practice, 10,* 456–467.

Ponterotto, J. G., Fuertes, J. N., & Chen, E. C. (2000). Models of multicultural counseling. In S. D. Brown (Ed.), *Handbook of counseling psychology* (3rd ed., pp. 639–669). Hoboken, NJ: Wiley.

Pope-Davis, D. B., & Coleman, H. L. K. (1997). Multicultural counseling competencies: Assessment, education and training, and supervision. *Multicultural aspects of counseling series.* Thousand Oaks, CA: Sage.

Porter, N., Garcia, M., Jackson, H., & Valdez, D. (1997). The rights of children and adolescents of color in mental health systems. *Women and Therapy, 20,* 57–74.

Porter, R. Y. (2000). Clinical issues and interventions with ethnic minority women. In J. F. Aponte & J. Wohl (Eds.), *Psychological intervention and cultural diversity* (pp. 183–199). Needham Heights, MA: Allyn & Bacon.

Pumariega, A. J. (2003). Cultural competence in systems of care for children's mental health. In A. J. Pumariega & N. C. Winters (Ed.), *The handbook of child and adolescent systems of care: The new community psychiatry* (pp. 82–104). San Francisco: Jossey-Bass.

Quinones-Mayo, Y., Wilson, K. B., & McGuire, M. V. (2000). Vocational rehabilitation and cultural competency for Latino populations: Considerations for rehabilitation counselors. *Journal of Applied Rehabilitation Counseling, 31,* 19–26.

Raja, S. (1998). Culturally sensitive therapy for women of color. *Women and Therapy, 21,* 67–84.

Reynolds, A. L. (1995). Challenges and strategies for teaching multicultural counseling courses. In J. G. Ponterotto (Ed.), *Handbook of multicultural counseling* (pp. 312–330). Thousand Oaks, CA: Sage.

Richardson, T. Q., & Molinaro, K. L. (1996). White counselor self-awareness: A prerequisite for multicultural competence. *Journal of Counseling and Development, 74,* 238–242.

Ridley, C. R., Baker, D. M., & Hill, C. L. (2001). Critical issues concerning cultural competence. *Counseling Psychologist, 29,* 822–832.

Rogler, L. H., Malgady, R. G., Costantino, G., & Blumenthal, R. (1987). What do culturally sensitive mental health services mean? The case of Hispanics. *American Psychologist, 42,* 565–570.

Rowe, D. M., & Grills, C. (1993). African-centered drug treatment: An alternative conceptual paradigm for drug counseling with African-American clients. *Journal of Psychoactive Drugs, 25,* 21–33.

Ruiz, P. (2004). Addressing culture, race, and ethnicity in psychiatric practice. *Psychiatric Annals, 34,* 527–532.

Salvendy, J. T. (1999). Ethnocultural considerations in group psychotherapy. *International Journal of Group Psychotherapy, 49,* 429–464.

Serrano, A., & Hou, S. (1996). Culture and ethnicity. In P. Kymissis & D. A. Halperin (Eds.), *Group therapy with children and adolescents* (pp. 329–335). Washington, DC: American Psychiatric Association.

Siegel, C., Davis-Chambers, E., Haugland, G., Bank, R., Aponte, C., & McCombs, H. (2000). Performance measures of cultural competency in mental health organizations. *Administration and Policy in Mental Health, 28,* 91–106.

Singh, N. N., McKay, J. D., & Singh, A. N. (1998). Culture and mental health: Nonverbal communication. *Journal of Child and Family Studies, 7,* 403–409.

Sue, D. W., Arredondo, P., & McDavis, R. J. (1992). Multicultural counseling competencies and standards: A call to the profession. *Journal of Counseling and Development, 70,* 477–486.

Sue, S. (1998). In search of cultural competence in psychotherapy and counseling. *American Psychologist, 53,* 440–448.

Sue, S. (1999). Science, ethnicity, and bias: Where have we gone wrong? *American Psychologist, 54,* 1070–1077.

Sue, S. (2003). In defense of cultural competency in psychotherapy and treatment. *American Psychologist, 58,* 964–970.

Sue, S. (2006). Cultural competency: From philosophy to research and practice. *Journal of Community Psychology, 34,* 237–245.

Sue, S., & Lam, A. G. (2002). Cultural and demographic diversity. In J. C. Norcross (Ed.), *Psychotherapy relationships that work: Therapist contributions and responsiveness to patients* (pp. 2401–2421). New York: Oxford University Press.

Sue, S., & Zane, N. (1987). The role of culture and cultural techniques in psychotherapy: A critique and reformulation. *American Psychologist, 42,* 37–45.

Sue, S., & Zane, N. (1995). The role of culture and cultural techniques in psychotherapy: A critique and reformulation. In N. R. Goldberger & J. B. Veroff (Eds.), *The culture and psychology reader* (pp. 767–788). New York: New York University Press.

Sue, S., Zane, N., Levant, R. F., Silverstein, L. B., Brown, L. S., Olkin, R., et al. (2006). How well do both evidence-based practices and treatment as usual satisfactorily address the various dimensions of diversity? In J. C. Norcross, L. E. Beutler, & R. F. Levant (Eds.), *Evidence-based practices in mental health: Debate and dialogue on the fundamental questions* (pp. 329–374). Washington DC: American Psychological Association.

Swanson, G. M., & Ward, A. J. (1995). Recruiting minorities into clinical trials toward a participant-friendly system. *Journal of the National Cancer Institute, 87,* 1747–1759.

Szapocznik, J., Santisteban, D., Rio, A., Perez-Vidal, A., & Kurtines, W. M. (1989). Family effectiveness training: An intervention to prevent drug abuse and problem behaviors in Hispanic adolescents. *Hispanic Journal of Behavioral Sciences, 11,* 4–27.

Tanenbaum, S. J. (2005). Evidence-based practice as mental health policy: Three controversies and a caveat. *Health Affairs, 24,* 163–173.

Taylor, B. A., Gambourg, M. B., Rivera, M., & Laureano, D. (2006). Constructing cultural competence: Perspectives of family therapists working with Latino families. *American Journal of Family Therapy, 34,* 429–445.

Thomas, A. R., & Cobb, H. C. (1999). Culturally responsive counseling and psychotherapy with children and adolescents. In H. T. Prout & D. T. Brown (Eds.), *Counseling and psychotherapy with children and adolescents: Theory and practice for school and clinical settings* (pp. 49–73). Hoboken, NJ: Wiley.

Vargas, A. M., & DiPilato, M. (1999). Culture-focused group therapy: Identity issues in gang-involved youth. In C. W. Branch (Ed.), *Adolescent gangs: Old issues, new approaches* (pp. 159–173). Philadelphia: Brunner/Mazel.

Vega, W. A. (2005). Higher stakes ahead for cultural competence. *General Hospital Psychiatry, 27,* 446–450.

Wade, P., & Bernstein, B. L. (1991). Culture sensitivity training and counselor's race: Effects on Black female clients' perceptions and attrition. *Journal of Counseling Psychology, 38,* 9–15.

Wallace, B. C. (1996). Women and minorities in treatment. In A. M. Washton (Ed.), *Psychotherapy and substance abuse: A practitioner's handbook* (pp. 470–492). New York: Guilford Press.

Wang, M., McCart, A., & Turnbull, A. P. (2007). Implementing positive behavior support with Chinese American families: Enhancing cultural competence. *Journal of Positive Behavior Interventions, 9,* 38–51.

Wright, D. J. (1999). Group services for students of color. In Y. M. Jenkins (Ed.), *Diversity in college settings: Directives for helping professionals* (pp. 1149–1167). Florence, KY: Routledge/Taylor & Francis.

Xiong, W., Phillips, M. R., Hu, X., Wang, R., Qinqing, D., Kleinman, J., et al. (1994). Family-based intervention for schizophrenic patients in China: A randomized controlled trial. *British Journal of Psychiatry, 165,* 239–247.

Culturally Adapted Interventions

Acosta, F. X., Yamamoto, J., Evans, L. A., & Skilbeck, W. M. (1983). Preparing low-income Hispanic, Black, and White patients for psychotherapy: Evaluation of a new orientation program. *Journal of Clinical Psychology, 39,* 872–877.

Arean, P., & Miranda, J. (1996). The treatment of depression in elderly primary care patients: A naturalistic study. *Journal of Clinical Geropsychology, 2,* 153–160.

Armengol, C. G. (1999). A multimodal support group with Hispanic traumatic brain injury survivors. *Journal of Head Trauma Rehabilitation, 14,* 233–246.

Banks, R., Hogue, A., Timberlake, T., & Liddle, H. (1998). An Afrocentric approach to group social skills training with inner-city African American adolescents. *Journal of Negro Education, 65,* 414–423.

Banks, S. R. (1998). *The impact of social support and active coping on enhancing mental health and employability outcomes among African-Americans and Latinos with disabilities: A community based group intervention.* Washington, DC: George Washington University Press.

Bass, C. K. (2000). *Effects of a culturally relevant intervention of the academic achievement of African American male adolescents.* Unpublished doctoral dissertation.

Belgrave, F. Z. (2002). Relational theory and cultural enhancement interventions for African American adolescent girls. *Public Health Reports, 117,* S76–S81.

Belgrave, F. Z., Chase-Vaughn, G., Gray, F., Addison, J. D., & Cherry, V. R. (2000). The effectiveness of a culture- and gender-specific intervention for increasing resiliency among African American preadolescent females. *Journal of Black Psychology, 26,* 133–147.

Bernal, G., Bonilla, J., & Bellido, C. (1995). Ecological validity and cultural sensitivity for outcome research: Issues for the cultural adaptation and development of psychosocial treatments with Hispanics. *Journal of Abnormal Child Psychology, 23,* 67–82.

Botvin, G. J., Schinke, S. P., Epstein, J. A., & Diaz, T. (1994). Effectiveness of culturally focused and generic skills training approaches to alcohol and drug abuse prevention among minority youths. *Psychology of Addictive Behaviors, 8,* 116–127.

Castro, F. G., Barrera, M., & Martinez, C. R. (2004). The cultural adaptation of prevention interventions: Resolving tensions between fidelity and fit. *Prevention Science, 4,* 41–45.

Cervantes, R. C., Kappos, B., Dueñas, N., & Arellano, D. (2003). Culturally focused HIV prevention and substance abuse treatment for Hispanic women. *Addictive Disorders and Their Treatment, 2,* 69–77.

Cherry, V. R., Belgrave, F. Z., Jones, W., Kennon, D. K., Gray, F. S., & Phillips, F. (1998). NTU: An Africentric approach to substance abuse prevention among African American youth. *Journal of Primary Prevention, 18,* 319–339.

Coard, S. I., Wallace, S. A., Stevenson, H. C., & Brotman, L. M. (2004). Towards culturally relevant preventive interventions: The consideration of racial socialization in parent training with African American families. *Journal of Child and Family Studies, 13,* 277–293.

Comas-Diaz, L. (1981). Effects of cognitive and behavioral group treatment on the depressive symptomatology of Puerto Rican women. *Journal of Consulting and Clinical Psychology, 49,* 627–632.

Costantino, G., Malgady, R. G., & Rogler, L. H. (1986). Cuento therapy: A culturally sensitive modality for Puerto Rican children. *Journal of Consulting and Clinical Psychology, 54,* 639–645.

Costantino, G., Malgady, R. G., & Rogler, L. H. (1994). Storytelling through pictures: Culturally sensitive psychotherapy for Hispanic children and adolescents. *Journal of Clinical Child Psychology, 23,* 13–20.

Dai, Y., Zhang, S., Yamamoto, J., Ao, M., Belin, T. R., Cheung, F., et al. (1999). Cognitive behavioral therapy of minor depressive symptoms in elderly Chinese Americans: A pilot study. *Community Mental Health Journal, 35,* 537–542.

Falconer, J. (2002). *The effectiveness of a culturally relevant eating disorder prevention intervention with African American college women.* Unpublished doctoral dissertation, University of Missouri-Columbia, Columbia.

Fisher, D. G., Lankford, B. A., & Galea, R. P. (1996). Therapeutic community retention among Alaska Natives: Akeela House. *Journal of Substance Abuse Treatment, 13,* 265–271.

Flaskerud, J. H. (1986). The effects of culture-compatible intervention on the utilization of mental health services by minority clients. *Community Mental Health Journal, 22,* 127–141.

Flaskerud, J. H., & Akutsu, P. D. (1993). Significant influence of participation in ethnic-specific programs on clinical diagnosis for Asian Americans. *Psychological Reports, 72,* 1228–1230.

Flaskerud, J. H., & Hu, L.-T. (1994). Participation in and outcome of treatment for major depression among low income Asian-Americans. *Psychiatry Research, 53,* 289–300.

Gallagher-Thompson, D., Arean, P., Rivera, P., & Thompson, L. W. (2001). A psychoeducational intervention to reduce distress in Hispanic family caregivers: Results of a pilot study. *Clinical Gerontologist, 23,* 17–32.

Gonzalez, M. A. (2003). *The effectiveness of a culturally based social work activity group in the promotion of ethnic identity and adaptive behaviors: A study of Puerto Rican children.* Unpublished doctoral dissertation, Catholic University of America, Washington, DC.

Gonzalez, M. A. (1999). *Patterns of mental health service utilization and treatment outcome in a community sample of Hispanic adults.* Unpublished doctoral dissertation, California School of Professional Psychology, Los Angeles.

Griner, D., & Smith, T. B. (2006). Culturally adapted mental health interventions: A meta-analytic review. *Psychotherapy: Theory, Research, Practice, Training, 43,* 531–548.

Grodnitzky, G. R. (1993). *Hero modeling versus non-hero modeling as interventions for Puerto-Rican and Anglo adolescents exhibiting behavior problems.* Unpublished doctoral dissertation, Hofstra University, Hempstead, NY.

Guinn, B., & Vincent, V. (2002). A health intervention on Latina spiritual well-being constructs: An evaluation. *Hispanic Journal of Behavioral Sciences, 24,* 379–391.

Gutiérrez, L. M., & Ortega, R. (1991). Developing methods to empower Latinos: The importance of groups. *Social Work With Groups, 14,* 23–43.

Hammond, W. R., & Yung, B. R. (1991). Preventing violence in at-risk African-American youth. *Journal of Health Care for the Poor and Underserved, 2,* 359–373.

Hansen, D. J., Zamboanga, B. L., & Sedlar, G. (2000). Cognitive-behavior therapy for ethnic minority adolescents: Broadening our perspectives. *Cognitive and Behavioral Practice, 7,* 54–60.

Harvey, A. R., & Hill, R. B. (2004). Africentric Youth and Family Rites of Passage Program: Promoting resilience among at-risk African American youths. *Social Work, 49,* 65–74.

Heppner, M. J., Neville, H. A., Smith, K., Kivlighan, D. M., Jr., & Gershuny, B. S. (1999). Examining immediate and long-term efficacy of rape prevention programming with racially diverse college men. *Journal of Counseling Psychology, 46,* 16–26.

Hinton, D. E., Pham, T., Tran, M., Safren, S. A., Otto, M. W., & Pollack, M. H. (2004). CBT for Vietnamese refugees with treatment-resistant PTSD and panic attacks: A pilot study. *Journal of Traumatic Stress, 17,* 429–433.

Hwang, W.-C. (2006). The psychotherapy adaptation and modification framework: Application to Asian Americans. *American Psychologist, 61,* 702–715.

Hwang, W.-C., Wood, J. J., Lin, K.-M., & Cheung, F. (2006). Cognitive-behavioral therapy with Chinese Americans: Research, theory, and clinical practice. *Cognitive and Behavioral Practice, 13,* 293–303.

Jackson, P. A. (1997). *The effect of exposure to culturally relevant/historically based material on level of frustration tolerance, level of depression, and mediation of anger in African-American young males.* Unpublished doctoral dissertation, California School of Professional Psychology, Alameda.

Jackson-Gilfort, A. M. (1997). *The relationship of cultural theme discussion to engagement with acting out: African American male adolescents in family therapy.* Unpublished doctoral dissertation, Temple University, Philadelphia.

Jackson-Gilfort, A. M., Liddle, H. A., Tejeda, M. J., & Dakof, G. A. (2001). Facilitating engagement of African American male adolescents in family therapy: A cultural theme process study. *Journal of Black Psychology, 27,* 321–340.

Kim, B. S. K., Omizo, M. M., & D'Andrea, M. J. (1998). The effects of culturally consonant group counseling on the self-esteem and internal locus of control orientation among Native American adolescents. *Journal for Specialists in Group Work, 23,* 145–163.

King, B. S. (1999). *The effect of a cultural-based life skills curriculum on American Indian adolescent self-esteem and locus of control.* Unpublished doctoral dissertation, University of Arkansas.

Kohn, L. P., Oden, T., Muñoz, R. F., Robinson, A., & Leavitt, D. (2002). Adapted cognitive behavioral group therapy for depressed low-income African American women. *Community Mental Health Journal, 38,* 497–504.

Kopelowicz, A., Zarate, R., Smith, V. G., Mintz, J., & Liberman, R. P. (2003). Disease management in Latinos with schizophrenia: A family-assisted, skills training approach. *Schizophrenia Bulletin, 29,* 211–228.

Kumpfer, K. L., Alvarado, R., Smith, P., & Bellamy, N. (2002). Cultural sensitivity and adaptation in family-based prevention interventions. *Prevention Science, 3,* 241–246.

Lau, A. S., & Zane, N. (2000). Examining the effects of ethnic-specific services: An analysis of cost-utilization and treatment outcome for Asian American clients. *Journal of Community Psychology, 28,* 63–77.

Lau, A. S. (2007). Making the case for selective and directed cultural adaptations of evidence-based treatments: Examples from parent training. *Clinical Psychology: Science and Practice, 13,* 295–310.

Lewis, S. Y. (1994). Cognitive-behavioral therapy. In L. Comas-Diaz & B. Greene (Eds.), *Women of color: Integrating ethnic and gender identities in psychotherapy* (pp. 223–238). New York: Guilford Press.

Lin, J. C. H. (1994). How long do Chinese Americans stay in psychotherapy? *Journal of Counseling Psychology, 41,* 288–291.

Lin, Y. N. (2001). The application of cognitive-behavioral therapy to counseling Chinese. *American Journal of Psychotherapy, 55,* 46–58.

Liu, E. T.-H. (2007). Integrating cognitive-behavioral and cognitive-interpersonal case formulations: A case study of a Chinese American male. *Pragmatic Case Studies in Psychotherapy, 3,* 1–33.

Longshore, D., & Grills, C. (2000). Motivating illegal drug use recovery: Evidence for a culturally congruent intervention. *Journal of Black Psychology, 26,* 288–301.

Longshore, D., Grills, C., & Annon, K. (1999). Effects of a culturally congruent intervention on cognitive factors related to drug use recovery. *Substance Use and Misuse, 34,* 1223–1241.

Malgady, R. G., Rogler, L. H., & Costantino, G. (1990). Culturally sensitive psychotherapy for Puerto Rican children and adolescents: A program of treatment outcome research. *Journal of Consulting and Clinical Psychology, 58,* 704–712.

Malgady, R. G., Rogler, L. H., & Costantino, G. (1990). Hero/heroine modeling for Puerto Rican adolescents: A preventive mental health intervention. *Journal of Consulting and Clinical Psychology, 58,* 469–474.

Martinez, C. R., & Eddy, J. M. (2005). Effects of culturally adapted parent management training on Latino youth behavioral health outcomes. *Journal of Consulting and Clinical Psychology, 73,* 841–851.

Mathews, C. A., Glidden, D., & Hargreaves, W. A. (2002). The effect on diagnostic rates of assigning patients to ethnically focused inpatient psychiatric units. *Psychiatric Services, 53,* 823–829.

Mathews, C. A., Glidden, D., Murray, S., Forster, P., & Hargreaves, W. A. (2002). The effect on treatment outcomes of assigning patients to ethnically focused inpatient psychiatric units. *Psychiatric Services, 53,* 830–835.

McCabe, K. M., Yeh, M., Garland, A. F., Lau, A. S., & Chavez, G. (2005). The GANA program: A tailoring approach to adapting parent–child interaction therapy for Mexican Americans. *Education and Treatment for Children, 28,* 111–129.

McGrogan, K. L. (1998). *The development and pilot test in a community center of a Latino parenting group for limited literacy: Spanish speaking families with children at risk.* Unpublished doctoral dissertation, Rutgers University, New Brunswick, NJ.

Mickens-English, P. (1996). *The efficacy of an Afrocentric/holistic group psychotherapy approach for Black women.* Unpublished doctoral dissertation, Kent State University, Kent.

Miranda, J., Green, B. L., Krupnick, J. L., Chung, J., Siddique, J., Beslin, T., et al. (2006). One-year outcomes of a randomized clinical trial treating depression in low-income minority women. *Journal of Consulting and Clinical Psychology, 74,* 99–111.

Moran, J. R. (1999). Preventing alcohol use among urban American Indian youth: The seventh generation program. *Journal of Human Behavior in the Social Environment, 2,* 51–67.

Myers, H. F., Alvy, K. T., Arrington, A., Richardson, M. A., Marigna, M., Huff, R., et al. (1992). The impact of a parent training program on inner-city African-American families. *Journal of Community Psychology, 20,* 132–147.

Normand, W. C., Iglesias, J., & Payn, S. (1974). Brief group therapy to facilitate utilization of mental health services by Spanish-speaking patients. *American Journal of Orthopsychiatry, 44,* 37–42.

Nyamathi, A. M., Leake, B., Flaskerud, J. H., Lewis, C., & Bennett, C. (1993). Outcomes of specialized and traditional AIDS counseling programs for impoverished women of color. *Research in Nursing and Health, 16,* 11–21.

Ochoa, M. L. (1981). *Group counseling Chicana troubled youth: An exploratory group counseling project.* Unpublished doctoral dissertation, University of Massachusetts, Amherst.

Organista, K. C., & Dwyer, E. V. (1996). Clinical case management and cognitive-behavioral therapy: Integrated psychosocial services for depressed Latino primary care patients. In P. Manoleas (Ed.), *The cross-cultural practice of clinical case management in mental health: Haworth social work practice* (pp. 119–143). New York: Haworth Press.

Organista, K. C., & Muñoz, R. F. (1996). Cognitive behavioral therapy with Latinos. *Cognitive and Behavioral Practice, 3,* 255–270.

Organista, K. C., Muñoz, R. F., & González, G. (1994). Cognitive-behavioral therapy for depression in low-income and minority medical outpatients: Description of a program and exploratory analyses. *Cognitive Therapy and Research, 18,* 241–259.

Palmer, S. (2000). Developing an individual therapeutic programme suitable for use by counselling psychologists in a multicultural society: A multimodal perspective. *Counselling Psychology Review, 15,* 32–50.

Perez, J. E. (1999). Integration of cognitive-behavioral and interpersonal therapies for Latinos: An argument for technical eclecticism. *Journal of Contemporary Psychotherapy, 29,* 169–183.

Pina, A. A., Silverman, W. K., Fuentes, R. M., Kurtines, W. M., & Weems, C. F. (2003). Exposure-based cognitive-behavioral treatment for phobic and anxiety disorders: Treatment effects and maintenance for Hispanic/Latino relative to European-American youths. *Journal of the American Academy of Child and Adolescent Psychiatry, 42,* 1179–1187.

Prizzia, R., & Mokuah, N. (1991). Mental health services of Native Hawaiians: The need for culturally relevant services. *Journal of Health and Human Resources Administration, 14,* 44–61.

Raymond, M. J. (1996). *Analysis of Native American cultural practices used as a treatment modality for alcohol addiction.* Unpublished doctoral dissertation, Pacific Graduate School of Psychology, Palo Alto, CA.

Robbins, M. S., Szapocznik, J., Santisteban, D. A., Hervis, O. E., Mitrani, V. B., & Schwartz, S. J. (2003). Brief strategic family therapy for Hispanic youth. In A. E. Kazdin & J. R. Weisz (Eds.), *Evidence-based psychotherapies for children and adolescents* (pp. 2407–2424). New York: Guilford Press.

Robinson, W. L., Harper, G. W., & Schoeny, M. E. (2003). Reducing substance use among African American adolescents: Effectiveness of school-based health centers. *Clinical Psychology: Science and Practice, 10,* 491–504.

Rossello, J., & Bernal, G. (1996). Adapting cognitive-behavioral and interpersonal treatments for depressed Puerto Rican adolescents. In E. D. Hibbs & P. S. Jensen (Eds.), *Psychosocial treatments for child and adolescent disorders: Empirically based strategies for clinical practice* (pp. 157–185). Washington, DC: American Psychological Association.

Rossello, J., & Bernal, G. (1999). The efficacy of cognitive-behavioral and interpersonal treatments for depression in Puerto Rican adolescents. *Journal of Consulting and Clinical Psychology, 67,* 734–745.

Santisteban, D. A., Coatsworth, J. D., Perez-Vidal, A., Mitrani, V., Jean-Gilles, M., & Szapocznik, J. (1997). Brief structural/strategic family therapy with African American and Hispanic high-risk youth. *Journal of Community Psychology, 25,* 453–471.

Satterfield, J. M. (1998). Cognitive behavioral group therapy for depressed, low-income minority clients: Retention and treatment enhancement. *Cognitive and Behavioral Practice, 5,* 65–80.

Schinke, S. P., Orlandi, M. A., Botvin, G. J., Gilchrist, L. D., Trimble, J. E., & Locklear, V. S. (1988). Preventing substance abuse among American-Indian adolescents: A bicultural competence skills approach. *Journal of Counseling Psychology, 35,* 87–90.

Schinke, S. P., Schilling, R. F., Palleja, J., & Zayas, L. H. (1987). Prevention research among ethnic-racial minority group adolescents. *Behavior Therapist, 10,* 151–155.

Schwarz, D. A. (1989). *The effect of a Spanish pre-therapy orientation videotape on Puerto Rican clients' knowledge about psychotherapy, improvement in therapy, attendance patterns and satisfaction with services.* Unpublished doctoral dissertation, Temple University, Philadelphia.

Shin, S.-K. (2004). Effects of culturally relevant psychoeducation for Korean American families of persons with chronic mental illness. *Research on Social Work Practice, 14,* 231–239.

Shin, S.-K., & Lukens, E. P. (2002). Effects of psychoeducation for Korean Americans with chronic mental illness. *Psychiatric Services, 53,* 1125–1131.

Smith, D. C., Leake, D. W., & Kamekona, N. (1998). Effects of a culturally competent school-based intervention for at-risk Hawaiian students. *Pacific Educational Research Journal 9,* 3–15.

Sobol, D. A. (2000). *An adolescent–parent conflict resolution training program for ethnically diverse families.* Unpublished doctoral dissertation, University of Southern California, Los Angeles.

Szapocznik, J., Feaster, D. J., Mitrani, V. B., Prado, G., Smith, L., Robinson-Batista, C., et al. (2004). Structural ecosystems therapy for HIV-seropositive African American women: Effects on psychological distress, family hassles, and family support. *Journal of Consulting and Clinical Psychology, 72,* 288–303.

Szapocznik, J., Rio, A., Perez-Vidal, A., Kurtines, W., Hervis, O., & Santisteban, D. (1986). Bicultural Effectiveness Training (BET): An experimental test of an intervention modality for families experiencing intergenerational/intercultural conflict. *Hispanic Journal of Behavioral Sciences, 8,* 303–330.

Szapocznik, J., Santisbetan, D., Hervis, O., & Spencer, F. (1981). Treatment of depression among Cuban American elders: Some validational evidence for a life enhancement counseling approach. *Journal of Consulting and Clinical Psychology, 49,* 752–754.

Szapocznik, J., Santisbetan, D., Kurtines, W. M., Hervis, O., & Spencer, F. (1982). Life enhancement counseling and the treatment of depressed Cuban American elders. *Hispanic Journal of Behavioral Sciences, 4,* 487–502.

Tacher, R. D. (1987). *Traditional vs. culturally sensitive family therapy sessions: A comparison of ratings by Cuban immigrants.* Unpublished doctoral dissertation, University of Texas, Austin.

Takeuchi, D. T., Sue, S., & Yeh, M. (1995). Return rates and outcomes from ethnicity-specific mental health programs in Los Angeles. *American Journal of Public Health, 85,* 638–643.

Thomas, K. A. (1995). *A comparison of counseling strategies reflective of cultural value orientations on perceptions of counselors in cross national dyads.* Unpublished doctoral dissertation, University of Minnesota, St. Paul.

Timberlake, T. L. (2000). *A comprehensive approach to social skills training with urban African American adolescents.* Unpublished doctoral dissertation, Temple University, Philadelphia.

Tom, L. M. (1989). *Psychoeducational approach with chronically mentally ill Chinese Americans: A cultural framework.* Unpublished doctoral dissertation, City University of New York.

Tucker, S. T. (1973). Action counseling: An accountability procedure for counseling the oppressed. *Journal of Non-White Concerns in Personnel and Guidance, 2,* 35–41.

U.S. Department of Health and Human Services. (2001). *Mental health: Culture, race, and ethnicity—a supplement to mental health: A report of the Surgeon General.* Rockville, MD: U.S. Department of Health and Human Services, Public Health Service, Office of the Surgeon General.

Weersing, V. R., & Weisz, J. R. (2002). Community clinic treatment of depressed youth: Benchmarking usual care against CBT clinical trials. *Journal of Consulting and Clinical Psychology, 70,* 299–310.

Yeh, M., Takeuchi, D. T., & Sue, S. (1994). Asian-American children treated in the mental health system: A comparison of parallel and mainstream outpatient service centers. *Journal of Clinical Child Psychology, 23,* 5–12.

Zane, N., Aoki, B., Ho, T., Huang, L., & Jang, M. (1998). Dosage-related changes in a culturally-responsive prevention program for Asian American youth. *Drugs and Society, 12,* 105–125.

Zane, N., Enomoto, K., & Chun, C.-A. (1994). Treatment outcomes of Asian- and White-American clients in outpatient therapy. *Journal of Community Psychology, 22,* 177–191.

Zane, N., Hatanaka, H., Park, S. S., & Akutsu, P. (1994). Ethnic-specific mental health services: Evaluation of the parallel approach for Asian-American clients. *Journal of Community Psychology, 22,* 68–81.

Zhang, N., & Dixon, D. N. (2001). Multiculturally responsive counseling: Effects on Asian students' ratings of counselors. *Journal of Multicultural Counseling and Development, 29,* 253–262.

Zhang, Y., Young, D., Lee, S., Li, L., Zhang, H., Xiao, Z., et al. (2002). Chinese Taoist cognitive psychotherapy in the treatment of generalized anxiety disorder in contemporary China. *Transcultural Psychiatry, 39,* 115–129.

Evidence-Based Practices

Ackerman, S. J., Benjamin, L. S., Beutler, L. E., Gelso, C. J., Goldfried, M. R., Hill, C., et al. (2001). Empirically supported therapy relationships: Conclusions and recommendations for the Division 29 Task Force. *Psychotherapy: Theory, Research, Practice, Training, 38,* 495–497.

Beutler, L. E. (2004). The empirically supported treatments movement: A scientist-practitioner's response. *Clinical Psychology: Science and Practice, 11,* 225–229.

Beutler, L. E., Moleiro, C., Malik, M., & Harwood, M. (2003). A new twist on empirically supported treatments. *International Journal of Clinical and Health Psychology, 3,* 423–437.

Beutler, L. E., Moleiro, C., & Talebi, H. (2002). How practitioners can systematically use empirical evidence in treatment selection. *Journal of Clinical Psychology, 58,* 1199–1212.

Chambless, D. L., Crits-Christoph, P., Wampold, B. E., Norcross, J. C., Lambert, M. J., Bohart, A. C., et al. (2006). What should be validated? In J. C. Norcross, L. E. Beutler, & R. F. Levant (Eds.), *Evidence-based practices in mental health: Debate and dialogue on the fundamental questions* (pp. 191–256). Washington, DC: American Psychological Association.

Chambless, D. L., & Hollon, S. D. (1998). Defining empirically supported therapies. *Journal of Consulting and Clinical Psychology, 66*(1), 7–18.

Chambless, D. L., Sanderson, W. C., Shoham, V., Bennett Johnson, S., Pope, K. S., & Crits-Christoph, P. (1996). An update on empirically validated therapies. *Clinical Psychologist, 29,* 5–18.

Choi, Y.-J., & Lee, K.-J. (2007). Evidence-based nursing: Effects of a structured nursing program for the health promotion of Korean Women with Hwa-Byung. *Archives of Psychiatric Nursing, 21,* 12–16.

Chorpita, B. F., Daleiden, E. L., & Weisz, J. R. (2005). Identifying and selecting the common elements of evidence-based interventions: A distillation and matching model. *Mental Health Services Research, 7,* 5–20.

Chorpita, B. F., Yim, L. M., Donkervoet, J. C., Arensdorf, A., Amundsen, M. J., McGee, C., et al. (2002). Toward large-scale implementation of empirically supported treatments for children: A review and observations by the Hawaii Empirical Basis to Services Task Force. *Clinical Psychology: Science and Practice, 9,* 165–190.

Chu, B. C. (2007). Considering culture one client at a time: Maximizing the cultural exchange. *Pragmatic Case Studies in Psychotherapy, 3,* 34–43.

Cochrane, S. V. (2005). Evidence-based assessment with men. *Journal of Clinical Psychology, 61,* 649–660.

Flannery-Schroeder, E. C., & Kendall, P. C. (2000). Group and individual cognitive-behavioral treatments for youth with anxiety disorders: A randomized clinical trial. *Cognitive Therapy and Research, 24,* 251–278.

Goldman, H. H., Ganju, V., Drake, R. E., Gorman, P., Hogan, M., Hyde, P. S., et al. (2001). Policy implications for implementing evidence-based practices. *Psychiatric Services, 52,* 1591–1597.

Hall, G. C. N. (2001). Psychotherapy research with ethnic minorities: Empirical, ethical, and conceptual issues. *Journal of Consulting and Clinical Psychology, 69,* 502–510.

Hunsley, J., & Johnston, C. (2000). The role of empirically supported treatments in evidence-based psychological practice: A Canadian perspective. *Clinical Psychology: Science and Practice, 7,* 269–272.

Jackson, Y. (2002). Exploring empirically supported treatment options for children: Making the case for the next generation of cultural research. *Clinical Psychology: Science and Practice, 9,* 220–222.

Malik, M. L., Beutler, L. E., Alimohamed, S., Gallagher-Thompson, D., & Thompson, L. (2003). Are all cognitive therapies alike? A comparison of cognitive and noncognitive therapy process and implications for the application of empirically supported treatments. *Journal of Consulting and Clinical Psychology, 71,* 150–158.

Messer, S. B. (2004). Evidence-based practice: Beyond empirically supported treatments. *Professional Psychology: Research and Practice, 35,* 580–588.

Miranda, J., Schoenbaum, M., Sherbourne, C., Duan, N., & Wells, K. (2004). Effects of primary care depression treatment on minority patients' clinical status and employment. *Archives of General Psychiatry, 61,* 827–834.

Muñoz, R. F., Lenert, L. L., Delucchi, K., Stoddard, J., Perez, J. E., Penilla, C., et al. (2006). Toward evidence-based Internet interventions: A Spanish/English Web site for international smoking cessation trials. *Nicotine and Tobacco Research, 8,* 77–87.

Norcross, J. C., Beutler, L. E., & Levant, R. F. (2006). *Evidence-based practices in mental health: Debate and dialogue on the fundamental questions.* Washington, DC: American Psychological Association.

O'Donohue, W., Buchanan, J. A., & Fisher, J. E. (2000). Characteristics of empirically supported treatments. *Journal of Psychotherapy Practice and Research, 9,* 69–74.

Siegel, C., Haugland, G., & Schore, R. (2005). The interface of cultural competency and evidence-based practices. In R. E. Drake, M. R. Merrens, & D. W. Lynde (Eds.), *Evidence-based mental health practice: A textbook* (pp. 273–299). New York: Norton.

Smith, J. C. (1999). *ABC relaxation theory: An evidence-based approach.* New York: Springer.

Tanenbaum, S. J. (2005). Evidence-based practice as mental health policy: Three controversies and a caveat. *Health Affairs, 24,* 163–173.

Task Force on Promotion and Dissemination of Psychological Procedures. (1995). Training in and dissemination of empirically-validated psychological treatments: Report and recommendations. *Clinical Psychologist, 48,* 3–23.

Thyer, B. A. (1991). Diagnosis and treatment of child and adolescent anxiety disorders. *Behavior Modification, 15,* 310–325.

Wampold, B. E., Mondin, G. W., Moody, M., Stich, F., Benson, K., & Ahn, H.-N. (1997). A meta-analysis of outcome studies comparing bona fide psychotherapies: Empirically, "all must have prizes." *Psychological Bulletin, 122,* 203–215.

Weisz, J. R., Doss, A. J., & Hawley, K. M. (2005). Youth psychotherapy outcome research: A review and critique of the evidence base. *Annual Review of Psychology, 56,* 337–363.

Whaley, A. L., & Davis, K. E. (2007). Cultural competence and evidence-based practice in mental health services: A complementary perspective. *American Psychologist, 62,* 563–574.

This list of references was compiled by Dr. Fernando Ortiz of Alliant International University.

INDEX